ECONOMICS

Understanding the Market Process

Henry Demmert
Santa Clara University

Harcourt Brace Jovanovich, Publishers
and its subsidiary, Academic Press
San Diego New York Chicago Austin Washington, D.C.
London Sydney Tokyo Toronto

For Emily and Brian

The goal of the economist is not merely to train a new generation in his arcane mystery: it is to understand this economic world in which we live and the other ones which a million reformers of every description are imploring and haranguing us to adopt. This is an important and honorable goal.

GEORGE STIGLER, 1982 Nobel Laureate in Economics

ISBN: 0-15-518911-5

Library of Congress Catalog Card Number: 90-82386
Printed in the United States of America

P R E F A C E

Not long ago, I visited some close friends whose son was home on vacation from college. I knew he had recently completed his first course in economics and I was interested in his reaction. What, I wondered, does a very bright undergraduate attending a college with a national reputation for superior teaching really bring away from his introductory economics course? As it turned out, his strongest impression—and probably his most enduring, for he never took another economics course—was that economics was mainly about graphs and curve shifting!

Needless to say, I was dismayed. But given the increasing incursion of formalism and technique into the teaching of undergraduate economics I suppose I should not have been too surprised. As teachers of economics we can avoid this kind of outcome and provide students with a lasting appreciation for the power of the economic way of thinking if only we would appeal as much as possible to their intuition and to their experience. We need not deny theory its proper role in the introductory economics course; we need only present it as systematic common sense. It is in that spirit that I have written *Economics: Understanding the Market Process* for the first college course in economics. I have sought to show how a few simple but powerful principles can help make sense of the incredibly rich but otherwise mystifying diversity of economic life. I have included numerous examples and applications to support and demonstrate this proposition. Contrary to the current fashion in textbook publishing, however, I have chosen to weave them into the fabric of the text itself rather than pull them out and highlight them in separate boxes. I believe the result is not only sound pedagogy but also a more coherent and readable text. (A list of these examples can be found after the Table of Contents.)

Economics: Understanding the Market Process is divided into three main sections: an introduction (Chapters 1–5), a microeconomics core (Chapters 6–14) and a macroeconomics core (Chapters 15–23). It concludes with a chapter on international economics (Chapter 24). As a relatively short book it can be used in a one-semester survey course covering both micro and macro; but, because it covers all of the essential topics in both areas, it can also be used in place of more encyclopedic principles textbooks by an instructor who wishes to emphasize depth rather than breadth in a two-semester (or two-quarter) course. The text has been constructed to provide the option of either a micro–macro or a macro–micro sequence. Additional flexibility is provided by the fact that some chapters, such as the one on international economics, can pretty much stand alone after the introductory material has been covered. (See the *Instructor's Manual* for more details on coverage and sequence options.)

Chapter 1 introduces the student to the nature of economic problems and methods. In the next three chapters, the standard material on supply and demand (Chapter 3) is preceded by an analysis of the logic of individual specialization and exchange (Chapter 2) and followed by an extensive discussion of the role of market processes in solving the immense coordination problems in a world of continuous change (Chapter 4). By proceeding from the level of the individual to that of the market and on to that of a system of interdependent markets, this arrangement effectively demonstrates the power of the "invisible hand" in coordinating the world's economic activity. Chapter 5 discusses the economic role of the command processes available to governments as an alternative to market coordination. On the normative side, it covers the standard material on market failure; on the positive side, it introduces the economic theory of public choice, which is then used throughout the remainder of the text as a framework for understanding why government does what it actually does (which, of course, is frequently inconsistent with what the normative theory says it should do). Without such a consistent theory of government behavior, the reasons for so many questionable economic policies escape the student. "If economics says trade protection (or rent control, etc.) is so harmful, why does the government do it?" Public choice theory provides a set of consistent answers.

Drawing a line between the introduction and the micro core after Chapter 5 is somewhat arbitrary, for either Chapter 6, or 7, or both can be treated as part of the introductory material. Chapter 6 introduces and applies the concepts of demand and supply elasticity, and Chapter 7 explores the logic and implications of augmenting market coordination with managerial coordination within business firms, focusing particularly on those firms organized as corporations. Chapter 8 considers the firm's production and cost functions as a prelude to the analysis of price and output determination in price takers' markets (Chapter 9) and price setters' markets (Chapter 10). Although the complete models of pure competition and monopoly are developed in Chapters 9 and 10, respectively, theoretical formalism is minimized in coverage of the intermediate cases of "imperfect competition." Instead of constructing elaborate theoretical models of oligopoly and monopolistic competition, the text discusses the nature of rivalrous competition and the conditions necessary for collusion in concentrated markets (Chapter 11) and focuses on the process of innovation, experimentation, and discovery in markets with differentiated products (Chapter 12). Chapter 13 looks at antitrust, regulatory, and environmental policies from both a normative and positive (public choice) viewpoint, and Chapter 14 introduces the general economics of factor markets and income distribution, focusing primarily on the labor market. (Although Chapter 14 concludes the micro core, it is a stand-alone chapter that can be assigned at any time after the introductory material has been covered.)

The macro core begins in Chapter 15 with a general overview of macroeconomic issues that provides the student with a perspective on recent macroeconomic history and a frame of reference for organizing the material that follows. After presenting the standard material on the national income accounts (Chapter 16) and the banking system and money creation (Chapter 17), the book turns to a historical overview of the classical–Keynesian debate in Chapter 18. I believe that an appreciation of the roots of this debate is crucial for understanding the issues of modern macroeconomics. Having illustrated the macroeconomic importance of wage adjustments in Chapter 18, the book goes on to provide a comprehensive overview of the aggregate labor market in Chapter 19 where modern job search and contract theories of unemployment and wage adjustment are developed. These theories are then integrated into the modern theory of aggregate supply and the business cycle in Chapter 20. Together Chapters 19 and 20 provide a firm foundation for the treatment of the monetary (Chapter 21) and income–expenditure (Chapter 22) theories of aggregate demand. Monetary and fiscal policies, the basics of which are introduced in Chapters 21 and 22, respectively, are then subjected to a more critical evaluation in Chapter 23, which concludes with an application of public choice theory to macroeconomic policy.

I have chosen to use the aggregate supply–aggregate demand apparatus (which I take great care to distinguish from the market supply–demand model) as the principal analytical framework throughout the macro core. In so doing, I have confined the Keynesian income–expenditure model, which in some textbooks is still the dominant mode of macroeconomic analysis, to a single chapter (Chapter 22), where I treat it as simply one framework for the analysis of aggregate demand. The equation of exchange is given equal billing as a framework for analyzing the monetary aspects of aggregate demand in Chapter 21.

Chapter 24 covers international economics. I should, however, emphasize that it is not the student's first encounter with the world economy; numerous examples and applications throughout the text highlight the international dimensions of economic issues. The logic of international trade shows up as early as Chapter 2. In Chapter 4 I have deliberately chosen examples of market interdependence that extend across international borders. In Chapter 5 I apply public choice theory to protectionism. Differences in employment practices between American and Japanese firms highlight an example in Chapter 9, which concludes with an application of the purely competitive model to the international market for oil tanker services. Chapter 11 discusses some international cartels. Chapter 16 introduces the concept of trade balances and examines their relationship to domestic saving and investment in the context of national income accounts. Chapter 22 shows how trade flows affect aggregate demand and domestic GNP. Chapter 24 simply wraps the international economy into a single neat package which, as noted, can stand pretty much on its own after the introductory material has been covered.

Economics has changed dramatically over the past quarter century. Transactions costs, incomplete information, efficient capital markets, property rights, public choice, agency costs, search costs, implicit contracts, customer markets, rational expectations, and the political business cycle are all relatively new concepts that have contributed greatly to our ability to make sense of otherwise mystifying economic phenomena. What makes this a truly modern textbook is that it introduces such concepts on the ground floor, making them integral elements of the analysis rather than simply grafting them on as afterthoughts.

Economics: Understanding the Market Process is available in a complete package including the textbook, a *Study Guide* prepared by Saul Kaufler of Los Angeles Pierce College, an *Instructor's Manual* (containing for each chapter an annotated outline, a list of distinctive features and points to emphasize, teaching suggestions, and answers to end-of-chapter questions), a *Test Bank* (in both paperback and computerized versions), and a set of *Transparency Masters*.

This book has been more than eight years in preparation, having been revised and rewritten numerous times. Among those who deserve my thanks for their helpful comments and suggestions on various versions of the manuscript are the following reviewers: Gerald Breger, University of South Carolina; William Davis, Western Kentucky University; Stephen Sacks, University of Connecticut-Storrs; Richard Towey; and Donald Wells, University of Arizona.

Finally, I would like to thank my family for helping me to ride out the many highs and lows that inevitably accompany a project like this, and to survive with my sanity nearly intact.

CONTENTS

Chapter 19 Employment, Unemployment, and the Labor Market 452

Chapter 20 Aggregate Supply and Aggregate Demand: The Modern Theory 476

APPLICATIONS IN ECONOMICS

CHAPTER	SUBJECT
1	Opportunity costs versus monetary outlays. Economic systems and ecological systems.
2	Cartels: the rise and fall of OPEC. Middlemen: supermarkets, department stores, financial intermediaries, business firms in general.
3	Inflation versus relative price changes: nominal and real price changes, 1970–89.
4	Market interdependence: the effects of a rise in the price of crude oil. Risk allocation: hedging in futures markets. Price floors: minimum wages, agricultural crop restrictions. Price ceilings: rent controls, gas lines, WWII ration tickets. Comparative economic systems: the collapse of socialism and the prospects for market capitalism in the Soviet Union and Eastern Europe.
5	Political tradeoffs: regulatory policy; foreign trade policy; environmental policy. Interest groups: the political economy of automobile import restrictions.
6	Price elasticity and expenditure changes: agricultural crop restrictions; the dilemma for drug enforcement policy. Elasticity and tax incidence.
7	Integrated production: how to produce a book. Present value: the determinants of stock and bond prices. Corporate finance. The stock market and capital allocation. The corporate takeover market and its colorful language.
8	Experience effects in the production of microchips.

9 The shutdown decision: car assembly plants during recessions; why Japanese firms continue production while their U.S. competitors shut down.
Entry and exit: competition in the supertanker market.

10 Exclusive monopoly rights and their economic value.
Price discrimination: airline pricing; college financial aid; coupon clipping; NFL season ticket packages; deBeers diamond "sightings."
Monopoly versus competition: the effects of eliminating the NCAA's monopoly over college football telecasts.

11 Rivalrous competition: IBM, Apple, and the microcomputer industry; Coke, Pepsi, and the soft drink industry.
Collusion: OPEC; the International Air Transport Association (IATA); the electrical equipment conspiracy; marketing diamonds through deBeers.
Professional codes of conduct: noncompetition among lawyers.

12 Innovation and imitation: Lite beer and its imitators.
Innovation and risk: RCA's video disk; IBM's PCjr; the "new" Coke.
Planned obsolescence: Does it pay?
Lemons markets: used cars.
Economic functions of brand names: rescuing the Tylenol name.
Advertising and prices: eyeglasses; legal services.

13 Merger policy: the Justice Department's merger guidelines; megamergers of the 1980s.
Antitrust and single-firm monopoly: Kodak, DuPont, and AT&T.
Vertical restraints: resale price maintenance (RPM); exclusive territories for beer and soft drink distributors.
Regulation and deregulation: airlines; broadcasting and telecommunications.
Environmental policy: command and control regulation by the EPA; marketable pollution rights.

14 Comparable worth and the gender gap.
Minimum wage laws.
Economic rent: the earnings of sports and entertainment superstars.
Factor market monopoly: labor unions; occupational licensure.
Monopsony: the reserve system and collusion in major league baseball.
Poverty: the high cost of escaping poverty; the political economy of the welfare system.

15 Economic growth: estimates of contributing factors.
Inflation versus one-shot changes in the price level: the effects of oil price shocks.
Anatomy of the recession of '82.
The Great Depression.
The German hyperinflation.
Stagflation during the 1970s.
What happened to the Phillips curve?

16 Measuring aggregate economic activity: the underground economy; illegal activity.

17 Financial intermediaries and deregulation of financial markets.
Monetizing government deficits.

18 Using Keynesian theory to explain the Great Depression.

19 Why people become unemployed.
Unemployment duration and the natural rate of unemployment.
Recent change in the natural rate of unemployment.
Job search theory and unemployment differentials.

20 Accelerating inflation during the 1960s.
The inflationary recession of 1970.
The supply shock recessions of 1973–75 and 1979–80.
Recession and recovery during the 1980s.
The Phillips curve revisited.

21 Credit cards and the demand for money.
Monetary growth and inflation between 1960 and 1982.
Recent changes in velocity and their implications.

22 Empirical estimates of the autonomous spending multiplier.

23 Information problems for policy makers: the stock market crash of 1987.
Monetary policy in practice.
Government deficits as future taxes.
Fiscal policy: the structural budget since WWII.
Fiscal policy and aggregate supply: the "supply side" tax cuts of the 1980s.
Political business cycles: unemployment, inflation, and the presidential election cycle from 1948 to 1988.

24 Sources and consequences of foreign trade deficits. Measuring the costs of protectionism: estimates for 15 industries.
Strategic trade policy: lessons from Japan's MITI?

C H A P T E R 1

Economic Problems and the Economic Approach

The basic problems of economics are simple; the hard part is to recognize simplicity when you see it.

HARRY G. JOHNSON *

Our wants are boundless and diverse. They range from basic desires for food, shelter, and other necessities of survival to the loftiest aspirations of our emotions and intellects. Not since the Garden of Eden, however, have we been able to fully satisfy all of these wants. This hard fact of life is the starting point for the study of economics.

SCARCITY, CHOICE, AND COST

Scarcity exists whenever available resources are insufficient to satisfy all wants or achieve all goals.

Natural resources are the productive resources available in the natural environment.

Economic problems are problems that confront all of us as we cope with the fundamental fact of **scarcity**. Scarcity exists because for all practical purposes human wants are limitless, whereas the productive resources available to satisfy those wants are limited. Productive resources include **natural resources** such as land, forests, rivers, and even time itself; man-made **capital goods** such as factories, machinery, and other "tools"; and **human resources** in the form of people's abilities, skills, and knowledge.

Productive resources are combined to produce **goods**. Anything that satisfies a human want is considered a "good" in economics. Goods can be material

* "The State of Theory," *American Economic Review: Papers and Proceedings* (May 1974), p. 324.

Capital goods are productive resources that are themselves produced.

Human resources include people's abilities, skills, and knowledge available for use in production.

A **good** is anything that satisfies a human want.

objects, such as food and clothing, or they can be intangibles such as entertainment, health care, and education. Occasionally the phrase "goods and services" is used to distinguish between physical commodities and intangibles, but the concept of goods is a perfectly general one, applying equally to material objects and desirable intangibles.

As it is used in economics, the term "good" conveys no ethical or moral connotation. If someone wants something, then that something qualifies as a good for that person. Cocaine is no less a good in this sense than are coconuts. Moreover, goods themselves have no intrinsic value; they have value only insofar as someone finds them, for whatever reason, desirable.

The combination of unlimited human wants and limited productive resources means that there will never be enough goods for everyone to have as much of everything as he or she wants. In other words, goods will always be scarce relative to the human wants they can satisfy.

Do not confuse scarcity with poverty. Poverty implies the inability to satisfy even the "basic necessities." Scarcity is both a more general concept and a more pervasive phenomenon than poverty. Wherever there are unsatisfied wants—whether they involve the most vital requirements for survival or the indulgence of the most trivial luxury—there is scarcity. As such, scarcity is a universal characteristic of the human condition. It is a problem that has of necessity been confronted by all people, rich or poor, in all societies, from subsistence to affluent, throughout history.

Scarcity Means Choice

Because our limited resources are insufficient to satisfy all of our wants, we must inevitably choose among our wants to determine which ones will be satisfied and to what extent. Choice is therefore an inescapable consequence of scarcity.

The choices demanded by scarcity pervade our lives at every level. The very fact that you are reading this book at this moment reflects a number of choices. The resources used to produce the book might have been used instead to produce detective novels (not to mention more leisure for its author). The money you spent to buy this book could have been spent on something else. You could be using your scarce time to watch TV, or sleep, or study calculus, or any number of other things. (But aren't you glad you chose to read an economics text instead?)

Think of the range of choices continuously confronting almost every family. How much of our limited budget should we spend on food? How much on entertainment? On education? Should we take a vacation at the beach this summer or have the roof repaired instead? Or should we turn down the thermostat and wear heavy sweaters during the winter so that we can afford both the summer vacation and the roof repair?

Consider some of the choices confronting a business firm. How many (and which) of the productive resources under its control should it devote to producing each good in its product line? How many to developing new products? How many to quality control? To marketing and distribution? To after-sale service?

Every day, in every business firm, from Mom-'n'-Pop operations to industrial giants like General Motors and IBM, choices must be made to answer these questions and hundreds of others like them.

Finally, consider the allocation of the federal government's budget. Every year thousands of political choices must be made about how to spend literally hundreds of billions of dollars. Choices must first be made among broad categories of federal government commitments such as defense, social programs, and revenue sharing with the states. Then choices must be made among the many alternatives within each category: aircraft carriers versus cruise missiles, food stamps versus medicare, California versus Connecticut. To the dismay of many a politician, even with hundreds of billions of dollars to spend, we can't have it all!

As these examples illustrate, the choices demanded by the fact of scarcity range from the personal choices of our daily lives to the far-reaching decisions that affect the well-being, perhaps even the survival, of millions of people. Economic problems and the choices they impose are truly universal facts of human life.

Choice Means Cost

The very idea of choice implies the sacrifice of some desirable alternatives in favor of others. The value we place on those foregone alternatives determines the **opportunity cost** of our choice. More specifically, the opportunity cost associated with any choice is the value of the *best* alternative foregone when that choice is made.

Opportunity cost is the value of the best alternative foregone when a choice is made.

Your opportunity cost of going to the movies is determined by the value you place on whatever else you would have chosen to do with your time and money had you not gone to the movie. The opportunity cost of using aluminum to produce bicycles is determined by the values people place on the thousands of other things—from baseball bats to engine blocks—that could have been produced instead with that aluminum. The opportunity cost of any government program is determined by the most valuable alternative use, whether in the private sector or the public sector, of the resources it absorbs.

Whenever there is a choice there is a cost. The old adage that "there ain't no such thing as a free lunch" is a fundamental truth in economics. Moreover, all costs are subjective. In choosing among alternatives, it is not a matter of comparing the value of each with some objective measure of its cost, for that cost is determined by the values the choice-maker places on the other alternatives.

Opportunity Costs and Monetary Outlays

But what about money? Aren't we talking dollars and cents when we talk about costs? Yes and no. Money does provide us with a common denominator for measuring and comparing costs, but monetary outlays are not themselves costs. If you spend $10 to go out for pizza with your friends, for example, your opportunity cost is not literally the $10 bill you must part with, but rather the other things you could have bought with that $10 had you not spent it on pizza. The use of money as the common measure of prices and costs provides you with an easy way to determine what those foregone options are. If the price of a movie ticket is $5, for example, you know that you have sacrificed the equivalent of two movies for your pizza. Furthermore, because the pizza parlor used money to hire labor, and purchase materials and other resources—in effect, bidding them away from alternative uses—its dollar costs of making the pizza reflect the value of the other goods that could have been produced with the same resources.

There are some cases, however, in which monetary outlays may not truly reflect the corresponding opportunity costs. For example, it might appear cheaper in money terms to dump industrial waste into the local lake than to haul it away in trucks and bury it. But if using the lake for waste disposal means that it can't be used for swimming and fishing, then the full cost of dumping the waste into the lake includes the value of the lost swimming and fishing opportunities. When the value of these foregone alternatives is taken into account, as it should be, using the lake as a waste disposal system may well be more costly than trucking the waste away. Looking only at monetary outlays can be misleading in such a case because it ignores part of the real cost.

THE PROCESS OF CHOICE

It should be clear by now that in the study of economics, the key element of human behavior is choice. As an inescapable consequence of scarcity and the fundamental basis of cost, choice deserves a closer look.

Who Chooses?

All choices are ultimately made by *individuals*. Committees, business firms, legislatures, and other groups and organizations do not choose. Although we often speak of "decisions by business firms" or "policies adopted by government," these are merely shorthand ways of summarizing the outcome of some group decision process. For example, to say that "the electorate chose candidate Smith over candidate Jones" is really to say that a majority of the *individuals* in the electorate chose to vote for Smith rather than Jones. Majority rule is just a way of aggregating individual choices to arrive at a collective decision.

In formal organizations such as legislatures, committees, and business firms, the process for converting individual choices into a group decision is usually spelled out explicitly. Within other groups, such as the family, the process is usually more flexible and thus better accommodates the desires of the particular individuals involved. Whatever the process, however, every group decision is ultimately traceable to the choices and preferences of individuals.

Although individual choice is the basic building block of economic analysis, there are many contexts in which little is lost by treating an organization—a family, a business firm, a government agency—as a decision-making black box.* In some cases, however, it is necessary to open the black box and inspect the specific forces affecting individual choices to understand how and why group decisions are made.

How Do Individuals Choose?

Individuals can make their choices in any number of ways. They can choose randomly by rolling dice or drawing straws; they can choose according to some rule of thumb such as first come, first served; or they can let tradition and habit dictate their choices. Economics, however, is concerned only with *purposeful choice*. In short, economics assumes that individuals act rationally in accordance with what they perceive as their own self-interest.

Because the assumption of rational self-interest is often a source of confusion among those unfamiliar with its role in economic analysis, it is important that we clarify just what it does, and does not, mean.

Rational self-interest means that people try to do the best they can given their circumstances and the means available to them. They will never knowingly choose a less preferred alternative over a more preferred one, nor will they ever choose a higher cost means of achieving a given end when a lower cost means is available. In formal terms, they will *maximize* the difference between the expected benefits and the costs of their choices.

Rational self-interest implies that people respond predictably to changes in benefits and costs. If the cost of driving an automobile rises, people will drive less; if the punishment meted out to robbers is reduced, there will be more robberies; if one economics instructor gives lower grades than the others (while not teaching any more effectively), enrollment in her courses will be lower.

Rational self-interest is not synonymous with selfishness. For each of us there are others whose well-being is a direct concern. It is therefore quite rational to take their welfare into consideration when making choices. To deny this would be to deny the existence of charitable donations and other forms of altruism, which would be absurd. But note that rational self-interest *does* imply that even altruistic choices are affected by costs and benefits. It implies, for example, that if tax deductions for charitable contributions are eliminated, such contributions will fall.

Rational self-interest does not mean that people are motivated solely by a quest for material goods. While economics certainly accepts the fact that many of our choices are meant to alleviate material wants, it does not deny that many choices—some of which require the sacrifice of material goods—are motivated by a quest for love, justice, honor, revenge, and other intangibles.

Rational self-interest does not mean that people don't make mistakes. All choices are made in the light of available information, and information itself is

**Black box* is the term often applied to a device whose performance characteristics are known even though its internal workings and means of operation may not be observed or known. For most of us, television sets, computers, and automobile engines are black boxes.

a scarce and costly good. Rarely will someone find it rational to incur the costs of acquiring *all* of the relevant information bearing on any particular choice; as a result, mistakes will occasionally be made. For example, before you pay to see a movie you may read newspaper reviews of it, talk to friends who have seen it, and so on. This is rational behavior; but, as you are surely aware, it does not guarantee that you will not be disappointed.

Rational self-interest does not mean that people always consciously calculate costs and benefits before making choices. The caricature of "economic man" as a coldly and efficiently calculating "utility maximizer" misses the point.* Rationality is intended to describe people's *behavior*, not their *thought processes*. And there is a difference. Consider how a physicist might describe the behavior of a pool player. He might use mathematical equations relating mass, velocity, and momentum transfer. This would provide a very accurate description of what happens on the pool table, but it would hardly describe the thought processes of the typical pool player. In other words, the successful pool player acts *as if* he makes detailed physical and mathematical calculations when *in fact* he does not. So it is in economics: People are assumed to behave *as if* they are rational; their thought processes, however, are not assumed to match those of a computer.

In some contexts, the consequences of choice may be great enough relative to the cost of detailed calculations that such calculations make sense. For example, it might make sense for the managers at NASA to calculate the expected consequences of their choices down to the *n*th decimal place before risking a billion dollar space shuttle and the lives of its crew. Often, however, information is simply too costly relative to the benefits for precise calculations to make sense. In such cases it is quite rational to rely on experience, rules of thumb, or rough-and-ready impressions of costs and benefits.

Finally, we must emphasize that rational self-interest is an assumption about the way people *actually do* behave. It is not a prescription about the way people *should* behave. As such, its validity rests ultimately on an appeal to the facts. Economic analysis has indeed found that people's behavior over a very wide range of activities—from market transactions to political choices to criminal behavior—is broadly consistent with rational self-interest.

ECONOMIC PROBLEMS AND ECONOMIC SYSTEMS

An **economic system** is a social system for coordinating individual choices in the face of scarcity.

We may make our choices as individuals, but we do not make them in isolation. All of us are members of social groups in which the alternatives available to each depend on choices made by others. To take a very simple example, you and I cannot choose to consume six apples each if only ten are available. There must be some way of coordinating our individual choices so that they are mutually consistent. This is the function of an **economic system**.

* *Utility* is simply a synonym for satisfaction.

The Fundamental Economic Problems

Every economic system, whatever its form, must provide a means for answering the questions raised by certain fundamental problems. These problems are *resource allocation, production techniques, distribution, temporal allocation*, and *risk allocation*.

Resource allocation: What goods will be produced and in what amounts? Any economic system must determine how scarce productive resources are to be allocated among the millions of different goods and services they can produce. Given the limited productive resources available, more of one good necessarily means less of some other. More Wheaties means less cornflakes; more TV sets means fewer stereos; more guns means less butter.

Production techniques: How will each good be produced? There are always many ways to produce a good, each utilizing a different mix of resources. Automobiles can be custom produced by skilled craftsmen or they can be mass produced by industrial robots; energy can be produced from petroleum, sunshine, or atomic nuclei; buildings can be made from wood, metal, concrete, glass, and plastics in an almost infinite variety of combinations. Every economic system must provide a means for choosing among the many possible production techniques available for each good.

Distribution: Who will get what? Once an economic system has decided what goods to produce and how to produce them, it must determine who will get them and in what amounts. In effect, it must determine who becomes rich and how, who is poor and why, and how big the differences are.

Consumption satisfies current wants.

Investment adds to the stock of productive resources to satisfy future wants.

Temporal allocation: When will goods become available? The problem of temporal allocation requires choices between **consumption** and **investment**. Consumption uses scarce resources to satisfy current wants; investment uses them to increase our productive capacity, and thus our ability to satisfy future wants. Investment includes activities as diverse as searching for new deposits of oil or minerals that add to our stock of natural resources, the production of buildings and machinery that add to our stock of capital goods, and the acquisition of new knowledge and skills that add to our stock of human resources. (This latter is sometimes called "investment in human capital." You probably weren't aware that you are investing in human capital as you read this!) When investment in new knowledge leads to better production techniques and improved products, the result is technological progress.

Investment is the source of our material progress, but such progress does not come free. The time, effort, and other resources used to produce capital goods, to acquire new skills, or to advance technology could always be used to satisfy more immediate wants. (You could be out earning money or enjoying yourself, for example, were you not investing in your human capital.) Every economic system must therefore provide a way of choosing between satisfying current wants and expanding future opportunities.

Risk allocation: Who will bear the consequences of uncertainty? Because our knowledge of the future is necessarily imperfect and incomplete, we must make many choices in an environment of uncertainty. The ultimate results of such choices may be quite different—either better or worse—from those we anticipate. They therefore carry an element of risk. A college student who chooses a major with an eye toward future employment, a scientist who chooses a research program hoping that it will result in fruitful new knowledge and applications, and an entrepreneur who commits money and effort to a new business venture are but a few examples of choices in which risk is an important consideration. Until someone invents an accurate crystal ball or reliable way of reading tea leaves, risk and uncertainty will remain permanent fixtures of the economic environment. Every economic system must therefore allocate the unexpected consequences, *both good and bad*, of risky choices.

Economic systems differ in their approaches to solving these problems, but the problems themselves are common to all systems.

Types of Economic Systems

All economic systems use a mix of two basic elements, *market* and *command*, in solving the basic economic problems. The essential difference between these elements lies in the constraints they place on individual choice. In a sense, the difference lies not so much in *how* choices are made, but in *who* makes them. **Market processes** solve economic problems by relying on the decentralized choices of individuals. **Command processes**, by contrast, subordinate individual choices to the decisions of some central authority.

Market processes rely on decentralized individual choices and voluntary exchange to solve economic problems and coordinate economic activity.

Command processes rely on centralized authority to solve economic problems and coordinate economic activity.

Just how the market coordinates the choices of millions of independent, self-interested individuals without collapsing in a spasm of chaos is perhaps the central mystery of economics. Because a significant portion of this book is devoted to unravelling that mystery, we shall not go into details at this point. Be content, if you can, with the famous analogy supplied by the father of economics, Adam Smith, more than 200 years ago when he observed that in a market system, each individual is guided "as if by an invisible hand to promote an end which was no part of his intention." (See what we mean by a mystery?)

It is easier to envision how a command system coordinates economic activity. The centralized authority—central planners in a socialist economy, the "boss" in a business firm, or whoever—decides what goods are to be produced, how they will be produced, and so on. These decisions are then carried down the chain of command to the level at which they are actually executed. If economic choices are guided by an "invisible hand" in a market system, they are guided by the "visible hand" of authority in a command system.

Neither market nor command exists in pure form. All real-world economic systems combine these two elements in some proportion. In *capitalist* systems, most productive resources are owned and controlled by private individuals who choose how those resources will be used, and who personally bear the consequences of their choices. Capitalist systems therefore tend to rely primarily on the market for economic coordination. In *socialist* systems, most productive resources are owned in principal by society but controlled in practice by the state. Since the state typically uses some form of centralized planning process to determine how those resources are used, command elements are of primary importance in socialist economies.

Economic Systems and Ecological Systems

An *ecological system* is a system in which interdependent biological organisms interact with one another and with their environment. Although an economic system is distinguished from a purely biological system by the element of conscious choice, there are nevertheless some interesting parallels between the two.

In an economic system, as in an ecological system, the ultimate effects of some change usually extend far beyond its immediate impact. In an ecological system, for example, a change in the population of one species in the food chain has consequences for the populations (and perhaps even the survival) of all of the other species in the system. So it is in an economy. One small change can send enough repercussions through the entire system that its ultimate effects are difficult or even impossible to anticipate. This point becomes particularly important where government policies are concerned, for the full effects of such policies are often unanticipated and sometimes even contrary to its original purposes. Rent controls and minimum wage laws provide a pair of good examples. As we shall see, economic analysis tells us that rent controls intended to make housing affordable may well reduce the amount of housing available at any price and that minimum wage laws intended to increase the earnings of unskilled workers may leave such workers unemployed with no earnings at all. If we are to understand the full effects of government policies and other changes in the economic environment, we must always look beyond their nominal intent and trace their repercussions as they work their way through the system.

Evolution is another property shared by ecological systems and economic systems. Given the uncertainty inherent in the economic environment, economic decisions, like biological mutations, are often part of a larger trial-and-error process. Within this process, natural selection tends over time to weed out those economic practices that are systematically more likely to fail than to succeed and to replace them with others better adapted to their environment. This process is most obvious in the marketplace's natural selection of business firms. Firms that operate efficiently and produce goods that people want survive and prosper; firms that operate inefficiently or produce products that no one wants face bankruptcy and extinction.

Much of the order we observe in an economic system is not the result of a conscious, comprehensive plan but of a process of economic evolution and natural selection that no one could have anticipated—"the result of human action, but not of human design."*

THEORIES, MODELS, AND FACTS

Our economic system is so complex and rich in detail that the only way we can hope to understand it is to abstract—separate key elements from irrelevant de-

*This phrase is attributed to the Scottish philosopher, Adam Ferguson, a countryman and contemporary of Adam Smith.

A **theory** is a general explanation applicable to a wide range of particular circumstances.

Empirical verification means testing a theory to determine whether its predictions are consistent with available facts.

tails—and to search for general patterns. The process of abstraction and generalization—in short, the search for order amidst complexity, leads to a **theory**.

The development of theories is one of the defining characteristics of the scientific approach. The other is **empirical verification**. Empirical verification is the process by which theories are evaluated in light of observed facts. Scientific generalizations that have survived many empirical tests and become widely accepted often come to be called "laws" of physical or social sciences. But they are not absolute truth. Neither economics nor any other science is a static body of truth; it is a continuing process by which the successive generalizations that enable us to order and understand our world are tested and revised in the light of new information. Those generalizations that fail the empirical test are discarded; those that pass are accepted, perhaps as laws, but even then only conditionally. New observations and new information may someday require that these laws also be discarded or at least modified.

Models

A **model** is an abstract representation of some particular facet of reality.

When our theorizing focuses on some particular real-world phenomenon, we are building a **model**. A model is an abstract representation of some particular facet of reality—a way of thinking about that reality that is intended to convey information about its essential properties.

We are all familiar with a variety of models, not all of them scientific, that are commonplace in our daily lives. We are using a model whenever we use a map. Fashion models convey information about how articles of clothing might look on us. Model children embody those characteristics that make them pleasant for adults to be around. A model airplane or an architect's model provides a miniature representation of some aspects of its real-world counterpart.

Models are useful because they simplify. They allow us to ignore irrelevant details and to focus our attention on the more important aspects of the reality under consideration. As Albert Einstein once said, however, "everything should be made as simple as possible—but not more so." How simple is appropriate? How do we know which details are important and which can be safely omitted from the model as irrelevant? How far can abstraction proceed before distortions, rather than useful simplifications, are introduced into the way we think about the world? The answer to these questions is, "It depends." Specifically, it depends on the uses for which the model is intended. If, for example, we intend to use a map of the United States to illustrate only its geographical boundaries, then a simple outline will suffice. However, if we intend to drive from Los Angeles to New York, we need a map that includes details like highways, a mileage scale, and the locations of towns and cities along the way. A backpacker's map, on the other hand, can safely omit information about cities and highways, but it must include things like elevation contours and the locations of lakes and rivers. In constructing economic models, we apply the same principles. The degree of abstraction—the elements of reality to be included and those to be dismissed as irrelevant—depends on the nature of the questions that the model is intended to address.

Economic Models

Economic models have some distinguishing characteristics that reflect the special nature of economic problems and the economic approach to the study of individual and social behavior.

Constrained Choice

As we have seen, the basic economic problem is that of rational choice in the face of scarcity. Accordingly, economic models usually begin by specifying the alternatives open to choice and the scarcity constraints that limit the range of choice. In the economic model of consumer spending decisions, for example, the starting point is the consumer's limited budget, the prices of the goods available for purchase, and some information about the consumer's tastes and preferences.

Maximizing Behavior

As we have seen, rational behavior implies that people do the best they can given their objectives and the options available to them. In other words, they attempt to *maximize* the difference between the benefits and costs of their choices. The interpretation of rational choice-making as maximizing behavior is a defining characteristic of economic models. In the model of consumer expenditure decisions, for example, it is assumed that the consumer attempts to maximize satisfaction, or "utility." Business firms are assumed to make their output, employment, and other decisions in a manner that maximizes their profit. In many economic models of political behavior, elected officials are assumed to make choices that will maximize their chances of reelection.

Decisions at the Margin

Decisions at the margin are decisions made by considering the effects of small changes on benefits and costs.

Marginal benefit is the benefit associated with a small change.

Marginal cost is the cost associated with any small change.

Economists generally model maximizing behavior as if people make **decisions at the margin**. This means that they consider successive small, or *marginal*, changes in the variables under their control. If the **marginal benefit** of the change exceeds its **marginal cost**, then the change will be made; if the marginal cost exceeds the marginal benefit, the change will not be made. The decision maker has maximized only when all adjustments for which the marginal benefit exceeds marginal cost, and none for which the reverse is true, have been made.

As a simple illustration of a marginal adjustment, consider how the owner of a profit-maximizing business firm might decide whether to increase output by a small amount, say, one unit per day. If producing one more unit per day adds $95 to the firm's costs, then that is the marginal cost of the change. If the extra unit brings in an additional $100 in revenues when it is sold, then that amount is its marginal benefit (specifically, its marginal revenue in this example). Because the marginal benefit exceeds the marginal cost, the firm's owner will find it profitable to produce the extra unit. On the other hand, if the extra unit of output brought in less than $95 in revenues, the marginal cost would exceed the marginal benefit and the extra unit would not be worth producing.

The comparison of marginal benefits and costs is not necessarily meant to be a literal description of the way people go about making choices. (Recall the distinction between people's behavior and their thought processes.) Decision making at the margin is simply a convenient and useful way of thinking about maximizing behavior.

Equilibrium

Equilibrium describes a state from which, unless disturbed, no further change will occur.

Equilibrium is a concept describing a state of rest and a balance of forces—a situation in which, unless disturbed, no further change will occur. Equilibrium exists in an economic model when the individuals whose behavior is being modelled have maximized—that is, when there are no additional actions that those individuals can take to further their objectives. If such additional actions were available, individuals would adjust to take advantage of the opportunities they present. A consumer is in equilibrium when his or her spending pattern maximizes utility; a business firm is in equilibrium when there are no further options available for increasing profits. As we shall see, equilibrium analysis is very useful in predicting how people respond to changes in the economic environment.

The **long run** is a period of time long enough for all adjustments to a change to work themselves out.

The **short run** is a period of time long enough for only some of the adjustments to a change to work themselves out.

It is often useful to distinguish between *long-run* and *short-run* equilibria. As these terms are used in economics, they refer not to specific calendar times, such as a year or a week, but to analytical concepts. Specifically, the **long run** is a period of time long enough for *all* adjustments to a change in the economic environment to work themselves out, whereas the **short run** is long enough for only *some* of those adjustments to work themselves out. For example, in our analysis of production, we assume that a business firm can change its rate of output by varying all of its resource inputs in the long run, but that it considers some of those inputs—usually buildings and other heavy capital—to be fixed in the short run. A short-run equilibrium is therefore only a partial equilibrium—an analytical stepping stone on the way to a final long-run equilibrium.

Evaluating Economic Models

As with the broader body of economic theory, a particular model is useful only if its predictions are consistent with observed facts. When that is the case, the model is accepted, but only conditionally, not as proven truth. A model that proves useful in some applications and in light of some facts might eventually fail the empirical test in other applications or in light of new facts. A model that fails in one application may still be useful in others, however. For example, the geocentric (earth-centered) model of the universe, although not very good at explaining the movement of the planets, is still used for navigation at sea. A model is not something that is true or false; it is a way of thinking about some particular aspect of reality.

Positive and Normative Economics

Positive economics attempts to explain economic processes and verify the explanations in the light of facts.

The process of constructing and testing economic models is known as **positive economics**. Because positive economics attempts to explain the way the world actually works, its conclusions can be shown to be true or false in light of observed facts.

Sometimes, however, economists (like everyone else) are concerned not so much with the way the world actually *is* as with the way it *should be*. They may want to determine whether one economic outcome is better than another, or to suggest which economic policy should be adopted in a given situation. Such concerns bring us into the realm of **normative economics**. Because normative economics atttempts to judge and evaluate economic phenomena, its conclusions cannot be shown to be true or false by an appeal to the facts; they are ultimately based on value judgments—that is, on someone's particular criterion for evaluating good and bad. We may agree or disagree with the criterion, but we cannot prove it to be true or false.

Normative economics evaluates economic conditions according to some subjective criterion; it cannot be shown to be true or false in light of facts.

Because it is not subject to empirical verification, normative economics is not truly scientific. This is not to say that it is not useful or necessary. However, it is extremely important that we are able to distinguish between normative conclusions based on untestable value judgments and positive conclusions that can be empirically tested. As an illustration of the distinction, consider the following set of assertions:

> Taxpayer subsidization of public transit systems would allow those systems to cover their costs with lower fares. Lower fares would increase ridership and reduce traffic on city streets and freeways. We should, therefore, subsidize public transit systems to reduce traffic congestion.

The first two sentences are positive because they are assertions of factually verifiable relationships. The third sentence, because it recommends the adoption of a policy ("We should . . . subsidize . . ."), is a normative statement. It is based upon the speaker's opinion of what constitutes acceptable levels of congestion. You may agree with the statement; others—perhaps the taxpayers who are to provide the subsidy—may not. The point is that there is no objective criterion for determining how much congestion is too much, or too little, or just the right amount. This judgment depends on the observer.

Positive Economics and Economic Policy

Positive and normative economics probably are most often confused in discussions of government economic policy. By its very nature, policy making requires that alternative courses of action be evaluated in light of some normative criterion. However, this does not mean that positive economics cannot also contribute to the policy-making process and our understanding of it. Positive economics is related to economic policy in two important ways.

First, positive economic analysis is necessary to predict the affects of various policies. It can tell policy makers which objectives are compatible and where tradeoffs are necessary. It can predict, for example, that an increase in the legal minimum wage will not only increase the earnings of some workers but that it will also make it more difficult for other workers, especially young, unskilled workers, to find jobs. It can predict that some policies intended to reduce interest rates may have the effect of increasing the rate of inflation. Whatever the particular normative criteria on which policy decisions are ultimately based, this kind of information is certainly valuable, if not indispensable, for intelligent policy making.

Second, positive analysis can be used to explain why certain policies are adopted and to predict which policies will most likely be adopted in a given set of circumstances. The simple assumption that government policies are always intended to serve the "public interest" (if indeed the public interest can even be unambiguously determined in any specific policy context) is naive and inconsistent with observed facts. Our government has at times adopted policies that have sanctioned the destruction of agricultural crops, prevented businesses from offering lower prices to consumers, and encouraged producers to adopt inefficient and wasteful production techniques. These policies have not generally been the results of mistakes, stupidity, or malicious intent on the part of government policy makers and bureaucrats, whose behavior is likely to be neither more devious nor more noble than that of the rest of us. In short, positive economics recognizes that government policy makers, like other economic decision makers, are rational people who respond predictably to the incentives confronting them. As such their behavior can be explained with the same economic theory that explains how consumers respond to a change in the price of a product or how business firms react to a new technology.

Economics as a Science

The natural sciences have been enormously successful in advancing our knowledge of our physical environment and in discovering widely applicable laws of nature. Economics, even though it is the most advanced of the social sciences, is more modest in its claims. This is due, at least in part, to the fact that it is a relative newcomer to the family of sciences. Formal theorizing about economic phenomena (as opposed to practical knowledge of economic affairs) is only about two hundred years old. Systematic empirical verification in economics, though attempted sporadically as early as a century ago, did not begin in earnest until the last few decades when the development of computers began to make large-scale data analysis feasible. Many feel that in light of its relatively brief history, economics has indeed made impressive strides.

Human behavior is also much more subtle and complex than most physical phenomena. If the goal of economics, or indeed any of the social sciences, were to predict with accuracy how specific individuals would behave in particular circumstances, the task would indeed appear insurmountable. People presumably have free wills and are motivated by a variety of factors, including distinctly personal traits and preferences as well as fundamentally unpredictable elements of whim and fancy. But economics does not seek to predict the behavior of specific individuals in particular circumstances. Rather it attempts to discover and explain general patterns common to a broad range of human behavior, and to generate predictions about the general tendencies that such behavior will exhibit under a variety of conditions. Viewed in this context, the task of predicting human behavior, though less ambitious, is much more realistic.

Why Economists Sometimes Disagree

There is a well-worn joke that if you took all of the economists in the world and laid them end to end, they wouldn't reach a conclusion. While this tends to overstate the extent of disagreement among economists, they often do disagree. But this fact does not make economics any less scientific than if they all agreed.

Most disagreements among economists, and certainly most of those reported in the news media, boil down to differences of opinion about what constitutes fairness and equity in a given situation, or about the relative importance of economic security versus individual freedom. We should no more expect economists to agree on these normative issues than we would any other group of citizens. Like anyone else, every economist has his or her own philosophical and political views; we would be naive to think that those views don't influence one's position on matters of economic policy.

In addition, economics simply has not resolved a number of important questions. Rather than admit ignorance (and perhaps be forced to forego a handsome consulting fee or the prestige of testifying before a Congressional committee), economists often issue opinions based on incomplete and imprecise analysis. In such cases, disagreement should be expected (as perhaps should candor), but such disagreement should tend to disappear as explanatory theories and empirical evidence are improved. Genuine positive disagreements are a healthy antidote to complacency in any scientific field.

Because economic issues are so important and so pervasive in our daily lives, disagreements among economists receive more than their share of publicity. It is unfortunate that in the public's mind, these disagreements occasionally overshadow the genuine contributions economics has made to our understanding of human behavior and social organization.

Defining Economics

Economics is best defined by the kinds of problems it studies and by the distinctive way it approaches those problems. As we have seen, the basic economic problem is the problem of scarcity or, more specifically, the problem of choosing among competing goals when the resources that can be used to satisfy those goals are limited. The distinctive characteristic of the economic approach is its emphasis on the rational element of human behavior in coping with scarcity. It shares with all other sciences a method that involves the construction of theories and models, testing them in light of available facts, and revising or replacing them when they fail that test.

Having just been introduced to these concepts, it would be surprising if at this early point you could grasp the true nature of economic reasoning and the range of problems to which it can be applied. Your appreciation for this will undoubtedly increase as you study further. Nevertheless, for those readers who find the simplicity of one sentence definitions appealing, we propose the following:

> Economics is the scientific study of rational choice in the face of scarcity, and of the social consequences of such choice.

Microeconomics and Macroeconomics

If you found yourself in the middle of a dense forest, you would have a good view of the individual trees but probably little idea of its overall shape. If you observed the same forest from an airplane, on the other hand, you would have a clear view of its outline but would not be able to make out the details of the individual trees. Which of these perspectives is more useful therefore depends on whether your primary interest is in the forest or the trees.

Microeconomics is the study of the behavior and interaction of the individuals, households, business firms, and other decision-making units that make up the economy.

Macroeconomics is the study of the relations among economic aggregates such as the economy's total output, total level of employment, and average level of prices.

So it is with our perspectives on the economy. When we study the individual "trees"—the business firms, households, and other decision-making units that make up the economic "forest"—our perspective is that of **microeconomics**. When we study the broad outlines of the forest itself—when we ask, for example, what determines the economy's total annual output of goods, or its overall levels of employment and unemployment, or the rate of inflation in the average level of all prices—our perspective is that of **macroeconomics**. (The prefixes come from the Greek, *micro* meaning small and *macro* meaning large.) Microeconomics studies the economy "in the small" by focusing on the individual decision-making units, such as business firms and households, that make up the economic system. Macroeconomics is concerned with the broader outlines of overall economic performance.

You might reasonably ask how the macro behavior of the economy as a whole can be studied without close attention to the micro behavior of its components. After all, is the whole not just the sum of its parts? This is an important question, and one which economics has been forced to confront in recent years.

Consider the following analogy. Suppose you are driving a car. If your only concern is with the macro issues of its speed and direction, you have to know how to use only the gas pedal, the brake pedal, and the steering wheel. You need not become an expert about the micro workings of the engine, the transmission, the fuel system, and so on. But if the automobile starts misbehaving, sputtering in response to more pressure on the gas pedal, or not responding at all to the brake pedal or to the steering wheel, then it becomes necessary to investigate the car's inner mechanisms—its micro elements.

So it has been in economics. Until the late 1960s, macroeconomics did a pretty fair job of explaining unemployment, inflation, and recession simply by concentrating on a few broad measures of overall economic activity. But when the economy began sputtering and misbehaving in the 1970s, and when it did not respond as anticipated to economic policies, economists were forced to examine more closely the micro foundations of macroeconomics. Microeconomics and macroeconomics, though usually still taught separately, have much more in common today than they did ten or fifteen years ago.

CHAPTER SUMMARY

1. The fact of *scarcity*—the limited resources available to satisfy virtually unlimited human wants—requires that people make choices about which wants are to be satisfied and to what extent. Whenever a choice is made, an *opportunity cost* is incurred. Opportunity cost is determined by the most valuable alternative foregone when a choice is made.

2. All choices are ultimately made by individuals. Economics assumes that individuals generally choose *rationally* and in their perceived *self-interest.* This means that they try to do the best they can in any given set of circumstances, and it implies that they respond predictably to changes in the costs and benefits of their actions. Rational self-interest does not mean that people are selfish, or that they are motivated only by a quest for material goods, or that they don't make mistakes, or that they always consciously calculate costs and benefits before acting.

3. *Economic systems* exist to coordinate choices. All economic systems must provide means for allocating resources, choosing among production techniques, distributing goods, choosing between the present and future use of resources, and assigning risks. They do this using a mix of *market* elements and *command* elements.

4. Economists use *theories* and *models* as ways of thinking about economic relationships. Theories and models abstract from certain elements of reality to focus on the essentials of the phenomena being studied. Their usefulness is determined by how well their generalizations and predictions fit observed empirical facts.

5. *Positive economics* attempts to explain the world as it is; its conclusions can be shown to be true or false in the light of observed facts. *Normative economics* judges and evaluates economic phenomena; its conclusions cannot be shown to be true or false because they ultimately rest on value judgments.

6. *Microeconomics* studies the individual households, business firms, and other decision-making units that make up an economic system; *macroeconomics* focuses on the overall performance of the system.

Key Terms and Concepts

scarcity
natural resources
capital goods
human resources
good
opportunity cost
economic system
consumption
investment
market process
command process
theory
empirical verification
model
decisions at the margin
marginal benefit
marginal cost
equilibrium
long run
short run
positive economics
normative economics
microeconomics
macroeconomics

Questions for Thought and Discussion

1. What are some of the costs you incur by attending college? Are they all monetary costs?
2. Distinguish between self-interest and selfishness.
3. Ann, who intended to spend her last $5 on a movie, instead gives it to a beggar in a wheelchair. Later she sees the same man running and playing frisbee in the park. Has Ann behaved irrationally?
4. "War is irrational." Do you agree?
5. Lila Landlady, learning apartment rents have risen in her neighborhood, informs Tom Tenant that she is raising his rent. Tom argues that the rent increase is unfair because Lila's costs have not increased. As evidence he points out that her insurance, utilities, property taxes, and other expenses are the same as when he moved in. Lila argues that even though her out-of-pocket expenses have not risen, her opportunity cost of renting to Tom has. What is her argument?
6. It is sometimes argued that a drafted army is less costly than a volunteer army because a nation must pay more to attract volunteers than it would have to pay draftees. Is this argument correct?
7. A well-known economist has said that "while economic systems of various sorts boast of their achievements in bringing goods and services to people, what makes them all economic systems is that they have systematic procedures for *preventing* people from getting goods and services." (Thomas Sowell, *Knowledge and Decisions*, p. 45) What does he mean?
8. Both astronomy and astrology make predictions based on the movements and positions of stars and planets. Astronomy is a science; astrology is not. Why the difference?

9. In what sense are economic theories and models "figments of the imagination?"

10. Is the following statement positive, normative, or a mixture of the two? "Raising the cigarette tax will make cigarettes more expensive and therefore discourage smoking, especially among young people who are not yet addicted to cigarettes. Since cigarette smoking is unhealthy, a rise in the cigarette tax would therefore contribute to a healthier society."

APPENDIX

Understanding Graphs

This book, like almost every other undergraduate economics text, makes use of graphs. A graph presents a visual picture of the relation between two variables. In some cases, the relation is based on actual data; in others it is a theoretical one.

In all graphs, the value of one variable is measured upward along the **vertical axis**, and the value of the other variable is measured to the right along the **horizontal axis**. The intersection of the two axes is called the **origin** and is labelled with an "*O*." Combinations of the values of the two variables measured on the axes are represented by points between the two axes.

We can illustrate the construction and interpretation of a graph with a simple example. Suppose your economics instructor has told you that in order to score well on her exams, you must attend class regularly and study for the exams. In other words, she has expressed a relation among three variables: exam score, class attendance, and hours of study. Because the value of the first variable, your exam score, depends upon the other two—how long you study and how regularly you attend class—we call it the **dependent variable** in the relationship; the other two variables, are called **independent variables**.

Table 1A.1 quantifies the relationship among the three variables. Column 1 shows the amount of time you spend studying for your economics exam, column 2 shows your exam score if your class attendance is perfect, and column 3 shows your exam score if you miss 1/3 of the class meetings. For example, with perfect attendance and 2 hours of study, you can expect a score of 70; with perfect attendance and 4 hours of study, you can expect a score of 95; and if you study 4 hours but miss 1/3 of the class meetings, you can expect a score of 75.

There are three variables in this example, but since a graph has only two axes, we can plot only the relation between two of them while holding the other constant. Let us therefore initially hold class attendance constant and consider the relation between your study time and your exam score when you attend class regularly—that is, the relation between columns 1 and 2 of the table. This relation is shown in Figure 1A.1 where study time is measured along the horizontal

Table 1A.1

The relation among study time, class attendance, and exam score

	1	2	3
	Study Time (Hours)	***Predicted Score with Perfect Attendance (Percent)***	***Predicted Score When 1/3 of Classes Are Missed (Percent)***
	0	25	5
	1	50	30
Point *A* →	2	70	50
	3	85	65
Point *B* →	4	95	75
	5	100	80

Figure 1A.1

The relation between study time and exam score (perfect attendance assumed)

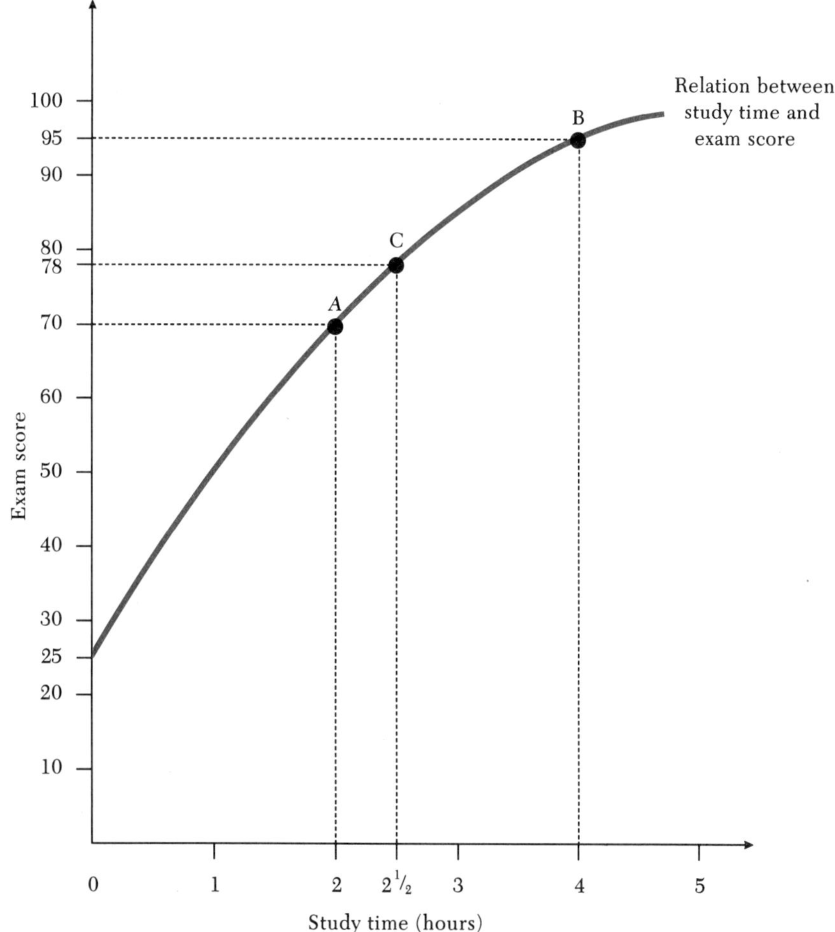

axis and exam score along the vertical. Each combination of study time and exam score can be represented by a point on the graph. For example, the combination of 2 hours of study and the resulting exam score of 70 is labelled point *A*, while the combination of 4 hours of study and the resulting exam score of 95 is labelled point *B*.

The graph actually gives us more information than is contained in the table because the smooth curve enables us to read study time-exam score combinations that are not shown in the table. For example, point *C* on the curve shows that 2-1/2 hours of study results in an exam score of 78.

Handling More Than Two Variables: Movements Versus Shifts

But what about the other variable, class attendance? More generally, how do we handle relations with three or more variables in a graph with only two dimensions? To answer these questions, consider what happens when we vary class attendance by changing our assumption that you attend class regularly. When you miss 1/3 of the class meetings, the relation between your study time and your exam score is no longer given by columns 1 and 2 in Table 1A.1, but by columns 1 and 3. We have plotted this relationship, along with the original one, in Figure 1A.2. As you can see, we get a new curve. The fact that it lies entirely below the original one tells us that the decrease in your class attendance decreases your exam score regardless of how long you study.

We can generalize from this example: *A single curve in a graph shows the relation between the dependent variable and one independent variable; movements along this curve show how the dependent variable changes in response to changes in that independent variable. On the other hand, changes in other independent variables shift the curve to a new position.* This distinction between movements along a curve and shifts in the curve is an important one, and we shall encounter it many times in the chapters that follow.

Slope

As we move from one point to another along a graphic relationship, the ratio of the change in the variable on the vertical axis to the change in the variable on the horizontal axis measures the **slope**. To see this, consider the two relations graphed in Figure 1A.3 on page 24. Part (a) shows a hypothetical relation between the Smith family's income and its expenditures. According to the graph, if the family's income is $35,000 per year, its annual expenditures will be $33,000; if its income rises by $5,000 to $40,000 per year, its expenditures will rise by $4,000 to $37,000 per year. The slope of the line is the ratio of the $4,000 increase in expenditures on the vertical axis to the $5,000 increase in income on the horizontal axis. Its numerical value is 4/5 or 0.8.

Part (b) of the same diagram shows the relation between the price of eggs and the quantity of eggs the Smith family will purchase each month. It shows that if

Figure 1A.2

The effect of a change in class attendance on the relation between study time and exam score

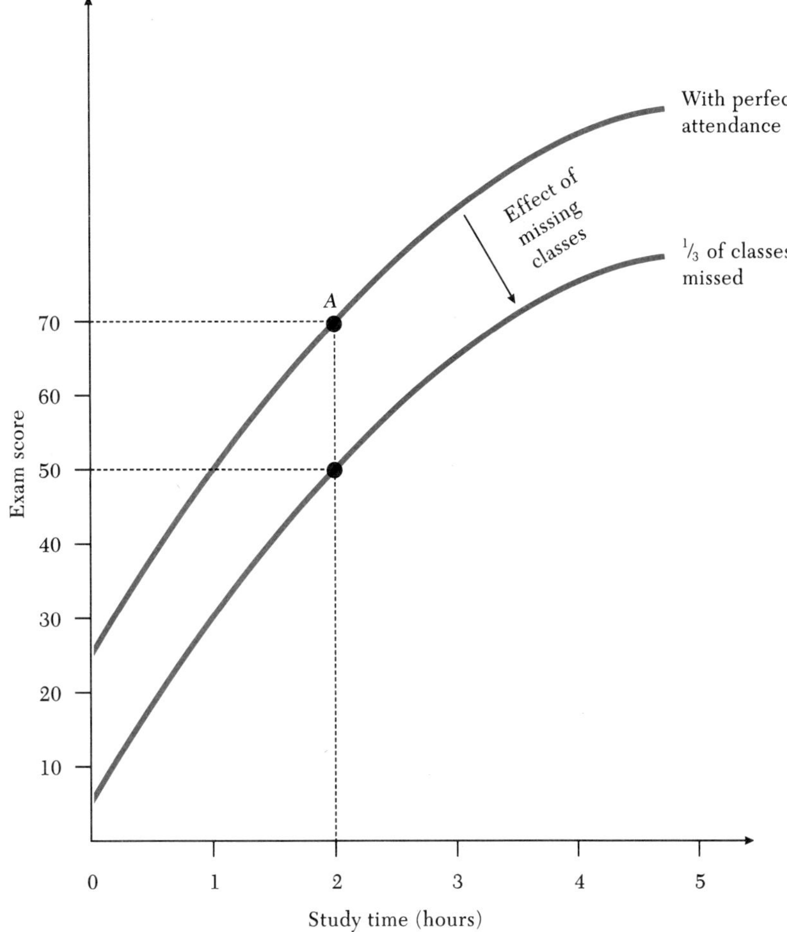

the price of eggs goes up by \$0.40 per dozen, the family's egg purchases will fall by 2 dozen per month. The slope of this line is the ratio of the \$0.40 increase in price to the 2 dozen decrease in quantity purchased, or $+0.40/-2 = -0.2$.

Both of the relationships in Figure 1A.3 are **linear** (straight lines). The slope of a linear relation is constant—that is, the same between any two points on the line. By contrast, slope changes as we move along a **curvilinear** relationship. Such a relationship is shown on page 25 in Figure 1A.4, which relates a factory's daily output rate to the number of workers it employs. Between points *A and B* on the curve, the number of workers rises by 5 (from 10 to 15), and as a result output increases by 20 units per day (from 90 to 110). The slope in that interval is therefore 20/5 = 4. Between points *A* and *C*, the number of workers rises by 10 (from 10 to 20), and output increases by 35 units per day (from 90 to 125).

Figure 1A.3

Calculating slope

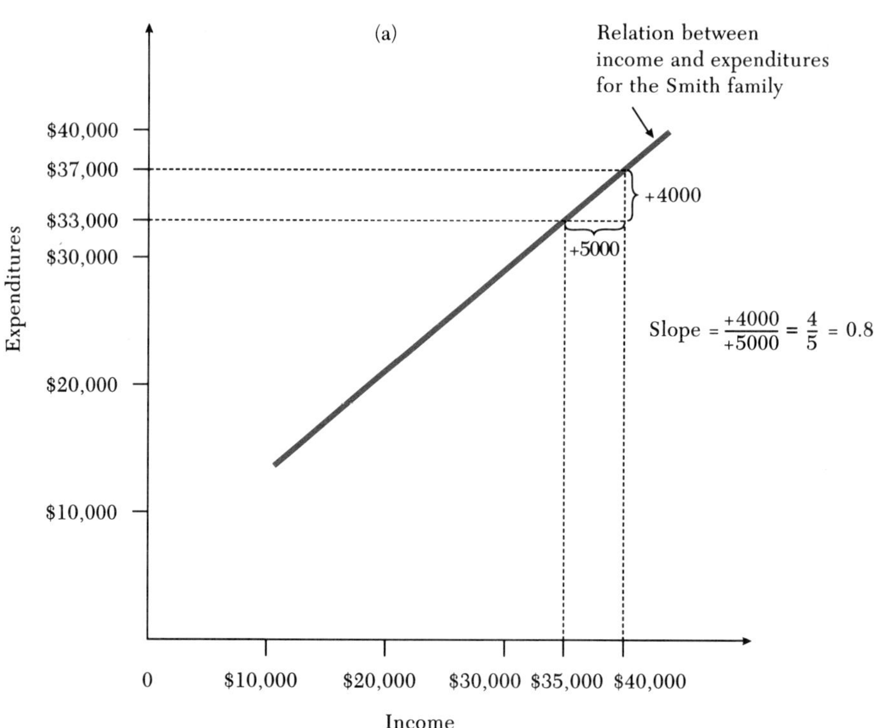

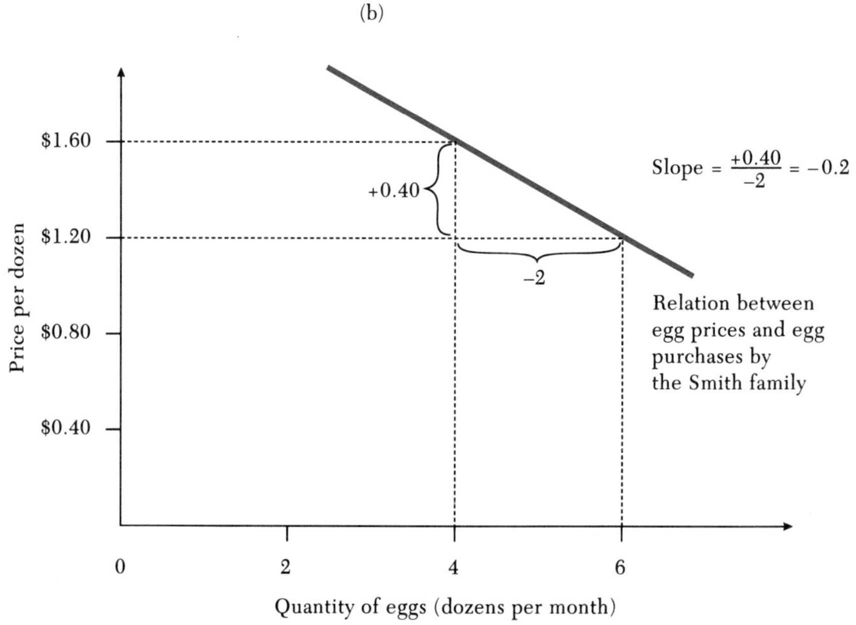

Figure 1A.4

Calculating slope for a curvilinear relationship

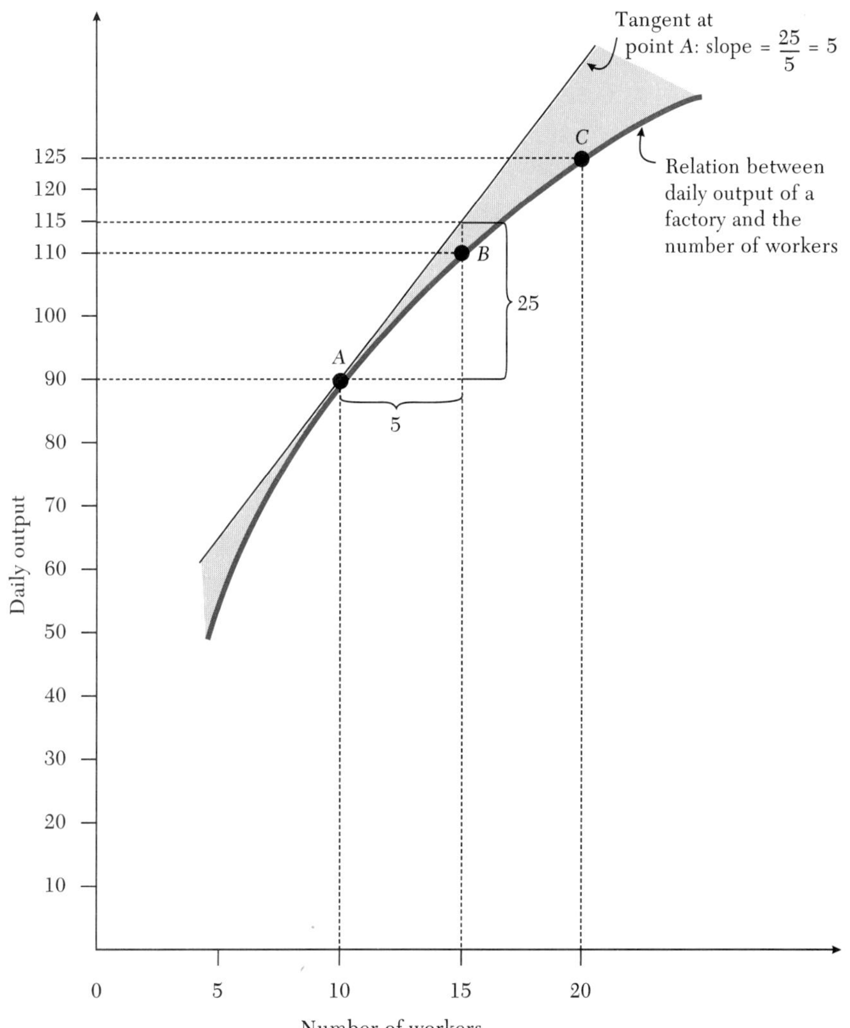

The slope in that interval is 35/10 = 3.5. As this example illustrates, the slope of a curvilinear relationship varies as we move along the curve, and it also depends on the magnitude of the changes in the variables. To avoid the potential confusion this ambiguity might cause, we generally measure the slope of a curvilinear relationship at a given point. To do so we use the slope of its tangent at that point. (The tangent is the straight line that just touches the curve at a single point.) In Figure 1A.4, the slope of the tangent at point A is (115 − 90)/(15 − 10) = 25/5 = 5.

Positive (Direct) Relationships and Negative (Inverse) Relationships

When the relationship between two variables is such that they move in the same direction, rising or falling together, it is said to be a **positive** or **direct relationship**. When the relationship between two variables is such that they move in opposite directions, it is said to be a **negative** or **inverse relationship**. Graphically, a positive (direct) relationship always has a positive slope and a negative (indirect) relationship always has a negative slope. In the foregoing examples, the relationship between your study time and your exam score, between the Smith family's income and its expenditures, and between the factory's output rate and the number of workers were all positive (direct) relationships. The relationship between the price of eggs and the Smith family's monthly egg purchases was a negative (inverse) relationship: When the price of eggs goes up, the quantity of eggs the family purchases goes down, and vice versa.

Areas in Graphs

It is often useful to interpret the *areas* formed by graphed lines and curves. Consider Figure 1A.5, which depicts the same linear relation between the price of eggs and the quantity of eggs purchased by the Smith family that we used in our discussion of slope. We have picked one point on the graph, namely, the Smith family's purchase of 6 dozen eggs per month at the price of $1.20 per dozen, and shaded the rectangular area formed by that point, the origin, and the corresponding points on the two axes. Since the area of a rectangle is equal to its base times its height, and since the height of the shaded rectangle is the price of eggs and the base is the quantity purchased, its area represents the product of

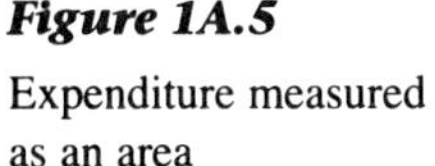

Figure 1A.5
Expenditure measured as an area

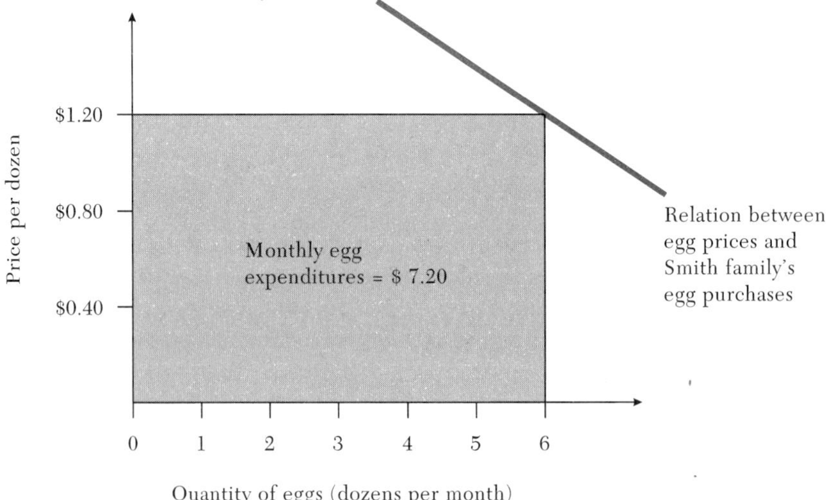

Figure 1A.6

A theoretical graph

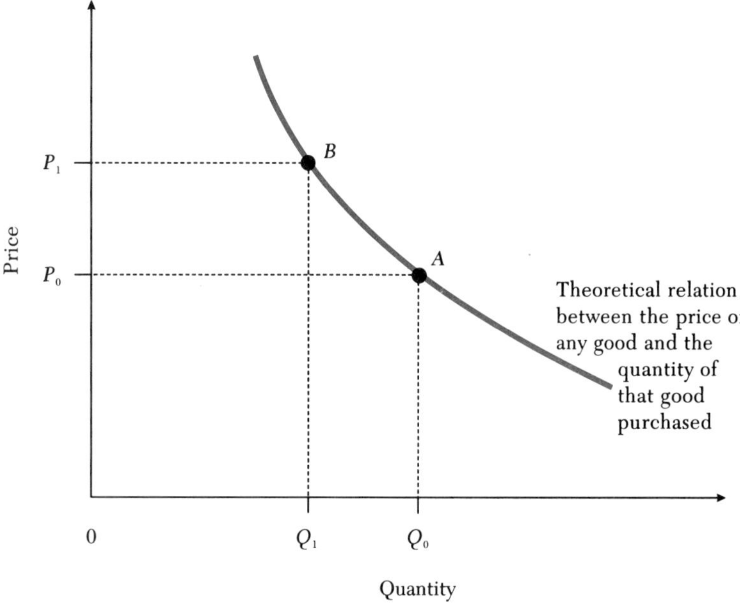

the price of eggs and the quantity purchased per month. This is equal to the Smith family's monthly expenditures on eggs. Specifically, the purchase of 6 dozen eggs per month at a price of \$1.20 per dozen means that the family spends \$7.20 (= 6 × \$1.20) per month on eggs. That amount is represented by the shaded rectangle.

Theoretical Graphs

All of the graphs used in the foregoing examples have used concrete numbers on the axes. Often, however, we use graphs that illustrate theoretical relationships without showing actual numerical values of the variables represented. For example, we might wish to convert the association between egg prices and the Smith family's egg purchases into a more general theoretical relationship that says that the higher the price of any good, the less people will want to purchase. Since this implies an inverse relation between price and quantity purchased, we can represent it by any negatively sloped line such as the one in Figure 1A.6. Although no numerical values are given on either of the axes, the graph's labels do tell us that at price P_0 people will want to purchase Q_0 units of the good, while at a higher price, P_1, they will want to purchase only Q_1 units. Moreover, at the price P_0, total expenditures on the good can be represented by the area of the rectangle whose height is equal to distance OP_0 and whose base is equal to distance OQ_0. Since the four corners of this rectangle are the points labelled O (the origin), P_0, A, and Q_0, we shall refer to it as rectangle OP_0AQ_0.

CHAPTER 2

Specialization, Exchange, and Transactions Costs: The Fundamentals of Economic Organization

It is not from the benevolence of the butcher, the brewer, or the baker that we expect our dinner, but from their regard for their own interest.

ADAM SMITH*

Think for a moment about the immense variety of goods you and your family regularly consume: the myriad different foods you eat in a week; the closet full of clothes you choose from every morning; the house, apartment, or dorm room in which you live, along with all its furnishings and appliances; your many sources of entertainment, transportation, medical, dental and personal care.

How many of these goods and services do you literally produce for yourself? If you are at all typical, your answer is: very, very few. Oh sure, you cook some of your own meals, maybe wash your own car now and then, perhaps even change its oil yourself. But for the most part you rely on the productive efforts of literally millions of other people for the vast majority of the goods you consume. Of course, those people do not provide you with all those goodies for free;

* *The Wealth of Nations* (Modern Library ed., 1937), p. 14.

they expect to be paid. And where do you get the money with which to pay them? You get it in exchange for the productive services you (or your family) provide in a process that ultimately produces the goods which they in turn wish to consume. In a nutshell, therefore, the activity that takes place in an economic system involves an elaborate network in which millions of people are continuously exchanging their productive services (through the medium of money) for the goods they desire as consumers.

In subsequent chapters we shall see how the market organizes and coordinates all of this activity and in the process "solves" the economic problems we introduced in Chapter 1. In this chapter we lay the foundations for that analysis by exploring some of the fundamental elements that drive the incredibly complex system of production and exchange we have been describing. So that the logic of the analysis is not lost amid a clutter of detail, we consider a very simple economy in which there are only two persons, whom we call Jack and Jill, and two goods, bread and beer. Both Jack and Jill produce and consume each good, but they differ in their abilities as producers and in their subjective tastes as consumers. These differences provide the basis for much of our analysis.

COMPARATIVE ADVANTAGE, SPECIALIZATION, AND EXCHANGE

Jack and Jill can utilize their time and other resources to produce bread, beer, or various combinations of both. Some of the possible output combinations that each can produce per week are shown in Table 2.1 and plotted in Figure 2.1 on page 30. We have assumed that Jill has more productive resources than Jack and is therefore more productive in absolute terms. This is reflected in both the table and the diagram, which show that Jill can produce more bread, more beer, or combinations with more of both goods than Jack.

In addition to the difference in absolute productivity, Jack and Jill also have different relative, or *comparative*, abilities, as reflected in the different production trade-offs with which they are confronted. As Table 2.1 shows, Jack must reduce his bread production by 5 loaves for each additional bottle of beer that he produces, while the corresponding trade-off for Jill is 3 loaves of bread per bottle of beer.

These trade-offs determine opportunity costs. Specifically, the *marginal cost* of 1 bottle of beer is 5 loaves of bread if produced by Jack and 3 loaves of bread if produced by Jill. Conversely, the marginal cost of each additional loaf of bread is 1/5 of a bottle of beer if produced by Jack and 1/3 of a bottle of beer if produced by Jill. We say that the lower marginal cost producer of a good has a **comparative advantage** in its production. Accordingly, in our two-person economy Jack has a comparative advantage in the production of bread and Jill has a comparative advantage in the production of beer.

Comparative advantage is the efficiency advantage enjoyed by the lowest marginal cost provider of a good or productive service.

Table 2.1

Possible production combinations

JACK		JILL	
Bread (Loaves/Week)	***Beer (Bottles/Week)***	***Bread (Loaves/Week)***	***Beer (Bottles/Week)***
15	0	18	0
10	1	15	1
5	2	12	2
0	3	9	3
		6	4
		3	5
		0	6

Figure 2.1

Output combinations for Jack and Jill

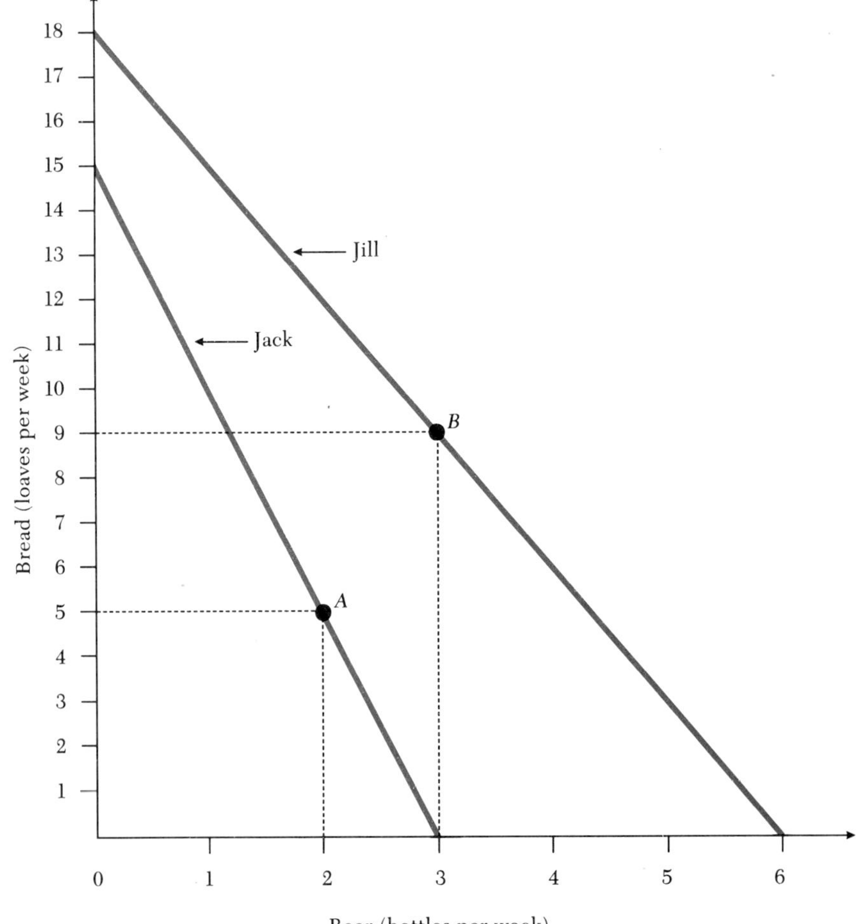

Table 2.2

Comparative advantage at work

	1 INITIAL OUTPUT		2 OUTPUT CHANGES		3 FINAL OUTPUT	
	Bread	***Beer***	***Bread***	***Beer***	***Bread***	***Beer***
Jack	5	2	+5	−1	10	1
Jill	9	3	−3	+1	6	4
Total	14	5	+2	0	16	5

The Law of Comparative Advantage

Suppose we start from an initial situation in which Jack and Jill each produce a mix of both beer and bread. In particular, suppose Jack initially produces a combination of 5 loaves of bread and 2 bottles of beer per week, and Jill produces a combination of 9 loaves of bread and 3 bottles of beer. These combinations are represented by points *A* and *B* in Figure 2.1 and are shown under Initial Output in Table 2.2. If they start from these initial output combinations, Jack and Jill can increase total output if each produces more of the good in which (s)he has a comparative advantage and less of the other good. If, for example, Jack produces 5 more loaves of bread, 1 bottle of beer is lost; but Jill can more than compensate by producing 1 more bottle of beer at a cost of only 3 loaves of bread. The result, shown under Output Changes Table 2.2, is a net increase in total output of 2 loaves of bread.*

The **law of comparative advantage** says that the total output available from a given amount of resources increases when they are used according to their comparative advantages.

This example illustrates a very famous proposition known as the **law of comparative advantage**. The law says that total output increases when resources—in the foregoing example, Jack's and Jill's resources—are used according to their comparative advantages.

The law of comparative advantage has many applications in economics, but its fundamental message is the same in every context: Organizing production according to comparative advantage makes more goods available from our limited productive resources.

*We could just as well have used comparative advantage to increase bread output or, for that matter, the output of both goods simultaneously. For example, maintaining the 5-to-1 trade-off for Jack and the 3-to-1 trade-off for Jill, reorganize production as follows:

	Change in Bread Output	***Change in Beer Output***
Jack	+2.5 loaves	−0.5 bottles
Jill	−2.1 loaves	+0.7 bottles
Net	+0.4 loaves	+0.2 bottles

For the purpose of illustration, the example here allows us to deal in whole numbers and keeps things simpler.

Figure 2.2

Production possibilities curve for Jack and Jill

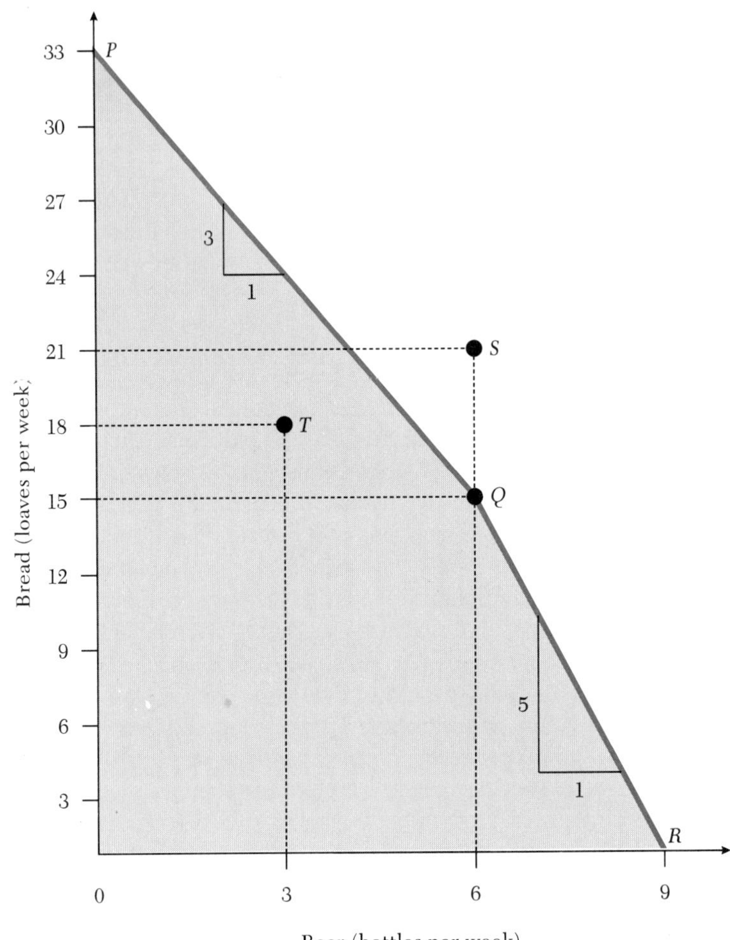

Production Possibilities

Now consider the various combinations of bread and beer that Jack and Jill can produce if they combine their resources in a manner consistent with the law of comparative advantage.

If all of their resources are devoted to bread production, Jack can produce 15 loaves and Jill 18 for a total of 33 loaves. If they produce only beer, they can produce a total of 9 bottles (3 by Jack and 6 by Jill). These bread-only and beer-only total outputs are labelled points *P* and *R* on the respective axes of Figure 2.2.

Now suppose that starting from point *P* where they produce only bread, Jack and Jill decide they would like to wash down their bread with a bottle of beer. If that bottle of beer is to be produced with the smallest possible sacrifice of bread, it must be produced by Jill because she has the comparative advantage in beer

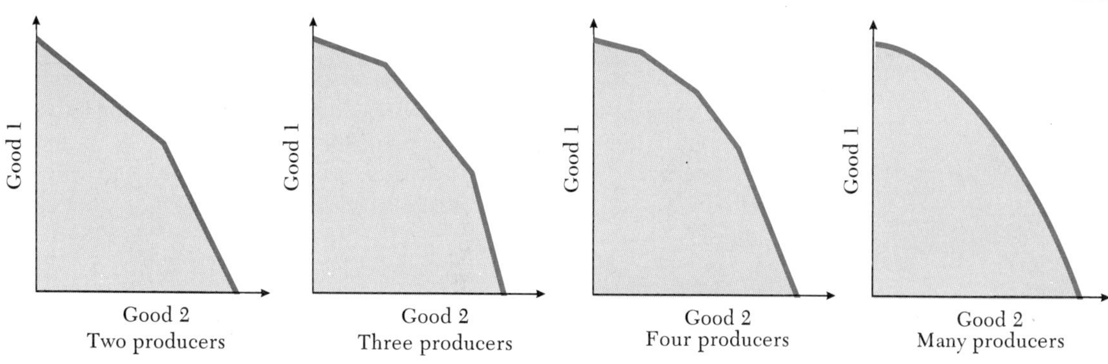

Figure 2.3

Production possibilities curves

production. In fact, any beer up to Jill's maximum output of 6 bottles per week should be produced by Jill, while Jack specializes in bread production in accordance with his comparative advantage. Increasing beer output from nothing up to 6 bottles thus moves us along line segment *PQ* in Figure 2.2. The −3 slope of that line segment reflects the fact that each additional bottle of beer has a marginal cost of 3 loaves of bread when it is produced by Jill.

If more than 6 bottles of beer are to be produced, they must be produced by Jack at a marginal cost of 5 loaves of bread per bottle. That would move us along line segment *QR* (whose slope of −5 reflects the higher marginal cost) until we reach point *R*, where both Jack and Jill are producing only beer and where the total output is 9 bottles of beer per week.

The **production possibilities curve (PPC)** shows the various combinations of two goods that can be produced when resources are used fully and efficiently.

Figure 2.2 is called a **production possibilities curve**, or *PPC* for short. It shows the output combinations that can be produced when productive resources are used fully and efficiently—that is, according to their comparative advantages.

Points outside the production possibilities curve, such as *S*, are unattainable given the available resources and existing technology. (To satisfy yourself that this is true, try to come up with a combination of Jack's and Jill's outputs that gives the total output shown by point *S*. You will find it impossible.) In this sense, the PPC represents an output *frontier* beyond which our economy cannot operate. Although this frontier is fixed at any given time, it can shift outward over time to encompass points like *S* if investment makes more productive resources available or if technological progress allows Jack and Jill to squeeze more output from the same resources. Points inside the PPC represent output combinations associated with inefficient resource use. For example, if we were to ignore comparative advantage and have Jack produce only beer and Jill only bread, we would end up at point *T* inside the PPC frontier.

As we move from this simple case of two producers to the more realistic case of many producers, the kinks in the PPC (such as the one at point *Q* in Figure 2.2) become more and more numerous and the PPC tends to smooth out as illustrated in Figure 2.3. However, the characteristic convex (bowed out) shape of the curve, which implies that the more of a good produced the higher its marginal cost, remains.

Subjective Tastes and Production Choices under Autarky

The production possibilities curve shows the output combinations that *can* be produced with efficient use of our limited resources and available technology; it does not tell us anything about which combination *will* be produced, or about how such a determination is made. The output mix that is actually chosen will depend not only on the objective abilities of Jack and Jill as producers but also on their subjective tastes as consumers.

To illustrate the relationship between tastes and abilities, let us first consider a world in which Jack and Jill are entirely self-sufficient, each producing only for his or her own consumption. The term used to describe such self-sufficiency is *autarky*. Although literal autarky is virtually nonexistent in reality, it provides a useful starting point for our analysis.

We assume that Jack's subjective tastes are such that he would be willing to exchange bread and beer at the rate of 6 loaves of bread for 1 bottle of beer. We can say that the **marginal value** of beer to Jack is 6 loaves of bread: He is willing to give up *at most* 6 loaves of bread to get 1 additional bottle of beer, and he would require *at least* 6 loaves of bread to willingly part with 1 bottle of beer.*

Marginal value is the subjective value of one more unit of a good to some individual.

Jill's subjective tastes, like her productive abilities, differ from Jack's. In particular, the marginal value of beer to Jill is 2 loaves of bread. She is willing to exchange bread and beer at the rate of 2 loaves of bread for 1 bottle of beer.

The combination of their abilities as producers and tastes as consumers allows Jack and Jill each to benefit from an independent change in production and consumption. As a consumer, Jack is willing to give up 6 loaves of bread in return for 1 bottle of beer, but his abilities as a producer enable him to do better than that. He need only reduce his bread production by 5 loaves to produce another bottle of beer. In other words, the marginal value of an additional bottle of beer exceeds its marginal cost when he produces it himself.

Just the opposite is true for Jill. She is willing to give up 1 bottle of beer if she can get at least 2 loaves of bread in return, but as a producer she can obtain 3 more loaves of bread if she reduces her beer production by 1 bottle. She can therefore come out ahead by producing more bread for herself.

Specialization and Exchange

The foregoing example illustrates why people often produce goods for their own consumption: why, for example, some people grow their own vegetables, make their own car repairs, and in a few cases even build their own houses. Whenever the value of the goods produced exceeds the opportunity cost of the producer's own time, effort, and other resources, self-production can provide a means of improving one's economic welfare. As we noted at the outset, however, although we all rely on our own productive activities to satisfy some wants, we are by no

*Alternatively, we could say that the marginal value of a loaf of bread to Jack is 1/6 of a bottle of beer. However, since it is easier to deal with whole numbers, we confine ourselves to dealing with bread values of beer.

Table 2.3

Autarky at work

	1 INITIAL OUTPUT		2 OUTPUT CHANGES		3 FINAL OUTPUT	
	Bread	***Beer***	***Bread***	***Beer***	***Bread***	***Beer***
Jack	5	2	−5	+1	0	3
Jill	9	3	+3	−1	12	2
Total	14	5	−2	0	12	5

means self-sufficient. Even in those areas in which we do rely heavily on our own production—in cooking a meal, for example—we invariably utilize many resources supplied to us by others. A closer look at the preceding autarky example provides a clue as to why this is so.

Although leaving both parties better off, Table 2.3 shows that the proposed changes in Jack's and Jill's production also reduce total output because the changes are just the opposite of those dictated by the law of comparative advantage. Though not a logical necessity in the two-person, two-good world of Jack and Jill, it is almost inevitable as a practical matter that any significant degree of autarky in the real world would entail the sacrifice of many of the potential benefits of comparative advantage. To produce for ourselves even a small fraction of the goods we consume would require that we produce most of them at a comparative *dis*advantage relative to other, less costly, producers.

Our autarky example illustrates an important point, however. Even though Jack and Jill can increase total output by following their respective comparative advantages, that alone does not guarantee an improvement in their economic welfare. In fact, just the reverse is true. Although comparative advantage requires that Jack reduce his beer production by 1 bottle to produce 5 more loaves of bread, his subjective tastes demand at least 6 additional loaves of bread to compensate him for the loss of that bottle of beer. And although comparative advantage requires that Jill incur a cost of 3 loaves of bread to produce another bottle of beer, its personal marginal value to her is only 2 loaves of bread. Given our assumptions about their subjective tastes, simply following their comparative advantages would leave both Jack and Jill worse off despite the fact that it leads to greater total output!

Exchange means the voluntary giving of one thing in return for another.

The missing link in our example, the element that allows individuals to reap the full benefits of their comparative advantages in production, is trade, or **exchange**. The introduction of exchange takes us out of the realm of autarky and brings us into an economic environment that more closely resembles our own. Most of us find it advantageous to follow our comparative advantages as producers—thus concentrating our productive efforts in one or a few areas—but only because we can exchange the fruits of that specialization for the many goods we desire as consumers. Because opportunities for exchange allow the larger total output made possible by comparative advantage to be reallocated in a manner

Table 2.4

Specialization and exchange

	1 INITIAL OUTPUT		2 OUTPUT AFTER SPECIALIZATION		3 FINAL DISTRIBUTION	
	Bread	***Beer***	***Bread***	***Beer***	***Bread***	***Beer***
Jack	5	2	15	0	3	3
Jill	9	3	0	6	12	3
Total	14	5	15	6	15	6

consistent with people's tastes, specialization and exchange go hand-in-hand in the organization of any economic system.

Table 2.4 illustrates the benefits of combining specialization and exchange in our simple two-person, two-good world. The Initial Output combinations are the same as in our autarky example in Table 2.3. If Jack and Jill specialize according to their respective comparative advantages, the result is a total output of 15 loaves of bread and 6 bottles of beer. After specialization, Jack and Jill can work out a mutually beneficial exchange. For example, Jill might offer to trade Jack a bottle of beer in return for 4 loaves of bread, an exchange that would more than compensate her for the value she places on the beer (and covers her cost of production as well). If Jack can obtain a bottle of beer, which he values at 6 loaves of bread, for only 4 loaves of bread in trade with Jill, he would be foolish to produce it himself at a cost of 5 loaves. Both would therefore benefit from exchange at the 4-bread-for-1-beer trading ratio. (As you can probably see, any trading ratio between 5-for-1 and 3-for-1 would work. Anything more than 5-for-1 would lead Jack to produce beer for himself rather than trade for it; anything less than 3-for-1 would lead Jill to produce additional bread herself rather than trade for it.)

To conclude our comparison with autarky, suppose three trades are made at the 4-for-1 ratio, Jack thereby giving up a total of 12 loaves of bread to Jill in return for 3 bottles of beer. The last two columns of Table 2.4 show the resulting distribution of output. A comparison with the final output combinations in the autarky example in Table 2.3 shows clearly that the combination of specialization and exchange is preferable for both parties. Jack ends up with the same amount of beer, but 3 loaves of bread rather than none, whereas Jill ends up with same amount of bread, but 3 bottles of beer rather than 2.

Relations between Specialization and Exchange

The amount and variety of goods available to each of us as consumers are a direct consequence of combining specialization and exchange. Without exchange, each of us would have to be a "jack (or jill?) of all trades" just to satisfy even a small portion of our wants. As a result, the potential gains from comparative advantage would be lost. With exchange, however, people can specialize in those relatively few things they do best as producers and trade the fruits of that specialization for the great variety of goods they value as consumers. In reality, a baker trades his bread not just for beer but for shelter, clothing, entertainment, medical care, and the numerous other goods he values as a consumer but which he has no comparative advantage in producing.

When exchange is possible, rational self-interest automatically provides each individual with an incentive to find and pursue his own comparative advantage. No one need gather information about the talents and capacities of various individuals and assign each to the tasks for which he is best suited. Each person will find it in his own interest to find and pursue those productive activities in which he or she is relatively most efficient because the payoffs that result—payoffs that can be exchanged for those things that he or she wants most to consume—will be maximized. Economics predicts, in the absence of restrictions on individual choice, therefore, that people will be drawn into productive endeavors in a manner broadly consistent with their comparative advantages.

A more subtle, but at least as important, effect of specialization and exchange is that together they enable us to economize tremendously on knowledge and information. Imagine how much you would have to know to do even the simplest things for yourself. Do you know how to make bread? Really make it from start to finish? Do you know how to grow the wheat that goes into bread? To mill that wheat into flour? To mine, refine, and shape the metal that goes into the baking pan? To design and build an oven that achieves and maintains just the right temperature for baking bread? Of course you don't! None of us possesses even the tiniest fraction of the knowledge that goes into the simplest commodities we consume, let alone such modern technological marvels as our cars, cameras, and computers. *Exchange permits us to purchase that knowledge already embodied in the goods we buy.* When we buy a loaf of bread at the grocery store, for example, we are buying not just the physical commodity but also the knowledge of thousands of specialists—wheat farmers, millers, bakers, metallurgists, engineers, and on and on—whose efforts directly and indirectly got it there. Without specialization and exchange, the incredible variety and complexity of the products we take for granted would be literally unthinkable.

Subjective Values and the Gains from Trade

Recall that the value of a good is determined not by some intrinsic property of that good but rather by the subjective value someone places on it. The particular someone who determines that value is the one who possesses the good. When a bottle of beer is traded from Jill, who values it at only 2 loaves of bread, to Jack, who values it at 6 loaves of bread, it literally increases in value by 4 loaves of bread. This 4 loaves of bread, which reflects the difference between the marginal values they place on beer, is a measure of the *gains from trade* when Jill trades a bottle of beer to Jack.

With the 4-for-1 exchange ratio we used in the preceding examples, the gains from trade were divided equally between Jack and Jill. In giving up 4 loaves of bread to get a bottle of beer he values at 6 loaves of bread, Jack gains the equivalent of 2 loaves of bread. When Jill obtains 4 loaves of bread for a bottle of beer she values at only 2 loaves of bread, she also gains the equivalent of 2 loaves of bread. The total gains from trade resulting from the exchange are therefore equal to 4 loaves of bread.

With a different exchange ratio, the total gains would remain the same but they would be divided differently between the two traders. If, for example, the bread price of beer were 5 loaves, then Jack's gain would be 1 loaf of bread on each bottle of beer traded (which is the same as if he produced it himself) and Jill's would be 3 loaves. Clearly, Jill, as the seller of beer, would prefer the higher price, while Jack, as the buyer, would prefer a lower price; but whatever price they settle on, both benefit from trade.

TRANSACTIONS COSTS AND MIDDLEMEN

Transactions costs are costs that arise in the process of exchange.

Exchange is not always simple and straightforward. There are often **transactions costs** that must be overcome if trade is to take place. The need to transport goods between traders is a fairly obvious source of transactions costs. The *information, negotiations*, and *enforcement* that some exchanges require are less apparent sources of transactions costs but can be just as important.

Information costs are the costs of acquiring information useful in exchange.

Information costs exist when the characteristics of the goods to be exchanged, or of one or the other of the parties to the exchange, are unknown. To make an intelligent purchase, for example, you often have to devote time and other resources to gathering information about the quality, reliability, and other characteristics of various goods and about the prices charged and services offered by various sellers. For some goods, a simple inspection may provide you with all the information you need. To tell whether the banana you are about to buy is ripe, for example, all you have to do is look at its color. For other goods, however—customized computer systems, used cars, and medical care come to mind—the cost of acquiring useful and accurate information may be considerably higher. Information about the seller, in addition to information about the good itself, can be particularly important when such things as after-sale service and technical support are important. If you know the seller's reputation, that alone may provide you with all of the information you need. In some cases, however, you may have to do considerable shopping around to determine which seller supplies the particular mix of services you want.

Sellers can also incur information costs. When you buy goods on credit, for example, the seller must obtain information about your income, credit record, and other debts to determine whether you are likely to meet your future payment obligations.

Negotiation costs are the costs of negotiating the terms of an exchange.

Negotiation costs include the costs of arriving at an agreement on price and other terms of the exchange. Like information costs, negotiation costs are negligible in some transactions. You don't walk up to the supermarket clerk and negotiate the price of a loaf of bread, for example. By contrast, some exchanges require formal contracts that explicitly spell out the rights and duties of the parties involved. For example, if you hire a building contractor to build a house, you (and the contractor) would be well advised to draw up a contract that not only includes such obvious details as price, number of square feet, and expected date of completion, but also specifies how various unforeseen contingencies, such as bad weather, a carpenter's strike, or a fire that destroys your half-completed house, would be handled. Negotiating a myriad of contractual provisions like these can be a costly process, often requiring the services of lawyers and other third parties as well as the primary parties to the exchange.

Enforcement costs are the costs of enforcing the terms of an exchange.

Finally, once an agreement is reached, it may be necessary to incur **enforcement costs** to insure that commitments are met. Some transactions create incentives for opportunistic, or even fraudulent, behavior on the part of one or the other of the parties involved. For example, what if the building contractor you hire to build your house takes your initial down payment and skips town? Some of the costs of preventing such behavior are borne by government agencies that enforce laws against fraud and theft. Other enforcement costs must be borne by the parties to the exchange. Alarm systems, door locks, insurance policies, guard dogs, and private security police are all examples of costly ways of protecting the property we obtain in transactions.

Transactions Costs in the Simple Exchange Model

To analyze some of the implications of transactions costs, let us return to our two-good economy. So that we may focus our attention on the role of transactions costs in exchange, however, we now use only Jack's and Jill's subjective marginal values and ignore their abilities as producers. Furthermore, we assume that the source of the transactions cost in this pure exchange economy is a language barrier: Jack speaks only English and Jill speaks only French. It is therefore difficult for them to communicate with one another, and if they cannot communicate, they cannot trade. What can be done to make trade possible?

One possibility is for either Jack or Jill to learn the other's language. Learning a language is costly but would be worth it if those costs do not exceed the potential gains from trade. (Why else do Japanese and American businesspeople learn one another's language?) However, there may be another, less costly, option. Suppose there is a third party—call him Max—who already speaks both English and French and can therefore translate for Jack and Jill. His comparative advantage in language translation makes him an ideal middleman, or *intermediary*, through whom Jack and Jill can lower transactions costs.

Having agreed to serve as translator, Max proposes the following: He offers (in English) to sell Jack 1 bottle of beer for 5 loaves of bread, and he offers (in

French) to pay Jill 3 loaves of bread for 1 bottle of beer. Since Jack is willing to pay 6 loaves of bread for a bottle of beer, and Jill is willing to accept 2 loaves of bread for a bottle of beer, both feel that Max has presented them with an attractive offer and both therefore accept. Max thus takes the 5 loaves of bread from Jack, hands 3 of them to Jill in return for a bottle of beer which he then hands to Jack, keeping 2 loaves of bread for himself.

Seeing Max walk off with 2 loaves of bread, Jack and Jill might feel that he has exploited them. But Max can point out that he has just enabled Jack and Jill to work out a trade that would have been even more costly, perhaps impossible, without his services. Furthermore, he might point out that his time and talents have an opportunity cost for which he expects compensation if he is to perform that service. Max has "exploited" Jack's and Jill's ignorance of one another's language only in the same sense that a doctor "exploits" his patients' ignorance of medicine. They have the choice of "cutting out the middleman" and presumably would do so if they could perform Max's services at a lower cost than the 2 loaves of bread he charges them. If, however, he has a comparative advantage in overcoming the language barrier, then all parties, Jack and Jill included, come out ahead by using his services.

The Ubiquitous Middleman

Direct transactions between final consumers and the primary suppliers of productive services are the exception rather than the rule in all modern economies. Virtually all trade utilizes the services of intermediaries in the process by which goods ultimately find their way from resource suppliers to final consumers.

Intermediaries appear in a variety of forms. Stockbrokers, real estate agents, used car dealers, and building contractors are fairly obvious examples. So are ticket "scalpers." All sorts of retail sellers also qualify. Supermarkets are intermediaries between farmers, ranchers, dairymen, and other producers of primary food products and the consumers of food. Department stores, by stocking their shelves with various brands of clothing, appliances, housewares, and so on, and by providing information and other point-of-sale services, act as intermediaries between the manufacturers of these goods and final consumers. In financial markets, banks and other so-called "financial intermediaries" provide the link between lenders (savers) and borrowers. Indeed, in a fundamental sense, every business firm is an intermediary specializing in bringing productive resources together, coordinating their activities, and turning out a final product. Without firms, consumers would have to deal separately and directly with individual workers, owners of raw materials, suppliers of financial capital, and so forth to obtain the goods they desire. Imagine how much more costly it would be for you to obtain a consumer good—even a simple one like a loaf of bread, let alone something like your car or stereo—in a world without business firms.

Of course, like Max, business firms and other intermediaries do not perform their services for free; their costs must be covered in the prices that they charge. However, they could not continue to exist if the agents they link together were willing to do without their services—or could provide those services themselves at lower cost.

Open Markets and Competition

An **open market** is a market in which anyone is free to compete.

Returning to our simple economy, suppose that the 2 loaves of bread Max charges for his services more than cover his cost so that he is making a profit. If language translation is an **open market** in which anyone is free to compete, Max's profits will attract competitors. To examine some of the implications of this, let us assume that a translator named Milly arrives on the scene and attempts to capture the market from Max. Milly offers to sell beer to Jack for 4.5 loaves of bread per bottle and to buy it from Jill for 3.5 loaves per bottle. By offering better terms to Jack and Jill—and thus taking a smaller cut of only 1 loaf of bread for herself—Milly could capture the translation business from Max.

Of course, nothing prevents Max from responding to Milly's competition. For example, he might counter by offering to buy beer for 3.75 loaves of bread per bottle, and to sell it for 4.25 loaves per bottle, thus reducing his cut to only 0.5 loaf of bread per transaction.

As competition between Max and Milly continues, the gap between the buying and selling price for beer narrows and the middleman's profits shrink. This is clearly beneficial to both Jack and Jill, but their benefits are ultimately limited by the fact that any intermediary must cover its opportunity cost. If the cost to Milly of providing the translation service is less than 0.5 loaf of bread per transaction, she can retaliate by further undercutting Max and still cover her costs. If Max's costs are even lower, he would have an incentive to further undercut Milly. Ultimately, only the lowest cost translator will be left serving the market and all of the cost savings will have been passed on to Jack and Jill in the form of lower prices for what they buy and higher prices for what they sell. So it is in reality. Competition benefits the ultimate parties to an exchange—the sellers of productive services and buyers of consumer goods—while at the same time squeezing the profits of business firms and other intermediaries.

Cartels

Although competition is in the interest of both Jack and Jill, Max and Milly could gain from its elimination. Because it reduces their profit to zero, each has an incentive to eliminate or suppress that competition. For example, Max might threaten Milly with violence if she tries to cut in on his turf. Although illegal, this technique is used by organized crime to protect its profitable markets from competition.

Collusion means agreeing not to compete.

Alternatively, Max might convince Milly that they would both be much better off **colluding** rather than competing. They might, for example, both agree to buy beer from Jill for a price she will just barely accept—say, 2.1 loaves of bread per bottle—and sell it to Jack for a price he will just barely accept—say 5.9 loaves of bread per bottle. Then they could split the 3.8 loaves difference, leaving both better off than they were when they were competing.

A **cartel** is an association formed to limit or eliminate competition among its members.

Max and Milly's collusive agreement is an example of a **cartel**. Although Max and Milly both profit from the cartel, Jack and Jill are worse off because their total gains from trade, net of the middleman's take, are less when they deal with the cartel than when they dealt with competitive intermediaries. Their incentives as producers are also negatively affected. Jill's incentive to produce beer is reduced because the cartel is paying her a lower price for each additional bottle she produces; Jack's incentive to produce bread is reduced because at the cartel's prices he can buy less beer with each loaf of bread he produces. Total production and trade might thus be reduced as a result of the cartel.

Cartels are generally illegal in the United States. In many other countries cartels are legal for some purposes—for example, among firms producing goods for export. In the international arena, cartels like the Organization of Petroleum Exporting Countries (OPEC) are effectively beyond the authority of law. Even in the absence of legal restrictions on collusion, however, the Max–Milly translators' cartel could run into difficulties. Max and Milly are probably not the only people who speak both French and English, and to prevent other translators from undercutting the cartel and capturing its market, Max and Milly would have to either compete with them or accept them into the cartel. The first option defeats the entire purpose of the cartel, and the second means splitting its profits into a larger number of smaller shares.

Moreover, the cartel's potential competition is not restricted to those who are already bilingual. Other parties, seeing the profits to be made in the French-English translation business, might decide to learn both languages. Each time another competitor appears, the cartel faces the same dilemma: either compete with the newcomer or allow him to join the cartel, further diluting its profitability.

The point is that if a cartel is to succeed for any length of time, it must be able to block new competition. Even in the case of OPEC, a cartel that once controlled virtually all of a truly vital natural resource, time and ingenuity have led to the emergence of more and more competition. In response to the extraordinarily high world oil prices of the 1970s, U.S. oil companies found it profitable to go to the north slope of Alaska for oil, while Britain found it profitable to extract oil from the North Sea. Investment in a search for new deposits of oil paid off for Mexico and other non-OPEC countries whose known reserves increased many fold. Other competition took the form of less direct substitutes for OPEC oil. These included everything from more efficient automobiles and insulated houses to the development of nuclear power—all of which were motivated to some extent by the high prices charged by the cartel. By the middle 1980s, a combination of internal bickering and external competition had virtually destroyed the once powerful OPEC cartel.

Money, Barter, and Transactions Costs

The economy that we have thus far been describing is an example of a *barter economy*, that is, one in which goods are traded directly for goods without the intervening use of money. Virtually all real-world economies, however, are *money economies*. As a generally acceptable means of payment—a common *medium of exchange*—money makes possible a substantial reduction in transactions costs. It does so by eliminating the "double coincidence of wants" as a prerequisite for mutually beneficial exchange. For example, if a plumber in a barter economy wants a steak for dinner, he has to find a butcher who needs his plumbing fixed. If the butcher doesn't need plumbing repairs but does want his car repaired, the two of them could search for an auto mechanic with a plumbing problem to work out a three-way exchange. The plumber could fix the mechanic's plumbing, the mechanic could repair the butcher's car, and the butcher could give the plumber 20 pounds of steak. As you can imagine, there is a pretty good chance the plumber wouldn't get his steak in time for dinner.

In a money economy, by contrast, the plumber just finds a butcher—any butcher will do—and pays him with money. Whether that butcher wants his plumbing fixed is of no concern. With money as a common medium of exchange, the butcher can simply use it to buy whatever he wants. Money therefore greatly reduces transaction costs, facilitates exchange, and permits much greater specialization than would be possible in a barter economy.

Relative Prices and Nominal Prices

Absolute (nominal) prices are prices expressed in money terms.

Relative (real) prices are the trading ratios between goods.

In a money economy, prices are quoted in monetary units like U.S. dollars, Japanese yen, or British pounds sterling. What is important in production decisions and in exchange relationships, however, is not the monetary amounts—the **absolute** or **nominal prices**—but the real exchange ratios between goods. These exchange ratios reflect the **relative** or **real prices** of goods. For example, if the nominal price of a loaf of bread is $1.00 and the nominal price of a bottle of beer is $0.50, the relative prices are such that 1 loaf of bread is equivalent in value to 2 bottles of beer. It is not the dollar amounts themselves, but the 2-for-1 exchange ratio that measures the real opportunity cost of purchasing one or the other of those goods.

Note that nominal prices can change without any effect on relative prices. For example, a proportional 50 percent increase in the nominal prices of bread and beer to $1.50 and $0.75, respectively, leaves their relative prices unchanged. When all, or nearly all, nominal prices increase together, the result is *inflation* in the general price level. As the preceding discussion suggests, it is logically possible (although unlikely) for inflation to raise the general level of money prices without effecting relative prices.

SOME NORMATIVE CONSIDERATIONS

So far we have used our simple model to address only questions of positive economics. Why, for example, does exchange take place? What is the connection between exchange and specialization? Why are intermediaries so prevalent?

But what about normative evaluation? Is it "good" that comparative advantage raises total output? Is exchange a "desirable" activity? Should competition be promoted and cartels discouraged?

It is important to reemphasize that answers to normative questions like these ultimately rest on fundamental value judgments, which, even if accepted as valid, cannot be established as factually true. It is one thing, for example, to observe that someone's behavior is generally consistent with his wanting more of some good rather than less; it is quite another to conclude that he *should* have more rather than less. The former is simply a statement of fact; the latter requires some criterion for judging better and worse.

One criterion used extensively in normative economics simply relies on an individual's own judgment in evaluating his or her own circumstances. If someone believes that he is better (or worse) off as a result of some economic change, then he is assumed to in fact be better (or worse) off. If we accept this normative premise, then several important conclusions follow. Consider, for example, a normative evaluation of exchange. If exchange is truly voluntary—that is, if each party to the exchange is free to decline any offer made by the other—then each presumably feels that he or she will be made better off as a result of the exchange. Consequently, if we accept individuals' evaluations of their own economic welfare as valid, and if no third parties are adversely affected by exchange, then we would conclude that exchange is a desirable economic activity.

Normative evaluation becomes more complicated when some parties are adversely affected by a change that benefits others. Suppose, for example, that the extra beer Jack obtains in his trade with Jill is just enough to get him drunk and, as a result, he drives his car through his neighbor's flower garden. Now there is an ambiguity in the effects of the exchange. Jack and Jill may still feel that they have benefitted from the exchange, but Jack's neighbor certainly does not. Jack's purchase of beer, whatever it did for Jack, has resulted in the destruction of the neighbor's flower garden.

In cases like this where there are losers as well as gainers, normative evaluation requires that we compare the benefits to the gainers with the costs to the losers to come up with some measure of the net effect. Suppose, for example, that we are willing to treat all of the affected parties equally, and that the value Jack's neighbor places on his flower garden is equivalent to 6 loaves of bread. We might conclude that the exchange is no longer beneficial on balance because the trading gains to Jack and Jill (which we measured as 4 loaves of bread) are less than the value of the lost flower garden.

This sort of comparison of benefits and costs is typical of normative economics. Specifically, economists generally regard an economic change as an improvement whenever the sum of all the benefits to those favorably affected exceeds the costs to those adversely affected. In practical applications of this **economic efficiency criterion,** benefits and costs are usually measured in monetary amounts. However, despite the apparent precision implied by a "hard" dollars-and-cents figure, the monetary amounts used to measure benefits and costs still reflect the judgments of individuals, as registered through the marketplace, as to how they can best earn and spend their money. The efficiency criterion accepts these judgments as valid. Moreover, it treats a dollar's worth of benefits (or of costs) the same regardless of the identity of the gainer (or loser).

The **economic efficiency** criterion is a normative criterion which holds that something is desirable if its benefits exceed its costs.

Often we find it desirable to differentiate among individuals or groups: rich versus poor, consumers versus producers, labor versus management, or whatever. In such cases, we are concerned not only with the magnitude of benefits and costs but also with their *distribution*. We might, for example, consider a $100 cost imposed on a poor person to be a greater burden than the same cost imposed on a rich person. Or we might think that benefits to consumers count for more than benefits to producers.

Unfortunately, economics itself tells us virtually nothing about how costs and benefits should be distributed. This is not to say that distribution is not an important normative issue. It just means that judgments about distribution inevitably reflect the personal views of particular individuals about what constitutes "fairness," "equity," or "justice." These are elusive concepts which, like beauty, lie in the eye of the beholder. And, when it comes to such judgments, the economist's eye is no sharper than anyone else's.

CHAPTER SUMMARY

1. The lowest marginal cost producer has a *comparative advantage* in its production. The *law of comparative advantage* says that the economy's total output of goods will rise when each person produces more of those goods in which he has a comparative advantage and less of other goods.

2. The *production possibilities* curve (PPC) shows the output combinations of two goods that can be produced using all resources fully and in accordance with their comparative advantages. Output combinations represented by points inside the PPC reflect inefficient resource use; combinations outside the PPC are unattainable with available resources and current technologies. Investment in new resources and technological progress shift the PPC outward over time.

3. Mutually beneficial exchange is made possible by differences in people's subjective preferences. A person's subjective preferences can be represented by the *marginal values* he places on different goods.

4. In an economic system in which individuals are free to pursue their own interests, comparative advantage, specialization, and exchange are closely interrelated. Specialization in accordance with comparative advantage leads to increases in total production; exchange, in turn, not only allocates that product in a way that reflects differences in personal tastes but also provides the fundamental incentive for each individual to pursue his or her comparative advantage in the first place.

5. *Transactions costs* are the costs of engaging in exchange. They include the costs of obtaining information about exchange opportunities, the cost of negotiating the terms of the exchange, and the costs of enforcing rights to the goods obtained in an exchange.

6. Intermediaries, or "middlemen," are parties to many exchanges. Their function is to reduce transactions costs; if they do not, the ultimate parties

to the exchange will find it to their advantage to "cut out the middleman" and deal directly with one another.

7. Competition among intermediaries raises the prices of the things they buy and lowers the prices of the things they sell, thus benefitting the ultimate parties to the exchange. Because competition also lowers the profits of middlemen, they may try to form a cartel. However, successful cartels are unlikely where markets are open to entry by new competitors.

8. The use of money as a common medium of exchange substantially reduces transactions costs below what they would be in a barter economy. It is important to distinguish between *absolute (nominal) prices* and *relative (real) prices* in a money economy.

9. The basic normative criterion of *economic efficiency* is one that compares benefits and costs. Benefits and costs are usually measured in money amounts and reflect the judgments of individuals, as registered through the marketplace, as to how they can best earn and spend their money. Normative economics cannot address *distributional* issues without additional value judgments.

Key Terms and Concepts

comparative advantage
law of comparative advantage
production possibilities curve
marginal value
exchange
transaction costs
information costs
negotiation costs
enforcement costs
open market
collusion
cartel
absolute (nominal) prices
relative (real) prices
economic efficiency criterion

Questions for Thought and Discussion

1. It takes Stan 40 minutes to cook a meal and 20 minutes to do the dishes. It takes his roommate, Ollie, 45 minutes to cook a meal and 30 minutes to do the dishes. Which of the two has the comparative advantage as cook and which as dishwasher?
2. In the land of Oz, with its poorly educated and unskilled labor force, it takes 4 hours to produce a widget and 8 hours to produce a gizmo. In Wonderland, with its highly educated and skilled labor force, it takes only 1 hour to produce a widget and only 3 hours to produce a gizmo. Use comparative advantage to show how both nations could benefit from trade with one another.
3. Most colleges and universities base faculty tenure and promotion decisions on both teaching and research, and they usually apply the same, uniform standards in evalu-

ating all faculty. Does such a policy lead to a mix of teaching output (e.g., educated students) and research output (e.g., published papers) on the university's PPC?

4. The marginal value of a fish to Garfield is 7 bowls of milk; the marginal value of a fish to Odie is 2 bowls of milk. Identify a mutually beneficial trade between Garfield and Odie.

5. "Economic analysis tells us that people with different tastes can obtain mutual benefits from trade with one another. It therefore concludes that trade is good." The foregoing statement is a mixture of positive (first sentence) and normative (second sentence) elements. Change the second sentence so that it is entirely positive.

6. Since the "energy crises" of the 1970s, politicians and others have argued that the United States must become energy self-sufficient. What does the analysis in this chapter suggest to you about such a goal?

7. Why should you be wary of ads that promise lower prices because the seller has "cut out the middleman?"

8. Anyone selling a house can do so simply by putting up a FOR SALE BY OWNER sign. Yet relatively few people do this, choosing instead to use the services of an intermediary, specifically a realtor, who charges a commission that typically runs into thousands of dollars. What services does the realtor provide that makes these services worth so much to so many house sellers?

9. When a sure-sellout rock concert comes to town, it is not uncommon for teenagers to wait hours in line to obtain tickets, only to resell them to 20–30 year olds. In effect, the teenagers act as intermediaries between ticket brokers and young adult rock fans. Can you explain this phenomenon in terms of comparative advantage and exchange?

10. The kind of competition we described in this chapter involved making better exchange offers (prices) than one's competitor to potential buyers and sellers. Can you think of any other forms of competition that are used to attract business in the real world?

11. The following table shows the percentage increases in the absolute prices of various consumer goods (actually categories of consumer goods) between 1985 and 1989. It also shows the percentage increase in the average of all consumer prices during the same period.

Consumer Goods	*Price Increase*
Food	+18%
Housing	+14%
Transportation	+ 7%
Medical care	+32%
Entertainment	+11%
Average of all consumer goods	+15%

What happened to the relative prices of transportation and entertainment between 1985 and 1989? For which categories of consumer goods did the real price (measured as the price relative to all other consumer goods) increase? Decrease?

12. Can you think of some circumstances in which you would *not* accept the normative value judgment that an individual is the best judge of his own economic well-being?

CHAPTER 3

Demand, Supply, and the Market Mechanism

The price system is just one of those formations which man has learned to use (though he is still very far from having learned to make the best use of it) after he had stumbled upon it without understanding it.

FRIEDRICH A. HAYEK*

In this chapter we introduce the basic model of demand and supply. As a framework for thinking about an extensive range of economic and social phenomena, this model is certainly the most useful and widely applicable one in all of economics. It also forms the basis for much of the analysis which we develop in the chapters that follow.

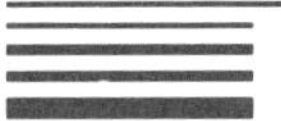

MARKETS

The **market** for a good includes all of the contacts between buyers and sellers of that good.

We often think of a **market** as a particular place where buyers and sellers meet to exchange goods. A specific location may have been an important attribute of markets until the last century or so, but with modern systems of communication, contact between buyer and seller is no longer limited to face-to-face meetings. Accordingly, in modern economics the concept of a market encompasses the entire set of relationships among buyers and sellers of a good.

* "The Use of Knowledge in Society," *American Economic Review* (September 1945).

Market characteristics can vary across a broad spectrum. To illustrate the range of possibilities, consider two quite different examples of actual markets, the market for used cars and the New York Stock Exchange (NYSE). The goods traded in the used car market are physical commodities with characteristics that vary considerably from unit to unit: A used 1985 Chevrolet is not likely to be identical to any other used car, even another used 1985 Chevrolet. Whether the ultimate buyer and seller of a used car meet face-to-face (via a newspaper classified ad, for example) or whether they utilize the services of a middleman such as a used car dealer, price is typically determined through direct negotiations between the parties involved. Moreover, they may find it useful to have some knowledge of one another's personal characteristics, such as the buyer's credit record or a used car dealer's reputation for honesty.

By contrast, the goods traded on the NYSE are shares of corporate stock, intangible legal rights of ownership in corporations, with each share of stock in any given corporation identical to every other share. On the NYSE, buyers and sellers almost never meet and are usually completely unaware of, and unconcerned with, one another's identity. All trades are made at arm's length through a series of intermediaries, such as stockbrokers, who are in turn linked together only by telephone or other long distance communications media. Unlike the used car market, the NYSE is *impersonal:* Neither the buyer, the seller, nor the intermediary has any personal influence on the price at which shares of stock are traded. Finally, modern systems of communication make the NYSE virtually international in scope and instantaneous in its adjustment to changes in economic conditions, whereas used car markets tend to be localized markets in which changes in the economic environment are more slowly digested.

The demand–supply market model that we are about to develop abstracts from many of these descriptive features of particular markets to focus on the fundamental determinants of price and quantity traded in any market.

Demand, Supply, and Market Intentions

Demand refers to the purchase plans of buyers.

Supply refers to the sales plans of sellers.

Our analysis is organized around the plans or intentions of market participants. In particular, we use the concept of market **demand** to describe the purchase plans of potential *buyers* and the concept of market **supply** to describe the sales plans of potential *sellers*. Demand and supply thus provide two distinct categories into which we can mentally file all of the factors that might affect the planned actions of market participants.

It is very important to keep in mind that demand and supply do not refer to specific amounts of a good. Neither buyers nor sellers plan to buy or sell a given amount of a good regardless of market conditions. Their plans depend on many variables. Buyers' purchase plans, for example, might depend on their incomes; sellers' plans might depend on the cost of making the good available for sale; the plans of both are influenced by the price at which goods are traded. When these or other factors change, so also will the plans of buyers and sellers. In other words, the concepts of demand and supply express *relationships* between plans to buy or sell and the variables that affect those plans.

Our model focuses on the determination of one particular variable that affects both the supply and the demand for any good, namely, its price. By reconciling the plans of buyers and sellers, market price adjustments coordinate exchange and determine how much of a good will be traded.

Before turning our attention to this coordinating function of price, we must first examine in more detail each of the two building blocks of our model.

DEMAND

Price reflects the market value of the alternatives that must be sacrificed in order to purchase a good and thus serves as a monetary measure of the good's opportunity cost to the buyer. Rational behavior implies that, other things being equal, the higher its opportunity cost, the less likely an alternative is to be chosen. Accordingly, we would expect the planned purchases of a good—the *quantity demanded*—to be inversely related to its price: the higher the price, the smaller the quantity demanded, and the lower the price, the larger the quantity demanded. This hypothesis, perhaps the most important in all of economics, is known as the **law of demand**.

The **law of demand** states that, other things being equal, more of a good will be demanded at a lower price than at a higher price, and vice versa.

The law of demand is a perfectly general proposition that applies to all kinds of human choice. It predicts, for example, that if the price of steak falls, other things being equal, people (though perhaps not every individual person) will demand more steak. If the cost of medical care rises, people will demand less medical care. If wages fall, employers will demand more labor. If fines for traffic violations are increased, there will be less speeding and reckless driving. The applications of the law of demand are limitless.

There are a number of things that we should emphasize with respect to the law of demand.

First, the law of demand is not just a statement about what people want or desire; it is a proposition about what they actually intend to do. Simply wanting a good does not constitute an effective demand for that good. As the term is used in economics, demand implies a willingness to buy a good and an ability to pay for it.

Second, the law of demand is an other-things-equal proposition. While many factors other than the price of a good affect the quantity of that good demanded, the law of demand isolates the relation between quantity demanded and price, abstracting from (holding constant) all other factors that might affect demand. (We postpone for a moment our discussion of the effects of these other factors.)

Third, the law of demand is a proposition about trade-offs at the margin. It recognizes that because there are substitutes for anything—including getting by with less or even doing entirely without—people will substitute away from higher priced alternatives in favor of lower priced ones when relative prices change. The notion of "absolute necessities"—fixed amounts of some goods for which there are "no substitutes" and which people will demand regardless of the opportunity cost—is completely foreign to the economic way of thinking. If it were literally true, as many people claim, that there is no substitute for good health, then we would be at a loss to explain why people eat rich food, smoke cigarettes, and avoid regular exercise. These are all substitutes for good health, substitutes that many people in fact choose over good health. The law of demand tells us that people would choose more good health if it were less costly to do so.

Fourth, the law of demand applies to all goods, from primary productive resources to final consumer goods. Because all productive activity is undertaken ultimately to satisfy consumer demand, the demands for productive resources and for intermediate inputs are often referred to as *derived* demands. The demand for farm land and for the implements with which to till it and harvest its fruits, for example, derives ultimately from the demand for food. The demand for a college education derives, at least in part, from the demand for the higher levels of future income which that education is expected to generate.

Finally, the law of demand is positive, not normative. It makes no judgment about what goods people *should* want, how much of any good they *should* have, or what price they *should* pay for it. In a positive sense, a big spender's willingness to pay $1,000 for a few ounces of cocaine or a wino's determination to spend his last panhandled dollar on a bottle of cheap Tokay are no less expressions of demand than your purchase of a pound of hamburger or a college education.

The Demand Curve

A **demand curve** shows the quantity of a good demanded at each price when all factors other than the good's price are held constant.

We depict the relation between price and quantity demanded graphically in the **demand curve**. The market demand curve for a good shows the quantity of that good buyers would want to purchase at various prices, other things being equal.

Table 3.1 on page 52 shows the quantity of gasoline demanded at various prices in some hypothetical market. The same information is plotted as the demand curve labelled *D* in Figure 3.1 on the same page. The curve shows the quantity of gasoline demanded, *Q*, as a function of its price, *P*, assuming that all other factors affecting demand are held constant as the price of gasoline varies. Since the amount purchased depends on the time period over which the purchases are to be made, the units of measurement on the horizontal axis are quantity demanded per unit time, in this case, per day. The negative (or downward) slope of the demand curve, which shows that larger quantities are demanded at lower prices, reflects of the law of demand.

The demand curve can be interpreted in either of two ways:

The demand curve shows the quantity demanded at each price. Pick any price on the vertical axis, and from that price on the demand curve read the corresponding quantity demanded on the horizontal axis. For example, in Figure 3.2(a) on page 53 we pick the price of $1.20 per gallon, go across to the demand curve and then down to the horizontal axis to find that 3,000 gallons per day are demanded at that price.

Table 3.1

A hypothetical demand schedule for gasoline

PRICE *(Dollars per Gallon)*	QUANTITY DEMANDED *(Gallons per Day)*
$2.00	2,000
1.80	2,100
1.60	2,300
1.40	2,600
1.20	3,000
1.00	3,500
0.80	4,100
0.60	4,800
0.40	5,600
0.20	6,500

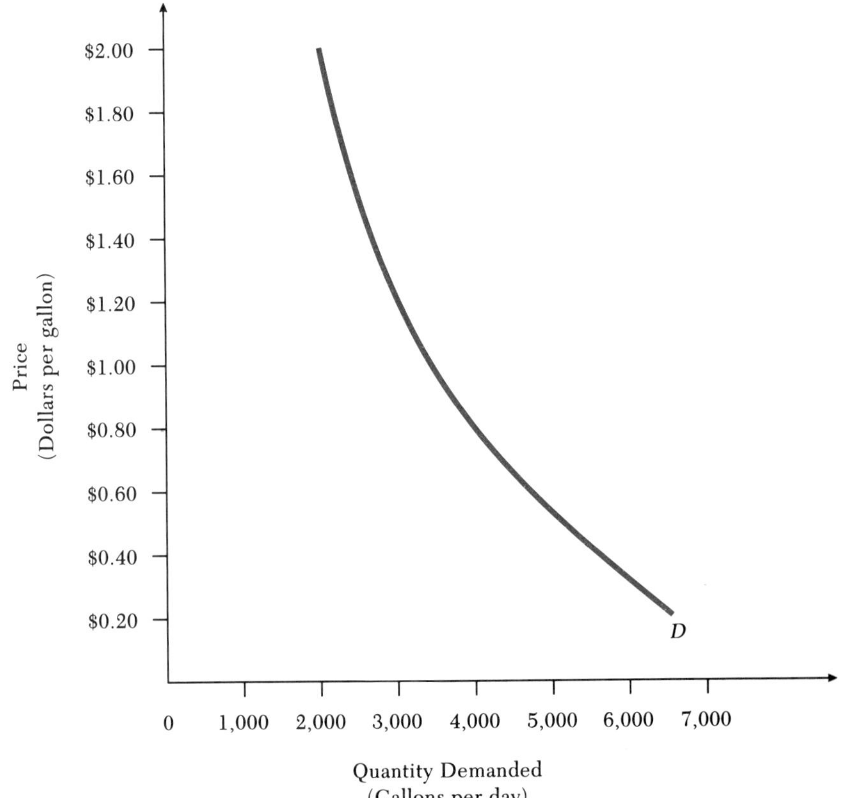

Figure 3.1

A hypothetical demand curve for gasoline (based on the data in Table 3.1)

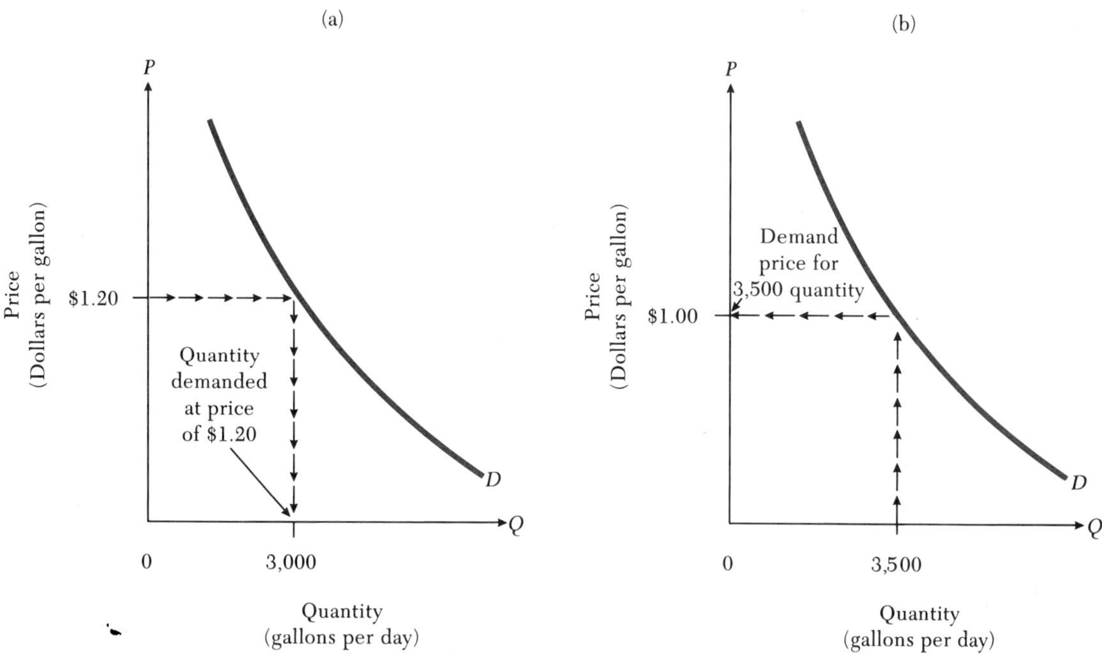

Figure 3.2

Two ways to interpret the demand curve

The **demand price** for each unit of a good is the maximum price any buyer is willing to pay for that unit and is equal to its marginal value.

The demand curve also shows the maximum price at which any particular quantity will be demanded. Pick any quantity on the horizontal axis, and from the demand curve determine the corresponding **demand price** on the vertical axis. In Figure 3.2(b), for example, we pick 3,500 as the quantity, go up to the demand curve and across to the vertical axis to find that the demand price for that quantity is $1.00. The information that 3,500 gallons would be purchased at a price of $1.00 per gallon but not at any price above that tells us that the maximum amount anyone is willing to pay for that 3,500th gallon of gasoline per week is $1.00. The demand price is therefore the marginal value of the last unit demanded at that price. If the price were $1.01 maybe 3,499 gallons would be purchased, but not 3,500.

Other Factors Affecting Demand

As we have already noted, price is only one of many factors that can effect the demand for a good. In order to avoid mistakes in analysis, we must carefully distinguish between the effects of price changes and the effects of changes in the other variables that affect demand.

The effect of a change in the price of the good itself can be interpreted as a movement from one point to another along its demand curve. We call this movement along a given demand curve in response to a change in price a *change in the quantity demanded.* For example, according to the demand curve in Figure

3.1, a fall in the price of gasoline from $1.20 to $1.00 per gallon increases the quantity of gasoline demanded from 3,000 gallons per day to 3,500 gallons per day. Similarly, a rise in the price from $0.60 to $0.80 per gallon decreases the quantity demanded from 4,800 to 4,100 gallons per day.

Remember that the price-quantity relationship shown by the demand curve is an other-things-equal relationship—that is, one for which all potential influences on demand other than the price of the good itself are held constant. If some other relevant factor changes, the whole relationship between price and quantity demanded is affected. Graphically, this means a shift of the entire demand curve.

To illustrate the effect on demand of a change in some factor other than price, suppose that someone invents a cheap, easily installed device that doubles the fuel efficiency of any car or truck. Table 3.2 and the corresponding diagram, Figure 3.3, shows what happens to the demand for gasoline when this device is installed by all of the drivers in the market. At each pricc the amount of gasoline demanded is cut in half and the demand curve shifts from the original one labelled *D* to a new one labelled *D'*. We call this inward shift of the demand curve a *decrease in demand* to distinguish it from a *decrease in quantity demanded*, which results from a rise in price. Similarly, if something other than the price of gasoline raised the amount demanded at each price, the demand curve would shift to the right and there would be an *increase in demand*.

In our terminology, therefore, a *change in the price of the good* leads to a *change in the quantity demanded* and a *movement along* a given demand curve. A *change in any other relevant factor* leads to a *change in demand* and a *shift* in the demand curve. The distinction may seem like nit-picking, but it is very

Table 3.2

A decrease in the demand for gasoline

PRICE *(Dollars per Gallon)*	INITIAL QUANTITY DEMANDED *(Gallons per Day)*	FINAL QUANTITY DEMANDED *(Gallons per Day)*
$2.00	2,000	1,000
1.80	2,100	1,050
1.60	2,300	1,150
1.40	2,600	1,300
1.20	3,000	1,500
1.00	3,500	1,750
0.80	4,100	2,050
0.60	4,800	2,400
0.40	5,600	2,800
0.20	6,500	3,250

Figure 3.3

A decrease in the demand for gasoline

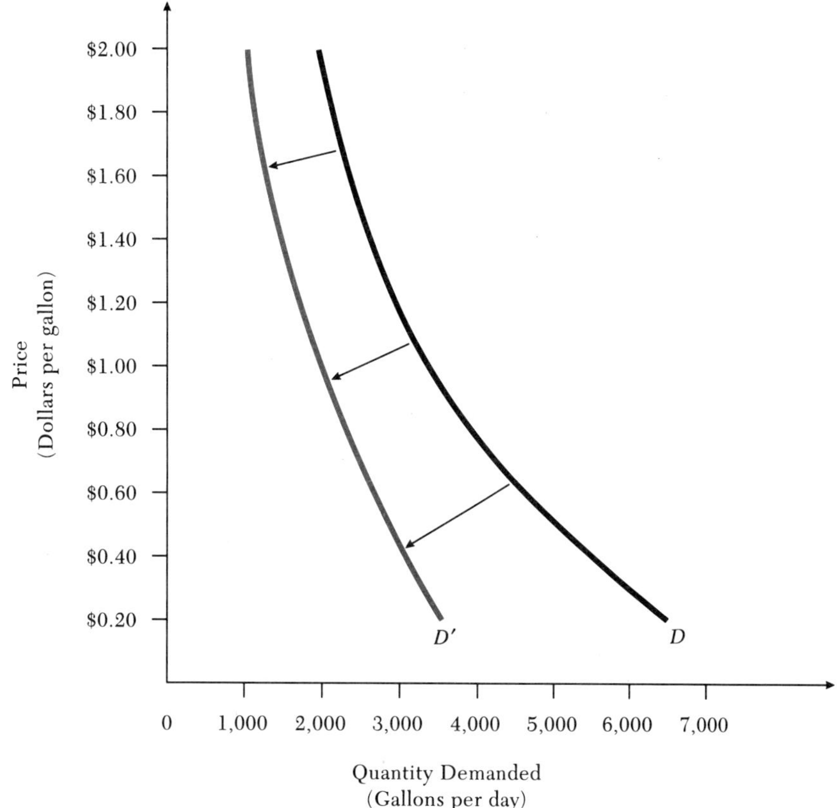

important. Confusion between movements along a curve and shifts in the curve is probably the principal source of error among beginning students of economics. You will be on safe ground if you remember that a curve depicting the relationship between any two variables—such as that between price and quantity demanded along the demand curve—does not shift as a result of changes in those variables alone. It shifts only in response to changes in other relevant factors not shown explicitly on the axes of the diagram.*

*Mathematically, we can write the overall demand function as

$$Q^d = Q^d(P, \text{other variables})$$

where Q^d is the quantity demanded, $Q^d(\ldots)$ is the demand function, P is the price of the good, and the other variables in the demand function include any factors other than the price of the good itself which might affect demand. In constructing the demand curve, the other variables are all held constant as price varies. In the jargon of mathematics, there is therefore actually a family of demand curves for any good, each of which shows the price–quantity relation that holds for some particular set of values for all of the other variables affecting demand. When these other variables change, the price–quantity relationship shown by the demand curve shifts.

What Other Factors Are We Talking About?

The factors other than a good's price which affect its demand depend on the nature of the particular good. The following is a short list of the main categories into which these other factors fall. Changes in any of them will shift the demand curve, either increasing demand (shifting the demand curve upward and to the right) or decreasing demand (shifting the demand curve downward and to the left).

Income The demand for most goods is positively related to buyer income: An increase in income increases demand and shifts the demand curve to the right; a decrease in income shifts the demand curve to the left.

Size of the Market Demand is positively related to the number of potential buyers (as measured by market population, for example).

Prices of Related Goods Related goods consist of *substitutes* and *complements*. Substitutes are goods that perform similar functions and can be used in place of one another. Examples of substitutes include coffee and tea, VCRs and movie theaters, Chevrolets and Toyotas, and electricity, coal and natural gas. The demand for any good is positively related to the prices of its close substitutes. An increase in the price of Toyotas, for example, will increase the demand for Chevrolets. *Complements* are goods that are used together to fulfill the same want. Pizza and beer, gasoline and automobiles, computer hardware and software, and lectures and textbooks are all examples of complementary goods. (Note, however, that a textbook can sometimes also be a substitute for a lecture.) The demand for any good is inversely related to the prices of its complements. A reduction in the price of computer hardware will increase the demand for software; a rise in the price of pizza will reduce the demand for beer.

Tastes and Preferences Although our underlying subjective preferences, as well as our basic biological and psychological wants, remain relatively stable over time, their particular manifestation as market choices is subject to the influence of a variety of cultural and environmental factors. These include such things as fashion trends, fads, peer pressure, and emulation effects ("keeping up with the Joneses").

Information The demand for a good is affected by the amount and kind of information available to potential buyers. A favorable review in *Consumer Reports*, for example, increases the demand for a product, whereas a government announcement that it poses a health hazard decreases the demand. Advertising attempts to increase the demand for a product by providing favorable information about it and (either explicitly or implicitly) unfavorable information about the products of competitors.

Expectations The current demand for a good, particularly a nonperishable good, may depend on expectations of future changes in its price, quality, or other attributes. Expectations that housing prices are about to rise will stimulate the current demand for houses; expectations that housing prices are about to fall will decrease current demand.

Transactions Costs To the extent that transactions costs are borne by the buyer, they have a negative affect on demand. Other things being equal, the more costly it is for buyers to acquire information about a good, negotiate with the seller, or enforce the rights they acquire in an exchange, the lower the demand will be. Conversely, the demand for a relatively complex good like a sophisticated camera or a personal computer is increased when the seller provides information in the form of demonstrations, users' manuals, and training. Similarly, the demand for goods that are subject to high enforcement costs—car stereo systems and property in high crime neighborhoods, for example—will be lower as a result of those high costs.

Government Policies Government policies such as taxes and subsidies affect demand for many goods. For example, the deductibility of mortgage interest in computing personal income taxes increases the demand for home ownership; government programs such as medicare and food stamps increase the demand for medical services and food, respectively, by subsidizing certain buyers of those goods.

SUPPLY

Almost all of what we have said about demand on the buyers' side of the market has a parallel on the supply, or sellers', side. This shows up first in the similarity between the concept of a demand curve and that of a supply curve.

The Supply Curve

The **supply curve** shows the quantity of a good supplied at each price when all factors other than the good's price are held constant.

Just as the demand curve shows the relation between price and the quantity demanded by buyers, the **supply curve** shows the relation between price and the quantity supplied by sellers. In particular, the market supply curve for any good shows the quantity of that good sellers will offer for sale at various prices, other things being equal.

Since price is a measure of the benefit to the seller in an exchange, and since rational behavior implies that people respond positively to benefits, it seems reasonable to conclude that the higher the price, the greater the quantity supplied. (Note that the quantity that sellers supply—that is, the quantity they *offer for sale*—at any price is not necessarily the quantity they can *actually sell* at that price. The latter depends also on demand.) Behind this intuitive explanation, however, lies an important relationship among price, marginal cost, and the supply decision of the individual seller.

Marginal Cost and the Supply Curve

A seller will supply a unit of a good only if its price covers the marginal cost of supplying it. We can use a simple example to illustrate why this is so.

Table 3.3 on the next page shows a hypothetical schedule of the various

Table 3.3
Widget supply and marginal cost

QUANTITY SUPPLIED	TOTAL COST	MARGINAL COST
0	$ 0	—
1	10	$10
2	22	12
3	36	14
4	52	16
5	70	18
6	90	20
7	115	25

amounts of widgets that could be supplied per day by Wally the Widgetmaker, the corresponding total costs Wally would incur at each supply rate, and the marginal cost of each additional unit supplied. (Widgets are generic, make-believe goods that occasionally show up in our analyses.) Since the marginal cost of each unit is the amount that unit adds to total cost, the numbers in the marginal cost column are just the successive differences between the numbers in the total cost column. This same relation between quantity supplied and marginal cost is plotted graphically in Figure 3.4.

Now suppose that Wally can sell his widgets at a price of $15 each. A look at Table 3.3 indicates that this price would cover his marginal cost for each of the first 3 units, but not for the 4th, 5th, or 6th. Wally would supply at least 3 widgets per day because each additional widget he supplies up to and including the 3rd adds more to his revenues (namely, $15) than to his costs, and thus increases his profits. But he would not supply more than 3 widgets per day because each additional widget beyond the 3rd would add more to his costs than to his revenues and thus reduce his profits. At a price of $15, therefore, Wally would supply exactly 3 widgets per day. This combination of price and quantity supplied is labelled point *A* in Figure 3.4.

Extending this line of reasoning, we can see that, at any price, the corresponding quantity supplied can be read directly from the marginal cost curve. For example, at a price of $17 the marginal cost of each of the first 4 widgets is covered so Wally would supply 4 as shown by point *B* in the diagram. If the price were $20, he would supply a 5th widget as well; he would be indifferent about supplying the 6th because the $20 price would just cover its marginal cost. To avoid ambiguity in this kind of situation, we arbitrarily assume that a unit for which price and marginal cost are equal will be supplied. Accordingly, point *C* indicates that Wally would supply 6 widgets per day at a price of $20. In effect, the stepped line relating marginal cost to quantity supplied in Figure 3.4 is Wally's supply curve. We would obtain the *market* supply curve for widgets by simply adding the amounts supplied at each price by Wally and all of the other

Figure 3.4

Marginal cost and the supply decision

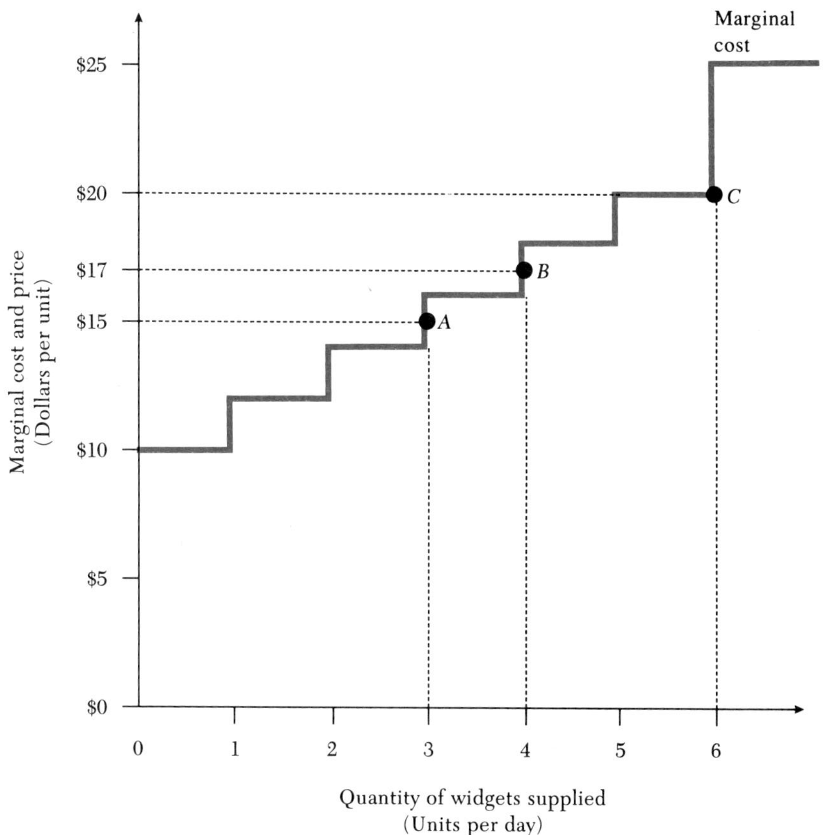

widget makers in the market. For all practical purposes, we can consider the quantity supplied in the market to be continuously variable, and so we generally draw the market supply curve as a smooth curve like the one labelled *S* in Figure 3.5 on the next page.

As was the case with demand curve, there are two equally valid ways to interpret the supply curve.

The supply curve shows the quantity supplied at each price. Pick any price on the vertical axis and, at that price on the supply curve, read the corresponding quantity supplied on the horizontal axis.

The supply curve also shows the *minimum* price at which any particular quantity will be supplied. Pick any quantity on the horizontal axis and determine from the supply curve the corresponding **supply price** on the vertical axis. It follows from our derivation of the supply curve that the supply price of any unit is equal to its marginal cost.

The **supply price** for each unit of a good is the minimum price any seller is willing to accept for that unit and is equal to its marginal cost.

Like the demand curve, the supply curve is strictly a positive construct. It shows only the amount that *will* be supplied at various prices. It provides no basis for normative evaluation of which goods *should* be supplied, in what

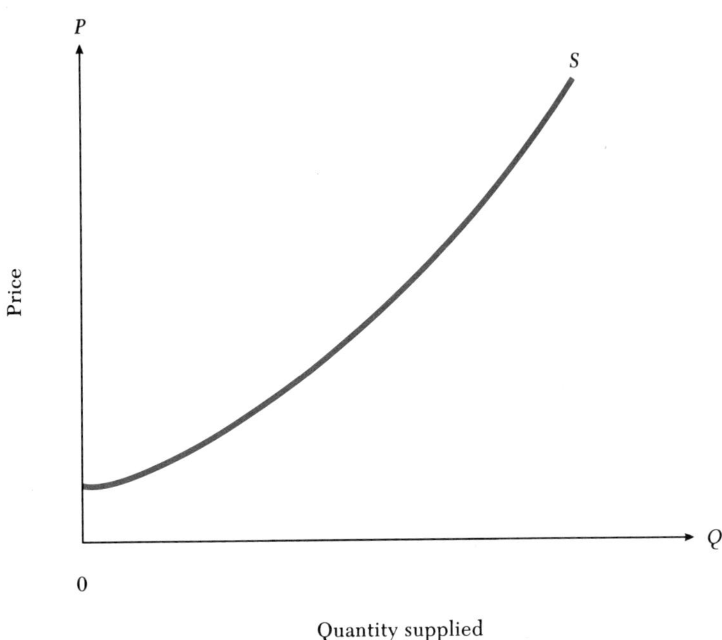

Figure 3.5

A market supply curve

amounts they *should* be made available, or what price suppliers *should* receive for them.

Other Factors Affecting Supply

As with demand, there are a number of factors other than the price of the good itself that can affect the supply decision.* In order to distinguish the effect of price from the effects of these other factors, we must again distinguish between movements along a curve and shifts in the curve. Specifically, a *change in the price* of a good, other things being equal, results in a movement from one point to another along its supply curve. For example, the increase in the price of widgets from \$15 to \$17 in the preceding example moved us from point *A* to point *B* on Wally's supply curve. We call this *movement along the supply curve* a *change in the quantity supplied.* A change in any of the other factors that affect supply leads to a *shift of the supply curve,* which we refer to as a *change in supply.* Specifically, because a rightward (or downward) shift of the supply curve

*The general supply function can therefore be written as

$$Q^s = Q^s(P, \text{other variables})$$

where Q^s is the quantity supplied, $Q^s(\ldots)$ is the supply function, P is the price, and the other variables include all other factors that might affect the supply decision.

indicates that more will be supplied at each price, it represents an *increase in supply*; a leftward shift represents a *decrease* in supply. (Note that an *increase in supply*, because it implies that any given amount will be supplied at a lower price, is equivalent to a *decrease in the supply price*; correspondingly, a *decrease in supply* is equivalent to an *increase in the supply price*.)

The following are some of the other factors—that is, factors other than the price of the good itself—that can shift the supply curve.

Input Prices Increases in the price of labor, raw materials, or any other inputs used in the production of a good increase its marginal costs (and thus its supply price) and shift the supply curve upward and to the left. Decreases in input prices would do the opposite.

Number of Sellers An increase in the number of sellers in the market would increase market supply, and a decrease in the number of sellers would reduce it.

Prices of Technologically Related Goods Goods are related technologically when they are produced using similar resources and production techniques. For example, if both wheat and rye can be grown on the same farmland, an increase in the price of rye would reduce the supply of wheat as farmers respond to the higher price of rye by planting more rye and less wheat.

Technological Change Technological improvements that reduce the marginal cost of producing a good increase the supply of that good (reduce its supply price).

Expectations If sellers expect higher prices in the future, they may hold their current supply off the market in anticipation of selling later at a higher price. Thus anticipation of higher *future* prices may lead to a reduction in *current* supply. This is especially likely for nonperishable goods that can be stored over time. Conversely, expectations of lower future prices might lead to an increase in current supply as sellers try to sell off inventories before prices fall.

Transactions Costs To the extent that transactions costs are borne by the seller, they tend to reduce the supply (raise the supply price). For example, if the seller must do a credit check on the buyer, then that cost (as well as the costs associated with the risk of the buyer defaulting) must be covered in the supply price. Similarly, the cost of preventing shoplifting—as well as the cost of the shoplifting that doesn't get prevented—is included in the supply prices of goods sold in department stores.

Government Policies Government policies such as taxes, subsidies, and business regulations can affect supply. Taxes levied on sellers, such as those on cigarettes and gasoline, increase sellers' marginal costs and reduce supply. Subsidies, such as those given to the producers of various agricultural crops, increase supply. Government license requirements, such as those for TV and radio stations, taxicabs, and liquor stores, often reduce supply by legally limiting the number of sellers in the market.

MARKET PRICE DETERMINATION

The demand curve provides us with information about all of the price–quantity combinations consistent with the market plans of buyers, and the supply curve provides information about all of the price–quantity combinations consistent with the market plans of sellers. If we combine the information contained in the two curves, we find that there is only one price–quantity combination consistent with the market plans of both buyers and sellers. This unique combination lies at the intersection of the demand curve and the supply curve.

The **market-clearing price** is the price that equates the quantities demanded and supplied. Graphically, it occurs at the intersection of the demand and supply curves.

Because the price determined by this intersection is the only one at which the quantity of the good that sellers offer to sell is exactly equal to the quantity that buyers are willing to purchase, it is called the **market-clearing price**.

Table 3.4 shows the quantities of gasoline demanded and supplied at various prices, and Figure 3.6 plots the corresponding demand and supply curves. The market-clearing price of gasoline is $1.00 per gallon, for at that price, and only at that price, is the quantity of gasoline demanded equal to the quantity supplied.

Shortages and Surpluses

At any price other than the market-clearing price, there is either a *shortage* or a *surplus*.

A **shortage** is the amount by which quantity demanded exceeds quantity supplied when price is below its market-clearing level.

A **shortage** results whenever a price is below its market-clearing level. At a price of $0.60 per gallon in Table 3.4, for example, 4,800 gallons are demanded per day but only 1,000 gallons are supplied. The magnitude of the shortage can be measured by the difference between the quantity demanded and the quantity supplied—in this case, 3,800 gallons per day. This shortage corresponds to distance *AB* in Figure 3.7(a) on page 64.

Table 3.4

Hypothetical demand and supply schedules for gasoline

PRICE *(Dollars per Gallon)*	**QUANTITY DEMANDED** *(Gallons per Day)*	**QUANTITY SUPPLIED** *(Gallons per Day)*
$2.00	2,000	5,600
1.80	2,100	5,500
1.60	2,300	5,300
1.40	2,600	4,900
1.20	3,000	4,300
1.00	3,500	3,500
0.80	4,100	2,500
0.60	4,800	1,000
0.40	5,600	0
0.20	6,500	0

Figure 3.6
Equilibrium in the gasoline market (based on Table 3.4)

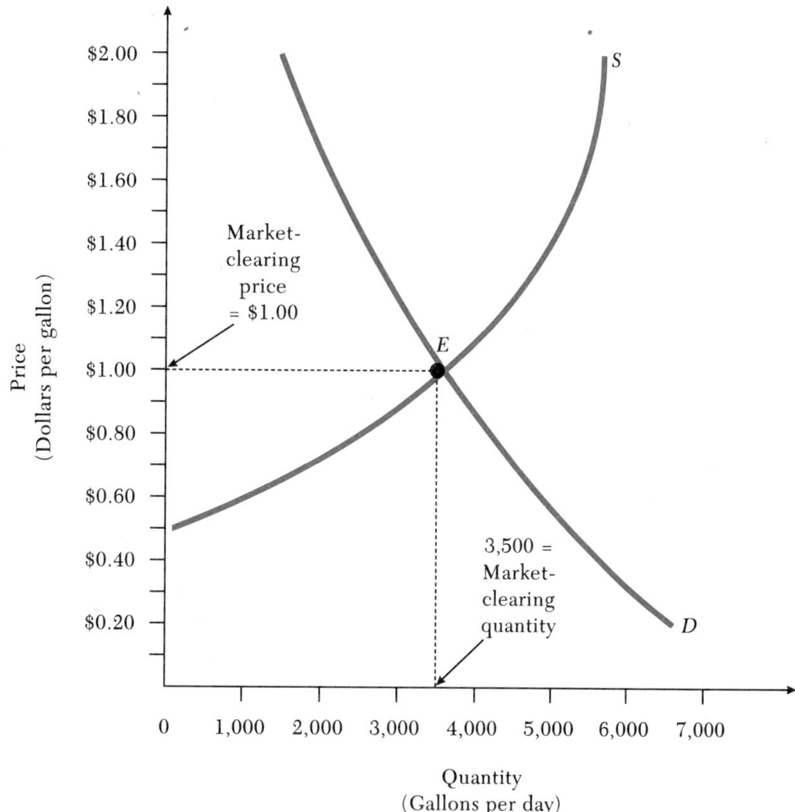

A **surplus** is the amount by which quantity supplied exceeds quantity demanded when price is above its market-clearing level.

A **surplus** results whenever a price is above its market-clearing level. At a price of $1.40 per gallon, sellers would offer 4,900 gallons per day for sale but buyers would purchase only 2,600 gallons per day. The resulting surplus of 2,300 gallons per day can be measured as distance *CD* in Figure 3.7(b) on page 65.

Given the nature of the demand and supply curves, a shortage can occur only when the price is below its market-clearing level, and a surplus can occur only when the price is above its market-clearing level. Shortages and surpluses therefore are not absolute; they exist only in relation to prices that fail to clear the market.

Market Equilibrium

If a price is initially below its market-clearing level, the resulting shortage implies that there are at least some potential buyers unable to purchase the amount of the good they want. In other words, there are some buyers for whom the marginal value of additional units of the good exceeds the current price, but who are unable to obtain those additional units at that price. Those frustrated buyers have an incentive to offer higher prices in an effort to outbid other buyers and

Figure 3.7

(a) Shortage of gasoline at \$0.60 per gallon price, (b) Surplus of gasoline at \$1.40 per gallon price

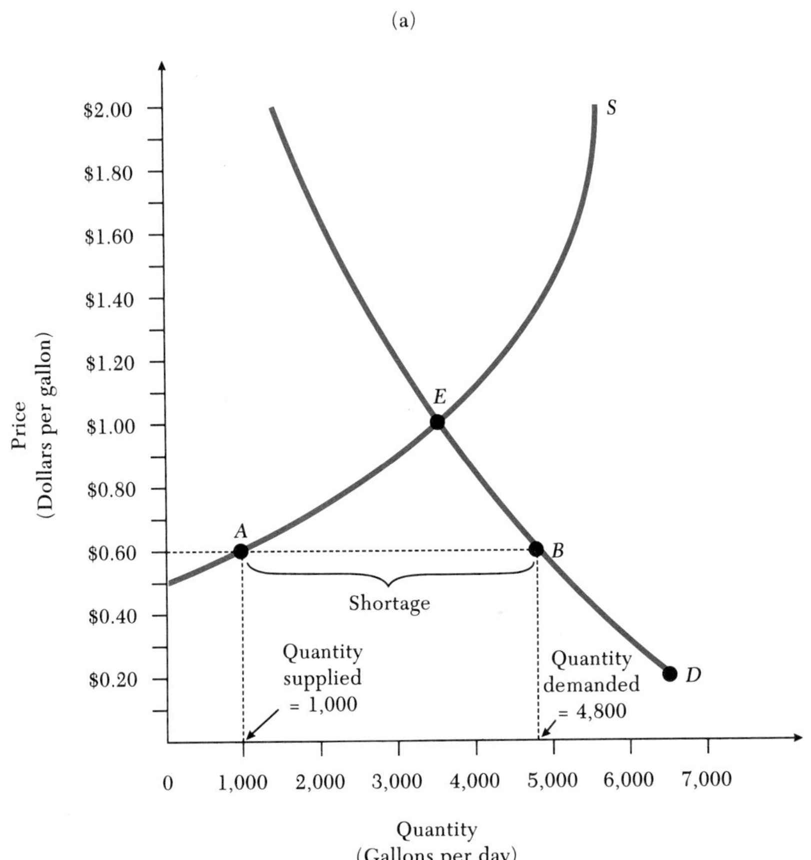

thus obtain more of the good. In the presence of a shortage, therefore, competition among buyers with unmet demands will bid up the price of the good. As the price rises, the quantity demanded will decrease and the quantity supplied will increase until the shortage, and the accompanying upward pressure on price, is eliminated at the market-clearing price.

If a price is initially above its market-clearing level, the resulting surplus implies that there are at least some sellers unable to sell all they would like to sell. Since the price more than covers the marginal cost of supplying the unsold units (otherwise they would not have been offered for sale in the first place), sellers have an incentive to offer lower prices to attract buyers. In the presence of a surplus, therefore, competition among sellers unable to sell all they want at the prevailing price will lead to downward pressure on price. The falling price will increase the quantity demanded, decrease the quantity supplied, and reduce the surplus until it is eliminated at the market-clearing price.

To summarize: If a price is not at its market-clearing level, the resulting shortage or surplus generates market forces that move it toward that level. Conversely,

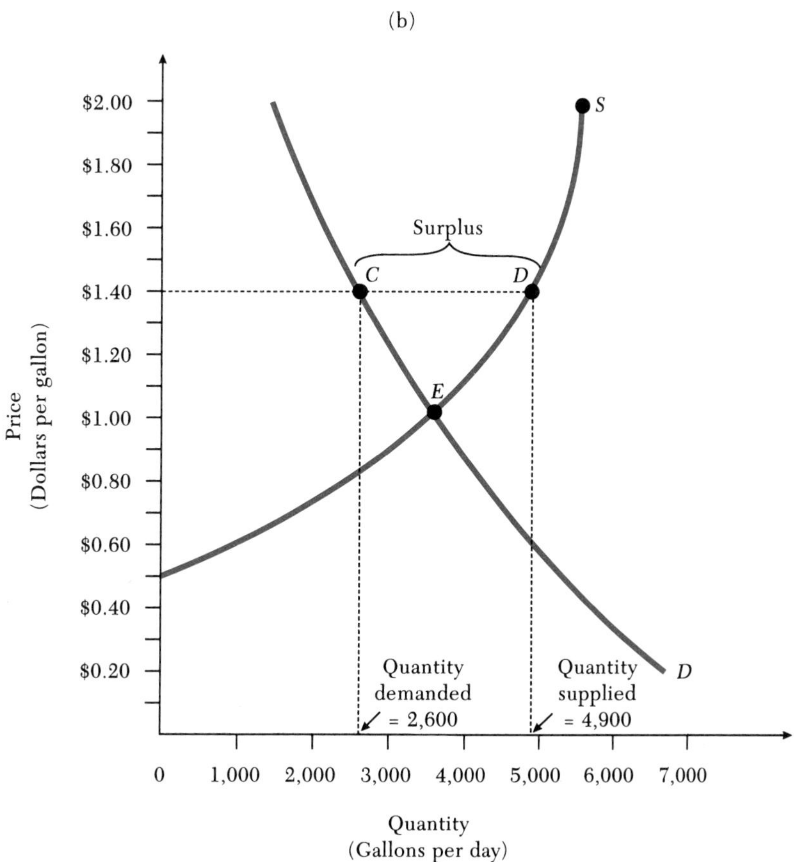

if a price is at its market-clearing level, the resulting equality between quantities demanded and supplied means that there will be no tendency for that price to change. Price will therefore always tend toward an *equilibrium* that clears the market and insures that the plans of buyers and sellers are mutually consistent. This is the fundamental coordinating function of price in a market economy.

Predicting with the Demand–Supply Model

The preceding analysis is *not* meant to suggest that markets simply adjust to an equilibrium that, once achieved, lasts forever. Quite the contrary; the value of the equilibrium concept is that it enables us to explain and predict the *changes* in price and quantity that result from a wide variety of factors affecting demand, supply, or both.

The simplest approach to such prediction is to start from an initial equilibrium and then determine whether the factor whose influence is to be analyzed will shift the demand curve or the supply curve. After such a shift there will be a new

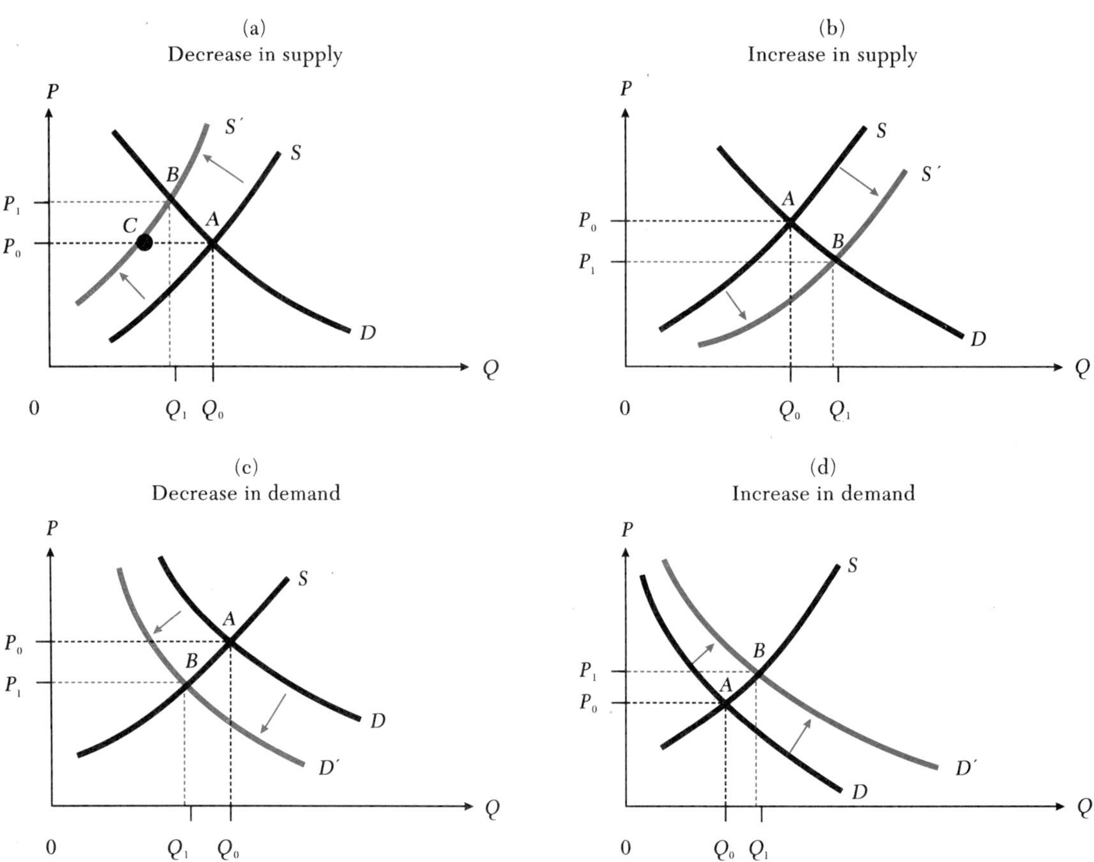

Figure 3.8

Changes in supply or demand. (a) Decrease in supply, (b) Increase in supply, (c) Decrease in demand, and (d) Increase in demand

equilibrium. By comparing it with the initial equilibrium, we can deduce the expected effects on the market price and the quantity traded.

To take a concrete example, suppose we want to predict the effect on the gasoline market of an increase in the price of crude oil. Because crude oil is an important input in the production of gasoline, an increase in its price will increase the marginal cost, and thus the supply price, of gasoline, thereby shifting the supply curve upward and to the left. If the gasoline market was initially in equilibrium at point *A* in Figure 3.8(a) with Q_0 gallons of gasoline produced and consumed per day at a price of P_0 per gallon, the shift of the supply curve from S to S' will create an initial shortage equal to distance *AC*. As a result, price will be bid up until the shortage is eliminated and a new equilibrium is established at point *B* with a new price of P_1 and quantity of Q_1. The supply–demand model thus predicts that the effect of the higher price of crude oil on the gasoline market will be higher gasoline prices and less gasoline produced and consumed.

Note again the difference between shifts in curves and movements along curves. There has been a *decrease in supply*—a leftward shift of the supply curve—due to a change in something other than the price of gasoline—namely, the higher price of crude oil. But there has been only a *decrease in the quantity of gasoline demanded*—a movement along the demand curve from point *A* to point *B* as the price rises from P_0 to P_1. The increase in the price of crude oil has not reduced the demand for gasoline; rather it has reduced the supply, and that in turn has driven up the price, thereby reducing the quantity of gasoline demanded.*

An increase in supply—resulting from, say, a reduction in the price of crude oil or an improvement in refining technology—has just the opposite effect, which is illustrated in Figure 3.8(b) where point *A* is again the initial equilibrium. The supply curve shifts rightward (downward), and a surplus is created at the initial price, P_0. As a result, the price falls and the quantity traded rises until a new equilibrium is established at point *B*, where the price is lower (P_1) and the quantity traded is greater (Q_1).

The same approach can also be used to derive the effects on price and quantity of changes in factors that affect demand. For example, a device that increases gas mileage would reduce the demand for gasoline, shifting the demand curve to the left as shown in Figure 3.8(c). The decrease in demand would cause an initial surplus of gasoline and exert downward pressure on gasoline prices until a new equilibrium is reached at point *B*, with both price and quantity lower than in the initial equilibrium. Conversely, an increase in demand—due, for example, to stricter emission control requirements that reduce the fuel efficiency of cars—would lead to increases in both price and quantity as shown in Figure 3.8(d).

Finally, consider the model's predictions regarding the effects of simultaneous changes in demand and supply. In particular, suppose that higher crude oil prices reduce the supply of gasoline at the same time that stricter emission controls increase the demand. As the foregoing analysis suggests, these changes will be reflected in a simultaneous rightward shift of the demand curve and a leftward shift of the supply curve. This is illustrated on page 68 in Figure 3.9, where the initial equilibrium is at point *A* and the final equilibrium at point *B*. Since both the demand curve and supply curve have shifted up—that is, since both the demand price and the supply price have risen—it is clear that the final equilibrium price (P_1) must be above the initial price (P_0). The effect on the quantity traded, however, is ambiguous. In Figure 3.9 it has fallen from Q_0 to Q_1 because in that diagram the reduction in supply has more than offset the increase in demand. If the increase in demand had more than offset the reduction in supply, the equilibrium quantity traded would have risen.

In general, when demand and supply change simultaneously, the supply–demand model can predict the effects on either price or quantity, but not both. Without additional information regarding the relative magnitudes of the shifts in the demand and supply curves, the effect on the other variable is ambiguous.

*Note that *after* the shift of the supply curve, there is also an increase in the *quantity* supplied—a movement from point *C* to point *B* along *S'*—in response to the rising price.

Figure 3.9

Effects of a simultaneous increase in demand and decrease in supply

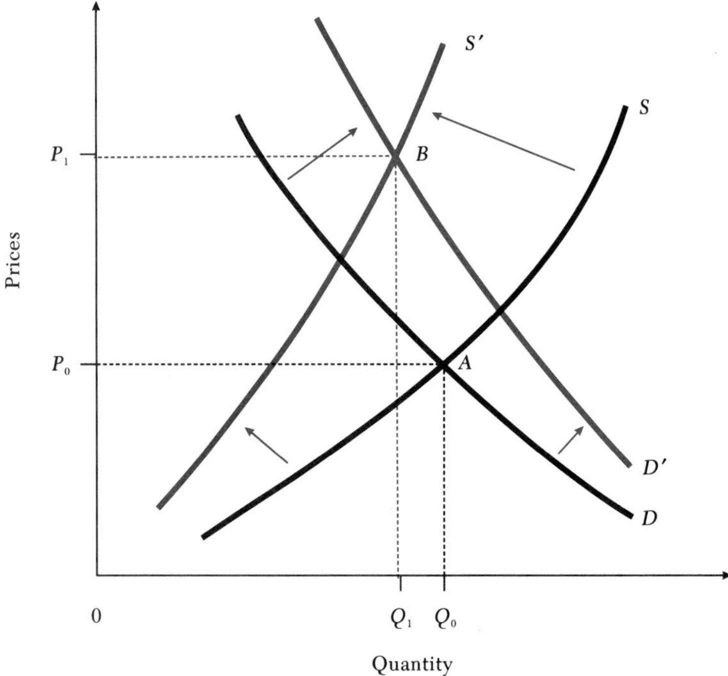

The effects of all of the possible combinations of changes in demand and supply are summarized in Table 3.5. Test your understanding by working through each case independently, explaining the economic processes by which the predicted adjustments occur. Although diagrams are useful in such an exercise, the important point is not simply to become familiar with the mechanics of curve shifting, but rather to understand the interactions between buyers and sellers that are summarized in the supply–demand model.

Table 3.5

Summary of effects of changes in demand and supply

	ASSUMED CHANGE IN:		PREDICTED EFFECT ON:	
	Demand	***Supply***	***Price***	***Quantity***
(a)	0	–	+	–
(b)	0	+	–	+
(c)	+	0	+	+
(d)	–	0	–	–
(e)	+	+	?	+
(f)	+	–	+	?
(g)	–	+	–	?
(h)	–	–	?	–

0 = no change; + = increase; – = decrease; ? = ambiguous effort

	ABSOLUTE (NOMINAL) PRICES				RELATIVE (REAL) PRICES*			
Time period →	*1970–74*	*1975–79*	*1980–84*	*1985–89*	*1970–74*	*1975–79*	*1980–84*	*1985–89*
All consumer goods	**+34**	**+47**	**+43**	**+15**	**n.a.**	**n.a.**	**n.a.**	**n.a.**
Food and beverages								
At home	+50	+43	+26	+19	+12	−3	−12	+3
Restaurant	+43	+52	+37	+18	+6	+3	−4	+3
Housing								
Home ownership	+35	+53	+48	+21	0	+4	+3	+5
Rent	+23	+35	+42	+20	−8	−9	−1	+4
Fuel and utilities	+45	+59	+62	+1	+8	+8	+13	−12
Furnishings	+26	+41	+28	+7	−6	−4	−11	−7
Apparel	+22	+22	+20	+13	−9	−17	−16	−2
Transportation								
New cars	+12	+41	+26	+12	−16	−4	−12	−3
Used cars	+19	+64	+87	+6	−12	+11	+31	−8
Gasoline	+53	+66	+40	−12	+14	+13	−2	−23
Public transit	+31	+35	+93	+17	−2	−8	+35	+2
Medical care	+33	+59	+58	+32	−1	+8	+11	+15
Entertainment	+26	+35	+35	+17	−6	−8	−5	+2

*Price changes relative to all other consumer goods

Table 3.6

Percentage changes in nominal and relative prices of selected consumer goods, 1970–1989

Relative Prices, Absolute Prices, and Inflation

In the last chapter we introduced the distinction between absolute (or nominal) prices and relative (or real) prices. Absolute prices—the monetary amounts listed on the price tags of goods—reflect not only the forces of supply and demand but also the effects of inflation and deflation. The basic market model developed in this chapter abstracts from inflation and deflation, and therefore provides an explanation of *relative* prices only.

It is easy to confuse changes in nominal prices with changes in relative prices when nearly all nominal prices are rising during a period of inflation. In an inflationary world, a change in the relative price of any good can be determined only with reference to changes in the general price level (which measures the average of all nominal prices). If, for example, the nominal price of steak has risen by only 5 percent while at the same time inflation pulled the general price level up by 10 percent, then steak has become less expensive relative to other goods. Put somewhat differently, the real opportunity cost of buying steak has fallen because less of those other goods must be sacrificed in order to purchase a pound of steak. By the same token, if the nominal price of steak has risen by 15 percent while the general price level has risen by 10 percent, then the real price of steak has increased.

Table 3.6 shows the actual changes in both nominal and relative prices for selected groups of consumer goods during five-year intervals between 1970 and 1989. As you can see from the columns titled Absolute (Nominal) Prices, inflation pushed up the average nominal price of all consumer goods, as well as nominal prices in nearly all of the groups of goods listed, during each period. The lone exception was the fall in the price of gasoline during 1985–89. The numbers in the columns titled Relative (Real) Prices have been adjusted to eliminate the effects of inflation. As such, they show the percentage changes in the prices within each group relative to the average price of all consumer goods. These are the price changes that can be explained with the basic demand–supply model. For example, the large increase in the real price of gasoline during the 1970s was primarily the result of OPEC actions that increased the cost of crude oil, an important input in gasoline production. The fall in the price of gasoline after 1980 reflects the collapse of OPEC and the resulting drop in crude oil prices. The rise in the real price of medical care reflects (at least in part) the increase in demand resulting from greater coverage of government-subsidized health care.

Preview

In the next chapter, we see how this system of markets and prices—of demand and supply—coordinates economic activity and, in the process, solves the basic economic problems we introduced in Chapter 1. We also see what happens when it is prevented from doing so by artificial restrictions on price adjustments.

CHAPTER SUMMARY

1. The *market* for a good consists of the set of all relationships linking buyers and sellers of that good.
2. *Market demand* relates the purchase plans of buyers to all of the factors that affect those plans; *market supply* relates the sales plans of sellers to all of the factors that affect those plans. *Market price* is common to both demand and supply because it affects the plans of both buyers and sellers.
3. The *law of demand* states that, other things being equal, there is an inverse relation between the price of a good and the quantity of that good demanded. That is, more will be demanded at lower prices than at higher prices.
4. The *demand curve* is a graphic representation of the relation between price and quantity demanded. The curve can be interpreted in either of two ways: It shows the quantity demanded at each price; it also shows the demand price for each quantity.
5. The *demand price* for each unit of a good is the maximum price any buyer in the market is willing to pay for that unit. As such, it is equal to the marginal value of that unit.

6. The effect of a change in the price of a good is represented graphically by a movement from one point to another along a given demand curve for that good. Such a movement is called a *change in the quantity demanded*. The effect of a change in any other factor that influences the demand for that good is to shift its demand curve. Such a shift is called a *change in demand*.

7. The *supply curve* is a graphic representation of the relation between price and quantity supplied. The curve can be interpreted in either of two ways: It shows the quantity supplied at each price; it also shows the supply price for each quantity.

8. The *supply price* for each unit of a good is the minimum price any seller in the market is willing to accept for that unit. As such, it is equal to the marginal cost of that unit.

9. The effect of a change in the price of a good is represented graphically by a movement from one point to another along a given supply curve for that good. Such a movement is called a *change in the quantity supplied*. The effect of a change in any of the other factors that influence the supply of that good is to shift its supply curve. Such a shift is called a *change in supply*.

10. The *market-clearing price* is the only price at which quantities demanded and supplied are equal. Graphically, it occurs at the intersection of the demand and supply curves.

11. At any price above the market-clearing price, there is a *surplus* that exerts downward pressure on price. At any price below the market-clearing price, there is a *shortage* that exerts upward pressure on price. When prices are free to adjust, the tendency of a price always to move toward its market-clearing level establishes the market-clearing price as the *equilibrium price*. The corresponding quantity is the quantity traded in equilibrium.

12. Changes in factors other than the price of the good itself can affect both demand and supply. The demand–supply model enables us to predict the effects that changes in these other factors have on the equilibrium price and quantity traded.

Key Terms and Concepts

market
demand
supply
law of demand
demand curve
demand price
supply curve
supply price
market-clearing price
shortage
surplus

Questions for Thought and Discussion

1. "The law of demand couldn't possibly apply to goods such as food or water, which are vital to survival." Do you agree?
2. "Because the quantity of any good bought must obviously always be equal to the quantity sold, it follows that the quantity demanded and the quantity supplied are always equal and the market is always in equilibrium." What is wrong with this statement?
3. "If the supply of gasoline increases, its price will fall. However, the lower price of gasoline will encourage more driving, thereby increasing the demand for gasoline and driving its price back up again. Therefore, we cannot tell whether an increase in the supply of gasoline will ultimately raise, lower, or not affect the price of gasoline." Where does this analysis go wrong?
4. Critique the following newspaper headline: "Stock prices tumble as a wave of selling hits Wall Street!"
5. Every so often we encounter doomsday predictions that the world is about to run out of one or another natural resource such as crude oil or natural gas. These predictions of shortages are usually based on extrapolation of past and current trends in "supply" and "demand" into the future. Often they are illustrated by a diagram like the one in Figure 3.10. What is wrong with predicting shortages in this manner?
6. What is the difference between *scarcity* of a good and a *shortage* of a good?
7. "Allowing the price of a good to rise when there is a shortage is unfair because some people, especially poor people, won't be able to afford it at the higher price." Do you agree? What issues are raised by this objection to using market price to ration goods.

Figure 3.10

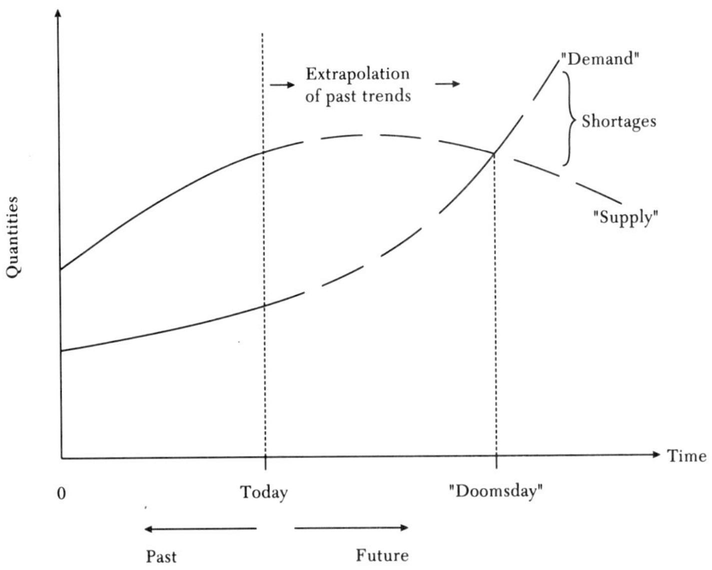

8. Landing slots, which allow an airline to take off or land a flight at a particular time of day, are granted to airlines at little or no charge by most airports. As a result, there is a shortage of landing slots at nearly all major airports. Predict the consequences of changing all this and allocating all landing slots by supply and demand.

9. During the 1970s, the price of natural gas was being set by federal government regulators rather than by supply and demand. Those regulators computed the average cost of producing domestic natural gas and, in order to encourage increased production of natural gas, set a price well above that average cost. They were then surprised when production did not increase. Can you tell them why it didn't?

10. It is sometimes claimed that the introduction of VisiCalc, the first spreadsheet program for personal computers, was the critical element in the early success of the Apple II computer on which it was designed to run. Use demand and supply to explain the logic of this claim.

11. Starting from an initial equilibrium, draw a diagram to show what will happen in the widget market as a result of each of the following:
    a. The price of gadgets, which most consumers consider a good substitute for widgets, falls.
    b. The government levies a $1 per unit tax on widgets, collecting the tax from widget sellers.
    c. The price of kryptonite, an essential input in widget production, rises.
    d. A respected widget market analyst and guru forecasts higher prices for widgets (which are durable, nonperishable goods) in the future.
    e. The market for widgets expands as both the number of widget buyers and widget sellers increases.

CHAPTER 4

The Price System and Economic Coordination in the Dynamic Economy

At the heart of economics is a scientific mystery: How is it that the pricing system accomplishes the world's work without anyone being in charge? . . . How is order produced from freedom of choice?

VERNON L. SMITH*

An economic system is an immensely complex set of social relationships. In the U.S. economy, for example, there are nearly 250 million people in some 80 million households. They supply labor, capital, and other productive resources to about 15 million business enterprises which, along with their counterparts in dozens of other countries around the world, provide food, shelter, clothing, entertainment, medical care, education, and the countless other goods we all consume. The basic task of the economic system is to coordinate the actions of these hundreds of millions of people and the millions of producing units into which they are organized.

The people whose behavior must be coordinated have different tastes and preferences, different talents and abilities, and are usually far removed from one another. As consumers, they are generally unaware of either the identity of the suppliers of the resources used to produce the goods they consume or the technologies by which those productive resources are combined. As producers, they

*Vernon L. Smith, "Microeconomic Systems as an Experimental Science," *American Economic Review*, Vol. 72 (December 1982), p. 952.

tend to specialize. As we have seen, specialization increases productive efficiency, but it also makes it rare for any single person to comprehend an entire production process from start to finish.

To take a concrete example, consider the production of a common consumer good, say a television set. To produce a TV, raw materials like crude oil, silicon, various metals, and forest products must be extracted from the physical environment. Then those raw materials must be refined and transformed into the wire, nuts, bolts and screws, glass, wood, and plastic parts that are in turn used to construct the cabinet, the picture tube, the tuner, the circuit boards, and the other components. The set is then assembled and transported to the point of retail sale, where its availability, price, and other characteristics are advertised to potential buyers, and where those buyers can come to inspect it and compare it with other brands.

This production process involves thousands upon thousands of individual producers, from miners and loggers to foundrymen and machinists, from engineers and truck drivers to salespersons and advertising account executives. Most of them neither know one another nor have any idea of one another's role in the production process. The final consumer hasn't the slightest idea of who mined the copper ore for the wires in his TV, nor does he know how to train an engineer competent to design its circuits, or, most importantly, how to coordinate all of the activities necessary to create the television set. That coordination is carried out through a series of transactions involving the exchange of human resources (labor, knowledge, technical skills, and so on), capital services (both real and financial), and natural resources (mineral and forestry rights, for example) that culminates in the television set. Blissfully unaware of this complex process, the consumer need merely push a button to enjoy "Monday Night Football" or "All My Children."

Our task in this chapter is to gain a perspective on how the market coordinates the complex chain of events by which productive resources are supplied, combined, and transformed into the final goods we all consume.

THE MARKET SYSTEM

The Circular Flow of Economic Activity

Economists often describe the workings of the economy in terms of a *circular flow* of economic activity. Such a circular flow representing the private sector of a market economy is pictured in Figure 4.1 on page 76. Two sets of economic agents—households and business firms—are shown linked by two sets of markets—markets for final goods and markets for productive resources. Because productive resources are often referred to as "factors of production," markets for productive resources are also called **factor markets**.

Factor markets are the markets in which productive resources (labor, capital, etc.) and their services are exchanged.

The household sector supplies labor, capital, and other productive resources to the business firms that demand those resources for use in production. The

Figure 4.1

The circular flow of economic activity

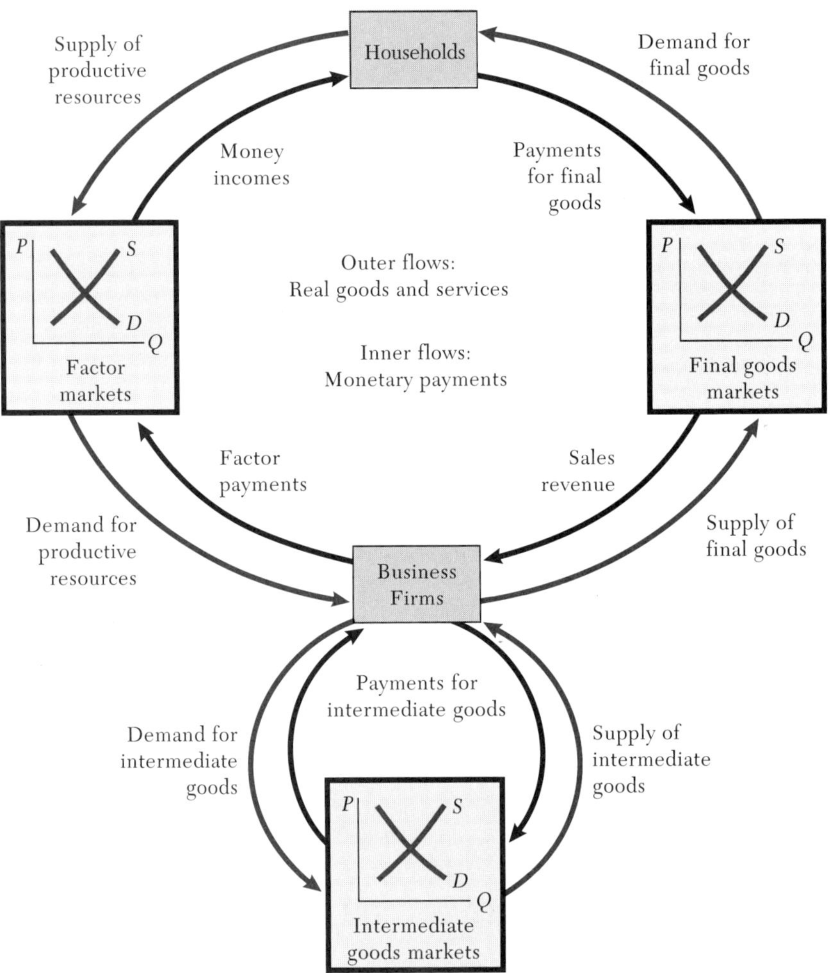

process is coordinated through the factor markets where relative price adjustments equate the supply and demand for each productive resource and allocate those resources among various producers. Monetary *factor payments* for the use of resources flow through the factor markets in the opposite direction—from firms to households. These payments are the source of household incomes. The factor markets therefore determine how productive resources are allocated and what their relative prices are, as well as the incomes of those who supply them.

On the right-hand side of Figure 4.1, household demand for final goods generates a flow of money payments from households to firms and a corresponding real flow of final goods from firms to households. The amounts of each of the various final goods produced, their prices, and their distribution among households are determined by supply and demand in the final goods markets.

Intermediate goods are goods used up in the production of other goods.

Many transactions involve exchanges of **intermediate goods** within the business sector rather than exchanges between households and business firms. These exchanges are shown by the separate circular flow at the bottom of Figure 4.1; they begin and end in the business sector. Transactions involving such things as raw materials, semifinished goods, components, business services, and other inputs used in the production process, as well as transactions between manufacturers, distributors, and retailers, take place in the intermediate goods markets. These markets exist because firms, like individuals, often find it advantageous to specialize in their production. In so doing, they must buy many of their inputs from other firms. Television manufacturers, for example, do not mine the copper, aluminum, and silicon they use in the production of a TV set, nor do they cut down the trees for its wooden cabinet. In fact, most do not even make their own picture tubes, and a few simply purchase all of their components from other manufacturers and specialize solely in assembling and marketing the final product.

The process of production and exchange can thus be described as a circular flow of transactions leading from households in their role as suppliers of primary productive services, to the business firms that purchase those services and combine them with the intermediate goods supplied by other business firms, and then back again to the households in their role as demanders of final goods. The entire process is coordinated by markets in which relative price adjustments insure that quantity supplied is equal to quantity demanded for each productive resource, intermediate good, and final good.

Market Interdependence

Markets are not isolated and insulated from one another. They are linked together in an interdependent system in which adjustments in any one market have repercussions in many other markets, some closely related and others apparently far removed.

To illustrate the nature of this interdependence, consider the effects of a reduction in the world supply of crude oil. The reduction in supply will increase the market price of crude oil, but that is only the first-order effect. Secondary effects will be felt in the markets for heating oil, gasoline, and all other commodities that use crude oil as an intermediate input. The higher price of crude oil will mean higher marginal costs and thus higher supply prices for those commodities. These second-round price increases will in turn have further effects on the markets for still other related goods. The rise in the price of heating oil, for example, will increase the demand for substitutes, including natural gas, electricity, and solar panels. The rise in the price of gasoline will increase the demand for smaller, more fuel-efficient cars relative to the demand for large gas guzzlers. Markets even farther removed will also be affected. The higher overall cost of heating homes and other buildings, for example, will increase the demand for wool sweaters, resulting in a rise in the price of wool. If the higher wool price persists, there will eventually be a shift in the use of ranch land from raising cattle to raising sheep. And that will cause the price of lamb chops to fall relative to the price of steak!

This hypothetical chain of events, which has carried us from a reduction in crude oil supplies to a fall in the relative price of lamb chops, illustrates an important point: In an interdependent system like a market economy, virtually everything affects everything else. The ripple and feedback effects of any significant change are so widespread, and extend so far beyond the initial impact, that they are virtually impossible to fully anticipate in advance. Moreover, the kinds of external economic shocks that can affect the adjustment process—wars, variations in weather, international cartels, technological breakthroughs, the discovery of new raw material deposits, and shifts in government policy, to mention just a few—are themselves often unanticipated and their effects compounded, so that before the chain reaction of effects from any one disturbance has worked its way through the system, another has begun to be felt.

Market Prices as Social Coordinators

As you might imagine, if any individual, or group of individuals, were assigned the responsibility for anticipating all of the ramifications of an economic disturbance, and for planning the economic adjustments needed to accommodate it, the task would be virtually insurmountable. The chronic shortages and surpluses of goods, the mismatches between input allocations and production goals, and the extreme vulnerability of economic plans to unforeseen shocks—all of which are daily facts of life in societies, such as the Soviet Union, that have relied heavily on centralized economic planning—provide ample evidence on this point.

In a market directed economy, however, such massive information requirements are fortunately unnecessary. A market system allows both the information and the decision-making authority necessary to coordinate economic adjustments to remain decentralized. Coordination is achieved not through central directives but through adjustments in relative prices. In this capacity, relative prices perform two crucial functions:

First, relative price changes convey to individual decision makers (buyers and sellers, producers and consumers) the *information* necessary for them to adapt to a change in economic conditions. An increase in the relative scarcity of any good or productive resource—due either to a reduction in its supply or to an increase in the demand for it—is communicated to buyers and sellers as an increase in its price. Conversely, the information that a something has become relatively more abundant is communicated by a fall in its price.

Second, relative price changes provide decision makers with the *incentive* to alter their behavior and adapt to changes in economic conditions. A higher price not only informs the potential consumer of an increase in the relative scarcity of a good, it also provides an incentive to reduce the consumption of that good in favor of substitutes. In addition, higher prices give suppliers an incentive to expand production of both the original good and the substitutes for which consumer demand has increased. A higher price for a productive resource creates an incentive for producers to adopt, or to develop, production techniques that economize on its use. Lower prices, signalling greater relative abundance, provide the opposite set of incentives.

The coordinating role of relative prices can be illustrated in the context of the foregoing example of the effects of a reduction in the supply of crude oil. If relative prices are allowed to adjust freely to this economic shock, no one has to order or exhort consumers to reduce their consumption of gasoline or heating oil, for the rising prices of those commodities automatically provide consumers with an incentive to do just that. No central authority need inform the producers of natural gas that more gas is desired as a substitute for petroleum-based energy sources, for the rising price not only tells them that is the case, it also provides them with an incentive to tap natural gas deposits that would have been uneconomical at lower prices. In response to the higher prices of all energy sources, the market will automatically channel productive resources into the search for new deposits and new technologies, and it will allocate those resources only to areas in which the expected value of the results at least covers their opportunity cost. Finally, no bureaucrat need send a memo explaining the energy situation to a rancher in the Australian outback, requesting him to raise more sheep for wool production. All that rancher and thousands of others like him need to know is that the real price of wool has risen, and they will respond by increasing the amount of wool they supply.

By way of contrast, it is interesting to note what happened during the late 1970s when the federal government, responding to a reduction in international crude oil supplies, tried to use its centralized authority to allocate gasoline rather than rely on the market. Armed with volumes of statistics, a well-trained staff, and a considerable budget, and having to deal with only a single commodity, the government nonetheless succeeded in creating huge shortages and long gas lines on the West Coast while the Midwest and East were relatively unaffected. The market solves millions of infinitely more complex allocation problems every day with hardly any notice.

WHAT, HOW, AND FOR WHOM? MARKETS AND THE BASIC ECONOMIC PROBLEMS

In Chapter 1 we identified five fundamental problems that any economic system must solve: resource allocation, choice of production techniques, distribution, temporal allocation, and risk allocation. Let us now consider how these problems are solved in a market economy. The basic demand–supply model developed in

Chapter 3 can be applied directly to analyze the role of the market in resource allocation, the choice of production techniques, and distribution. The analysis of the market's role in temporal allocation and risk allocation will require some extensions of our basic model.

Resource Allocation: What Is Produced?

The demand–supply model tells us that the market allocates productive resources among goods by comparing the marginal value of each good (its demand price) with its marginal cost (its supply price). Moreover, because market adjustments tend to equate the demand price and the supply price, the quantity of each good produced in equilibrium is that amount for which the marginal cost of the last unit produced equals its marginal value. The result is an output mix that maximizes the total economic value of the goods we produce with our scarce resources.

To illustrate the logic of this assertion let us consider the allocation of resources to widget production. Suppose that at the current rate of output in the widget market say, Q_1 in Figure 4.2, the marginal value of the last widget

Figure 4.2

Market allocation: comparing marginal value and marginal cost

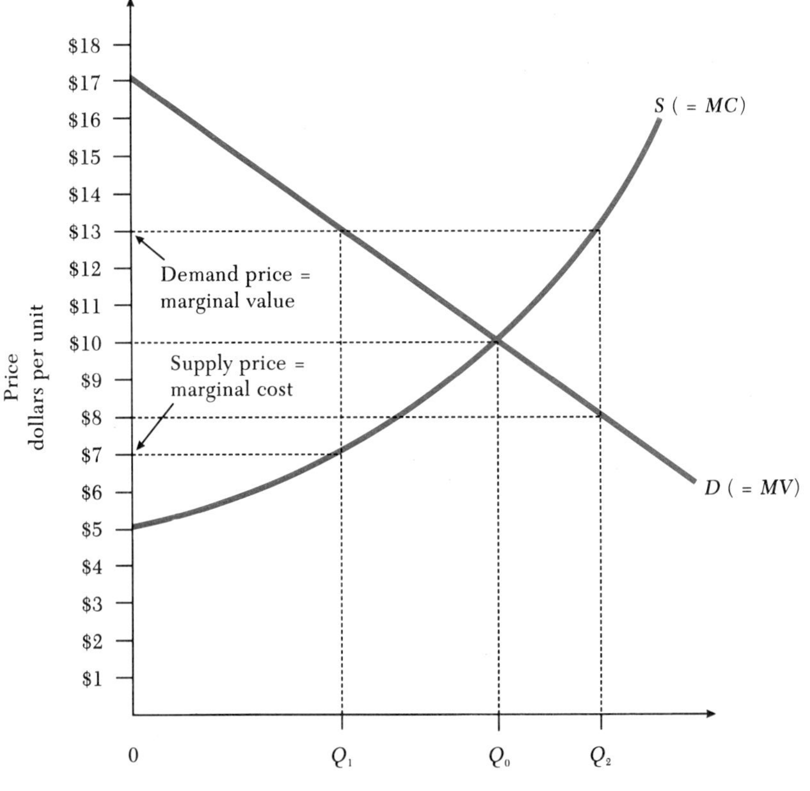

produced is $13 and its marginal cost is $7. Since opportunity cost measures the value of foregone alternatives—in this case, the value of the other goods that must be sacrificed to produce that widget—the $6 difference between its marginal value and its marginal cost measures the excess of its value over the value of what we give up to get it. This $6 increase in value is therefore the gain in economic value from using our resources to produce that last widget rather than something else.

Up to the market-clearing output rate of Q_0, the marginal value of each additional widget traded exceeds its marginal cost. Thus, stopping anywhere short of Q_0 would mean a failure to capture some potential benefits, such as the $6 gain in the preceding example. On the other hand, it is not worth producing more widgets than Q_0 because their marginal costs would exceed their marginal values. For example, if the output rate were Q_2 in Figure 4.2, the last widget produced would have a marginal cost of $13 and a marginal value of only $8, so that its production would reduce by $5 the economic value we get from our scarce resources.

It follows that total economic value is at a maximum and, equivalently, resources are efficiently allocated, only when the marginal value of the last unit of each good produced and exchanged is equal to its marginal cost. This is exactly what the market achieves when it equates demand and supply in equilibrium.

In Figure 4.3(a) on page 82, the roughly triangular area labelled *ABE* represents the difference between the marginal values and marginal costs of all widgets traded in equilibrium. It thus provides a graphic representation of the net economic value created in the widget market. Figure 4.3(b) on the same page shows how that value is shared, as gains from trade, by buyers and sellers of widgets. The value captured by buyers, which we call **consumers' surplus**, reflects the difference between the marginal value of each widget purchased and its market price. For example, a buyer who values a widget at $13 and is able to obtain it at a price of $10 gains a consumer's surplus of $3 on the purchase. Total consumers' surplus in equilibrium—the excess of marginal value over price on all units traded—can be represented by the area below the demand curve and above the market price, or area AEP_0 in Figure 4.3(b).

Consumers' surplus is the difference between the maximum amount buyers are willing to pay for a good and the amount they actually pay for it; it measures the share of the gains from trade captured by buyers.

The value captured by sellers, which we call **producers' surplus**, reflects the difference between the market price and the marginal cost of each widget sold. For example, a seller who receives a price of $10 for a widget that costs $7 to supply gains a producers' surplus of $3 on the transaction. Total producers' surplus in equilibrium—the excess of price over marginal cost on all units traded—can be represented by the area above the supply curve and below the market price, or area P_0EB in Figure 4.3(b).

Producers' surplus is the difference between the minimum amount sellers are willing to accept for a good and the amount they actually receive for it; it measures the share of the gains from trade captured by sellers.

The sum of consumers' and producers' surpluses, which together make up the total gains from trade, is maximized when the market is in equilibrium.

Because the conditions underlying demand and supply are in reality always changing, an equilibrium may never actually be reached. The important point, however, is that the market is continually adjusting to change, comparing the values of all the different goods that could be produced with available resources, and shifting those resources from less valuable to more valuable uses. And it does this "without anyone being in charge!"

Figure 4.3

(a) Total value created in equilibrium and (b) Consumers' and producers' surplus

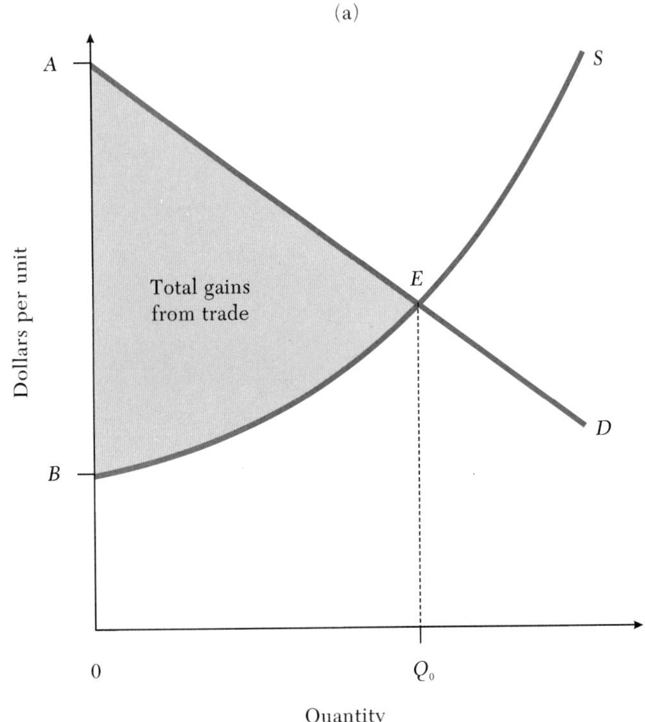

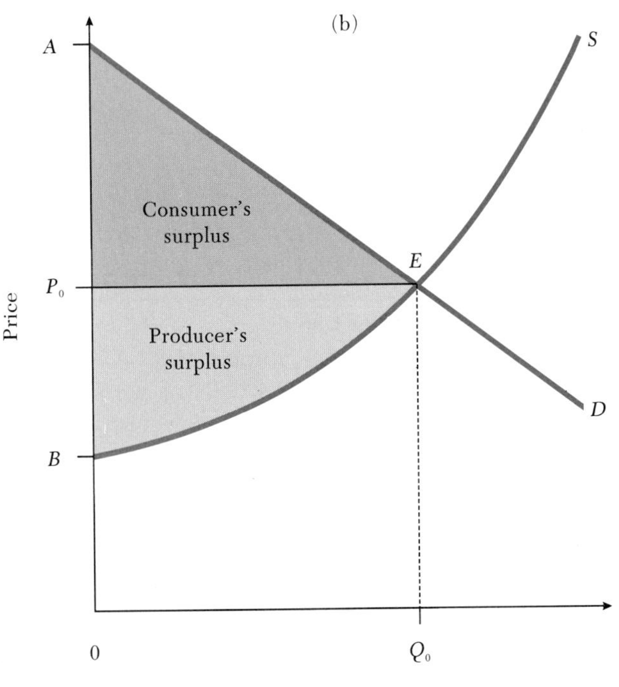

Production Techniques: How Is It Produced?

There are generally a number of different technologies available for the production of any particular good, each using a different mix of labor, capital, raw materials, and other resources. The relative prices of resources convey information about their respective opportunity costs and provide producers with an incentive to adopt those production techniques that use the least costly combination of resources. Because substitution is possible in production as well as in consumption, producers shift to production techniques that substitute lower priced resources for higher priced ones when relative prices change. If new deposits of aluminum are discovered, for example, aluminum will fall in price relative to copper, iron, and other metals, and will be substituted for them in a variety of production processes. If the price of labor rises relative to that of capital, producers will adopt more *capital intensive* technologies—that is, technologies that use a higher proportion of capital to labor. If the relative price of labor falls, producers will adopt more *labor intensive* technologies.

In a dynamic economy, the development and application of new technologies also reflect the relative prices of productive resources. For example, the continuing development of labor-saving production techniques, from the assembly line to robotics, is a response to the increasing real price of labor. Similarly, the main stimulus to the development of solar energy technology was the dramatic increase in the real prices of fossil fuels during the 1970s and early 1980s.

Distribution: Who Gets It?

In a market economy, goods are allocated on the basis of price. Since goods are available only to those willing to pay at least the market price, they are allocated to those who effectively value them most highly. If less of some good is available, its price will rise and those who are unwilling to pay the higher price will no longer consume it, or they will at least consume less of it.

Because effective demand implies the ability, as well as the willingness, to pay for a good, the distribution of goods also depends on the distribution of income and wealth in the economy. In a market economy, one's income depends on the amounts and kinds of productive resources he or she supplies and on the market prices those resources command. Changes in relative prices therefore also affect the distribution of income. For example, a fall in the relative price of computers increases the quantity of computers demanded, and this in turn increases the demand for software engineers to write the programs to run the computers. The result is an increase in the earnings of computer programmers.

Temporal Allocation: When Is It Available?

Markets not only allocate resources among different uses at any given time, they also allocate resources between the present and the future. The fundamental problem of temporal allocation is that of determining how much of our available productive capacity is to be used to produce goods for current consumption and how much is to be used for the investment that will enable us to produce more in the future.

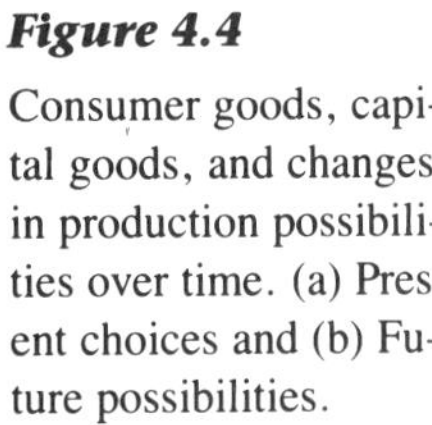

Figure 4.4

Consumer goods, capital goods, and changes in production possibilities over time. (a) Present choices and (b) Future possibilities.

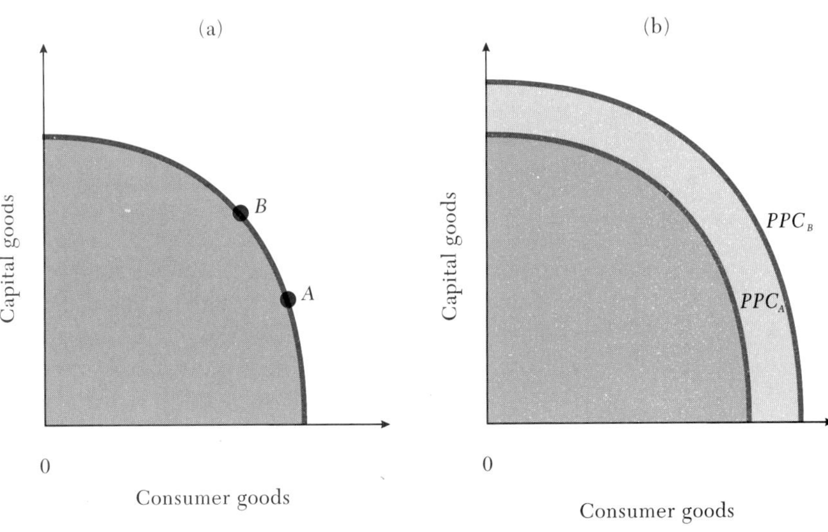

The nature of the temporal allocation problem can be illustrated with the aid of the production possibilities curve. Figure 4.4(a) depicts a hypothetical production possibilities curve showing the various combinations of consumer goods and capital goods that can be produced with an economy's current productive capacity. At point *A* on the curve, a relatively large proportion of that capacity is devoted to the production of consumer goods and a relatively small proportion to the production of capital goods—that is, to current investment. Point *B* represents a current output mix with fewer consumer goods but more capital goods. Figure 4.4(b) shows the alternative *future* production possibilities curves that would result from the *current* choice of points *A* and *B*, respectively. As the two graphs indicate, a choice to invest more now [point *B* in Figure 4.4(a)], although it means less current consumption, also means that production possibilities will be expanded in the future [PPC_B in Figure 4.4(b)]. The reason is that the capital goods produced today are part of the productive capacity of the future.

Capital markets are the markets that coordinate saving and investment decisions and, in the process, determine how much of our productive capacity is to be used for current consumption and how much is to be used for adding to our capital stock.

To see how choices between points like *A* and *B* are made in a market economy, we must understand the workings of the economy's **capital markets** which coordinate saving and investment decisions.

The Basic Economics of Capital Markets

A **financial intermediary** specializes in channelling funds from lenders/savers to borrowers/investors.

As our discussion of the circular flow indicated, households are the ultimate source of all productive resources, including the capital goods used by business firms. However, households rarely supply physical capital directly to firms. Rather, both make use of **financial intermediaries** that specialize in channelling savings from households to business firms. Banks are the most common form of financial intermediary. In effect, households lend to banks when they deposit funds in their passbook savings accounts and the various money market accounts banks offer. Banks then use those deposits to make loans to business firms to finance the purchase of capital goods. Savings and loan associations, brokerage firms, life insurance companies, and other financial intermediaries provide similar services. All convert the *financial investments* that households make when they save into the *real investments* that business firms make when they acquire capital goods. The extra future output made possible by the additional capital enables business firms to reimburse households (again, usually through financial intermediaries) for their original financial investments and to pay them a premium as well. This premium can take the form of a promise of a specified future amount, in which case it is called *interest*, or it can be a share of the business' future *profits* (if any). Accordingly, we can divide the capital markets into the **credit market**, in which savers receive interest, and the **equities market**, in which they receive claims on future profits. Since such claims typically take the form of shares of stock in business corporations, we postpone our discussion of the equities (stock) market until Chapter 7, where we consider the economics of the modern corporation. Here we concentrate on the credit market and the role of interest rates in coordinating choices between present and future.

The **credit market** is the market in which funds are loaned out in return for the promise of future repayment with interest.

The **equities market** is the market in which investment funds are supplied in return for a claim on future profits.

Interest Rates as Relative Prices

The interest premium is the cost a borrower incurs to have purchasing power available sooner rather than later and, correspondingly, the reward the saver (lender) reaps by postponing access to that purchasing power. In a very fundamental sense, therefore, the interest rate is a measure of the value of the present relative to the future. As with other relative prices, its function is to coordinate the allocation of scarce resources; in the case of the interest rate, this means coordinating choices between the present and future use of resources.

(The interest rate is sometimes referred to as the "price of money" and the credit market as the "money market." This terminology is misleading, however. Interest is not a payment for money per se; it is like rent paid for the temporary use of money. As such, it is no more the "price of money" than Hertz' car rental rate is the price of a new Ford.)

Why There Are Interest Rates

The existence of interest rates rests on two fundamental factors: *subjective time preference* and the *productivity of capital*.

Subjective Time Preference If you were to give someone $100 today in return for a promise to repay $100 1 year from today, you would not come out even. You would have given up the alternative of buying and enjoying $100 worth of goods *this* year, an alternative that cannot be restored by the $100 repayment you receive *next* year. It is gone forever! That is why most people demand a premium to postpone their use of purchasing power. In other words, their subjective tastes exhibit preference for earlier availability of goods over later availability.

As with other subjective tastes, we can express time preference in terms of a trade-off—in this case, a trade-off between present and future. Suppose, for example, that Jack would be just as happy with a promise of $105 one year from now as he would be with $100 in his pocket right now. We would say that his rate of subjective time preference is 5 percent per year because that is the premium (expressed as an annual rate) that he would require to postpone his consumption of $100 worth of goods and services for one year. If Jill would be equally satisfied with $100 now or $110 one year from now, then her rate of subjective time preference is 10 percent.

The difference between Jack's and Jill's rates of subjective time preference is the basis for a mutually beneficial exchange. If, for example, Jack gives Jill $100 now, and Jill gives Jack her promise to repay him $108 at the end of one year, then both come out ahead: The $108 more than compensates Jack (he would have accepted as little as $105) and at the same time is less than the $110 maximum that Jill would have been willing to pay for the use of $100 for a year.

This exchange between Jack and Jill is, of course, just a one-year loan of $100 from Jack to Jill at an 8 percent rate of interest. (As you can probably see, any interest rate between 5 percent and 10 percent would work in this example.) Differences in subjective time preferences among individuals thus provide one reason for borrowing and lending. People with higher rates of time preference can borrow from those with lower rates of time preference and both can come out ahead.

The Productivity of Capital Capital includes all of the tools, both physical and intellectual, that we use in production. Because resources must first be used to produce the tools before the tools can be used to produce final goods, production using capital goods is a *roundabout* process. Roundabout production methods delay the availability of the final product, but they also lead to greater output than more direct methods using less capital. By first constructing a printing press, for example, we can ultimately produce many more books than we could lettering them by hand. By first learning to use a computer, we can solve many more problems, and more difficult problems, than we could with just a pencil and paper. Constructing the printing press and learning to use the computer take time, but the increased future output made available by such methods can more than compensate for the wait. In other words, after allowing for all of their costs, capital goods can still have a *positive net productivity*.

The productivity of capital is the principal source of the demand for credit. If a business firm anticipates that a capital good costing $100,000 will enable it to produce an additional $20,000 per year worth of output (net of other costs) into the indefinite future, it would be willing to pay up to 20 percent interest to borrow the $100,000 to purchase that capital good.

The Credit Market and the Interest Rate

Figure 4.5 shows the supply and demand for credit (sometimes called *loanable funds*). The supply of credit reflects the time preferences of households. Other things being equal, the higher the interest rate, the greater the incentive of households to save, the less incentive for them to borrow, and the greater the net supply of credit to businesses. The demand for credit on the part of businesses reflects the expected productivity of new capital investments. The lower the interest rate,

Figure 4.5

The credit market

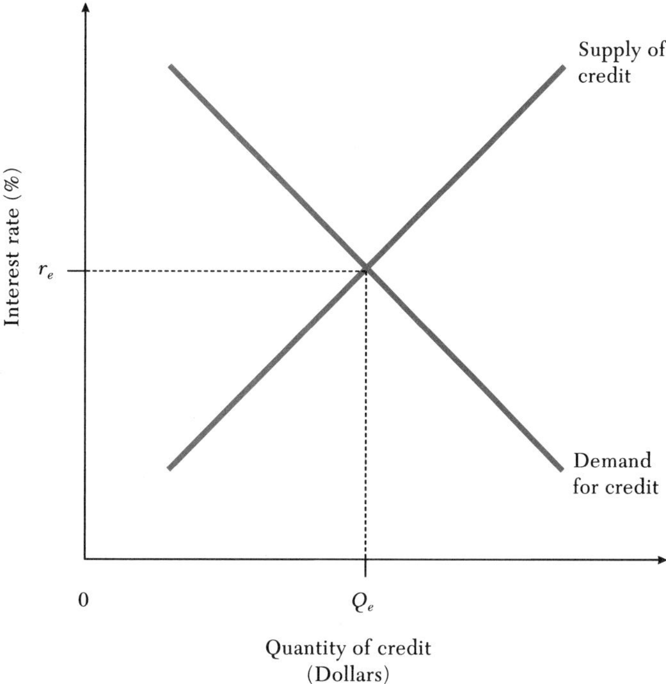

the less the opportunity cost of borrowing, the more businesses will want to invest in new capital goods, and the greater the volume of credit they will demand.

If the interest rate in Figure 4.5 were above its market-clearing level (r_e), the supply of credit would exceed the demand, there would be a surplus of credit, and competition among lenders would force the interest rate down to its market-clearing level. Conversely, if the interest rate were below its market-clearing level, there would be a shortage of credit, and competition among borrowers would force the rate up to its market-clearing level. By continuously adjusting to clear the credit market, the interest rate coordinates the lending and borrowing choices of millions of households and business firms.

Other Factors Affecting Interest Rates

The **pure rate of interest** is the rate of interest determined by subjective time preference and the productivity of capital.

The interest rate that would be determined solely by the interaction between subjective time preference and the productivity of capital is known as the **pure rate of interest**. The interest rates we actually observe in the credit market reflect the influence of many other factors. Among the most important of these are *transactions costs*, *risk*, and *inflation*.

Transactions Costs For the same reason that retail prices are higher than wholesale prices, financial intermediaries charge borrowers higher interest rates than they pay to lenders (savers): The intermediaries must cover the costs of the services they provide. These costs differ for different types of borrowing and lending. For example, the interest rate bankers pay on accounts from which funds can be withdrawn on short notice is generally less than what they pay on accounts that require funds to be deposited for a longer period of time. The bookkeeping and other transaction costs are much higher for the former because of the more frequent turnover of funds. Similarly, loans requiring more servicing, such as extensive credit checks, monthly billings, and detailed record-keeping, are supplied only at higher interest rates than loans requiring less servicing. This is why a simple 90-day business loan to a borrower with whom the bank has a continuing relationship is usually made at a lower interest rate than, say, a car loan requiring a credit check and three or four years of monthly billing and record-keeping.

Default risk is the risk that the borrower in a credit transaction will not fully repay his debt.

A **risk premium** is an addition to the interest rate to compensate the lender for the possibility that the borrower might default.

Risk Differentials Because many loans are never fully repaid, every credit transaction carries an element of **default risk**—the risk that the borrower may fail to meet some or all of his future payment obligations. Figure 4.6 shows how risk affects interest rates. Because of the potential losses default risk imposes on lenders, their supply price of credit to risky borrowers is higher than to riskless borrowers, and the higher supply price results in a higher market interest rate for risky borrowers. The difference between the interest rate on loans to risky borrowers (r_1) and the interest rate on loans to riskless borrowers (r_0) is called a **risk premium**. The higher the risk, the greater the risk premium. Different risk premiums account for much of the variation in interest rates that we observe at any given time in the credit markets.

The **nominal interest rate** includes a premium for expected inflation; it is equal to the sum of the real interest rate and the expected rate of inflation.

The **real interest rate** is the interest rate that would exist if no inflation were expected.

Inflation The rate of inflation is the rate at which the general level of nominal prices rises over time, or equivalently, the rate at which the purchasing power of money declines over time. To the extent that lenders expect inflation, they demand higher interest rates to compensate for the lower purchasing power of the dollars with which they will be repaid. Similarly, borrowers who expect inflation are willing to pay higher interest rates to obtain money now because they expect its purchasing power to be less in the future. Expectations of inflation therefore increase both the supply price and the demand price for credit, as illustrated in Figure 4.7 on page 90. As a result, the expected rate of inflation is incorporated into market rates of interest. Specifically, the **nominal interest rate** that the market establishes is equal to a **real interest rate**—the rate that would clear the market in the absence of inflationary expectations—plus the *expected rate of inflation*. Other things being equal, the higher the expected rate of inflation, the higher the nominal interest rate.

To take a concrete example, suppose that the market would establish a real interest rate of 3 percent in the absence of inflation. If borrowers and lenders expect a 5 percent rate of inflation, then the nominal interest rate will be 8 percent. (The repayment of 8 percent more dollars, each with 5 percent less purchasing power, is exactly equivalent to the repayment of 3 percent more dollars in the absence of inflation.) If a 7 percent rate of inflation is anticipated, then the

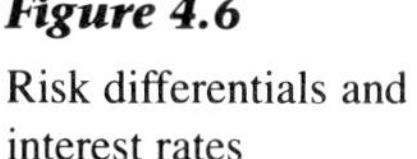

Figure 4.6

Risk differentials and interest rates

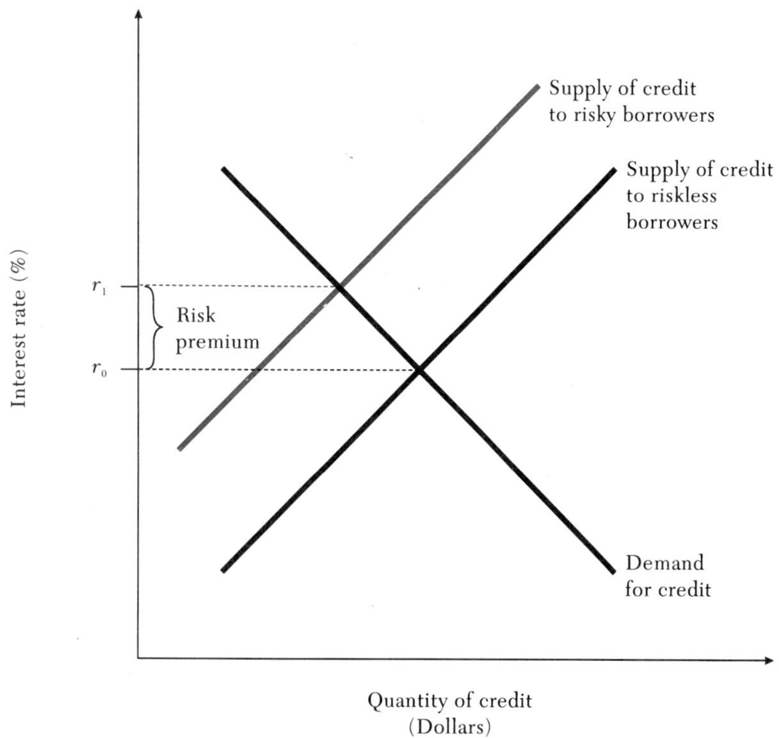

nominal rate will be 10 percent. If no inflation is anticipated, then the nominal rate will be the same as the real rate, namely, 3 percent.

The Credit Market, Interest Rates, and Allocation over Time

To see how the credit market coordinates temporal allocation, consider the effects of a change in saving. Specifically, suppose that people decide to save more now in order to consume more in the future. It is one thing to want more future consumption; it is quite another to shift the use of productive resources from present to future so that future consumption opportunities will actually expand. This shift is accomplished through the credit market, which transmits the greater demand for future consumption from savers to producers and simultaneously provides the latter with an incentive to create the capacity to meet that future demand. Specifically the rise in saving leads to an increase in the supply of credit. This reduces the market-clearing interest rate and encourages businesses to borrow to invest in new capital goods. The result is an increase in future productive capacity—precisely what is needed to meet the future consumption demands implied by the increase in current saving.

Figure 4.7

Real interest rates, nominal interest rates, and expected inflation

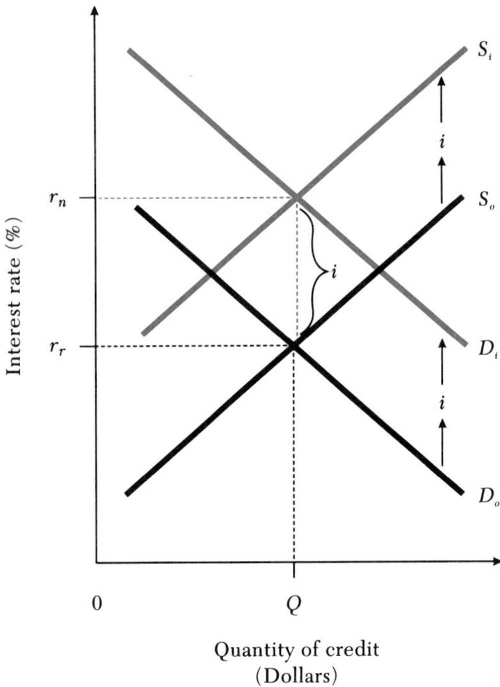

D_o = Demand for credit when no inflation is expected
S_o = Supply of credit when no inflation is expected
$i = r_n - r_r$ = expected rate of inflation
D_i = Demand for credit when i% inflation is expected
S_i = Supply of credit when i% inflation is expected
r_r = Real rate of interest
r_n = nominal rate of interest

Risk Allocation: Who Bears the Risk Inherent in Economic Activity?

As we have seen, many economic choices are accompanied by an element of risk. People differ in their attitudes toward risk. Some pay a premium to avoid risk; others willingly accept risks when they feel that the reward for success is sufficient. Just as the market allows people to trade on differences in their subjective tastes, including time preferences, it also allows them to trade on differences in their attitudes toward risk. As in other market processes, the mechanism for allocating and shifting risk is voluntary exchange and the relative prices that are established in the course of exchange.

How the Market Allocates Risk

Let us briefly consider some of the ways in which the market allocates risks. This set of examples is meant to be representative, but by no means exhaustive, of the various market processes for allocating risk.

Risk Premiums in Relative Prices Risk transfers are sometimes implicit in the prices we pay for goods. As we have seen, for example, borrowers who are perceived by lenders to have a higher risk of default generally have to pay higher interest rates to obtain credit. The higher interest rate compensates the lender for the risk that he will not be fully repaid. When we buy a brand name product with a well-known reputation for quality and reliability rather than a generic substitute with an unknown reputation, the higher price we pay is in effect a premium for insurance against disappointment. A seller who offers a warrantee with his product explicitly accepts the risk of something going wrong with that product and charges accordingly. In effect, he is selling insurance along with his product.

Variations in Contractual Forms In some transactions one party is guaranteed a fixed payment and the other party claims whatever remains after that payment is made. A party whose return is guaranteed in an exchange is called a **contractual claimant**; the party who takes what, if anything, is left, and thus bears the risk, is called the **residual claimant**.

A **contractual claimant** is one whose claim on some economic gain is promised by contract.

A **residual claimant** is one whose claim on some economic gain takes the form of a share of the residual, if any, that is left after all contractual claims are met.

As an illustration, consider some of the possible agreements between a landowner and a farmer. Because of the vagaries of the weather, the possibility of pests and crop disease, and the unpredictability of agricultural prices, farming is a risky business. If the farmer rents the land from the landowner for a fixed amount, intending to sell his crop for whatever it will bring, then the landowner is the contractual claimant and the farmer is the risk-bearing residual claimant. If the landowner pays the farmer a fixed wage to farm the land and sells the crop for whatever it will bring, then the farmer is the contractual claimant and the landowner bears the risk. If they agree to divide whatever revenues the crop brings, then they are both residual claimants sharing the risks.

Futures Markets Markets in which agreements are made today for the delivery of some good at a future date are called **futures markets**. There are futures markets for most agricultural commodities, primary metals and other raw materials, semi-finished goods such as plywood and cloth, and many financial assets. Futures markets permit the exchange of risk between those who wish to avoid risk (or *hedge*) and those who wish to gamble (or *speculate*).

A **futures market** is a market in which buyers and sellers agree now to a price at which they will exchange goods at some specified future date.

To see how this works, consider the example of a farmer who plants his corn in March not knowing what price it will bring when it is harvested in September. The corn futures market enables him to avoid that risk by locking in a price in March for the corn he will harvest in September. In effect, he enters a contract with a speculator who agrees to buy the farmer's corn at a predetermined price. If this price is \$3.00 per bushel, the speculator will buy the corn for that amount when it is harvested in September and then resell it for whatever it will bring. If the price of corn turns out to be \$3.25 in September, the speculator will make a profit of $0.25 per bushel; if the price turns out to be $2.75 per bushel, he will suffer a loss of $0.25 per bushel. In any case, however, the $3.00 price is guaranteed to the farmer.*

Innovation, Risk, and Entrepreneurship

Entrepreneurship is the undertaking of risky ventures for the sake of possible profit.

Choice is not always just a mechanical process of selecting from among known alternatives bound by given constraints. Often it involves alertness to new opportunities or a creative and innovative search for new alternatives and new ways of overcoming constraints. The exploration of untested alternatives, the discovery of previously unknown opportunities—in short, the search for new things to do and better ways to do old things—is called **entrepreneurship**.

Entrepreneurship is critical for technological and economic progress but, because it abandons the tried-and-true for new-and-untested waters, it is inevitably risky. In a market system, the incentive to innovate is provided by the promise of the profits. Because there is almost always an element of luck involved in entrepreneurial success, profits may appear in retrospect to be just a windfall to the successful entrepreneur. It is important to remember, however, that the *prospect* of profits plays a critical role in encouraging innovation: Without a prize for the winner, few would play the game.

It is also important to remember that in a market economy, unsuccessful entrepreneurs pay the price for their failures. The incentive to innovate is therefore tempered by the realization that the entrepreneur must provide not just something new, but also something of economic value, or suffer the consequences.

OVERRIDING THE MARKET

Markets are not always left free to perform their coordinating function and to solve the basic economic problems. Even in so-called free market economies, we can find many examples of legal restrictions on market price adjustments, as well as numerous instances in which market coordination is rejected in favor of coordination by command. Let us consider some examples and their consequences.

Price Floors

A **price floor** is a legal minimum price.

A **price floor** establishes the minimum price at which a good can be legally traded. Examples of price floors include minimum wage laws, many agricultural support prices set by government, liquor prices in many states, and the price of taxi service in most cities.

*The actual futures market transaction is more complex than this in practice. The farmer and speculator never actually meet and negotiate the terms of their agreement; they deal through a broker at terms established by the market. This simplified description of an exchange between the farmer and the speculator, however, illustrates the logic of risk shifting through the futures markets.

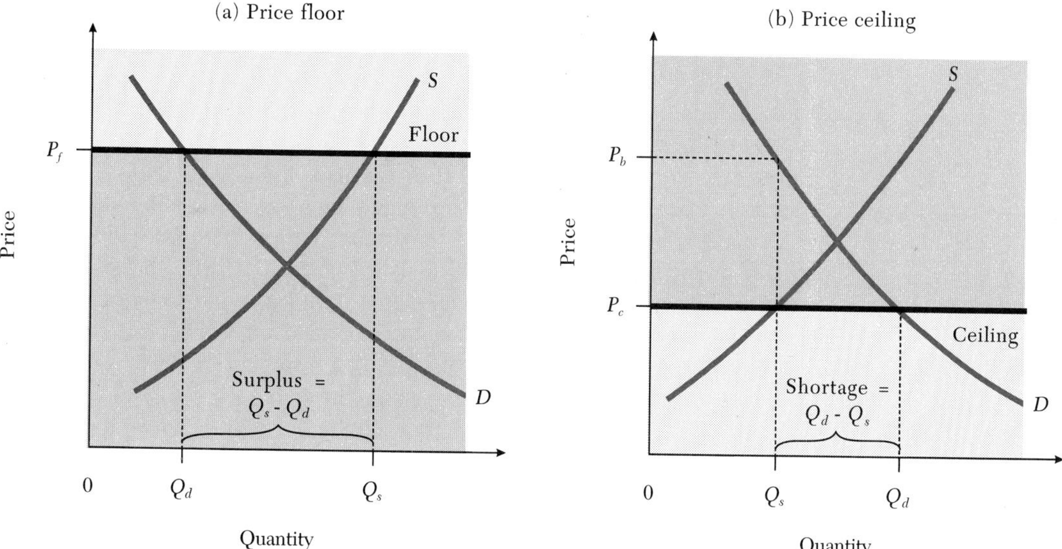

Figure 4.8

The effects of price controls

Since there is no tendency for the price of a good to fall below its market-clearing level, a price floor has an effect on the market only when it is set above the market-clearing price. This is the case with the price floor labelled P_f in Figure 4.8(a). At that price sellers are willing to supply an amount equal to Q_s, whereas buyers demand only Q_d. The surplus of $Q_s - Q_d$ would ordinarily be eliminated by a falling price, but since the price floor prevents such an adjustment, the surplus would persist indefinitely (or at least until changes in supply and demand raised the market-clearing price above P_f). The effect of a price floor set above the market-clearing price of a good is therefore to create a persistent surplus of that good.

The labor market surplus created by the minimum wage, for example, manifests itself in higher unemployment rates among workers who offer to supply more labor services than potential employers demand at the minimum wage. The unemployment induced by the minimum wage falls heavily on unskilled and inexperienced workers whose services are not worth the legal minimum wage to potential employers. In many agricultural markets, the government must either purchase (and occasionally destroy) the surpluses created by its price floors or pay farmers not to produce. In the cases of liquor and taxicabs, the government generally attempts to eliminate the surplus by requiring a license to sell liquor or drive a cab and then limiting the number of licenses it issues.

Price Ceilings

A **price ceiling** is a legal maximum price.

A **price ceiling** establishes the maximum price at which a good can be legally traded. In practice, these have included not only ceilings on specific prices, such as rent controls, but also the kind of economy-wide price controls that are used by most governments in time of war and occasionally in misguided and inevitably unsuccessful attempts to eliminate inflation. Our last bout with such economy-wide price controls in the United States occurred in the early 1970s.

Since there is no tendency for a price to rise above its market-clearing level, a price ceiling prevents market adjustments only when it is set below the market-clearing price. When this is the case, as it is with the price ceiling labelled P_c in Figure 4.8(b) on the previous page, the result is a shortage equal to $Q_d - Q_s$. Under such circumstances, buyers who value the good more than its price, but who cannot obtain it in the amounts they desire, would ordinarily bid its price up, and the rising price would eliminate the shortage. But with a price ceiling in effect, the shortage would persist indefinitely (or at least until changes in supply and demand establish a market-clearing price below the ceiling price). The effect of a price ceiling set below the market-clearing price is thus to create a persistent shortage of the good whose price is subject to the ceiling.

It is important to recognize that a price ceiling does not eliminate the market forces that would otherwise raise that price. When the legal price is prevented from rising to allocate a good, higher (legal) price bids are inevitably replaced by other forms of competition among buyers. Some might be spontaneous responses to the persistent shortage conditions in the legal market, while others might represent a deliberate attempt by government authorities to substitute political decisions for market decisions.

Each of the following has been observed at one time or another in response to price ceilings on legal market transactions.

Black Markets A black market is one in which the good is traded illegally at prices above the legal ceiling. Because there is no supply response to the higher black market price (black market prices are generally not paid to the actual producers of the good), the price on the black market will not only be higher than the legal ceiling price, it will also be higher than the market-clearing price in the absence of price controls. In Figure 4.8(b), if the quantity supplied at the ceiling price (Q_s) were sold on the black market, the price on those illegal transactions would be P_b. This explains why, for example, the interest rates charged by so-called loan sharks are so much higher than market rates. Loan sharking is simply lending at very high, black market interest rates, usually to high risk borrowers who cannot obtain credit through legitimate financial institutions because of *usury* laws limiting the rate of interest such institutions can charge. Without such laws, there would be no loan sharks, and high-risk borrowers would be able to obtain credit through legitimate channels at interest rates well below those charged by loan sharks. (But at higher rates, of course, than would be charged to low-risk borrowers.)

Official Rationing Programs When economy-wide price controls were in effect during World War II, the federal government rationed available supplies of meat, sugar, butter, gasoline, and many other commodities by distributing ration tickets entitling each household to a limited amount of each commodity. The cost of administering this program was quite high; it involved the government in arbitrary decisions regarding fairness and equity in the distribution of goods; and it did not prevent black markets from arising.

One way to eliminate black markets under a ration ticket approach would be to allow the tickets to be bought and sold. Thus, for example, all automobile owners might be given ration tickets allotting them 30 gallons of gasoline per month at the official ceiling price. Those drivers who chose to use fewer than 30 gallons could then sell a portion of their ration tickets to others who wanted to use more than 30 gallons per month. There would be a legal "white market" in which ration tickets would be traded at prices higher than the official price of gasoline—the actual commodity being rationed. But because this higher price is paid to other ticket holders, and not to the producers of gasoline, there would be no incentive to increase the quantity supplied in response to the higher price. The white market price in ration tickets would therefore approach the black market price, P_b, in Figure 4.8(b).

Queuing One spontaneous manifestation of the shortage created by a price ceiling is the *queue*: Potential buyers wait in line to obtain a good, with available supplies allocated to those willing to wait the longest. This was the case with the notorious gasoline lines that accompanied interruptions of crude oil supplies in 1974 and 1979 when there was a price ceiling on gasoline. Queuing is also common in cities with rent controls where waiting periods of years are not uncommon to obtain an apartment. In some cities with rent controls, potential renters must wait until the occupants of a rent-controlled apartment die in order to move up in the official queue. Waiting in line has also been the standard procedure for obtaining consumer goods in the Soviet Union where official prices have been kept below market-clearing levels.

Quality and Service Deterioration With a greater quantity demanded than they can meet at the legal price ceiling, sellers may find it to their advantage to allow quality to deteriorate, especially in cases where quality is costly to maintain. Thus, despite a severe housing shortage—and because of the rent controls that have caused the shortage—a city like New York must condemn literally thousands of living units each year as unfit for habitation. Similarly, engine oil checks, cleaned windshields, and general "service with a smile" disappeared during the gas lines of the 1970s. The decline in quality is an effective increase in the real price: The buyer pays the same amount of money but gets less in return.

Side Payments Placing a ceiling on the price of a good may be ineffective when the seller can accept other forms of payment. Under rent controls, for example, landlords often require renters to pay "key money" to obtain the keys to enter their apartments, or to pay additional rent for a parking space—even if they don't own a car. During the gasoline shortages of the 1970s, many motorists found that if they had their cars serviced at the local gas station—and were willing to pay higher than "normal" prices for such services—they could get their tanks filled without waiting in line.

Seller Preferences Sellers, forbidden to accept higher money prices, may simply ration available supplies among preferred customers. The preferences may be determined by long-standing business relationships, or they may reflect nothing more than the seller's own prejudices on otherwise irrelevant grounds like the race, religious belief, or ethnic background.

Price ceilings almost always represent political attempts to make costly things cheaper, and therein lies their political appeal. But if something is costly, that fact cannot be legislated out of existence. Price controls can force us to bear the cost in a different way—by waiting in line, accepting lower quality, suffering arbitrary discrimination, or simply doing without—but they cannot make the high cost disappear. Do any of us really believe that we would be able to enjoy filet mignon and lobster for every meal, drive a different car every day of the week, and live in a mansion with an olympic-size swimming pool if only the government would pass a law making all of those goodies "affordable"? Probably not. (If you answered yes, however, I think I can also get you a pretty good deal on a bridge.) It is a testament to hope, if not to reason, that we nonetheless keep trying.

Market versus Command

As we saw in Chapter 1, the alternative to coordination of economic activity by the market is coordination by *command*. Whereas the market is a decentralized system in which decision-making authority rests with individuals, coordination by command relies on a centralized authority to make decisions that are binding on all affected parties. In every economic system, from the family to the world economy, we can find both the voluntary elements of the market and the authoritarian elements of command. Pure forms do not exist in the reality. Moreover, economics alone cannot tell us which particular mix of market and command elements is most appropriate. Normative issues of individual freedom and social responsibility must inevitably be involved in any such evaluation. But economics can contribute greatly to an understanding of the role of market and command elements in an economic system, and of the consequences of using one or the other to make economic decisions.

Coordination by command characterizes the internal workings of any organization in which there is a hierarchy of authority. All family members, for example, must abide by the decisions made by the head of the household; the boss in a business firm issues orders that apply to all subordinates. Because of its far-reaching authority, however, government is the most visible source of command elements in any economic system. Its role in coordinating economic decisions can range from supplementing the market, as is usually the case in the United States, Japan, and most Western European economies, to largely supplanting the market, as has been the case in the centrally planned, command economies of the Soviet Union, Cuba, and, until very recently, the Soviet-bloc countries of Eastern Europe.

In a command economy, the central authority of government replaces the decentralized voluntary exchange of the market in attempting to solve the basic economic problems. Government planners determine what goods are to be produced, and how, by issuing orders to the managers of state-owned enterprises. Government price and wage controls, as well as control over entry into most occupations, effectively determine how the fruits of economic activity are to be distributed. Government planners replace the capital markets in determining how much productive capacity is to be devoted to current consumption and how much to investment for the future. Those same planners decide where and how investment funds are to be used. Finally, since the means of production are owned by the state, most of the risks inherent in economic activity are borne by the state—which really means that they are spread among all citizens.

In recent years, it has become overwhelmingly evident that economic systems that have relied primarily on command have become inefficient and backward in comparison with those that have relied primarily on the market. The former have become notorious for worker absenteeism, shoddy goods, shortages and surpluses (both chronic and periodic), a general lack of innovation in products and production techniques, and many other forms of inefficiency. By the end of the 1980s, living standards in the command economies of the Soviet Union and Eastern Europe were about half what they were in the market economies of the United States, Japan, and Western Europe. It is hardly surprising that, where given the chance, the citizens of countries whose communist regimes supported such command systems have voted overwhelmingly to replace those regimes with democratic governments more favorable to market capitalism.

The pace of change has been incredibly swift, and it is difficult to predict where it will ultimately lead. In the Soviet Union and in some Eastern European countries, such as Romania, the absence of a democratic tradition and the virtual elimination of market institutions under communism will probably make the road to economic reform a long and rocky one. Even with *perestroika*, the much publicized Soviet economic reforms intended to decentralize economic decisions and introduce market-style incentives, the Soviet economy has a long, long way to go before it even faintly resembles the market economies of the West. In other countries, such as Poland, Czechoslovakia, and Hungary, where market institutions were never entirely eliminated under communism, and where political democracy has seemingly taken stronger hold, the prospects for success appear brighter, as they also do in a united Germany.

In all cases, however, the key to reform is not access to Western capital or Western technology. Nor is it so much the establishment of such basic market institutions as private property and freedom of contract, indispensible as they are. Rather, the most important ingredient appears to be the cultivation of attitudes conducive to a market order: individual initiative and responsibility, a willingness to take risks, and a tolerance of income disparities reflecting differences in effort, and even luck. Whether such attitudes can take root where they have been discouraged for decades and, if so, how long it will take, remains to be seen.

CHAPTER SUMMARY

1. We can think of market activity as a *circular flow* of transactions leading from households in their role as suppliers of primary productive services, to the business firms that purchase those services and combine them with the intermediate goods supplied by other business firms, and then back again to the households in their role as demanders of final goods. The entire process is coordinated by markets in which relative price adjustments insure that quantity supplied is equal to quantity demanded for each productive resource, intermediate good, and final good.

2. Markets are not isolated and insulated from one another. They are linked together in an interdependent system in which adjustments in any one market have repercussions in many other markets.

3. Market prices are social coordinators that convey to individual decision makers (buyers and sellers, producers and consumers) *information* about changes in economic conditions and, at the same time, provide them with *incentives* to adapt to those changes.

4. The market solves the problem of *resource allocation* (What is produced?) by allocating resources to each good up to the point at which its marginal value (demand price) is equal to its marginal cost (supply price). In so doing, it maximizes the total value of the goods we squeeze out of our scarce resources.

5. The market solves the problem of choosing *production techniques* (How is it produced?) by giving producers an incentive to adopt the technique using the least costly combination of resources. When relative prices change, producers substitute lower priced resources for higher priced resources.

6. The market solves the problem of *distribution* (Who gets it?) by allocating goods to those people willing and able to pay their market prices. A person's ability to pay those prices depends primarily on the market prices of the productive resources that person supplies.

7. The problem of *temporal allocation* (When is it available?) is solved through the economy's *credit market* in which financial intermediaries convert the financial investments that households make when they save into the real investments that business firms make when they acquire capital goods. In so doing, the credit market coordinates choices between present and future consumption.

8. *Interest rates* measure the value of the present relative to the value of the future. The *pure rate of interest* is a theoretical concept that reflects only subjective time preference and the productivity of capital goods. Actual interest rates set in the credit market reflect the influence of transactions costs, risk, and inflationary expectations as well.

9. The market allows people to trade on differences in their attitudes toward risk. As in other market processes, the mechanism for allocating and shifting risk is voluntary exchange and the relative prices that are established in the course of exchange.

10. A *price floor* is a legal minimum price. If a price floor is set above the market-clearing price of a good, the result is a persistent surplus of that good.

11. A *price ceiling* is a legal maximum price. If a price ceiling is set below the market-clearing price of a good, the result is a persistent shortage of that good.

Key Terms and Concepts

factor markets
intermediate goods
consumers' surplus
producers' surplus
capital markets
financial intermediary
credit market
equities market
pure rate of interest
default risk
risk premium
nominal interest rate
real interest rate
contractual claimant
residual claimant
futures market
entrepreneurship
price floor
price ceiling

Questions for Thought and Discussion

1. Pick a simple consumer good, say, the shirt on your back. Do you think you could list all of the people involved, both directly and indirectly, in its production? Try it!
2. Access to many of the goods you use is not allocated by the market; that is, the market does not set a price for their usage. Examples include freeways and city streets, most public parks, libraries, classes taught by popular professors at popular hours, and parking spaces on some college campuses and in the downtown areas of major cities. What do all of these goods have in common, and what does the common element have to do with the absence of market allocation?
3. Is it irrational for low-income countries with high population densities to use labor-intensive production techniques when more modern, capital-intensive techniques are available?
4. Karl Marx proposed the following rule for determining the distribution of society's goods: "From each according to his abilities, to each according to his needs." Do

you think the market distribution of goods conforms to this rule? Do you see any practical problems in implementing such a rule?

5. Who do you think would have the higher rate of subjective time preference, a 20-year-old or a 70-year-old?
6. The federal government can borrow money at lower interest rates than can private businesses. Why do you think that this is the case?
7. In the text you read how a farmer who expects to *sell* wheat in the future can use the futures market to eliminate the risk of future price fluctuations. How might a baker, who expects to *buy* wheat in the future, use the futures market to protect against the risk of future price fluctuations?
8. Coordination by command has proven to be very ineffective in the centrally planned economies that rely heavily on it. On the other hand, we take it for granted that command is the best way to allocate goods within a family. After all, no one would seriously suggest that Mom, Dad, and the kids bid against one another to see who will get the most desert, or who will get to watch what program on television. Rather Mom and/or Dad use their authority to make these decisions for the family. What characteristics of the family differentiate it from a national economy and make it particularly suitable for coordination by command?

CHAPTER 5

The Public Sector: An Overview of Political Economy

There cannot be many things in man's political history more ancient than the endeavor of governments to direct economic affairs.

GEORGE STIGLER*

The public sector, or government, plays a fundamental role in every economic system. Even in an economy like that of the United States, which relies primarily on the market for economic coordination, the influence of government is felt in virtually every private sector economic decision from household budgeting to corporate investment strategies. To speak of government intervention in the economy as if the public sector were some separate entity that could be divorced from the rest of the economic system is misleading: Government does not intervene in the economy; it is part of the economy—a very large and important part.

The federal government, the fifty state governments, and the nearly 80,000 local government units in this country employ about one-sixth of the work force (not including the military), absorb about one-fifth of our total annual output of goods and services, and collect annual revenues equal to about one-third of all earned incomes. Government produces (or finances the production of) billions of dollars worth of goods and services each year: Education, defense, roads and bridges, police and fire protection, parks, and sports stadiums are but a few examples. Government also implements a myriad of policies intended to modify the results of the private marketplace. It taxes some goods (like liquor, cigarettes, and gasoline) and subsidizes others (like housing, medical care, and cer-

* *The Citizen and the State* (University of Chicago Press, 1975), p. ix.

tain agricultural products). It regulates employment conditions, product safety characteristics, and the potentially polluting by-products of industrial and agricultural activity. It adopts some policies that promote competition and others that discourage competition. Finally, government policies almost always redistribute income and wealth. In some cases, the redistribution is the primary intent of the policy, as with food stamps, welfare payments, and agricultural subsidies, while in many other cases the redistribution is only a side effect of a policy with a different explicit goal.

Economic analysis can contribute to our understanding of the role of government in the economy in two ways.

First, economics can predict conditions under which the private marketplace, if left to itself, is unlikely to perform well, and it can suggest government policies that might improve that performance. This is a fundamentally *normative* approach to the economics of the public sector.

Second, economic analysis provides us with a tool for explaining and predicting the actual affects of government policies—which may or may not coincide with the announced intentions of those policies—and, more generally, why the government does what it does. This is a fundamentally *positive* approach to the economics of the public sector.

In this chapter we consider both approaches.

WHAT GOVERNMENT SHOULD DO: THE NORMATIVE ECONOMICS OF THE PUBLIC SECTOR

The Legal Framework: Property Rights

Imagine a farmer who wants to raise and sell corn but who fears that before he can harvest his crop, it will be picked and hauled away by someone else. The farmer could arm himself and use force (or at least the threat of force) to stop anyone who attempts to take his corn, or he could take other security measures—barbed wire, guard dogs, or electronic alarm systems, for example—to protect his crop. But all of these actions are costly, and they would result in a smaller supply of corn than if the farmer did not have to worry about the loss of his crop. The costs of protecting his crop from pillage by outsiders could be so high that the farmer might not even bother to grow any corn at all.

If our farmer does succeed in growing and protecting his corn crop, he might want to exchange some of it for cattle so that he can consume milk and meat as well as corn. If he would have to shoulder the additional burden of warding off cattle rustlers, however, he might just forget about having any variety in his diet. Certainly he would have a greater incentive to devote his time and other costly resources to the production of corn if he could be sure of reaping the fruits of his efforts.

As this example illustrates, in a world in which there are no rights to exclude others from the use of scarce resources—or more accurately, in a world in which private individuals like our hypothetical farmer must personally bear the costs of establishing and enforcing whatever rights exist—incentives for production and exchange are significantly weakened. One of the most fundamental economic functions of government, therefore, is to provide the framework of legal rights that allow individuals to secure the rewards of their productive activities and force them to bear the costs associated with the use of scarce resources. this legal framework the economy's system of **property rights**. The rights it establishes cannot just be moral or philosophical abstractions; to be effective they must be real claims that can and will be enforced by the powers of government.

Property rights are the legal rights of an owner to use goods, to exclude others from their use, and to transfer ownership to others.

Because property rights are best understood as the rights associated with the use and control of goods, they are more accurately and usefully defined in relation to people's *behavior* than in relation to physical objects. Take, for example, the property rights associated with your ownership of a car. Besides the physical piece of machinery on wheels—and in fact what gives your ownership of that piece of machinery any meaningful content—you possess a bundle of rights, enforceable by government, regarding the use of the car. In particular, you have the exclusive right to drive the car or to determine who can. You have the right to change its form or appearance, by painting it, for example, or by modifying its engine. And finally, you have the right to transfer (sell, rent, or give) any or all of these rights to someone else.

All property rights are limited rather than absolute. Although you have the exclusive right to drive your own car, for example, you do not have the right to drive it through a red light or down the wrong side of the street. Your right to change its form does not include the right to remove its muffler or emission control system. And you cannot transfer the right to drive the car to a 10-year-old child.

Some property rights are private in that they are held by private individuals or groups of private individuals such as a family or a business partnership. Other property rights are nominally assigned to society in general, with control over the goods to which they apply effectively vested in the hands of government decision makers. In any case, government aids in the enforcement of property rights and provides a judicial arena for resolving disputes about those rights.

Sources of Market Failure

In Chapter 4 we showed that efficient resource allocation requires that the marginal value of the last unit of each good produced and consumed equals its marginal cost. Usually the market achieves this ideal automatically when it equates demand price and supply price in equilibrium. However, there are some conditions under which this will not be the case.

Market failure refers to the failure of a real-world market to achieve ideal economic efficiency.

Market failure is the term economists sometimes apply to situations in which real-world markets fail to duplicate the conditions of ideal economic efficiency. In a literal sense, markets always "fail" simply because economic efficiency is an artificial construct based on a normative ideal of how the world should be.

Perfect economic efficiency is, quite literally, a figment of the economist's imagination. It is not meant to describe reality, and it is quite unlikely that reality could ever be made to conform exactly to that ideal.*

There are cases of market failure, however, in which the departure from the ideal is so extreme, and the corrective policy sufficiently accessible, that most economists would agree that some government action is desirable. Although there is far from complete agreement on the specific, real-world instances of significant market failure, and perhaps even less on the nature of the appropriate government policy in each instance, nearly all economists recognize a number of general areas of market failure where government actions can potentially improve matters.

Public Goods

Suppose that the river Alph flows through the middle of the city of Xanadu and that it periodically overflows its banks and floods the city, damaging property and threatening lives. A private contractor proposes to build an upstream dam to control the flow of water through the city, thereby eliminating the threat of flooding. Knowing that her dam would be of immense value to the citizens of Xanadu, she sets out to solicit payment from them to finance the construction of the dam. But, in spite of the fact that the value of the dam to the citizenry is considerably greater than its construction cost, the contractor finds that she is unable to collect nearly enough to pay that cost. Why?

A **free rider** is a person who enjoys the benefits of a good while bearing little or none of the costs of providing it.

A **public good** provides benefits that are *indivisible* and *nonexclusive*—that is, benefits that can be enjoyed jointly and simultaneously by a number of consumers, and from which those consumers cannot be excluded once the good is provided.

A **private good** is a good whose benefits are confined to a single consumer and from which other consumers can be excluded at low cost.

The reason is that if the dam is built and the flood threat eliminated, everyone in Xanadu will benefit *whether or not he has contributed to the cost of building the dam*. Any individual citizen, therefore, has the incentive to get a free ride by not contributing to the construction of the dam (or contributing only a token amount) in the hopes that others will contribute enough for the dam to be built. Were that to happen, the **free rider** would enjoy the benefits of flood protection at little or no personal cost. The problem is that everyone has some incentive to free ride so that the amount collected by the private contractor will not reflect the true value of the dam to the citizens of Xanadu.

The dam and the flood protection it would provide is an example of a **public good**. Public goods have two defining characteristics. First, consumption of the benefits of public goods is *indivisible*. Once the good is provided, its benefits can be enjoyed jointly and simultaneously by a number of consumers. Second, the benefits provided by a public good are *nonexclusive* in the sense that nonpayers cannot be excluded (except at high cost) from their enjoyment.

A public good is different from **private goods** such as hamburgers, jeans, and computer time. The enjoyment of consuming a private good such as hamburger is confined to a single person. (Or more accurately, if it is shared by more than one person, more for one means less for another.) A person who does not fork

*Some economists refer to these departures from the ideal as "theory failure" rather than "market failure," thus emphasizing a belief that when reality cannot be changed to conform to the theory's ideal, then the theory, not reality, has failed. The point is well taken, but here we adopt the conventional terminology of market failure, recognizing nonetheless that in order to be of any use in the formulation of government policy, even normative economics must start by taking the world as it is and not by doggedly pursuing an unattainable ideal.

over a dollar or so to Ronald McDonald is excluded from the delights of a Big Mac.

Returning to our example of the flood control dam, suppose now that the city government of Xanadu steps into the picture. The government has the power to levy taxes to finance construction of the dam and, unlike the voluntary payments sought by the private contractor, taxes are mandatory. If the citizens express a desire for flood control, whether through the ballot box or some other means of political expression, the government can use its powers of taxation to overcome the free rider problem.

It is important to recognize that the economic argument is an argument that government must *finance* the provision of public goods; it is not an argument that government itself must actually *produce* those goods. In the preceding example, the government of Xanadu could use its tax revenues to purchase materials and capital goods and to pay public employees to construct the dam, or it could simply use the same tax revenues to pay a private construction firm to build the dam. On normative grounds the choice should be determined on the basis of the lower cost alternative.

Although there are relatively few examples of *pure* public goods—flood control, air pollution control, and national defense probably come as close as anything—there are nonetheless many examples of goods that have enough of the characteristics of public goods to qualify them for government provision on the grounds of economic efficiency. One could charge prices for police services, for example, and private security forces do just that. But police protection provides some indivisible benefits that cannot be charged for, such as the generally safer environment for all who live in a well-policed area. A similar argument can be made for public education if we accept the premise that there are gains to society in general, over and above the gains to the educated individual, from having an educated population. As in the case of police protection, however, educational services are provided not only by government but also by private educational institutions, from preschools to graduate and vocational schools, all of which offer their services through the private marketplace. Because the distinction between public and private goods is not always clearly and finely drawn, therefore, the choice between public and private provision of many goods is often ambiguous on normative grounds.

Externalities

Market equilibrium results in an economically efficient outcome only if all benefits and costs are reflected in demand and supply prices, and thus registered in the marketplace. Sometimes this is not the case. Occasionally economic activity creates **externalities**, that is, benefits or costs that are not captured by the market and therefore not reflected in the prices that buyers are willing to pay or the costs that suppliers must cover.

An **externality** is a positive or negative spillover from market activity.

The most important and widespread example of an externality problem is the problem of pollution. Pollution is the result of a negative externality, or **external cost**. To take a concrete example, consider a factory that produces some good, say widgets, and in the process drains industrial waste into the Alph river that flows nearby. Although the owners of the factory must pay for the labor, raw

An **external cost** is a cost that is not reflected in market prices; it is a negative spillover from market activity.

materials, and other inputs used in the production of widgets, they may not have to pay for the use of the river. The river is nonetheless a scarce resource, and dumping waste into it is not costless. Using it for waste disposal reduces opportunities for fishing and recreation and spoils its aesthetic qualities as well. The sacrifice of these valuable alternatives represents an opportunity cost, but one which the factory does not pay, and which, therefore, will not be reflected in the supply price of its product.

The problem reflects a fundamental defect in the system of property rights: If no one owns the river, no one has the right to charge for its use as a waste disposal system. As a result, the factory tends to use the river as if it were a free and abundant resource when in fact it is scarce and its use costly.

To illustrate the problem graphically, consider Figure 5.1 in which *D* is the demand curve for widgets and *S* is the supply curve. As we have seen, the supply curve reflects marginal cost, but only the **private cost** that is actually borne by the supplier. If widget production generates external costs, then the *external marginal cost* must be added to the private marginal cost to obtain a measure of the **social cost** of producing widgets. The curve labelled *SMC* in Figure 5.1 represents the social marginal cost of widget production.

A **private cost** is a cost borne directly by the economic decision maker responsible for it.

Social cost is the sum of the private cost borne by the economic decision maker and external cost borne by others.

When we compare the social marginal cost of widgets with their marginal value (demand price), we find the efficient widget output to be equal to the amount labelled Q_E in the diagram. The market equilibrium, however, is at output Q_0 and price P_0 as determined at the intersection of the demand and supply curves. The price that the market establishes for widgets does not reflect the external costs that widget production generates, and as a result too many widgets are produced and consumed relative to the efficiency ideal.

Figure 5.1

External costs

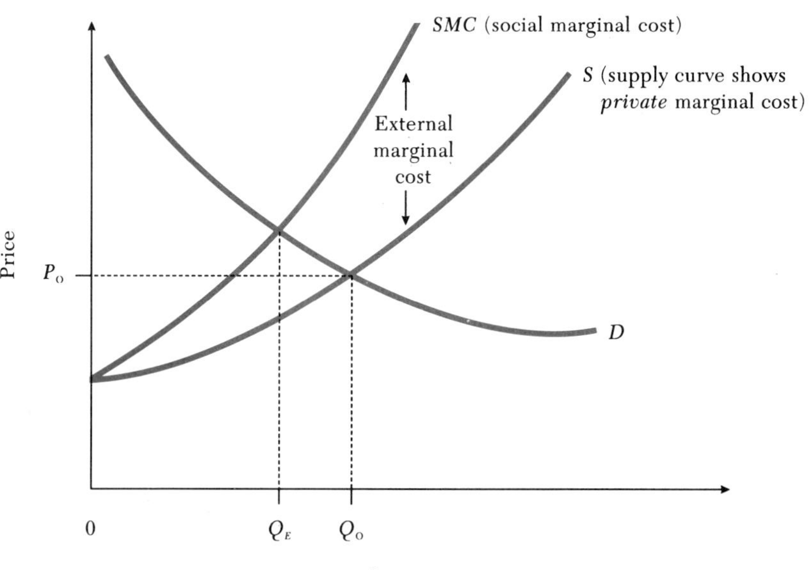

The appropriate government response to this problem is to *internalize* the externality—that is, to shift the external costs onto those whose activities generate such costs. This gives such parties an incentive to take into account in their decision making *all* of the costs that their actions impose on others. Externalities can be internalized in a number of specific ways, but in general government must establish rights to the goods—water, air, blessed silence, or whatever—whose free use is the source of the external cost, and then charge for the use of those rights.

One possibility is for government to appropriate the right to itself, in the name of society in general, and then to levy a charge on the activity generating the externality. For example, the government of Xanadu could tax anyone who discharges waste into the river Alph. If the tax is set to reflect the external marginal cost created by such discharges, then it will create incentives to make efficient use of Alph, balancing its value as a waste disposal system against its value in commercial fishing and as a recreational and aesthetic resource.

Another possibility is for the government to use its judicial powers to establish property rights to the goods affected by the externality and to assess damages against anyone who violates those rights. The court system of Xanadu, for example, might allow those claiming harm as a result of the disposal of industrial waste into Alph to establish those claims in a court of law and sue for damages. If the damages established in court accurately reflect the external costs, they will have an effect similar to that of the tax, namely imposing the external costs on those who use Alph for disposal of waste.

It is important to note that economic efficiency does not require that no waste be disposed into the river, only that those who would do so are confronted with the costs of their actions.

An **external benefit** is a positive spillover from market activity.

Not all externalities are negative. Some activities generate **external benefits** rather than external costs. External benefits are the positive side effects that are not captured by the market. If, for example, a family keeps its children inoculated against contagious diseases, those actions benefit not only that family but those of its children's playmates. For an economically efficient decision to be made, *all* benefits should be weighed against the costs of inoculation. The problem from the standpoint of economic efficiency is that when the family makes a decision about inoculating its children, it may have little incentive to consider the potential benefits to its neighbors.

Positive externalities are very similar to public goods in that they are the result of indivisible and nonexclusive benefits. The family that has its children inoculated, for example, cannot charge its neighbors for the indivisible benefits that spill over to them, or threaten to withhold those benefits unless the neighbors contribute to its medical costs. The government policies that normative economics suggests for dealing with positive externalities are therefore quite similar to those it proposes for public goods. In the case of inoculation against contagious disease, for example, the government might underwrite some or all of the costs of the inoculation program. Whether this amounts to provision of a public good or the subsidization of a private good is little more than a semantic distinction. In general, the difference between public goods and private goods that generate external benefits is primarily a matter of degree.

Monopoly and Collusion

The marketplace produces ideally efficient results only when it is driven by competition; when elements of monopoly or collusion are present, efficiency may be compromised. Although most markets tend naturally toward competition, they are not immune from the threat of collusion or other monopolistic practices. Nearly all economists agree that government should promote competition and discourage monopoly and collusion. To understand the reasoning behind this position, let us consider the effects of monopoly elements on output and pricing.

In Figure 5.2 the competitive market equilibrium would be established at point A with a price equal to P_C and Q_C units exchanged. If, however, sellers in that market collude with one another and agree to support prices above the competitive level, say at P_M, this will necessitate a reduction in output to an amount equal to Q_M, which is the most that buyers will purchase at the collusive price. The essence of collusion and other forms of monopolistic behavior is an increase in price above the competitive level and a reduction in trade below the competitive level. As a result, some potential benefits from production and exchange are lost: In the output range between Q_M and Q_C in Figure 5.2, the marginal value of each additional unit exceeds its marginal cost, yet under conditions of monopoly none of those units would be supplied. (The value of the lost trade opportunities can be approximated by the area *ABC* in the diagram.)

The example of the early days of the OPEC cartel provides an extreme, but striking, example of the effects of monopoly. Before OPEC, the price of a barrel of imported crude oil was less than $3.50, reflecting its marginal cost of production and transportation. Almost overnight the cartel, by imposing maximum pro-

Figure 5.2

The effects of monopoly and collusion

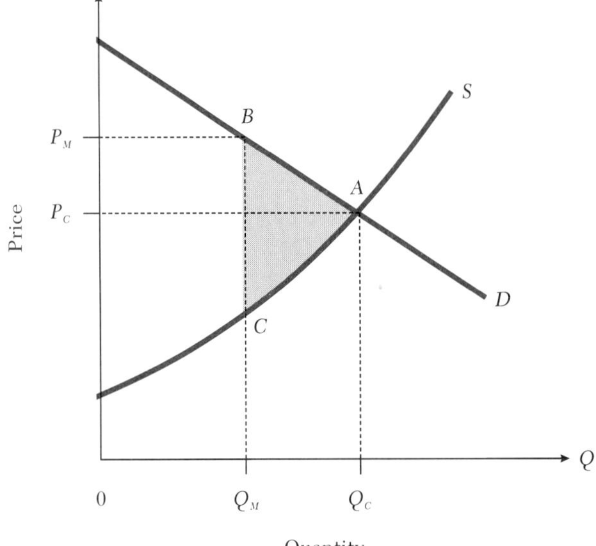

duction limits on each of its members, was able to drive that price up to nearly $12. This spread between marginal value and marginal cost meant that there were suddenly many uses of crude oil which people valued at more than the $3.50 marginal cost—warm houses, Sunday drives, vacation trips in recreational vehicles to mention a few of the more obvious—but which were unavailable at prices less than $12.

Economists have suggested two basic approaches for government to deal with the potential problem of monopoly. In those markets where the technology permits more than one supplier to serve the market, the government should assist in the maintenance of competition by punishing collusion and other forms of anticompetitive behavior. This is the purpose of our federal and state *antitrust laws*.

In some cases, however, the technology of production and distribution is such that the market will support only a single supplier. This is thought to be the case in many *public utilities*, such as local telephone service and the distribution of water and electrical power, where duplication of capital equipment like telephone lines and water pipes would be too costly to support more than a single supplier in any given geographic market. For these so-called *natural monopolies*, some economists have proposed government regulations designed to emulate the competitive market by setting prices equal to marginal cost and permitting the owners of the firm only a competitive return on their investment.

Information

Information is essential to the efficient functioning of markets: Unless the parties to a market transaction have all the relevant information about the goods and services in which they are trading, the proposition that there are mutual benefits from exchange is open to question. However, information can be considered a public good, or a good which generates external benefits. Once provided, it can be shared by any number of people, and once in the public domain it is very costly, if not impossible, to exclude anyone from using it. Since the supplier of information might not be able to capture all of the benefits which that information provides, normal market incentives might be inadequate for the efficient provision of certain types of information. When a new drug is discovered, for example, the producer might not have sufficient incentive to explore all of its long-term side effects before releasing it to the market. Similarly, an employer might not have an incentive to discover and publicize among his employees the long-term health hazards associated with working with certain materials; or the manufacturer of a consumer product might not have an interest in advertising injury risks or health hazards associated with use of that product.

On the basis of this argument, many economists would argue that government has a role in discovering and disseminating various kinds of information relevant to market transactions. For example, the government might provide (or require private parties to provide) information about the harmful side effects of drugs, tobacco, alcohol, or other potentially dangerous substances. It might investigate and publicize information about the safety characteristics of automobiles, microwave ovens, and other consumer products. It might also gather and publicize the health and safety aspects of various types of employment.

Strictly speaking, if we accept the proposition that an individual is the best judge of his or her own welfare, then the preceding argument concerns only the *provision of information* by the government; it is not an argument that the government, having provided the relevant information to market participants, should further *regulate their behavior*. Given that people have accurate information about the consequences of their actions, there is no economic argument for preventing them from consuming dangerous substances, accepting risky employment, or purchasing potentially hazardous products. (This assumes that the risks are confined to the person actually making the decision. If that is not the case, then externalities exist, and there may be an economic argument for expanding the role of government beyond the mere provision of information.)

Macroeconomic Instability: Inflation and Unemployment

Market economies have historically experienced periodic *recessions*, during which total output falls and unemployment rises. They are also prone to occasional bouts of *inflation*, during which nearly all nominal prices rise and the value of money (and money-denominated financial assets) falls. In recent years, we have found that it is even possible to have the worst of both worlds: simultaneous recession and inflation.

The federal government has assumed responsibility for dealing with these problems of macroeconomic instability. The tools it uses are *monetary* and *fiscal* policies. We discuss these stabilization policies in detail in the macroeconomic section of this book but, in a nutshell, monetary policies are those through which the government manages the size and growth of the nation's money supply and fiscal policies as those affecting the size and financing of the federal government's budget.

There is considerable disagreement among economists on the relative importance and appropriate approach to monetary and fiscal stabilization policies. Indeed, some contend that they have been part of the problem, rather than part of the solution when it comes to macroeconomic instability. All agree, however, that such policies have a significant impact on the macroeconomic performance of the economy.

Equality and Security

One of the most important and growing areas of government economic activity during the past half century has been the active redistribution of income and wealth and the provision of income security *safety nets* as they have come to be called. Income redistribution is implicit in the progressive structures of the federal income tax and most state income taxes and in government programs such as food stamps and rent subsidies.* Income security is sought through programs like social security, unemployment compensation, and medicare, which shift

*A progressive tax is one that increases more than proportionately with income. For example, the current federal income tax levies a 15 percent tax on taxable incomes up to $29,750 for married couples ($17,850 for single individuals), and a 28 percent tax on income beyond that amount.

to society (that is, to taxpayers in general) many of the risks inherent in economic life.

Although economics itself provides no normative basis for this role of government, it can contribute to our understanding of the effects of such programs and of their impact on other normative goals. In particular, economics forces us to confront the possible trade-offs between efficiency and widely shared views of fairness and equity. There is evidence, for example, that unemployment compensation tends to prolong unemployment by reducing its costs, that the tax-funded retirement benefits of the social security system tend to reduce private saving and capital formation, and that a steeply progressive tax structure tends to reduce incentives to work and earn.

Just what constitutes an equitable distribution of income or a fair division of risk between the individual and society, and to what extent these goals should be pursued in light of the costs they impose, however, are questions that must ultimately be resolved through the political process, not by economic analysis.

The Costs and Benefits of Government

Attempts by government to remedy market imperfections are themselves necessarily imperfect. This is true even for a government selflessly and single-mindedly devoted to improving market efficiency or to altering the market's distribution of income or risk at the lowest possible cost. Like the market, the real public sector inevitably "fails" when measured against the ideal. Because costs as well as benefits arise whenever the government acts to correct market imperfections, there is no guarantee that the net effect will be beneficial. There are undoubtedly many cases where the cure has been worse than the disease.

Besides the opportunity costs of the labor and other resources that the public sector must employ simply to function at all, there are other costs inherent in government decisions. Government policies are almost always coordinated by command processes, and such processes have several disadvantages relative to market processes.

First, command decisions are generally less flexible and less able to discriminate among individual differences in taste, ability, or environment than are market decisions. Federal air pollution controls, for example, impose the same emissions requirements on automobiles driven daily in the Los Angeles basin as on those driven rarely and only in the Nevada desert. In the former case, the cost of the controls may well be economically justified, while in the latter it is almost certainly not. In principle, the distinction between Los Angeles and Nevada could be made and the emission control requirement adjusted accordingly, but these are clearly only two extremes, and the costs of differentiating among the thousands of intermediate cases are simply prohibitive for government policy makers.

Other examples of this inherent defect in the command approach abound: Unemployment compensation makes no distinction between those unemployed who have accumulated substantial savings to fall back on and those for whom government benefits are the sole source of subsistence; public elementary and secondary schools rely heavily on uniform curricula and standard texts with little attention to the needs and abilities of different students; consumer product safety regulations make no distinctions between the careful and informed consumer and the careless and uninformed.

This inflexibility and inability to allow for differences in individual circumstances is probably the single greatest source of complaints about government bureaucracy.

Second, command decisions require a greater centralization of information than do market decisions. In the market, individuals need know only their own tastes and the options confronting them in order to make choices. The command decisions made by government require that someone in authority—a federal regulatory board, a municipal zoning commission, the Congress of the United States—gather, interpret, and act on what can be an immense amount of information, often conflicting, and concerning which they may have no particular expertise. The market, by imposing much more limited information requirements on decentralized economic agents—the decision makers who have the most direct and least costly access to relevant information—is generally more efficient in utilizing information than a large-scale command system.

Third, a command approach to economic decisions is less responsive to costs and benefits than is the market. When resources are allocated through the market, their relative prices and the relative prices of the goods they can produce provide suppliers with the information they need about the costs and benefits of the alternatives open to them. But because the benefits generated by most government programs are not sold, there is no corresponding measure of value to guide public sector decision makers. If, for example, the local school board is trying to determine whether to devote more resources to developing reading skills or to increasing emphasis on social studies, it has no hard indicator of the comparative values of these alternatives to its students.

In addition, the simple fact is that the relevant benefits and costs are rarely borne directly by the government decision makers themselves. As a result the political process is less direct and precise in registering costs and benefits than is the market. The incentive to maximize the difference between benefits and costs—the market's bottom line—is therefore much weaker in the public sector than in the private, and the chances of weeding out inefficient programs are correspondingly diminished.

We therefore conclude that, while the market alone is not likely to achieve the normative ideal of economic efficiency, neither are the remedies realistically available to the public sector. The normative approach to the role of the public sector in the economy is necessarily one of *second best*—that is, of choosing the best from among the realistically available options, given that the ideal (first best) is not attainable in practice.

Though this rule is conceptually simple, its practical application is not. In some cases—where property rights are well defined, where there are no significant externalities, and where markets are reasonably competitive—it may be fairly clear that the role of the public sector can be minimized. In other cases—where there are public goods or significant external effects, for example—it may be equally clear that the public sector should play a substantial role. It is the intermediate cases, however, that present the greatest difficulties in drawing the line between the responsibilities of the public sector and those of the private sector.

WHAT GOVERNMENT DOES: PUBLIC CHOICE THEORY AND THE POSITIVE ECONOMICS OF THE PUBLIC SECTOR

To view government as a neutral and disinterested institution, however imperfect, for correcting market failures and implementing widely shared views of equity and fairness is to seriously misperceive the true nature of the political process. The government policies that we actually observe, whether or not narrowly economic, are the outcome of a process in which the interests of the general public, organized interest groups, elected representatives, and a permanent government bureaucracy are all played out. Though most of the institutional details of this process are beyond the scope of this book, economic analysis can shed considerable light on some of its essential characteristics.

Public Choice Theory

In recent years, economists have taken the same analytical tools they use to study market processes and applied them to the study of political processes in an effort to understand why government does what it does. The result is the economic theory called **public choice theory**. Here we summarize the basic elements of that theory; in subsequent chapters we apply it to a variety of government policies.

Public choice theory is a positive economic theory of government behavior.

Government Authority as a Scarce Resource

The starting point for public choice theory is a recognition that government authority is a scarce and valuable resource that must be allocated among a variety of alternative uses. Only government has the legitimate authority to force people to do things they would otherwise choose not to do—pay taxes, obey laws and regulations, and so on. Government can use this power in many ways, but it cannot be all things to all people. There are inevitably conflicting goals and constituencies among which political choices must be made. The following three examples, drawn from different areas of government activity, illustrate the general nature of the trade-offs involved in political decisions.

1. **Foreign Trade Policy.** Domestic producers often seek, and frequently obtain, government protection from foreign competition. In recent years, for example, the federal government of the United States has placed limitations

on imports of automobiles, television sets, steel, shoes, clothing, computer memory chips, and dozens upon dozens of other products. Such trade restrictions benefit those groups directly associated with the protected industry, such as its managers, stockholders, and employees. Accordingly, it is by no means surprising that we find such groups in the forefront of political activity to limit foreign competition. However, by reducing the supply of imported goods, trade protection almost always raises prices to consumers.

2. **Business Regulation.** When the government regulates private business firms, the regulatory process tends to become a forum in which the interests of the regulated firms, their employees, their competitors, and the consumers they serve are all weighed. Although the stated purpose of regulation is almost always to benefit consumers, the interests of consumers are in fact often subordinated to those of the regulated firms or other affected groups. There is ample evidence, for example, that federal regulation of railroads, airlines, ocean shipping, long-distance telephone service, radio and television broadcasting, and other industries generally favored the regulated firms and their employees at the expense of consumers.

3. **Environmental Externalities.** Government authority over air and water quality, federal lands (including national parks), and other environmental resources often necessitates political trade-offs between the aesthetic and healthful qualities of our physical environment and other desirable economic goods. Reducing air pollution may require not only more costly automobiles but also closed factories and fewer industrial jobs. Drilling for oil and natural gas off the California coastline may compromise the beauty of the coast, and perhaps even threaten some of its wildlife, but it also produces a valuable energy resource. Prohibitions on strip mining may preserve the aesthetic beauty of a region, but they also raise the supply price of many minerals. Government decisions affecting the quality of the environment must therefore inevitably weigh the interests of consumers, industry, labor, and advocates of environmental preservation.

Rationality in the Public Sector

As the foregoing examples make clear, decision makers in the public sector must make choices among valuable, but competing, alternatives. Public choice theory assumes that rational self-interest is no less a factor there than it is in choices made by individuals, households, and businesses in the private sector. In particular, the theory assumes that voters, politicians, government bureaucrats, and all others whose choices affect public policy attempt to maximize the difference between the benefits and costs to themselves of the various alternatives open to choice. Voters vote in accordance with their perceived interests; politicians attempt to maximize their chances of being elected (or re-elected); and government bureaucrats attempt to maximize their security and independence. Indeed, it is the assumption of rational self-interest that makes public choice theory an *economic* theory of the political process.

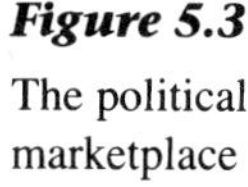

Figure 5.3

The political marketplace

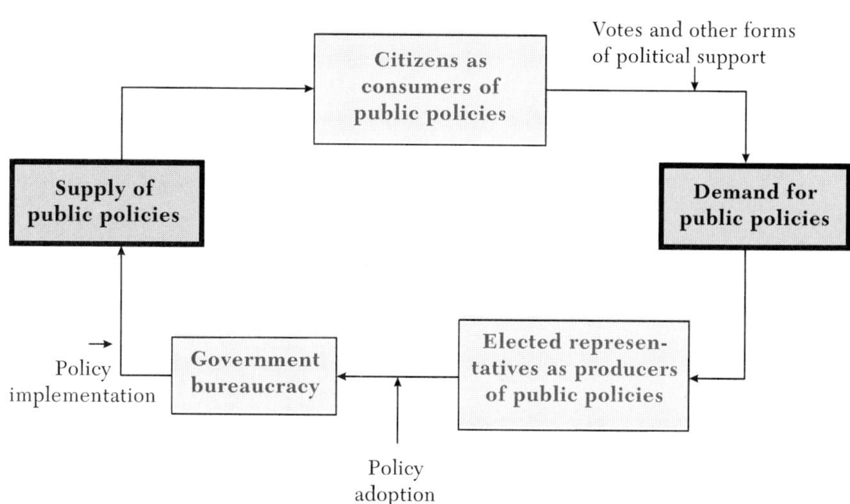

Although the costs and benefits of public sector decisions are expressed through a political process rather than through the market process, the fundamental concepts of supply and demand still apply. Figure 5.3 illustrates how the supply and demand for public policies interact in the democratic political process. The demand for public policies is transmitted from citizens to their elected representatives through votes and other forms of support in the political marketplace. Those representatives then determine which policies to supply by comparing the political costs and benefits of various alternatives. Between the citizens and their elected representatives stands a group of political intermediaries—the permanent government bureaucracy consisting of the various departments and agencies that actually implement public policies.

The theory of public choice predicts that the policies adopted will be those for which the demand *as expressed through the political process* is high relative to the political costs. Given the nature of the process by which information and incentives are transmitted from citizens to government, however, the benefits and costs as seen by elected representatives and government bureaucrats are often distorted. In a sense, the political process acts as a lens through which the costs and benefits affecting some groups appear to be magnified, while those affecting other groups appear diminished. Especially significant in this respect is the difference between the individual citizen-voter and the organized political interest group.

The Rational Ignorance of Individual Citizens

The average citizen is confronted with an enormous variety of political issues that affect his or her welfare. The issues are often complex and their effects uncertain. Moreover, even if an individual citizen knew those effects, his impact

The **rational ignorance effect** occurs when individual citizens find it rational to remain relatively uninformed about public policies because the costs of becoming informed are high relative to the benefits.

on the political outcome is usually limited to casting an intelligent vote or writing a letter to his representative in Congress. Though many votes and letters taken together may have an effect on political decisions, one person's vote or letter is not likely to have much of an impact. Given the large costs and relatively small benefits of becoming informed about all of the government policies that affect his personal welfare, the individual citizen may find it quite rational to remain uninformed on a variety of political issues. This **rational ignorance effect** implies that, *as individuals*, many citizens in a democracy, especially those whose time has valuable alternative uses, have little incentive to participate actively in the political process.

The Role of Interest Groups

An **interest group** is a group of citizens who share a common and well-defined position on some political issue.

In contrast to the rational ignorance of the individual citizen, a group of citizens who share a common and well-defined position on an issue or set of issues, will find it advantageous to join together in an organized political **interest group**. Examples include the AFL-CIO and other organized labor groups, the National Rifle Association, the Sierra Club, the National Association of Manufacturers, The Urban League, and the many so-called political action committees (PACs). Groups such as these can spread the costs of acquiring and disseminating information about government activities, as well as the costs of funding and coordinating lobbying efforts, campaign support, and other activities intended to influence political decision makers, over their entire membership. The ability to economize on the costs of influencing government decisions gives organized interest groups a comparative advantage, relative to individual citizens, in the democratic political process. It should come as no surprise, therefore, that such groups play an important role in shaping government policies.

Applying Public Choice Theory: Automobile Import Restrictions

As an application of public choice theory, consider foreign trade policy with respect to automobile imports. When formulating such policy, political decision makers—in this case, the Congress—must choose between the interests of prospective car buyers and those of domestic automobile producers and the United Auto Workers (UAW), the union that supplies labor to the domestic automobile industry. A policy permitting unlimited foreign competition benefits consumers through lower prices and greater variety, but it may also threaten profits, wages, and job security in the domestic auto industry. On the other hand, a policy that restricts imports protects the jobs and earnings of UAW members and favors the stockholders of General Motors, Ford, and Chrysler, but it also reduces the total supply of automobiles and raises their price to the consumer.

Economics can demonstrate that the costs of import restrictions almost always exceed the benefits. But public choice theory explains why such policies are nonetheless frequently adopted.

To the political decision maker, such as a member of Congress about to vote on a trade bill, the economic interest of consumers, although large in the aggregate, is diffuse and unorganized. Individual car buyers typically have little or no idea of the costs they will bear as a result of import restrictions, and they have even less incentive to find out what those costs might be. Domestic automobile producers and the UAW, on the other hand, are organized interest groups with well-defined and narrowly focused goals. As such, their interests are likely to be much more visible and immediate. It may be fairly easy, for example, for the UAW to channel funds into campaign contributions and for its spokespeople to articulate its position for the news media. The political process therefore tends to magnify the value of protection to organized industry and labor groups and discount the costs such protection imposes on consumers in general. It follows that, although import restrictions are economically inefficient, they may well be adopted—and, in fact, are frequently adopted—as public policy.

Public Interest versus Special Interests

To some, it may seem that public choice theory takes a rather cynical view of the political process. What about the public interest? Does it not play an important role in the formation of government policies? Should it not? All of us would agree that the answer to the latter question is yes. The problem is reaching an agreement on just what constitutes "the public interest." At any rate, public choice theory is a positive model of what government does, not a normative model of what government should do.

But what about the positive question of whether something called the public interest actually influences public policy. To answer this question, we require a working definition of the public interest, something which is not so easy to come by. But let's try anyway.

Inevitably government policies create both gainers and losers. Although there is bound to be an element of arbitrariness in evaluating the gains and losses, normative economics does suggest one possible criterion for doing so—namely, the basic economic efficiency criterion. In particular, we may consider a policy to be in the public interest if the benefits to the gainers exceed the costs imposed on the losers. This definition has a unique appeal in that the gainers could *in principle* compensate the losers and still come out ahead, so that everyone could be at least as well off with the policy as without it. (Since compensation would in general be a practical impossibility, however, the hypothetical compensation is admittedly of little consolation to the losers!)

A **special interest** is an interest which, when served, generates more total costs than benefits but concentrates large individual benefits on a relatively few persons while spreading the costs over many.

By contrast, a policy serves a **special interest** when it creates more total costs than benefits, but spreads the costs over a large number of people, each of whom bears a relatively small individual cost, while concentrating the benefits on a small number of people, each of whom receives a relatively large individual benefit. The import restrictions we previously discussed would be an example of such a special interest policy: The total costs of import restrictions exceed the total benefits, but those costs are spread over millions of consumers, while the benefits are concentrated on a few domestic producers and their employees.

As part of a positive model, our analysis of the role of organized interest groups in the political process does not distinguish between special interests and the public interest; it simply concludes that interest groups are likely to play an important role in public sector decisions. It does not imply that the goals of organized interest groups are necessarily inconsistent with our definition of the public interest and, while it recognizes the potential impact of organized special interests as a fact of life, it does not imply that they dominate the political process to the exclusion of policies that are in the public interest. Which interest group, if any, will prevail on any particular policy issue, and whether or not its interests are consistent with the public interest as we have defined it, are questions to which public choice theory provides no general answer.

CHAPTER SUMMARY

1. One of the fundamental economic functions of government is to provide the legal framework of transferable *property rights* within which production and exchange take place.
2. *Market failure* occurs when real-world markets fail to meet the conditions of economic efficiency. In a literal sense, markets always "fail" simply because perfect economic efficiency is an ideal, unattainable in reality. However, when the market's departure from efficiency is substantial, government action might improve things.
3. *Public goods* are goods that provide simultaneous joint benefits to many consumers and for which it is difficult to exclude consumption by nonpayers. To overcome the potential *free rider* problem that is created by the combination of joint consumption and difficult exclusion, we can rely on the government's authority to levy taxes to finance the provision of public goods.
4. *Externalities* are benefits or costs that are not captured by the market and therefore not reflected in the prices that buyers are willing to pay or the costs that suppliers must cover.
5. When the production or consumption of some good generates *external costs*, social costs exceed private costs and the market produces too much of the good at too low a price. Normative economics suggests government policies that internalize such externalities by shifting the external costs onto those whose activities generate such costs.
6. *External benefits* are analytically very similar to public goods in that they are the result of indivisible and nonexclusive benefits. The government policies that normative economics suggests for dealing with external benefits are therefore quite similar to those it proposes for public goods, namely, the subsidization (or outright provision) of goods whose consumption generates such benefits.

7. *Collusion* and other forms of *monopolistic* behavior increase price above the competitive level and reduce trade below the competitive level. As a result, some potential benefits from production and exchange are lost when markets are monopolized. Normative economics therefore suggests that government policies should encourage competition and discourage monopoly.

8. *Information* has certain characteristics that make it similar to a public good. Accordingly, some economists argue that government should produce and disseminate certain types of information such as that about the safety and health characteristics of goods.

9. Government has used its *monetary and fiscal policies*, with varying degrees of success, to deal with macroeconomic problems of unemployment and inflation.

10. In recent years, government has been called on to provide greater income *equality and security* than might be forthcoming from the market.

11. Like the market, the real public sector inevitably "fails" when measured against the ideal. The real choice that must be made in choosing between the private sector and the public sector in any particular instance is not a choice between two ideals, nor is it a choice between an imperfect market and a perfect government, but rather a choice between an imperfect market and an imperfect government.

12. *Command decisions* by government are generally less flexible, require more centralized information, and are less responsive to costs and benefits than are market decisions.

13. *Public choice theory* is a positive theory of government behavior. It views government authority as a scarce and valuable resource that must be allocated among competing alternatives by rational, self-interested, public sector decision makers.

14. The combination of *rational ignorance* on the part of individual voters and the economic advantages of organized political *interest groups* suggests that the former will play an important role in the political process.

15. A government policy serves a *special interest* when it creates more costs than benefits but spreads the costs among many while concentrating the benefits on a few.

Key Terms and Concepts

property rights
market failure
free rider
private cost
social cost
external benefit

public good
private good
externality
external cost
public choice theory
rational ignorance effect
interest group
special interest

Questions for Thought and Discussion

1. Sunshine Beach is city owned and operated and is open to the public. Is it a public good?
2. Suppose that the marginal cost of producing one more gizmo is $20. The marginal value of one more gizmo is $10 to Ann, $12 to Ben and $15 to Clare. Is it worth producing another gizmo if gizmos are a private good that can be consumed by only one person? If they are a public good whose consumption can be enjoyed simultaneously by Ann, Ben, and Clare?
3. What characteristics of radio and TV broadcasts make them essentially public goods? If they are public goods, how is it that privately owned networks such as ABC, CBS, and NBC produce them? Is the programming of cable networks, such as ESPN and HBO, also a public good?
4. We said that to overcome the free rider problem, government might have to use its taxing authority to finance the provision of public goods, but it need not produce them. Consider national defense as a public good. What aspects of national defense does the federal government actually produce? What aspects does it simply finance with tax revenues?
5. What are some of the private costs you incur when you drive your car? What are some of the external costs your driving imposes on others?
6. We pointed out that external benefits are similar to public goods. In what sense are large-scale external costs due to air pollution an example of a "public bad?"
7. During the late 1980s, the federal government budgeted between $4 and $5 billion annually for the Environmental Protection Agency. Do you think that amount is an accurate measure of the value of resources devoted to producing a cleaner environment?
8. What are some examples of federal government programs whose primary purpose is to increase economic equality and security? Must such programs be provided by the public sector, or would the private sector provide substitutes in the absence of government provision?
9. What does public choice theory imply about the size of government? In terms of resource allocation, will the public sector consume too many, too few, or just about the right amount of resources relative to the private sector?
10. It is sometimes argued that government is inefficient because it attracts people who are lazier and less competent than those employed in the private sector. Is this argument consistent with public choice theory?
11. Would a more educated citizenry cure the problem of rationally ignorant voters?
12. Can you give a definition of the *public interest* with which everyone would agree?

C H A P T E R 6

Elasticity of Demand and Supply

Elasticity is a measure of how sensitive one variable is to a change in another, related variable. It is equal to the ratio of the percentage (or proportionate) change in the dependent variable to the percentage (or proportionate) change in the independent variable.

What would happen to the enrollment at your college or university if tuition were increased by 10 percent? If a firm wants to raise its total sales revenue, can it do so simply by raising the prices of the products it sells? Or must it cut prices to stimulate sales? If congress were to raise the tax on gasoline, how much of the tax increase would be passed on to consumers in the form of a higher price? Would consumers spend more or less on gasoline as a result of the higher price? How would the higher price of gasoline affect ridership on the local mass transit system?

The answers to questions like these depend on something called **elasticity**. Elasticity is a measure of how sensitive one variable, such as the quantity of a good demanded or supplied, is to changes in another variable, such as the good's price. In this chapter, we introduce this important and useful concept and apply it to both the demand and supply sides of the market.

DEMAND ELASTICITY

Demand elasticity (or more formally, the *price elasticity of demand*) is a numerical measure of how sensitive the quantity demanded is to price. It is defined as the ratio of the percentage (or proportional) change in the quantity of a good demanded to the percentage (or proportional) change in its price, other

Demand elasticity measures the sensitivity of the quantity of a good demanded to changes in its price. It is equal to the ratio of the percentage change in quantity demanded to the percentage change in price, other things being equal.

things being equal.* The other-things-equal qualification insures that all other factors which might affect demand, and which would shift the demand curve if they changed, are held constant. Demand elasticity thus measures the influence of a change in price on quantity demanded as we move along a given demand curve.

Since changes in price and quantity always have opposite signs as we move along the demand curve, the simple ratio of the two always yields a negative number. To avoid this, and to convert demand elasticity into a positive number, we take the absolute value of the ratio of the quantity change to the price change. We can therefore write the general formula for the price elasticity of demand as

$$E_d = \left| \frac{(\text{\% change in quantity demanded})}{(\text{\% change in price})} \right|$$

where E_d is the price elasticity of demand and the vertical bars indicate absolute value. For example, if a 10 percent increase in the price of apples reduces the quantity of apples demanded by 15 percent, then the elasticity of demand for apples is 1.5 (= 15/10). If a 10 percent drop in the price of bananas leads to a 5 percent increase in the quantity of bananas demanded, then the elasticity of demand for bananas is 0.5 (= 5/10).

The more sensitive the quantity demanded to a change in price, the greater the numerical value of demand elasticity and the *more elastic* the demand. Conversely, the less sensitive the quantity demanded is to a change in price, the smaller the numerical value of demand elasticity, and the *less elastic* (or the *more inelastic*) the demand. In the foregoing examples, the demand for apples is more elastic than the demand for bananas.

Calculating Elasticity along the Demand Curve

Elasticity can be measured either at a single point on the demand curve or between two points on the curve. Calculating elasticity at a point requires the use of calculus, which we shall mercifully spare you.† Calculating it between two points requires a rule for converting absolute changes in price and quantity into percentage (or proportional) changes.

Suppose, for example, that we want to calculate the demand elasticity between points *A* and *B* on the demand curve in Figure 6.1. Point *A* indicates that

*A percentage change is simply a proportional change multiplied by 100. For example, a proportional change of 75/100 (expressed as a fraction) or 0.75 (expressed as a decimal) is equivalent to a percentage change of 75. As long as we express both numerator and denominator in the same way, either as proportions or as percentages, it makes no matter which we use to calculate elasticity. In most of our sample calculations, we use proportional changes expressed as fractions.

†If you insist, however, the formula for the elasticity at a point on the demand curve is

$$E_d = \frac{dQ/Q}{dP/P} = \frac{P}{Q} \cdot \frac{dQ}{dP}$$

where *P* and *Q* are the price and quantity and dQ/dP is the derivative of the quantity demanded with respect to price at that point on the demand curve.

Figure 6.1

Absolute and proportional changes

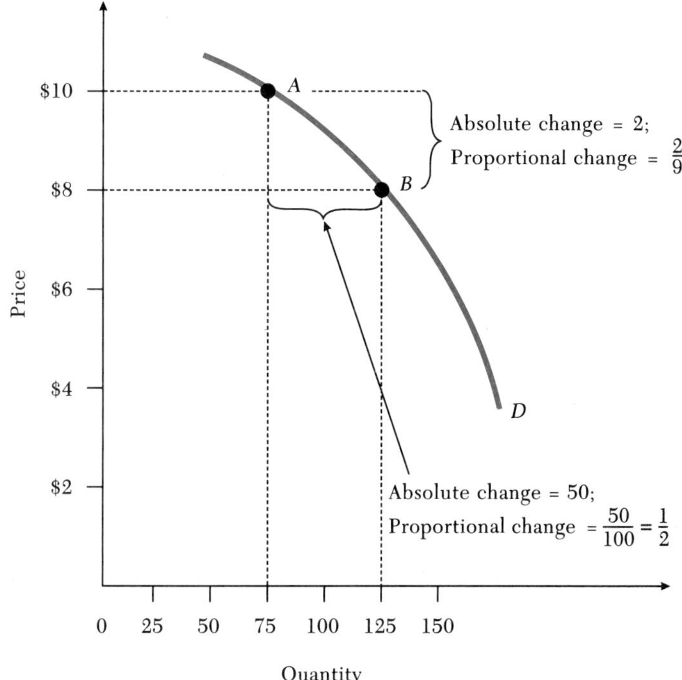

75 units will be demanded at a price of \$10, and Point *B* indicates that 125 units will be demanded at a price of \$8. The absolute changes in price and quantity between these two points are clear: \$2 (= \$10 − \$8) for price and 50 units (= 125 − 75) for quantity demanded. However, the percentage changes are ambiguous. Using the \$10 price as the base for calculating the percentage change in price implies that the \$2 change is a 20 percent (= 2/10) change. On the other hand, using the \$8 price as the base implies that the same \$2 change is a 25 percent (= 2/8) change. We encounter the same ambiguity in calculating the percentage change in quantity demanded: Is the 50 unit change from 75 to 125 a 67 percent change (= 50/75) or a 40 percent change (= 50/125)? If we try to resolve these problems with a rule such as "always use the initial values of price and quantity as the basis for calculating proportional changes," we introduce another source of ambiguity: Between the same two points on the demand curve, elasticity would have a different value when calculated for a fall in price than it would for a rise in price.

We avoid all of these problems by using neither the initial nor the final value, but rather the *average of the two values* as the base for calculating a proportional or percentage change. Accordingly, the formula we use for calculating the elasticity between two points on the demand curve is

$$E_d = \left| \frac{\Delta Q_d / \bar{Q}_d}{\Delta P / \bar{P}} \right|$$

where ΔQ_d and ΔP are the absolute changes in quantity demanded and price, respectively, and $\bar{Q}_d$ and $\bar{P}$ are the averages of their initial and final values. Note that it makes no difference which set of values is called *initial* and which *final*; the computed value of elasticity will be the same.

We can now use the preceding formula to calculate the elasticity between points A and B on the demand curve in Figure 6.1. Since the average of the two prices is \$9 [= (10 + 8)/2] and the average of the two quantities demanded is 100 [= (75 + 125)/2], the proportional changes in price and quantity demanded are 2/9 (or equivalently, 22 percent) and 50/100 (or 50 percent), respectively. Thus the elasticity of demand between points A and B is

$$E_d = \left| \frac{50/100}{2/9} \right| = \frac{450}{200} = 2.25$$

Elasticity and Slope

Like elasticity, *slope* is also a measure of how sensitive one variable is to changes in another variable. For example, if the slope of the demand curve is -2, that tells us that a \$2 increase (decrease) in price leads to a one-unit decrease (increase) in quantity demanded. Elasticity is not the same thing as the slope, however. Elasticity is a ratio of *proportional* changes; slope is a ratio of *absolute* changes.

Because it depends on proportional changes, the value of elasticity, unlike that of slope, is independent of the units of measurement. A given change in price is the same proportional change whether we measure it in dollars, cents, or pesos; a given change in quantity of, say, some liquid, is the same proportional change whether we measure it in barrels, gallons, liters, or pounds. Absolute changes, and therefore the numerical value of slope, *do* depend on the units of measurement.

In addition, elasticity generally varies along a demand curve, even one with a constant slope. Consider, for example, the straight-line demand curve shown in Figure 6.2. Since each \$2 change in price leads to a ten-unit change in quantity demanded, this demand curve has a constant slope of $-1/5$. However, its elasticity depends on where we are on the curve. As the calculations accompanying the diagram indicate, the elasticity between points A and B (= 3) is not the same as the elasticity between points C and D (= 1/3), even though the absolute changes in price and quantity are the same in each interval.*

*Elasticity is relatively high in the interval between points A and B because the ten-unit absolute change in quantity is large in proportion to the average quantity of 25 in that interval, while the \$2 absolute change in price is small in proportion to the \$15 average. Between C and D, however, the same ten-unit change in quantity is smaller in proportion to the 75 unit average, while the same \$2 change in price is larger in proportion to the \$5 average price. Thus, in the interval between A and B, the larger *proportional* change in quantity divided by the smaller *proportional* change in price results in a larger value of elasticity than in the interval between C and D.

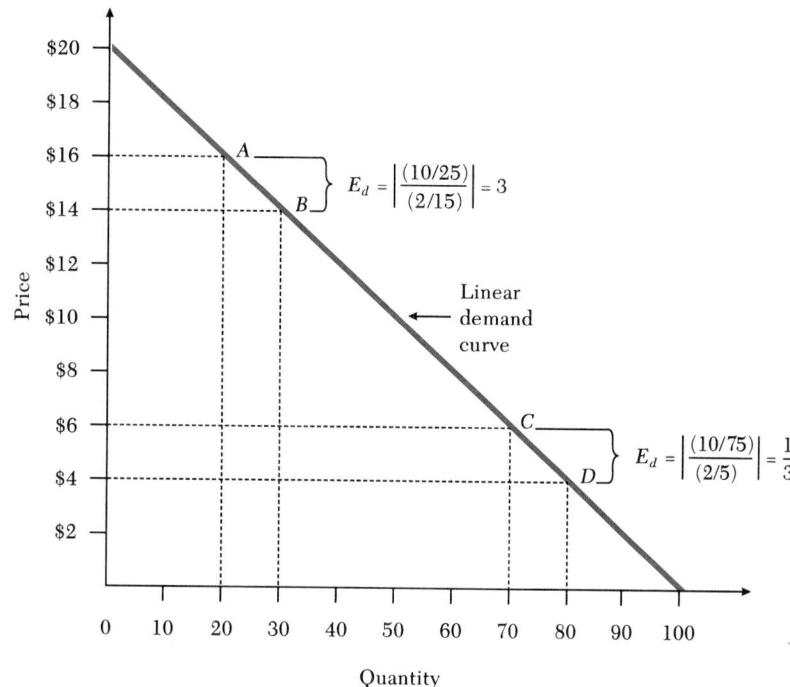

Figure 6.2

Elasticity varies along a demand curve

For linear demand curves, like the one in the foregoing example, there is a simple relation between the numerical value of elasticity and the price interval over which it is measured. In any price range above the midpoint of a linear demand curve, elasticity is greater than one; in any price range below the midpoint, elasticity is less than one; and at the midpoint (or between any two points symmetric about it), elasticity is equal to one. This is illustrated in Figure 6.3, where the point labelled M is the midpoint between the intercepts on the two axes, points P' and Q', respectively.

Elasticity and slope are not completely unrelated, however. Given the units of measurement of price and quantity, the steeper the demand curve in any particular price range, the less its elasticity; the flatter the demand curve, the greater its elasticity. Accordingly, we often find it convenient for purposes of illustration to portray differences in elasticity as differences in slope.

Classifying Demand According to Its Elasticity

Depending on the numerical value of elasticity, demand can be classified as *perfectly inelastic, relatively inelastic, unitary elastic, relatively elastic,* and *perfectly elastic*. These five possibilities are represented in Figure 6.4 on p. 126.

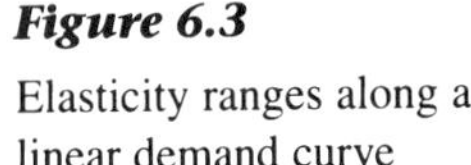

Figure 6.3

Elasticity ranges along a linear demand curve

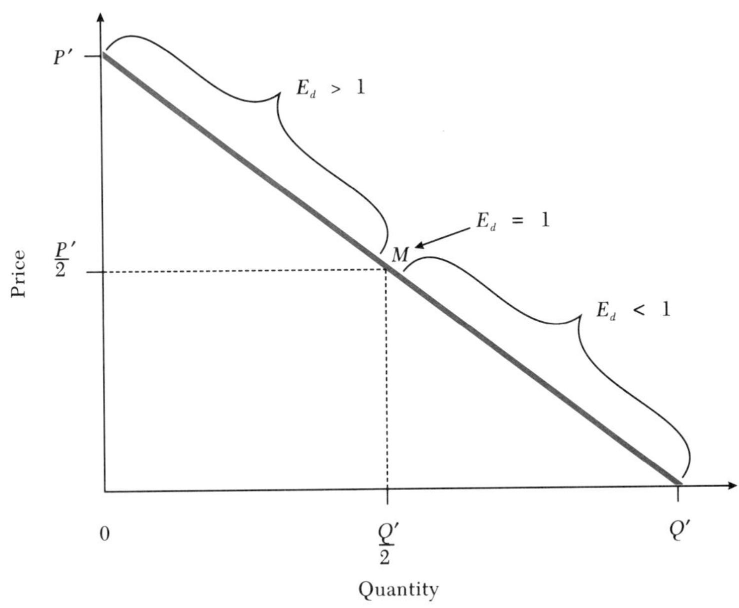

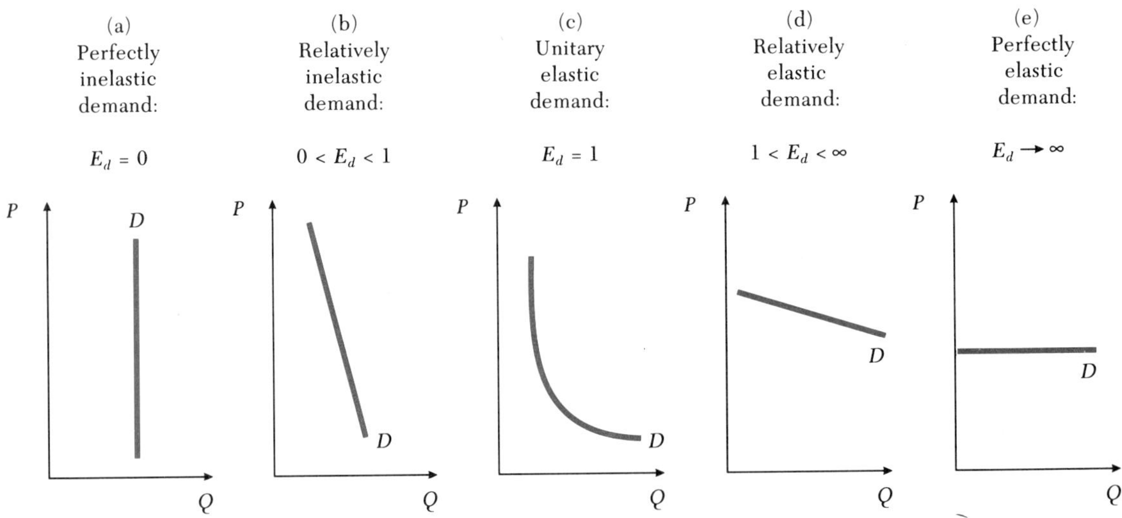

Figure 6.4

Classifying demand by elasticity.

Perfectly Inelastic Demand: $E_d = 0$

The case of **perfectly inelastic** demand is illustrated in Figure 6.4(a). The demand curve is vertical because the zero value of the elasticity coefficient means that changes in price have no effect on the quantity demanded. Demand could conceivably be perfectly inelastic in a relatively narrow price range in certain

A **perfectly inelastic** relationship between two variables is one for which the value of elasticity is zero, implying that a change in the independent variable has no effect on the dependent variable.

An **inelastic** relationship betwen two variables is one for which the value of elasticity is less than one, implying that a change in the independent variable leads to a less than proportionate change in the dependent variable.

rare circumstances, but no demand curve could be perfectly inelastic throughout. Quantity demanded must eventually fall as price rises, if for no other reason than the fact that at a high enough price, people would literally be unable to afford as much of the good as at lower prices.

Inelastic Demand: $0 < E_d < 1$

Demand is **inelastic** when the value of elasticity is less than one. This will be true whenever a given percentage change in price results in a smaller percentage change in quantity demanded. For example, if a 10 percent increase in price leads to a 7 percent decrease in the quantity demanded, then demand is inelastic ($E_d = 0.7$).

The case of inelastic demand is illustrated in Figure 6.4(b) where the steep slope of the demand curve indicates that quantity demanded is relatively insensitive to price. (Remember, however, that elasticity is not slope. If we moved far enough up the linear demand curve in part (b), we would eventually reach a region above its midpoint where elasticity is greater than one.)

A **unitary elastic** relationship between two variables is one for which the value of elasticity is equal to one, implying that a change in the independent variable leads to an equal proportionate change in the dependent variable.

Unitary Elasticity: $E_d = 1$

Demand is **unitary elastic** whenever a given percentage change in price results in an equal (and opposite) percentage change in quantity demanded: for example, when a price increase of 10 percent leads to a 10 percent reduction in the quantity demanded. As we have seen, a linear demand curve is unitary elastic at its midpoint. There is also a special case, illustrated in Figure 6.4(c), in which demand elasticity is unitary along the entire demand curve. We explain its shape below.

An **elastic** relationship between two variables is one for which the value of elasticity is greater than one, implying that a change in the independent variable leads to a more than proportionate change in the dependent variable.

A **perfectly elastic** relationship between two variables is one for which the value of elasticity approaches infinity, implying that a very small change in the independent variable has a very large effect on the dependent variable.

Elastic Demand: $E_d > 1$

Demand is **elastic** when the value of elasticity is greater than 1: that is, when a given percentage change in price results in a larger percentage change in quantity demanded. For example, if a 10 percent increase in price leads to 12 percent decrease in the quantity demanded, then demand is elastic ($E_d = 1.2$).

The case of elastic demand is illustrated in Figure 6.4(d). The demand curve is drawn with a flat slope to indicate that quantity demanded is relatively sensitive to changes in price. (But again bear in mind that the slope of the curve notwithstanding, if we extended the linear demand curve in part (d) far enough out to the right, we would eventually reach a region of inelastic demand below its midpoint.)

Perfectly Elastic Demand: $E_d = \infty$

A **perfectly elastic** demand curve is horizontal as shown in Figure 6.4(e). This is another extreme case, one in which even the slightest change in price causes an infinitely large change in the quantity demanded.

What Determines the Price Elasticity of Demand?

The most fundamental determinant of the elasticity of demand for any good is the availability of substitutes for that good. In general, the more and better substitutes there are for any good, the more sensitive buyers are to a change in its price and the more elastic its demand. For example, if people consider Pepsi a good substitute for Coke, then a relatively small increase in the price of Coke would cause many buyers to switch to Pepsi, thereby significantly reducing the quantity of Coke demanded. Conversely, a small decrease in the price of Coke would attract many Pepsi drinkers and significantly increase the demand for Coke. Thus the demand for Coke is more elastic to the extent that people consider Pepsi a good substitute.

Note that the overall demand for a particular kind of good, such as cola soft drinks, is generally less elastic than the individual demands for the particular brands of that good, such as Coke or Pepsi. Noncola soft drinks such as Seven-Up are not as good a substitute for cola as Coke is for Pepsi. Similarly, while there are few good substitutes for a car, there are many good substitutes for Fords, namely, Chevrolets, Toyotas, and Plymouths, to mention just a few. Thus the demand for cars in general is much less elastic than the demand for Fords in particular.

The elasticity of demand also depends on the time horizon over which the effects of changes in price are observed. In particular, since a longer period of time allows buyers greater flexibility in adjusting to a change in price, demand is generally more elastic in the long run than in the short run. For example, when gasoline prices rose dramatically during the 1970s, people with gas guzzling cars at first found it difficult to reduce their gasoline consumption by even a small amount. As a result, demand was quite inelastic in the short run. However, as smaller, more efficient automobiles eventually replaced the gas guzzlers—largely in response to high gasoline prices, we should note—gasoline consumption fell much further and demand was accordingly more elastic.

Table 6.1 shows some estimates of the price elasticity of demand for a variety of different categories of goods. These estimates tend to confirm that the longer the time allowed for adjustment to a change in price, the more elastic the demand.

Buyer Expenditures, Seller Revenues, and Elasticity

If consumers buy fewer units of a good in response to its higher price, will their total expenditures on that good increase or decrease? If a seller cuts price to sell more units, will total sales revenue increase or decrease?

Since a dollar of expenditure from the buyer's standpoint is the same as a dollar of revenue from the seller's standpoint, these are really just two ways of asking the same question: What happens to buyer expenditures, or equivalently, to seller revenues, when the price of a good changes? Other things being equal,

Table 6.1

Some estimated price elasticities of demand

Good	ELASTICITY *Short Run*	*Long Run*
Alcoholic beverages	0.92	3.63
Beer	1.13	n.a.
Sports equipment	0.88	2.39
Movies	0.87	3.67
Medical care	0.31	0.92
Owner-occupied housing	0.04	1.22
Bus travel (local)	0.77	3.54
Bus travel (intercity)	0.20	2.17
Rail travel	0.54	1.70
Air travel (foreign)	0.70	4.00
Natural gas	0.15	10.74
Electricity	0.13	1.90
New cars	1.35	n.a.
Gasoline	0.15	0.78

SOURCES: T. F. Hogarty and K. G. Elzinga, "The Demand for Beer," *The Review of Economics and Statistics,* May 1972; H. S. Houthakker and L. S. Taylor, *Consumer Demand in the United States,* 2 ed. (Harvard University Press, 1970); U.S. Senate Subcommittee on Antitrust and Monopoly, *Administered Prices: Automobiles* (Washington, D.C.: U.S. Government Printing Office, 1958); James L. Sweeney, "The Demand for Gasoline: A Vintage Capital Model," Department of Engineering Economics, Stanford University.

a higher price means that more will be spent on each unit purchased but that fewer units will be purchased. Conversely, a lower price means that the seller will take in less revenue on each unit sold but will sell more units. The relative magnitudes of the price and quantity effects, and thus which of the two will predominate, depends on the elasticity of demand.

In particular, if demand is *inelastic* in the region of a price change, the change in price is proportionately larger than the corresponding change in quantity demanded. As a result, *total buyer expenditures (seller revenues) change in the same direction as price.* For example, if the short-run elasticity of demand for gasoline is equal to 0.15, then a 10 percent increase in price more than offsets the resulting 1.5 percent reduction in the amount of gasoline purchased. The price increase is therefore accompanied by an increase in consumer expenditures on gasoline.

If demand elasticity is *unitary* in the region of the price change, the equal and opposite changes in price and quantity exactly offset one another so that *buyer expenditures (seller revenues) remain constant when the price changes.* For example, a 10 percent price increase, if matched by a 10 percent reduction in quantity demanded, has no effect on total buyer expenditures or seller revenues. Were the demand curve unitary elastic throughout, this would imply that buyers spend the same total amount on the good regardless of its price. The equation of such a constant-expenditure demand curve is $P \times Q = K$, where K is the constant level of expenditures. This is the equation of a "rectangular hyperbola," and that is what we have in Figure 6.4(c).

Finally, if demand is *elastic* in the region of the price change, the change in quantity demanded is proportionately larger than the corresponding change in price. As a result, *total buyer expenditures (seller revenues) change in the opposite direction from the change in price.* For example, if the elasticity of demand for Chevrolet Camaros is equal to 2.5, a 10 percent reduction in the price of Camaros would lead to a 25 percent increase in the number sold. Because the increase in the number of units sold more than offsets the decrease in price, the price cut is accompanied by an increase in General Motors' revenues from the sale of Camaros.

We can use the relation between demand elasticity and revenues (expenditures) to explain certain economic aspects of two diverse areas of government policy, namely, agricultural policy and drug enforcement policy.

Agricultural Crop Restrictions

For more than half a century, the federal government of the United States has encouraged farmers to limit their production of a variety of agricultural crops. These policies have almost invariably received the political support of farmers and farm-state legislators. To explain such support we must ask how it is that farmers can gain by *not* producing?

The answer lies in the elasticity of demand for the crops subject to supply restrictions. In particular, the restricted supply leads to a higher price and, as long as the demand for the affected crops is *inelastic*, the higher price means higher total revenues for farmers. (Not only are farm revenues higher, but with less to plant and harvest, farm costs are also lower. Thus the crop restrictions raise the overall profits of the affected farmers. Were the demand for the restricted crops elastic, supply restrictions would reduce farm revenues and possibly profits as well.)

An apparent paradox arises, however, when we recognize that the government often has to *pay* farmers to restrict their output. If the restricted supply means higher revenues, why do farmers need such an inducement to go along with the government's crop restriction program? The answer lies in the distinction between the *market demand* and the *demand for the output of an individual farmer*. While the overall market demand for a crop such as wheat is relatively inelastic, the demand for the wheat produced by an individual wheat farmer is virtually *perfectly elastic* because there are many other farmers producing perfect substitutes for his crop. Were he to attempt to charge a higher price than other wheat farmers, no one would buy his wheat. However, if all wheat farmers together restrict output, the market supply of wheat falls and the market price rises. When this happens, each individual farmer has an incentive to free ride on the supply restrictions of the others by producing as much as possible to take advantage of the higher price. Of course, were they all to do this, market supply would expand rather than contract, the price would fall rather than rise, and, because demand is inelastic, revenues would fall. This is why the government, in order to insure the success of its crop restriction programs, must often literally pay farmers not to produce.

The Dilemma for Drug Enforcement Policy

Successful drug raids by law enforcement agencies always make the prime-time newscasts. Whenever the Coast Guard intercepts a shipment of cocaine, for example, or whenever Drug Enforcement Agency officials burn a clandestine marijuana plantation, reporters and camera crews are on the scene. Crimes such as burglary, robbery, and auto theft are also newsworthy, especially when they are reflected in a rise in the overall crime rate. Economic analysis suggests, and the evidence tends to confirm, that these events are not unrelated.

By intercepting, confiscating, and destroying supplies of illegal drugs and imprisoning their suppliers, drug enforcement policy tends to focus primarily on the supply side of the market. As in any market, a reduction in supply drives up the price. Whenever there is a major drug bust, therefore, the street price of the confiscated drug rises (see Figure 6.5). Since the demand for illegal drugs tends to be *inelastic*, especially among addicts, total expenditures by users of the drug

Figure 6.5

Supply-side drug enforcement policy

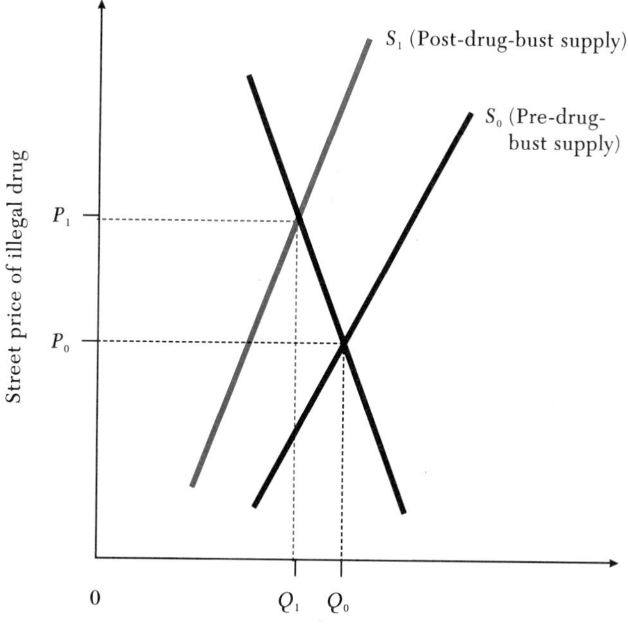

rise in response to the higher price. Unfortunately, the source of the additional expenditures is all too often crimes of another sort—namely, burglary, robbery, auto theft, and other so-called crimes against property—committed by the users of illegal drugs. There is indeed statistical evidence confirming that property crime rates in large cities tend to rise following a major drug bust. Note that if the demand for illegal drugs were elastic, drug busts would complement, rather than confound, efforts to reduce property crime. As it is, the two are often at odds with one another.

Given the inelastic demand for most illegal substances, economic analysis suggests that the ideal drug enforcement policy would be one that reduces the demand for illegal drugs rather than (or along with) the supply. Unfortunately, economists are no better at suggesting how to reduce the demand than are criminologists, sociologists, and psychologists.

Other Elasticities Related to Demand

The demand for a good depends on many factors in addition to its price, and we could define an elasticity corresponding to each of those factors. Two of the most important are income elasticity and cross elasticity.

Income elasticity measures the sensitivity of demand to a change in buyers' income. It is equal to the ratio of a percentage change in demand to a percentage change in buyer income, other things being equal.

A **normal good** is one for which the demand increases when buyers' incomes increase.

An **inferior good** is one for which the demand decreases when buyers' incomes increase.

Income elasticity measures the sensitivity of demand to changes in buyer income. It is defined as the ratio of the percentage change in demand to the percentage change in buyer income, other things being equal. Using E_I to denote the income elasticity of demand, therefore,

$$E_I = \frac{(\%\text{ change in quantity demanded})}{(\%\text{ change in income})}$$

A good for which demand increases when income rises and decreases when income falls is called a **normal good**. Accordingly, income elasticity for a normal good is positive. By contrast, a good for which the demand decreases when buyer income increases (and vice versa) is called an **inferior good**. The income elasticity of demand for inferior goods is negative. For example, suppose that in response to a 10 percent increase in buyer incomes, the demand for steak rises by 6 percent and the demand for hamburger falls by 8 percent. It follows that steak is a normal good with an income elasticity of $+0.6$ and hamburger is an inferior good with an income elasticity of -0.8.

Normality or inferiority are not inherent characteristics of goods. Whether or not a particular good is normal or inferior for any particular consumer depends, among other things, on that consumer's income level. For someone who is poor and can afford very little meat, a cheap grade of hamburger may be a normal good. If that same consumer's income rises enough so that any further increase would lead her to buy sirloin steak instead of hamburger, then hamburger will have become an inferior good for her and sirloin a normal good. If her income were to rise so high that any further increase would induce her to switch from sirloin to filet mignon, then sirloin would also have become an inferior good. Indeed, even things that most of us consider luxury goods may be considered inferior by someone who is very wealthy. The man who uses an increase in his income to replace his Mercedes Benz with a Rolls Royce, for example, considers the Mercedes to be an inferior good.

Cross elasticity measures the sensitivity of the demand for one good to a change in the price of another, related good. It is equal to the ratio of the percentage change in the quantity demanded of one good to the percentage change in the price of a related good, other things being equal.

Cross elasticity measures the sensitivity of the demand for one good to the price of some other good. It is defined as the ratio of the percentage change in demand for one good to the percentage change in the price of some other related good, other things being equal. Using E_{xy} to denote the cross elasticity of the demand for good X with respect to the price of good Y, we can express cross elasticity as

$$E_{xy} = \frac{(\text{\% change in quantity of X demanded})}{(\text{\% change in price of Y})}$$

The cross elasticity of demand between two goods that are *substitutes* is positive because an increase (decrease) in the price of one of them will increase (decrease) the demand for the other. For example, if a 10 percent increase in the price of IBM personal computers increases the demand for Apple Macintosh computers by 5 percent, then the cross elasticity of demand for the Macintosh with respect to the price of an IBM PC is equal to +0.5.

The cross elasticity of demand between two goods that are *complements* is negative because an increase in the price of one will decrease the demand for the other, and vice versa. For example, if a 10 percent decrease in the price of personal computers leads people to buy more computers and thereby increases the demand for computer software by 15 percent, then the cross elasticity of the demand for software with respect to the price of computers is equal to −1.5.

Notice that we do not take the absolute value when computing either income or cross elasticity because the sign itself tells us something about the nature of the demand for the good. In the case of income elasticity, it tells us whether the good is normal or inferior; in the case of cross elasticity, it tells us whether the goods are substitutes or complements.

SUPPLY ELASTICITY

Supply elasticity measures the sensitivity of the quantity of a good supplied to changes in its price. It is equal to the ratio of the percentage change in quantity supplied to the percentage change in price, other things being equal.

As with most of the concepts applicable to the demand side of the market, elasticity can also be applied to the supply side. In particular, we define **supply elasticity** (or more formally, the *price elasticity of supply*) as

$$E_s = \frac{(\text{\% change in quantity supplied})}{(\text{\% change in price})}$$

where E_s is the price elasticity of supply. For example, if a 10 percent increase in the price of a good leads to a 15 percent increase in the quantity supplied, the elasticity of supply is 1.5. (Here again we do not take the absolute value of the ratio of the quantity and price changes as we did with the price elasticity of demand because a price change generally changes the quantity supplied in the same direction.)

Figure 6.6

Computing supply elasticity

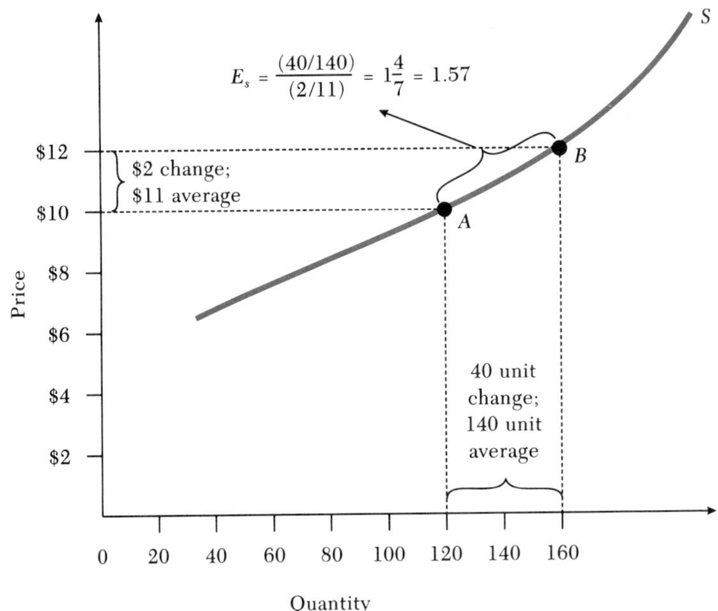

As with demand elasticity, supply elasticity is an other-things-equal measure; that is, it must be computed between two points along a given supply curve. Figure 6.6 shows such a computation using a formula analogous to the one we used in computing demand elasticity, namely,

$$E_s = \frac{\Delta Q_s / \bar{Q}_s}{\Delta P / \bar{P}}$$

where the $\bar{Q}_s$ and $\bar{P}$ are averages of quantity supplied and price, respectively.

Supply elasticity is not the same thing as the slope of the supply curve. As with demand elasticity, however, for given units of measurement and within any given price range, the *flatter the supply curve*, the *more elastic is supply* with respect to price; the *steeper the curve*, the *more inelastic the supply* with respect to price.

As we know, the supply curve reflects marginal cost. Accordingly, supply elasticity is determined by factors that affect the relation between marginal cost and the amount supplied. These factors include the technology of production, the behavior of input prices as supply is varied, and the time allowed for suppliers to respond to price changes. In general, the smaller the rise in marginal cost as the quantity supplied increases, the more *elastic* will be supply; the greater the rise in marginal cost, the more *inelastic* (less elastic) will be supply. At one extreme, supply is *perfectly elastic* ($E_s = \infty$) when the quantity supplied can be increased at constant marginal cost. At the other extreme, supply is *perfectly inelastic* ($E_s = 0$) if the quantity supplied cannot be increased regardless

Figure 6.7

Elasticities of supply

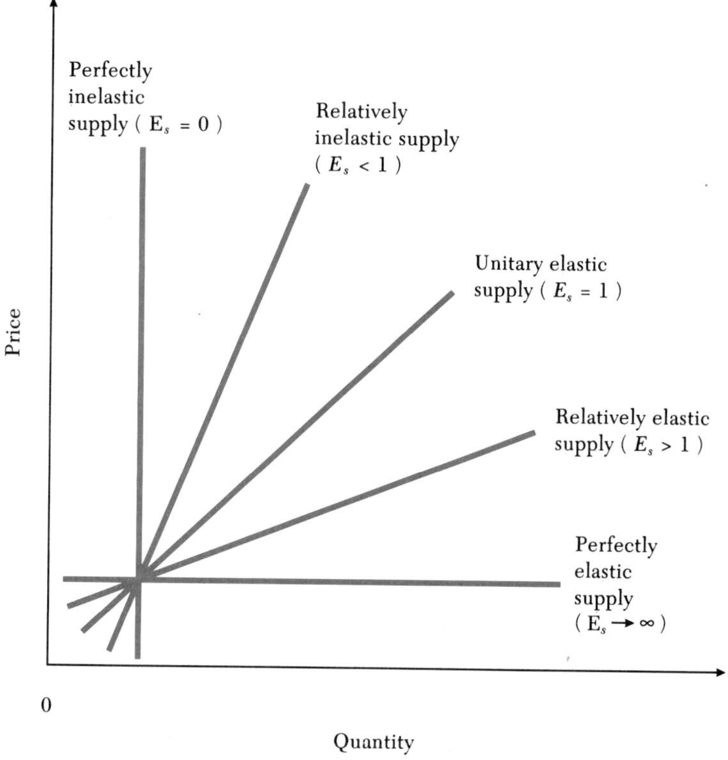

of how high the price rises. (For example, the world's supply of original van Gogh paintings is perfectly inelastic.) These extremes, as well as the intermediate possibilities, are depicted in Figure 6.7.

A Final Application: Elasticity and Tax Incidence

When the government levies a tax on market transactions, such as a sales tax, it typically collects the tax revenues directly from sellers. In the literal sense of who actually hands over the money to the government, therefore, sellers pay the tax. However, to the extent that the tax raises the market price, part of the actual tax burden is passed on to buyers. Other things being equal, the division of the tax burden between sellers and buyers—what economists call the **tax incidence**—depends on the elasticities of both demand and supply.

Tax incidence refers to the division of the tax burden between the buyers and sellers of the good on which the tax is levied.

To see why, let us consider the effects of a tax on gasoline. Figure 6.8 on the next page shows supply and demand in the market for gasoline; D_0 is the demand curve for gasoline and S_0 (= MC) is the pretax supply curve. We have assumed that with no tax the market-clearing price of gasoline would be $1.00.

Figure 6.8

Incidence of a tax on gasoline

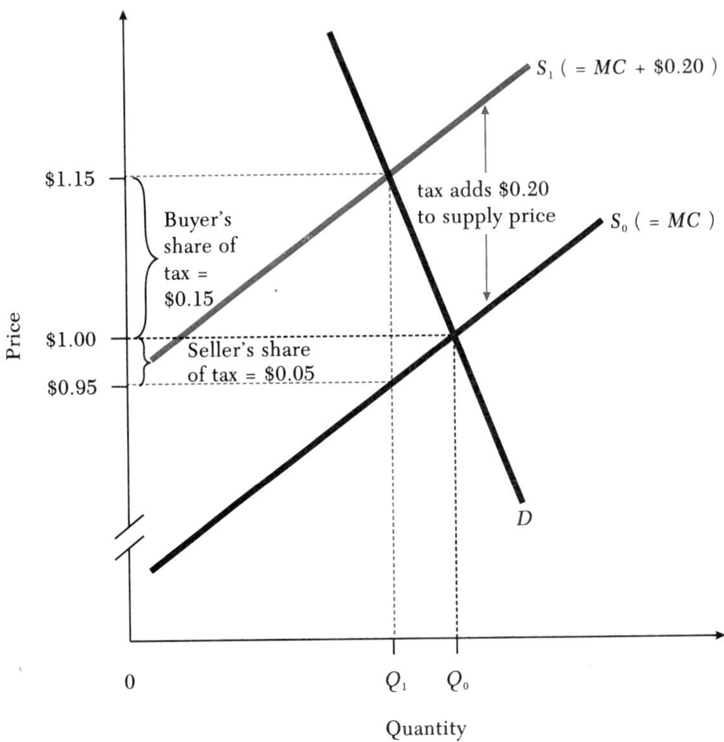

Now suppose that a tax of \$0.20 per gallon is levied on gasoline retailers. Since retailers must now hand over \$0.20 to the government for each gallon of gas they sell, they will add that amount to marginal cost in determining their supply prices. The tax therefore shifts the supply curve vertically upward by \$0.20 to S_1 (= MC + \$0.20). The market-clearing price rises, but *not* by the full amount of the tax. As you can see from the diagram, if sellers simply add the \$0.20 per gallon tax to the original \$1.00 price and charge \$1.20 per gallon, the fall in quantity demanded would create a surplus of gasoline. The final, after-tax price must therefore be somewhere between \$1.00 and \$1.20. In Figure 6.8 we have assumed it to be \$1.15. In effect, this implies that buyers pay \$0.15 of the \$0.20 tax on each gallon of gas.

For their part, sellers receive a price of \$1.15 per gallon, but after paying the \$0.20 tax they are left with only \$0.95 per gallon. Because this is \$0.05 per gallon less than they received before the tax was imposed, their share of the tax burden is \$0.05.

In general, therefore, both buyers and sellers share in the burden of a tax on market transactions. Just how much of the tax is paid by each depends on the elasticities of demand and supply.

Figure 6.9 (a)

Demand elasticity and tax incidence

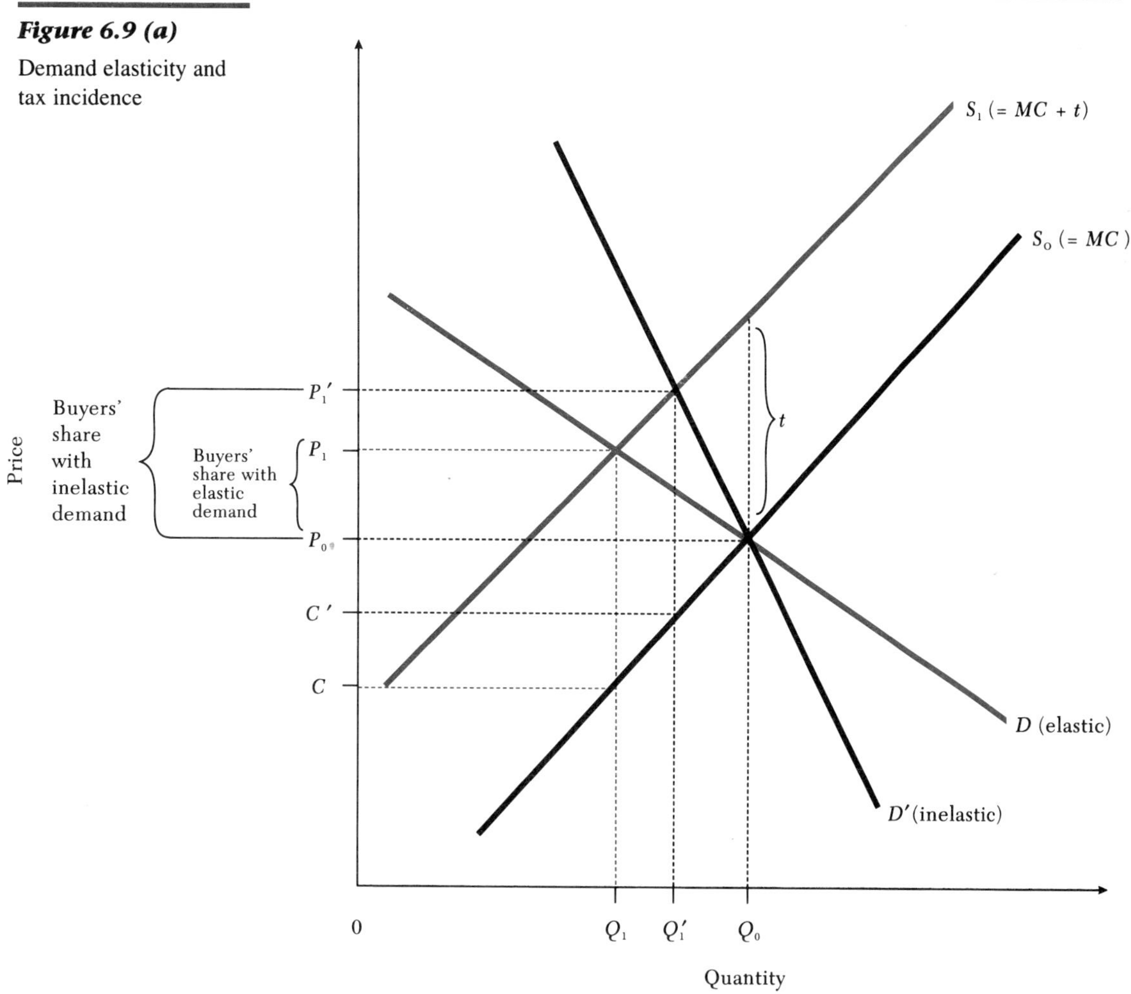

Figure 6.9(a) illustrates the role of demand elasticity in allocating the tax burden. It includes two demand curves, one labelled D and the other D'. Given the pretax supply curve, S_0 (= MC), the initial market-clearing price is P_0 with either demand curve. However, the demand curve labelled D is more elastic at that price than is the one labelled D'. When a tax of $\$t$ per unit is imposed, the supply curve shifts up by that amount to S_1 (= $MC + t$). As you can see, the more elastic the demand, the less the increase in price and the smaller the share of the tax borne by buyers. In particular, buyers pay $(P_1' - P_0)$ of the $\$t$ tax when demand is given by D', but only $(P_1 - P_0)$ when demand is given by D. Correspondingly, the sellers' share of the tax is lower when demand is less elastic $(P_0 - C')$ than when it is more elastic $(P_0 - C)$.

Figure 6.9 (b)

Supply elasticity and tax incidence

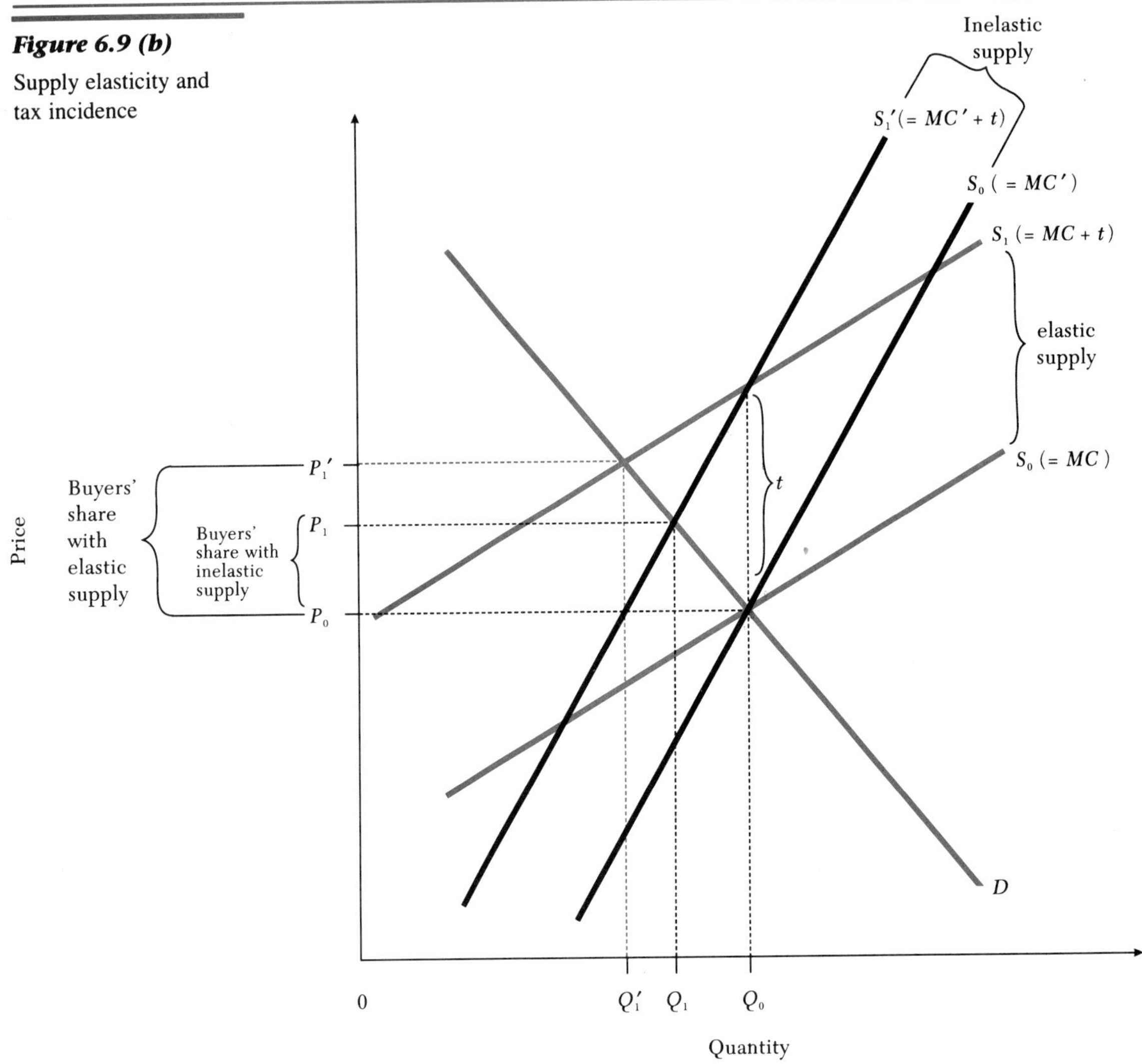

Figure 6.9(b) shows the role of supply elasticity in allocating the tax burden. The before- and after-tax supply curves labelled S_0 and S_1, respectively, are more elastic than those labelled S_0' and S_1'. As you can see from the diagram, the increase in price, and thus the share of the tax burden borne by buyers, is greater with the more elastic supply.

In summary, then, the burden of a tax will fall more heavily on buyers to the extent that demand is inelastic and supply is elastic. It will fall more heavily on sellers to the extent that demand is elastic and supply is inelastic.

CHAPTER SUMMARY

1. *Demand elasticity* (formally the *price elasticity of demand*) is the ratio of the percentage (or proportional) change in the quantity of a good demanded to the percentage (or proportional) change in its price, other things being equal.

2. Demand is *perfectly inelastic* if the numerical value of demand elasticity is 0, (relatively) *inelastic* if it is between 0 and 1, *unitary* if it is equal to 1, (relatively) *elastic* if it is greater than 1, and *perfectly elastic* if it is infinite.

3. The principal determinants of the elasticity of demand for any good are the *availability of substitutes* for that good and the *time allowed for an adjustment* to a change in its price. The more and better substitutes and the longer the time to adjust to a price change, the more elastic will be demand.

4. If demand is inelastic ($E_d < 1$), seller revenues (or equivalently, buyer expenditures) will change in the same direction as a change in price. If demand is elastic ($E_d > 1$), seller revenues (buyer expenditures) will change in the opposite direction from a change in price. If demand elasticity is unitary, seller revenues (buyer expenditures) will not change when price changes.

5. *Income elasticity* is defined as the ratio of the percentage change in demand to the percentage change in buyer income, other things being equal. It measures the sensitivity of demand to changes in buyer income. Income elasticity is positive for *normal goods* and negative for *inferior goods*.

6. *Cross elasticity* is defined as the ratio of the percentage change in the demand for one good to the percentage change in the price of some other related good, other things being equal. It measures the sensitivity of the demand for one good to changes in the price of some other good. Cross elasticity is positive when the two goods are *substitutes* and negative when they are *complements*.

7. *Supply elasticity* (formally the *price elasticity of supply*) is the ratio of the percentage (or proportional) change in the quantity of a good supplied to the percentage (or proportional) change in its price, other things being equal.

8. The burden, or *incidence*, of a tax will fall more heavily on buyers to the extent that demand is inelastic and supply is elastic. It will fall more heavily on sellers to the extent that demand is elastic and supply is inelastic.

Key Terms and Concepts

elasticity
demand elasticity
perfectly inelastic
inelastic
unitary elastic
elastic
perfectly elastic
income elasticity
normal good
inferior good
cross elasticity
supply elasticity
tax incidence

Questions for Thought and Discussion

1. The local transit district discovers that ridership falls from 12,000 per week to 6,000 per week when it raises the basic bus fare from $1.00 to $1.50. What is the slope of the demand curve for bus rides in this price range? What is the elasticity of demand in this price range? Did transit system revenues go up or down as a result of the fare increase?
2. Using the estimates of the demand for rail travel given in Table 6.1, tell what advice you would give the management of Amtrak (the passenger rail service in the United States) when they ask Congress for an additional subsidy to cover their costs.
3. "Since there is no substitute for water, the demand for water must be perfectly inelastic." Do you agree?
4. What would be the sign of the cross elasticity of demand between each of the following?
   a. Tires and gasoline
   b. Pepsi and Seven-Up
   c. Theater movies and rental movies
   d. Rental movies and VCRs
5. We used the example of paintings by Van Gogh as an example of a good with a perfectly inelastic supply. Is there a sense in which this example is incorrect?
6. There is good evidence that the demand for gasoline is relatively inelastic, even in the long run. There is also evidence that the long-run supply is fairly elastic. If Congress actually does raise the gas tax, who will bear the lion's share of the burden—motorists or gasoline producers?
7. Henry George, a famous economist of about a century ago, proposed that government raise all revenues by levying a tax on land. How do you think his proposal was received by landowners?

CHAPTER 7

Business Firms and the Organization of Production

A fundamental characteristic of organization in Western economies has been decentralization—a diffusion of authority and responsibility and a limitation of the pyramiding of managerial hierarchies to cases where the hierarchy clearly pays its way.

NATHAN ROSENBERG AND L. E. BIRDZELL*

As we have seen, final consumers rarely enter into direct exchanges with suppliers of labor and other productive resources to obtain the goods they demand. Instead, the bulk of productive activity is channelled through intermediaries that we call *firms*. Our primary concern in this chapter is the *capitalist business firm* that is organized and operated to make a profit.

Why do firms exist? What do they contribute to the process of transforming energy, materials, and human effort into final goods? What different organizational forms do they take, and why has one form in particular, the private corporation, become so important in the economies of advanced industrial nations?

In this chapter we try to answer these and other questions about the nature and functions of the modern business firm.

* *How the West Grew Rich* (Basic Books, 1986), p. 297.

THE ORGANIZATION OF PRODUCTION

How to Produce a Book: An Illustration of Two Alternatives

By way of introduction, let us examine two alternative ways of organizing and coordinating a concrete production process, namely, the process that led ultimately to the book you are now reading. A partial list of the people who supplied labor and other productive resources along the way includes the owners of standing timber, loggers, paper millers, editors, graphic artists and layout designers, typesetters and printers, bookbinders, truck drivers, employees of the college bookstore, and (ahem!) the author. This brief list overlooks many other contributors—from the people who extract the dyes from which ink is made to those who write computer software for word processing—but let's try to keep things simple.

Production without Firms

It is possible (though unlikely) that the entire production process leading to this book could take place without any coordinating element other than the signals and incentives created by market price adjustments. Each individual logger with an axe and a chain saw could operate as an independent contractor (or jobber) who purchases rights to cut and sell timber from the owners of forest lands and then sells that timber to other individuals who convert it into paper. The author could buy the paper from them, hire someone to read and edit his manuscript, someone else to design a cover and lay out a format, someone to set the type, someone to do the printing, and someone to do the binding. He could then rent warehouse space to store the book while he toured college campuses trying to convince economics professors to adopt his book for use in their classes. Finally, he could hire someone with a truck to deliver it to those who did so.

Each step in this hypothetical production process could thus be accomplished by means of a market transaction between two parties—timber owner and logger, logger and paper maker, paper maker and author, and so on. There would be no business firms involved, only individuals who act as independent suppliers of productive services and whose activities are coordinated only by market price adjustments that equate quantities supplied and demanded at each step along the way.

Business Firms and Integrated Production

But, of course, that is not the way this book or any other actually does get produced. Typically, the services of loggers, the rights to cut timber, and the capital, knowledge, and skills necessary to convert it into paper are all combined within a firm specializing in the production of forest products. Weyerhauser and Georgia Pacific are two examples of such firms. The functions of editing, graphics and layout design, as well as the distribution of textbooks to professors, are

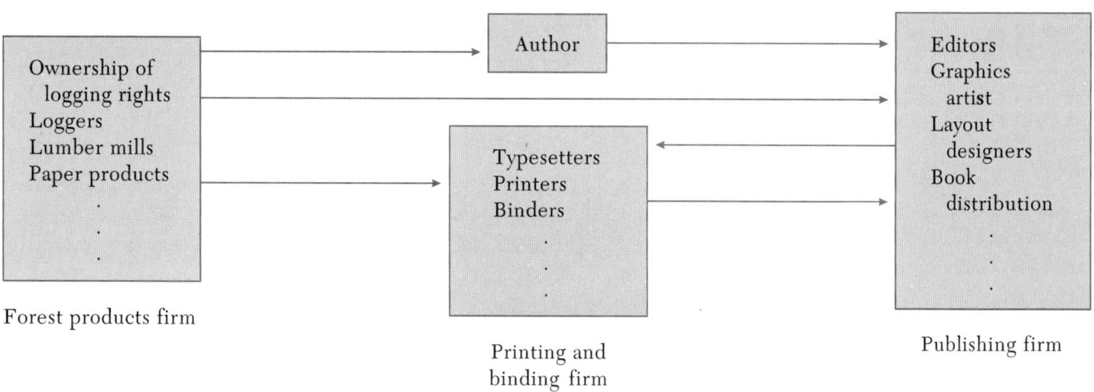

Figure 7.1

Integrated production

all coordinated within a publishing firm such as Harcourt Brace Jovanovich, Inc., the publisher of this book. Typesetting, printing, and binding might be combined within another firm, and storage and delivery within still another. Such a production process is illustrated in Figure 7.1.

Horizontal integration combines productive activities at the same stage of a production process within a single firm.

Vertical integration combines productive activities at successive stages of a production process within a single firm.

Because a number of production activities are joined together within each firm, the production process is said to be *integrated*. There are two kinds of integration, **horizontal integration** and **vertical integration**. Horizontal integration combines a number of suppliers of the same productive service or resource within a single firm. If, for example, two loggers join forces to cut and sell trees instead of competing with one another, the result is horizontal integration. Writing a book with a coauthor, employing twenty typesetters, and owning a fleet of trucks are all examples of horizontal integration. Vertical integration combines two or more successive steps in the same production process within the same firm. If the logging firm also owns a lumber mill, then it is vertically integrated. If typesetting, printing, and bookbinding are all done by the same firm, then that firm is also vertically integrated. Different firms display different degrees of horizontal and vertical integration, but integrated production itself is a defining characteristic of all firms.

Markets and Managers

Market coordination is coordination achieved through market price adjustments.

Managerial coordination is coordination achieved within a firm by managerial authority.

In their *external* relations with one another and with final consumers, the activities of firms are subject to **market coordination**: Price adjustments in factor markets, intermediate goods markets, and final goods markets determine the allocation of the inputs that firms purchase and the allocation of the outputs that they produce. But the *internal* process by which inputs are transformed into outputs within the firm is primarily subject to **managerial coordination**. Managerial coordination relies on the discretionary authority of managers—supervisors, shop foremen, division heads, and ultimately the firm's owners—to allocate resources within the firm. Some manager in a forest products firm, for example, must determine how much of the company's cut timber is to be allocated to the production of plywood, how much to the production of cardboard boxes, and how much to the production of paper. Another must determine how many of the firm's loggers are to be employed in the Pacific Northwest and how many in the Southeast.

Why Firms?

To see why managerial coordination replaces market coordination at various stages of the production process, we must examine the advantages of production within firms.

Team Production

Moving a piano up a flight of stairs can be accomplished by two men, but it cannot be accomplished by one man alone, even if he works twice as long and hard. Piano moving is an example of *team production*. Team production exists whenever two or more people can accomplish more by coordinating their efforts and working together than they can by working as separate individuals. In other words, in team production the whole is more than just the sum of its individual parts.

The analogy with an athletic team is instructive. A football team, for example, must be more than just a bunch of big, strong men if it is to "produce" more points than its opponents. It must be a group with a common purpose and with different special talents that mesh in an appropriate manner. So it is with team production. By working together and specializing according to their respective comparative advantages, people can often contribute more as members of a team than they could acting as individuals.

Long-Term Contracts

Long-term contracts, whether formal or implicit, are another important characteristic of the firm. Neither a football team that breaks in a new quarterback every game nor a rock group that uses a different drummer for each concert is likely to be very successful. Similarly, effective team production requires continuity and familiarity among team members. Moreover, such continuity is achieved with lower transactions costs when the suppliers of the cooperating productive resources are bound together by long-term contracts than when agreements must be renegotiated for each round of production. Indeed, it is only the long-term nature of the association among resource suppliers that enables us to speak meaningfully of them as constituting a firm at all.

Managerial Coordination

Without its management, a firm would be like a ship without a rudder. Decisions about what goods to produce, how to produce them, how to market them—in short, decisions about the allocation of the resources under the control of the firm—all fall within the scope of managerial discretion.

Figure 7.2

The pyramid of authority

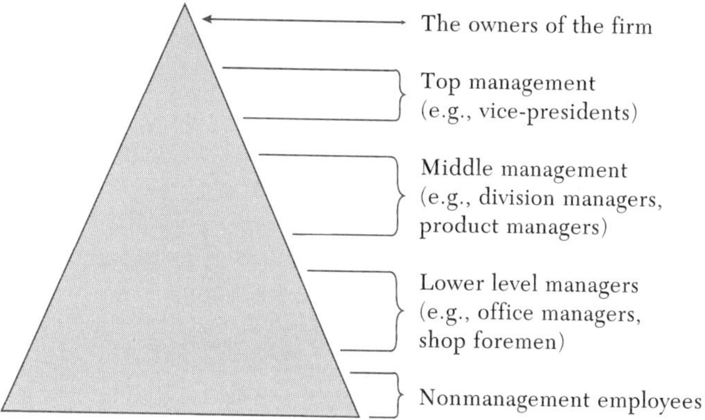

In addition, management must monitor team production. Were it possible to pay each worker strictly according to his contribution to *output*, the incentive to loaf, or *shirk*, on the job would be minimized because less productive effort would mean less pay. But when production is carried out by a team, it is often difficult to identify the separate contribution of each team member to final output. To prevent shirking in team production, therefore, it is usually necessary to monitor the *input* of each team member and to reward him or her accordingly. This requires that someone in the firm have the authority to assign tasks, hire and fire employees, and to promote or demote them. In short, it requires a boss.

But what is to keep the managers from shirking their duties? In other words, who is to monitor the monitors? A partial answer lies in the fact that there are many levels of management in most firms. As Figure 7.2 illustrates, the structure of authority and responsibility within a firm can be thought of as a pyramid. At the bottom of the pyramid are the firm's nonmanagerial employees. Next come the lower levels of management such as office managers and shop foremen, then product managers, section managers, division managers, and so on up to the firm's owners at the pinnacle of the pyramid. Not only do higher levels of management monitor lower levels, but the reverse is often implicitly true as well. Specifically, much of the pressure on higher level managers to perform well comes from people below them trying to work their way up the pyramid of authority.

Ownership, Profit Maximization, and Risk Bearing

Another set of incentives comes into play when we reach the level of ownership in a capitalist firm. The firm's owners are *residual claimants*: They claim whatever remains of the firm's revenues after its *contractual claimants*—its employees, suppliers, creditors, and anyone else to whom its payments are legally obligated—have been paid. The residual is, of course, the firm's (that is, the owners') *profit* or *loss*. Because the owners' rewards are directly linked to the overall performance of the firm, they have the ultimate incentive to monitor its employees, including its managers.

Profit maximization means that decisions are made with the objective of increasing profits or reducing losses.

Economists generally assume that the goal of the capitalist firm is **profit maximization**. This simply means that the decisions made within the firm—whether regarding production, pricing, employment, product quality, or any other aspect of its operation—are made with the objective of increasing profits (or, equivalently, reducing losses, if any).

Because the owners of the firm claim any residual profits, they clearly have an incentive to make those profits as great as possible. However, firms, especially large ones, are complex organizations involving hundreds, perhaps even thousands, of managerial decision makers. Even if the ultimate owners of the firm are interested solely in maximizing profits, that in itself does not ensure that all of the decisions made by their subordinates will reflect that goal. As we shall see, this applies especially to the modern corporation.

In any case, production always carries an element of risk. Today's managerial decisions regarding what to produce, how to produce it, and so on come to fruition only after the final product reaches the market. In the interim, market demands can shift, new technologies can make products and production techniques obsolete, input prices can fluctuate, and conditions of competition can change. As residual claimants, the firm's owners bear most of these risks. Accordingly, we can think of their profits as the market's reward for successful risk bearing and their losses as its penalty for unsuccessful risk bearing.

The Limits of the Firm

If the combination of integrated production, managerial coordination, and risk-bearing ownership is such an efficient way of organizing production, then why does all production not take place within one gigantic firm? Indeed, why not organize the entire economy as a single, huge firm and dispense with market coordination altogether?

While it is true that up to a point the substitution of managerial coordination for market coordination economizes on the transactions costs of organizing production, exclusive reliance on managerial control also introduces costs and inefficiencies of its own. As a firm grows in scale and scope, the base of the authority pyramid expands and becomes farther and farther removed from the firm's owners and top managers. Information filtering up from the bottom of the organization to its top managers becomes more and more distorted, while orders filtering down from the top become more and more difficult to enforce. The resulting loss of information and control are important sources of inefficiency, which become magnified as the size and complexity of the organization increase. In effect, the firm's top management is spread more and more thinly and begins to lose touch with its expanding base of operations. At some point the marginal cost of further expansion exceeds the marginal benefit, and the firm has reached its limit as an efficient means of organizing production.

We have observed the most dramatic illustrations of the kinds of problems that arise when very large-scale production relies almost exclusively on managerial control in the command economies of the Soviet Union and other Eastern European states. Until very recently, the role of market coordination was minimized in those economies, and it is not much of an exaggeration to characterize them as having been managed like gigantic, completely integrated (both horizontally and vertically) firms. The managers were the state planning committees and the various levels of government bureaucracy that administered the plans and attempted to coordinate nearly all official economic activity. As we noted Chapter 4, these economies were notorious for worker absenteeism, shoddy goods, shortages and surpluses, lack of innovation, and many other forms of inefficiency.

THE MODERN CORPORATION

Forms of Business Organization

Like snowflakes, no two business firms are ever quite the same. They range from small "Mom 'n' Pop" operations with few employees and little capital to multinational giants with world operations, such as IBM, Exxon, and General Motors. However, nearly all of them can be sorted into three basic categories: *proprietorships, partnerships*, and *corporations*. Figure 7.3 on the following pages shows the number of firms, their share of total business revenues, and average revenue per firm in each of the three categories in the U.S. economy in 1985, the latest year for which data are available.

Proprietorships

A **proprietorship** is a firm owned and operated by a single individual.

A **proprietorship** is a firm that is owned and operated by a single individual—the proprietor—who is typically responsible for the firm's day-to-day operations, receives all of its profits, and bears all of its losses. The proprietor is personally liable for all debts incurred by his firm. Should his business fail, the firm's creditors can claim not only the assets of the business itself but also the owner's personal assets such as his home, his car, and family savings account. The amount of financial capital that a sole proprietorship can raise is thus limited by the owner's personal wealth. As a result, the average proprietorship is relatively small. As you can see from Figure 7.3, although 71 percent of all firms were proprietorships in 1985, together they accounted for only about 6 percent of all business revenues, averaging only $45,000 per firm.

Because of its legal simplicity and the owner's direct control of the entire business, the proprietorship is often well suited to the needs of small businesses. In larger organizations, however, the advantages of direct control are more than

Figure 7.3

Types of firms by number, total business revenues, and revenue per firm. (All data for 1985.)

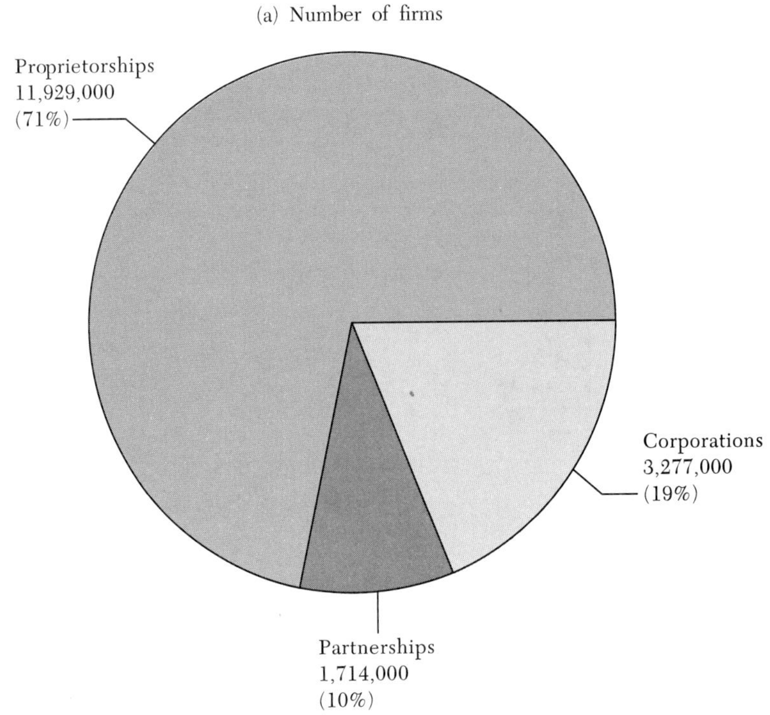

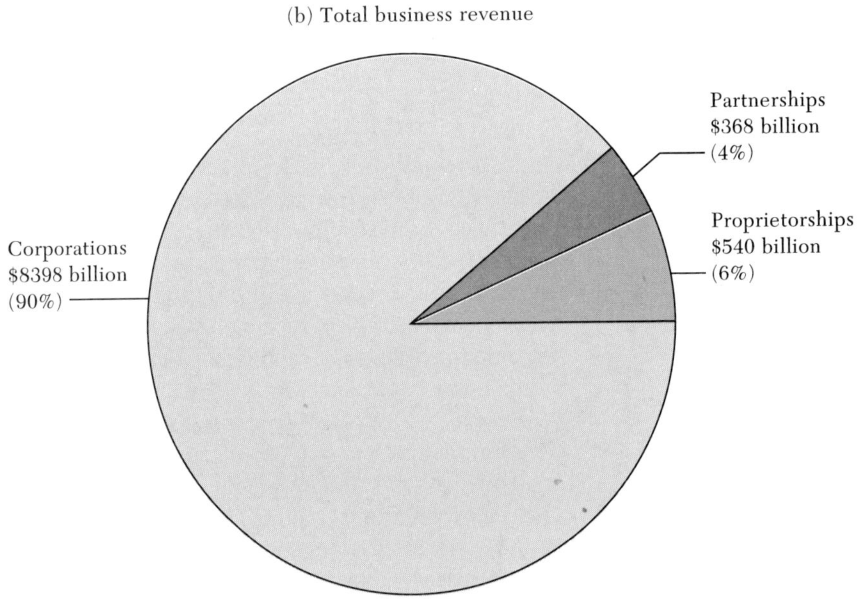

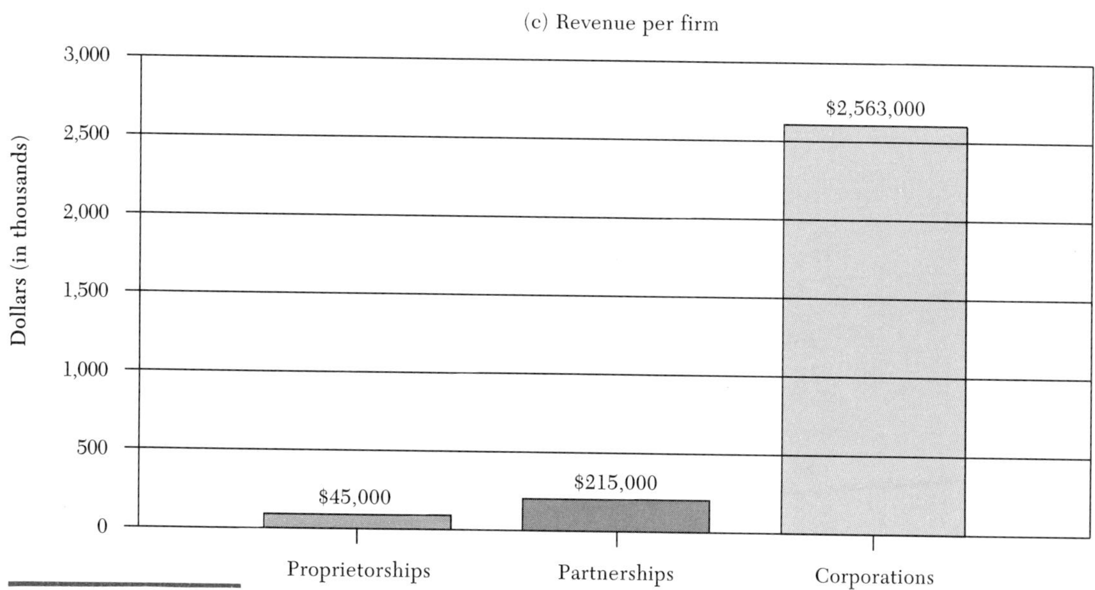

Figure 7.3
(*continued*)

offset by the need to raise substantial amounts of capital and to decentralize and specialize managerial functions.

Partnerships

A **partnership** is a firm owned and operated by two or more individuals.

A **partnership** is a firm owned and operated by two or more individuals. As Figure 7.3 shows, partnerships are the least common form of business enterprise. With the exception of multiple ownership and its implications, the characteristics of the partnership are much the same as those of the sole proprietorship. Like the sole proprietor, the partners are responsible for the firm's day-to-day operations, they receive all of its profits, and they bear all of its losses. Multiple ownership gives the partnership potential advantages over the proprietorship in raising capital and dividing managerial responsibilities, but it also leads to certain drawbacks. For example, each owner remains personally liable for the firm's debts, including debts incurred by his partners in the name of the firm. In addition, because important decisions require agreement among all partners, significant disagreements can lead to dissolution of the partnership and perhaps even the demise of the firm. In short, partnerships have most of the drawbacks of sole proprietorships and not many advantages.*

*In the past, most partnerships were formed by professionals such as doctors and lawyers for whom state laws restricted incorporation. These restrictions have been relaxed in recent years and, as a result, medical, legal, and other professional corporations are replacing partnerships in many states.

Corporations

A **corporation** is a form of business organization that combines joint ownership and professional management, and in which owners have limited liability and marketable ownership rights (corporate stock).

The predominant form of business organization in modern industrial economies is the **corporation**. Although there are only about one-fourth as many corporations as there are proprietorships and partnerships in the United States, they account for nearly 90 percent of all business revenues. Using revenue per firm as a measure of size, you can see from Figure 7.3(c) that the average corporation is considerably larger than the average proprietorship or partnership.

The corporate form of business organization has four distinguishing characteristics: *joint ownership, limited owner liability, easily marketable ownership rights*, and *professional management*.

A share of **stock** is a share of corporate ownership.

Joint Ownership Like a partnership, a corporation has many legal owners. They become owners by purchasing shares of **stock** in the corporation. Each share of stock is a share of corporate ownership, and the stockholders, like the owners of other kinds of firms, are residual claimants who are legally entitled to the corporation's profits and obligated to bear its losses. In many large corporations there are millions of stockholder-owners.

Professional Management Although the stockholders are the legal owners of the corporation, typically very few of them, if any, participate in its day-to-day management. Instead the managerial function is delegated to salaried professionals whose duty it is to run the corporation in a manner consistent with the interests of the stockholders. The corporation's managers may own shares of its stock, and thus be owners as well as managers, but the functional difference between ownership and management is nonetheless quite clear in a corporation.

Limited Liability Unlike the joint owners of a partnership, the liability of corporate stockholders is limited to their investment in the firm. Because the corporation itself is considered a legal entity separate from its owners, debts incurred in its name are not the personal liabilities of its stockholders. If you invest $1,000 in the stock of a corporation that later goes bankrupt, you will lose your $1,000 investment, but the corporation's creditors cannot take your personal savings to pay its debts.

Marketable Ownership Rights In most partnerships, an owner cannot sell his share of the firm without the permission of all of the other partners. By contrast, corporate stockholders can buy and sell shares of stock as they desire without having to obtain the permission of, or even notify, any other stockholders. Indeed, the stock of many corporations is traded daily on organized stock markets such as the New York Stock Exchange, the American Stock Exchange, and the National Over-the-Counter Market.

Why Corporations?

Our answer to this question is that the corporate form of business has become prominent because it is particularly well suited to the needs of modern, large-scale production and distribution. Large-scale production requires large amounts of capital, usually far beyond any amount that could be supplied by even the wealthiest of individuals. The corporation overcomes this problem by aggregating small amounts of capital supplied by many individual investors who are given ownership rights (shares of stock) proportionate to the size of their investment. By then delegating discretionary authority to salaried professional managers, the corporation minimizes one of the major problems inherent in multiple ownership, namely, the transactions costs of reaching an agreement among a large number of owners. It would be virtually impossible for even a few hundred stockholders, let alone the millions that share in the ownership of many corporations, to actively participate in the management of the firm. Just the costs of informing so many owners about day-to-day operations, let alone the negotiation costs of arriving at joint decisions about how it should be run, would be prohibitive. Nor is there any reason to presume that those who provide financial capital and bear risk as residual claimants have any particular expertise in actually running the business. Such expertise is instead provided by managerial specialists.

If this were the end of the story, a significant problem would still remain. Stockholders would have turned over a share of their wealth, perhaps a significant share, to a group of managers whom they do not know and over whom they have virtually no personal control. What if the managers do such a poor job of running the corporation that the stockholders' return is negative? What if poor management results in corporate bankruptcy?

Agency costs are the costs of insuring that one's representative (agent) acts on one's behalf.

These potential problems are the result of **agency costs**. In the context of corporate organization, agency costs are the costs to stockholders of insuring that their agents, the corporation's managers, operate it in accordance with the stockholders' interests. The provisions of limited liability and share marketability are organizational features intended to minimize the problem of agency costs. The former limits the stockholders' maximum potential loss to their investments in the firm; the latter allows stockholders dissatisfied with the return on their investment to simply sell their shares and invest elsewhere. (More on the implications of this later.)

Some people mistakenly believe that the corporation is merely a "creature of the state." This view is based on the observation that a corporation can be legally brought into existence only by obtaining a charter from one of the fifty state governments. But state charters of incorporation merely reduce transactions costs by providing a uniform set of standards and requirements that do not have to be renegotiated every time a group of individuals wishes to form a corporation. The state no more creates the corporation with its charter than it creates a marriage by issuing a marriage license.

Corporate Finance: The Basics

One of the distinctive features of the corporate form of business lies in its financial structure. This structure is a reflection of the manner in which corporations attract financial capital and allocate risk among investors.

Raising Financial Capital

Retained earnings are the portion of corporate profits that are kept within the corporation rather than distributed to stockholders.

Dividends are those corporate profits that are paid out to stockholders.

A **bond** is a financial instrument that promises the holder specified future payments at specified future dates.

For small capital expenditures, and for the ordinary maintenance and replacement of its capital stock, a corporation might use its **retained earnings**. Retained earnings are profits that have not been distributed to stockholders as **dividends**. (Although a corporation's profits are legally owned by its stockholders, management generally decides whether those profits will be reinvested in the firm or distributed as dividends.) For major investment projects, however, the corporation usually turns to external sources for financing.

Like a partnership or a proprietorship, it can borrow from financial intermediaries such as banks. In addition, a corporation can raise financial capital by issuing and selling **bonds**. A corporation's bond represents its promise to pay the bondholder specific amounts at specific future dates. For example, a bond might promise the holder \$1,000 per year for each of the next five years. When a corporation sells a bond, it is in effect borrowing from the buyer an amount equal to the bond's sale price in return for a promise to repay the future amounts specified by the bond. Accordingly, raising capital through the sale of new corporate bonds is known as *debt financing*.

Finally, a corporation can raise financial capital by issuing and selling new shares of corporate stock. Unlike bonds, stock shares do not promise the holder any specific payments—only a share of future profits, *if there are any*. Since shares of stock are shares of ownership, or equity, in the corporation, the sale of new shares of stock is known as *equity financing*.

Present Value

Present value is the value today of an amount available in the future; it is equal to the sum that would have to be invested today, at today's interest rate, in order to have that amount in the future.

Bonds and shares of stock both represent claims on the future income of the corporations that issue them. In the case of bonds, the claim is contractual; in the case of stock, the claim is residual. Regardless of the form of the claim, however, its value depends on the amount and timing of the future income it is expected to generate. To see how the market determines the value of claims to future income, and thus how much financial capital a corporation can raise by selling new stock or bonds, we must introduce the important concept of **present value**. The present value of any future amount is the sum that would have to be invested today, at today's interest rate, to have that amount in the future. Let's illustrate with an example.

Suppose that Megabux, Inc., an imaginary corporation, is attempting to raise financial capital by selling a simple bond that promises the holder \$100 at the end of 1 year. What will this bond be worth?

To answer this question, we must ask how much we would have to invest today in order to have \$100 at the end of 1 year if we *didn't* buy the bond. Clearly, this depends on today's interest rate. For example, if the interest rate is 10 percent, we could invest \$90.91 today, earn \$9.09 in interest, and have \$100 (= \$90.91 + \$9.09) at the end of 1 year. In that sense, having \$90.91 today is equivalent to having \$100 at the end of the year. Since Megabux's bond is simply a promise of \$100 after 1 year, its market value today—its present value—would therefore be \$90.91.

Algebraically, if we start with an amount V today and invest it at an interest rate r (where r is expressed as a decimal value rather than a percent), then we will have a future amount F after 1 year, consisting of the principal V plus interest rV for a total of $V(1 + r)$. The relation between the future amount, its present value, and the interest rate is therefore $F = V(1 + r)$. Solving for V gives the formula for the present value of an amount available after one year, namely,

$$V = \frac{F}{(1 + r)}$$

Applying this formula to the foregoing example, we can calculate the present value of Megabux's \$100, 1-year bond when the interest rate is 10 percent as $V = \$100/(1.10) = \$90.91$. Were the interest rate only 5 percent, the present value of the same bond would be $V = \$100/(1.05) = \$95.24$.

We can use the same basic logic to determine the present value of amounts more distant than 1 year into the future. Suppose, for example, that we want to determine the present value of an amount to be available 2 years from now. With interest compounded annually, the relation between the present value, the future amount, and the interest rate is given by*

$$F = V(1 + r)^2$$

Solving for V, the present value, we obtain

$$V = \frac{F}{(1 + r)^2}$$

Thus, if Megabux's bond promises the holder \$100 after 2 years, rather than after 1 year, its value when the interest rate is 10 percent will be $\$100/(1.10)^2 = \$82.64$. (You might want to do some calculations to confirm that if you start with \$82.64 now and earn 10 percent compound interest, you will have \$100 after 2 years.)

The general formula for the present value of an amount available t years into the future is

$$V = \frac{F_t}{(1 + r)^t}$$

where F_t signifies a future amount available after t years.

The **discount factor** is the factor by which a future amount is multiplied to determine its present value.

The factor $[1/(1 + r)^t]$ by which we multiply the future amount to obtain its present value is called the **discount factor**. Table 7.1 on the following page shows the discount factors for a number of different interest rates and future time periods. To find the present value of any future amount, we simply multiply that amount by the appropriate discount factor from the table. For example, the value of \$500 available at the end of 10 years at an interest rate of 7.5 percent is

*After 1 year we would have $V + rV$, or $V(1 + r)$. Compounding interest for a second year, we would have $V(1 + r) + rV(1 + r)$, which is equal to $V(1 + r)^2$. Each time we compound interest for another year we multiply again by $(1 + r)$ to obtain the future amount.

Table 7.1

Discount factors for computing present value

YEARS INTO FUTURE / INTEREST RATE →	2.5%	5.0%	7.5%	10.0%	12.5%	15.0%
1	0.9756	0.9524	0.9302	0.9091	0.8889	0.8696
2	0.9518	0.9070	0.8653	0.8264	0.7901	0.7561
3	0.9286	0.8638	0.8050	0.7513	0.7023	0.6575
4	0.9060	0.8227	0.7488	0.6830	0.6243	0.5718
5	0.8839	0.7835	0.6966	0.6209	0.5549	0.4972
6	0.8623	0.7462	0.6480	0.5645	0.4933	0.4323
7	0.8413	0.7107	0.6028	0.5132	0.4385	0.3759
8	0.8207	0.6768	0.5607	0.4665	0.3897	0.3269
9	0.8007	0.6446	0.5216	0.4241	0.3464	0.2843
10	0.7812	0.6139	0.4852	0.3855	0.3079	0.2472
11	0.7621	0.5847	0.4513	0.3505	0.2737	0.2149
12	0.7436	0.5568	0.4199	0.3186	0.2433	0.1869
13	0.7254	0.5303	0.3906	0.2897	0.2163	0.1625
14	0.7077	0.5051	0.3633	0.2633	0.1922	0.1413
15	0.6905	0.4810	0.3380	0.2394	0.1709	0.1229
⋮	⋮	⋮	⋮	⋮	⋮	⋮
20	0.6103	0.3769	0.2354	0.1486	0.0948	0.0611
25	0.5394	0.2953	0.1640	0.0923	0.0526	0.0304
30	0.4767	0.2314	0.1142	0.0573	0.0292	0.0151
35	0.4214	0.1813	0.0796	0.0356	0.0162	0.0075
40	0.3724	0.1420	0.0554	0.0221	0.0090	0.0037
45	0.3292	0.1113	0.0386	0.0137	0.0050	0.0019
50	0.2909	0.0872	0.0269	0.0085	0.0028	0.0009

($500)(0.4852) = $242.60. (The discount factor of 0.4852 comes from the 10-year row and 7.5 percent column in Table 7.1.) If we were to invest $242.60 today at 7.5 percent compound interest, we would have $500 at the end of 10 years.

As you can see from the table, the higher the interest rate and the more distant the future time at which an amount becomes available, the more heavily that amount is discounted; i.e., the smaller the discount factor. For example, at an interest rate of 2.5 percent, the promise of a dollar 20 years from now is worth about 61¢; at an interest rate of 15 percent, that same promise is worth about 6¢.

Bonds That Promise Many Payments

Unlike Megabux's simple bond promising a single payment after 1 year, most bonds promise many future payments spread over a number of years. We cannot add these payments together because that would be like adding apples and oranges. Rather, to determine the value of the bond, we must discount each of the future payments to its present value and then add them.

To illustrate, suppose that Megabux's bond promises a $100 payment at the end of each of the next 4 years, and then a final payment of $1,000 when the bond *matures* after 5 years. We can calculate the market value of this bond by again using the discount factors in Table 7.1. In particular, if the interest rate is 10 percent, we can use the first five discount factors in the 10 percent column of the table to calculate the market value of the bond, namely, $100(0.9091) + $100(0.8264) + $100(0.7513) + $100(0.6830) + $1000(0.6209) = $937.88. If the interest rate were 7.5 percent, the value of the same bond would be $1031.53; if the interest rate were 12.5 percent, it would be $855.46. (Can you verify these values using the discount factors in Table 7.1?)

(This process of converting a stream of future payments into a single present value is called *capitalization*. The market implicitly capitalizes the future payments promised in a bond when it determines the value of that bond. The opposite of capitalization is *amortization*. Just as capitalization collapses a series of future amounts into a single present value, amortization spreads a single present amount over a series of future payments. For example, a loan is amortized when the amount borrowed today (the principal) is repaid (with interest) in a series of future payments.)

Stock Shares as Perpetuities

Unlike a bond, a share of stock is not paid off and redeemed at some definite future date. Rather, it entitles the stockholder to share in the corporation's profits (or losses) for as long as the corporation exists, which may be a very, very long time. We can approximate the value of a share of corporate stock by treating it as a **perpetuity**. A perpetuity is something that pays the same amount every year, year in and year out, forever.

A **perpetuity** is something that generates periodic income payments forever.

What is the present value of a perpetuity of, say, $100 per year, if the interest rate is 10 percent? To answer this, ask yourself the following equivalent question: What amount would you have to invest today at 10 percent interest to withdraw $100 per year forever? Clearly, $1,000 would do the trick. At 10 percent interest, $1,000 would generate $100 per year in interest, which you could withdraw each year forever without ever touching the principle.

Algebraically, the present value of a perpetuity paying an amount A per year forever is*

$$V = A/r$$

Although a share of stock in a corporation is not a true perpetuity—no corporation literally lasts forever and corporate profits vary from year to year—the preceding formula provides a good rule of thumb for estimating the value of

*For the mathematically inclined, A/r is the sum of the infinite geometric series, $A[1/(1 + r) + 1/(1 + r)^2 + 1/(1 + r)^3 + \cdots + 1/(1 + r)^t + \cdots]$.

corporate stock. For example, suppose that Megabux is expected to generate average net earnings for its stockholders of $5 million per year into the indefinite future. At an interest rate of 10 percent, the present value of those earnings would be $50 million (= $5 million/0.1). Thus, if Megabux has 1 million shares of stock outstanding, its value will be $50 per share.

As this example suggests, the market value of a corporation's stock reflects the present value of its expected future earnings. When people buy and sell shares of stock they are therefore trading in expectations of the future. An investor who expects that the future holds improved performance for a particular corporation can buy shares of its stock from those who feel otherwise. For example, an investor who believes that Megabux's future earnings will average $6 million per year rather than $5 million per year implicitly expects the stock price to rise from $50 per share to $60 per share. If he acts on this belief and it turns out to be correct, he will make $10 per share in *capital gains*. If he turns out to be wrong, he will make nothing, or perhaps even suffer a *capital loss* if the value of the stock drops.

The Efficiency of Financial Markets

Many economists believe that the stock markets (as well as other financial markets) process new information so efficiently and so rapidly that it is almost instantly reflected in stock prices. To the extent that this true, only the very first traders to acquire and act on new information affecting the value of a corporation's stock can expect to profit from that information. For example, if you read in the morning paper that Megabux has just discovered oil in its parking lot (the kind in the ground, not the kind that drips from its employees cars), it will almost certainly be too late for you to profit from that information. If you call your stockbroker to place an order, you will probably find that the price of Megabux stock has already risen in response to the company's unexpected good fortune.

This does not mean that the average investor cannot make an occasional "killing" in the stock market; it only means that such an occurrence is almost invariably the result of luck. Only those investors who obtain and act on valuable information *before* anyone else has a chance to use it are guaranteed a sure, quick payoff. The rest of us must be content with stock market returns that average about what we can earn on other types of investments.

Present Value and Investment Decisions

In the foregoing examples, we focused on the determinants of the value of corporate stocks and bonds. The concept of present value is perfectly general, however. It can be used to estimate the value of anything that generates future income or services.

To illustrate, suppose that Megabux is considering investing in some new capital good, a $25,000 computer system. It expects the computer to generate end-of-year cost savings of $15,000 during the first year, $10,000 during the second year, and $5,000 during the third year. (For simplicity, we assume that after the third year the computer will be obsolete and worthless.) The value of the computer to Megabux is the present value of these future cost savings. If the interest rate is 10 percent, that value (using the first three discount factors in the 10 percent column of Table 7.1) is ($15,000)(0.9091) + ($10,000)(0.8264) + ($5,000)(0.7513) = $25,657. If the interest rate were 12.5 percent, the computer's value to Megabux would be only $24,746 [= ($15,000)(0.8889) + ($10,000)(0.7901) + ($5,000)(0.7023)]. The computer system is therefore a good investment for Megabux if the interest rate is 10 percent (because its $25,657 value would be greater than its $25,000 purchase price), but it would not if the interest rate were 12.5 percent (because the computer's $24,746 value would be less than its purchase price).

The Corporate Balance Sheet

A corporation's **assets** are the things it legally owns.

A corporation's **liabilities** are the obligations it owes to others.

A corporation's **net worth** is the difference between its assets and its liabilities.

Stockholder equity is the aggregate value of the stock held by corporate stockholders.

Table 7.2 shows Megabux's *balance sheet*. The balance sheet summarizes the corporation's **assets** (what it owns), its **liabilities** (what it owes to others), and its **net worth** (the difference between assets and liabilities). Net worth is entered on the liability side of the balance sheet, not because it represents an obligation in any real sense, but because placing it there makes the balance sheet balance. Net worth is a measure of what stockholders actually own, over and above the legal obligations of the corporation. It is sometimes referred to as **stockholder equity**.

When a corporation acquires a new capital good, such as the computer system in the foregoing example, its purchase price is entered on the asset side of the balance sheet. Because the balance sheet must continue to balance, either the liabilities side must increase by exactly the same amount, or some other category on the asset side must decrease by that amount. The possibilities are illustrated in Table 7.3 on the following page. If the new capital is financed through retained earnings, another asset, perhaps cash holdings, will decrease. If it is financed by borrowing—through the sale of bonds, for example—liabilities will increase. If

Table 7.2

The Megabux corporate balance sheet

ASSETS *(Millions)*		LIABILITIES *(Millions)*	
Cash	$ 20	Debt	$100
Plant and equipment	140	Other liabilities	15
Inventories	30		
Other assets	10	Total liabilities	115
		Net worth	85
Total assets	200	Liabilities + net worth	200

Table 7.3

Financing a capital investment: effects on the corporate balance sheet

(A) RETAINED EARNINGS

Assets		*Liabilities*	
Cash	− 25,000		
Plant and equipment	+ 25,000		
		Total liabilities	(no change)
		Net worth	(no change)
Total assets	(no change)	Liabilities + net worth	(no change)

(B) SELLING NEW BONDS (DEBT)

Assets		*Liabilities*	
Plant and equipment	+ 25,000	Debt	+ 25,000
		Total liabilities	+ 25,000
		Net worth	(no change)
Total assets	+ 25,000	Liabilities + net worth	+ 25,000

(C) SELLING NEW STOCK (EQUITY)

Assets		*Liabilities*	
Plant and equipment	+ 25,000		
		Total liabilities	(no change)
		Net worth	+ 25,000
Total assets	+ 25,000	Liabilities + net worth	+ 25,000

the capital is financed through the sale of new stock, net worth (stockholder equity) will increase.

Capital Structure and Risk Allocation

If a corporation's net worth becomes negative, the corporation cannot meet its legal obligations even if all of its assets are sold off (*liquidated*). In this case, it is technically *bankrupt*. Bondholders and other creditors of a bankrupt corporation cannot recover all of what is owed them because their claims exceed the assets of the corporation and because limited liability prevents them from claiming any of the personal assets of its stockholders. The limited liability of stockholders does not eliminate the risk of business failure; it just shifts some of that risk from stockholders to bondholders.

Does this mean that the limited liability provision is unfair to bondholders and other corporate creditors? Not at all. Bondholders and other creditors make their loans voluntarily in full awareness of the limited liability provision. Moreover, a corporation's balance sheet and other pertinent financial information is by law a matter of public record. If potential bond buyers feel that there is a significant risk of the corporation defaulting on its loan obligations, they will demand a higher interest rate—a risk premium—to compensate them for that risk. Only those lenders willing to accept the risk premium established by the market will purchase the corporation's bonds.

Other things being equal, the higher the ratio of a firm's liabilities to its net worth—or, as it is commonly called, its *debt/equity* ratio—the greater will be the risk to its bondholders, and the higher will be the risk premium it must pay to borrow funds. This premium thus limits the ability of the corporation to expand by borrowing alone.

On the other hand, if a corporation's future earnings prospects suddenly improve, the value of its stock will rise, its stockholder equity will increase, and its debt/equity ratio will fall. For example, if investors suspect that Megabux has developed a potentially profitable new product, they will bid up the price of its stock, thereby lowering its debt/equity ratio. As a result, Megabux will find that it can borrow at a lower risk premium or, alternatively, sell new stock at a higher price. In any case, it will have cheaper access to the capital and other resources necessary to produce and market its new product. It is in this way that the stock and bond markets continuously shift financial capital, and ultimately real capital, to those corporations with the most profitable investment prospects.

WHO REALLY RUNS THE CORPORATION, AND FOR WHAT END?

In a small proprietorship, the interests of the owner and the manager typically coincide, for they are one and the same person. In a large corporation, however, the numerous stockholder-owners are almost always far removed from its day-to-day management. Moreover, the sheer size of many corporations means that many managerial decisions often have far-reaching consequences for groups other than the corporation's stockholders.

These observations raise two important issues, one positive and one normative, regarding the behavior of corporate managers. The positive issue is whether corporate managers actually do act in the interest of stockholders; the normative issue is whether they should serve other constituencies as well.

The Issue of Corporate Control

As the corporation's residual claimants, stockholders are entitled to its profits. They obtain those profits in the form of dividends distributed out of the corporation's current earnings or in the form of capital gains that result when the market price of their stock appreciates. Either way, the interests of stockholders are best served by a management that maximizes profits.

Do corporate managers actually maximize profits in accordance with the interests of stockholders? Or are agency costs so high that managers can pursue goals more consistent with their own personal interests, such as higher salaries and larger staffs of assistants, than are consistent with profit maximization?

Although some degree of managerial discretion undoubtedly exists, a number of factors serve to limit that discretion and channel it into the service of stockholder interests. These include pay packages that make the managers themselves owners and competition in the markets for managerial talent and corporate control.

Making Managers into Owners One way to make managerial interests consistent with stockholder interests is to make the managers stockholders. It is standard practice in large corporations, for example, for top management to receive pay packages that include **stock options** in addition to salaries. A stock option is an option to buy the firm's stock at some predetermined price. To illustrate, suppose that a manager is given an option, which she can exercise at the end of the year, to buy 1,000 shares of her corporation's stock at the current price of $50 per share. If her actions as a manager prove to be so effective that the price of the stock rises to $75 by the end of the year, she can exercise her option by buying 1,000 shares for $50,000 and then reselling them for $75,000. Her stock option is therefore worth $25,000. On the other hand, if the stock price falls during the year, her option is worth nothing. A manager who owns stock (or options to buy stock) in the corporation she manages thus becomes, like other stockholders, a residual claimant with a personal stake in its profitability.

A **stock option** is an option to purchase shares of corporate stock at some predetermined price.

The Market for Managerial Talent Managerial salaries, like other resource prices, are determined in a competitive market. Because the talents and abilities of top management are gauged primarily by the profitability of the corporations they manage, a manager with a good track record will command a higher salary in the market for corporate managers than will one with a poor track record. In a sense, this fact makes top managers residual claimants even if they own no stock in the companies they manage: Although their *current* earnings may be fixed by contract, their *future* earnings depend on the profits they generate for the corporation.

The Market for Corporate Control An individual stockholder who becomes disgruntled with the return on his investment can do little but sell his stock. If many stockholders become disgruntled and sell, however, the market price of the stock will fall and the firm may become the target of a *takeover* bid.

Table 7.4

The language of the corporate takeover market

Term	Definition
Corporate raider	One who seeks corporations that are undervalued because of poor management, buys a controlling interest, and replaces the management.
Tender offer	An offer to purchase shares of corporate stock at a specified price per share. Often the first step in a takeover attempt.
Leveraged buyout	Using the corporation's assets as collateral to obtain financing for acquiring a controlling interest. (Known in the trade as an LBO.) Often used by threatened managers to obtain control of the corporation themselves and preserve their jobs.
Poison pill	Special new stock issued by a corporation's management at so high a price that a takeover becomes unattractive.
Blank check	Special new stock issued by a corporation's management to friendly buyers, and carrying two, three, or more votes per share. Makes it more difficult for the corporate raider to obtain a controlling interest.
White knight	An outsider who purchases a controlling interest in the corporation in a *friendly* takeover—that is, one in which incumbent management is retained—to prevent a *hostile* takeover.
Greenmail	Payment made by a corporation's managers to a would-be raider so that the raider will not take over their firm.
Golden parachute	A provision in a manager's contract that pays him a large amount should he lose his job in a corporate takeover.
Scorched earth	The selling off of valuable assets to so lower the value of the corporation that the would-be raider finds it unattractive.

A **corporate takeover** occurs when someone obtains control over a corporation by acquiring 50+ percent of its voting stock.

A **corporate takeover** occurs when a third party—an individual corporate raider, a group of investors, or another firm—identifies a corporation whose stock price appears to be depressed because of poor management, acquires controlling interest in that corporation by purchasing at least 50 percent of its voting stock, and uses that controlling interest to replace the firm's management. Of course, the incumbent managers often try to protect their jobs by resisting a takeover, in which case the takeover is a *hostile* one. However, it is important to recognize that the hostility comes not from stockholders but from management, who, quite naturally, will try to prevent such a takeover. (Table 7.4 lists some "colorful" tactics that incumbent managers use in an effort to preserve their jobs.) If the takeover succeeds, and if the takeover group was correct in its assessment of the previous management, the new managers will be able to increase the firm's profitability. This in turn will increase the stock price and generously reward the takeover group with capital gains.

Although takeovers are risky and can involve high transactions costs, they occur regularly. Indeed, the very threat of a takeover often provides a powerful stimulus to corporate management to act in the interest of stockholders.

While competition for managerial talent and corporate control serve to limit management's discretion in pursuing goals inconsistent with the interests of stockholders, there is undoubtedly some slippage. The real question is, therefore, an empirical one: How important is managerial discretion and does it lead to significant departures from profit maximization? While the available evidence is not conclusive, it provides no grounds for rejecting the assumption (or more accurately in the current context, the hypothesis) of profit maximization.

The Issue of Corporate Social Responsibility

An important normative question has crystallized in recent years in the debate over *corporate social responsibility*. In essence, this is a debate over whether corporate managers should be responsible to constituencies other than the corporation's stockholders. On one side are those who argue that corporate management is responsible, within the boundaries of law, solely to its stockholders, and that profit maximization in the interests of those stockholders should therefore be its overriding goal. On the other side are those who argue that because the actions of a large corporation affect so many people who are not its stockholders—its employees and citizens of the communities in which it operates, for example—it should also weigh the interests of those constituencies in making its decisions.

Even if a corporation's only explicit goal is to maximize the profits and wealth of its shareholders, competitive market forces always induce it to serve many constituencies. If its customers want safe and durable products, the market provides it with a profit incentive to produce such products, for if it acquires a reputation for producing dangerous and shoddy products, it will not be able to sell them. If the corporation's employees want a reasonably safe and healthy work environment, the market provides it with a profit incentive to provide such an environment, for if it does not, it will have to pay higher wages to attract employees.

As we have seen, however, markets rarely work in a manner that everyone considers ideal. Upon closer examination, therefore, many criticisms of corporate behavior as "irresponsible" really involve the identification of areas where the market fails to achieve an ideal outcome, rather than an indictment of the profit motive itself. Industrial air and water pollution, for example, are not so much the result of corporate profit-seeking per se as they are a consequence of the market's inability to impose the costs of such pollution on the corporations whose activities contribute to it. Where such costs can be imposed, profit-maximizing firms do have an incentive to help maintain a clean environment to avoid those costs.

Instances of market failure such as environmental pollution can be dealt with most effectively without attempting to change the goals of the firm. Since 1970, for example, the Environmental Protection Agency (EPA) of the federal government has issued clean air and water standards and has levied fines on those firms that violate the standards. Corporations have reduced their polluting activities, not because they have become more socially responsible than they were during the 1950s and 1960s, but because it is now often more profitable to avoid the fines than to pollute. Although the specific methods used by the EPA and other government regulatory bodies are often criticized by economists, the point is that, whatever their methods, these bodies are more effective in attaining social goals when they harness the profit motive rather than ignore it.

The arguments for corporate social responsibility often go beyond a desire to improve the performance of markets or to channel profit incentives into socially desireable outcomes. As we noted earlier, there are those who claim that a corporation should pursue goals other than that of maximizing the wealth of its stockholders. Two specific constituencies often mentioned as candidates for corporate favoritism in addition to (or even in place of) its stockholders are the firm's employees and the communities in which its major operations are located. We can best examine the implications of placing the interests of these constituencies above that of the corporation's stockholders in the context of a concrete example.

Suppose that Megabux, Inc. is trying to decide whether to shut down its unprofitable assembly plant in Snowville to take advantage of the lower labor costs in Sunbelt City. Because the Snowville plant generates higher costs and lower profits than the Sunbelt City alternative, shutting it down would benefit the firm's stockholders, as well as the consumers of its product. But the shutdown would also entail laying off many workers in Snowville and harming the local economy. If Megabux places the interests of its Snowville employees and the local merchants above that of its stockholders and thus decides to keep the plant open, it will in effect transfer wealth from its stockholders (and also from workers and merchants in Sunbelt City) to workers and merchants in Snowville. The higher costs it incurs will also mean higher prices for its customers. We leave the normative evaluation of these results up to you. The point is that corporate social responsibility, however one defines it, is likely to create costs as well as benefits.

There is a still more fundamental problem, however. If Megabux *consistently* places other interests above those of its stockholders, it will put itself at a permanent competitive disadvantage vis-à-vis its competitors. Consequently, it will have difficulty raising funds for capital replacement and expansion, and the market value of its stock will fall until it either faces bankruptcy or is the target of a takeover by a group that places greater emphasis on profits.

Finally, we should note that there are some who feel that the very terminology "corporate social responsibility" is contradictory. They view the corporation as a fundamentally private institution in a society where social policy is the legitimate province only of government. Thus they believe that social policies should be formulated and implemented through the political process rather than by individuals whose primary expertise is in the management of private businesses.

Because it is a normative question, economics cannot tell us what a corporation *should* do. It can, however, predict the consequences of pursuing different goals, including goals not strictly in accordance with the interests of corporate stockholders. Whether corporations should aspire to social responsibility by pursuing such goals depends on *how* one evaluates those consequences—and on *who* is doing the evaluating.

CHAPTER SUMMARY

1. Business firms combine *integrated production* with *managerial coordination*. This combination enables them to reap the advantages of team production with long-term contracts and to allocate much of the risk inherent in production to the firm's owners.

2. *Proprietorships* are firms with a single owner who typically manages the firm's day-to-day operations and, as the residual claimant, receives all of its profits and bears all of its losses. The proprietor is personally liable for all of the firm's debts. *Partnerships* are similar to proprietorships except that they have multiple owners.

3. Corporations are the predominant form of business organization in modern industrial economies. The corporate form of business organization has four distinguishing characteristics: *joint ownership, limited liability*, readily *marketable ownership rights*, and *professional management*. This combination of characteristics is particularly well suited to large-scale production.

4. In addition to retained earnings and borrowing from financial intermediaries, corporations can use *equity financing* (stock sales) or *debt financing* (bond sales) as sources of financial capital.

5. The present value of any future amount is what would have to be invested today at the current interest rate in order to have that amount in the future. Present value can be calculated by multiplying the future amount by a discount factor equal to $1/(1 + r)^t$, where r is the interest rate (expressed as a decimal value) and t is the number of years into the future that the amount becomes available.

6. The limited liability of a corporation's stockholders implies that a portion of the risk of bankruptcy is borne by the corporation's bondholders. Other things being equal, the higher the corporation's debt/equity ratio, the greater the risk borne by bondholders.

7. The interest of corporate stockholders is best served by management that maximizes profits. *Stock options* give management an incentive to maximize profits by rewarding them for doing so. The way in which managerial salaries are set in the *market for managerial talent* and the threat of hostile takeover in the *market for corporate control* also provide management with an incentive to act in the best interest of stockholders.

8. The issue of *corporate social responsibility* boils down to a debate over whether corporate managers should be responsible to constituencies other than the corporation's stockholders—for example, to its employees or the citizens of the communities in which its operations are located.

Key Terms and Concepts

horizontal integration
vertical integration
market coordination
managerial coordination
profit maximization
proprietorship
partnership
corporation
stock
agency costs
retained earnings
dividends
bond
present value
discount factor
perpetuity
assets
liabilities
net worth
stockholder equity
stock option
corporate takeover

Questions for Thought and Discussion

1. Who provides the managerial coordination for a football team? For a symphony orchestra?
2. A merger takes place when two firms combine their operations. Given the terminology introduced in the text, what do you think distinguishes a horizontal merger from a vertical merger?
3. Do you think it is unfair that despite their legal status as owners of the corporation, stockholders typically cannot participate in its management?
4. Corporations can borrow for very long periods of time. It is not unusual for a corporation to issue bonds that do not mature for 20 or 30 years. By contrast, most proprietorships and partnerships can borrow only for much shorter periods of time. Why do you think this is the case?
5. Your rich uncle has died and left you $100,000 in his will. There is a catch, however: You cannot take possession of the money until your 25th birthday. Having just turned 20, you will have to wait 5 years for your inheritance. Impatient, you offer your inheritance to whomever will give you the most money right now. How much do you think you will get if the interest rate is 7.5 percent?
6. The owner of a small business asks your advice on a prospective capital investment. In particular, he is considering the purchase of a computer to track his inventory,

which he records at the end of each year. He anticipates that the computer will save him $300 in labor costs this year, $350 next year, and $400 two years from now, at which time he plans to retire and sell the computer. He expects its resale value then to be $1500. Its purchase price now is $2500. What advice would you give him if the current interest rate is 10 percent? If the interest rate is 5 percent?

7. A 30-year-old professional baseball player signs a contract that pays him a $100,000 signing bonus, a $300,000 per year salary (payable at the beginning of the season) for 3 years, and a deferred payment of $200,000 when he turns 40. He is reported in the press to have signed a contract worth $1.2 million [= $100,000 + (3)($300,000) + $200,000]. What is his contract really worth? (Assume an interest rate of 10 percent.)

8. Suppose you own an oil well that is expected to pump $50,000 worth of oil each year for the indefinite future. What is the value of your well if the interest rate is 12.5 percent?

9. When the stock market sets the price of a share of stock in an individual corporation, it equates the quantities demanded and supplied. In what sense is the market also balancing the bets that the stock price will rise against the bets that it will fall?

10. Draw an analogy between the ability of a corporation's stockholders to control its management and the power of voters to control their elected politicians.

CHAPTER 8

Production, Costs, and Profits

Steel, plastic, glass, and other materials can be combined with engineering know-how and technical skills to produce an automobile. An empty stage, a script, and a few actors can be transformed into a hit Broadway play. Textbooks and lectures, combined with hours of study and reflection, can produce an educated person.

In each of these cases, something of lesser value is converted into something of greater value. We call such a conversion *production*. In this chapter we examine the nature of the production process within a firm, the implications for the behavior of firm's costs, and the relation between costs and profits. Having examined the organizational nature of the firm in the previous chapter, we shall simplify it here by treating it like a black box that simply transforms inputs into outputs.

THE PRODUCTION FUNCTION

A **production function** shows the relation between the amount of inputs used in a production process and amount of output that results.

Fundamental to any production process is the conversion of inputs—materials, energy (including human effort), and the services of capital goods—into outputs. The relation between inputs and outputs is described by the **production function**.

Table 8.1 shows the production function for Widgetek, Inc., a hypothetical world leader in the manufacturing of widgets. We have kept things simple by assuming that Widgetek uses only two inputs, labor and capital. Its labor input

Table 8.1

Widgetek's production function (weekly output rates)

LABOR INPUT	CAPITAL INPUT		
(Worker-Weeks)	*1 Unit*	*2 Units*	*3 Units*
0	0	0	0
1	50	55	60
2	104	115	126
3	161	179	197
4	220	246	272
5	280	315	350
6	339	385	430
7	396	454	511
8	450	521	591
9	500	585	669
10	545	645	744
11	584	700	815
12	616	749	881
13	640	791	941
14	655	825	994
15	660	850	1039

is measured in units called *worker-weeks*, which is 1 person working for 1 week. The first column of the table lists various possible inputs of labor from 0 to 15 worker-weeks. For now, let us think of Widgetek's capital input as the amount of widget-making machinery that its labor force has to work with. The top row of the table shows three alternative capital inputs: 1 unit, 2 units, and 3 units, respectively. (We'll refine this rather hazy definition of the capital input later.)

The entries in the remaining rows and columns represent the quantity of widgets that Widgetek can produce per week using the corresponding inputs of labor and capital. For example, if Widgetek hires 8 workers and provides them with the services of 2 units of capital, it can produce a total of 521 widgets per week. An increase in either input results in an increase in output: The same 8 workers can produce 591 widgets per week, for example, if Widgetek provides them with 3 units of capital to work with. Alternatively, Widgetek can increase its output to 585 widgets per week if it employs 9 workers rather than 8 with the same 2 units of capital.

This example illustrates an important property of production: Any given output can be produced with more than one combination of inputs. In other words, inputs can be substituted for one another in the production process.

Although this fact may not be obvious from the table, which shows only discrete input amounts, it can easily be illustrated in a diagram. In Figure 8.1 we have plotted Widgetek's production function as a set of three curves, one for each amount of capital it might employ. According to the diagram, the output rate of 600 widgets per week can be produced by combining 11.5 worker-weeks

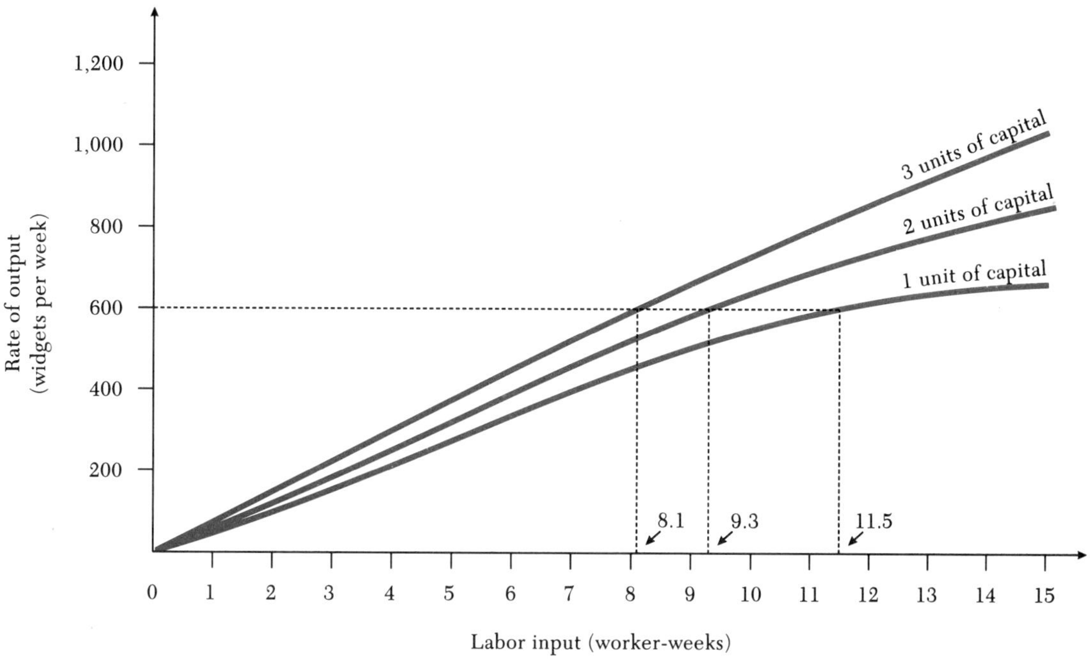

Figure 8.1

Widgetek's production function

of labor with 1 unit of capital, 9.3 worker weeks of labor with 2 units of capital, or 8.1 worker weeks of labor with 3 units of capital. The particular input combination that the producer actually chooses depends on the relative costs of the two inputs. Specifically, a profit maximizing firm will seek the least costly combination of inputs to produce any given output.

Marginal Product and Diminishing Returns

The **marginal product** of an input is the addition to total output that results when one more unit of that input is added to the production process.

The contribution of an additional unit of any input to total output is that input's **marginal product**. Assuming 2 units of capital, for example, the marginal product of the first unit of labor is 55 widgets because it raises Widgetek's total output from 0 to 55 widgets per week. The second unit of labor raises output from 55 to 115 widgets per week, so its marginal product is 60 widgets. The marginal product of the third unit of labor is 64 widgets, and so on. The marginal product schedules for labor combined with 1, 2, and 3 units of capital, respectively, are shown in Table 8.2 and plotted in Figure 8.2, both on the following page.

Note the behavior of the marginal products as the labor input (and thus the rate of output) increases while the amount of capital is held constant: Each marginal product increases, reaches a maximum, and then declines. It initially rises because, up to a point, the given capital stock is more efficiently utilized by a larger labor force. The marginal product of a second worker might be higher

Table 8.2

Labor's marginal product (change in weekly output rate)

LABOR INPUT	CAPITAL INPUT		
(Worker-Weeks)	*1 Unit*	*2 Units*	*3 Units*
1	50	55	60
2	54	60	66
3	57	64	71
4	59	67	75
5	60	69	78
6	59	70	80
7	57	69	81
8	54	67	80
9	50	64	78
10	45	60	75
11	39	55	71
12	32	49	66
13	24	42	60
14	15	34	53
15	5	25	45

Figure 8.2

The marginal product of labor

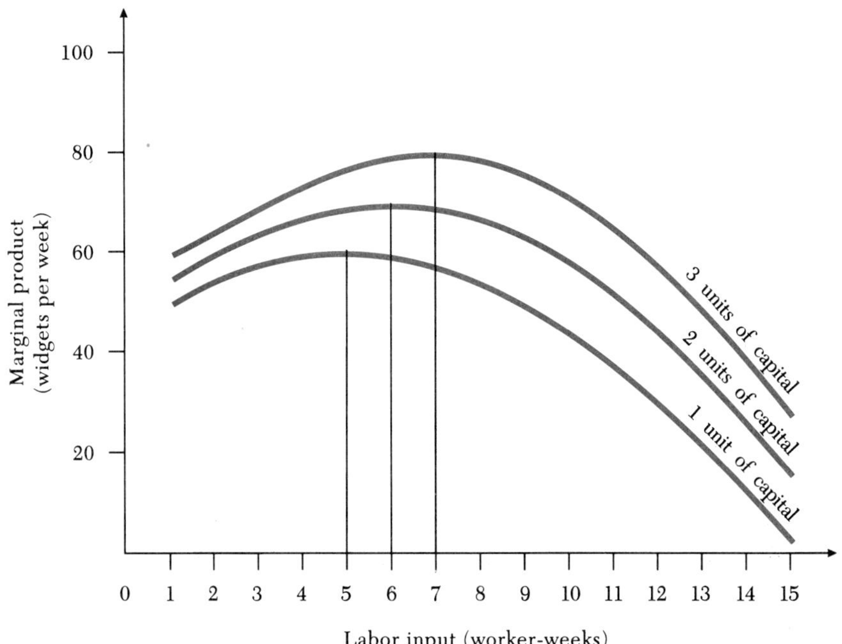

than that of the first, for example, because two people can specialize their functions and make more effective use of the available capital. A third person might contribute even more because of still further specialization, and so on. This is the range of *increasing returns* to labor.

Beyond some point, however, opportunities for teamwork and additional specialization are reduced as the fixed amount of capital is spread more and more thinly. As additional units of labor are added, their marginal product begins to fall. This is the range of *diminishing returns* to labor. Note that the greater the amount of capital, the greater the employment (and output) rate that can be attained before diminishing returns to labor set in. With Widgetek's hypothetical production function, for example, diminishing returns set in beyond the fifth unit of labor when 1 unit of capital is available, beyond the sixth unit of labor when 2 units of capital are available, and beyond the seventh unit of labor when 3 units of capital are available.

A little reflection suggests why diminishing returns must hold, not only for variations in the amount of labor combined with a fixed amount of capital, but for variations in any input used in conjunction with a fixed amount of any other input. If there were no diminishing returns, the entire world output of corn could be grown on a single acre of land—indeed in a flower pot—simply by adding enough labor, fertilizer, and other variable inputs. If there were no diminishing returns, production in a single factory could be expanded indefinitely just by adding enough workers, materials, and machinery.

The **law of diminishing returns** holds that, other things being equal, the marginal product of a variable input eventually declines as more of that input is added to a fixed amount of some other input.

Because diminishing returns is such a universal phenomenon, it has been given the status of a "law" of production, namely, the **law of diminishing returns**. According to this law, if successive amounts of a variable input are added to a fixed amount of other inputs, other things being equal, beyond some point the marginal product of the variable input will begin to decline.

There are three important points that should be emphasized with respect to the law of diminishing returns.

First, the law assumes that at least one input is fixed in amount. If all inputs can be varied simultaneously, diminishing returns might be avoided. From Table 8.2, for example, if Widgetek were to simultaneously increase its labor input from 8 to 9 to 10 worker-weeks and its capital input from 1 to 2 to 3 units, the marginal product of its labor would rise from 54 to 64 to 75.

Second, the law of diminishing returns does not depend on intrinsic differences in productivity. In our hypothetical production function, for example, the marginal product of the fifteenth worker is less than the marginal product of the fifth worker, not because the fifteenth worker is any less skilled or hardworking than the fifth, but because, when a fifteenth worker is added, the available capital is spread thinner than when the fifth worker is added.

Finally, the law of diminishing returns assumes a given technology. If increases in the variable input are accompanied by simultaneous advances in technology, diminishing returns might not be observed. During most of the twentieth century, for example, a growing world population has pressed its demand for food on a relatively constant amount of farm acreage. However, what would otherwise have been diminishing returns to labor employed in agriculture have been much more than offset by advances in agricultural technology.

The Short Run and the Long Run in Production

The possibility for input substitution implies that a producer can vary its rate of output in many ways. For example, we have seen how Widgetek can vary its weekly output of widgets by changing its labor input, its capital input, or both. As a practical matter, however, Widgetek or any other producer is more likely to achieve short-term variations in output by varying some inputs while holding others constant. In other words, it is likely to operate with both *fixed* and *variable* inputs. There are three reasons for this.

First, input variation is itself costly. Changing the amount of any input generally involves transactions costs over and above the costs of the inputs themselves. In addition to the wage costs of hiring new workers, for example, are the costs of selecting and training them. When such workers are fired or laid off, the firm must balance the loss of trained and experienced human capital against the savings in wage costs. Increasing the input of physical capital such as machinery imposes transactions costs of delivery, installation, and set up.

Second, the shorter the time period over which variations in input usage occur, the more costly they are likely to be. Increasing labor input within a very short period of time, for example, might require payment of high overtime rates. More intensive use of machinery can result in wear and tear and breakdowns that can be avoided if time is allowed for the acquisition of new machines.

Third, the costs of varying some inputs are greater than the costs of varying others. For example, short-term variations in output can generally be accomplished at a lower cost by varying the amounts of labor, energy, and raw materials used than by changing inputs of fixed capital such as buildings and heavy machinery.

The differential transactions costs of varying inputs over short periods of time are the basis for the distinction between the *short run* and the *long run* as these concepts apply to production and costs. In the short run, the costs of varying some inputs are high enough that those inputs can be considered fixed, while the costs of varying other inputs are low enough that those inputs can be considered variable. By contrast, in the long run, the firm has sufficient flexibility to vary all of its inputs.

There is no simple period of calendar time, such as a month or a year, that divides the short run from the long run. For a street-corner hot dog vendor using only his own labor and a few simple inputs, the long run might be no more than a week; for an industrial giant like General Motors, it might be a decade or more. Moreover, we cannot identify specific inputs that are always fixed in the short run and others that are always variable. Which inputs are fixed and which are variable depend on the particular production process, the kinds of inputs used, and the time period considered. We can simplify by using the concept of the **plant** to describe the set of inputs that are fixed in the short run. In most cases,

A firm's **plant** includes all of its fixed inputs.

we can think of the plant as consisting of buildings, heavy machinery, and the specialized human capital (such as a firm's top management and other highly trained and experienced personnel) which it is costly to vary within a short period of time.

SHORT-RUN COSTS

Variable costs are the short-run costs attributable to a firm's variable inputs. These costs vary with the firm's output rate.

Fixed costs are the short-run costs attributable to a firm's fixed inputs. These costs do not vary with the firm's output rate.

In the short run, a firm changes its output rate by altering the amount of variable inputs used in conjunction with its fixed plant. Corresponding to these variable and fixed inputs are its **variable costs** and its **fixed costs**. A firm's variable costs are those attributable to its variable inputs. Since the firm's short-run output depends on how much of these inputs it uses, variable costs vary with its rate of output. Fixed costs are the costs attributable to the firm's fixed inputs; as such, they are constant and independent of the firm's rate of output. Variable costs typically include the costs of energy, raw materials, and intermediate goods, as well as most of the firm's labor costs. Fixed costs typically include such things as rental costs and property taxes, insurance, security, general maintenance, and other expenses related to the plant, as well as the opportunity cost of the funds tied up in the plant. In a sense, we can think of the firm's fixed costs as those associated with the plant itself and its variable costs as those that arise in the operation of the plant.

Capital Goods and Short-Run Costs

We can identify the short-run costs associated with the plant and its components in the context of a simple example.

Suppose that Widgetek's management has just purchased a sophisticated $100,000 computer to control and coordinate all of the machinery in its factory. Because the computer represents an addition to Widgetek's fixed plant, can we conclude that the $100,000 expenditure is now a part of Widgetek's fixed costs? Perhaps surprisingly, the answer is no. To see why, consider the following analogy.

Suppose you spend $1,000 to buy a bond. Does your expenditure represent a cost? Not if the bond is still worth $1,000 after you buy it. Since you can resell the bond for $1,000, you have sacrificed no alternatives and therefore have incurred no real opportunity costs. You have just converted one form of wealth (money) into another form of wealth (the bond). A capital good such as Widgetek's computer system is analogous to a bond: Each retains value after it is purchased. The purchase price of the computer, like that of the bond, therefore represents an *investment* rather than a cost.

There are, however, some real costs associated with both the bond and the computer. First, there are the transactions costs of the purchase itself. In the case of the bond, they consist of brokerage fees and other expenses involved in buying and selling financial assets. In the case of Widgetek's computer, they include such things as the sales tax, the costs of delivery and set up, and the costs of programming the computer to meet Widgetek's particular needs. We call these costs **acquisition costs**. Like brokerage fees in the case of the bond, acquisition costs cannot be recovered by reselling the computer. Accordingly, they are measured by the difference between the original expenditure on a capital good and its immediate resale value. For example, if, having taken delivery of its $100,000 computer, Widgetek could resell it for only $90,000, the acquisition cost would be $10,000. It is primarily because of such costs that capital goods like Widgetek's computer become fixed inputs once purchased. It would simply be too costly for a firm to buy more of them each time a temporary increase in output is called for and then resell them when a reduction in output is warranted.

Acquisition costs are the nonrecoverable transactions costs of acquiring a capital good or other asset.

Another cost associated with Widgetek's new computer is its **possession cost**. Possession costs reflect the foregone interest on funds tied up in capital goods. For example, if Widgetek has the option of selling its computer for $90,000 and investing the proceeds at an interest rate of 10 percent, then it would be sacrificing $9,000 per year in interest by choosing to keep the computer rather than sell it. Widgetek's possession cost is therefore $9,000 per year in foregone interest. This cost is fixed.

Possession costs are opportunity costs of ownership in the form of foregone interest on funds tied up in capital goods or other assets.

Finally, there are the **operating costs** associated with Widgetek's new computer. These might include the costs of the electrical power needed to run it, the salary of the computer operator, and depreciation due to use. Operating costs are generally variable because they depend on whether, and to what extent, a capital good is used.

Operating costs are the costs of operating a capital good.

Opportunity Costs versus Sunk Costs

Before Widgetek purchased the computer, all of these costs—acquisition, possession, and operating—were open to choice. Consequently, all were opportunity costs that could be avoided simply by choosing not to purchase the computer. Once the purchase has been made, however, only the possession and operating costs are opportunity costs; the acquisition cost is *sunk*. **Sunk costs** are bygones: They cannot be avoided, and since they are not open to choice, they are not opportunity costs. As such, they are irrelevant for current and future decisions.

Sunk costs are costs that are unavoidable bygones of past decisions.

The irrelevance of sunk costs is perhaps best illustrated by means of an example from the world of gambling. Suppose that you are playing poker and, believing that you have a winning hand, you have bet heavily on your first few cards. On the next card dealt, however, you realize that one of the other players almost certainly has a better hand than yours. What should you do? Should your reasoning be: "I've already bet a lot on this hand. I have too much invested to drop out of the game now so I'll meet the next bet and stay in"? Or should it be: "I've bet heavily on what I mistakenly thought was a good hand. It would be foolish to throw good money after bad, so the best thing to do now is to fold this hand and cut my losses"?

If you think the first response is the better one, we strongly advise you to stay out of poker games! The bets that you have already made on what now appears to be a losing hand are sunk costs. In retrospect, they might have been a mistake, but they are a mistake that cannot be undone; they are lost regardless of the choices you make now. Your current bet, however, is an opportunity cost; it is a cost that you can avoid simply by folding your hand. The sensible thing to do at this point is to avoid whatever additional losses you can and hope for better cards on the next deal.

The same reasoning applies to economic decisions. We can always learn from the past, especially from past mistakes, but the sunk costs associated with past decisions are irrelevant from the standpoint of current and future choices. Once Widgetek has purchased its computer, therefore, the only relevant costs associated with it are its possession and operating costs. If the computer generates enough revenue to cover those costs, Widgetek will keep and use it; if it does not, then Widgetek will eventually sell the computer and avoid both the possession and operating costs.

But suppose a *temporary* slump in business reduces the computer's contribution to revenues below the sum of its possession and operating costs. Widgetek could sell the computer to cut its immediate losses, but it might want to take a longer term view of its predicament. In particular, if Widgetek thinks the slump in business is only temporary, it might decide to keep the computer it already has to avoid the acquisition costs of buying a new one again when business recovers. Once it commits to keeping the computer, the fixed costs of continued possession can also be considered sunk for all practical purposes.

Once Widgetek has committed to keeping its computer, therefore, its decision to use it will depend only on operating costs. If use of the computer is expected to generate enough revenue to cover its operating costs, it will be used; if it does not, it will be *shut down* and allowed to sit idle until either business conditions improve or Widgetek decides to sell it.

Costs and the Rate of Output in the Short Run

To see how short-run costs vary with the rate of output, we assume that Widgetek's fixed input—its plant—is the amount of capital it uses. Furthermore, we shall reinterpret the three capital inputs in Tables 8.1 and 8.2 as three different scales of plant: One unit of capital now represents a *small-scale* plant; 2 units of capital, a *medium-scale* plant; and 3 units of capital, a *large-scale* plant. We assume that Widgetek is initially operating with a medium-scale of plant. Accordingly, its short-run output rate is determined by the amount of labor it employs with that plant.

Widgetek's production function relates its inputs to its outputs; its cost functions relate outputs to costs. To bridge the gap between the two, we need to know the prices of inputs. We therefore assume that a worker-week of labor costs $400 and that (fixed) plant costs are $2,000 per week in a medium-scale plant. Given

1 Labor Input (L)	*2* Marginal Product (MP)	*3* Output Rate (q)	*4* Total Variable Cost (TVC)	*5* Total Fixed Cost (TFC)	*6* Total Cost (TC)	*7* Average Variable Cost (AVC)	*8* Average Fixed Cost (AFC)	*9* Average Total Cost (ATC)	*10* Marginal Cost (MC)
0		0	$ 0	$2000	$2000	$ —	$ —	$ —	$ —
1	55	55	400	2000	2400	7.27	36.36	43.64	7.27
2	60	115	800	2000	2800	6.96	17.39	24.35	6.67
3	64	179	1200	2000	3200	6.70	11.17	17.88	6.25
4	67	246	1600	2000	3600	6.50	8.13	14.63	5.97
5	69	315	2000	2000	4000	6.35	6.35	12.70	5.80
6	70	385	2400	2000	4400	6.23	5.19	11.43	5.71
7	69	454	2800	2000	4800	6.17	4.41	10.57	5.80
8	67	521	3200	2000	5200	6.14	3.84	9.98	5.97
9	64	585	3600	2000	5600	6.15	3.42	9.57	6.25
10	60	645	4000	2000	6000	6.20	3.10	9.30	6.67
11	55	700	4400	2000	6400	6.29	2.86	9.14	7.27
12	49	749	4800	2000	6800	6.41	2.67	9.08	8.16
13	42	791	5200	2000	7200	6.57	2.53	9.10	9.52
14	34	825	5600	2000	7600	6.79	2.42	9.21	11.76
15	25	850	6000	2000	8000	7.06	2.35	9.41	16.00
16	15	865	6400	2000	8400	7.40	2.31	9.71	26.67
17	4	869	6800	2000	8800	7.83	2.30	10.13	100.00

Table 8.3

Cost functions: medium-scale plant

these input prices, Table 8.3 shows the relation between Widgetek's labor input, its weekly output, and its short-run costs. The first three columns of the table, which show labor input, marginal product, and weekly output, have been taken directly from the production functions of Tables 8.1 and 8.2.

Total Cost Functions

Columns 4–6 of Table 8.3 are Widgetek's *total cost functions*.

Total variable costs (*TVC*) in column 4 were obtained by multiplying the number of units of labor employed (column 1) by the $400 cost per unit. For example, the total variable cost of producing 645 widgets per week in a medium-scale plant is $4,000 per week because it requires 10 workers costing $400 per week each. The curve labelled TVC in Figure 8.3 plots Widgetek's total variable cost as a function of its rate of output (not as a function of its labor input).

Total fixed cost (*TFC*) in column 5 is the total cost attributable to Widgetek's plant. Since the plant is fixed in the short run, and since we have assumed a weekly cost of $2,000 for a medium-scale plant, total fixed costs are $2,000 regardless of Widgetek's weekly output rate. The total fixed cost "curve" is the horizontal line labelled TFC in Figure 8.3.

Total cost (*TC*) in column 6 is simply the sum of total variable cost and total fixed cost at each rate of output. Widgetek's total costs as a function of output

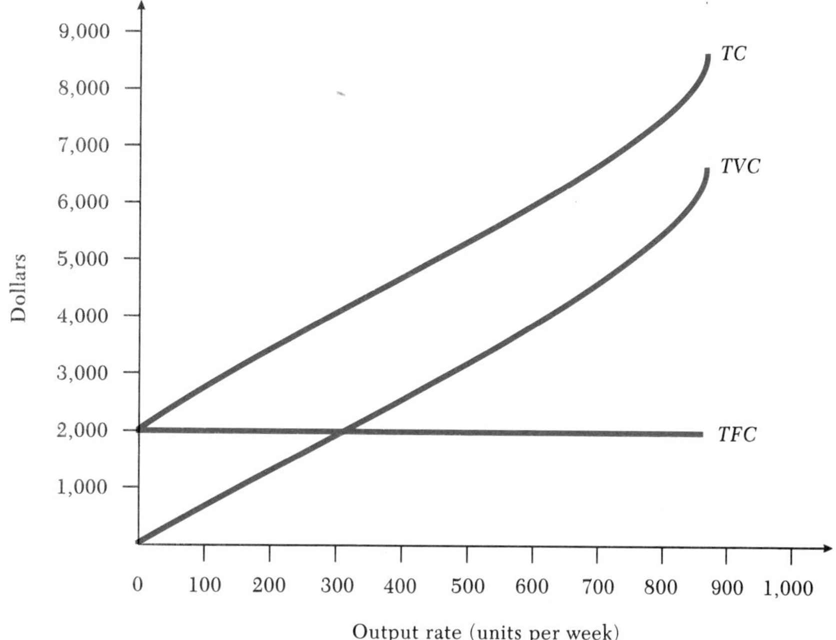

Figure 8.3

Widgetek's total cost functions

are plotted as the curve labelled TC in Figure 8.3. Geometrically, the total cost curve is the vertical sum of the TVC curve and the TFC curve.

Average Cost Functions

Columns 7–9 in Table 8.3 display Widgetek's *average cost functions*, that is, its variable, fixed, and total costs *per unit* of weekly output.

Average variable cost is the variable cost per unit of output.

Average variable cost (*AVC*) in column 7 is obtained by dividing total variable cost in column 4 by the corresponding rate of output in column 3. For example, the average variable cost at an output rate of 645 widgets per week is $4,000 divided by 645, which is equal to $6.20 per widget as shown in the table. Widgetek's average variable cost curve is labelled AVC in Figure 8.4 on p. 178.

Average fixed cost is the fixed cost per unit of output.

Average fixed cost (*AFC*) in column 8 is obtained by dividing total fixed cost by the corresponding rate of output. Because we are dividing the constant total fixed cost by larger and larger rates of output, average fixed cost falls continuously as the rate of output rises, in effect spreading plant overhead over more and more units of output. The average fixed cost curve is labelled AFC in Figure 8.4.

Average total cost is the total cost per unit of output.

Average total cost (*ATC*) in column 9 is the total cost per unit of output. It can be calculated either by dividing total cost in column 6 by the corresponding rate of output in column 3, or by adding the average variable cost in column 7 to the average fixed cost in column 8. At an output rate of 645 widgets per week, for example, average total cost is $9.30, which is equal to $6,000 divided by

Figure 8.4

Widgetek's unit (average and marginal) cost curves

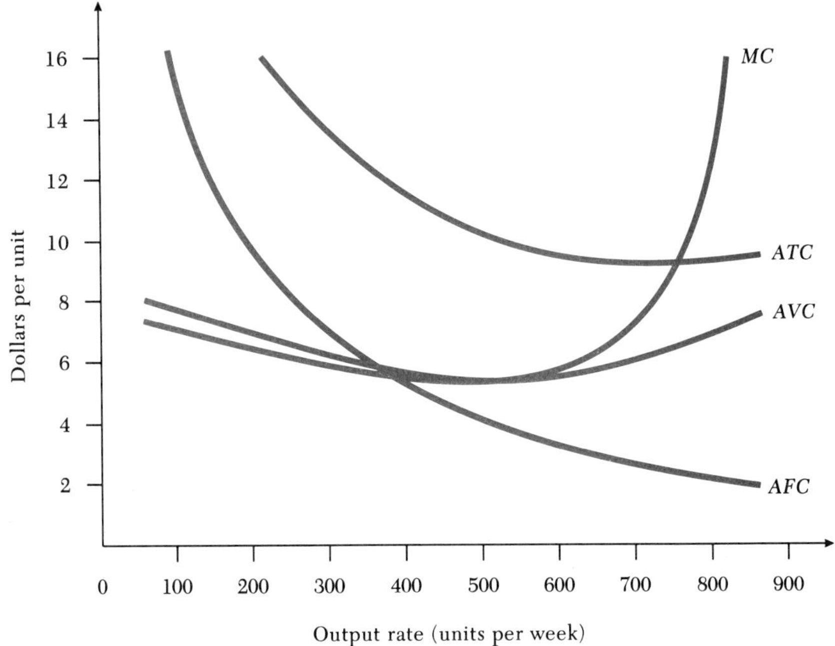

645 and also equal to $6.20 plus $3.10. (Some ATCs in column 9 are not exactly equal to AVC + AFC because of rounding.) The average total cost curve is labelled ATC in Figure 8.4. Notice that it is U shaped: Average total costs at first fall, reach a minimum of $9.08 per unit at an output rate of 749 widgets per week, and then rise with further increases in output. We examine the reasons for this shape later.

Marginal Cost

The last column of Table 8.3 shows marginal cost (*MC*) at various output rates. As we defined it in previous chapters, marginal cost is the change in total cost due to a 1 unit change in output. Because single unit changes in output are not shown in the table, however, the marginal cost figures shown in column 10 are calculated over output intervals of more than 1 unit. We have calculated these amounts by dividing the change in total cost in each output interval by the corresponding change in output. For example, if the rate of output is increased from 585 to 645, total costs rise by $400. Dividing this change in total costs by the 60-unit increase in output gives the marginal cost *per additional widget produced* between 585 and 645 widgets per week. This amount is $6.67 as shown in the table. The curve labelled MC in Figure 8.4 shows what marginal cost would look like if we calculated it for continuous variations in output.

Three characteristics of the short-run marginal and average cost curves bear further explanation: the shape of the marginal cost curve, the relation between marginal costs and average costs, and the shape of the average total cost curve.

The Shape of the Marginal Cost Curve

The behavior of marginal costs is inversely related to the behavior of marginal product. To see why, let us again turn to Table 8.3. In particular, suppose Widgetek increases its labor input from 9 workers to 10 workers in its medium-scale widget plant. The table shows that output rises by 60 widgets per week, the marginal product of the 10th worker, while total costs rise by $400, the weekly wage the firm must pay to employ that extra worker. The cost to the firm *per additional unit of output* is therefore the $400 increase in wage costs divided by the 60 unit marginal product, or $6.67 per unit. But, as we have already seen, this is just the marginal cost in that output range. In general, *the marginal cost at each rate of output is equal to the price of the variable input divided by its marginal product.* Assuming that the input price remains constant, it follows that, where marginal product is rising, marginal cost must be falling; conversely, where marginal product is falling—that is, where diminishing returns are at work—marginal cost must be rising. To verify that this is the case, compare columns 2 and 10 of Table 8.3. Also look at Figure 8.5 on the following page. It plots marginal product and marginal cost with matching scales on the horizontal axes. The marginal cost curve is a mirror image of the marginal product curve. *Falling marginal product and rising short-run marginal cost are, therefore, equivalent expressions of the law of diminishing returns.*

The Relation between Marginal and Average Values

Suppose your grade point *average* (GPA) is 3.2 on a 4-point scale. What will happen to your GPA if you get an A in the next (i.e., *marginal*) course you take? Your GPA will rise, of course. If you get a C in your next course, your GPA will fall.

Suppose you play basketball and are *averaging* 12 points a game for the season. What will happen to your scoring average if you are held to only 4 points in your next (i.e., *marginal*) game? It will go down, of course. If you score 20 points in your next game, your scoring average will rise.

These are but two examples of the logical relation between marginal and average values of any variable. Whenever the marginal value is greater than the average value, adding another unit will pull the average up; whenever the marginal value is less than the average value, adding another unit will pull the average down. This relationship is rooted, not in economics or technology, but in simple arithmetic.

Look again at the marginal cost, the average variable cost, and the average total cost curves in Figure 8.4. The marginal cost curve intersects the average variable and average total cost curves at their respective minimum points—at the

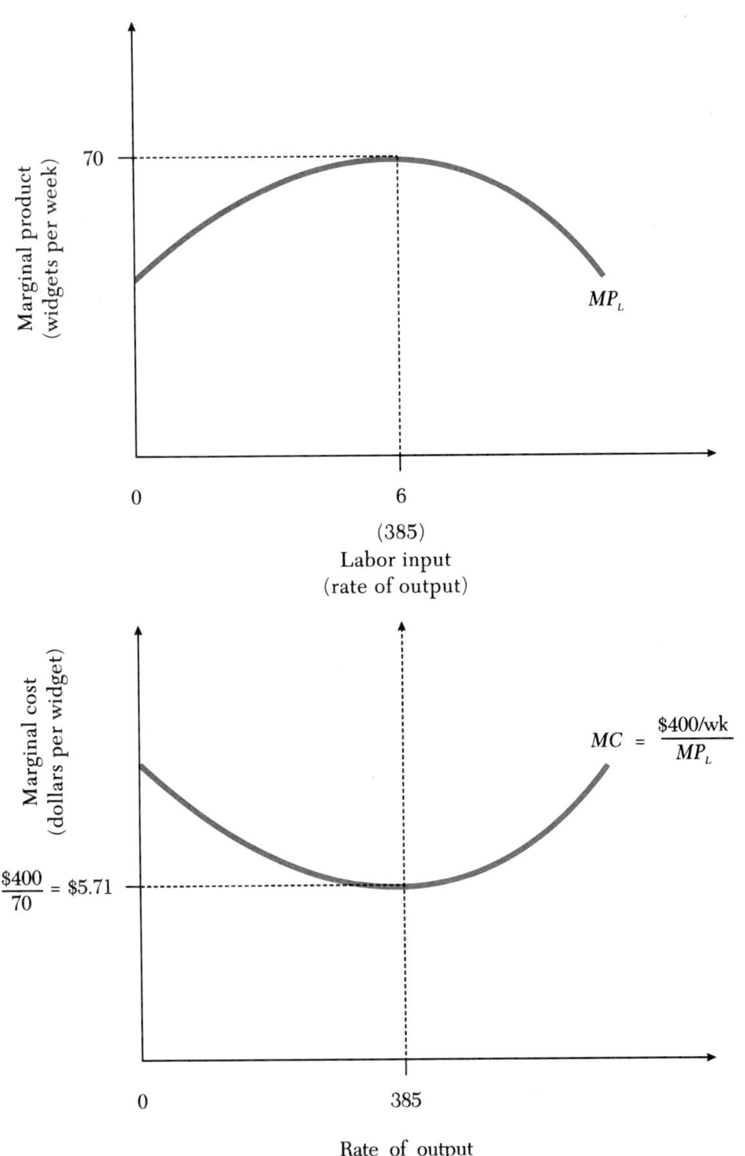

Figure 8.5

Marginal product and marginal cost

bottom of the U so to speak. This is not just a coincidence. At lower rates of output, marginal cost is less than average cost, so producing another unit will reduce the average. At higher rates of output, marginal cost is greater than average cost, so producing another unit will increase the average. Accordingly, the average variable and average total cost curves must be falling up to the point at which they cross the marginal cost curve and rising beyond that point. It follows that the marginal cost curve must cut the average variable cost and average total cost curves in their respective minimum points. (This relationship does not hold for average fixed costs because total fixed costs are constant, and average fixed costs are therefore not affected by marginal costs.)

The Shape of the Short-Run Average Total Cost Curve

As the rate of output is increased, the average total cost initially declines for two reasons: (1) Average fixed costs fall as fixed (overhead) costs are spread over more units, and (2) the impact of diminishing returns has not yet been felt on average variable costs, which are also falling. Because both average fixed cost and average variable cost are falling as the rate of output rises, average total cost, which is the sum of the two, must also be falling.

At greater rates of output, however, diminishing returns lead to higher marginal costs, which pull up average variable costs and eventually offset further reductions in average fixed costs. The result is that average total costs eventually rise with increases in the rate of output. If you study Table 8.3 closely, you will see this process at work.

THE LONG RUN

Scale adjustments are long-run variations in all inputs used in production.

While short-run variations in Widgetek's output rate must be achieved through changes in the amount of labor it employs, in the long run it can also vary the size of its plant. Long-run adjustments in the size of plant, accompanied by changes in the other inputs that are also variable in the short run, are called **scale adjustments**. If, for example, Widgetek doubles all of its inputs—the amount of labor it employs, the size of its plant, and everything else—then it has doubled its scale of operations.

A firm's long-run cost functions show how its costs vary with output when its entire scale of operations is changing. To take a concrete example, let us return to Widgetek's production function in Table 8.1. Based on the information in that table, *and* assuming that Widgetek was operating in a medium-size plant, we derived Widgetek's short-run cost functions. One of those cost functions, the average total cost, is plotted again in Figure 8.6 on the following page. Now, however, it is labelled ATC_M to distinguish it from the average total cost curves associated with other scales of plant. The short-run average total cost curves for both the small- and large-scale plants are also plotted in Figure 8.6. They are labelled ATC_S and ATC_L, respectively. All of these cost curves reflect the assumption that Widgetek must pay $400 per week for labor. In addition, we assume that Widgetek's fixed costs are $1,000 per week in a small-scale plant, $2,000 per week in a medium-scale plant (as previously assumed), and $3,000

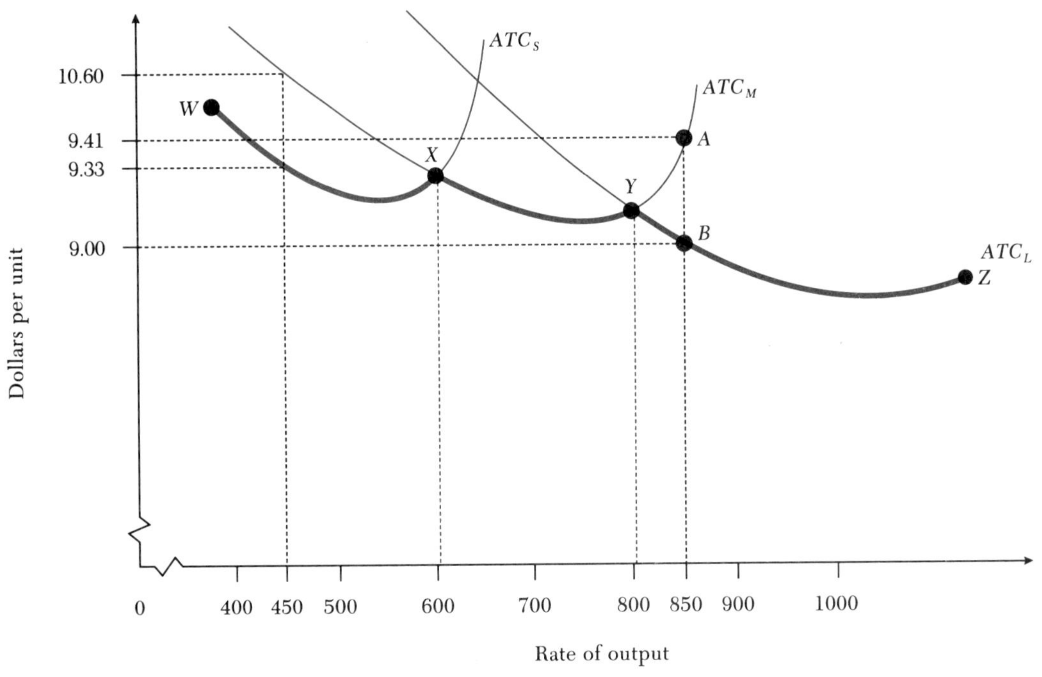

Figure 8.6

Widgetek's long-run average cost

per week in a large-scale plant. The cost functions for small- and large-scale plants are also shown in Tables 8.4A and 8.4B, respectively.

Scale Adjustments and the Long-Run Average Cost Curve

Suppose that Widgetek's market forecasting division estimates that, over the long run, the firm can expect to sell about 850 widgets per week. Widgetek can produce 850 widgets per week in its current (medium-scale) plant at an average total cost of $9.41 each. This output-cost combination is depicted by point *A* on ATC_M in Figure 8.6. One of Widgetek's options, therefore, is to continue to produce in its medium-scale plant, maintaining that plant as long as possible, and replacing it with another medium-scale plant when it wears out. In other words, Widgetek could make a long-run decision to continue to operate in a medium-scale plant.

Note, however, that Widgetek could produce the same 850 widgets per week at a lower average total cost—somewhere between $8.85 and $9.08 according to Table 8.4B—if it moved to a large-scale plant. Thus, if Widgetek anticipates a long-run output rate of 850 widgets per week, it will eventually move its operations into a large-scale plant rather than keeping and replacing its medium-scale plant. The long-run average cost of producing 850 widgets per week—that is, the lowest average cost that can be achieved for that output rate when all inputs are variable—is therefore determined by point *B* on ATC_L. It is approxi-

Table 8.4

Cost functions for small- and large-scale plants

(A) COST FUNCTIONS: SMALL-SCALE PLANT

1 Labor Input (L)	*2* Marginal Product (MP)	*3* Output Rate (q)	*4* Total Variable Cost (TVC)	*5* Total Fixed Cost (TFC)	*6* Total Cost (TC)	*7* Average Variable Cost (AVC)	*8* Average Fixed Cost (AFC)	*9* Average Total Cost (ATC)	*10* Marginal Cost (MC)
0			$ 0	$1000	$1000	$ —	$ —	$ —	$ —
1	50	50	400	1000	1400	8.00	20.00	28.00	8.00
2	54	104	800	1000	1800	7.69	9.62	17.31	7.41
3	57	161	1200	1000	2200	7.45	6.21	13.66	7.02
4	59	220	1600	1000	2600	7.27	4.55	11.82	6.78
5	60	280	2000	1000	3000	7.14	3.57	10.71	6.67
6	59	339	2400	1000	3400	7.08	2.95	10.03	6.78
7	57	396	2800	1000	3800	7.07	2.53	9.60	7.02
8	54	450	3200	1000	4200	7.11	2.22	9.33	7.41
9	50	500	3600	1000	4600	7.20	2.00	9.20	8.00
10	45	545	4000	1000	5000	7.34	1.83	9.17	8.89
11	39	584	4400	1000	5400	7.53	1.71	9.25	10.26
12	32	616	4800	1000	5800	7.79	1.62	9.42	12.50
13	24	640	5200	1000	6200	8.13	1.56	9.69	16.67
14	15	655	5600	1000	6600	8.55	1.53	10.08	26.67
15	5	660	6000	1000	7000	9.09	1.52	10.61	80.00

(B) COST FUNCTIONS: LARGE-SCALE PLANT

1 Labor Input (L)	*2* Marginal Product (MP)	*3* Output Rate (q)	*4* Total Variable Cost (TVC)	*5* Total Fixed Cost (TFC)	*6* Total Cost (TC)	*7* Average Variable Cost (AVC)	*8* Average Fixed Cost (AFC)	*9* Average Total Cost (ATC)	*10* Marginal Cost (MC)
0		0	$ 0	$3000	$3000	$ —	$ —	$ —	$ —
1	60	60	400	3000	3400	6.67	50.00	56.67	6.67
2	66	126	800	3000	3800	6.35	23.81	30.16	6.06
3	71	197	1200	3000	4200	6.09	15.23	21.32	5.63
4	75	272	1600	3000	4600	5.88	11.03	16.91	5.33
5	78	350	2000	3000	5000	5.71	8.57	14.29	5.13
6	80	430	2400	3000	5400	5.58	6.98	12.56	5.00
7	81	511	2800	3000	5800	5.48	5.87	11.35	4.94
8	80	591	3200	3000	6200	5.41	5.08	10.49	5.00
9	78	669	3600	3000	6600	5.38	4.48	9.87	5.13
10	75	744	4000	3000	7000	5.38	4.03	9.41	5.33
11	71	815	4400	3000	7400	5.40	3.68	9.08	5.63
12	66	881	4800	3000	7800	5.45	3.41	8.85	6.06
13	60	941	5200	3000	8200	5.53	3.19	8.71	6.67
14	53	994	5600	3000	8600	5.63	3.02	8.65	7.55
15	45	1039	6000	3000	9000	5.77	2.89	8.66	8.89
16	36	1075	6400	3000	9400	5.95	2.79	8.74	11.11
17	26	1101	6800	3000	9800	6.18	2.72	8.90	15.38
18	15	1116	7200	3000	10200	6.45	2.69	9.14	26.67
19	3	1119	7600	3000	10600	6.79	2.68	9.47	133.33

mately \$9.00 per unit. In fact, the long-run average cost for any output rate greater than about 800 widgets per week (corresponding to point *Y*, the intersection of ATC_M and ATC_L in the diagram) would be given by the corresponding point on ATC_L.

On the other hand, output rates of less than about 600 widgets per week (corresponding to point *X* in the diagram) can be produced with the lowest average total cost in the small-scale plant. For example, a weekly output of 450 widgets can be produced at an average total cost of \$9.33 in the small-scale plant and about \$10.60 in the medium-scale plant. The long-run average cost for any output rate from 1 to 600 widgets per week is therefore given by the corresponding point on ATC_S. Finally, because output rates between 600 and 800 (between points *X* and *Y*) can be produced at the lowest cost in the medium-scale plant, the long-run average costs for those outputs are given by the corresponding points on ATC_M. Widgetek's entire long-run average cost curve is therefore the scallop-shaped curve consisting of segment *WX* of ATC_S, segment *XY* of ATC_M, and segment *YZ* of ATC_L. It shows the minimum average cost of producing any given output when Widgetek has enough time to adjust the scale of its plant as well as the amount of labor it employs. (Since all inputs, and therefore all costs, are variable in the long run, there is no long-run distinction between fixed and variable costs. We can simply refer to "long run average costs" and leave it at that.)

Figure 8.7 shows what happens to the long-run average cost curve (*LRAC*) as we allow more and more scale possibilities until ultimately scale is continuously variable. In part (c) the long-run average cost curve becomes a smooth "envelope" curve tangent to each of the infinite number of possible short-run average total cost curves at a single point.

Economies and Diseconomies of Scale

Figure 8.8 on page 186 shows a long-run average cost curve with the same U shape that characterizes the short-run average total cost curve. The factors that may cause the long-run average cost curve to have this shape, however, are *not* the same as the factors that explain the shape of the short-run average total cost curve. Short-run average total costs initially decline as fixed overhead costs are spread and then rise as diminishing returns take effect. Both of these factors rely on the existence of at least one fixed input. In the long run, however, all inputs are variable so that we must look elsewhere for an explanation of the behavior of long-run average costs. In particular, we must look to something called economies and diseconomies of scale.

Economies of Scale

Economies of scale lower long-run average cost as the scale of a firm's operations increases.

In almost any production process, average costs can be reduced, at least up to a point, by expanding the scale of operations. We refer to this phenomenon as **economies of scale**. It applies not only to the physical production of goods within a firm, but to many of the firm's other functions as well—including pur-

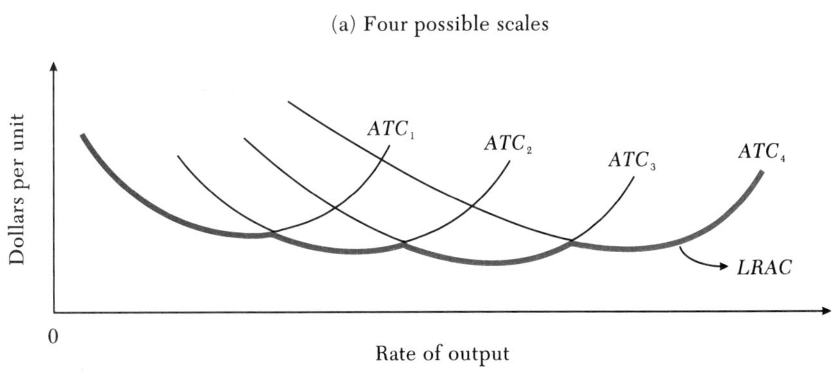

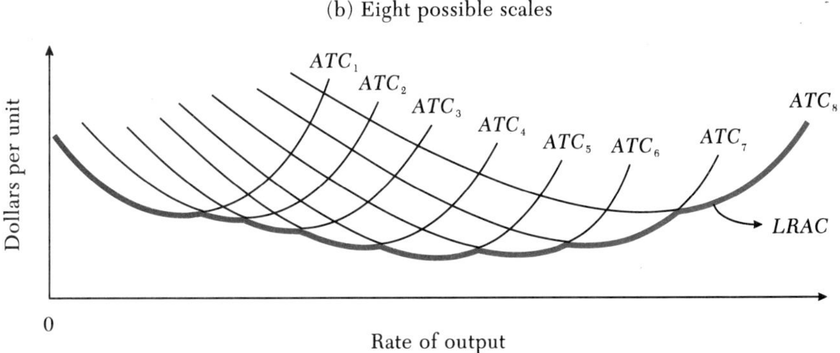

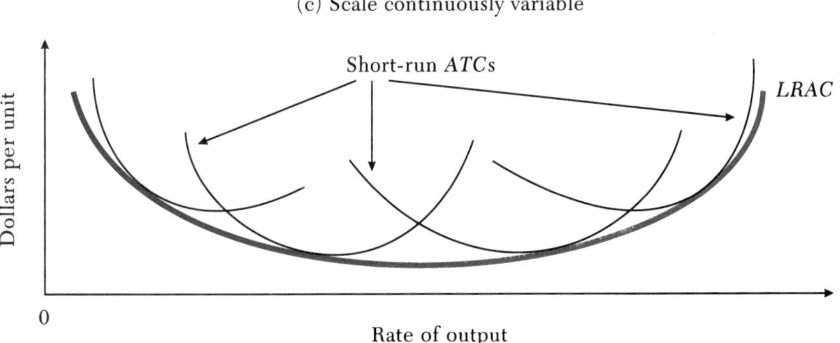

Figure 8.7

Scale variations and long-run average cost. (a) Four possible scales, (b) Eight possible scales, and (c) Continuously variable scale.

chasing, marketing, distribution, and research and development. Economies of scale can have a number of sources.

Specialization We have already seen how specialization can increase productivity when different inputs are allocated according to their comparative advantages. The larger the scale of operations, the greater the opportunities for

Figure 8.8

Economies and diseconomies of scale.

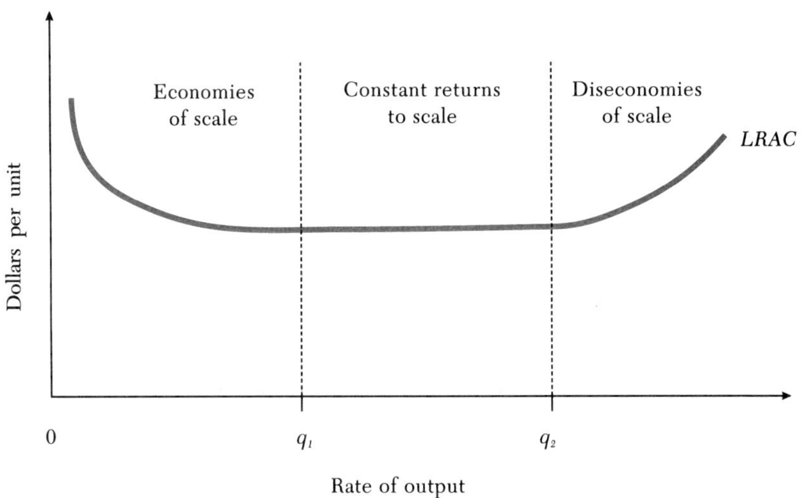

specialization of labor, capital, and other inputs within a firm. The resulting increases in productivity are reflected in lower unit costs. The epitome of specialization is the assembly line, where workers and equipment are specialized down to the smallest of tasks in the overall production process. Assembly line production becomes feasible only at a relatively large scale of operations.

The Indivisibility of Capital Many of the greatest cost saving innovations of the last century have been embodied in relatively large-scale capital equipment. Because these units of capital are *indivisible* (in the sense that a producer cannot purchase them in fractional units), their efficient use generally requires some minimum scale of operations. For example, it would hardly pay an automobile producer to use a $20 million sheet metal press capable of stamping out 1,000 automobile bodies per day to produce an output of only fifty cars per year. Without such a press, the producer might have to form the bodies by hand at a much higher cost per unit.

Diversification A larger scale of operations allows a firm to diversify its product line and to carry on its production in a variety of different locations—even in different countries. Such a firm does not have "all its eggs in one basket." If one of its products fails in the marketplace, it can fall back on others rather than closing up shop and going out of business. If a strike or fire disrupts production at one of its plants, it can carry on in other locations. Other things being equal, such diversification reduces the risk to investors and may enable the firm to raise capital more cheaply than it otherwise could.

Diseconomies of scale raise long-run average cost as the scale of a firm's operations increases.

Diseconomies of Scale

Long-run average costs eventually rise with increases in scale because of **diseconomies of scale**. The principal source of diseconomies of scale is to be found in the control and information loss that results when managerial coordination begins to reach its effective limits. If a firm becomes too large, it begins to experience inefficiencies in internal coordination and control, and these inefficiencies show up as higher costs.

Constant Returns to Scale

Constant returns to scale keep long-run average cost constant when a firm's scale of operations changes.

There may be a range of output over which there are neither economies nor diseconomies of scale (or over which their effects cancel out) so that long-run average costs remain constant. The result is **constant returns to scale**, which are represented by the horizontal portion of the long-run average cost curve between the output rates q_1 and q_2 in Figure 8.8.

Constant returns to scale imply that changing all inputs in proportion changes total output in the same proportion. For example, doubling all inputs would result in a doubling of output so that cost per unit would remain the same. Thus a firm that can change its scale simply by replicating its existing operation—including its entrepreneurial and managerial inputs—would face constant returns to scale.

Other Factors Affecting Costs

Changes in the *rate of output*, whether the result of short-run changes in one or more variable inputs, or of long-run changes in the entire scale of operations, move us from one point to another *along a given cost curve*. The affects of *other factors* show up as *shifts in the cost curves*. Among the more important of these factors are changes in input prices, technological progress, and experience effects.

Changes in Input Prices

An increase in the price of any input will shift the firm's average total cost curve upward; a decrease will shift it downward. If the input whose price is changing is a variable input, then both the marginal and average total cost curves will shift (as will the average variable cost curve); if it is a fixed input, the average total cost curve (as well as the average fixed cost curve) will shift, but the marginal cost curve will not. These effects are illustrated in Figures 8.9(a) and (b) on the next page for an increase in input prices.

Technological Progress

Technological progress alters costs via its impact on the production function. An advance in technology that enables us to squeeze more output from given inputs would increase some or all of the total output amounts in Table 8.1. Other things being equal, getting more output from the same amount of inputs, or equivalently, getting the same amount of output from a smaller amount of inputs, leads to a reduction in costs and a downward shift in the cost curves. Technological progress can also reduce costs by introducing new production techniques that

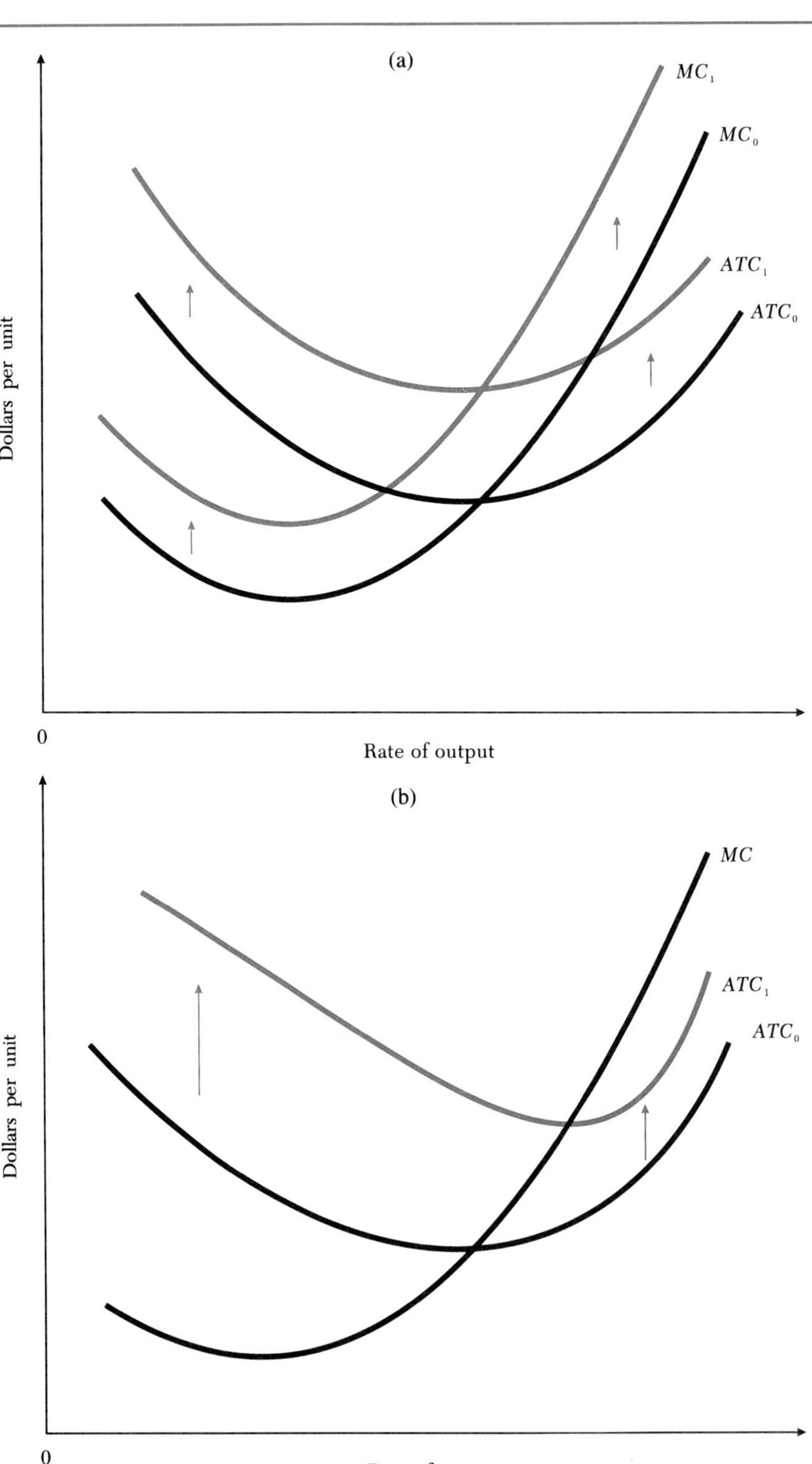

Figure 8.9

(a) The effect on the firm's unit cost curves of an increase in the price of a *variable* input and (b) The effect on the firm's unit cost curves of an increase in the price of a *fixed* input.

Figure 8.10

The effect of technological progress on the firm's unit cost curves.

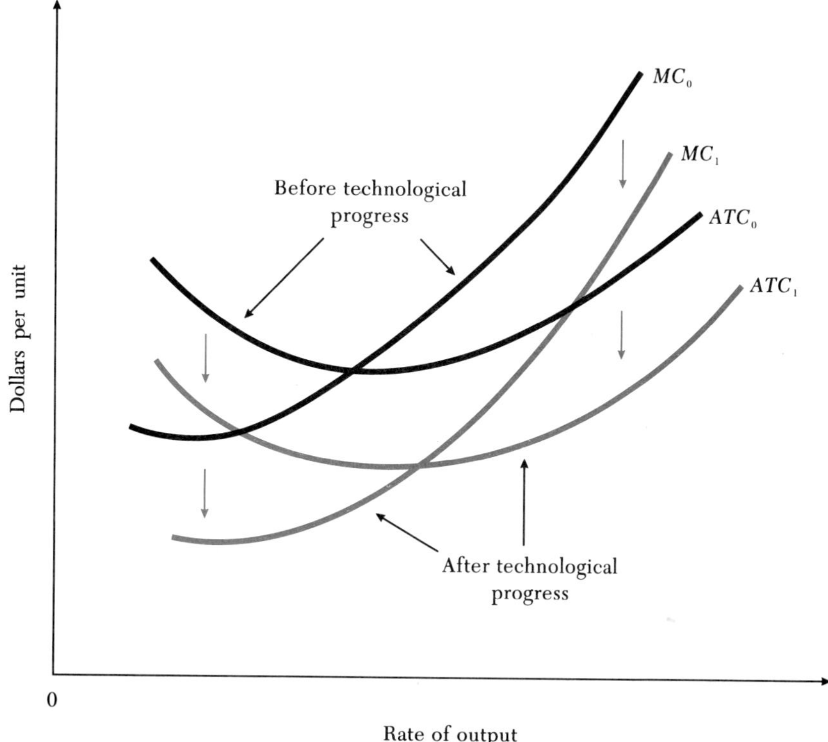

substitute less costly for more costly inputs. The effects of technological progress are illustrated in Figure 8.10.

Experience Effects

All of our cost curves relate costs to the *rate* of output, that is, the flow of output per day, week, or other interval of time. Costs may also depend on the cumulative *volume* of output produced, independently of the rate at which it is produced. The cumulative experience of past production enables producers to identify and overcome the inevitable bugs that accompany any new production process. In addition, observation, experimentation, and just plain trial-and-error eventually lead to the discovery of more efficient ways of doing things. Graphically, the impact of these **experience effects** on the unit cost curves is similar to that of technological progress in Figure 8.10.

Experience effects are the effects of past production experience in reducing costs. They are usually related to the cumulative volume of past production.

Perhaps nowhere are experience effects as pronounced as in the production of the microelectronic chips, the thumbnail-sized integrated circuits used in computers, digital watches, and virtually all modern electronic appliances. The increased yields and reliability that have come with experience in the microscopic production process by which these chips are made tend to reduce costs by about 30 percent for each doubling of cumulative production.

COSTS AND PROFITS

Economic profit is the difference between a firm's revenues and all of its opportunity costs.

The difference between a firm's total revenues and its total opportunity costs is its **economic profit**. Although this definition seems obvious enough, its application is not always so simple.

Explicit Costs and Implicit Costs

Explicit costs are costs for which there is an actual market transaction.

Implicit costs are the opportunity costs of owner-supplied resources not obtained in market transactions.

Typically, most of the resources used by firms are obtained in market transactions. For example, a firm hires labor and purchases energy, raw materials, and intermediate goods from other firms. Costs such as these for which there is a corresponding monetary payment are the **explicit costs** of production. Explicit costs are opportunity costs because the owners of the firm could spend the money on other things. Furthermore, because the market prices of productive resources reflect their value in alternative uses, the explicit monetary outlays made to acquire them are also a measure of their opportunity cost to society.

Some resources used in production are not acquired in market transactions, but rather are supplied directly by the owners of the firm. For example, the owner might work in her own business, or she might use capital goods which she herself owns. Although no market transaction takes place, and thus no monetary outlay is recorded, there is nonetheless an opportunity cost because such resources have alternative uses. The opportunity costs of owner-supplied productive resources are **implicit costs** of production. Total opportunity cost includes both explicit costs and implicit costs.

An Example

To see the relevance of the distinction between explicit and implicit costs, let us for the moment turn our attention away from the high-tech, corporate world of Widgetek, Inc. and focus on the operations of a small proprietorship.

Hamilton Q. Smith is the owner of a fast food restaurant, Ham's Burger Delight. He has two full-time employees, and he purchases all of his beef, buns, and other ingredients from outside suppliers. Together these two expense categories make up Ham's explicit costs as shown in Table 8.5. (All costs shown in the table are measured on an annual basis.)

Ham also works in his own business as manager and part-time cook. In addition, he owns the building in which his restaurant is located, and he has a secret special sauce recipe that Ronald McBurger has expressed an interest in obtaining for use in his own chain of fast food places. In order to calculate the implicit costs Ham incurs in his business, we must determine the opportunity cost of his own labor, his building, and his secret sauce recipe.

If Ham didn't work in his own restaurant, he could get a job managing one of Ronald McBurger's restaurants at a salary of $25,000 a year. If that is the best alternative open to him, then it represents the opportunity cost of Ham's labor in his own business. In addition, if Ham were not using his building for his own business, he could rent it to someone else for $500 per month. The opportunity

Table 8.5

Explicit and implicit costs for Ham's Burger Delight

Explicit Costs		
Wages and salaries	$ 35,000	
Ingredients	50,000	
Total explicit costs		$ 85,000
Implicit Costs		
Ham's own labor (forgone wages)	25,000	
Ham's own building (foregone rent)	6,000	
Ham's secret special sauce recipe (foregone interest)	1,000	
Total implicit costs		32,000
Total Opportunity Cost		$117,000

cost of occupying his own building for a year is therefore $6,000 (= 12 × $500). Finally, because Ronald McBurger has offered Ham $10,000 for his secret sauce recipe, Ham's decision to keep and use the recipe himself costs him the foregone interest he could have earned on $10,000. Assuming a 10 percent rate of interest, this represents an annual cost of $1,000. The total annual implicit cost incurred by Ham in running his own business is therefore $32,000 (= $25,000 + $6,000 + $1,000). Adding this amount to his explicit costs of $85,000 gives his total costs for the year as $117,000.

Now suppose that over the course of the year Hamilton's business generates total revenues of $115,000. According to our definition of economic profit, Ham has suffered a *loss* equal to $2,000 (= $115,000 − $117,000). But after he has paid $35,000 to his employees and $50,000 to his ingredient suppliers, he still has $30,000 of his $115,000 revenues left in the till which, as owner of the business, he can call his own. How can we say that he has lost money?

The apparent paradox can be cleared up by asking what Ham would have earned had he taken advantage of the best available alternatives to running his own business. As we have seen, he could have earned $25,000 in salary, $6,000 in rent, and $1,000 in interest, for a total of $32,000. By operating his own business, he has earned only $30,000. Thus, compared with the other alternatives open to him, Ham has ended up $2,000 to the worse. In that sense, he has indeed suffered a $2,000 loss. Hamilton's economic losses are therefore a signal to him that he could have done better by using his labor and other productive resources elsewhere than in his own business.

If Hamilton's revenues had been $120,000 for the year, he would have made a pure economic profit of $3,000 (= $120,000 − $117,000). Accordingly, the $35,000 he would have left after meeting his explicit obligations is $3,000 more than the $32,000 he and his assets could have earned in alternative employment. The positive profit would therefore be an indication to Ham that his labor and other resources had earned more in his own business than he could have earned in the best available alternatives.

Finally, if Hamilton's revenues had been exactly $117,000, he would have broken even. The zero economic profit would indicate to him that he had earned just as much by running his own business as he could have earned by taking advantage of the best alternatives open to him.

To summarize: Economic profit is a measure of the performance of an enterprise relative to the best alternative uses of the owner's resources. Positive profits indicate that those resources are earning more than they would in alternative uses; negative profits (losses) indicate that they are earning less than they would in alternative uses; zero profit (breaking even) indicates that they are earning the same as they would in alternative uses.

Economic Profit and Accounting Profit

One of the implications of the preceding example is that Hamilton Q. Smith would continue to operate his business indefinitely if it earned zero profits. If he broke even year in and year out, he would earn just as much as he would if he sold his business, secret sauce recipe and all, and went to work for someone else. So breaking even would be enough to keep him in business. Ask the owner of any business if he can survive without profits, however, and the response is sure to be, "No way!".

Accounting profit is the difference between a firm's revenues and its explicit costs.

The apparent discrepancy can be resolved by noting the difference between *economic profit*, upon which our example is based, and **accounting profit**, which is what the business owner undoubtedly has in mind when he says he cannot survive without a profit. Unlike the economist, the accountant generally does not consider all of the implicit costs of owner-supplied resources in computing profit. In the preceding example, when Hamilton has revenues of $117,000, he is breaking even in the sense that his economic profit is zero. His accountant, however, would review Ham's payroll records and receipts for the purchase of ingredients, deduct these explicit costs from the $117,000 in revenues Ham has recorded for the year, and report a profit of $32,000.

Accounting profit is always larger than economic profit because the former does not reflect the implicit opportunity costs of owner-supplied resources. There is no inconsistency, therefore, between the economist's conclusion that a firm must earn at least zero *economic profits* to remain in business, and the business owner's contention that a firm must earn positive *accounting profits* to remain in business. Zero economic profits indeed imply positive accounting profits.

Risk Bearing and the Opportunity Cost of Capital

In a corporation such as Widgetek, where management is carried out by salaried professionals rather than by the stockholder-owners, the major element of Hamilton Q. Smith's implicit costs—the cost of owner-supplied labor—is zero. The primary owner-supplied factor of production in a corporation is capital, and the major implicit cost is the foregone interest on the owners' financial investment in the corporation.

To illustrate, suppose that stockholder equity in Widgetek, Inc. is $100 million. If Widgetek earns accounting profits of $13 million per year, it has an accounting profit rate (return on equity) of 13 percent. But if its stockholders could have earned a 10 percent return in alternative investments, Widgetek's economic profits are only $3 million per year ($13 million minus the $10 million implicit opportunity cost of the $100 million invested by shareholders) for an economic profit rate of 3 percent.

Introducing the inevitable element of risk complicates the picture somewhat. Since most people prefer to avoid risk, risk bearing is a cost for which stockholders (or for that matter, the owners of any firm) must be compensated if they are to continue to supply it with capital. Thus, if investment in Widgetek is riskier than the alternative with the 10 percent return, some or all of the extra $3 million may be compensation for risk bearing rather than pure economic profit. After adjusting for risk, Widgetek's economic profit is therefore less than $3 million; it could conceivably be negative in spite of the positive profits its accountants report.

The main difference between economic profit and accounting profit when applied to the corporation, therefore, is that accountants do not account (no pun intended) for the opportunity cost of the capital and risk bearing supplied by stockholders. The opportunity costs of capital and risk bearing are sometimes referred to as a "normal (accounting) profit," even by economists. It is important to realize, however, that these are real costs of production, costs which, if not covered by the firm's revenues, will lead to capital being withdrawn from the firm and invested elsewhere in the economy where returns are higher.

Why the Difference?

Why do economists and accountants define and measure profit differently? The reason lies in the different uses for which the two measures are intended. The economists' profit concept is useful for their purposes because it enables them to explain the dynamics of resource allocation, especially the allocation of capital and entrepreneurial effort. (We shall see the significance of this momentarily.) Accountants, on the other hand, must come up with real numbers! Their function is to report on the historical performance of the business firm, and the only cost categories of any use to them are those that can actually be measured. Many of the implicit costs economists include *in theory* as part of opportunity costs are difficult or impossible for accountants to measure *in practice*. It might be impossible, for example, to determine what portion of net revenues is compensation for risk bearing, or to determine the implicit opportunity cost of an advantageous location or a well-known brand name. For this reason, many kinds of implicit costs are simply ignored by accountants.

Profits, Losses, and Resource Allocation

Are economic profits just a ripoff whose only function is to enrich greedy capitalists? Should people be protected against losses, even if those losses are the result of their own choices? Many people would answer yes to either or both of these questions. Economic analysis, however, suggests that profits and losses perform a vital function in a market economy. We examine this function in some detail in subsequent chapters, but it is worth presenting a general overview here.

As we have seen, positive economic profits imply that the capital and entrepreneurial effort (and perhaps other resources as well) are earning more than they would earn in alternative uses. Economic losses indicate that the reverse is true. Thus profits and losses are market indicators of the comparative value of resources in alternative uses. Even more importantly, profits and losses provide incentives for the owners of capital and other resources to continuously transfer those resources to sectors of the economy where they are most valuably employed. If profits are greater in the production of computers than in the production of steel, for example, investment will be channeled, via the financial markets, from steel production into computer production, and the process will continue until the expected returns on investment in the two industries are equal.*

Profits and losses are not just window dressing. Like prices, they provide the kinds of signals and incentives necessary to coordinate the allocation of scarce resources and are thus fundamental to the market's ability to adjust to changing economic conditions.

CHAPTER SUMMARY

1. The firm's *production function* relates its inputs to its outputs. It also shows how different inputs can be substituted for one another in the production process.

2. The *law of diminishing returns* says that, as successive amounts of a variable input are added to a fixed amount of other inputs, other things being equal, the marginal product of the variable input will begin to decline beyond some point.

3. In the *short run*, some inputs are fixed and some are variable; in the *long run*, all inputs are variable. Accordingly, in the short run there are both *fixed costs* and *variable costs*, while in the long run all costs are variable.

4. *Acquisition costs* are the transactions cost of acquiring a capital good; *possession costs* are the foregone interest on the funds tied up in that capital good; and *operating costs* are the costs of actually using it.

*The mechanism by which capital is withdrawn is the sale of stock by shareholders. This increase in the supply of the corporation's stock depresses the stock's price and reduces the market value of the corporation until the return on equity, the ratio of profits to market value, rises to the competitive level. Similarly, the stock of a firm that is expected to earn positive pure profits increases in value until it also is earning a competitive return.

5. *Sunk costs* are bygones; they cannot be avoided, and since they are not open to choice, they are not opportunity costs. Sunk costs are irrelevant for current and future decisions.

6. A firm's short-run unit costs consist of *marginal cost* (MC), *average variable cost* (AVC), *average fixed cost* (AFC), and *average total cost* (ATC).

7. *Diminishing returns* are reflected in rising marginal costs as the rate of output rises. As long as marginal cost is less than average total cost (or average variable cost), increasing the rate of output will lead to a reduction in average total cost (or average variable cost). If marginal cost is greater than average total cost (or average variable cost), increasing the rate of output will lead to a rise in average total cost (or average variable cost). Accordingly, the average total cost and average variable cost curves are U shaped; the marginal cost curve cuts each at its minimum point.

8. Long-run changes in all inputs, including those that are fixed in the short run, are called *scale adjustments*. The firm's *long-run average cost curve* shows the minimum average cost of producing any given output when all inputs can be varied.

9. *Economies of scale* lead to falling average cost as the scale of operations is increased; *diseconomies of scale* lead to rising average cost as the scale of operations is increased; *constant returns to scale* imply that average cost is not affected by changes in the scale of operations.

10. Changes in input prices, technological progress, and experience effects shift the firm's cost curves.

11. *Explicit costs* are costs for which a market transaction takes place; *implicit costs* are the costs of owner-supplied resources not acquired through a market transaction.

12. A firm's *economic profit* is equal to the difference between its revenues and all of its opportunity costs, both explicit and implicit. It is a measure of the performance of an enterprise relative to the best alternative uses of the resources supplied by its owner. Positive profits indicate that those resources are earning more than they would in alternative uses; negative profits (losses) indicate that they are earning less than they would in alternative uses; zero profit (breaking even) indicates that they are earning the same as they would in alternative uses.

13. A firm's *accounting profit* is the difference between its revenues and its explicit costs. Accounting profit is always greater than economic profit.

Key Terms and Concepts

production function
marginal product
law of diminishing returns
plant
variable costs
fixed costs
acquisition costs
possession costs
operating costs
sunk costs
average variable cost
average fixed cost
average total cost
scale adjustments
economies of scale
diseconomies of scale
constant returns to scale
experience effects
economic profit
explicit costs
implicit costs
accounting profit

Questions for Thought and Discussion

1. Suppose that you bought a new car last year for $10,000. It is now worth $8,000 in the used car market. When you drive it, it depreciates at the rate of 20 cents per mile. The car gets 20 miles to the gallon and gasoline costs $1.00 per gallon. Your insurance is $1,000 per year, and the state license fee is $200 per year. The interest rate is 10 percent.
   a. Which, if any, of the costs associated with your car are sunk?
   b. What are the fixed and variable costs associated with your car?
   c. What are the explicit and implicit costs associated with your car?
   d. What is the marginal cost of driving 1 more mile?
   e. What is the average total cost per mile of driving another 10,000 miles during the next year?
2. A business firm has purchased a piece of machinery for $20,000 using funds it otherwise would have invested at 12 percent annual return. Having taken delivery of the machine, the firm can either resell it for $15,000 or keep and use it, thus incurring an additional $2,000 per year in operating costs. Are any of the costs associated with this machine sunk? How much must the machine add to revenues if the firm is to keep and use it?
3. A producer incurs short-run total costs of $40 if she shuts down her plant and produces nothing. If she produces 1 unit, her total cost is $48, for 2 units it is $56, and for 3 units it is $70. What is the marginal cost of the third unit and the average variable cost of 3 units?
4. It is believed by some that existing business firms that own their plant and equipment outright have a cost advantage over new firms that must borrow, and thus pay interest on, the funds to finance their plants. Why is this belief wrong?
5. Give an example of each of the following as they might apply to a small proprietorship:

a. Explicit fixed costs
b. Implicit fixed costs
c. Explicit variable costs
d. Implicit variable costs

6. Can you supply the information missing from the following table of short-run costs?

q	FC	VC	TC	AFC	AVC	ATC	MC
0	$200	$—	$200	$—	$—	$—	$—
1	200	50	250	200	50	250	50
2	200	80	280	100	40	140	30
3	200	100	300	66.67	33.33	100	20
4	200	120	320	50	30	80	20
5	200	140	340	40	28	68.00	20

7. Assume that you quit your $18,000 per year job and invest $20,000 of your own money (withdrawn from your 10 percent money market account) to start your own business. After 1 year you sell your business for $35,000 and go back to your old job. What is your economic profit for this 1-year business venture?

8. Suppose that Megabux, Inc. has 5 million shares of stock outstanding at a current price of $10 per share. Its total net income (accounting profit) last year was $4 million. In addition, the interest rate in the economy last year was 10 percent. What was Megabux's total economic profit or loss last year? Assuming the interest rate remains the same, what will happen to the price of a share of Megabux stock if the company is expected to continue earning a net income of $4 million per year for the foreseeable future?

CHAPTER 9

The Model of Pure Competition

Competition may be the spice of life, but in economics it has been more nearly the main dish.

GEORGE STIGLER*

We all know what it means to compete. It means to strive to do something better than someone else. To run faster or jump higher, to score higher on an examination, to gain more votes in an election, to be more attractive to members of the opposite sex—these are all forms of competition with which we are familiar. Like it or not, competition in one form or another is an important part of virtually everyone's life.

THE COMPETITIVE PROCESS VERSUS THE MODEL OF PURE COMPETITION

In the economic sphere, competition assumes an incredibly rich variety of forms. This variety is especially apparent in competition among business firms. Firms compete with one another by trying to offer products and services with the style, features, convenience, and degree of quality and reliability that will most appeal to buyers—all at prices that buyers are willing to pay. They introduce new products, new technologies, and even open up whole new markets. In a world of uncertainty, economic competition is a dynamic process of trial and error, of success and failure, a process wherein the market rewards the successful entrepreneur with profits and punishes the unsuccessful with losses.

The successful entrepreneur often achieves advantages over his less successful

* *The Organization of Industry* (University of Chicago Press, 1983), p. 5.

competitors. For example, since consumers are willing to pay a premium for high-quality, reliable products, a firm that establishes a reputation for quality and reliability is in a position to charge higher prices than its competitors.

Moreover, profits can sometimes be made by *not* competing. For example, in Chapter 2 we saw how a cartel can raise prices and generate profits for the parties involved. Exclusive legal rights—a license or a patent, for example—can protect firms from competition and have much the same effect on prices and profits as a cartel.

Because the market rewards the successful entrepreneur with advantages vis-à-vis less successful competitors, and because it provides incentives both to compete and not to compete, it should come as no surprise that the nature and extent of competition vary from market to market in the real world. In this chapter we focus on an extreme case, an economic model called **pure competition**. Like all models, this one is an abstraction and, indeed, it abstracts a lot from what we have just described as the competitive process. In particular, it abstracts from the entrepreneurial search for new products and new ways of producing them; it assumes that all competitors produce the same product, have access to the same information, and enjoy no competitive advantages vis-à-vis one another. In effect, competition is "pure" because the competitors are assumed to be equal in all respects.

Pure competition is an economic model in which firms are assumed to be numerous and small in relation to the total market and produce a homogeneous product, in which all relevant information is costlessly available to all buyers and sellers, and in which there are no artificial restrictions on market entry or exit.

Although a few real-world markets do approximate the conditions of pure competition, the model is not intended to be a literal description of the competitive process. Its usefulness is to get us started on our study of the microeconomics of market structure by isolating a few of the essential features of that process. That is our purpose in this chapter. In Chapter 10 we focus on the essential features of pure monopoly, which is the antithesis of pure competition. Then in subsequent chapters we see how elements of both competition and monopoly interact in the real-world competitive process.

The Assumptions of the Model of Pure Competition

The model of pure competition is based on four key assumptions: that all buyers and sellers are small in relation to the total market; that the good traded is standardized, or homogeneous; that information is costless; and that the market is open to anyone who wants to participate.

Small Relative Size In a purely competitive market there are numerous producers, each of which is small in relation to the total market. Although we cannot specify the exact number of producers or their maximum relative size consistent with pure competition, the essential idea behind this assumption is that each individual supplier is so small that, were it to vanish from the market, the impact on total market supply would be negligible. This is very nearly the case, for example, in many agricultural markets: Even the largest wheat or corn farmer contributes such a small fraction of total market supply that its disappearance would have a negligible effect on the market. By contrast, the assumption of small relative size would not apply to the markets for automobiles or crude oil.

If General Motors or Saudi Arabia disappeared tomorrow, there would be a noticeable effect on market supply.

Homogeneous products are products that are the same in the eyes of buyers regardless of their particular producers.

Homogeneous Products In a purely competitive market, the product of any one seller is indistinguishable in the eyes of buyers from that of every other seller. In this sense, the good traded is a **homogeneous product**. There are no brand names, no quality differentials, no differences in service or convenience—in short, nothing that would lead any buyer to prefer the product of one seller to that of any other. The products of the various sellers in a purely competitive market are, therefore, *perfect substitutes* for one another.

A certain type of wheat or a particular grade of coal are examples of homogeneous products. Buyers neither know nor care about the identity of the producer. Automobiles, toothpaste, and college educations, on the other hand, are examples of *differentiated products* because the producer's identity might make a difference to the potential buyer. Fords and Chevrolets are *close* substitutes, but in the eyes of most buyers they are not *perfect* substitutes.

Costless Information Each buyer and seller in a purely competitive market knows the price, quality, and all other relevant characteristics of the goods being traded. In addition, all sellers share the same knowledge of buyer preferences and of the technologies available to meet those preferences. This assumption, combined with the assumption of homogeneous products, leaves no room for entrepreneurial activity on the part of firms. They do not search for better products or better ways of meeting buyer demand—in short, they don't innovate. Nor do consumers search for lower prices, higher quality, or better service, for there is no variation in price, quality, or service among sellers.

Here again, these conditions are approximated in only a few real-world markets. For example, in a centralized market such as the New York Stock Exchange or the Chicago Mercantile Exchange, buyers and sellers typically care not a whit about one another's identity, and information about prices is disseminated instantly to all potential traders. If you want to buy a share of IBM stock or a bushel of corn, all it takes is a simple call to a stock or commodities broker to find the current price and place an order. By contrast, if you want to buy a new car, it may take a considerable amount of shopping around to find which dealer has the model you want at the most attractive price, the cheapest credit terms, and the best reputation for after-sale service.

Open Markets Finally, the purely competitive model assumes that the market is *open*. An open market is one in which there are no artificial restrictions on the movement of resources. In particular, firms are free to *enter* the industry in search of profits or to *exit* from the industry to avoid losses. This freedom does not imply that there are no costs associated with entry and exit, for such costs always exist. It only rules out *artificial* restrictions on entry, exit, or resource mobility in general. Artificial restrictions on entry include private, collusive attempts to exclude potential competitors from a market, as well as legal or governmental restrictions such as patents and license requirements. Government subsidies or bailouts intended to keep firms in business, on the other hand, are examples of artificial restrictions on exit.

CASH PRICES

Wednesday March 28, 1990
(Quotations as of 4 p.m. Eastern time)

GRAINS AND FEEDS	Wed	Tues	Yr.Ago
Barley, top-quality Mpls., bu	2.75-.90	2.75-.90	4.35
Bran, wheat middlings, KC ton	76.00	76.00	100.00
Corn, No. 2 yel. Cent-Ill. bu	bp2.50	2.51½	2.59½
Corn Gluten Feed, Midwest, ton	79.-116.	84.-116.	109.00
Cottnsd Meal, Clksdle,Miss. ton	147½-150	147½-150	198.75
Hominy Feed, Cent-Ill. ton	84.00	84.00	86.00
Meat-Bonemeal, 50% pro. Ill. ton.	205.-210.	210.00	262.50
Oats, No. 2 milling, Mpls., bu	n1.57	1.57	2.42½
Sorghum, (Milo) No. 2 Gulf cwt	4.75	4.78	5.00
Soybean Meal,			
Decatur, Illinois ton	160½-170½	164½-170½	231.50
Soybeans, No. 1 yel Cent.-Ill. bu	5.68	5.80	7.47½
Wheat,			
Spring 14%-pro Mpls. bu	3.95	3.97½	4.51
Wheat, No. 2 sft red, St.Lou. bu	bp3.73	3.84	4.35½
Wheat, No. 2 hard KC, bu	4.01½	4.05¼	4.53¼
Wheat, sft wht, del Portland Ore.	3.73	3.74	4.60
FOODS			
Beef, 700-900 lbs. Mid-U.S.,lb.fob	n.a.	1.13	1.13
Broilers, Dressed "A" NY lb	.6011	.6036	.6192
Butter, AA, Chgo., lb.	1.07¾	1.07¾	1.30½
Cocoa, Ivory Coast, $metric ton	g1,346	1,279	1,763
Coffee, Brazilian, NY lb.	n.83	.83	1.28
Coffee, Colombian, NY lb.	n.99	.98¼	n.a.
Eggs, Lge white, Chgo doz.	.82-.88	.82-.88	.77½
Flour, hard winter KC cwt	9.95	10.15	10.80
Hams, 17-20 lbs, Mid-US lb fob	n.a.	.73	n.a.
Hogs, Iowa-S.Minn. avg. cwt	52.00	52.50	38.75
Hogs, Omaha avg cwt	52.00	52.00	38.50
Pork Bellies, 12-14 lbs Mid-US lb	n.a.	.43	.29
Pork Loins, 14-17 lbs. Mid-US lb	n.a.	1.16	n.a.
Steers, Tex.-Okla. ch avg cwt	79.50	79.50	79.75
Steers, Feeder, Okl Cty, av cwt	93.00	93.00	92.25
Sugar, cane, raw, world, lb. fob	.1548	.1523	.1173
FATS AND OILS			
Coconut Oil, crd, N. Orleans lb.	xxn.18	.18	.26⅜
Corn Oil, crd wet mill, Chgo. lb.	25¾	.26¼	.22
Corn Oil, crd dry mill, Chgo. lb.	.26¼	.26¼	.22½
Cottonseed Oil, crd Miss Vly lb.	.22½	.22½	n.a.
Grease, choice white, Chgo lb.	.12¼	.12¼	.13
Lard, Chgo lb.	.13¼	.13¼	.14¼
Palm Oil, ref. bl. deod. N.Orl. lb.	n.15⅛	.15¼	.32½
Soybean Oil, crd, Decatur, lb.	.2230	.2282	.2165
Tallow, bleachable, Chgo lb.	n.13	.13	.14¾
Tallow, edible, Chgo lb.	n.15	.15	.16¼

FIBERS AND TEXTILES	Wed	Tues	Yr.Ago
Burlap, 10 oz 40-in NY yd	n.2875	.2875	.2830
Cotton 1 1/16 str lw-md Mphs lb	.6763	.6751	.5775
Wool, 64s, Staple, Terr. del. lb.	3.00	3.00	4.18
METALS			
Aluminum			
ingot lb. del. Midwest	q.73-.75	.73-.75	.92
Copper			
cathodes lb.	p1.25½-.28	1.24½-36	1.45½
Copper Scrap, No 2 wire NY lb	k.90	.86	1.01
Lead, lb.	p.55-.57	.55-.57	.35
Mercury 76 lb. flask NY	q285-295	285.-295.	325,00
Steel Scrap 1 hvy mlt Chgo ton	98.-103.	98.-103.	115.50
Tin composite lb.	q3.9188	3.8857	5.5533
Zinc Special High grade lb	p.83½	.83½	.95¼
MISCELLANEOUS			
Rubber, smoked sheets, NY lb.	n.46	.46	.55⅞
Hides, hvy native steers lb., fob	.98	.98	.94
PRECIOUS METALS			
Gold, troy oz			
Engelhard indust bullion	373.28	369.28	384.25
Engelhard fabric prods	391.94	387.74	403.46
Handy & Harman base price	372.00	368.00	382.95
London fixing AM 373.30 PM	372.00	368.00	382.95
Krugerrand, whol	a372.50	371.00	383.25
Maple Leaf, troy oz.	a382.50	382.25	394.75
American Eagle, troy oz.	a382.50	382.25	394.75
Platinum, (Free Mkt.)	475.00	477.50	522.75
Platinum, indust (Engelhard)	473.25	474.75	522.50
Platinum, fabric prd (Engelhard)	573.25	574.75	622.50
Palladium, indust (Engelhard)	130.25	126.50	155.00
Palladium, fabrc prd (Englhard)	145.25	141.50	177.00
Silver, troy ounce			
Engelhard indust bullion	4.960	4.990	5.815
Engelhard fabric prods	5.307	5.339	6.222
Handy & Harman base price	4.910	4.950	5.765
London Fixing (in pounds)			
Spot (U.S. equiv. $5.0010)	3.0760	3.0660	3.4565
3 months	3.1925	3.1825	3.5680
6 months	3.3105	3.3010	3.6785
1 year	3.5510	3.5395	3.9095
Coins, whol $1,000 face val	a3,520	3,550	4,225

a-Asked. b-Bid. bp-Country elevator bids to producers. c-Corrected. d-Dealer market. e-Estimated. f-Dow Jones International Petroleum Report. g-Main crop, ex-dock, warehouses, Eastern Seaboard, north of Hatteras. j.-f.o.b. warehouse. k-Dealer selling prices in lots of 40,000 pounds or more, f.o.b. buyer's works. n-Nominal. p-Producer price. q-Metals Week. r-Rail bids. s-Thread count 78x54. x-Less than truckloads. z-Not quoted. xx-f.o.b. tankcars.

Table 9.1

Commodity prices set by market demand and supply

Source: Reprinted by permission of *The Wall Street Journal*, © Dow Jones & Company, Inc., 1990. All rights reserved worldwide.

Price Takers: Perfectly Elastic Firm Demand

A **price taker** is a seller whose independent actions have no affect on market price.

Each firm in a purely competitive market is a **price taker**. A price taker cannot affect the price of its product by its own independent actions.* The first three assumptions of the purely competitive model—namely, small relative size, a homogeneous product, and costless information—insure that this will be the case. Because buyers know all prices and consider the products of different sell-

* Sellers who do have some control over the price of their product are called **price setters**. The case of the price setter is introduced and analyzed in Chapter 10.

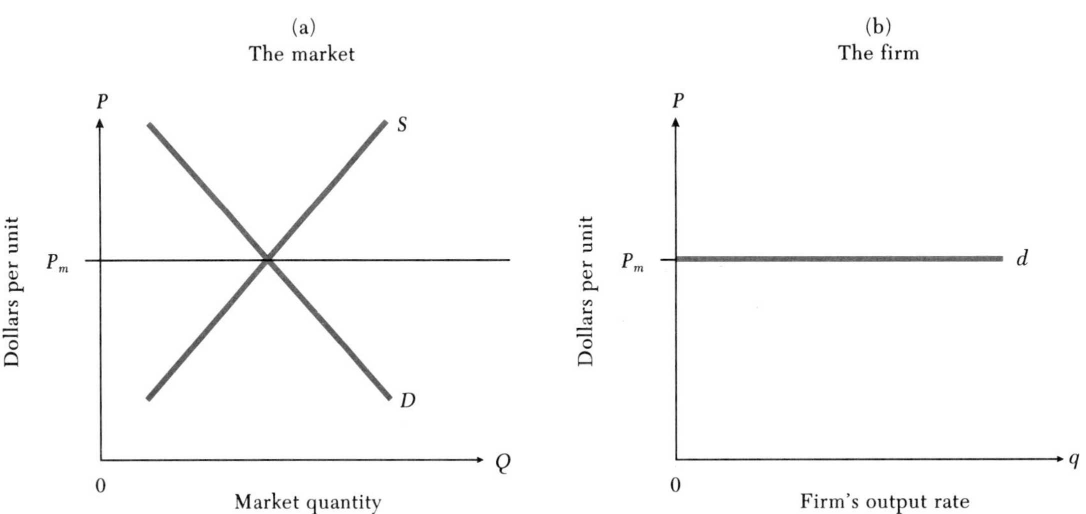

Figure 9.1

The individual firm's demand curve in pure competition.

ers to be perfect substitutes for one another, no seller can hope to sell anything if it charges a price higher than its competitors. All sellers must therefore charge the same price. Moreover, because each is very small in relation to the total market, variations in its output have a negligible effect on market supply, and thus on price.

Where, then, does the price come from if it is not set by any individual seller (or buyer)? The answer is that it is set by the impersonal market, that is, by supply and demand. Look, for example, at the commodity prices reported in the business and financial section of any metropolitan newspaper. (See Table 9.1 on the previous page for an example.) The prices quoted for a bushel of wheat or corn, or for a pound of copper, are not set by individual farmers or miners; they are set by supply and demand on so-called commodity exchanges where offers to buy and sell are continually balanced by price adjustments.

The situation is illustrated in Figure 9.1 where part (a) on the left-hand side of the diagram depicts the market and part (b) on the right depicts the individual firm. (Throughout our microeconomic analysis, we represent market quantity by an upper case Q and the quantity produced by an individual firm by a lower case q.) Market supply (S) and market demand (D) set a price of P_m, and that price is given for the individual firm. Because the firm can produce and sell as much or as little as it chooses at the market price without affecting that price, the horizontal line labelled d and corresponding to the market price is the demand curve *from the perspective of the individual firm*. In a perfectly competitive market, the demand for the output of any individual producer—which is distinct from the market demand for the good itself—is therefore *perfectly elastic*.

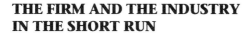

THE FIRM AND THE INDUSTRY IN THE SHORT RUN

An **industry** is a group of firms selling products that are close substitutes for one another.

We define an **industry** as a group of firms that sell products that are close substitutes for one another. For example, Ford, Chrysler, and Toyota are all in the automobile industry; Pepsi, Coca-Cola, and Canada Dry are all in the soft drink industry. From what we have already said, a purely competitive industry represents the extreme case in which the products of different firms are not only close substitutes, but perfect substitutes.

In the last chapter we saw that a firm can vary its scale in the long run but operates with a given scale in the short run. We can also distinguish the short run from the long run in terms of industry adjustments. In particular, we assume that firms can enter or exit an industry in the long run, but the number of firms in the industry is fixed in the short run.

Short-Run Profit Maximization

Because the purely competitive firm is a price taker, its only short-run decisions are whether to produce at all and, if so, how much to produce. We assume that the firm's goal in making these decisions is to maximize its profits (or minimize its losses).

To illustrate the nature of the profit-maximizing supply decision, let us consider the operations of Acme Gizmo, a hypothetical producer in the purely competitive gizmo market. Acme's revenues and costs are shown in Table 9.2 on the following page. Column 1 shows the various daily output rates at which Acme can operate in the short run. In constructing columns 2 and 3, we assumed that the market price for gizmos is $18. Because Acme is a price taker, this price is given and does not vary with its rate of output. Each unit produced and sold thus adds $18 to its total revenues. For a price taker, therefore, the **marginal revenue** from the sale of each additional unit of output is the same as the market price.

Marginal revenue is the addition to a seller's revenue when one more unit is sold.

Columns 4 and 5 show Acme's total cost and marginal cost for each output rate. These include both explicit and implicit costs. The $35 total cost at the zero rate of output reflects the fixed costs that Acme continues to incur in the short run even if it produces nothing.

One way to approach profit maximization is to determine total revenues and total costs at each rate of output, calculate profit as the difference between the two, and then find the output rate at which the calculated profit is highest. We did this in column 6, which shows that Acme's most profitable output rate is either 14 or 15 units per day and its corresponding total profit is $60 per day.

To see the logic of profit maximization—as opposed to the mere arithmetic of calculating profits—we must use a different approach, however—namely, a comparison of marginal revenue and marginal cost. Suppose, for example, that Acme initially produces 11 gizmos per day and earns profits of $54 per day. A comparison of marginal revenue and marginal cost tells Acme that increasing its

Table 9.2

Revenues, costs and profits for Acme Gizmo, a price taker (price = $18)

1 Rate of Output (q)	2 Total Revenue (TR)	3 Marginal Revenue (= Price) (MR)	4 Total Cost (TC)	5 Marginal Cost (MC)	6 Profit (+) or Loss (−)
0	$ 0	$—	$ 35	$—	$−35
1	18	18	45	10	−27
2	36	18	53	8	−17
3	54	18	60	7	−6
4	72	18	67	7	5
5	90	18	75	8	15
6	108	18	84	9	24
7	126	18	94	10	32
8	144	18	105	11	39
9	162	18	117	12	45
10	180	18	130	13	50
11	198	18	144	14	54
12	216	18	159	15	57
13	234	18	175	16	59
14	252	18	192	17	60
15	270	18	210	18	60
16	288	18	229	19	59
17	306	18	249	20	57
18	324	18	270	21	54
19	342	18	292	22	50
20	360	18	315	23	45

output rate from 11 to 12 gizmos per day would add to its profits. Why? Because the marginal revenue brought in by the twelfth gizmo ($18) exceeds the marginal cost ($15) of producing it. As you can see from the table, increasing output from 11 to 12 gizmos per day increases Acme's profits from $54 to $57, an increase that is exactly equal to the $3 excess of marginal revenue over marginal cost.

Increasing the rate of output from 12 to 13 gizmos per day would increase Acme's profits by another $2 because the marginal revenue of the thirteenth gizmo exceeds its marginal cost by that amount. A fourteenth gizmo would add another $1 to Acme's daily profits; a fifteenth would have no effect on profits because its marginal revenue just offsets its marginal cost. Production of a sixteenth gizmo per day, however, would reduce profits because it would add more to Acme's costs ($19) than to its revenues ($18). Given the $18 market price, therefore, Acme would increase its rate of output up to, but not beyond, 15 gizmos per day.

In general, therefore, if the marginal revenue from an additional unit of output exceeds its marginal cost, its production and sale will increase profits; if the reverse is true, its production and sale will decrease profits. From this follows the general rule for determining the profit-maximizing rate of output: A firm maximizes profits at the output rate where marginal revenue and marginal cost are equal.

Note that the last unit produced under this rule—the one for which marginal revenue and marginal cost are exactly equal—leaves profit unchanged. In the case of Acme Gizmo, that unit is the fifteenth gizmo per day; Acme would earn its maximum profit of $60 per day whether it stopped at 14 gizmos per day or produced the fifteenth as well. Accordingly, we could restate the preceding rule to say that profits are maximized "at an output rate where marginal revenue and marginal cost are equal, *or at an output rate which is lower by 1 unit.*" But why complicate matters? Since it doesn't really make any difference, we always use the simpler *equality* of marginal revenue and marginal cost as the rule for profit maximization.

Depicting the Output Decision Graphically

Acme's profit-maximizing output decision is illustrated in Figure 9.2, where the cost curves have been derived from the information in Table 9.2 and where we once again assume a market price, and therefore a marginal revenue, of $18 per gizmo. (Note that the price taker's marginal revenue curve corresponds to its perfectly elastic demand curve.) Graphically, the equality between marginal revenue and marginal cost occurs at the intersection of the marginal revenue line and the marginal cost curve. This intersection corresponds to an output rate of

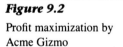

Figure 9.2

Profit maximization by Acme Gizmo

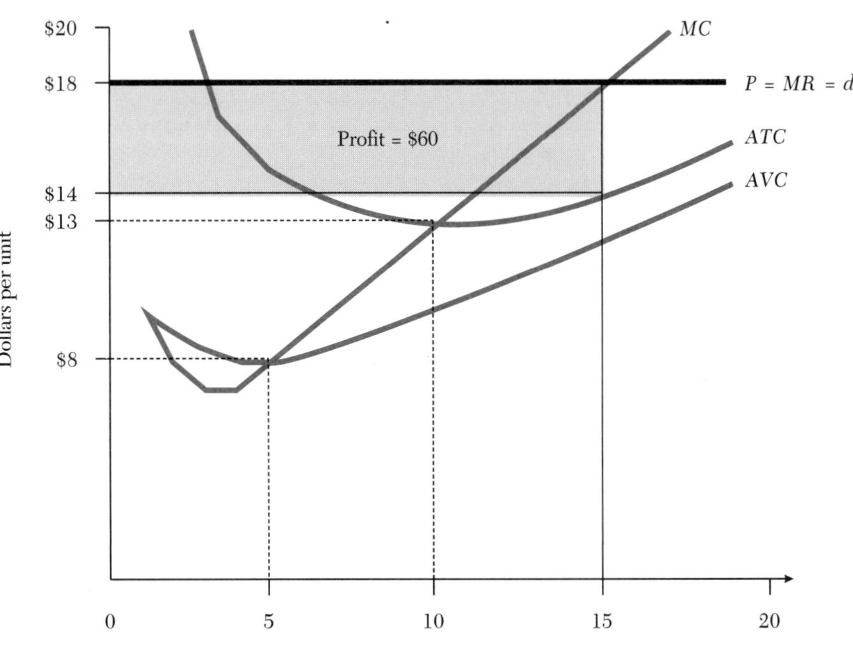

15 gizmos per day on the horizontal axis. At that output rate, average total cost is $14 per unit (= the $210 total cost divided by the 15 gizmo rate of output). Acme's *profit per unit* is the $4 difference between the $18 price and its $14 per unit average total cost. Its *total profit* is the profit per unit times the number of units sold, or $60 (= $4 per unit times 15 units). This total profit is represented graphically as the shaded rectangular area whose height is equal to profit per unit (price minus average total cost) and whose length is equal to the number of units produced and sold per day.*

(Note that Acme maximizes *total* profit, not profit per unit, or *average* profit. The latter is always greatest at the output rate where average total cost is minimized. In this example, the ATC reaches its minimum value of $13 per gizmo at an output rate of 10 gizmos per day. With a market price of $18, an average profit of $5 per gizmo (= $18 − $13), and an output of 10 gizmos per day, Acme's total profit would be only $50 per day. As our preceding example has shown, total profits are greater if Acme's output is increased to 15 gizmos per day. At that output rate, the lower profit per unit is more than offset by the additional number of units sold.)

Dealing with Losses: Produce or Shut Down?

Now suppose that the gizmo market turns sour and the price per gizmo falls to $10. This situation is illustrated in Figure 9.3 where Acme's cost curves are exactly the same as in the previous diagram but the marginal revenue line is drawn at the new market price of $10. The fact that the average total cost curve lies entirely above the $10 price means that Acme will lose money regardless of the output rate it chooses. If it expects these losses to persist indefinitely, it will sell its plant (or not bother to replace it when it wears out) and eventually go out of business. But that is a long-run decision. The crucial question in the short run is whether it is better for Acme to continue production at a loss or to temporarily **shut down** its operations and wait for an increase in gizmo prices. Note that shutting down is not the same as going out of business. In a shut down, the firm produces nothing ($q = 0$ in Table 9.2), but it nonetheless retains possession of its idle plant and continues to bear the fixed costs associated with that plant. According to Table 9.2, these fixed costs are $35.

A **shut down** is a situation in which a firm minimizes short-run losses by producing nothing.

Table 9.3 compares the short-run alternatives open to Acme when the market price of gizmos falls to $10. If it shuts down, it will have no revenue but it will avoid its variable costs. Acme's daily loss during a shut down will therefore be equal to its $35 fixed costs. If, on the other hand, Acme continues to produce, it should again select the output rate that equates marginal revenue and marginal cost. According to Table 9.2, the output rate at which marginal cost equals the new $10 marginal revenue is 7 gizmos per day. (Disregard columns 2 and 3,

*Profits can also be calculated as the difference between the total revenue rectangle (whose base is 15 units and whose height is the $18 market price) and the total cost rectangle (whose base is 15 units and whose height is the $14 average total cost).

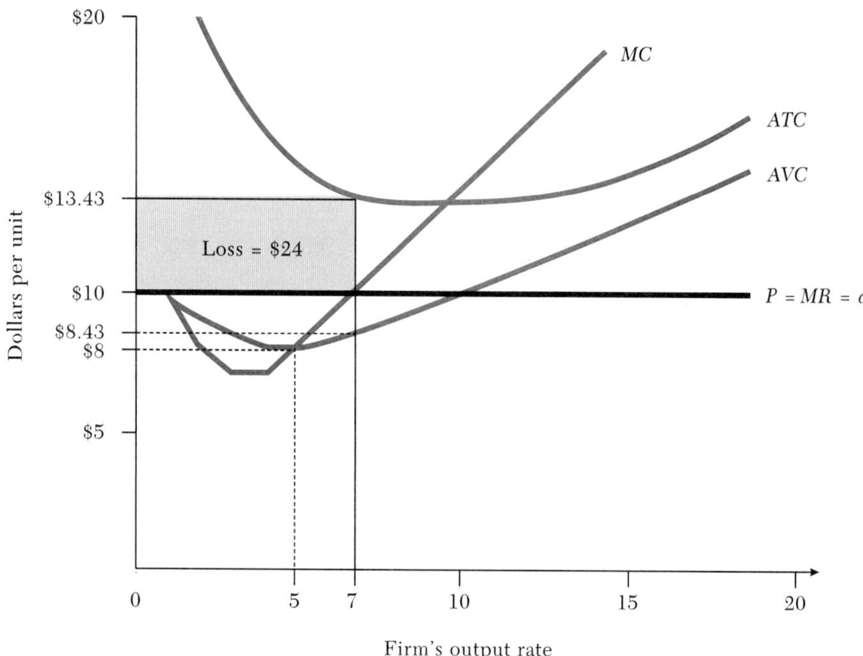

Figure 9.3

Loss minimization by Acme Gizmo

Table 9.3

Shut down versus continued production at Acme Gizmo at price = $10

		SHUT DOWN ($q = 0$)		PRODUCE ($q = 7$)
Total revenues		$ 0		$70
Variable costs	0		59	
Fixed costs	35		35	
− Total costs		−35		−94
= Profit		−35		−24

which assume a price and marginal revenue of $18.) Producing 7 gizmos per day and selling them at the $10 market price results in revenues of $70 per day and total costs (also from Table 9.2) of $94 per day. Acme's daily loss from continued production would therefore be $24, which is less than its loss from shutting down.

A closer look at Table 9.3 shows why Acme minimizes its losses by continuing to produce. The only differences between shutting down and continuing production are in the entries for revenues and variable costs. If Acme shuts down, both are zero; if it continues to produce, revenues are $70 per day and variable costs are $59 per day. The $11 difference between the two is exactly the amount by which continued production reduces Acme's loss. The crucial question is therefore whether Acme's revenues from continued production are sufficient to cover its variable costs. Unlike fixed costs, variable costs can be avoided by choosing not to produce. Thus, if the revenues from continued production at least cover the resulting variable costs, then continued production is preferable to shutting down. On the other hand, if revenues do not cover variable costs, then losses are minimized by shutting down.

Figure 9.3 analyzes Acme's choice between continued production and shutting down at the $10 price in terms of its unit cost curves. For revenues to cover variable costs, the market price (which is the same thing as *average revenue*) must cover the average variable cost. According to the diagram, the average variable cost is $8.43 at the 7 gizmo per day rate of output (= $59 total variable cost divided by the rate of output of 7 gizmos per day). The $10 price therefore does cover the average variable cost and so, as we concluded earlier, Acme minimizes its losses by continuing to produce. The resulting $24 daily loss is represented by the shaded rectangle whose height is equal to the $3.43 loss per unit (= the $13.43 average total cost minus the $10 price) and whose base is the 7 produced per day.

According to Figure 9.3, Acme's minimum average variable cost is $8 per unit at an output rate of 5 gizmos per day. At any market price below $8, Acme would therefore shut down its plant because revenues would not be sufficient to cover its variable costs. Under such circumstances, it would be better to shut down and incur only its $35 per day fixed costs.

Some Examples

We can illustrate the shut-down decision by means of a pair of examples. During severe recessions, automobile manufacturers typically shut down some of their assembly plants based on the judgement that revenues from continued operation would not cover the costs of the labor, materials, and other variable inputs needed to operate the plants. As a result, plants representing multimillion dollar capital investments stand idle for months at a time until they are eventually reopened when market conditions improve.

Our second example involves a contrast frequently observed in markets where U.S. firms compete with Japanese firms.* When the market price declines, the U.S. firms often shut down while the Japanese continue to produce. This happened a number of times, for example, in the market for steel during the 1970s and in the market for computer memory chips during the 1980s. Almost inevitably, U.S. firms cry foul, claiming that the Japanese are *dumping* their products

* See "Fixed Versus Variable Costs of Production: Crisis in the Steel Industry," Chapter 11 in Robert Paul Thomas, *Microeconomic Applications* (Wadsworth, 1981) for an in-depth analysis of this phenomenon.

below cost in a deliberate attempt to harm their U.S. competitors and perhaps even drive them out of business.

Whatever the merits of this dumping claim, economic analysis provides an alternative, more benign explanation of why the Japanese continue production at prices so low that their U.S. competitors find it better to shut down. The explanation has to do with differences in employment practices in Japan and the United States. When U.S. firms shut down, they typically lay off their production workers to save on labor costs. Labor costs are therefore a variable cost for U.S. firms. Japanese employment practices, by contrast, are such that workers are typically kept on the payroll through thick and thin. Accordingly, Japanese firms regard labor costs as essentially fixed. Given comparable levels of total costs, therefore, Japanese firms have lower variable costs and higher fixed costs than their U.S. competitors.

The result is illustrated in Figure 9.4. For simplicity we assume that U.S. and Japanese firms have the same average total cost curve. However, because labor costs are a variable cost in the United States but a fixed cost in Japan, the average variable cost curve for U.S. firms is above that for Japanese firms. Correspondingly, the shut-down price for U.S. firms (P_1) is above that for Japanese firms (P_2). At prices between P_1 and P_2, therefore, the U.S. firms shut down while their Japanese counterparts continue to produce.

Figure 9.4

Different AVCs mean different shut-down prices for U.S. and Japanese producers.

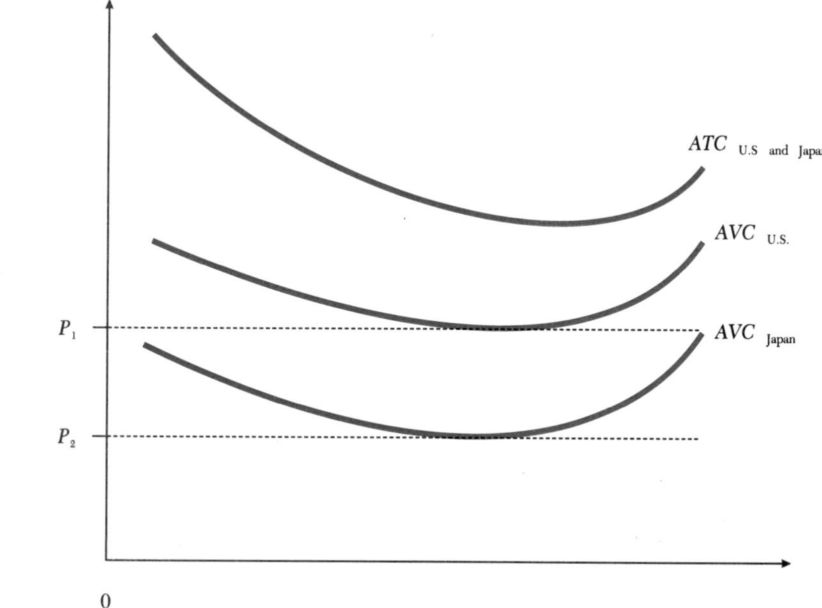

Short-Run Supply

The foregoing analysis enables us to derive the short-run supply curves for both the individual firm and the entire market.

The Short-Run Supply Curve of the Individual Firm

For prices below the minimum average variable cost, the firm will shut down and supply nothing in the short run. For prices above the minimum average variable cost, it will maximize profits (or minimize losses) by producing the output for which marginal cost equals marginal revenue, which is the same thing as price for the price taker. For any price above the minimum average variable cost, therefore, we can read the quantity supplied directly from the firm's marginal cost curve. In Figure 9.5, for example, q_1 units will be supplied at a market

Figure 9.5

The individual firm's short-run supply curve

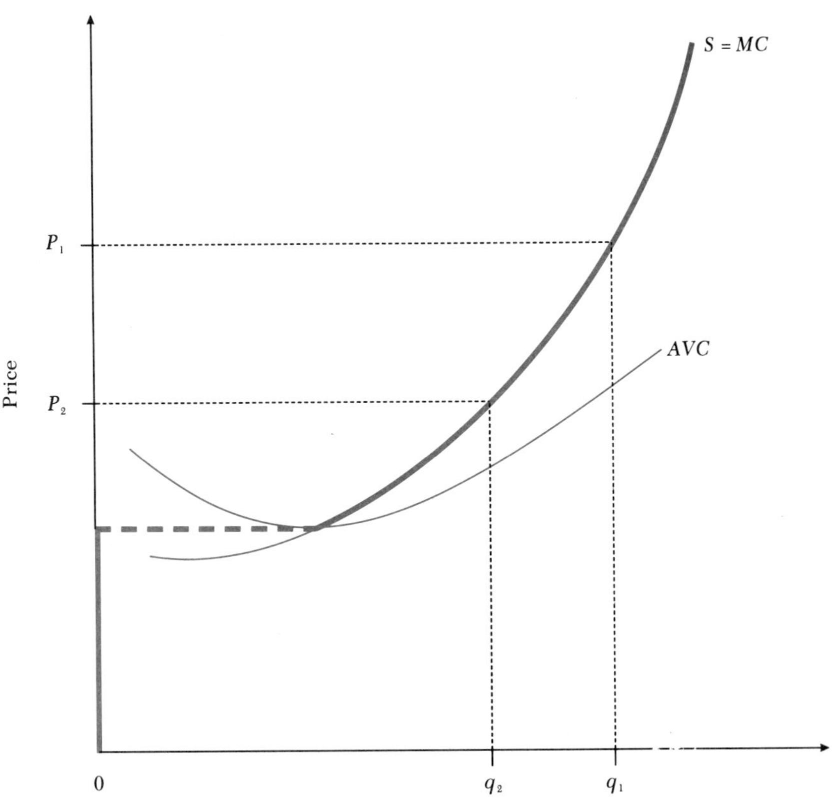

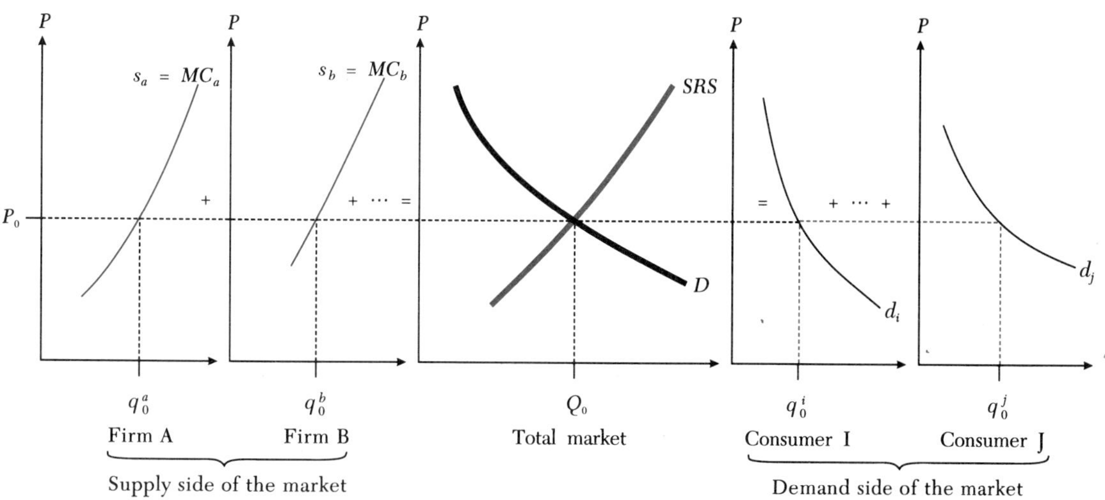

Figure 9.6

Short-run market equilibrium: the big picture

The **firm's short-run supply curve** is the portion of its marginal cost curve that lies above its average variable cost curve.

The **short-run industry supply curve** is the market supply curve in the short run when the number and size of the firm in the industry that supplies the market are fixed.

price of P_1, and q_2 units will be supplied at a market price of P_2. The **firm's short-run supply curve** is, therefore, that portion of its marginal cost curve that lies above the average variable cost curve.

Short-Run Market Equilibrium: The Big Picture

Figure 9.6 provides an overview of short-run equilibrium for the entire market. On the supply side, the total quantity supplied at any price is simply the sum of the quantities supplied by all of the individual firms in the market at that price. Accordingly, the **short-run industry supply curve** (*SRS*), which is also the market supply curve in the short run, is the horizontal sum of the supply (marginal cost) curves of all of the individual firms in the industry. On the demand side, the market demand curve is determined by summing the quantities demanded by all of the individual consumers in the market at each price. The market supply and demand curves together determine the market clearing equilibrium price, P_0, and the corresponding quantity traded, Q_0. At the market clearing price, Firm A supplies q_0^a units, Firm B supplies q_0^b units, and so on. Similarly Consumer I purchases q_0^i units, Consumer J purchases q_0^j units, and so on. The market clears because, given the construction of the market supply and demand curves, the sums of the individual quantities demanded and supplied, respectively, must both be equal to Q_0.

Although no individual producer or consumer in a purely competitive market can affect the market price, the interaction of all producers and all consumers together establishes an equilibrium price which in turn determines both the total amount produced and exchanged and its allocation among individual producers and consumers.

THE LONG RUN

When we shift our perspective from the short run to the long run, we must consider two new sources of adjustment: adjustments in the individual firm's scale of operations and adjustments in the number of firms in the industry.

Adjustments in the Firm's Scale of Operations

While the firm is confined to a given plant in the short run, it has the option of changing its scale of operations to a larger or smaller plant in the long run. Figure 9.7 plots a firm's long-run average cost curve (*LRAC*) and long-run marginal cost curve (*LRMC*) along with two short-run average total cost curves (ATC_1 and ATC_2) and their associated short-run marginal cost curves (MC_1 and MC_2). As we saw in the previous chapter, each of the short-run average total cost curves corresponds to a different scale of operations; in particular, ATC_2 corresponds to a larger scale of operations than ATC_1.

Suppose that, in the short run, the firm is operating with the scale corresponding to ATC_1. If the market price is P_m, short-run output will be at q_1 where the short-run marginal cost is equal to the price. But if the firm expects the market

Figure 9.7

Adjustments in the firm's scale

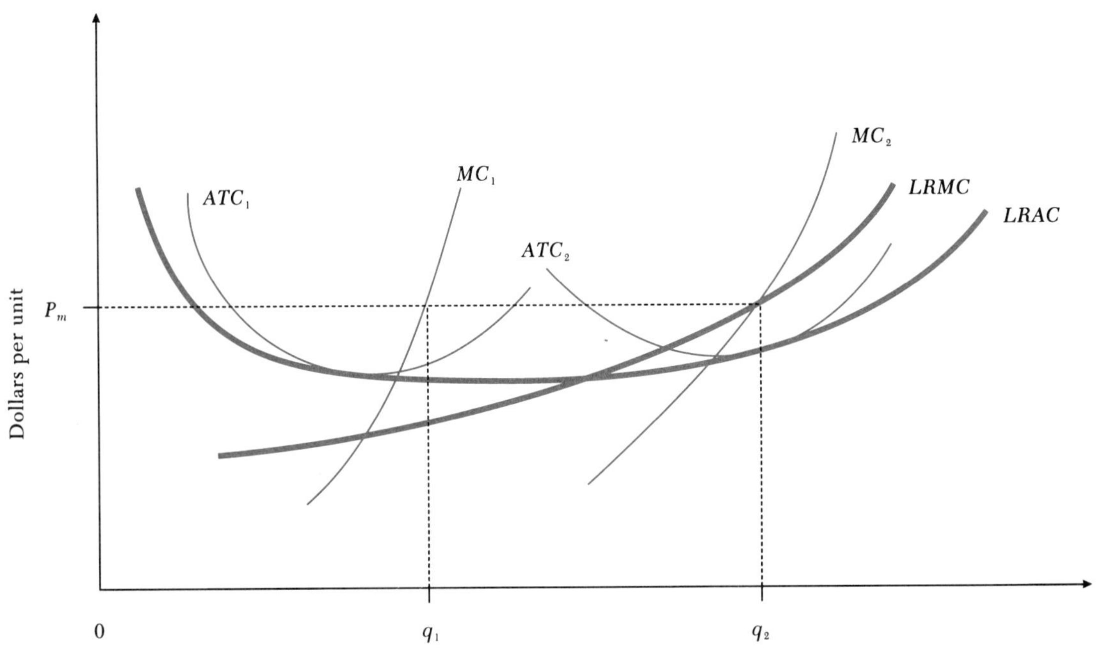

price to remain at P_m, it will eventually increase its output to q_2 where the long-run marginal cost is equal to that price. It will do this by moving to a larger size plant, namely, the one corresponding to ATC_2.

Don't be confused by the geometry! For most students it looks (and probably is) complex. The important point is that the underlying logic is exactly the same for the long-run output decision as for the short-run: If the marginal revenue (in this case, the price) is greater than the marginal cost at the current rate of output, profits can be increased by increasing the rate of output. The only difference is that the long-run marginal cost reflects the cost of increasing output, not just by adding more labor, materials, and other variable inputs to fixed plant, but by expanding the entire *scale* of operations—including the plant.

Long-Run Equilibrium

The *firm* is in long-run equilibrium only when there is no incentive for it to change either its rate of output or its scale of operations. In addition, the *industry* is in long-run equilibrium only when the firms in the industry are earning zero economic profits. If firms are earning positive profits, those profits will attract new firms into the industry; if firms are suffering economic losses, some of them will leave the industry. Long-run equilibrium in a purely competitive industry must therefore be a *zero-profit* equilibrium.

This zero-profit equilibrium is illustrated in Figure 9.8. The price P_0 determined by market supply and demand in part (a) on the left is the long-run equi-

Figure 9.8

Long-run equilibrium

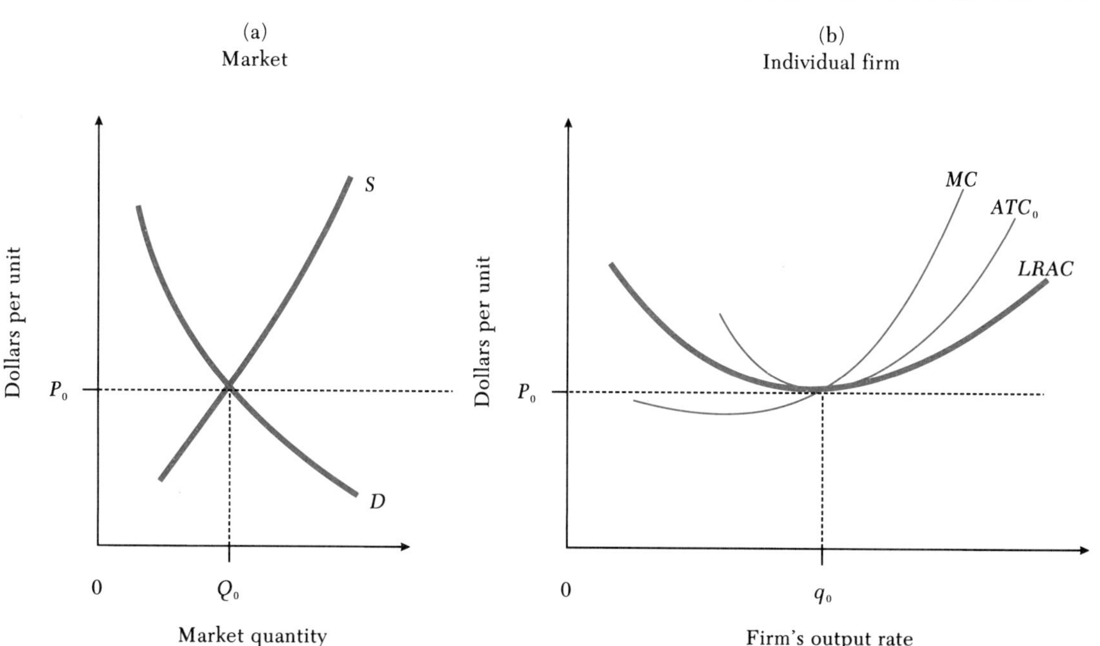

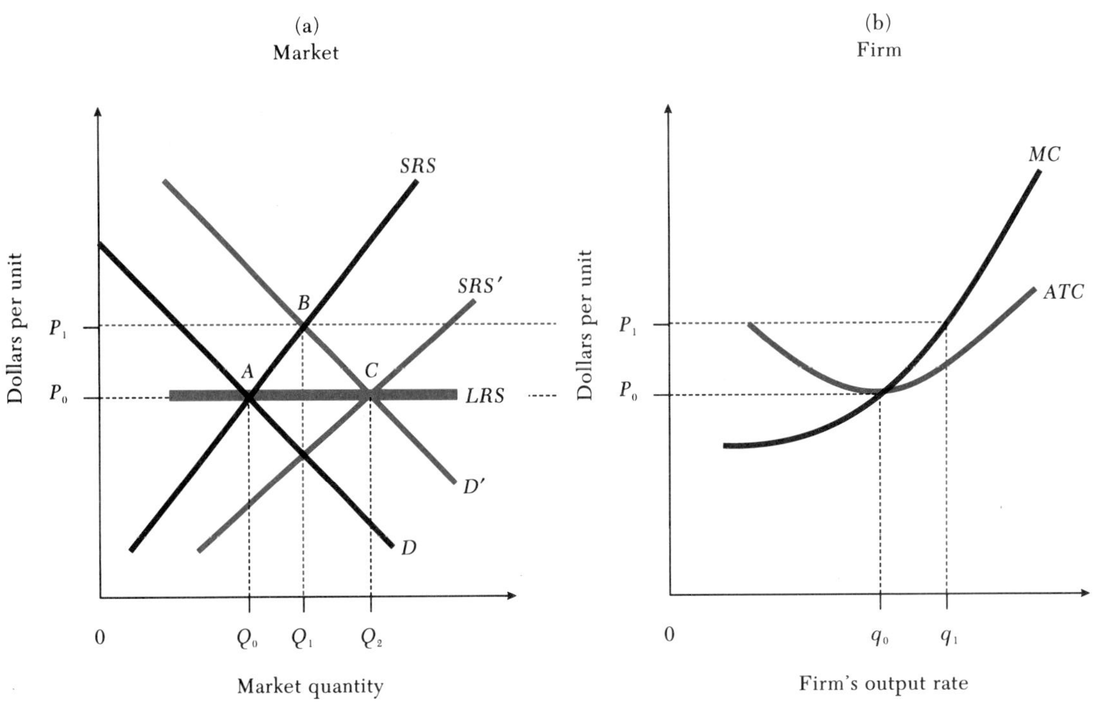

Figure 9.9

Adjustment to an increase in demand: constant cost industry.

librium price because the individual firm, shown in part (b) on the right, can just break even at that price. To do so, it must produce at that rate of output (q_0), and in that scale of plant (ATC_0), which minimizes long-run average cost. Producing at any other rate of output, or operating in any other scale of plant, would mean economic losses.

Long-Run Industry Adjustment to a Change in Demand

Long-run equilibrium is not meant to describe some state to which an industry adjusts once and for all. Technological progress, changes in demand, and a variety of other factors inevitably disturb any long-run equilibrium—in reality, probably before it is ever actually attained. Rather the value of the equilibrium concept lies in its implications for the way in which an industry adjusts to changes in the economic environment. To illustrate the nature of such adjustment, let us use Figure 9.9 to trace the long-run consequences of an increase in demand. Initially, we simplify our analysis by assuming that all firms in the industry are identical.

Part (a) on the left-hand side of Figure 9.9 shows the initial market demand curve (D) and short-run industry supply curve (*SRS*). (Ignore for the moment the curve labelled *LRS*.) The industry is in long-run equilibrium at point *A* with price P_0 and quantity Q_0 because each firm, as shown in part (b) on the right-hand side of the diagram, is just breaking even at that price. Starting from this initial equilibrium, market demand now increases from D to D'.

Short-Run Response

In the short run, the increase in demand moves the industry along its short-run supply curve and raises the price from P_0 to P_1. As each individual firm responds to the rising price by increasing its output rate from q_0 to q_1, the quantity supplied to the market increases from Q_0 to Q_1, and a new short-run equilibrium is established at point B. Since the price is above the average total cost, the firms in the industry are now earning positive economic profits.

Long-Run Response

In the long run, the profits attract new entrants into the industry. Such entry can take two forms: new firms can be literally started from scratch by investors who want a share of the industry's profits, or existing firms in other industries can expand into this now-profitable market. In either case, the entry of new producers increases supply, shifting the short-run market supply curve to the right and forcing price down until the opportunities for pure profit disappear. If we assume that entry does not affect costs, then the industry will be back in long-run equilibrium only when the short-run supply curve has shifted out to *SRS'* with a new zero-profit, long-run equilibrium established at point *C*. In the new equilibrium, the price will have returned to its original level and industry output will have increased to Q_2.

The effects of a decrease in demand are just the reverse. Starting from an initial equilibrium, there is a short-run decline in both price and quantity. The lower price means economic losses leading to the exit of firms from the industry and a shift of the short-run supply curve to the left until a new equilibrium is established at the original price and a lower quantity.

Long-Run Supply

The line labelled LRS, which connects the initial and final long-run equilibrium points *A* and *C* in Figure 9.9, shows what happens to price and quantity supplied after all adjustments to a change in demand have worked themselves out. As such, it is the **long-run industry supply curve**. Its shape depends on the effects of entry and exit on production costs. There are three possibilities:

The **long-run industry supply curve** is the market supply curve in the long run when the number and size of the firms in the industry that supplies the market are variable.

A **constant cost industry** is one in which the long-run supply price is constant because entry and exit do not affect production costs.

1. **Constant Cost Industries.** The horizontal long-run supply curve we have just derived is the defining characteristic of a **constant cost industry**. In our derivation, we assumed that the entry and exit of firms, or, more generally, the expansion and contraction of the industry, does not affect the cost curves of individual firms. Thus, for pure profits or losses to be eliminated and a new long-run equilibrium established after a change in demand, price must return to its original level. In a constant cost industry, therefore, the long-run supply curve is perfectly elastic (horizontal), indicating that costs, and thus the industry's supply price, remain constant as the industry ex-

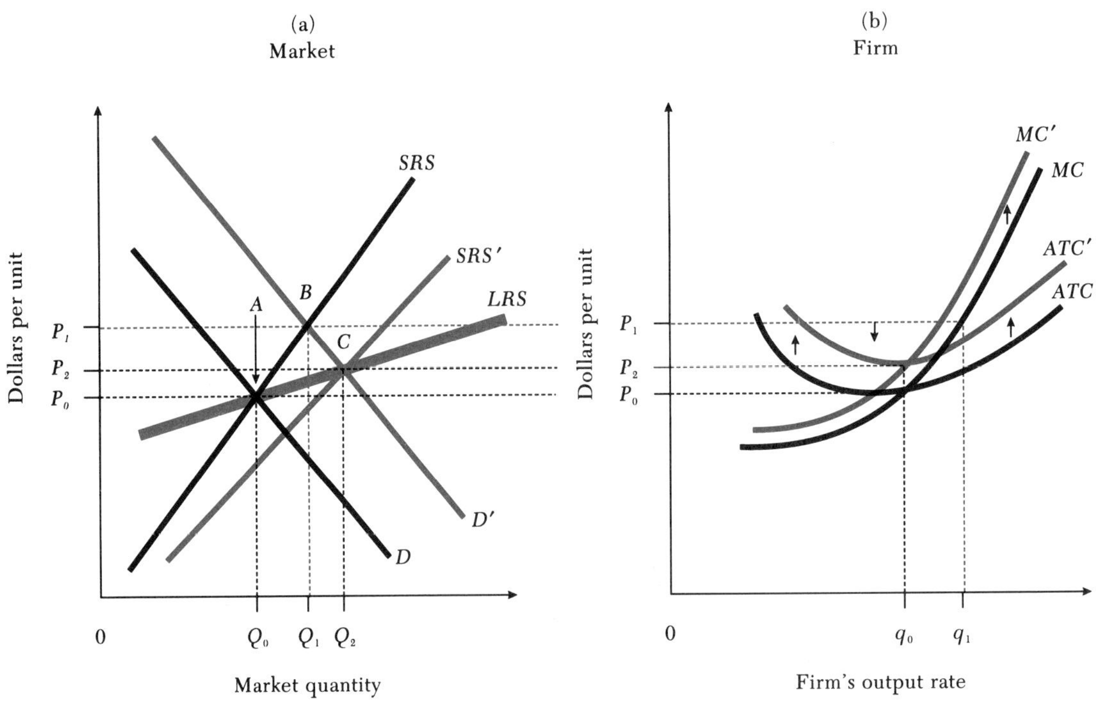

Figure 9.10

Adjustment to an increase in demand: increasing cost industry.

An **increasing cost industry** is one in which the long-run supply price rises as output increases because the entry of firms raises production costs.

pands. In such an industry, changes in demand have no long-run effect on price. (They do, however, have short-run effects as we have seen.)

2. **Increasing Cost Industries.** In many cases the production costs of individual firms rise as the industry expands and fall as the industry contracts. Such an industry is called an **increasing cost industry**. The most likely source of such changes in costs is a change in the prices of the industry's inputs. As the industry expands, its demand for inputs rises, and, unless those inputs are themselves in perfectly elastic (long-run) supply, the increase in demand will force their prices up causing production costs to rise.

An adjustment to an increase in demand under such circumstances is illustrated in Figure 9.10. In the short run, price rises from P_0 to P_1, and the resulting short-run profits attract new entrants, just as in the constant cost industry of our foregoing example. As entry proceeds, however, not only does the price of output fall because of the increased supply, but also costs increase because of rising input prices. The rising costs are indicated by the upward shift in the firm's cost curves. Profits are thus squeezed out by a combination of two factors, namely, falling output prices and rising production costs. The final long-run equilibrium price will be one like P_2, which is above the initial price P_0. In an increasing cost industry, therefore, the long-run supply curve has a positive slope, indicating that costs, and thus the supply price, rise as the industry expands.

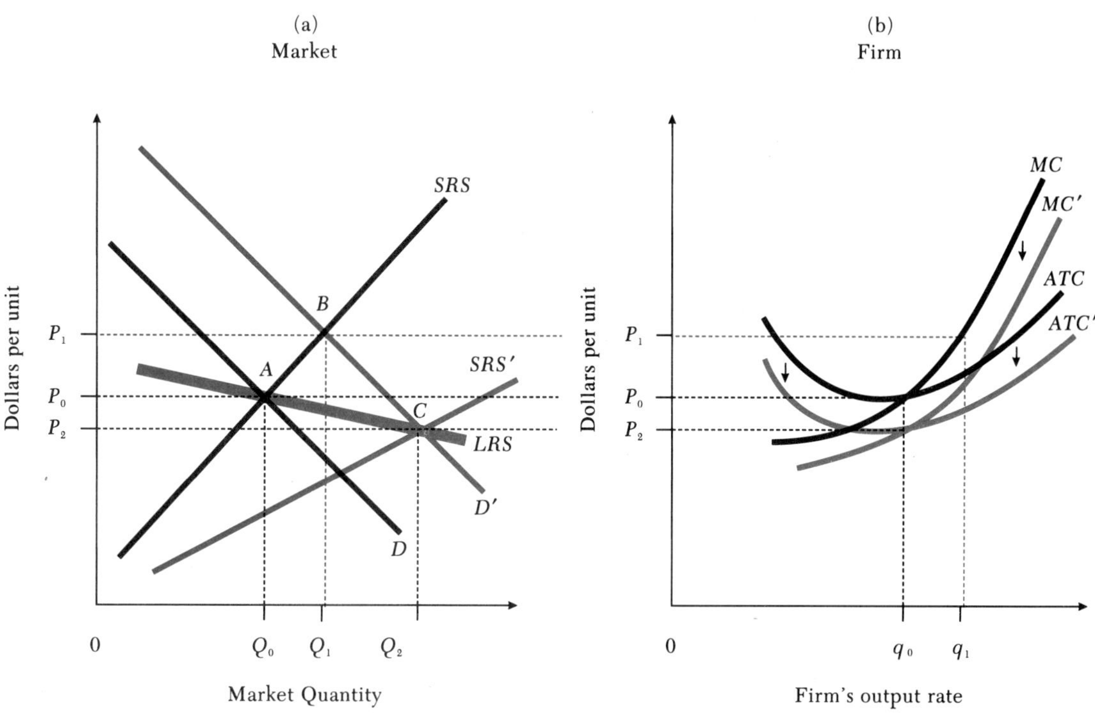

Figure 9.11

Adjustment to an increase in demand: decreasing cost industry.

A **decreasing cost industry** is one in which the long-run supply price falls as output increases because the entry of firms lowers production costs.

3. **Decreasing Cost Industries.** Finally, it is possible for production costs to fall as an industry expands. Such an industry is called (surprise!) a **decreasing cost industry**. For example, if there are economies of scale in the production of the industry's inputs, an expansion of the industry leads to lower input costs. A decreasing cost industry is illustrated in Figure 9.11 where, after the initial short-run increase in price occurs in response to the increase in demand, entry drives down both costs and prices. The result is that the final long-run equilibrium price P_2 is below the initial price. In a decreasing cost industry, therefore, the long-run supply curve has a negative slope, indicating that costs, and thus the supply price, fall as the industry expands.

Shifts in the Long-Run Industry Supply Curve

Long-run changes in industry output in response to changes in demand are represented by *movements along* the industry's long-run supply curve. Changes in costs resulting from factors other than changes in industry output, on the other hand, lead to *shifts* of the long-run supply curve. One such factor is technological progress. For example, technological progress has dramatically lowered the long-run supply curve for electronic computing power over the last three decades. The result, as illustrated in Figure 9.12(a), has been lower prices and greater utilization of computer services. Changes in input prices caused by fac-

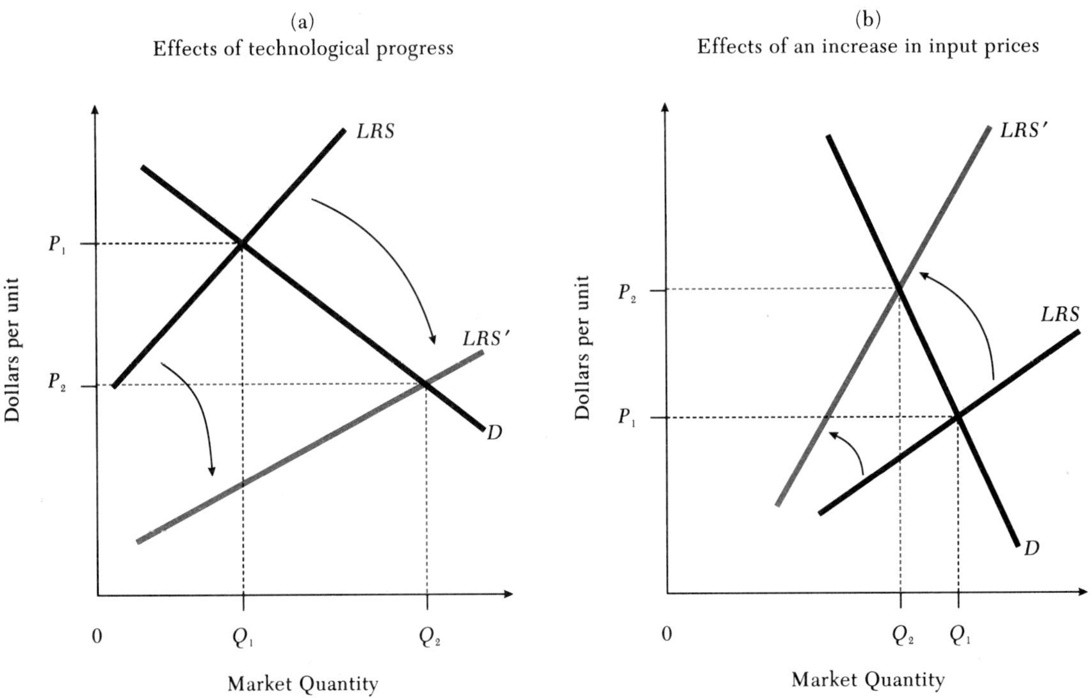

Figure 9.12

Shifts in the long-run industry supply curve.

tors other than expansion and contraction of the industry also shift the industry's long-run supply curve. The actions of the OPEC cartel in doubling and redoubling the world price of crude oil during the 1970s, for example, shifted up the long-run supply curves of many industries for which crude oil, or crude oil derivatives, are an important input. Given demand, this upward shift of the long-run supply curve increased the prices and reduced the consumption of many goods such as gasoline. This situation is illustrated in Figure 9.12(b).

Differential Rents

Let us now drop the assumption that all firms are identical. This simplifying assumption is quite unrealistic, even for industries whose other characteristics closely approximate those of pure competition. In agriculture, mining, and commercial fishing, for example, some farms are located on more fertile land than others, some mines have the advantage of extracting their ore from richer veins, and some fisheries have access to more plentiful lakes and rivers. What does this observation do to our conclusion that all firms earn zero economic profit in long-run equilibrium? Does it not imply, for example, that if Farmer Jones, who grows corn on land of average fertility, breaks even, then Farmer Brown, who grows corn on much more fertile land, will earn economic profits, even in the long run? Perhaps surprisingly, the answer to this question is no.

Suppose, for example, that Farmer Jones earns $25,000 per year while Farmer Brown earns $40,000 per year. Assuming that Jones and Brown are equally skilled as farmers, the $15,000 earnings differential reflects only the greater fertility of Brown's land. The fact that both Jones and Brown own their own land does not mean that their use of that land is free: Each could rent the land to someone else rather than farm it himself, and that foregone rent is an implicit opportunity cost that must be taken into account in determining their respective profits.

How much more annual rent do you think Brown could earn than Jones if each rented out his land rather than farming it himself? If you said $15,000, you are quite correct: In a competitive rental market, the owner of the superior land would capture the entire value of its greater fertility in the higher rent he would be able to charge. Farming the land himself rather than renting it out to some other farmer thus implicitly costs Brown $15,000 per year more than Jones. When this difference in implicit rental costs is taken into account, Brown's farm is no more profitable than Jones's.

"But," you might say with some skepticism, "common sense tells us that if Brown and Jones both work equally hard for a year doing the same thing, and if Brown ends up with $40,000 while Jones ends up with only $25,000, Brown is obviously better off. How can you say that his farm is not more profitable than Jones's?" Such skepticism is well founded, and common sense does indeed tell us that Brown is obviously better off in some sense than Jones. The problem is one of terminology: Given the definition of economic profit, Brown does not earn greater annual *profits* than Jones. He does, however, possess greater *wealth* than Jones, for he owns a more valuable piece of farmland. If Brown's extra wealth took the form of more money in the bank than Jones, he would earn more interest, but technically we would not refer to that extra interest as profit. Neither do we refer to Brown's additional income from his more fertile land as profit. The term economists apply to the returns, in excess of opportunity cost, to specialized and nonreproducible factors of production, such as Farmer Brown's more fertile land, is **economic rent**. The difference between Brown's and Jones' earnings is thus a reflection of *differential economic rents*.

Economic rent is income in excess of opportunity cost earned by a resource that is limited in supply.

Technological Change and Long-Run Adjustments

Long-run adjustments, both at the level of the individual firm and of the industry, are generally accompanied by technological change. As new firms enter an industry, they do so with more modern and technically advanced plants; as existing firms alter their scale of operations, they incorporate the latest technology in their new plant and equipment.

To illustrate the long-run effects of changing technology, let us assume that technological progress is a continuous process so that, at any point in time, many different "vintages" of plant and equipment are represented in the industry. Some firms possess the most modern and up-to-date plants, while others operate in older plants that embody obsolete technology. This is illustrated in Figure

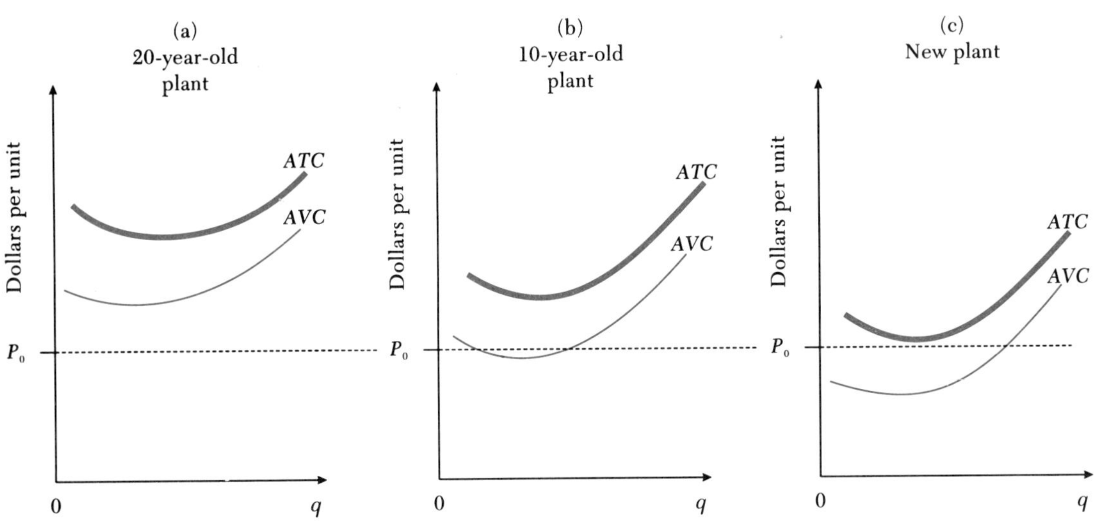

Figure 9.13

The effects of technological progress

9.13, which depicts the hypothetical cost curves associated with three different vintages of plant: a 20-year-old plant, a 10-year-old plant, and a new plant. Other things being equal, the newer the plant, the lower the costs of production.

Because entry will continue until the new plants embodying the latest technology can expect to just break even, competition will force the market price down to P_0, the minimum average total cost in those plants. The older vintage plants will therefore suffer economic losses as shown in the diagram. The 10-year-old plant would nonetheless continue in operation because it is covering its variable costs. To say that such a plant should be closed down because it is obsolete and "losing money" overlooks the fact that many of the costs associated with the plant are sunk and are therefore irrelevant for decisions regarding its continued operation in the short run. While it is true that such a plant must eventually be scrapped or replaced with a new one, it will continue in use as long as its variable costs can be covered. The 20-year-old plant, on the other hand, cannot even cover its variable operating costs and so it will be scrapped or replaced immediately.

An Application: Competition among the Supertankers *

We can use an application of the preceding analysis to consolidate and illustrate some of the major points we have been making.

Supertankers, the largest ships afloat, are the principal means of transporting crude oil from exporting countries in the Mideast and elsewhere to countries

*This example is based on information contained in "Perfect Competition Among the Supertankers," Chapter 14 in Robert Paul Thomas, *Microeconomic Applications* (Wadsworth, 1981).

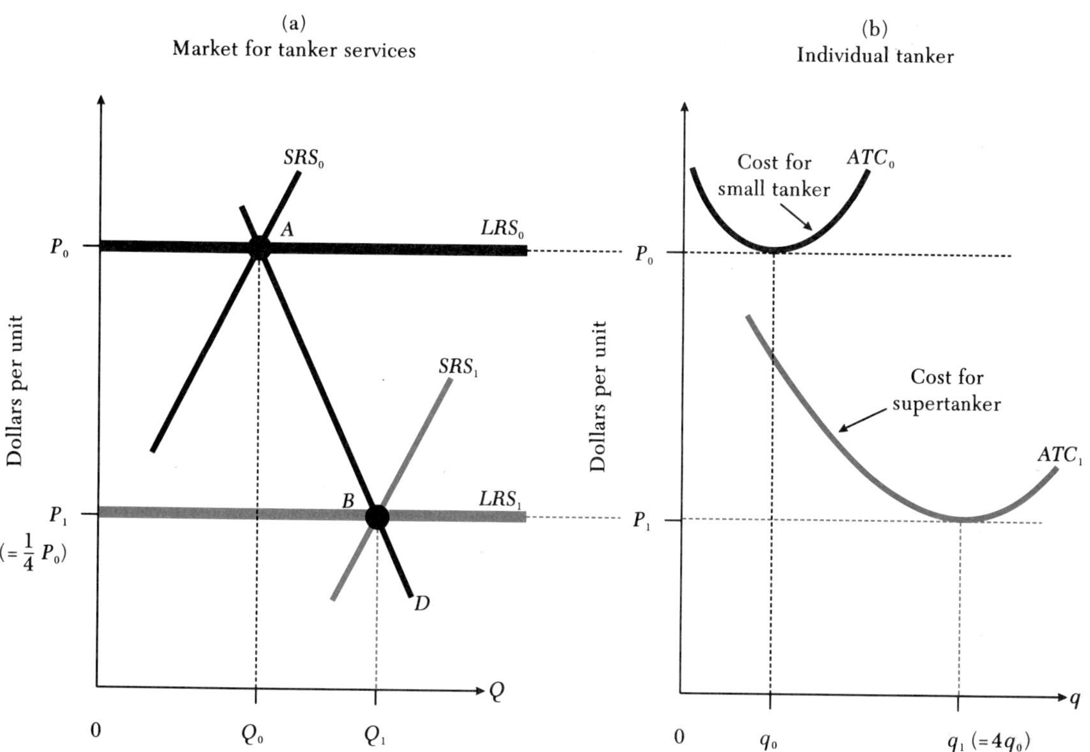

Figure 9.14

Adjustment to supertanker technology.

where it is refined and consumed. The first supertanker was launched in 1967; it had four times the capacity and was four times as efficient as the older, smaller ships which then made up the world's tanker fleet.

Figure 9.14 illustrates the impact of the new supertanker technology on the market for tanker services. Point *A* in part (a) on the left-hand side of the diagram represents the market's long-run equilibrium before the advent of the supertanker. In part (b) on the right-hand side, we can see that the equilibrium market price P_0 is just sufficient to cover the minimum average total cost, along ATC_0, of running one of the smaller tankers then in existence. (The horizontal long-run supply curve, LRS_0, implies that the fleet could have been expanded or contracted at a constant cost.) The new supertanker technology introduced a new average total cost curve, ATC_1, along which costs are minimized at four times the output rate and one-fourth the cost as under the old technology.

At the original market price, shipping crude oil by supertanker was clearly more profitable than shipping it in the smaller, less efficient ships. Our model predicts that those ships would be phased out and replaced by an expanding fleet of supertankers, and that is exactly what happened. In 1967 there was one supertanker afloat; in 1969 there were 63; in 1971 there were 287; and in 1973 there were 393, with about another 500 under construction or on order. Had this entry continued with no further disturbances, additions to the supertanker fleet

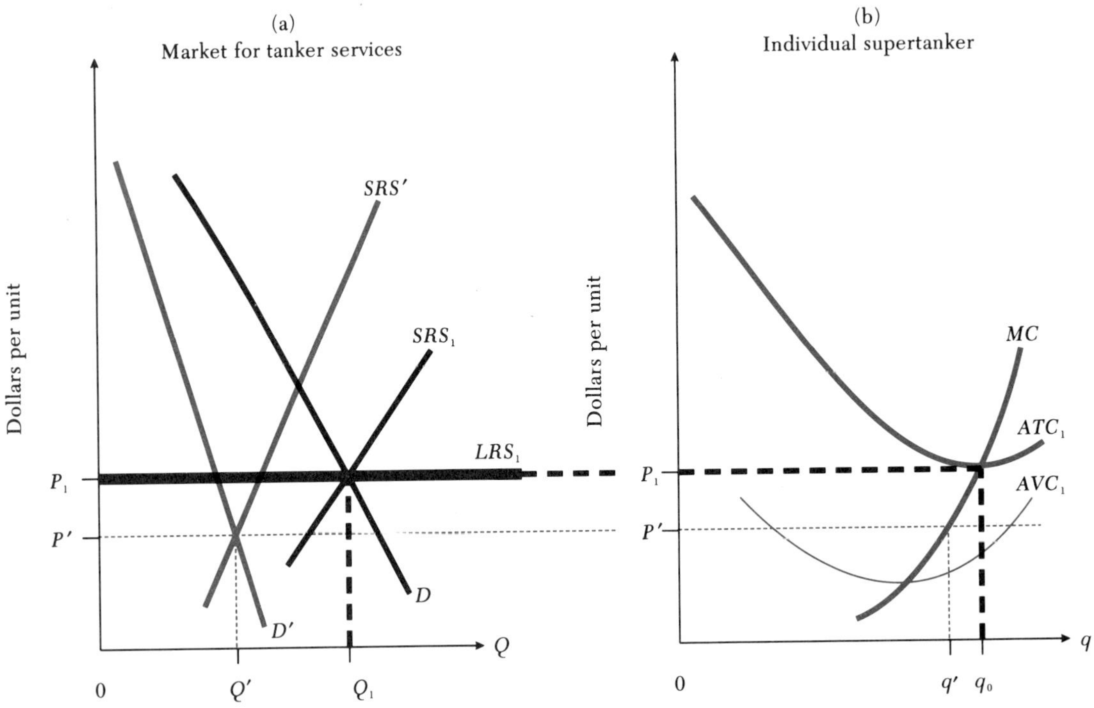

Figure 9.15

Impact of a fall in demand for tanker services.

would have continued to shift the short-run market supply curve rightward to SRS_1, decreasing the price of tanker services to P_1, a price that would just cover the minimum average total cost of operating a supertanker. The new long-run supply curve LRS_1 reflects this lower level of costs.

Before this new equilibrium was reached, however, the market for supertanker services was hit by a major shock. In late 1973, when the OPEC cartel drastically cut production of crude oil, the demand for the services of supertankers was suddenly and sharply reduced. The result is illustrated in Figure 9.15. The curves SRS_1, LRS_1 and D in part (a) and ATC_1 in part (b) are the same as in Figure 9.14. The short-run supply curve labelled SRS' represents the one to which the industry had adjusted in 1973. When demand suddenly fell from D to D', the price of tanker services fell along this supply curve to P', well below the level necessary to cover the cost of operating a supertanker.

Our model predicts both a short-run and a long-run response to the lower price. In the short-run, some supertankers already in service would continue to operate at a loss as long as price covered their average variable costs. Most of the costs associated with owning a supertanker are fixed possession costs. Perhaps the most significant of these is the enormous interest cost (either explicit or implicit) of the owner's multimillion dollar investment. Variable costs, which include the cost of the fuel to run the ship and the wages of its crew, are small relative to fixed costs. Indeed, the (minimum) average variable cost of operating a tanker was only about 30 percent of the (minimum) average total cost. Because the lower market price for tanker services covered these average variable costs, many supertankers continued to ply the seas at a loss. For example, one owner whose tanker cost him $2 million per year leased it to Exxon for only $900,000 per year, an amount that was sufficient to cover his variable costs.

The long-run response to the lower price was exit. Orders for new ships were cancelled and existing ships were scrapped—more than 200 in 1975 alone. Fortunes were lost as tankers were sold for scrap, returning their owners only a fraction of their original, multimillion dollar investments.

THE NORMATIVE IDEAL?

The model of pure competition is often used as the normative standard against which real-world markets are evaluated. This is because long-run equilibrium under conditions of pure competition satisfies some important conditions necessary for economic efficiency. Competition forces each firm in a purely competitive industry to minimize its long-run average cost by producing at the lowest cost rate of output in the most efficient scale of plant so that the industry's output is produced at the smallest possible cost. Moreover, the conditions of pure competition insure that the industry's output always tends toward that for which the marginal value of the last unit produced is equal to its marginal cost. As we saw in Chapter 4, this maximizes the value of the goods we produce with our scarce resources.

Some Qualifications

There is more to economic efficiency than producing the right amount of output at the lowest possible cost, however. Even if the world were purely competitive (which it is not), that in itself would not guarantee economic efficiency. When production and consumption of some good generate negative externalities, such as pollution, all costs are not captured and accounted for in the marketplace. Under such conditions, even a purely competitive world would not achieve complete efficiency. In addition, public goods may not be produced in purely competitive markets even if their value exceeds their costs. As we have seen, because nonpayers cannot be excluded from consuming such goods once they are provided, producers cannot charge for them and therefore have little economic incentive to supply them.

Perhaps most importantly of all, the model of pure competition focuses only on *static* conditions that minimize costs and allocate resources efficiently at a given moment in time. It tells us nothing about the kind of market conditions that promote the kind of *dynamic* efficiency that leads to innovation and economic progress. Such efficiency is a product of *entrepreneurial competition* whereby firms experiment with new products and new technologies in an attempt to discover new and better ways of meeting consumer wants. As we shall see, it may well be that some departures from the purely competitive "ideal" are more conducive to such progress.

Looking Ahead

Real-world markets are not, nor can they ever be, purely competitive, for pure competition is quite literally a figment of the economist's imagination. Remember, however, that the purpose of any model is to abstract from the details of reality, to simplify it and make it intellectually manageable. In this sense, the model of pure competition is very abstract. Nonetheless it provides the essential starting point for the study of other market structures and other forms of competition. Many of the tools we have developed in this chapter—the determination of a producer's profit-maximizing output by a comparison of marginal revenue and marginal cost, the short-run decision to operate or shut down, the effects of entry and exit, the analysis of rent differentials, and the effects of technological change, to name a few—are applicable to the analysis of firms and industries regardless of their particular market structure.

CHAPTER SUMMARY

1. A *purely competitive industry* is one in which there are large numbers of sellers, each small relative to the market, and in which the product is homogeneous, information is free, and entry and exit are unrestricted.

2. The combination of large numbers of small sellers, a homogeneous product, and free information imply that the individual firm in a purely competitive market is a *price taker*. A price taker can sell as much or as little as it wishes at the price set by market supply and market demand, but it cannot influence that price. In effect, it faces a perfectly elastic (horizontal) demand curve at the market price.

3. For the price taker, the market price is also the marginal revenue from the sale of each unit of output. As long as price is greater than average variable cost, its profits are maximized (or losses minimized) at the output rate for which marginal revenue and marginal cost are equal. If price is less than average variable cost, the firm will minimize short-run losses by shutting down.

4. The *short-run supply curve* of the individual firm is its marginal cost curve above the minimum average variable cost.

5. In the long run, positive economic profits attract new entrants into the industry, and economic losses force some firms to exit from the industry. Entry and exit of firms insure that pure profits and losses always tend toward zero in the long run.

6. If entry and exit have no effect on costs, the industry is a *constant cost industry* with a *perfectly elastic (flat) long-run supply curve*. If entry raises (lowers) costs, the industry is an *increasing (a decreasing) cost industry* with an *upward (downward) sloped long-run supply curve*.

7. At any given time, there will be variations in returns among firms because of differential *economic rent* earned by specialized and nonreproducible factors of production and because of different vintages of plant and equipment reflecting the effects of technological progress.

8. From the standpoint of *static efficiency*, the purely competitive industry is the normative ideal. However, the model of pure competition has nothing to say about the entrepreneurial competition that leads to *dynamic efficiency*.

Key Terms and Concepts

pure competition
homogeneous product
price taker
industry
marginal revenue
shut down
firm's short-run supply curve
short-run industry supply curve
long-run industry supply curve
constant cost industry
increasing cost industry
decreasing cost industry
economic rent

Questions for Thought and Discussion

1. Buyers, as well as sellers, may find themselves to be price takers in certain markets. Can you think of some markets in which you, as a buyer, are a price taker? Can you think of some in which you can influence the price of the goods you buy?

2. Refer to Table 9.2 and Figures 9.2 and 9.3 for the following questions.
   a. What would Acme's short-run output and profits (or losses) be if the market price for gizmos were \$15? \$12? \$9? \$7?
   b. Suppose that the gizmo industry is a constant cost industry and that Acme is already operating in its most efficient scale of plant. What is the long-run supply price of gizmos?
   c. Assume there are 100 identical firms (including Acme) in the gizmo industry. If 2,000 gizmos per day are demanded at a market price of \$18, would the market be in equilibrium at that price?

3. "A producer's marginal cost tells him *how much* to produce; his average cost tells him *whether* to produce at all." Explain.

4. The egg industry comes very close to being purely competitive. Using the theory developed in this chapter, see if you can reconstruct what happened in that industry

(in both the long run and the short run) when it became widely known that eggs are a source of cholesterol, which may contribute to heart disease.

5. Assume that a purely competitive industry is initially in long-run equilibrium. Compare the long-run and short-run effects of an increase in fire insurance rates (a fixed cost) for firms in the industry with those of an increase in the price of the raw materials (a variable input) they use in production.

6. Suppose that you own a yacht that you charter to adventurous vacationers. You financed the purchase of the yacht with a 10 percent loan for $200,000, so your interest payments are $20,000 per year (which works out to about $55 per day). Insurance on the yacht is $15,000 per year (or about $40 per day). It costs $400 per day for the fuel and crew to operate the yacht.

   a. If you anticipate that you will be able to charter your yacht for only 200 days each year, what is the minimum daily charter rate that will keep you in business?
   b. What is the minimum daily charter rate that you will accept to take a party of vacationers out to sea?
   c. What will you do if the highest charter rate you can get turns out to be between your answers to parts a and b?

CHAPTER 10

Price Setters: Market Power and Monopoly

A **price setter** is a seller with some control over the price of its product.

Contrary to the assumptions of the purely competitive model, most firms are not price takers, but **price setters**. A price setter is a seller with some individual control over the price of its product. Unlike the price taker which faces a demand curve that is perfectly elastic (horizontal) at a price determined by market forces beyond its control, the price setter faces a downward sloped demand curve for its product. That demand curve in turn constrains the price setter's control over price: It can charge a higher price, but only if it is willing to sell a smaller amount of output; or it can sell more output, but only if it is willing to accept a lower price. For most price setters, the trade-off between price and output along the demand curve is an uncertain one, and the process of selecting a "best" price is one of trial and error.*

Market power is the ability of a seller to control the price of its product—that is, the ability to act as a price setter.

Economists refer to the individual firm's control over the price of its product as **market power**. Market power is always a matter of degree: The more competition faced by the firm, the less its discretion in setting price and the less its market power. Conversely, the less competition faced by the firm, the greater its discretion in setting price and the greater its market power. The extreme case of a price setter facing no significant competition, and therefore possessing a great

*The term *price searcher* rather than *price setter* is often used to reflect this trial-and-error process. However, since we use the term *search* for other purposes in this chapter, we shall avoid confusion by using the term price setter.

deal of market power, is that of *monopoly*. Although, by definition, all price setters have some market power, very few qualify as monopolists.

In this chapter we analyze the determinants of market power and how it affects price and output in price setters' markets. We also examine some of normative implications of market power and monopoly.

SOURCES AND DETERMINANTS OF MARKET POWER

As we saw in Chapter 9, the purely competitive firm is a price taker because there are perfect substitutes for its product, because buyers have costless access to those substitutes, and because the firm is so small in relation to the total market that variations in its output have a negligible effect on market price. If any of these conditions are violated, the firm will be a price setter. Accordingly, there are three basic sources of market power for an individual seller: a product that is *differentiated* from that of other sellers, the existence of *search costs* for buyers, and *large size* relative to the total market. In addition, sellers might jointly exercise market power through *collusion*.

Differentiated Products

Differentiated products are products that are substitutes for one another but are not identical in the eyes of buyers.

Differentiated products are products that, while good substitutes for one another, are not identical in the eyes of buyers. Moreover the perceived differences among such products are the basis for differences in buyer preferences. Product differentiation can be due to physical differences, such as variations in quality, reliability, or styling, or it can be the result of differences in the conditions of sale, such as service or convenience. It can even be based on differences that exist only in the mind of the buyer: If buyers think there is a difference between Clorox bleach and Purex bleach, then Clorox and Purex are differentiated products—even if their chemical composition is identical.

The seller of a differentiated product generally has some market power simply because there are no perfect substitutes for its product. Aim and Crest are both toothpastes, for example, but they are not identical products in the eyes of most consumers. Because at least some consumers prefer the taste of Aim to that of Crest, or because some believe that Aim cleans their teeth or freshens their breath better than Crest, the producers of Aim may be able to charge a higher price than the producers of Crest and not lose all of their customers to Crest.

Similarly, a supermarket has some discretion in pricing because its unique combination of location, service, and convenience differentiate it from other supermarkets carrying otherwise identical products. Or a department store may be able to charge a higher price than a discount store for the same product because it provides more personal service, a more liberal return policy, or a more elegant shopping environment.

The important point is that product differentiation that appeals to differences in buyer preferences gives the seller some control over price: The seller of a differentiated product can charge a higher price and still retain some customers who prefer its product to the products of its competitors. Similarly, by charging a lower price, it might be able to attract some customers who would otherwise buy its competitors' products.

Search Costs

Even if there are perfect substitutes for its product, a seller may still have some market power if it is costly for buyers to find and purchase those substitutes—in other words, if shopping is costly. One supermarket may be able to charge a few cents more than another for the same brand of coffee simply because few coffee buyers find it worthwhile to shop around in search of a lower price. Or perhaps the supermarket may be able to charge more for the coffee because it charges less for ground beef, and the shoppers who come in to buy ground beef do not find it worth going to another supermarket just to save a few cents on a pound of coffee.

Search costs are the costs of finding and taking advantage of the best price or other product characteristics.

The costs of shopping for the best price are a form of **search costs**. As the preceding examples suggest, search costs include not only the costs of taking advantage of price differences—for example, the costs of travelling to the location where some good is available at the lowest price—but also the information costs of finding out about those price differences in the first place. In general, the higher the search costs relative to the price of the product, the less the incentive of potential buyers to shop around for a better deal, and consequently the greater the market power exercised by the seller.

Large Size Relative to the Market

A seller that produces a significant share of the total market supply of its product may be able to influence market price. For example, Saudi Arabia exercises market power in the international market for crude oil, not because Saudi oil is differentiated from Libyan oil or Mexican oil, nor because there are search costs of finding a lower priced seller, but because Saudi Arabia's production decisions have a significant impact on world supply, and hence on world crude oil prices.

Collusion

Finally, market power may result from collusion among otherwise independent sellers. In a market with fifty or a hundred relatively small sellers of a homogeneous product, no individual seller acting alone could exert a significant influence over the market price. However, if a number of those sellers coordinate their production and pricing decisions through collusion instead of competing with one another, together they may wield market power.

Market Power and Elasticity

Whatever its source, market power is never absolute, for every price setter is still constrained by the demand for its product. Other things being equal, therefore, charging a higher price always imposes a penalty in the form of lost sales.

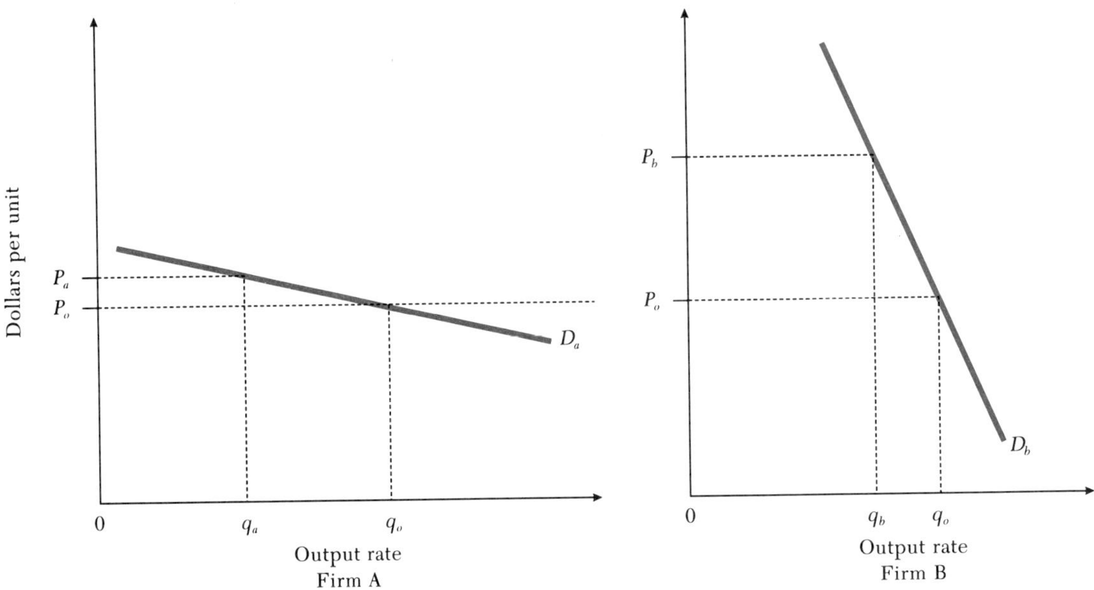

Figure 10.1
Elasticity and market power

The size of this penalty—that is, the degree to which a higher price reduces sales—depends on the price elasticity of demand. Other things being equal, the less elastic the demand for the product of an individual seller at the competitive price, the greater that seller's market power.

The relation between demand elasticity and market power is illustrated in Figure 10.1. The curves labelled D_a and D_b are the demand curves for the products of Firm A and Firm B, respectively, and P_0 is the competitive price for each.* Firm A faces a relatively elastic demand curve: Even a small increase in A's price above the competitive level—say to P_a—would result in a substantial loss of sales. Firm B, on the other hand, faces a very inelastic demand and thus can raise its price substantially above the competitive level—say to P_b—and still experience only a relatively small decline in sales. Because the penalty to Firm B of raising its price above the competitive level is less than the penalty to Firm A, Firm B has greater market power than Firm A.

This relation between market power and demand elasticity is directly related to the sources of market power just discussed. In particular, demand will be less elastic and a seller's market power will be greater (1) the greater the degree of product differentiation (that is, the fewer good substitutes there are for that sell-

*The competitive price is the price equal to minimum long-run average cost, that is, the price which would prevail in long-run, purely competitive equilibrium. We compare monopoly power by measuring elasticity at that price because, as we have seen, elasticity generally varies along the demand curve, and because the degree of monopoly power possessed by a seller is measured relative to pure competition. In other words, since a purely competitive price taker has zero monopoly power, pure competition provides a natural base from which to measure the monopoly power of a price setter.

er's product), (2) the higher buyers' search costs relative to the price of the product, and (3) the greater the seller's share of total market output.

Market Power in the Long Run: Entry Costs

In 1948 the Xerox Corporation introduced the first commercially useful dry copying process. Because the process was patented by Xerox, no one else was legally permitted to use it. As a result, there were no good substitutes for Xerox copiers: Carbon paper and a few "wet" copying processes, which produced literally wet copies of the original, were about the only alternatives. Xerox thus found itself with considerable market power, and it used that market power to maintain correspondingly high prices and profit levels. In time, however, as Xerox's patents expired and as new copier technologies were developed, IBM, Kodak, and many other manufacturers introduced their own dry copying machines and challenged Xerox in the lucrative office copier market. Their entry quickly reduced Xerox's market power, thereby forcing its prices and once substantial profit margins down to competitive levels.

This example conveys an important lesson: To the extent that market power is profitable, it contains the seeds of its own destruction in the competition it will attract from new entrants. Profitable market power can persist, therefore, only to the extent that the emergence of new competition is prevented or delayed either by *natural cost advantages of incumbent firms*—that is, firms already in the industry—or by *artificial entry restrictions*.

Natural Advantages of Incumbent Firms

Entry into an industry is never literally free. Any new business venture, whether intended to challenge incumbent firms at their own game or to strike out in an entirely new direction, requires some initial investment. This investment may include the costs of developing a new product or service and of setting up a system of production and distribution. While some portion of the initial investment can usually be recovered in the event of failure—for example, a physical plant and its equipment can often be resold—many of the expenditures required by entry are not recoverable and are thus true opportunity costs from the standpoint of the prospective entrant. To view all such costs as restrictions on entry, however, is misleading. While it is true that a new entrant may have to borrow funds to purchase the same plant and equipment that an incumbent firm already owns, the incumbent's implicit costs of continued possession are no less an opportunity cost than the new entrant's explicit interest payments. Entry is costly for the newcomer, but so also is staying in business costly for the incumbent.

To isolate those costs peculiar to entry itself, we must therefore focus on certain **natural cost advantages of incumbent firms** relative to new entrants. There are a number of potential sources of such advantages.

Natural cost advantages of incumbent firms are factors that enable firms already in an industry to produce at lower cost than new entrants.

Economies of Scale The existence of economies of scale implies that a producer must attain some minimum scale of operations to achieve the lowest possible average cost. In Figure 10.2, for example, the firm must attain a scale of

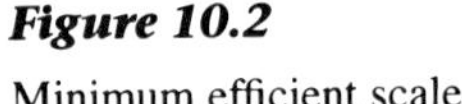

Figure 10.2

Minimum efficient scale

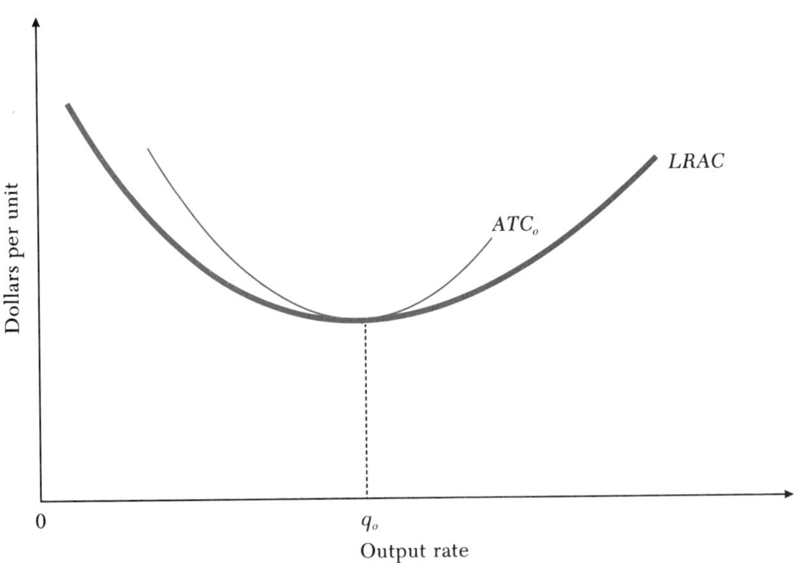

operations consistent with the rate of output given by q_0 to minimize unit costs. Incumbent firms, especially those that have survived for some time in the industry, have probably already attained an efficient scale. The new entrant, however, may have to start small, especially in markets where products are differentiated and brand identity is important. At least initially, therefore, economies of scale may force the new entrant to operate with higher unit costs than incumbents.

Experience Effects As we saw in Chapter 8, in any production process costs fall with experience. An incumbent with substantial cumulative past production experience may therefore have acquired valuable, cost-reducing know-how not immediately available to a new entrant.

Differences in the Cost of Capital As we have seen, the pattern of interest rates established in the capital markets reflects, in part, the market's assessment of risk. To the extent that the capital markets view entry as a risky venture, the cost of financial capital to the new entrant may be higher than its cost to incumbents. This is especially likely when the entrant is literally a new firm rather than an established firm branching into a new market.

Although this cost of entry is sometimes said to reflect "imperfections in the capital market," the actual case is quite the opposite. Only about half of all new firms remain in business beyond 5 years after their formation; the rest fail. If lenders could tell in advance which new entrants would succeed and which would fail, the former would be at no disadvantage relative to incumbents in raising financial capital. But of course lenders don't have crystal balls. To argue, therefore, that a *potentially* successful entrant pays "too high" a risk premium because of "imperfections" in the capital market ignores the fact that information about the future is costly and incomplete. Indeed, risk premiums exist, not because the capital markets are imperfect, but because those markets are doing the best job they can with the imperfect information that is available.

All of these natural entry costs can be overcome in time if the new entrant produces a product that is superior to the products of incumbents. Such an entrant will eventually capture enough of the market to overcome the incumbents' scale and experience advantages, and its capital costs will fall as risk premiums are adjusted in light of its success. Although entry may be delayed in the short run, therefore, only superior economic performance by incumbents in providing the products that people demand at the lowest possible cost can prevent entry in the long run.

Artificial Restrictions on Entry

Artificial entry restrictions are restrictions on entry unrelated to any cost or efficiency advantages of the firms already in an industry.

In addition to the natural costs of entry, there are often restrictions on entry unrelated to any cost or efficiency advantages of incumbents. These **artificial entry restrictions** fall into two categories: legal, government imposed restrictions and illegal, private coercion.

Legal Restrictions Perhaps the most frequently encountered restrictions on entry are those imposed by government. Examples include patents, license requirements, and exclusive government franchises. Both Xerox and Polaroid, for example, were able to maintain substantial market power as a result of patent protection. Government license and certification requirements limit entry into industries as diverse as banking, broadcasting, and marriage counselling. Amtrak and the U.S. Postal Service are examples of exclusive government franchises, as are most local public utilities, such as local telephone and power companies.

Illegal Private Coercion There are also private means, other than superior efficiency, to exclude potential competitors from a market. Organized crime, for example, uses violence (or threats of violence) to deter entry into its markets in gambling, drugs, and other illegal activities. Such tactics are the essence of "criminal" monopoly.

Potential Entry

Even if actual entry never takes place, the very threat of *potential entry* can reduce the market power of incumbents. By raising its price too high above unit costs, the incumbent signals the existence of pure profits and, in effect, invites entry and increased competition. Under such circumstances, the best strategy for the price setter may be to charge a lower price than it would in the absence of potential entry. If it has a cost advantage over potential entrants, it will still earn pure profits while deterring entry. For example, if the incumbent's average cost is $10 per unit compared to an entrants' $11 per unit, the incumbent can charge, say, $10.50 per unit, earn $0.50 per unit in pure profits, and not attract entry. As this example suggests, the smaller the natural cost advantage of the incumbent, the greater the effectiveness of potential entry in reducing market power.

Monopoly

When does a seller possess sufficient market power to be considered a literal *monopolist*? Most dictionaries define a monopolist as the sole seller of a product. According to this definition, however, virtually every seller would be a monopolist because the product of each is in some way unique. General Motors would be considered a monopolist, for example, because it is the only seller of Chevrolets. Even the gas station at the corner of Sixth and Main is a monopolist as the only seller of gasoline at that particular location. Clearly, however, since consumers have access to many substitutes for Chevrolets, as well as for the gasoline sold by the station at Sixth and Main, neither General Motors nor the local gas station is a monopolist in any useful sense of the term.

To get at the essence of monopoly, we must therefore rule out competition from producers of close substitutes. What makes markets competitive is the access of buyers to *substitutes* for the product of any one seller. In the case of pure competition, there are many sellers of goods that are *perfect substitutes* for one another, and the market is open to the entry of more such sellers in the long run. As the antithesis of pure competition, therefore, pure **monopoly** requires that there be a *single seller* of a product for which there are *no close substitutes* in the short run and *substantial entry costs* that close the market to new competition in the long run.

A **monopoly** is a single seller of a product with no close substitutes in a market with substantial entry costs.

In spite of this seemingly straightforward definition, the concept of monopoly inevitably becomes ambiguous when we try to apply it to concrete situations. How close, for example, is a "close substitute?" Is copper a close substitute for aluminum? Is electricity or coal a close substitute for natural gas? Is the telephone a close substitute for mail, and vice-versa? How difficult or costly must entry be for a market to be considered effectively closed? Is it sufficient that entry costs keep out new competitors for a month? A year? A decade? Because there are no clear answers to such questions, it is best to think of a pure monopoly simply as an extreme, limiting case in which the competition faced by a seller is negligible. About as close as we come in practice to the case of pure monopoly are the local public utilities that provide telephone service; distribute water, gas, and electricity; and whose exclusive government franchises protect them from new competition.*

The Value of Exclusive Rights

As the preceding discussion suggests, enduring market power, whether or not associated with literal monopoly, is based on some exclusive, legal right that prevents competitors from exactly duplicating the price setter's product. Examples of such rights include the government franchises already mentioned as well as licenses, patents, and other forms of legal protection from competition. To the extent that such rights increase the earnings of their holders, they are valuable economic assets.

*Most public utilities are regulated by government agencies, however, so that their behavior does not conform to the analysis of the unregulated monopolist developed in this chapter. We discuss public utility regulation and its effects in Chapter 13.

To illustrate, consider the hypothetical case of Mona Poley, inventor and patent holder for the amazing Doodad, the miracle household tool with a million-and-one uses. Mona's Doodad patent protects her from direct competition and thus enables her to earn $5,000 per year more than she would earn if she did not have patent protection. Since patent protection in the United States lasts for 17 years, the value of Mona's patent in a competitive market is equal to the present value of $5,000 per year for 17 years. Assuming an interest rate of 10 percent, this is approximately $40,000. Mona can either produce and market Doodads herself, thus taking her profits in the form of a flow of $5,000 each year for the next 17 years, or she can sell the patent to someone else for its equivalent $40,000 present value and take her profit in a single lump sum.

Note the close parallel between Mona's ownership of the Doodad patent and Farmer Jones's ownership of superior farmland that we discussed in the previous chapter. Each enjoys extra earnings because each owns something that cannot be duplicated by their competitors. In the case of Mona's patent, duplication is prohibited by law; in the case of Farmer Jones's land, it is prevented by the natural scarcity of fertile farm land. Like the extra earnings Farmer Jones enjoys because of his more fertile farm land, therefore, the extra $5,000 per year that Mona earns because of her patent is an *economic rent*. Indeed, what we often loosely refer to as monopoly profit is technically not profit at all but economic rent collected by the owners of exclusive legal rights.

Estimates of the economic value of a variety of exclusive rights, most of them rights granted by government, are shown in Table 10.1. As with Mona's patent,

Table 10.1

The value of monopoly rights

EXCLUSIVE RIGHT	SOURCE	MARKET VALUE	YEAR
New York taxicab licenses	City of New York	$68,000	1980
Television station licenses	Federal Communications Commission	$2–50 million	1979
Trucking rights per route	Interstate Commerce Commission	$5,000–2.5 million per route	1979
American League baseball franchises	Major League Baseball	$20–25 million	1981
Tobacco growing rights (per acre)	U.S. Department of Agriculture	$1,500–3,000	1960
New York Stock Exchange seats	Securities and Exchange Commission	$82,000–212,000	1979

Source: Heinz Kohler, *Intermediate Microeconomics: Theory and Applications* (Chicago: Scott, Foresman and Company, 1982), p. 344.

the values given in the table reflect the present value of the future profits that the corresponding right is expected to generate.

THE POSITIVE ECONOMICS OF MARKET POWER

The model of price setting behavior that we are about to develop focuses on the fundamental logic of price determination by an individual seller with market power. As such, it is applicable to any price setter, whether a pure monopolist or a firm whose market power is substantially limited by competition. It is not necessarily a literal description of the way business firms actually set prices, however, for they rarely have at their disposal all of the information we assume in our model. In the absence of such information, they must search for the most profitable prices to charge by using educated guesses and rules of thumb. For example, a department store may set the retail price of new merchandise by using a standard 30 percent markup over its wholesale cost. If the markup turns out to be too high, so that the merchandise does not move off the shelves quickly enough, the store may then put it on sale at a lower price. If the merchandise is snapped up immediately at the standard markup price, the store may decide to use a higher markup the next time around. Actual price setting is therefore often a process of trial and error. Whatever the process, however, once a firm finds the most profitable price, that price will be the one that satisfies the conditions of the model we are about to develop.

Demand and Marginal Revenue for the Price Setter

To illustrate the nature of the profit-maximizing pricing decision, let us consider our hypothetical Mona Poley. Columns 1 and 2 of Table 10.2 show the demand schedule for Mona's Doodads, and column 3 shows the corresponding total revenue (price times quantity) that Mona would receive at each price. Column 4 shows Mona's *marginal revenue*, the change in total revenue that results from each additional Doodad sold. Notice that, except for the first unit, *the marginal revenue associated with each quantity is less than the corresponding demand price for that quantity*. For example, Mona can sell 6 Doodads per day if she charges a price of $9, but her marginal revenue from the sale of the sixth Doodad is only $4, not $9.

To see why marginal revenue is less than price, let's assume that Mona initially charges a price of $10, sells 5 Doodads per day, and thus earns daily revenues of $50. If she wants to increase her sales to 6 Doodads per day, she must reduce her price to $9. The $9 price applies not just to the additional (sixth) Doodad Mona sells, however, but also to the 5 she could have continued to sell at the $10 price. Although the sixth Doodad itself adds $9 to her daily revenues,

Table 10.2

Demand, revenues, and cost for Mona Poley's Doodad Factory

DEMAND		REVENUES		COSTS		
1	2	3	4	5	6	7
Price (P)	*Quantity Demanded (q)*	*Total Revenue (TR)*	*Marginal Revenue (MR)*	*Total Cost (TC)*	*Marginal Cost (MC)*	*Total Profit (+) or Loss (−)*
$15	0	$ 0	$—	$20	$—	−20
14	1	14	14	21	1	− 7
13	2	26	12	23	2	+ 3
12	3	36	10	26	3	+10
11	4	44	8	30	4	+14
10	5	50	6	35	5	+15
9	6	54	4	41	6	+13
8	7	56	2	48	7	+ 8
7	8	56	0	57	9	− 1
6	9	54	−2	65	11	−11
5	10	50	−4	78	13	−28
4	11	44	−6	93	15	−49
3	12	36	−8	110	17	−74

selling the other 5 for $9 rather than $10 subtracts $5 from those revenues. The net effect is that Mona's revenue rises by $4 (= $9 − $5) from $50 per day to $54 per day. The marginal revenue contributed by the sixth Doodad is therefore $4.

The relation between Mona's demand curve and her marginal revenue is shown in Figure 10.3 on page 238. Both price and marginal revenue are measured along the vertical axis. The price at which any quantity of output can be sold is shown by the demand curve, whereas the marginal revenue corresponding to that quantity can be read from the marginal revenue (*MR*) curve. Because marginal revenue is less than price, the marginal revenue curve lies below the demand curve. For each demand curve there is a corresponding marginal revenue curve.

In the special case of a linear demand curve, there is a simple rule of thumb for locating the marginal revenue curve: The marginal revenue curve is also a straight line, and it has the same vertical intercept, but twice the slope, as the demand curve. The marginal revenue curve corresponding to a linear demand curve therefore lies halfway between the demand curve and the vertical (price) axis as shown in Figure 10.4 on page 239.

Profit Maximization for the Price Setter

Let us see how Mona Poley can maximize the profitability of her Doodad monopoly. The basic logic of profit maximization is the same for the price setter as it was for the price taker. It involves a comparison of marginal revenue and marginal cost for each possible increase in the rate of output.

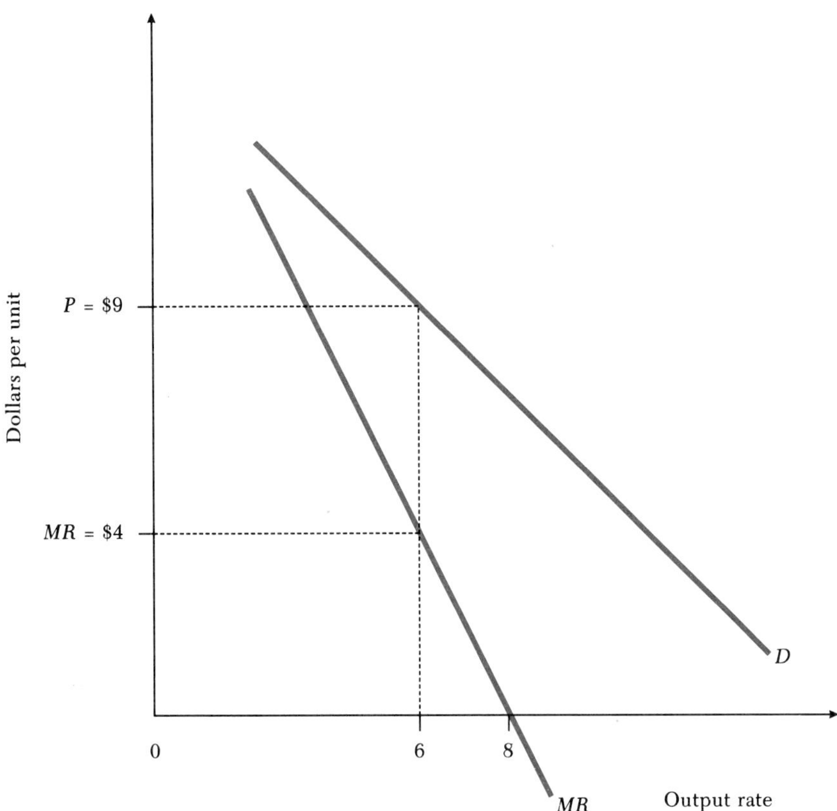

Figure 10.3

Demand and marginal revenue for Mona Poley's Doodads

Columns 5 and 6 of Table 10.2 show Mona's total costs and marginal costs, respectively, for output rates from 0 to 12 Doodads per day. Mona's maximum profit is attained at a price of $10 and an output (and sales) rate of 5 Doodads per day because the marginal revenue contributed by each additional Doodad up to, and including, the fifth exceeds its marginal cost. Each therefore increases total profit (or reduces losses) by an amount equal to the difference between marginal revenue and marginal cost. The fifth Doodad, for example, adds $6 to revenues but only $5 to costs. It therefore contributes an additional $1 to Mona's profit. (You can verify this by looking at column 7 in the table.)

Producing more than 5 Doodads per day, on the other hand, reduces Mona's profit because marginal cost exceeds marginal revenue. Producing a sixth Doodad per day, for example, results in only $4 of additional revenues but $6 of additional costs, thus reducing Mona's daily profit by $2. (Again, column 7 verifies that this is the case.)

The same rule therefore applies to the price setter as to the price taker, namely: Profits are maximized by producing all units for which marginal revenue at least covers marginal cost and none for which the reverse is true.

Figure 10.4

Locating the marginal revenue curve when the demand curve is linear

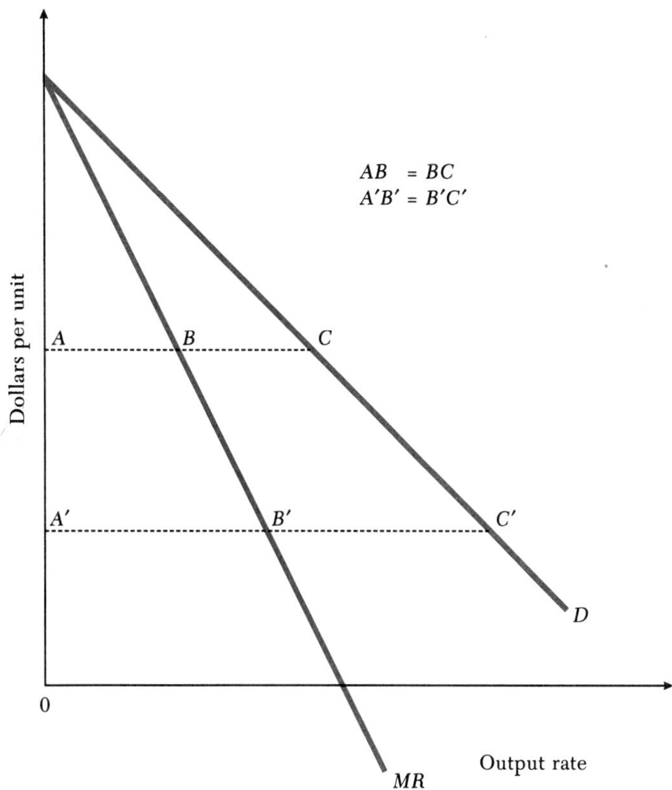

The only difference between the price taker's and the price setter's profit-maximizing output decision is that, for the price setter, marginal revenue is not the same as price.

Determining the Profit-Maximizing Price and Output Graphically

The price setter's profit maximum is illustrated in Figure 10.5 on the next page. Graphically, the marginal revenue curve lies above the marginal cost curve for output rates up to q_0. Each additional unit of output up to q_0 thus increases profits because the marginal revenue from its sale exceeds the marginal cost of producing it. Each additional unit of output beyond q_0 reduces profit because its marginal cost exceeds its marginal revenue. The profit-maximizing rate of output is therefore q_0. It is determined by the intersection of the marginal revenue and marginal cost curves at point E. The profit-maximizing price is P_0, the demand price corresponding to output q_0.

If we include the average total cost curve (ATC) in the diagram, as we have

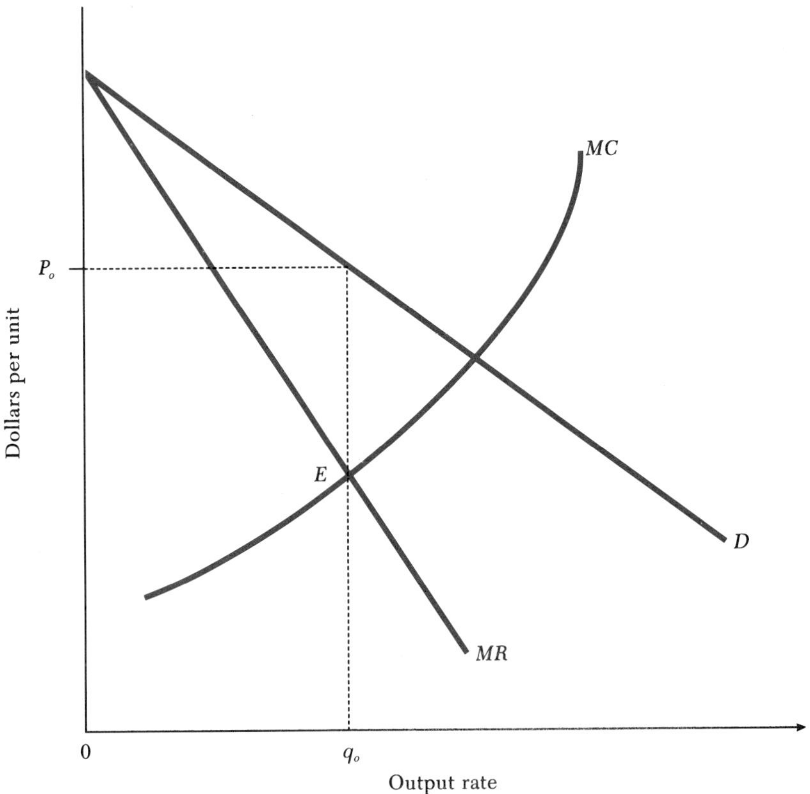

Figure 10.5

Profit-maximizing price and output for the price setter

in Figure 10.6, we can also represent the price setter's total profit graphically. In particular, total profit is given by the shaded rectangular area, P_0ABC, whose base is equal to the number of units supplied and whose height is equal to the profit per unit (the difference between price and average total cost).

Some Common Myths about Market Power

The ability to set price does *not* mean that a price setter can charge any price it wants. Any price setter, even the most powerful monopolist, is constrained by the demand for its product. Failure to recognize this elementary fact has led to a number of myths regarding the economic implications of market power.

Myth 1: A Price Setter Will Always Charge the Highest Price Possible The price setter maximizes profits by producing the output for which marginal revenue and marginal cost are equal, and by charging the *highest price at which that output can be sold*—that is, the corresponding price on the demand curve. But that is the "highest price possible" only in a trivial sense. The price setter

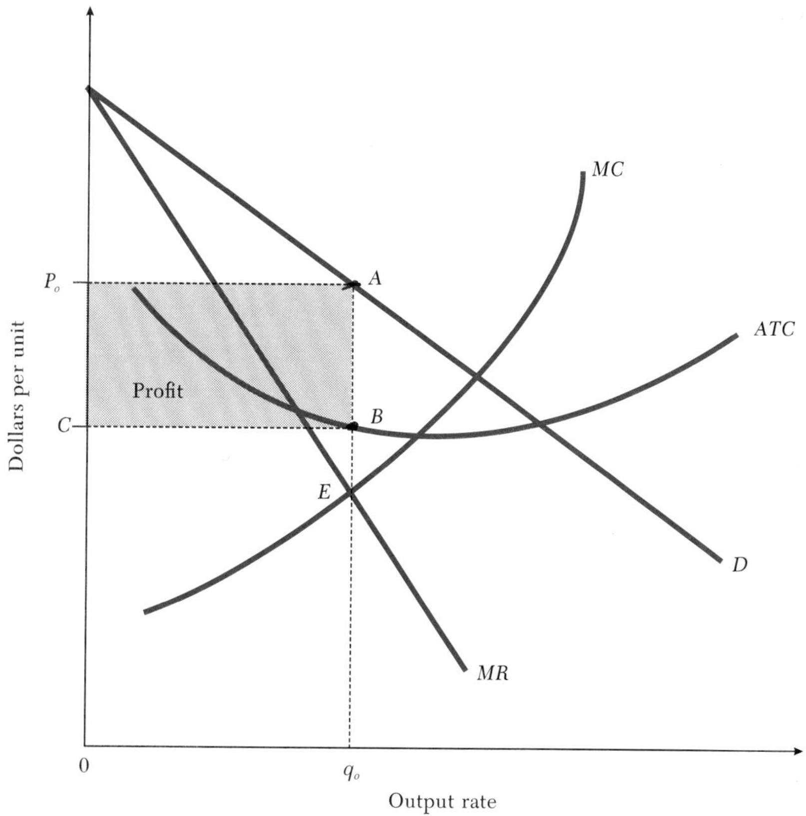

Figure 10.6

Measuring the price setter's profits

can always charge a higher price, sell fewer units, and earn less profit. However, economic theory tells us that it will not.

Myth 2: Market Power Guarantees Profitability If the price setter's costs are high enough relative to the demand for its product, the demand curve lies below the average total cost curve. In that case, as Figure 10.7 on the next page shows, there is no single price–quantity combination on the demand curve that enables the price setter to break even, let alone earn profits. If the price P_1 is above the average variable cost, as in Figure 10.7, the best the price setter can do is to produce output q_1 and incur a loss equal to the rectangular area P_1CBA. If P_1 were below the average variable cost, the price setter would shut down and incur a loss equal to its fixed costs. In either case, it will exit from the market in the long run unless demand increases or costs fall.

That market power does not guarantee profitability can perhaps best be seen from our patent system. In a typical year the U.S. Patent Office grants about 70,000–80,000 patents, each of which confers a legal "monopoly" on its holder. It has been estimated that fewer than 10 percent of those patents are ever

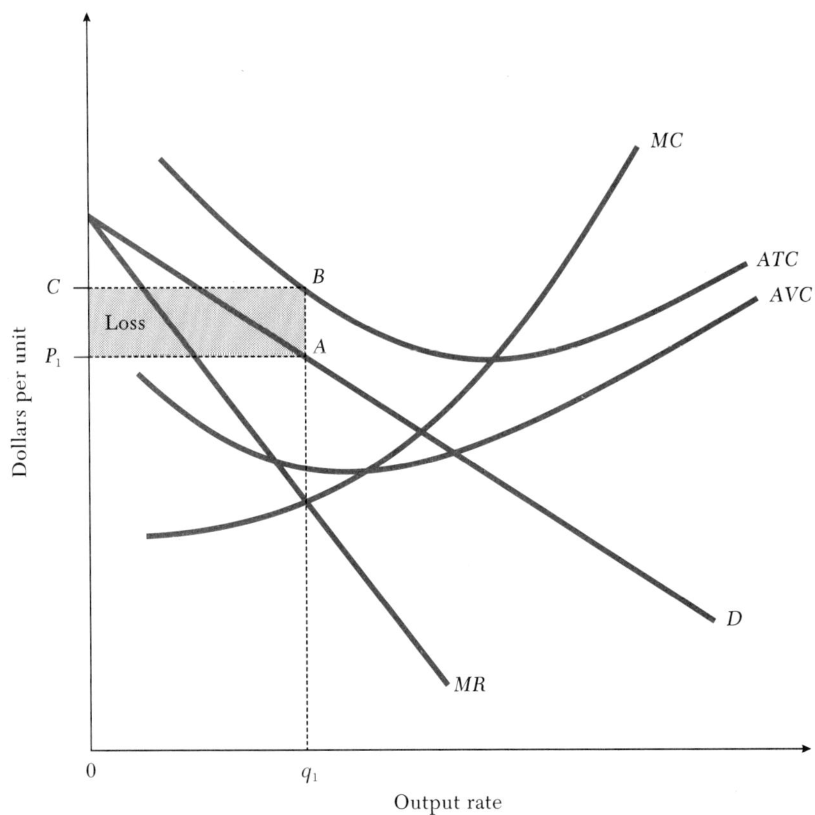

Figure 10.7

An unprofitable price setter

used commercially, and of those that are, probably only a small fraction result in any profits for the patent holder. To be profitable, any price setter, even a pure monopolist, must meet a market demand and meet it at a cost less than the price the market will bear.

Myth 3: Market Power Allows the Price Setter to Set Price without Regard to the Forces of Supply and Demand As we have seen, any price setter must take demand into account when determining price. Furthermore, although the price setter does not have a supply curve in the same sense as a price taker, it must still consider marginal cost in arriving at its profit-maximizing output rate. In fact, as Figure 10.8 shows, an increase in marginal costs has the same effect on the price setter that it would have in a purely competitive market—namely, an increase in price and a reduction in output. Thus demand and supply (marginal cost) are as relevant to the determination of price and output in a price setter's market as they are in a purely competitive market.*

*While changes in demand typically have the same effects on the price setter's price and quantity as they do on price and quantity in a purely competitive market, the effects are not quite as clear cut as

Figure 10.8

The effects of an increase in marginal cost

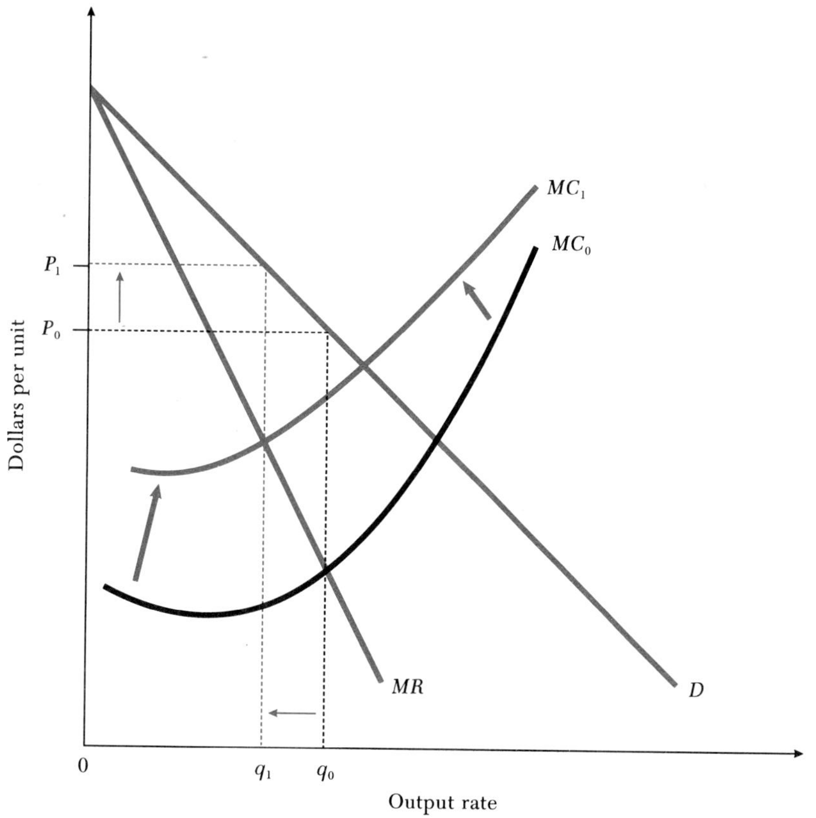

Price Discrimination

There are some circumstances in which a price setter, rather than charging a single price for each unit sold, can charge different prices to different buyers, or it can sell different amounts to the same buyer at different prices. We call such practices **price discrimination**.*

Price discrimination occurs when a seller charges multiple prices for the same product.

Price discrimination requires not only that the seller have some market power but also that it be able to keep its markets (or buyers) separated. Were this not the case, those buyers charged the lower price would be able to undercut the

those of a change in marginal cost. For example, although an increase in demand generally leads to an increase in the price setter's equilibrium price, it can lower that price if it is accompanied by an increase in demand elasticity or if marginal costs are falling as output is increased.

*Strictly speaking, the term *price discrimination* applies only to price differentials that do not reflect differences in cost. For example, to the extent that price discounts given to large-volume buyers reflect the lower unit costs of dealing in large-volume transactions, the discounts do not constitute price discrimination. Similarly, the higher interest rates that lenders charge to higher risk borrowers, or the higher premiums insurance companies charge riskier categories of drivers do not constitute price discrimination.

price discriminator by reselling the good to those who would otherwise have to pay the higher price. For example, suppose an apple monopoly announces that it will sell apples to women for 10 cents each and to men for 15 cents each. Before long some enterprising woman will discover the profitability of buying apples for 10 cents and reselling them to men at some price between 10 cents and 15 cents. In effect, if reselling apples is costless, any woman who buys apples from the monopolist at the lower price becomes its competitor in selling them to men. The competition would force the men's price down until it was equal to the women's price, and the monopolist's attempt to price discriminate would fail.

In general, therefore, price discrimination can succeed only when the transactions costs of reselling the product are high relative to the price differentials. This is the reason price discrimination is most frequently observed in the sale of services. Unlike physical commodities, services such as medical care, entertainment, and education cannot easily be resold by the original buyer.

Price discrimination can assume a variety of forms. Some take advantage of differences in demand elasticity; others differentiate among individual buyers on the basis of their demand prices; still others involve minimum purchase requirements or combine fixed and variable price components. Consider the following examples, each of which assumes that resale is too costly to undermine price discrimination.

Exploiting Differences in Demand Elasticity

When elasticities of demand differ across markets, the price setter will find it profitable to discriminate in price among those markets. In particular, the seller will maximize profits by charging higher prices in the markets where demand is less elastic and lower prices in the markets where demand is more elastic.

To illustrate, consider the two markets whose demand curves are shown in Figure 10.9 where, to keep things simple, we have assumed a constant marginal cost. The price setter maximizes profits by selling in each market an amount for which marginal revenue in that market is equal to marginal cost. Accordingly, in Market A, where demand is more elastic, q_a units will be sold at a price of P_a per unit, while in Market B, where demand is less elastic q_b units will be sold at a price of P_b per unit.

Differences in elasticity explain why sellers sell the same product at lower prices in markets where they face more competition. Other things being equal, the more competition, the more elastic the demand for the product of any one seller. For example, during the early 1980s Sony was selling identical television sets for nearly 50 percent less in the United States than in Japan. Sony's pricing policies reflected the fact that it faced more competition in the U.S. market than in the Japanese market.

Selective discounts, such as those given to coupon clippers and certain airline travelers, are also examples of price discrimination based on differences in demand elasticity. Shoppers who take the time to clip and file coupons for price rebates on groceries, toiletries and other household products are probably more

Figure 10.9

Price discrimination based on differences in elasticity

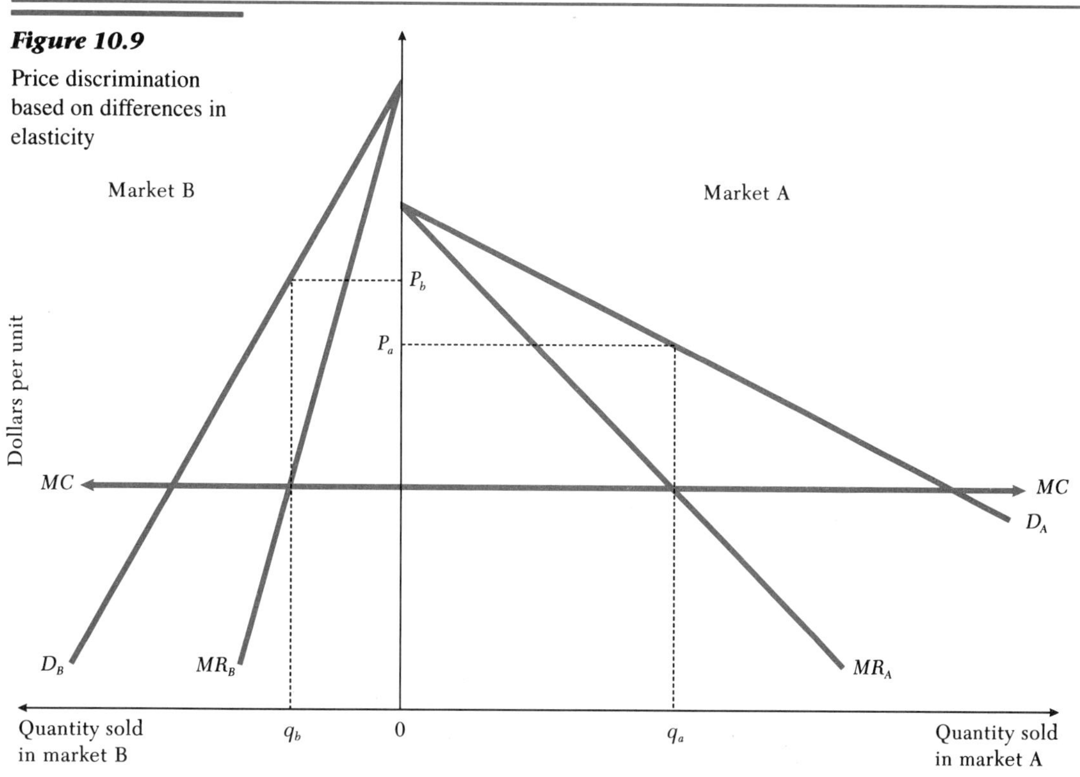

price-sensitive—that is, their demands are more elastic—than those for whom the coupons are too much trouble. The coupons thus enable the manufacturer to pass along selected price rebates, but only to those shoppers whose demand is more elastic.

In the case of air travel, airlines are aware that vacation travellers are generally more sensitive to price than business travellers. To take advantage of the difference in elasticity, they regularly offer discount fares, but only to passengers who purchase tickets well in advance of their flight and who remain at their destination for some minimum length of time—usually a week or more—before their return flight. Most vacation travellers can easily meet such conditions, but business travellers must typically fly on short notice and stay only a day or so at their destinations. The qualifications for the discount fare thus enable the airlines to charge lower prices to vacation travellers, while still maintaining the higher, "normal" prices for business travellers.

Other examples of price discrimination based on differences in elasticity include the higher prices movie theaters charge on weekends when demand is less elastic than on weekdays, and the lower telephone rates available after 5 P.M. and on weekends when demand is more elastic than during business hours.

Exploiting Differences in Demand Price

Sellers can sometimes gather enough information about individual demand prices to charge different individuals different prices for the same product. The pricing of a college education provides a good example of such price discrimination.

Suppose, for example, that prestigious Podunk University has an enrollment capacity of 10,000 students. As shown by the demand curve in Figure 10.10(a), one way for PU to fill its student body is to charge a flat tuition rate of $2,000 per year. This way generates annual tuition revenue of $20 million as represented by the shaded area.

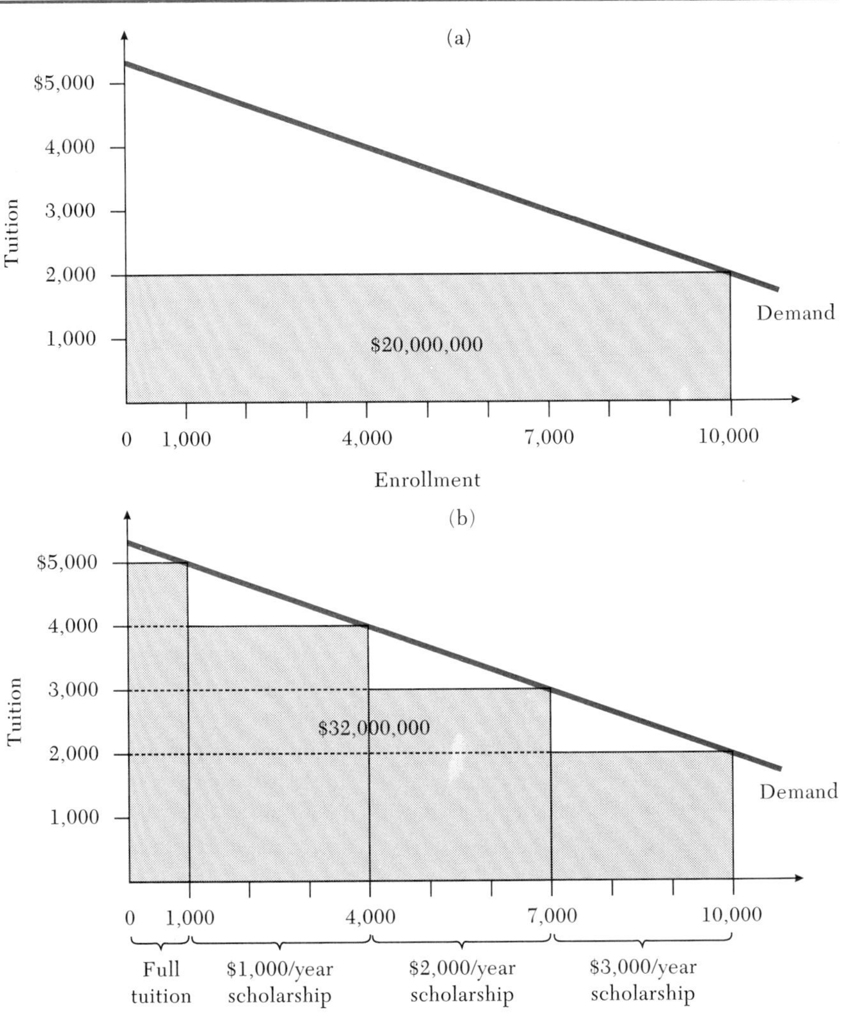

Figure 10.10
Price discrimination through financial aid. (a) Flat tuition: $2,000 per year and (b) Tuition $5,000 per year with financial aid

Alternatively, PU can charge a high base tuition of $5,000 per year, combined with selected "tuition rebates" in the form of financial aid. According to the demand curve in Figure 10.10(b), only 1,000 students per year are willing to pay full tuition to obtain a Podunk degree. However, PU can enroll an additional 3,000 students if it reduces their effective tuition to $4,000 by giving each a $1,000-per-year partial tuition scholarship. Another 3,000 students will enroll if they are given $2,000 per year in scholarship money, and still another 3,000 will enroll if they are given $3,000-per-year scholarships. Total enrollment will still be 10,000 students, but the total tuition revenues, as represented by the shaded area, are now $32 million. Combining a high base tuition with liberal financial aid therefore enables PU not only to fill its enrollment but also to raise an additional $12 million in tuition revenue.

Financial aid systems like the one just described are of course a form of price discrimination: Some students pay more than others for the same education. Although it is unlikely that any university can determine precisely the maximum tuition any particular student is willing to pay, and thus determine the size of the scholarship necessary to enroll that student, it can get at least a rough idea from information about the family's financial status. Since wealthier families are usually willing to pay more for education than poorer families, PU could grant financial aid in inverse proportion to family wealth. This is just what most universities actually do, and it is why they require each applicant for financial aid to submit a family financial statement. The resulting price discrimination allows the university to cover a greater portion of its costs with tuition revenues while simultaneously providing an education to students who would otherwise be unable to afford one.

Price discrimination based on income differentials occurs in other areas as well. There is some evidence that it is common in medical and dental care, legal services, and other areas where the seller solicits information about the client's occupation to obtain a rough gauge of his income. Even the American Economic Association determines its membership dues on the basis of the members' academic rank and annual income!

Package Deals

Price setters can also use package deals or all-or-nothing offers as a method of price discrimination. For example, most National Football League teams require fans to purchase tickets to the team's preseason exhibition games at the same price as its regular season games to qualify for season tickets. Note that in this form of price discrimination, the prices are the same but the value of the goods differs: Ticket buyers would not ordinarily be willing to pay as much for preseason games as for regular season games; they do so only to qualify for season tickets.

The DeBeers company, the international diamond monopolist, practices a similar form of price discrimination. It offers each wholesale diamond buyer a pouch of diamonds on a take-it-or-leave-it basis. The buyer is not given the option of haggling over the prices of the individual gems in the pouch but must pay a given price for the entire pouch.

Some package deals do entail different prices for essentially the same product. For example, children are often admitted at a discount rate to movies, the circus, ball games, and other family style entertainment, but only if accompanied by an adult paying the full admission price. Book and record clubs give members discount prices, but only in return for an agreement to buy some minimum number of books or records per year. Perhaps with a little thought you can come up with still other examples.

Fixed and Variable Price Components

Another common form of price discrimination combines a fixed charge, independent of the number of units purchased, with a price per unit of the good. The overall price of telephone service, for example, combines a fixed monthly fee with other charges based on the number of message units accumulated by the user. Restaurants and bars often levy fixed cover charges that are independent of the amount of food or drink purchased. Cable television services usually charge fixed fees for installation and rental of descrambling equipment and then sell special programming on a pay-per-view basis.

THE NORMATIVE SIDE: MARKET POWER, EFFICIENCY, AND EQUITY

Let us now consider the normative consequences of market power. We proceed in two steps, addressing, first, the positive question of how market power affects prices and outputs relative to pure competition and, second, the normative implications of those effects for economic efficiency. In subsequent chapters we examine government policies toward market power and monopoly; our purpose here is to introduce the normative model by which such policies can be evaluated.

Throughout this analysis we must bear in mind that pure competition, the standard against which we are evaluating the effects of market power, is an abstract ideal rather than a realistically attainable market structure. Some degree of market power is inevitable in any real economy, and government policies that fail to take this into account risk ineffectiveness or, worse, can even promote waste and inefficiency. Most economists feel that market power becomes a legitimate policy concern only in special or extreme circumstances—when it is the result of collusion or artificial entry restrictions, for example, or when its degree approaches that of pure monopoly.

Competition and Monopoly: A Comparison

To illustrate the effects of market power on price and output, let us suppose that the hypothetical widget industry is transformed from pure competition into a pure monopoly by the merger of all widget producers into a single firm. To

Figure 10.11

Pure competition and monopoly compared: the efficiency loss due to monopoly

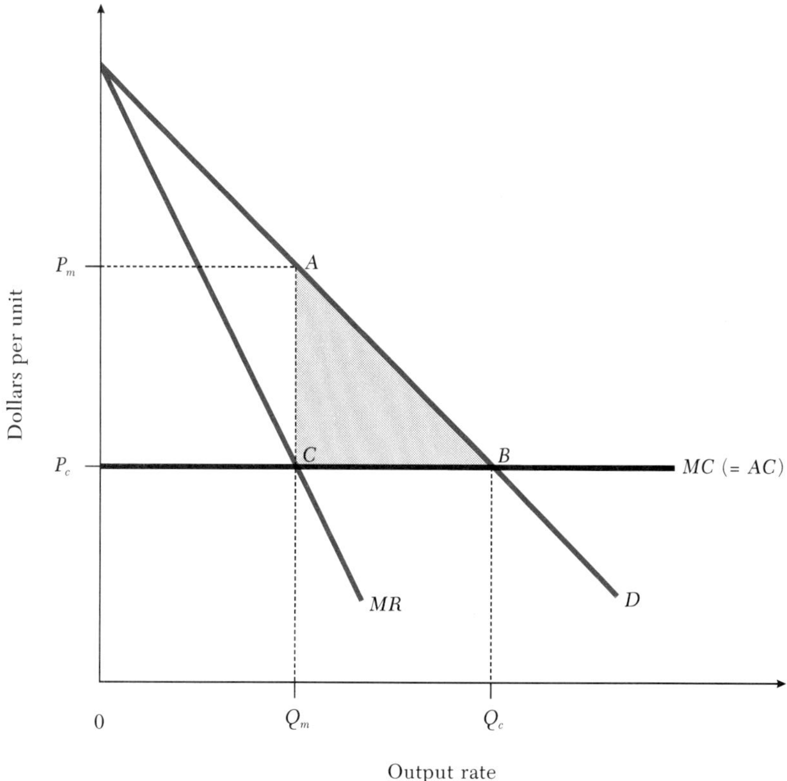

isolate the effects of market power per se, we assume that the costs of widget production are unaffected by the merger. Furthermore, we assume that marginal and average costs are constant (that is, widget production is a constant cost industry) and that the widget monopolist is unable to price discriminate.

The market demand curve for widgets is labelled D in Figure 10.11, and the marginal (and average) cost curve is labelled $MC(= AC)$. Since the industry's marginal cost curve is the market supply curve under conditions of pure competition, the price and quantity in purely competitive equilibrium would be P_c and Q_c, respectively. After monopolization, however, output is determined by the intersection of the marginal revenue and the marginal cost curves. Since the monopolist now serves the entire widget market, its marginal revenue curve is the marginal revenue curve derived from the market demand curve—namely, the curve labelled MR in the diagram. The monopolist therefore produces a quantity of widgets equal to Q_m and charges a price equal to P_m.

A comparison of prices and quantities shows that, other things being equal, price is higher and quantity supplied is lower under conditions of monopoly than under conditions of pure competition. In effect, the monopolist is able to charge a higher price because it restricts output below that which would be supplied under pure competition. It is this restriction of output—the creation of an *artificial scarcity*—that is the fundamental source of monopolistic inefficiency.

An Example: Monopoly, Competition, and College Football

The market for television rights to college football games provides a good illustration of the differences between monopoly and competition. All U.S. colleges and universities that field big-time collegiate football teams are members of the National Collegiate Athletic Association, or NCAA. Prior to 1984, the NCAA acted as a monopolist in the sale of the rights to televise college football games. A television network that wanted to broadcast a particular game could not purchase the rights directly from the schools involved (or from their athletic conference) but instead had to negotiate with the NCAA. The NCAA in turn used its monopoly position to restrict the number of games shown on a typical autumn Saturday to a select two or three for which it charged premium prices. The resulting revenues were divided among all NCAA members, including those without football programs.

This share-the-wealth arrangement was challenged in court by the University of Oklahoma and the University of Georgia, both of which wanted to sell the television rights for their high-powered football programs independently. In 1984, the U.S. Supreme Court ruled that they and other NCAA members could do so, thus effectively eliminating the NCAA's monopoly. Colleges and universities, acting both independently and as members of football conferences, immediately began competing to sell television rights to their football games. Rights were sold not only to ABC and CBS, the two networks with which the NCAA had been dealing, but also to cable networks and independent stations. As our analysis predicts, the number of games increased, and increased dramatically. Instead of only two or three games, viewers in most areas of the country can now watch as many as ten on a typical autumn Saturday (with a weekly Thursday night cable TV game thrown in for good measure). As competition increased the number of games shown on television, it also drove down the price of television rights. For example, CBS, which had paid $1.2 million to the NCAA for the right to televise the Michigan-Iowa game in 1983, was able to purchase the rights to that same game in 1985 for only $575,000.

The Efficiency Loss due to Monopoly

Returning to our hypothetical example of the widget market depicted in Figure 10.11, note that the economic cost of monopolizing the widget market cannot be measured simply by the value of the lost widget production, $Q_c - Q_m$. We must also recognize that the reduction in widget output frees resources for use in the production of other goods. To evaluate the overall effect of the widget monopoly, therefore, we must balance the value of the foregone widgets against the value of these additional other goods.

The value of the lost widget production can be represented by the area under the demand curve between Q_m and Q_c, namely area Q_mABQ_c. Furthermore, because opportunity cost represents the value of resources in alternative uses, the area under the marginal cost curve between Q_m and Q_c, namely area Q_mCBQ_c, measures the value of the other goods that can be produced with the resources freed by the widget monopoly.

The **monopolistic efficiency loss** is the net loss of economic value due to monopolistic output restriction.

As you can see from the diagram, the net effect of monopoly on resource allocation is negative: The value of the lost widget output (Q_mABQ_c) exceeds the value of the other goods that can be produced with the same resources (Q_mCBQ_c) by an amount equal to the approximately triangular area ABC. The area ABC represents the **monopolistic efficiency loss**. It reflects the fact that monopoly causes resources to be reallocated from higher valued uses to lower valued uses.*

Other Costs of Monopoly: Rent Seeking

Rent seeking means using scarce resources to seek exclusive monopoly rights and the economic rents that accompany such rights.

Some economists have argued that, at least in some cases, the efficiency loss triangle may understate the economic costs of monopoly. They point out that the very promise of monopoly profits, or rents, attracts resources into attempts to obtain the exclusive rights that are the source of such rents. Sometimes the resources devoted to such **rent seeking** are used productively. A patent, for example, is intended to reward successful innovation. Often, however, rent seeking simply uses the political process to create and enforce exclusive monopoly rights favoring some groups at the expense of others. For example, a would-be monopolist may use lawyers, lobbyists, and other resources to obtain government protection from competition. Since these resources have valuable alternative uses, using them to obtain a monopoly results in real opportunity costs. Moreover, if there is competition among rent seekers, these costs rise until they just offset any potential monopoly gains. In terms of Figure 10.11, the cost of the resources devoted to obtaining a monopoly can therefore be as great as the rectangular area, P_mACP_c that would otherwise be monopoly rents.

Price Discrimination and Economic Efficiency

Suppose that instead of charging the same price for all the widgets it sells, the widget monopolist in Figure 10.11 can price discriminate. Given this monopolist's market power, there are two ways price discrimination can increase economic welfare. First, it can provide an incentive to supply units of output that would not be supplied by a single price monopolist. As long as the demand price (marginal value) of those additional units exceeds their marginal cost, there are net efficiency gains from producing them.

Second, price discrimination may generate enough additional revenues to cover costs the seller could not cover by charging a single, uniform price. In such a case, *no* production would take place in the absence of price discrimination.

*An alternative (but equivalent) way of interpreting the welfare loss is that it reflects the difference between marginal value (demand price) and marginal cost (competitive supply price) summed over the interval between Q_m and Q_c. Because marginal value exceeds marginal cost for all units in that interval, not producing them results in a loss of potential gains from trade. This was the interpretation of monopolistic inefficiency given in Chapter 5.

Going back to Figure 10.7, for example, we saw that when the demand curve lies entirely below the average cost curve, there is no single price at which the price setter breaks even. Using price discrimination, however, the price setter may be able to raise enough revenues to cover costs and stay in business. This would be economically efficient because the value of what it supplies (which is at least as great as the revenues it can collect as a price discriminator) exceeds the cost. The problem is that, without price discrimination, it might be unable to capture enough of that value to stay in business.

The price discrimination embodied in universities' financial aid programs provides a good illustration of both of these sources of potential increases in economic welfare. The aid enables many students who could not pay full tuition, but to whom the marginal value a college education exceeds its marginal cost, to attend college. At the same time, the additional revenue generated by price discrimination enables the university to cover a larger share of its total costs—indeed, in many cases, to stay in business.

In some cases, however, price discrimination may reduce output further than single price monopoly and thus may compound, rather than reduce, monopolistic inefficiency. The efficiency effects of price discrimination therefore depend on the particular circumstances in which it occurs.

Market Power and Dynamic Economic Efficiency

The preceding arguments all relate to *static* efficiency, that is, to the allocation of resources at a given point in time. As we have seen, however, competition is, by its very nature, a *dynamic* process in which firms attempt to gain and maintain a competitive advantage through the continuing development of new products and new technologies. Many economists have stressed the links between market power and these innovative and entrepreneurial aspects of the competitive process. They point out that the promise of monopoly rents is itself a potential source of innovation and technological progress, and that the competitive advantage which results from successful innovation or entrepreneurship often contributes to market power.

The patent system provides perhaps the clearest example of the relation between market power and the incentive to innovate. An innovative idea, once discovered, is like a public good: It is costly for an innovator to prevent competitors from using his idea for their own commercial gain. The patent system remedies this by protecting the innovator from the unauthorized use of his ideas. As such, it strengthens the economic incentive to innovate. Although a patent holder's market power may result in static resource misallocation, *given that the patented innovation already exists*, the innovation may not have been forthcoming in the first place without the promise of a patent monopoly. To the extent that the benefits from the innovative activity which it encourages outweigh the static misallocation of resources it may also create, the patent system promotes rather than retards economic welfare.

A similar point can be made regarding trademarks. By granting a single producer the exclusive, legal right to use a brand name, such as Coke or Honda, a trademark prevents competitors from marketing an identical product. Trademarks thus contribute to increased product differentiation and, other things being equal, greater market power for the sellers of brand-name goods.

Other things are *not* equal, however, when we take a broader view of the trademark system. Although trademark protection for a particular *existing product* may mean a higher price for that product, the trademark system itself encourages the introduction *new products* by protecting the investments of those who introduce them. On balance, therefore, the system almost certainly stimulates competition.

Even in the absence of legal protection, innovative activity can sometimes lead to temporary market power. A firm that is first to introduce a new product may establish a reputation and a customer following that take time for its competitors to overcome. Or the innovator may be able to protect trade secrets long enough to get a jump on the competition.

In some cases, of course, the source of market power may be unrelated to innovation or any other socially productive activity—for example, when it is the result of collusion or when it is based on government grants of special privilege to successful rent seekers. An overall evaluation of the consequences of market power therefore requires not only an analysis of its implications for static resource allocation but also an examination of the nature of the process by which market power is attained and the implications of that process for dynamic economic progress.

Market Power and Distribution: Who Gains and Who Loses?

Market power affects not only the size and growth of the economic pie through its impact on resource allocation and technological progress but also the way in which that pie is cut and distributed among the members of society.

To the extent that market power creates or prolongs pure economic profits or rents, it transfers some of the trading gains from buyers to sellers. That statement is simple enough as far as it goes, but it doesn't go nearly far enough. Things begin to get complicated when we recognize that most people are both buyers (of final goods) and sellers (of productive services). For example, if the seller is a corporation, any monopoly profits it earns may accrue to the thousands or even millions of individuals who own its stock, either directly as personal investors or indirectly as participants in insurance and pension funds. In addition, the firm's employees, especially management and unionized labor, may also share in its monopoly profits. These same stockholders and employees may in turn purchase the products of other firms with market power, or even the products of the firm which they own or which employs them.

On balance, therefore, the net effect of market power on the distribution of economic welfare is difficult to unravel. Even if we had a standard for judging fairness and equity—and, as we have seen, economics has little to say about what such a standard should be—applying that standard to evaluate the effect of market power on the distribution of economic welfare would be extremely difficult, if not impossible.

CHAPTER SUMMARY

1. Unlike a price taker, a *price setter* has individual control over the price of its product. We refer to this control as *market power*. There are three basic sources of market power: a *differentiated product, search costs* for buyers, and *large size* relative to the total market. Sellers can jointly exercise market power through *collusion*.

2. Market power is a matter of degree. The more elastic the demand for the price setter's product, the less its market power; the less elastic, the greater the market power.

3. Profitable market power can persist in the long run only to the extent that the price setter is protected from entry.

4. Entry costs due to *natural advantages of incumbents* are the result of scale economies, experience effects, and higher costs of financial capital to the new entrant. All of these costs can be overcome if the new entrant produces a superior product to that of incumbents.

5. Most *artificial restrictions on entry* are legally imposed by government; however, they also include illegal private coercion.

6. *Potential entry* can be almost as effective as actual entry in keeping prices near competitive levels.

7. A pure *monopoly* exists when there is a *single seller* of a product for which there are *no close substitutes* in the short run and *substantial entry costs* that close the market to new competition in the long run.

8. The value of exclusive legal rights that protect a firm from exact duplication of its product by competitors is equal to the present value of the future economic rents they are expected to generate for their owners.

9. A price setter's marginal revenue curve is derived from the demand curve for its product. For the price setter, the marginal revenue curve lies below the demand curve—that is, for any given quantity demanded, marginal revenue is less than price.

10. The price setter's profits are maximized at an output rate, and a corresponding demand price, for which marginal revenue and marginal cost are equal.

11. Market power does not mean that the price setter charges the highest price possible, nor that it is guaranteed a profit, nor that it can set price independently of supply and demand.

12. *Price discrimination* is possible for a price setter when the transactions cost of reselling its product is high.

13. Price discrimination can take advantage of differences in demand elasticity (charging the higher price in the market where demand is less elastic) or

differences in individual demand prices. It can also take the form of an all-or-nothing offer or a combination of fixed and variable price components.

14. Other things being equal, price will be higher and output lower when a market is monopolized than when it is competitive. The monopolist's artificial restriction of output results in a static *monopolistic efficiency loss* reflecting the difference between the value of the lost output and the opportunity cost of producing it.

15. Many economists stress the positive links between market power and dynamic economic efficiency. Specifically, the promise of market power provides an incentive for innovation and technological progress, and the competitive advantage that results from successful innovation is often accompanied by market power.

Key Terms and Concepts

price setter
market power
differentiated products
search costs
natural cost advantages of incumbent firms
artificial entry restrictions
monopoly
price discrimination
monopolistic efficiency loss
rent seeking

Questions for Thought and Discussion

1. General Motors Corporation, a local Mom-'n'-Pop grocery store, and an independent craftsperson selling wares on the street are all price setters in their respective markets. What are the principal sources of market power for each?
2. A major league baseball team announces that it is raising ticket prices by 20 percent to cover escalating player salaries. Is the team a price setter? If so, why didn't it raise ticket prices by 30 percent and not only cover the higher player salaries but also increase its profits?
3. Only one daily newspaper is published in many U.S. cities. Are the publishers examples of pure monopolists? On what does your answer depend?
4. More often than not the source of monopoly is government. The historical examples are many. Nearly 500 years ago when the trade routes from Europe to the Far East were opening up, European governments granted exclusive monopoly licenses to private trading companies. Certain states in the United States, such as Massachusetts and Virginia, were founded by private monopolists (Massachusetts Bay Company, the Virginia Company) chartered by the British crown. Today, local governments grant exclusive franchises to suppliers of cable TV services. Can you guess at what motivates a government to grant monopoly franchises?

5. What are some of the substitutes for the products of the following government monopolies:
   a. The U.S. Postal Service
   b. AMTRAK
   c. The local power (electricity and gas) company
   d. The local school district
6. The manager of a department store explains to you how she sets prices: She marks up the wholesale cost per unit by 30 percent. Is this really an explanation? Why or why not?
7. In the example about Doodads, we said that Mona Poley could sell her patent for $40,000 rather than use it to generate an extra $5,000 per year in economic rent. Would the buyer of Mona's patent earn any rent?
8. A firm finds that at its current price and output rate, the price elasticity of demand for its product is 0.5. Have you any advice for its managers?
9. If a price setter hires a full-time production manager, she will be able to increase her output rate from 90 to 100 units per day. However, to sell the extra 10 units, she will have to lower her price from $70 per unit to $65 per unit. In addition, each unit of her product requires $5 worth of materials. What is the highest daily wage she would pay to hire the manager?
10. In many metropolitan areas, consumers now have the option of purchasing new cars from auto brokers. These brokers give price quotes over the telephone for the particular make and model of car the buyer is interested in. If the price is agreeable to the buyer, the broker then buys the car—either directly from the manufacturer or from dealer overstocks—and sells it to the buyer at the quoted price. How do you think this reduces market power in the new car market? What do you think it does to the spread of prices at which new cars are sold? There was recently an attempt in California to make auto brokerages illegal. Who do you think was behind this?
11. The Aluminum Company of America (Alcoa) once had a near monopoly on the production of new aluminum in the United States. Alcoa's near monopoly was based on its ownership of nearly all the U.S. reserves of bauxite, a mineral essential to the production of aluminum. Since Alcoa could obtain bauxite from itself at cost but would charge other producers a monopoly price for bauxite, it was argued that Alcoa's ownership of bauxite gave Alcoa a cost advantage over potential competitors and thus prevented entry into the aluminum market. Evaluate this argument.

CHAPTER 11

Concentration, Competition, and Collusion

As we have seen, pure competition—with its large number of small, independent suppliers—and pure monopoly—with its single seller insulated from competition—represent extreme cases. In this chapter, we consider the intermediate case of an industry whose structure lies somewhere between these extremes, namely, one in which there are a small number of firms, each of which is large relative to the total market. We call such an industry a **concentrated industry**.

A **concentrated industry** is one in which a small number of firms account for the bulk of sales.

As we shall see, there is no critical number of sellers—no magic degree of concentration—which divides competitive industries from industries that perform like monopolies. Nor is there a smooth and gradual transition from competitive results to monopolistic results as the number of sellers in the industry declines. The number of competitors in an industry is just one ingredient among many which determine how competitive it will be.

THE MEANING AND MEASUREMENT OF INDUSTRIAL CONCENTRATION

Measuring Concentration: The Concentration Ratio

An industry's **concentration ratio** measures the percentage of industry sales accounted for by a small number (typically four or eight) of the largest firms in an industry.

The most widely used measure of industrial concentration is the **concentration ratio**, which measures the percentage of total industry revenues accounted for by a small number of the largest firms in that industry. The U.S. Department of Commerce periodically calculates 4-, 8-, 20-, and 50-firm concentration ratios for a variety of U.S. manufacturing industries. Table 11.1 shows some of these concentration ratios for 1982, the latest year for which data are available. The table shows, for example, that the motor vehicle industry, in which the four

Table 11.1

Concentration ratios: 1982

	CONCENTRATION RATIO				*Total*
Industry	***4-Firm***	***8-Firm***	***20-Firm***	***50-Firm***	***Number of Firms***
Bottled and canned soft drinks	14	23	39	56	1,236
Newspapers	22	34	49	66	7,520
Pharmaceutical preparations	26	42	69	90	584
Petroleum refining	28	48	76	93	282
Bread, cake, and related products	34	47	60	73	1,869
Electronic computing equip.	43	55	71	82	1,520
Farm machinery and equipment	53	63	69	77	1,787
Soap and other detergents	60	73	83	90	642
Aircraft	64	81	98	99+	139
Tires and inner tubes	66	86	98	99+	108
Photographic equipment	74	86	91	94	723
Motor vehicles and car bodies	92	97	99	99+	284

Source: *Statistical Abstract of the United States, 1989.*

largest producers accounted for 92 percent of total sales revenue, was much more concentrated than the soft drink industry, in which the four largest producers accounted for only 14 percent of total revenue, and even the fifty largest accounted for only 56 percent.

Because of the problems inherent in defining markets, we must exercise caution in interpreting these numbers. For example, despite the relatively low concentration ratios for newspaper publishing, it would be a mistake to conclude that a large number of relatively small publishers compete for readers in the typical newspaper market. Quite the contrary: About three-fourths all newspaper markets are served by only a single daily newspaper. The problem is that the concentration ratios in Table 11.1 are based on national sales data, whereas the relevant market for most newspapers is local. Similarly, the overall concentration ratio reported for the aircraft industry obscures the fact that some aircraft producers, such as Boeing and McDonnell-Douglas, produce only large, commercial aircraft and thus serve an entirely different market from others, such as Cessna and Beach, which produce only small, general aviation aircraft. The relevant markets for aircraft are thus more concentrated than the overall concentration ratio suggests.

Another limitation of the concentration ratios reported in Table 11.1 is that they do not take into account foreign competition. Industries such as motor vehicles, photographic equipment, and tires would appear substantially less concentrated if imports were included in the market. For example, although General Motors, Ford, and Chrysler account for nearly 90 percent of U.S. sales of domestically produced new cars, the same three manufacturers account for less than 70 percent when imports are included in the market.

The Determinants of Concentration

What determines the number and relative size of firms in a market, and thus the extent of its concentration? Why are some markets—such as those for agricultural commodities, retail trade, and services—served by hundreds or even thousands of relatively small firms, while others—such as those for automobiles and aircraft—are served by only a few relatively large firms?

The answer lies in the relation between the size of the market on the one hand and economies of scale on the other. Other things being equal, the more significant the scale economies relative to the size of the market, the more concentrated the industry that supplies that market.

To illustrate the fundamental logic of the relation between market size and scale economies, let us first consider the simple case of a competitive market in which all firms have identical, U-shaped, long-run average cost curves. This curve is labelled *LRAC* in Figure 11.1(a) on the next page. It shows that an individual firm minimizes unit cost by adopting the scale of plant for which the short-run average cost curve is the one labelled *ATC** and by producing at an output rate of q^*. We know from Chapter 8 that the fall in unit costs up to that output rate is the result of scale economies. Thus the more important scale economies, the larger the output rate, q^*, that minimizes long-run average cost.

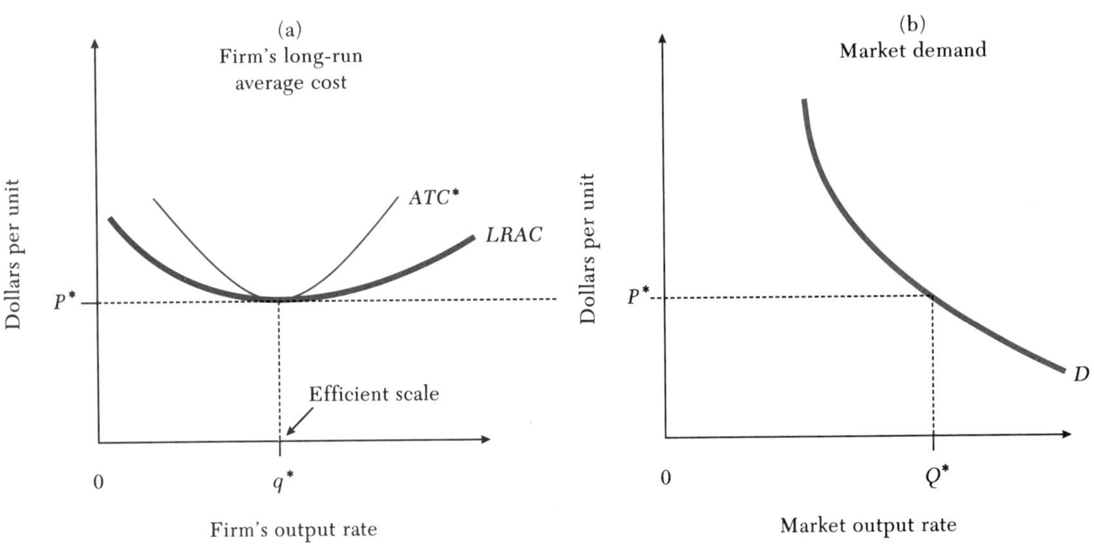

Figure 11.1

Individual firm economies of scale and market demand

The model of pure competition tells us that in the long run, the market price will tend toward P^*, a price that just covers minimum average cost and allows only efficient sized firms—that is, firms producing the output rate q^* in the most efficient scale of plant—to survive. According to the market demand curve in Figure 11.1(b), Q^* units are demanded at a price of P^*. Thus, with each individual firm producing q^* units, the number of firms serving the market in the long run can be approximated by the ratio of Q^* to q^*. For example, suppose that total quantity demanded at the competitive price is 100 million units per year ($= Q^*$). If efficient production requires that each individual firm produce 2 million units per year ($= q^*$), then the market can support 50 firms in the long run. On the other hand, if efficient production requires that each firm produce 20 million units per year, the market can support only 5 firms in the long run.

Of course in reality things can get a little more complicated than this simple example suggests. For one thing, there may be a range of efficient scales over which minimum average cost remains constant, rather than a single scale that minimizes long-run average cost. This possibility is illustrated in Figure 11.2, where q^* is the output rate associated with the *minimum* efficient scale, but where further increases in scale are accompanied by constant unit costs. In this case, the ratio of Q^* to q^* determines only the *maximum* number of firms in long-run equilibrium. To the extent that some firms expand beyond q^*, there will be fewer firms and the market will be correspondingly more concentrated.

Furthermore, even though firms in a given industry typically share a common core of technology, differences in managerial skills, experience, and other specialized factors of production can lead to differences in their cost curves. As a result, neither the efficient scale of operations nor the corresponding level of minimum average cost need be identical for all firms in an industry.

Figure 11.2

Long-run average cost with a range of efficient scales

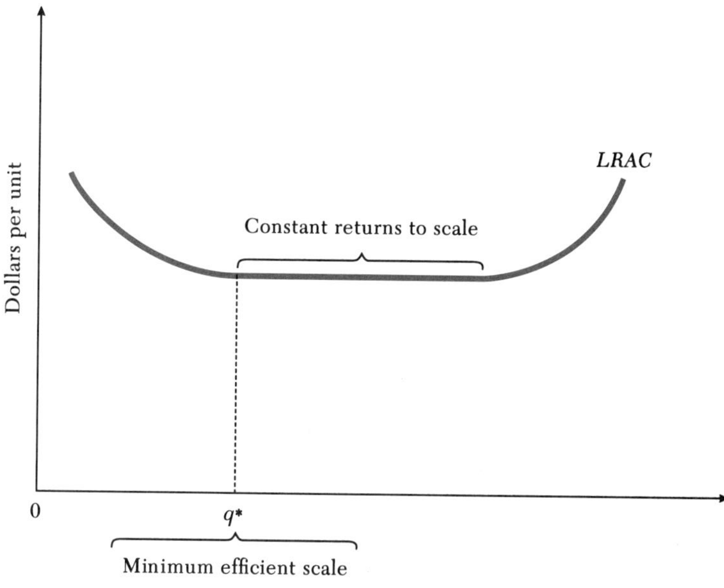

Finally, in some markets, market power may keep prices above the average costs of the most efficient producers. The resulting *umbrella effect* of such higher prices allows some less efficient producers to survive despite their higher costs, at least in the short run. In the long run, however, unless entry is completely blocked, competitive pressures eventually tend to weed out firms that fail to adopt the most efficient scale of operations.

The Survivor Principle

The foregoing analysis suggests that changes in technology and demand have predictable consequences for the evolution of an industry's structure over time. Suppose, for example, that market demand increases. As we have seen, this will lead to an increase in pure profits in the short run, and to the entry of new firms in the long run. If the efficient scale of operations remains the same, the entry of new firms will ultimately lead to a less concentrated industry.

On the other hand, if technological developments increase the efficient scale of operations relative to market demand, then firms that fail to expand will find themselves at a competitive disadvantage relative to those that do, and they will eventually be forced out of the market. Other things being equal, therefore, we would expect the size of the firms in the industry to increase and their number to fall. As a result, the industry will become more concentrated over time. The automobile industry provides a good example of just such an adjustment pattern. After Henry Ford's introduction of the assembly line as a means of large-scale, low-cost, mass production of automobiles, the number of significant automobile producers in the world declined from many hundreds to a relative handful within a matter of a few decades.

In the absence of artificial restrictions on entry and exit, therefore, an industry's structure, including its concentration, is the product of an evolutionary process based on survival of the fittest in the economic jungle. Appropriately, this way of viewing industrial structure has become known as the **survivor principle**. It applies not only to economies of scale per se, but to other characteristics of firms as well. If greater vertical integration leads to lower costs, for example, then competitive pressures lead firms to become more vertically integrated over time. If advertising is the most effective way to convey information to consumers, firms that do not advertise shrink in size and eventually disappear from the market. If diversification into many fields of business lowers the risk associated with an enterprise, and thus its cost of attracting capital, then firms become more diversified. And, by the same economic logic, if large-scale production offers cost advantages over small-scale production, markets become more concentrated as larger firms displace smaller firms.

The **survivor principle** holds that only those firms whose size and other characteristics are best suited to serve a market will survive in that market in the long run.

COMPETITION AS RIVALRY

Just as it takes only two to tango, it takes only two to compete. However, as the number of competitors in a market becomes smaller, at some point the nature of competition begins to change. Under the extreme conditions of pure competition, there are so many firms, and each is so small relative to the market, that the actions of any one have a negligible effect on the others. Pure competition is therefore *impersonal* competition. But in a market served by only a few firms, the actions of any one have significant effects on the others. The term that economists apply to industries characterized by such mutual interdependence is **oligopoly**. (The word's Greek roots mean "few sellers.") Oligopolistic competition is **rivalrous competition** because it takes on the characteristics of a contest among identifiable *rivals* who are aware of their mutual interdependence and who formulate business strategies based on that awareness. For example, when General Motors introduces a new model car, changes prices on its current models, or alters its advertising campaign, its competitors not only take notice, they typically respond by revising their own model lines, pricing policies, and marketing strategies. The management of General Motors in turn must anticipate these responses in formulating its own policies.

An **oligopoly** is an industry characterized by mutual interdependence among its firms.

Rivalrous competition is competition among identifiable rivals aware of their mutual interdependence.

Although oligopoly is often associated with big business, its defining characteristics lie not in the absolute size of firms but in their mutual interdependence. Three or four Mom-'n'-Pop grocery stores in a small town are as much oligopolists as are General Motors, Ford, Toyota, and their competitors in the U.S. automobile market.

We can illustrate some of the characteristics of rivalrous competition by means of a couple of examples.

Computer Wars

The personal computer industry has many of the characteristics of an oligopoly. Although there are many small producers, the bulk of sales are accounted for by a few large manufacturers, such as IBM, Apple, Tandy, and Compaq. The evolution of this industry provides a good example of the nature and results of competition in a relatively concentrated market.

In 1977 Apple, then a new company literally founded in a garage, began shipping the Apple II. At first, its principal competition came from Tandy's line of Radio Shack personal computers, as well as computers manufactured by Commodore and Atari. In 1982, sensing a profitable new market, computer giant IBM began shipping its own line of personal computers. There soon followed a wave of entry, including entry by other large and established firms, including Texas Instruments (TI), Digital Equipment Corporation (DEC), and AT&T. The market environment was quite different from one under conditions of pure competition: The product was differentiated and, because of its complexity, buyer search costs were relatively high. There were also a few large producers, such as most of those just mentioned, with considerable market power. Nonetheless, the results were much the same as we would expect under conditions of pure competition: Profits attracted entry and, with entry, output expanded and prices fell. For example, a basic IBM PC sold for about $3,500 when it was introduced in 1982; 5 years later, a much better and more powerful computer—an IBM clone—could be purchased for less than one-quarter of that price. Those firms that could produce an acceptable product at low cost survived; those that could not dropped out of the market. It is interesting to note that among the survivors were recent start-ups such as Apple and Compaq, while among those that eventually dropped out of the market were such large and established firms as TI and DEC.

It is also interesting to note the role of mutual interdependence and the rivalrous nature of competition in the personal computer market. When it became clear that IBM was setting the standard in that market, many firms realized that they could survive only by producing computers that were compatible with that standard. Some of them, including Tandy, AT&T, and a host of small clone producers, adopted a strategy of producing and selling IBM-compatible computers at lower prices than IBM. Others, such as Compaq, targeted the high end of the market by producing IBM-compatible computers that outperformed IBM's. Obviously, all of these firms must pay close attention to IBM prices and product characteristics in formulating their own strategies.

On the other hand, Apple decided early on to go it alone with its own, non-IBM-compatible line, the Macintosh. Apple's policies are nonetheless still heavily influenced by IBM—and vice-versa. Perhaps their greatest rivalry is in competition for the business market. Apple is well aware that the strength of

IBM lies in its large installed base of IBM computers, both PCs and mainframes, in many businesses. Realizing that few businesses are about to abandon the hundreds of computers they already have for the Macintosh, Apple has devoted a great deal of its corporate resources to insure that the Mac can communicate and exchange data with IBM and IBM-compatible PCs, as well as with IBM mainframe computers. For its part, IBM has recognized that the strength of the Macintosh lies in its simpler and graphically superior operating environment. (The operating environment is the basic computer screen from which the user selects programs and performs other essential tasks.) Accordingly, IBM, in partnership with software producer Microsoft, Inc., has developed a Mac-like operating environment for its PS-2 line of computers.

Clash of the Cola Titans

As long-time rivals in the cola segment of the soft drink market, Coca-Cola and Pepsi are well aware of their mutual interdependence. In developing the recipe for its New Coke, for example, Coca-Cola's principal criterion was to find a taste that Pepsi drinkers would prefer to Pepsi. Coke also employs an entire team of investigators whose only job is to travel around the country ordering Coke in various restaurants, and then sending samples of what they are served back to company headquarters in Atlanta for chemical analysis. If the sample turns out to be Pepsi (or some other cola), Coca-Cola informs the restaurant that it will sue unless the restaurant either serves "the real thing" or tells its customers who ask for a Coke that it serves only some other brand of cola.

Competition between the two cola titans often breaks out in price wars, as happened during the summer of 1988 in the Phoenix, Arizona metropolitan area.* Nationally, Coke accounts for about 31 percent of all cola sales and Pepsi for about 27 percent. In Phoenix, however, Pepsi was outselling Coke by about 35 percent to 29 percent. Trailing in market share and faced with excess capacity in its Phoenix-area bottling plant, Coca-Cola attempted to increase sales by drastically cutting price. To preserve its share of the Phoenix market, Pepsi responded with price cuts of its own. The price war was compounded as supermarkets and other retailers played the two cola giants off against one another, offering free advertising in their own local promotions to whichever would provide them with cola at the lowest wholesale price. As a result, the price of a six-pack of Coke fell to a low of $0.59 by midsummer.

It didn't take Coke and Pepsi long to realize how unprofitable their local price war had become. (In the national market, for example, each 1 percent cut in the price of Coke costs the company about $20 million in profits.) Eventually, Pepsi began raising its price, hoping that Coca-Cola would realize the futility of a continued price war and follow suit. Coke did, and soon the Phoenix-area prices of both Coke and Pepsi returned to "normal." But the underlying causes of the

*Timothy Tregarthen, "Coke vs. Pepsi: A Truce in the Cola Wars?" *The Margin* (March/April 1989).

price war—a heated rivalry and excess bottling capacity—made it likely that the cycle would soon be repeated, if not in Phoenix, then elsewhere.

Is There a Theory of Oligopoly?

Economists have had little success in developing a single, unified theory, like that of pure competition or monopoly, to explain the kinds of rivalrous competition just described. (For some attempts to do so, see the appendix to this chapter.) The problem, it seems, is that such a theory has to go beyond simple profit maximization to incorporate assumptions about how firms view their mutual interdependence. For example, to predict whether a firm will find it profitable to raise or lower prices may require an assumption about how it expects its rivals to react to such a change. Unfortunately, the appropriate assumptions appear to depend on the particular circumstances of oligopolistic interdependence, so that a general theory of oligopoly has proven to be an elusive goal for economic analysis.

CONCENTRATION AND COLLUSION

One characteristic of concentrated markets that has always held a special interest for economists is their susceptibility to *collusion*. As we saw in Chapter 2, collusion is the term applied to a voluntary agreement among competitors to eliminate or restrict market competition. In effect, it is a means by which otherwise competing sellers can obtain or increase market power by acting together.

Agreement, Coordination, and Enforcement

Price-fixing is a collusive agreement not to compete on the basis of price.

Effective collusion requires three basic ingredients: *agreement, coordination*, and *enforcement*. Suppose, for example, that the firms supplying the market pictured in Figure 11.3 on the following page *agree* to fix the price at P_f, which is above the competitive market price of P_c. By itself, this **price-fixing** agreement is ineffective without the ability of the group to restrict its total output to Q_f, the amount that can be sold at the higher price. Any greater output leads to surpluses, unwanted inventories, and downward pressure on price. To achieve this output restriction, the collusive group must thus *coordinate* its members' production, perhaps by assigning each a maximum output quota. For example, the firm in Figure 11.3(b) may be assigned a production quota of q_f, which is less than the amount q_c that it would produce under competitive conditions.

Finally, it is necessary to *enforce* compliance with a collusive agreement because such an agreement generally presents each party with an opportunity to profitably exploit the noncompetitive behavior of its fellow colluders. With price fixed at the artificially high level of P_f, for example, the individual colluder in Figure 11.3(b) finds that marginal revenue to be gained from independently in-

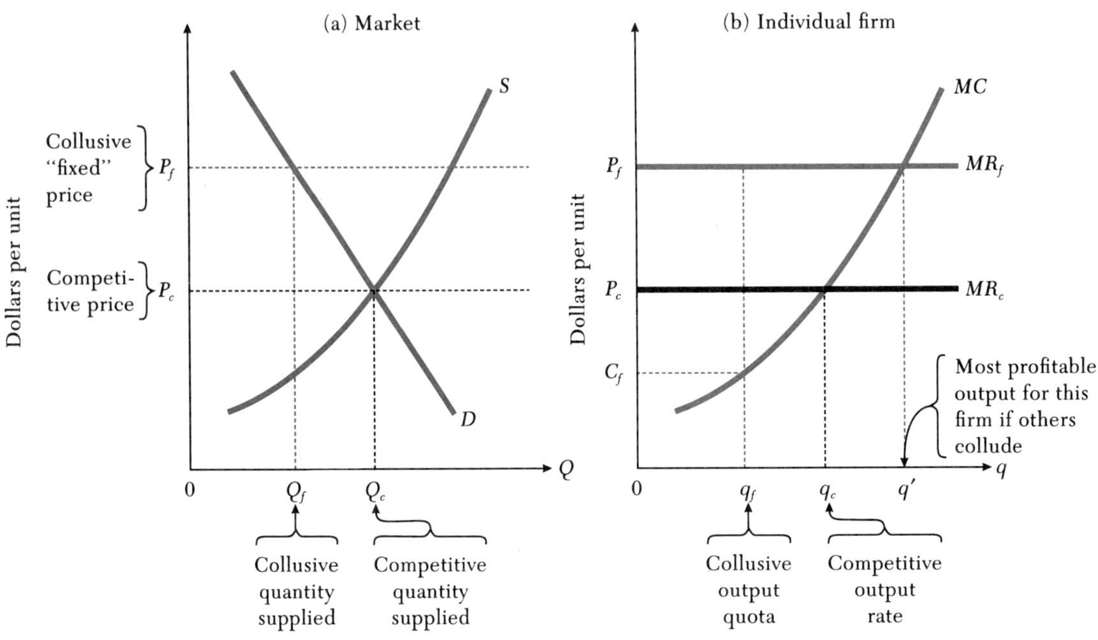

Figure 11.3

Effects of collusion

creasing output beyond its quota of q_f—indeed, beyond its previous competitive output rate of q_c—far exceeds the marginal cost. Thus, although collectively the colluders can all profit if all abide by the agreement to restrict output, individually each can profit even more by violating that agreement once it is in effect. The collusive agreement will eventually collapse, therefore, unless there is some means of detecting and punishing potential cheaters, or chiselers.

Other things being equal, the fewer the number of parties involved, the simpler and less costly it is for them to reach a collusive agreement, coordinate their behavior, and enforce compliance.* On the other hand, the collusive group must be large enough to include all significant sellers of a product (or of products that are close substitutes) if it is to exert significant market power. The fact that the collusive group must be small enough to be manageable, and yet not so small as to exclude significant competitors, suggests that collusion is most likely in markets where a relatively small number of firms account for a substantial share of total sales—that is, in concentrated markets.†

*A recent study of collusive price fixing, for example, found that the average number of firms involved was seven and that ten or fewer firms were involved in 80 percent of cases studied. See George A. Hay and Daniel Kelley, "An Empirical Survey of Price Fixing Conspiracies," *The Journal of Law and Economics* (April 1974), p. 20.

†Large numbers do not rule out all forms of collusion—only collusion based on voluntary, private agreement. Collusion can also be implemented through the use of the coercive power of government. For example, government can fix prices above competitive levels and then use its police powers to punish any firm that chisels. This is precisely what happens in many federal price support programs for agricultural products. In such markets, private collusion would be impossible because of the large number of producers involved. However, those producers have turned to the government as a source of coordination and enforcement to effectively collude.

Obstacles to Collusion

Don't get the wrong idea here: Concentration alone does *not* always lead to collusion. It simply makes collusion possible by lowering the costs of agreement, coordination, and enforcement. Many other factors can increase those costs and thus reduce the feasibility of collusion in even the most highly concentrated industries. The following are some of the more important of those factors.

Internal Bickering Even if collusion succeeds in completely eliminating *market competition* among sellers, it cannot eliminate their *internal competition* over the division of spoils. Conflicts over the allocation of profits, or over which colluder is to bear the brunt of the output restriction, increase the costs of maintaining a collusive arrangement and can become a serious threat to its survival. For example, when bickering among members of OPEC led to widespread violations of the cartel's production quotas in the mid-1980s, the price of crude oil on world markets quickly dropped $40 per barrel to less than $15 per barrel.

Entry Profitable collusion invites the entry of new competitors, and, unless such entry can be blocked, the new entrants must be taken into the collusive group—thus diluting profits until only a competitive return is earned—or the collusive group must compete with the new entrants—in which case collusion gives way to competition.

Differentiated Products Differentiated products reduce the possibilities for collusion in at least two ways. First, sellers of differentiated products are likely to have different costs and different demands, making agreement and coordination more difficult than they would be with homogeneous products. Second, differentiated products create opportunities for non-price competition. Any member of a collusive group has ample incentive and opportunity to try to increase sales by product improvement, more intensive advertising, more frequent model changes, or a more extensive product line. This kind of competition is virtually impossible for a collusive group to prevent and, because it is costly, it dissipates the pure profits that would otherwise result from collusion. At the same time, it increases the incentive for each individual seller to secretly chisel on price to expand sales without incurring the costs of non-price competition.

Technological Change Collusion is difficult in industries experiencing changes in technology. By continuously altering the nature of the product or the costs of production, technological change increases the costs of agreement, coordination, and enforcement, especially when its effects are unpredictable and vary among the parties to the collusive agreement.

The Effects of Collusion

We can illustrate the effects of collusion with the aid of Figure 11.4. Under competitive conditions, an industry's marginal cost curve (MC) is the market supply curve, and the equilibrium price and output are P_0 and Q_0, respectively. On the other hand, a collusive group maximizes the joint profits of its members by restricting total output to Q_1—the level that equates marginal revenue and

Figure 11.4

Competition, monopoly, and collusion

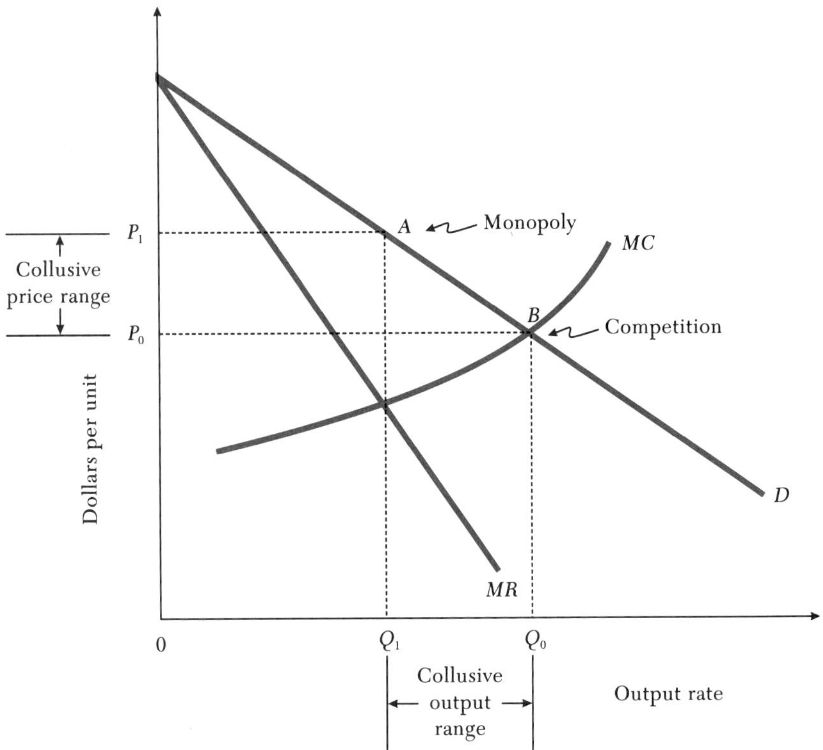

marginal cost—and charging the corresponding monopoly price P_1. In its most extreme form, therefore, collusion has the same effects as monopoly. However, because of the factors just noted, actual collusive arrangements are more likely to achieve results somewhat short of full-blown monopoly. Thus we can interpret actual collusion as leading to a price-quantity outcome somewhere between points *A* and *B* on the demand curve. The stronger the collusive agreement, the closer to the monopoly price at point *A*; the more costly and difficult are agreement, coordination, and enforcement, the closer to the competitive price at point *B*.

Explicit Collusion: The Cartel

As we saw in Chapter 2, a *cartel* is an association formed to limit or eliminate competition among its members. Private cartels are generally illegal in the United States and, to the extent that they exist in this country, they must rely on secrecy and conspiracy. In international markets and countries where cartels are legal, however, collusive agreements are often overt and above board. Whether overt or covert, cartels can take a variety of forms.

Price-Fixing Perhaps the most common type of cartel behavior is the price-fixing agreement just described. Certainly the most important price-fixing cartel in recent years has been that of the Organization of Petroleum Exporting Countries, or OPEC, to which we have referred on many occasions. The International Air Transport Association (IATA) provides another example of a price-fixing cartel. IATA openly sets airfares on all international routes flown by its member airlines, which consist of nearly all of the world's regularly scheduled, international commercial air carriers. IATA has effectively enforced its price-fixing arrangement by denying landing rights at major international airports to any airline that does not abide by its fare schedules.

Bid-Rigging Where contracts are awarded on the basis of a sealed bid, bidders may attempt to avoid competition by agreeing ahead of time on which of them is to submit the winning bid. Sealed bidding facilitates collusion by making it easy to detect cheating: If a party other than the collusively agreed-upon low bidder wins the contract, that in itself is clear evidence that that party has cheated.

One of the more famous cases of bid-rigging in U.S. history involved high level executives of a number of major electrical equipment suppliers—including General Electric, Westinghouse, and other respected manufacturers—who colluded in bidding on government contracts during the early 1960s. The participants used elaborate methods of communication to coordinate their actions: Calls were made from pay phones, notes were circulated in unmarked envelopes, and secret meetings were code named "choir practices." When the scheme was finally uncovered, the companies were fined millions of dollars and a number of top executives were sent to prison.

Market Division and Customer Allocation A cartel can also divide markets or customers among its members in such a way that each is effectively a monopolist in its own market. The territorial rights that major sports leagues typically grant to their individual franchises provide an example of market division intended to increase market power. In major league baseball, for example, territorial rights guarantee that no team can televise games in another team's home market without permission. As a result, each team has a monopoly in its local television market, thus enabling teams to sell local television rights at a higher price than would otherwise be the case.

Joint Sales Agencies In some cases a cartel channels its members' pooled output through a common sales agency, thereby eliminating competition in the sale of the product. The international diamond cartel, for example, relies on the fact that more than 80 percent of the world's annual production of uncut diamonds is marketed through De Beers Consolidated Mines, Ltd. As the sole broker between producers and dealers, De Beers effectively controls both the buying and selling prices of new diamonds and the total volume of new diamonds put on the market each year. This control greatly reduces the costs of agreement and coordination among individual diamond producers, wholesalers, and retailers. However, even De Beers must cope with the problem of enforcement. When the country of Zaire, a major producer of industrial grade diamonds, tried to circumvent the cartel and market its output independently in 1981, De Beers retaliated by dumping large quantities of industrial diamonds on the market, depressing their prices and eventually forcing Zaire to return to the fold.

Noncompetitive Codes of Conduct Many professions—law, medicine, dentistry, architecture, and others—have at one time or another promulgated codes of conduct that effectively suppressed competition among their members. Until recently, for example, lawyers were prohibited from advertising the prices of their services. After such restrictions were eliminated by a 1977 Supreme Court decision, the price of many standard legal services fell dramatically. Although the bar associations that enforced the prohibitions claimed that the lofty status of the legal profession would be tainted by the crass commercialism of advertising, it was apparently mainly the lofty status of legal fees that was undermined.

Tacit Collusion

Tacit collusion is collusion based on an implicit understanding, rather than on an explicit agreement.

Collusion need not always take the form of an explicit agreement. In principle, it can involve little more than an implicit recognition of the potential profits to be gained when no one rocks the boat by competing too vigorously and the willingness to behave accordingly. We refer to such behavior as **tacit collusion**. The lack of explicit agreements and formal methods of coordination and enforcement means that all of the obstacles to collusion discussed earlier are magnified when non-competitive behavior is based only on tacit agreement. This suggests that tacit collusion is possible only in highly concentrated industries and, even then, only under special circumstances. Although economists disagree over the frequency with which tacit collusion actually occurs and the extent to which it can effectively raise prices significantly above competitive levels, most agree that it cannot be ruled out entirely.

Concentration and Collusion: The Empirical Evidence

As we have already noted, economic theory does *not* imply that concentration always leads to collusion; it suggests only that concentration may facilitate collusion where other conditions are also conducive to such behavior. In other words, concentration may be a *necessary* condition for collusion, but it is not a *sufficient* condition. Whether or not there is, in reality, a systematic relation between concentration and collusion is an empirical question, and one to which economists have devoted much research. The earliest of this research, carried out during the 1950s, found a positive correlation between concentration and accounting profits in many industries.* Reasoning that firms in more concen-

*Joe S. Bain, "Relation of Profit Rate to Industry Concentration: American Manufacturing, 1936–1940," *Quarterly Journal of Economics* (August 1951).

trated industries can maintain high profit rates only through collusion, many economists interpreted this as evidence that concentration does indeed systematically lead to collusion. These economists tended to accept a view of competition that has come to be known as the **structuralist hypothesis**. According to this hypothesis, the more concentrated an industry's *structure*, the less competitive its *conduct*, and the closer its *performance* to that of monopoly. Indeed, some who accept the structuralist hypothesis in its most extreme form have described highly concentrated industries as *shared monopolies*.

The **structuralist hypothesis** holds that the structure of an industry—specifically, its concentration—is the principal determinant of the competitive conduct and performance of its members.

More recent research, using more extensive data and improved statistical techniques, has cast considerable doubt on the structuralist hypothesis, however. This research has revealed that the correlation between concentration and profits tends to become very weak, or even disappear, when differences in the absolute size of firms, advertising expenditures, and other factors are taken into account. It has also found that, within a given concentrated industry, larger firms tend to have higher than average profits while smaller firms do not.* If concentration leads to higher profits via collusion, this would not be the case: All firms in the concentrated industry would have higher than average profits because all would benefit from the umbrella of higher prices provided by collusion.

This recent evidence tends to support the position of those economists who have argued, contrary to the structuralist view, that concentration is more likely to be the *result of competition* than the *cause of collusion*.† According to this view, to the extent that significant economies of scale make larger firms more efficient than smaller firms, competition naturally leads, via the survivor principle, to higher concentration. On the other hand, if a few large but inefficient firms in a concentrated industry try to cover their higher costs by colluding, then smaller, more efficient firms will find it profitable to enter the market, underprice their larger, less efficient rivals, and eventually deconcentrate the industry. In the absence of artificial restrictions on entry and exit, therefore, an industry can become concentrated in the first place, and remain concentrated over time, only if concentration is consistent with efficient and competitive production. Conversely, by supporting a price umbrella that allows smaller, less efficient firms to survive, collusion can actually lead to *lower* levels of concentration than would otherwise be the case.

Although the debate over the link, if any, between concentration and collusion is far from resolved, it appears that those who view the link as a weak one have had the upper hand in recent years.

*Bradley T. Gale and Ben Branch, "Concentration versus Market Share: What Determines Performance and Why Does It Matter?" *Antitrust Bulletin* (Spring 1982).

†For a statement of this view, along with a summary of the controversy over the relationship between concentration and collusion, see John S. McGee, "The Concentration-Collusion Doctrine" in Fox and Halverson (Eds.), *Industrial Concentration and the Market System* (American Bar Association Press, 1979). For the opposing view see, Frederic M. Scherer, "Structure-Performance Relationships and Antitrust Policy" in the same volume.

CHAPTER SUMMARY

1. A *concentrated industry* is one in which a few relatively large firms account for a substantial share of market supply.
2. The *concentration ratio* is a simple way of measuring an industry's degree of concentration. It tells the percentage of industry sales accounted for by a small number (e.g., four, eight) of the largest firms in the industry. Concentration ratios should be interpreted with caution because they always depend on a necessarily arbitrary definition of the market.
3. Other things being equal, the more significant the scale economies relative to the size of the market, the more concentrated the industry which supplies that market.
4. According to the *survivor principle*, an industry's structure, including its concentration, is the product of an evolutionary process based on survival of the fittest in the economic jungle. The principle applies not only to fitness based on firm size and economies of scale, but to other characteristics of firms as well.
5. An *oligopoly* is a market in which there are only a few firms, each of whose actions affect the others. Competition in such a market tends to be *rivalrous* in the sense that each firm must take into account the actions and possible reactions of its identifiable competitors, or rivals, when formulating its policies.
6. Economists have had little success in developing a single, unified theory to explain rivalrous competition under conditions of oligopoly. Such a theory has to go beyond simple profit maximization to incorporate assumptions about how firms view their mutual interdependence.
7. Successful *collusion* must overcome the costs of reaching an agreement as well as coordinating and enforcing behavior consistent with the terms of that agreement. Enforcement is necessary because each party to collusion has an opportunity to profitably exploit the noncompetitive behavior of its fellow colluders by cheating on their agreement.
8. The fact that the collusive group must be small enough to be manageable, and yet not so small as to exclude significant competitors, implies that collusion is most likely in concentrated markets where a relatively small number of firms accounts for a substantial share of total sales.
9. Collusion is made more difficult by internal bickering among the colluders, threats of entry, differentiated products, and technological change.
10. To the extent that collusion succeeds, its effects on market price and quantity are similar to those of monopoly.

11. Explicit collusion, or *cartels*, can take many forms, including price-fixing, bid-rigging, market division, joint sales agencies, and noncompetitive codes of conduct.

12. *Tacit collusion*—that is, collusion without an explicit agreement—may be possible, but only in highly concentrated industries and, even then, only under special circumstances.

13. Recent empirical research has generally failed to support the structuralist hypothesis, which holds that the more concentrated a market's structure, the less competitive it is and the more its performance will resemble that of a monopoly.

Key Terms and Concepts

concentrated industry
concentration ratio
survivor principle
oligopoly
rivalrous competition
price-fixing
tacit collusion
structuralist hypothesis

Questions for Thought and Discussion

1. In addition to the concentration ratios for specific industries, measures of concentration have also been calculated for the U.S. economy as a whole. For example, in 1970 the 100 largest industrial corporations in the United States accounted for 62.3 percent of all domestic industrial sales. By 1980 that figure had grown to 67.6 percent, and by 1987 it had grown to 69.5 percent. What, if anything, does this tell you about what happened to the degree of competition in U.S. industry as a whole between 1970 and 1980?

2. In reporting market shares and concentration ratios, many textbooks use the terminology of *control*, as in "The four largest firms in the widget market control 80 percent of all widget sales." What does it mean to "control" a portion of market sales?

3. Will a firm in an oligopoly setting be more reluctant to raise its price if it believes its rivals will match its price increase or if it believes that its rivals will not respond at all? What about its incentive to lower price?

4. Collusion is a form of cooperation among firms that would otherwise be competitors. Is there a difference between collusive cooperation and other forms of cooperation, say, for example, firms pooling resources for research and development?

5. Widgets can be produced at a constant marginal and average cost of $3 per unit. (There are no fixed costs.) Assume that there are five firms in the widget industry, and use the information about the demand for widgets in the table to answer the following questions.

Demand Price	*Quantity*	*Total Revenue*	*Marginal Revenue*
$10	20	$200	
9	30	270	$7/unit
8	40	320	5/unit
7	50	350	3/unit
6	60	360	1/unit
5	70	350	– 1/unit
4	80	320	– 3/unit
3	90	270	– 5/unit
2	100	200	– 7/unit
1	110	110	– 9/unit

a. What will be the price of widgets, the total quantity of widgets produced, the quantity produced per firm, and the profits of each firm if they compete?
b. What will be the price of widgets, the total quantity of widgets produced, the output quota of each firm, and the profits of each firm if they act as a profit-maximizing cartel?
c. Assuming that four of the five producers abide by their output quotas in part b, approximately how much additional profit can the fifth make by cheating on its output quota and producing an extra unit?

6. We have argued that collusion is much more likely in concentrated markets than in unconcentrated ones. We also noted the use of noncompetitive codes of professional conduct as a means of collusion. As an example we cited the legal profession's ban on advertising prices (prior to 1977). But the legal profession is hardly a concentrated industry. There are thousands of independent lawyers and law firms, hundreds in most major metropolitan areas. How do you think such an unconcentrated industry overcame the costs of agreement, coordination, and enforcement to collude successfully for so long? (*Hint*: Have you ever heard of a bar association?)

7. Prior to 1890, the United States had no laws against collusion and cartels. Do you think that this invited the formation of cartels? Do you think that cartels flourished before 1890?

8. Many elite eastern colleges have in the past pooled information about common student applicants and jointly agreed on the amount of financial aid they needed. As a result, it was not uncommon for a student accepted at, say, both Harvard and Yale, to find that her tuition, net of financial aid, was the same at both institutions. Would you call this collusion?

9. Suppose you and your classmates decide to form a "student cartel." Reasoning that, because your instructor grades on a curve, if you and all of your classmates study only half as hard, then the curve will be only half as high. Each student will get the same grade he would otherwise have gotten, but with only half the study time. Describe the incentives to cheat on this student cartel. Do you think the student cartel would be more likely to succeed:

a. If the class is a small one or if it is a large one?
b. If the students in the class are all commuters or if they are all residents of the same dorm?
c. For the midterm exam or for the final exam?

APPENDIX

The Competitive Game

Rivalrous competition has much in common with games such as poker, chess, and bridge. Economic rivals, like the players in a game, must determine their moves and counter moves based on what they anticipate will be the reactions of their competitors. Their strategies must be formulated in the face of uncertainty, and the prizes—in this case, the profits—are distributed on the basis of a combination of both skill and luck. Elaborating on this analogy, an economist and a mathematician collaborated in 1944 to lay the foundations of *game theory*, a set of analytical tools for the study of rational behavior in the face of strategic interdependence.* Though the mathematics of advanced game theory is often quite formidable, we can capture its spirit in a simple example.

Suppose that Alpha, Inc. and Beta Co. are rivalrous competitors and that each is considering whether to raise its price, leave its price unchanged, or lower its price. The hypothetical outcomes corresponding to each possible combination of Alpha's and Beta's strategies are shown in the *payoff matrix* in Table 11A.1 on the following page. The first number in each box, or cell, in the matrix gives Alpha's payoff from the corresponding combination of strategies and the second number gives Beta's payoff. We can interpret the payoffs in this economic game as increases (+) or decreases (−) in profits. For example, cell i, the intersection of Alpha's "Raise Price" row with Beta's "Raise Price" column, shows that if Alpha and Beta both raise their prices the result is a $10 increase in profit for each. Cell ii, on the other hand, shows that if Alpha raises its price while Beta leaves its price unchanged, Alpha loses $5 while Beta gains $15. We might interpret this outcome as the result of Alpha's loss of customers to Beta when

*Oskar Morgenstern and John Von Neumann, *The Theory of Games and Economic Behavior* (Princeton University Press, 1944). Von Neumann was truly one of the foremost intellectuals of the twentieth century, making revolutionary contributions not only to mathematics but also to economics and computer science.

Table 11A.1

Payoff matrix for an economic "game"

		BETA		
		Raise Price	*No Change*	*Lower Price*
ALPHA	*Raise Price*	(i) +10, +10	(ii) −5, +15	(iii) −10, +5
	No Change	(iv) +15, −10	(v) 0, 0	(vi) −20, −5
	Lower Price	(vii) +5, −15	(viii) +10, −5	(ix) −15, −10

Alpha raises its price and Beta does not. Similarly, the mutual losses in cell ix can be interpreted as the result of a price war between the two rivals.

Suppose that Beta decides not to change its price. Then Alpha's best strategy is to lower its price, thus undercutting Beta and increasing its profit by $10. (To see this, look down the "No Change" column for Beta to find the highest corresponding payoff for Alpha.) On the other hand, if Beta decides to match any price change Alpha makes, the relevant cells for Alpha become those on the diagonal, namely, cells i, v, and ix, making Alpha's most profitable strategy to raise its price.

As these examples illustrate, the most profitable strategy for an oligopolist depends on the reactions it expects from its rivals. Accordingly, models of oligopoly typically begin with assumptions about the nature of those expectations and then deduce the behavior that follows. In some game-type situations, these expectations can be determined from the payoff matrix itself. In the payoff matrix in Table 11A.1, for example, Alpha could reasonably expect Beta to choose the "No Change" strategy. Why? Because that strategy gives Beta the highest payoff, regardless of the strategy chosen by Alpha. (To see this, compare Beta's payoff in the "No Change" column with its payoff in the other two columns for each of Alpha's three strategies. Regardless of Alpha's strategy, Beta's best response is to leave its price unchanged.) Knowing that Beta will not change its price, Alpha's best strategy is to lower its price. The economic game in Table 11A.1 therefore has an equilibrium outcome, namely, cell viii. Note that this equilibrium is based only on the standard economic assumption that both Alpha and Beta attempt to maximize profits (or minimize losses).

Now look at the payoff matrix in Table 11A.2 where Alpha's payoffs are the same as in Table 11A.1 but some of Beta's have been changed. In contrast to the original payoff matrix, there is no equilibrium in Table 11A.2 without further assumptions about the behavior of Alpha, Beta, or both. To see this, pick any strategy for Alpha, find Beta's best reaction to that strategy, and note that it gives

Table 11A.2

Payoff matrix without an equilibrium

		BETA		
		Raise Price	*No Change*	*Lower Price*
ALPHA	*Raise Price*	(i) +10, +10	(ii) −5, +15	(iii) −10, +5
	No Change	(iv) +15, −10	(v) 0, 0	(vi) −20, +10
	Lower Price	(vii) +5, −5	(viii) +10, −15	(ix) −15, −10

Alpha an incentive to switch strategy, which in turn gives Beta an incentive to switch, and so on *ad infinitum*. Unfortunately, most game-type situations—and virtually all realistic economic situations involving more than two rivals—are subject to problems of this sort. Predicting the behavior of firms in oligopolistic markets therefore usually requires assumptions over and above that of simple profit maximization. Although a complete survey of possible assumptions and of the numerous oligopoly models to which they lead is well beyond the scope of this book, a couple of representative examples illustrate their nature and limitations.

Price Leadership

One possible pattern of oligopolistic behavior is *price leadership*, whereby one firm—the price leader—assumes that its rivals will follow suit whenever it changes price. To see how price leadership might arise, look again at the payoff matrix in Table 11A.2. Starting from an initial position in cell v, suppose that Alpha raises its price. According to the table, it appears that Beta's best strategy is to leave its price unchanged, thereby enjoying a $15 profit increase (cell ii). However, Beta may recognize that its failure to match Alpha's price increase, by imposing a $5 loss on Alpha, would eventually force Alpha to retaliate by lowering its price back to the original level. The final result would thus leave both Alpha and Beta back in cell v where they began. Beta may therefore conclude that its best strategy is not to leave its price unchanged, but rather to follow Alpha's price increase with a price increase of its own and settle for a $10 increase in profits. Furthermore, if Alpha believes that Beta will match a price increase, then a price increase is indeed Alpha's best strategy.

Price leadership is likely to be a feasible and stable form of market behavior only if two conditions are present. First, the failure of a single oligopolist to match the price increases of the potential price leader must have a substantial adverse effect on the latter's profits; otherwise the potential price leader has no incentive to retaliate with a price cut. In the preceding example, Beta's incentive to follow Alpha's price increase comes from the losses it imposes on Alpha, and therefore the retaliation it invites, when it fails to do so. Second, retaliation must be swift; otherwise the interim profits available to an oligopolist who fails to follow a price increase create incentives not to follow the leader. Although these conditions may exist in certain circumstances—for example, in highly concentrated industries with homogeneous products such as steel—they are hardly universal characteristics of oligopolistic markets. In most cases, the potential benefits of undercutting the would-be price leader are simply too tempting for its rivals to ignore.

The Kinked Demand Model

Another model, and one that many economists once considered appropriate for the analysis of many oligopolistic markets, assumes that an oligopolist will expect its rivals to match a price cut but not a price increase. In effect, the oligopolist fears the worst when it comes to anticipating its rivals' reactions to a price change: If it raises its price, it will lose substantial sales to rivals who, by assumption, will not increase their prices. On the other hand, if it cuts its price in an attempt to expand sales, it will be frustrated by the matching price cuts of its rivals.

In terms of the payoff matrix in Table 11A.2, Alpha believes that Beta will match its price cut (cell ix), not match its price increase (cell ii), and presumably do nothing if Alpha does nothing (cell v). Comparing the outcomes of these three possibilities, we can see that Alpha's best strategy is "No Change" in its price. Furthermore, if Beta is assumed to have similar expectations about Alpha's reaction to a change in price, then Beta's best strategy is also "No Change" in price.

Interpreted graphically, the oligopolist's assumption that its rivals will match a price cut but not a price increase implies that it perceives its demand curve as less elastic for a price cut than for a price increase. The difference in elasticities results in a discontinuity, or *kink*, at the current price on the oligopolist's demand curve.

To illustrate the implications of this *kinked demand* model, let us assume that the oligopolist represented in Figure 11A.1 is initially maximizing its profits at a price of P_0 and an output rate of q_0. This price-output combination is represented by point K in the diagram. Part (a) shows two demand curves through point K: a more elastic demand curve labelled DD' and a less elastic demand curve labelled dd'. For each demand curve there is a corresponding marginal revenue curve. These marginal revenue curves are labelled MM' and mm', respectively.

In part (b) of the diagram, we have "erased" segment KD' of the more elastic demand curve below price P_0 and segment dK of the less elastic demand curve above price P_0. What remains is the demand curve DKd' which, as you can see, has a kink at point K. We have also erased those portions of the marginal revenue curves corresponding to the irrelevant segments of the corresponding demand

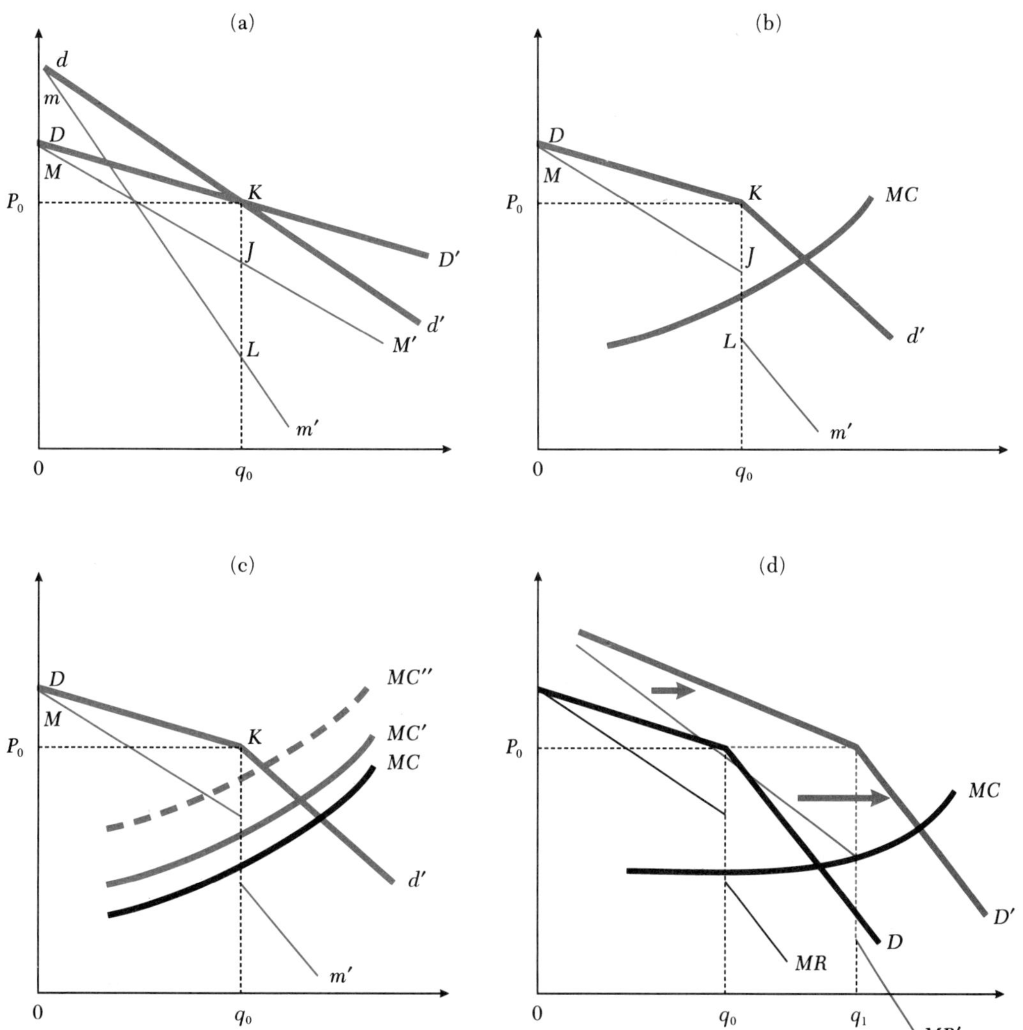

Figure 11A.1

The kinked demand model

curves, namely, segment *mL* of marginal revenue curve *mm′* and segment *JM′* of marginal revenue curve *MM′*. This leaves a marginal revenue curve given by *MJLm′* which has a vertical *gap* between points *J* and *L* directly below the kink in the demand curve.* Because we have assumed that q_0 is the profit-maximizing rate of output, the marginal cost curve must intersect the marginal revenue curve somewhere in this gap.

*Note that the segment of the marginal revenue curve corresponding to a given segment of the demand curve is determined with reference to quantity rather than price. For example, in determining the marginal revenue curve corresponding to demand segment *DA* we "erased" the portion of *DM* to the left of Q_0, not the portion above P_0, because the marginal revenue curve is drawn as a function of quantity rather than price.

Now suppose that costs change. In particular, suppose that the marginal cost curve shifts upward from *MC* to *MC′* as shown in part (c). Because the new marginal cost curve still passes through the gap in the marginal revenue curve, it intersects that curve at the same rate of output as before, namely q_0. Thus, despite the increase in its marginal costs, neither the profit-maximizing output nor the corresponding profit-maximizing price has changed for the kinked demand oligopolist. As you can see from the diagram, the marginal cost curve would have to shift by a larger amount, say to *MC″*, before the oligopolist would find it profitable to change its price and output. Similarly, an increase in demand as shown in part (d), would lead the kinked demand oligopolist to increase its sales to q_1 units but not to increase its price.

According to the kinked demand model, therefore, prices in oligopolistic markets do not respond to changes in cost and demand conditions unless those changes are relatively large. This hypothesis of *oligopolistic price rigidity* in effect suggests that oligopolistic industries are to some extent exempt from the laws of supply and demand.

As a general model of oligopolistic behavior, the kinked demand model has serious deficiencies. For one thing, it tells us nothing about how the rigid price is determined in the first place; it simply assumes an initial price and concludes that it will be rigid. Nor does it tell us anything about the effects of entry and exit, which would presumably take place if the rigid price leads to pure profits or losses. Most importantly, the kinked demand model fails the empirical test. Although the apparent stability of published *list prices* in some concentrated industries provided early empirical support for the model, subsequent investigation has shown that actual *transactions prices* (which take into account special discounts, variations in credit terms, and the like) actually tend to fluctuate *more* in markets with the characteristics of oligopoly than in markets that are virtually monopolized.* Thus the kinked demand model, like the price leadership model, describes at best a special case of oligopolistic behavior.

*See George J. Stigler, "The Kinky Oligopoly Demand Curve and Rigid Prices," *Journal of Political Economy* (October 1947); Julian L. Simon, "A Further Test of the Kinky Oligopoly Demand Curve," *The American Economic Review* (December 1969); Walter J. Primeaux and Mickey C. Smith, "Pricing Patterns and the Kinky Demand Curve," *The Journal of Law and Economics* (April 1976).

CHAPTER 12

Product Differentiation: Variety, Quality, and Advertising

Economists are at long last emerging from the stage in which price competition was all they saw. . . . [I]n capitalist reality as distinguished from its textbook picture, it is not that kind of competition which counts but the competition from the new commodity, the new technology, the new source of supply, the new type of organization . . . which strikes not at the margins of the profits and the outputs of the existing firms but at their foundations and their very lives.

JOSEPH A. SCHUMPETER*

The role of any model is to simplify. The models we have developed in the preceding three chapters simplified a great deal by focusing almost exclusively on the pricing dimension of the competitive process. To capture more of the richness and diversity of that process, we must go beyond these models to consider the product itself as an instrument of competition. In this chapter we therefore consider the economics of the product differentiation that leads to the incredible variety of goods and services offered in the marketplace and to the efforts of their producers to communicate their existence—and persuade us of their desirability—through advertising.

Monopolistic competition is a market structure in which there are a large number of firms selling differentiated products and in which there are no significant restrictions on entry.

We begin with an economic model with the oxymoronic (reach for your dictionary!) title of **monopolistic competition**. We then use the model's basic

* *Capitalism, Socialism and Democracy* (Harper & Row: Harper Torchbooks, 1962), p. 84.

insights, along with many of the analytical tools developed in previous chapters, to explore the sources, forms, and implications of product differentiation.

MONOPOLISTIC COMPETITION: THE BASIC MODEL

As the name suggests, the model of monopolistic competition is essentially a hybrid that combines elements of both pure competition and monopoly. Like pure competition, monopolistic competition assumes a large number of relatively small sellers competing in a market where there are no significant restrictions on entry. Unlike the pure competitor, the monopolistic competitor, by virtue of its differentiated product, is a price setter with some market power. However, that market power is limited by the many close substitutes produced by its competitors, including substitutes that may be introduced in the long run by new entrants. The monopolistically competitive firm is therefore "monopolistic" only in the very limited sense that no one produces a *perfect* substitute for its product.

Examples of markets that approximate the conditions of monopolistic competition include retailing (department stores, supermarkets, and gas stations, for example), and services (restaurants, movie theaters, law firms and building contractors, for example), as well as markets in housing, used cars, and most consumer goods.

As we saw in Chapter 10, products can be differentiated in a number of ways: There may be physical differences, such as differences in quality and reliability; differences in style, in service, location, and other conditions of sale; or any combination of these. Let us begin, however, with a simple case, namely, one in which the basis of product differentiation lies solely in differences in geographic location. In particular, we assume that we are dealing with the retail gasoline market in some metropolitan area, and that the only attribute which distinguishes one gas station from another in the eyes of consumers is its location. We begin with the market in long-run equilibrium and then examine the adjustments that take place when that equilibrium is disturbed.

The absence of entry restrictions in a monopolistically competitive industry guarantees that there are no economic profits (or losses) in long-run equilibrium. Such a zero-profit equilibrium can be interpreted graphically as the tangency of each firm's demand curve with its average total cost curve, as shown in Figure 12.1. Each firm's price just covers its average cost at the price-output combination corresponding to point E, the point of tangency; any other price-output combination consistent with demand lies below the average cost curve and thus results in losses. (Note that the intersection of the marginal revenue and marginal cost curves lies directly below the point of tangency. The reason is that profits are maximized—in this case at zero—at that point.)

Figure 12.1

Long-run equilibrium under monopolistic competition

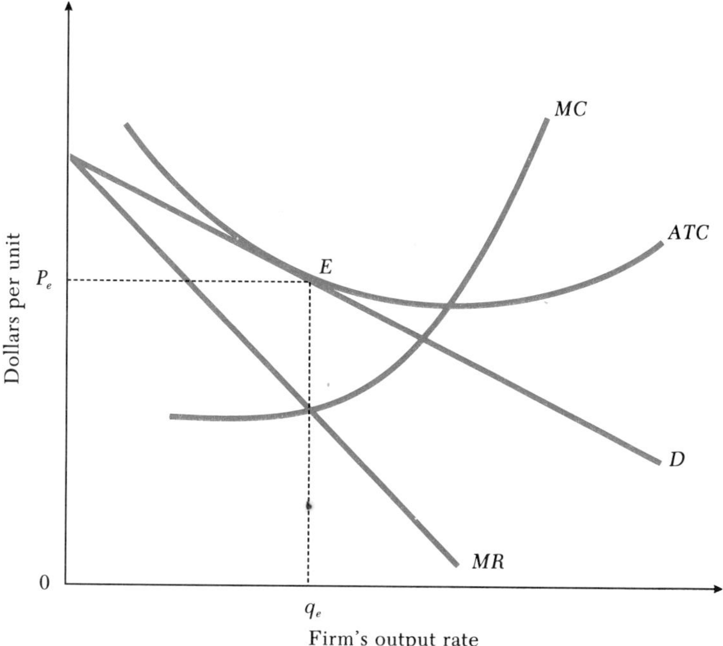

The Short Run

Now suppose that this equilibrium is disturbed. In particular, suppose that there is an unexpected shift in the metropolitan population from the central city to the suburbs. Assuming that people prefer to buy gasoline from gas stations close to their homes, this shift in population increases the demand for the gasoline supplied by suburban stations and decreases the demand for gasoline supplied by urban stations.

Figure 12.2 on the following page illustrates the situation in the suburban and urban markets after these changes in demand. The typical suburban gas station, shown in part (a), is now earning pure economic profits, and it is maximizing those profits by selling an amount equal to q_s and charging a price equal to P_s. The typical urban gas station, on the other hand, having suffered a decline in demand, is losing money as illustrated in part (b). Assuming that price still covers average variable cost, it minimizes those losses in the short run by producing output q_u and charging a price P_u.

Note that the determination of the profit-maximizing (or loss-minimizing) output and price is the same for the monopolistic competitor as it is for a monopolist or any other price setter: Output is determined at the intersection of the marginal revenue and marginal cost curves, and price at the corresponding point on the demand curve.

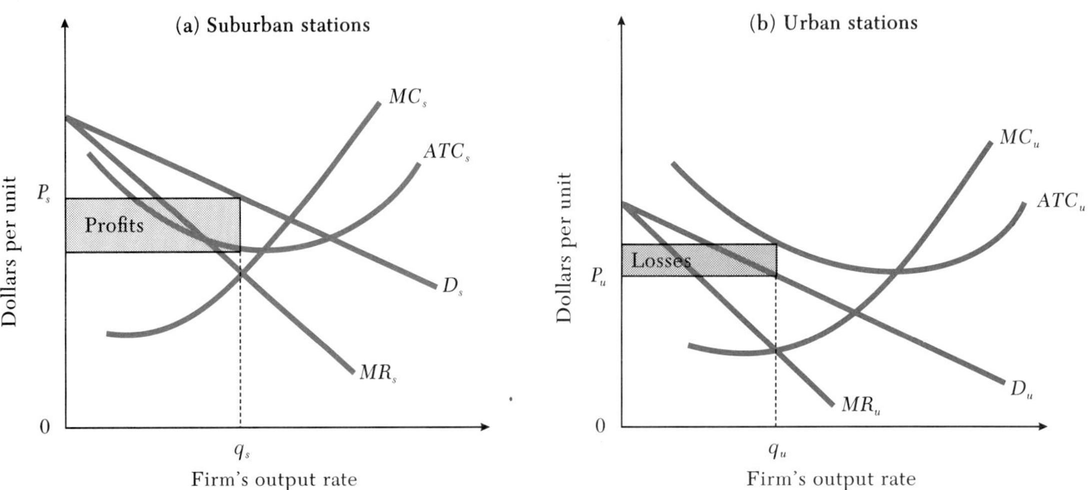

Figure 12.2

Short-run effects of population shift

The Long Run

Because profits and losses eventually result in entry and exit, the situation illustrated in Figure 12.2 is only a short-run equilibrium. In the long run, new gasoline stations will enter the suburban market while others will exit from the urban market.

As entry into the suburban market proceeds, the demand curves facing the suburban gas stations (incumbents as well as new entrants) will be affected in two ways. First, as the suburban market is divided among an increasing number of competitors, the demand for the gasoline sold by any one suburban station will be decreased. Second, because there will be more substitutes for the gasoline sold by each station—perhaps another gas station every couple of blocks rather than every couple of miles—the demand curve faced by each station will become more elastic. This simultaneous reduction in demand and increase in the price elasticity of demand is illustrated in Figure 12.3. Just the reverse will occur as gas stations exit from the urban market: The demand faced by the remaining urban stations will increase and become less elastic.

Entry and exit can also affect costs. In this particular example, suburban land costs may rise relative to urban land costs as the migration of gasoline stations (and, realistically, of other businesses as well) increases the demand for suburban commercial land relative to urban commercial land. Thus the cost curves in Figure 12.2(a) will shift upward while those in Figure 12.2(b) will shift downward.

These long-run demand and cost adjustments tend to reduce both the pure profits earned by owners of suburban gas stations and the losses suffered by the owners of urban gas stations. Other things being equal, the process will continue until all profits and losses—and thus any incentives for further entry or exit—are eliminated, and we are once again back in long-run equilibrium. The adjustments and the new equilibria are illustrated in Figure 12.4.

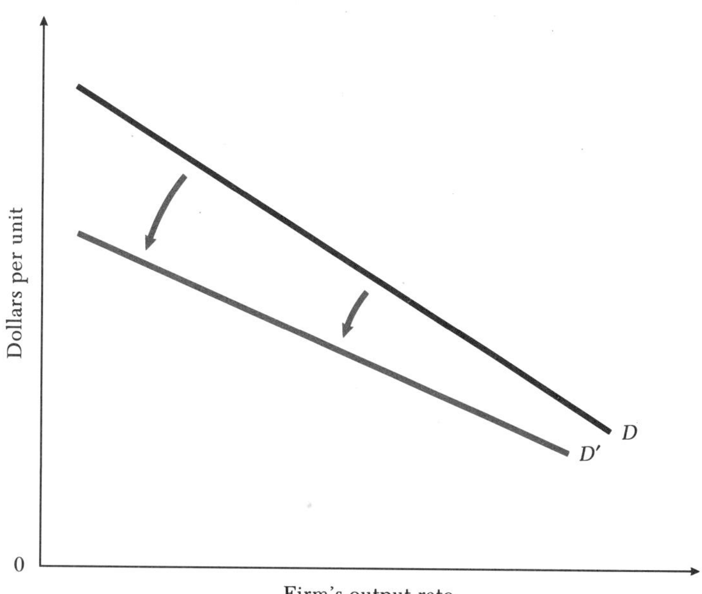

Figure 12.3

The effects of entry on demand: demand decreases and becomes more elastic

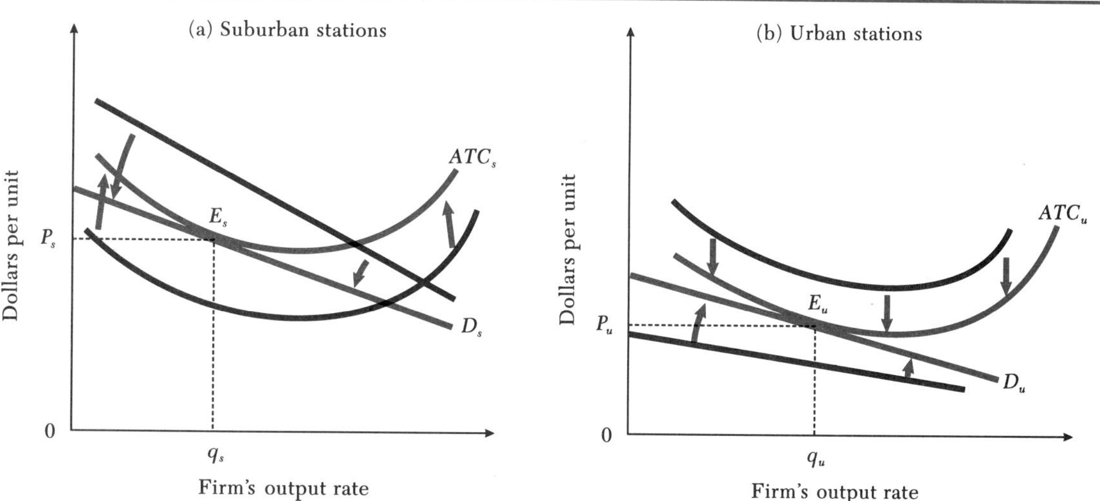

Figure 12.4

Adjustments to a new long-run equilibrium

The fact that all firms break even in a monopolistically competitive long-run equilibrium does *not* imply that all are charging the same price. Because products are differentiated, there are differences in costs and thus corresponding differences in price. In our particular example, gas stations located at busy intersections and along heavily travelled thoroughfares can charge higher prices because of greater demand, but they still only break even because of the higher rents they must pay for their prime locations.

Finally, we must once again emphasize a point we originally made in our earlier discussion of long-run equilibrium under pure competition. In any real-world market, a variety of factors that affect demand and cost conditions are continuously changing, so it is extremely unlikely that a long-run equilibrium will ever actually be attained. The *concept* of long-run equilibrium, however, is valuable because it enables us to predict the ultimate consequences of changes in factors that affect demand and cost. In the preceding example, the concept of long-run equilibrium enabled us to predict the effect of a shift in population on the geographic distribution of gas stations. Whether the actual distribution ever reaches a long-run equilibrium is immaterial to the fundamentals of the argument.

THE PRODUCT AS A VARIABLE

We can use the geographic distribution of gas stations in the preceding example as a metaphor for a much more general aspect of the competitive process. Just as competition among gas station owners involves the choice of location, so competition among the producers of any differentiated product involves the choice of those particular product characteristics that each hopes will be appealing to consumers. In other words, the product itself becomes a variable in this expanded view of the competitive process. In a world of costly information, competition involves not just the choice of prices and quantities, but the discovery of consumer preferences and the development of products that will meet those preferences. It also involves informing consumers, usually through advertising, about the nature and availability of such products. In the remainder of this chapter we examine these important aspects of the competitive process.

Imitation

In the marketplace, as in so many other areas of social interaction, success breeds imitation. Just as suburban market profits in the last example led to a migration of gas stations to the suburbs, any profitable product, regardless of the source of its differentiation, will attract imitators. The success of McDonald's, for example, led to the entry of other fast food chains—Burger King, Jack-in-the-Box, and Wendy's, to name just a few—offering the same general type of food, service, and convenience. The success of Lite Beer from Miller not only attracted a host of other low calorie beers introduced by Miller's competitors but also led to the production of "light" soft drinks, "light" wine, and even "light" potato chips. (Heavy potato chips, as any beer connoisseur knows, do not go well with light beer.) The introduction of close substitutes for successful products eventually reduces the market power and profits of their producers. Thus, while imitation may be the sincerest form of flattery, it is also costly for those who pioneer successful new products.

Innovation

Of course, not all new products are simply imitations of successful existing ones. Technological change is continuously opening up new production possibilities and producers are constantly searching for ways to incorporate those possibilities into new products and improved versions of old products. But since the particular product characteristics that will appeal most to consumers are rarely known by producers ahead of time, product innovation always involves an element of risk. A couple of examples serve as reminders that such risks exist for even the largest and most sophisticated innovators.

The Disappointing Disk

The video cassette recorder (VCR) was introduced in the mid-1970s. It is essentially a video tape recorder that allows the user to play prerecorded tapes and to tape and replay television programs. By the early 1980s, VCRs had become an established product in the consumer electronics market.

Just as VCRs were achieving their success, new technologies became available that allowed the storage of prerecorded programming on disks similar to phonograph records for playback on the television screen. (Indeed, the audio counterpart of the video disk is the compact disk, or CD, which has now virtually replaced the phonograph as a music medium.) Unlike VCRs, however, the video disk technology did not allow the consumer to record television programs. Gambling that the lower price, greater simplicity, and superior picture quality of video disks would outweigh this drawback, two major consumer electronics manufacturers, RCA and North American Phillips (the producer of Magnavox and Sylvania television sets), invested hundreds of millions of dollars in the development and marketing of video disk systems. By the mid-1980s, however, it became apparent that the systems would not be nearly as popular with consumers as these entrepreneurs had anticipated. RCA alone lost $575 million before it stopped manufacturing its video disk player.* Zenith, Pioneer, and other companies that had agreed to market the players under their own brand names also lost substantial sums of money on the venture.

On the brighter side, the technology that went into the video disk now shows immense promise in another quite unrelated area, namely, the storage of huge amounts of computer data. Moreover, as we enter the 1990s it appears that the videodisk technology may even be about to make a comeback in the consumer entertainment market.

Pulling the Plug on Junior

Buoyed by the phenomenal success of the personal computer it had introduced primarily for the business market in 1982, IBM introduced the PCjr home computer in 1983. Industry analysts confidently predicted that the "jr" would take the market by storm, leaving the competition in the dust. After all, they reasoned, IBM had never made a major marketing blunder in its corporate history,

* "$575 Million Loss Kills RCA Videodisc Player," *The Wall Street Journal*, April 5, 1984.

and the magical logo of IBM was itself sufficient to guarantee the success of the new product.

Surprise! The PCjr was a total flop, and IBM had to resort to rebates of up to 50 percent of the price and include free software with the machine just to move it off dealers' shelves. It finally admitted defeat when, after only sixteen months, it announced that it would discontinue production of the jr.*

From Reject to Classic

Early in the summer of 1985 the Coca-Cola company committed what one of its executives called the "largest faux pas in the history of marketing."† The company had worked for four-and-one-half years developing a replacement for its 99-year-old recipe for Coke, the world's largest selling soft drink. Its confidence bolstered by a $4 million testing program in which nearly three-quarters of more than 200,000 taste-testers preferred the new recipe, Coca-Cola withdrew the old recipe from the market and introduced the "new Coke" to great fanfare on Memorial Day, 1985. Despite one of the most exhaustive research efforts ever undertaken by a consumer products firm, the new Coke was an immediate disaster. Stunned executives at Coca-Cola rushed the old formula back into production under the name of Coca-Cola Classic.

Product Variety

Although we all share pretty much the same basic wants, the particular goods we choose to satisfy those wants vary considerably from person to person. Nearly everyone enjoys music, for example, but some like rock while others prefer classical; we all must eat, but some of us like Chinese food, while others like Mexican food, and still others like neither; some of us like to dress "preppie" while others prefer faded blue jeans and bare feet. In short, the myriad differences in consumer tastes create a demand for variety.

The market's response to that demand involves a balancing of two factors: *differences in individual preferences* and *economies of scale in production.* To illustrate their interaction, let us consider a simple example. In particular, suppose that there are 101 women, each willing to pay up to $200 for an evening gown. Each, however, has different tastes. One prefers floor length silk with a high neck, padded shoulders and long sleeves; another prefers a mid-length, backless, sleeveless satin design; still another prefers a mini-length chiffon with bouffant sleeves; and so on, through all of the 101 women with individually distinctive preferences.

If the cost of producing a single dress of each individual style were $150, the market response would be the production of 101 one-of-a-kind dresses, each tailored to meet the unique tastes of an individual woman. Because of scale

*"PCjr, Japanese to Change Market," *San Jose Mercury*, November 7, 1983, and "IBM to Halt PCjr Output Next Month," *The Wall Street Journal*, March 20, 1985.

†"Coca-Cola Faces Tough Marketing Task in Attempting to Sell Old and New Coke," *The Wall Street Journal*, July 12, 1985, and "How Coke's Decision to Offer 2 Colas Undid 4-1/2 Years of Planning," *The Wall Street Journal*, July 15, 1985.

economies, however, the cost of producing a single dress of each design is much higher than the cost per dress of producing a large number of the same style. For example, the cost of producing only one dress of a given style may be $300, while the cost of producing 50 or more of the same style may be only $150 per dress. The market balances the potential cost savings from large-scale production against each woman's willingness to pay for the specific styling characteristics she desires. If there are at least 50 women who want a floor length, silk dress with padded shoulders, and 50 who want a mid-length, backless satin dress, then those designs will be produced and sold for $150 each in a competitive market. If there is only one woman who wants a mini-length chiffon with bouffant sleeves, then that design will not be produced at all since only one woman wants that style and her demand price—by assumption, $200—is not enough to cover the $300 cost of one-of-a-kind design. Of course, if she were willing to pay the $300 cost, she would be able to buy her preferred style from a custom fashion designer. Otherwise, like everyone else, she must choose between floor length and mid-length dresses without bouffant sleeves.

Because of economies of scale, therefore, those product characteristics demanded by large numbers of consumers are generally available as standard features, while those characteristics for which the demand is limited relative to economies of scale are available only to those willing to pay the higher costs of small-scale production. This explains, for example, why there may be only three or four floor plans to choose from in a large housing development, and why automobiles come standard with radios (because only a few people *don't* want radios) but not with racing suspension (because only a few people *do* want racing suspension).

It also explains why the variety of programs is so limited on advertiser-supported television. The cost of an advertising message is generally fixed, so that the cost per viewer reached by the message falls as the size of the TV audience increases. Commercial television programming therefore tends toward a relatively few programs with broad-based appeal, rather than a great variety of programs appealing to more specialized tastes; the former are simply lower cost vehicles for getting across an advertising message. Thus, while few would contend that "LA Law" or "Roseanne" are of greater cultural importance than Shakespeare or *La Traviata*, simple economics explains why we rarely see the latter two on commercial television. Such programming is more often seen on networks that do not rely on advertising revenues, such as the government-subsidized Public Broadcasting System and cable systems that allow people to indulge their more specialized tastes by paying directly for the kinds of programming they most enjoy.

Product Quality

Distinct from the demand for a variety of products is the demand for product quality in the form of durability and reliability. Like greater variety, higher quality is generally more costly. In a competitive market, firms balance the costs of additional quality against what they believe consumers are willing to pay for it. Because people differ in their demands for additional quality, just as they differ with respect to other tastes and preferences, the market responds by providing a range of different qualities. It offers choices between Hondas and Hyundais, between Rolexes and Timexes, between Hyatts and Holiday Inns, and between Macy's and Marshall's. Of course the distribution of quality is generally consistent with the old maxim, "You get what you pay for," so the Hondas, Rolexes, Hyatts, and Macy's are usually more expensive than their lower quality counterparts.

Planned Obsolescence?

How many times have you heard it said that producers deliberately build *planned obsolescence* into their products? Their motivation presumably is that the faster their products wear out, the more frequently consumers will have to replace them, which in turn means more revenue for producers. On closer examination, however, this argument does not hold water. To see why, let us first make sure we are clear about the nature of the planned obsolescence argument. As we have seen, lower quality, less durable products generally cost less to produce than higher quality, more durable products. Thus, as long as some people are not willing to pay the higher cost of more durable products, then less durable products will survive in the marketplace. The planned obsolescence argument, however, goes further. It implies that firms will produce lower quality, less durable products *even if there are no cost savings from doing so*, because sales will be greater over time when products wear out faster.

The argument certainly does not apply in a competitive market, for any firm producing an inferior product—and not charging a commensurately lower price—will be driven out of the market by its competitors. But what about a monopolized market? Does a firm that is insulated from competition from higher quality products have an incentive to build in planned obsolescence as a means of increasing demand?

To take a concrete example, let us assume that a monopolist currently produces light bulbs that last 1 year and cost $0.50 each to produce. It sells 100 per day at a price of $0.75 each, so its profit is $25 per day [= 100 × (0.75 − 0.50)]. Now the monopolist discovers, and patents, a new light bulb that lasts 2 years and can be produced for $0.60 each. The new light bulb costs more to produce, and, since it lasts twice as long as the old one, the monopolist will sell only about half as many. Will it therefore use the patent to "deep six" the new technology?

The answer is no. Because each new light bulb will last twice as long, it is worth two of the old ones in the eyes of consumers. Thus, although the monopolist will sell the new light bulbs at the rate of only 50 per day (half the rate at which it sold the old ones), it can charge twice the price, or $1.50 per light bulb. Its profits will therefore be $45 per day [= 50 × ($1.50 − $0.60]. Clearly it is to the monopolist's advantage to produce the longer lasting light bulb.*

*In actuality, the monopolist in this example can generally increase profits to more than $50 per day by charging a price somewhat less than $1.50 and selling somewhat more than 50 of the new light bulbs per day.

In general, as long as the extra durability can be communicated to buyers, the seller can capture its value in the price of the product. Under these conditions, the deliberate production of less durable products without proportionately lower costs—which is what we mean by planned obsolescence—is not profitable.

Lemons Markets

A **lemons market** is a market in which low-quality products ("lemons") come to predominate because consumers cannot distinguish such products from high-quality products.

In markets where it is difficult and costly for buyers to identify product quality in advance, however, we might find what economists call a **lemons market**.* The classic example is the used car market. Buyers of used cars typically have little knowledge of how well a car has been maintained by its original owner and cannot easily distinguish between high-quality used cars and low-quality used cars ("lemons"). They are, therefore, only willing to pay a price reflecting what they perceive as the *average* level of quality in the market. While this price will certainly be acceptable to sellers of lemons, it will seem unreasonably low to sellers of high-quality used cars. As a result, there will be an overabundance of lemons in the used car market relative to the number there would be if buyers could distinguish quality differences.

Note, however, that sellers of high-quality used cars have an incentive to provide a signal to potential buyers about that quality. A dealer, for example, may offer a warranty on the used car. Or a private party may allow the prospective buyer to take the car to a mechanic of the buyer's choice for prepurchase inspection. The very willingness of the seller to offer a warranty or an independent inspection provides the buyer with some information about the probable quality of the car. It also enables the seller of a high-quality used car to obtain a price more in line with the quality of his product and, in so doing, reduces the prevalence of lemons in the market.

Brand Names as Low-Cost Conveyors of Information

Experience goods are goods whose quality becomes known only after they are purchased and consumed.

Inspection goods are goods whose quality can be determined by simple inspection prior to purchase.

A used car is an example of what economists call **experience goods**. It is a good whose quality (or other characteristics) cannot be fully evaluated by consumers prior to purchase. Only after buying and using (experiencing) it can they determine whether they have in fact gotten what they expected in the transaction. Other goods are such that their quality and other characteristics are readily apparent to consumers by simple inspection prior to purchase. Such goods are called, appropriately, **inspection goods**. The lemons problem does not arise with inspection goods because consumers know exactly what they are getting before they buy.

Most goods, even relatively simple consumer goods such as articles of clothing and food items, would ordinarily be experience goods were it not for the phenomenon of *brand names*. An established brand name gives consumers valuable information, at very low cost, about what to expect in a product. In effect,

*George A. Ackerlof, "A Market for 'Lemons': Quality Uncertainty and the Market Mechanism." *The Quarterly Journal of Economics*, August 1970, pp. 488–500.

it converts what would otherwise be an experience good into an inspection good. The name Sony on a television set, or the letters IBM on a computer, tell potential buyers a lot about what to expect in the way of the product's dependability and reliability, even if they know nothing about electronics. A pair of golden arches and the name McDonald's or the bright green script proclaiming Holiday Inn tell hungry or weary travellers just what to expect when they order hamburgers or check into a motel. In short, a brand name promises the customer no surprises.

Note that we are not saying that a brand name necessarily promises *high* quality; it only promises that the good will meet the consumer's *expectations* regarding its quality and other characteristics. Few would argue that a meal at McDonalds and a room at a Holiday Inn are superior to a meal at the Four Seasons and a room at the Ritz. However, all four of these brand names tell the consumer just what to expect, be it a palatable hamburger and a clean room or gourmet food and a view of Central Park.

Because of its efficiency in conveying information about a product, an established and well-known brand name is an asset of considerable value to a firm. As such, it creates an incentive for the firm to provide products that meet the consumer's expectations. A striking example of this was provided by the actions of McNEILAB, the makers of Tylenol, after several people died when Tylenol capsules were criminally laced with cyanide in the fall of 1982. In response, the company spent millions of dollars on protective packaging and other precautions—and millions more advertising these precautions—to re-establish consumer confidence in its product. It is doubtful that such vast expenditures would have been made had the Tylenol brand name not been so valuable; rather McNEILAB would simply have produced the same pain relief formula under a new name. For similar reasons, Apple Computer spent millions of dollars attempting to stop the sale of counterfeit Apples, not only because the counterfeits cut directly into sales of the genuine article but also because the poor reliability of the counterfeits diminished the value of the Apple brand name.

ADVERTISING

Producing a product that is somehow different from those of your competitors is one thing. Communicating its availability and its distinguishing characteristics to potential buyers may be something else again. For example, although differences in styling among various automobiles can be seen at a glance, less obvious features—a car's gas mileage, its trunk capacity, whether it has front- or rear-wheel drive—are less readily apparent. Similarly, although consumers know that hamburger is available at both Safeway and Alpha Beta, they may not know whether one or the other has it on sale this week. This kind of information is valuable both to sellers (who want consumers to be aware of their products) and to consumers (who want to be able to choose intelligently among those products). Because it is valuable, the market creates incentives to provide it.

Consumers themselves, of course, have an incentive to acquire information about what they purchase, and, up to a point, they will do so. However, given the extraordinary variety and complexity of the goods and services available to modern consumers, it is virtually impossible for them to personally investigate even the tiniest fraction of what the marketplace offers. Thus consumers often turn to specialists to obtain information about products. Consumer's Union is one example of such a specialist. It is an independent, not-for-profit organization that tests products ranging from frozen pies to new cars and sells the results in the form of a magazine, *Consumer Reports*. Many other magazines and books, especially those aimed at users of relatively complex products such as cameras, computers, and stereos, devote many pages to the testing and comparison of products. Used car buyers often hire a mechanic to check an automobile prior to purchase. Most of us consult friends and acquaintances about their experiences with various products before we ourselves decide which to purchase.

Other information, however, is provided by the seller. Sellers are well aware that search costs prevent buyers from directly examining every product on the market prior to purchase. The seller's incentive, therefore, is to provide the kind of information that will increase the chances that the buyer will notice, and ultimately purchase, its product. The vehicle by which a seller attempts to communicate information about its product is, of course, advertising. In 1988, nearly $120 billion was spent on advertising in the United States. Figure 12.5 shows how this expenditure was allocated among the major communications media.

Figure 12.5

Advertising expenditures by medium, 1988

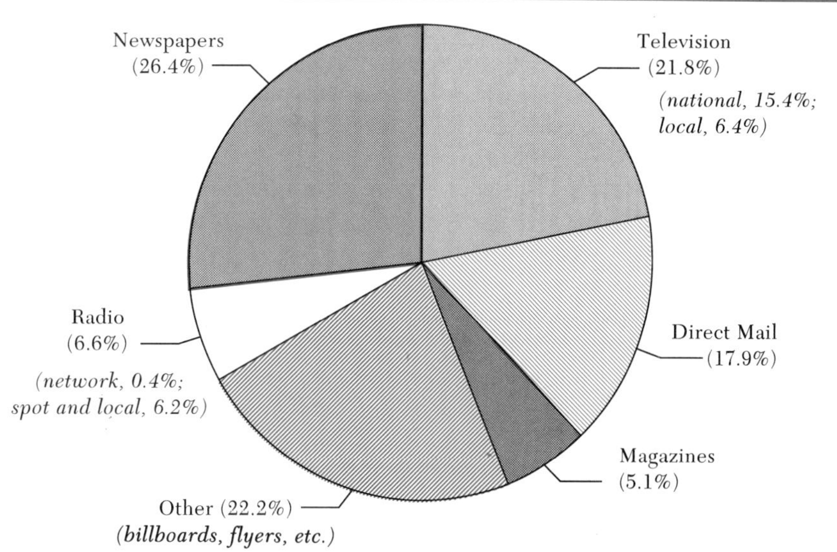

Source: *Statistical Abstract of the United States 1990*

Advertising as Information

Most consumers are well aware that the incentive of the seller is to promote its product and are thus justifiably skeptical about the claims made in advertisements. However, it does not follow that the information conveyed by advertising is always misleading, or at best, worthless, to the potential buyer.

Note from Figure 12.5 that the largest single advertising medium is the newspaper. A quick check of any daily newspaper will indicate that the staple of newspaper advertising is information about the prices and availability of products. Such information is especially valuable in reducing consumers' search costs. Most grocery shoppers, for example, would find shopping much more costly and inconvenient—and their food bills higher as well—were it not for information in newspaper ads about the weekly sales and specials available at local supermarkets. Virtually all direct mail ads, as well as much radio and TV advertising—especially the local ads that account for nearly half of all radio and TV advertising—provide similar information about a wide variety of products.

When it comes to claims about quality, reliability, performance, and other product characteristics, the seller's incentive is obviously to present its product in as favorable a light as possible. We would therefore be extremely naive to expect any *single* seller to present a completely objective and balanced assessment of its product. However, advertising by sellers of competing products provides additional information which, either directly or by implication, tells another side of the story. Pepsi and Coca-Cola, for example, may not have an incentive to advertise that their products contain caffeine, but Seven-Up, whose product does not contain caffeine, does. Butter producers may not have an incentive to tell consumers that butter is high in cholesterol, but margarine producers do.

Comparative ads showing a competitor's product in an unfavorable light were frowned on by the advertising industry and were not accepted by two of the three major broadcast networks until about a decade ago. Recently, however, such ads have become very popular and much more explicit in identifying competitors' brands. By 1981, comparative ads accounted for nearly one-fourth of all radio and television advertising.* They are probably even more prevalent today. While the consumer may have to sift through the claims of a number of competing advertisers to make an intelligent purchase, the information contained in such claims—as long as it is not blatantly false—reduces consumer search costs.

Truth in Advertising?

But what about false and deceptive advertising, the informational content of which is, by definition, worse than useless? Who or what protects the consumer from such misinformation? In part, protection is provided by "watchdogs" in both the public and private sector. At the federal level, the Federal Trade Commission is the government agency charged with enforcing legal prohibitions

* "Comparative Ads Are Getting More Popular, Harder Hitting," *The Wall Street Journal*, March 11, 1981.

against false and misleading advertising. Most states have similar agencies. In the private sector, organizations such as the Better Business Bureau and the consumer action services provided by many radio and television stations and newspapers also police advertising practices. Moreover, the market itself discourages false advertising by penalizing sellers who use such tactics. This is particularly true for sellers who rely on repeat purchases or have established brand names to protect.

If sellers are interested only in a fast buck, they may well be tempted to deceive their potential customers—to "take the money and run" so to speak. However, misleading claims are hardly the way to establish a loyal clientele and, to the extent that sellers rely on repeat purchases and the continued patronage of their customers rather than on one-shot sales, they have a strong incentive not to misrepresent their products.

In addition, we have seen that a brand name is a valuable asset to a seller only to the extent that it conveys reliable information to potential customers. To compromise the reliability of that information through false or deceptive advertising would seriously erode the value of the brand name and would rarely be profitable, especially in the long run.

Of course, neither market incentives nor watchdogs such as the Federal Trade Commission can ever completely eliminate false advertising. The foregoing discussion suggests that it is most likely to be a danger when the good in question is a non-brand name, experience good whose seller does not depend on repeat sales. In short, the lesson is: Never buy a generic home computer from a door-to-door salesperson!

Advertising and Competition

The effect of advertising on competition is an unresolved question in economics. On the one hand, some economists claim that advertising increases market power and acts as a "barrier to entry." In particular, they argue that, to the extent that advertising creates strong brand loyalty, it reduces the elasticity of demand for advertised products. As we have seen, the less elastic the demand for a product, the greater the seller's market power. In addition, it is sometimes argued that entry into markets with heavily advertised products is more difficult because a prospective new entrant must spend more on advertising than producers of established brands.

Other economists argue, to the contrary, that advertising promotes competition. They point out that in a market where products are differentiated, and where information and search are costly, advertising is the principal means by which consumers become aware of the alternatives available to them. Consumer awareness of these alternatives in turn reduces search costs and thus the market power of sellers. Furthermore, these economists maintain that, far from being a *barrier* to entry, advertising is more often an essential *vehicle* for successful entry. According to this argument, new firms would have a *more* difficult time entering a market if advertising were *not* available to them because there would be no way of informing consumers about the availability of their products and touting their advantages over the products of incumbents. Imagine, for example, how much more difficult it would be for the producer of the proverbial better mousetrap to crack the mousetrap market if it couldn't advertise its innovation. In this view, advertising itself is a *form* of competition, namely, a competitive response to costly information.

Because both of these positions are plausible on theoretical grounds, the actual effect of advertising on competition boils down to an empirical question that we can hope to answer only by looking at the facts. In particular, the view that advertising increases market power and discourages entry suggests that, other things being equal, profits will be higher in industries in which firms advertise heavily than in industries with little or no advertising. Initial investigations of the relation between advertising and profits indeed found evidence of a positive correlation between the two, thus tending to support the hypothesis that advertising reduces competition.*

Those who hold the pro-competitive view of advertising argue that these early studies confused economic profit with accounting profit. In particular, they point out that the studies were incorrect in treating advertising expenditures solely as a current expense. Because the goodwill and consumer awareness created by current advertising affect future sales as well as current sales, at least some portion of advertising expenditures should be treated as investment rather than as a current expense. In their failure to make this distinction, the early empirical studies mistakenly included as profit certain earnings that were actually a competitive return on past investment in advertising. When the data are adjusted to account for the long-term effects of advertising, profitability (as measured by rate of return on investment) appears to bear no significant relation to the level of advertising.

Those who hold the pro-competitive view of advertising also point out that advertising's effects in creating brand loyalty, and thus increasing the costs of entry, are questionable on other grounds as well. They point out that in markets where advertising expenditures are high relative to product price—beer and toiletries, for example—brand shares tend to be *less* stable, and brand loyalty therefore *less* pronounced, than in other markets.

Advertising's effects on competition may depend on the particular characteristics of the market. For example, there is some evidence that advertising has the clearly pro-competitive effect of reducing search costs in retail trade markets, whereas its effects on entry costs appear to be greater in markets for nondurable goods (toothpaste, breakfast cereals, and laundry bleach, for example) than in markets for durable goods (TVs and home computers, for example).

Advertising and Prices

What about the related question of the effect of advertising on prices? Does advertising lead to higher prices or lower prices? Certainly advertising is a cost of doing business and, as such, it must ultimately be covered in the price of the

*W. S. Comanor and T. A. Wilson, "Advertising, Market Structure and Performance," *Review of Economics and Statistics* (November 1967).

advertised product. Because it may also lower other costs, however, it does not necessarily follow that advertising always leads to higher prices. For example, where there are economies of scale in production, advertising can reduce unit costs by expanding the firm's market. If the reduction in production costs more than offsets the costs of advertising, total cost, and thus the competitive price, will fall. Furthermore, as we have seen, advertising can provide information that reduces buyers' search costs, thereby lowering prices by making markets more competitive. It hardly pays a seller to offer a lower price than its competitors if it cannot advertise that lower price to potential customers.

These considerations lead us to expect that, at least in some cases, the net effect of advertising is to lower prices. One well-known study of the market for eyeglasses discovered exactly such a case.* Prior to 1978, many states prohibited or otherwise restricted advertising of the price of eyeglasses; in other states, such advertising was permitted. In comparing the two groups, it was found that the price of eyeglasses was more than 25 percent higher on average in states that restricted advertising, and the price of eyeglasses and eye examinations combined was more than 10 percent higher. Moreover, a comparison of extremes showed that in the states with the most stringent restrictions on advertising, prices were more than twice as high for eyeglasses, and almost 70 percent higher for eyeglasses and eye examinations combined, than in states with no restrictions.

The price of legal services provides another example of the effects of advertising. As we saw in Chapter 11, lawyers' codes of professional conduct once prohibited advertising as "unethical." After this restriction was held to be illegal, the price of standard legal services soon fell dramatically. For example, in Phoenix, Arizona, where the lawyers who challenged the advertising restrictions practiced, the price of an uncontested divorce fell from $350 to $150.

Even where advertising results in higher dollar prices, however, it does not necessarily follow that the real cost to consumers is higher. Information about the characteristics and availability of various products is not free. The cost of such information is reflected either in the higher prices necessary to cover the advertising expenses of sellers, in the search costs borne by consumers themselves, or in both. Thus, unless advertising reduces search costs by more than it increases prices, it is in the interest of consumers to incur search costs themselves rather than pay the price differential necessary to cover advertising costs. Under such circumstances, firms that advertise will be driven out of the market by competition from firms that do not.

Thus, even where dollar prices are higher with advertising than they would be in an ideal, but imaginary, world of free information, the real cost to the consumer—including the costs of becoming informed—may well be less with advertising than without it.

*Lee Benham, "The Effect of Advertising on the Price of Eyeglasses," *The Journal of Law and Economics*, October 1972, pp. 337–52.

Advertising's Critics: Some Normative Questions

Nearly everyone agrees that advertising which provides useful information is valuable and that advertising which provides false or misleading information is undesirable. Many critics of advertising, however, point to what they see as its noninformational content—specifically, to messages they feel are meant to manipulate tastes and create artificial wants rather than to inform. Apparently these critics believe that people are borne with certain innate wants and needs which advertising then distorts into inaccurate—and illegitimate—market demands that only dimly reflect people's "true" wants and needs. The principle of consumer sovereignty thus becomes little more than a hollow slogan: Consumers are like sheep, being led and manipulated by the subtle messages of advertisers to purchase products they do not need and would not buy if it were not for advertising.

All advertising is meant to persuade, and it would be naive to deny that people are occasionally led by advertising into purchases that they later regret. However, the preceding view of the effects of advertising seems to some to be vastly overblown, if not downright wrong. These "critics of the critics" argue that advertising does not change people's wants in any fundamental way, it merely attempts to identify wants that already exist and channel those wants in the direction of specific products. The Miller Brewing Company, for example, probably did not create a demand for Lite Beer, it simply discovered that many beer drinkers would welcome fewer calories in their beer. The makers of Olympia Gold, Coors Light, and other low calorie beers then used their own advertising to compete for a share of the market that Miller had discovered.

To take another example, the domestic automobile industry has frequently been accused of using its advertising to foist large and inefficient automobiles on the American public. Its advertising, however, was unable to create a demand for the huge inventory of gas guzzlers it found itself holding when gasoline prices began rising dramatically in the mid-1970s. Nor was the industry able to manipulate consumer demand to insure the success of its smaller, more fuel-efficient cars when falling gasoline prices began leading consumers back to larger cars in the 1980s.

That the vast majority of advertising is devoted to discovering rather than creating wants is evidenced by the fact that market surveys play such a prominent role in product marketing. More than four out of every five technically feasible new products are never put on the market because market surveys indicate that they would not be accepted by consumers. Of those products that are introduced, a third to a half are withdrawn from the market within one year because they fail to sell in spite of advertising.* This would hardly be the case if advertising could be counted on to convert "losers" into "winners."

But what about the kinds of advertisements that seem to transmit no real information at all—inane jingles, athletes' or movie stars' paid endorsements,

*Heinz Kohler, *Intermediate Microeconomics: Theory and Applications* (Scott, Forseman, 1982), p. 369.

and so on? The immediate purpose of many ads is not to convey information about a product but rather to make consumers aware of its existence and to pique their interest so that they will try it once or at least investigate it further. To do this effectively, an advertisement often relies on a fundamental principle of mass communication: To be remembered, a message must be dramatic, simple, and repetitious. Politicians know this; preachers know it; and chanting political demonstrators know it. Should it surprise us that this principle has not been overlooked by Madison Avenue?

Finally, what about the issue of innate needs versus artificially created wants? Many argue that, aside from certain biological requirements, which in any case advertising cannot influence, there is no such thing as an innate need. All other wants, and especially the particular manifestation of those wants in the marketplace, are the product of our culture: of family, of schools, of church, and of scores of other social and economic institutions—including advertising. To profess to know which goods fulfill true and legitimate wants—Mozart concertos and "natural" foods, perhaps—and which satisfy wants that are only artificial and contrived—Kenny Rogers ballads and Big Macs, for example—smacks of a cultural elitism for which there is no objective basis. What these critics of advertising often really seem to be lamenting is that advertisers have discovered in the unwashed masses tastes and preferences that are different from (and of course inferior to) their own.

CHAPTER SUMMARY

1. A *monopolistically competitive* industry is like a perfectly competitive one in that there are many sellers, all small in relation to the market, and no entry or exit restrictions. Unlike pure competitors, however, monopolistic competitors are price setters because their products are differentiated from one another.

2. Profits and losses can exist in the short run in a monopolistically competitive market, but in the long run they are eliminated by entry and exit.

3. Product variety reflects a market balance between differences in individual preferences and economies of scale in production. Because of economies of scale, those product characteristics demanded by large numbers of consumers are generally available as standard features, whereas those characteristics for which the demand is limited relative to economies of scale are available only to those willing to pay the higher costs of small-scale production.

4. Like greater variety, higher quality is generally more costly, and firms must balance the costs of additional quality against what they believe consumers are willing to pay for it. Because people differ in their demands for additional quality, the market responds by providing a range of different qualities.

5. The *planned obsolescence* argument says that firms will produce lower quality, less durable products even if there are no cost savings from doing so, because sales will be greater over time when their products wear out faster. However, as long as the extra durability can be communicated to buyers, the seller can capture the value of the extra durability in the price of the product and planned obsolescence will not be profitable.

6. The *lemons market* is a market in which the quality of goods deteriorates over time because it is difficult and costly for buyers to obtain information about product quality and to pay accordingly.

7. *Brand names* are a low-cost way of providing consumers with information about the quality and other characteristics of goods before they buy. They are more important with respect to *experience* goods than *inspection* goods.

8. Sellers use advertising to communicate to potential buyers favorable information about their products, but the advertising of their competitors communicates, either implicitly or explicitly, unfavorable information as well.

9. To the extent that advertising increases brand loyalty or raises entry costs, it reduces competition. To the extent that it provides useful information, reduces search costs, or acts as a vehicle for entry, it increases competition.

10. As a cost, advertising must be covered in the money prices of advertised products. But to the extent that advertising enables a firm to reap economies of scale, or reduces buyer search costs, it leads to lower prices. This is especially true with respect to the real price, which includes search and information costs.

11. Advertising's critics argue that it is frequently used to manipulate and distort peoples innate wants and preferences. The "critics of the critics" argue that advertising does not change people's wants in any fundamental way; it merely attempts to identify wants that already exist and channel those wants in the direction of specific products.

Key Terms and Concepts

monopolistic competition
lemons market
experience goods
inspection goods

Questions for Thought and Discussion

1. A new car loses a substantial portion of its resale value as soon as it is driven out of the dealer's showroom—that is, as soon as it becomes a used car—even though it has been "used" hardly at all. How do you account for this?

2. I once bought a 13-inch Panasonic color TV for $225 when I could have bought a 13-inch Portland color TV for $150. Was I irrational? I also once ate many, many meals at McDonalds and other familiar fast-food restaurants on a driving trip across the United States. Does this mean that I prefer fast food to other highway cuisine?

3. Gasoline companies typically sell gas in metropolitan areas through stations that are operated by independent franchisees, but they own and operate their own stations on rural interstate highways. Why do you think they do this?

4. Which of the following brand names provide potential buyers with the most valuable information?
   Chiquita (bananas)
   Sunkist (oranges)
   Sony (television sets and stereos)
   Papermate (pens)
   Toyota (cars)
   IBM (computers)

5. Within a given metropolitan area, other things being equal, would you expect to find a greater dispersion of the prices of "big ticket" items, such as major appliances, or of the prices of everyday purchases, such as a pound of hamburger?

6. Retailers often claim they charge the lowest price in town. To back this up, some guarantee to make up the difference (sometimes even more than the difference) if, after purchase, the buyer finds the same item somewhere else at a lower price. Is the fact that retailers rarely have to make good on these price guarantees evidence that they do, indeed, have the lowest prices in town? Could it be evidence of something else?

7. Suppose that DuraReady Battery, Inc. has a monopoly on the battery market. The company currently charges $2.00 for a battery that costs $1.50 per unit to produce and has an average life of 3 months. One of DuraReady's engineers has come up with a design for a 1-year battery that can be produced at a cost of $3.00 per unit. DuraReady's management, fearing that the longerlived battery will reduce unit sales, is thinking about "deep sixing" the new design. Have you any advice for them?

8. What are some of the similarities, and some of the differences, between commercial advertising and political advertising?

CHAPTER 13

Government in the Marketplace: Antitrust Policy and Business Regulation

Antitrust policy is concerned with the degree of competition in the marketplace and with business conduct that might affect competition.

The **old style industrial regulation** involved government in regulating prices, profits, and entry conditions in specific industries.

The **new style social regulation** is concerned with environmental, health, and safety issues that cut across industry boundaries.

Government policies designed to influence market conditions and business behavior are an important part of our economic system. In this chapter we consider three types of government policy: **antitrust policy**, which is concerned with the degree of competition in the marketplace and with business conduct that might affect competition; **old style industrial regulation**, which seeks to alter prices, profits, and entry conditions in specific industries; and **new style social regulation**, which addresses issues, such as environmental quality, health, and safety, that cut across industry boundaries.

ANTITRUST POLICY

The Antitrust Laws of the United States

In 1890, Congress passed the *Sherman Antitrust Act*, the first and most important of our antitrust laws. The Sherman Act, which was to be enforced by the U.S. Department of Justice, declared illegal "every contract, combination . . . or conspiracy in restraint of trade or commerce" and prohibited every "attempt to monopolize . . . trade or commerce." Unfortunately, this sweeping language provided virtually no clue as to how such potentially ambiguous phrases as "restraint of trade" and "attempt to monopolize" were to be interpreted and applied in practice.

Largely because of this ambiguity, Congress passed two additional antitrust laws within a few days of one another in 1914: the *Federal Trade Commission Act* and the *Clayton Act*. The former established the Federal Trade Commission (the FTC, for short) and empowered it to find and prosecute "unfair methods of competition." The latter identified a number of specific business practices which it declared illegal, but only where they might "substantially lessen competition or tend to create a monopoly." But ambiguities still remained. What, for instance, constitutes an "unfair method of competition?" "Unfair" to whom? Consumers? Competitors? How "substantial" does a lessening of competition have to be for it to violate the Clayton Act? Is there a difference between "tending" to create a monopoly and actually creating one?

Because of ambiguities like these, it has ultimately fallen to the courts to interpret the language of the antitrust laws in the course of evaluating the competitive effects of concrete business practices. Modern antitrust policy has therefore been shaped at least as much by a century of judicial interpretation as by the original laws themselves.

The Goal of Antitrust Policy: A Fundamental Dilemma

Almost from its inception, antitrust policy has suffered from confusion regarding its goals. On the one hand, the laws themselves—especially the Sherman Act—clearly express a desire to promote competition in the marketplace. Many court decisions, however, appear to have been motivated, not so much by a desire to promote competition, as by a populist hostility to "big business." By seeking to promote the interests of small businesses regardless of the competitive consequences, such decisions have often confused the goal of *protecting competition* with that of *protecting competitors*. Not only are these goals different, they are often incompatible, for competition almost inevitably makes life uncomfortable for the competitors. However, it also insures that our wants are met as efficiently as possible by keeping costs and prices low, by fostering innovation, and by preventing monopolistic output restriction. Accordingly, most economists feel that the proper goal of antitrust policy is to protect competition, not competitors.

Per Se Illegality Versus the Rule of Reason

Not all restrictions on competition are contrary to the spirit of the antitrust laws, however. Consider, for example, the difference between a price-fixing agreement and a merger between two competitors. The price-fixing agreement simply eliminates competition; it makes no offsetting contribution to economic efficiency. A merger between competitors eliminates the competition between them, but, unlike the price-fixing agreement, it may also contribute positively to economic efficiency. For example, it may allow the merger partners to jointly reap economies of scale unavailable to either separately; or it may create a more efficient firm by integrating the best elements of each. The point is that the elimination of competition, while the fundamental purpose of the price-fixing agreement, can be (and usually is) merely an incidental side effect of the merger.

Good antitrust policy must therefore distinguish between those limitations of competition that simply increase market power with no offsetting benefits, and those that accompany the pursuit or exercise of superior economic efficiency. The former should be illegal *per se*, that is, *illegal in and of themselves, regardless of the circumstances in which they occur*. Price-fixing and other forms of explicit cartel behavior fall into the category of **per se illegality**.

Per se illegality means that a practice is illegal in and of itself without regard to circumstances in which it occurs.

A **rule of reason** approach determines the legal status of a business practice in light of the particular circumstances in which it occurs.

Clearly, however, a per se approach is not appropriate for dealing with those business practices, such as mergers, whose overall effects on competition can be beneficial, harmful, or neutral, depending on the circumstances. Such practices require an approach known as the **rule of reason**. Under a rule of reason, the actions in question are not considered illegal in and of themselves, but rather are evaluated in the light of the particular circumstances in which they occur.

In recent years, the courts have extended the rule of reason to more and more business practices once considered illegal per se, and in so doing they have relied increasingly on economic analysis. Let us examine the influence of that analysis in the evolution of three important areas of antitrust policy: mergers, single-firm monopoly, and vertical restraints.

Mergers

A **horizontal merger** is a merger between competitors.

A **vertical merger** is a merger between firms in a buyer-seller relationship.

There are three types of merger: **horizontal mergers** between competitors; **vertical mergers** between firms in a buyer-seller relationship; and *conglomerate mergers* between firms whose operations are unrelated. Because conglomerate mergers by their very nature have little if any impact on competition, antitrust policy has focused almost entirely on horizontal and vertical mergers. Accordingly, so shall we.

Horizontal Mergers

Most economists agree that antitrust policy should prohibit horizontal mergers that would lead to significant market power for the merged firm or that would significantly increase the chances of collusion by further reducing the number of firms in a highly concentrated industry. Antitrust policy toward mergers has not always been guided by these principles, however. Indeed, the Supreme Court once blocked a merger between two shoe manufacturers, not because it feared an increase in their market power, but because it feared that the merged firm would have lower costs, and thus be able to charge lower prices, than its competitors!* This was just one of a series of inconsistent and contradictory court rulings that created a climate of great uncertainty regarding not just merger policy, but antitrust policy in general, during the 1960s.

In 1968 the Department of Justice tried to introduce some semblance of order by issuing a set of *merger guidelines.* These guidelines limited the maximum acceptable market shares of merger partners. For example, the Department announced that it would challenge any attempt by a firm with a 4 percent or greater share of a highly concentrated market to acquire a competitor that also had a 4 percent or greater market share. (The Department defined a highly concentrated market as one with a four-firm concentration ratio of 75 or greater.) As a result of these relatively strict guidelines, as well as continued uncertainty over the position of the courts, there were very few horizontal mergers of any significance during the late 1960s and 1970s.

Then, in 1982 and again in 1984, the Department of Justice revised its merger guidelines. Under the new guidelines, concentration was measured somewhat differently, and the threshold of acceptable market shares was increased by a small amount.† More significantly, in placing greater emphasis on such factors as the extent of foreign competition, entry conditions and other characteristics of the particular industry, as well as a merger's potential contributions to efficiency, the Department's merger policy began to move away from a rigid "structural" approach in which market shares and concentration were of paramount importance.

Mergers that posed genuine threats to competition were still challenged under the new guidelines. In 1989, for example, the Justice Department blocked an attempt by American Airlines and Delta Airlines to merge their computer reservations systems. In 1986 the FTC halted mergers between Pepsi and Seven-Up and between Coca-Cola and Dr. Pepper. In addition, the Justice Department and the FTC often required changes in the mergers they did approve. For example, before approving a 1984 merger between Standard Oil of California (now Chevron) and Gulf Oil, the FTC required Gulf to sell more than 4,000 Gulf gas

* *Brown Shoe Co. v. U.S.* (1962). This was the classic example of protecting competitors at the expense of competition. In the words of the Court: "Of course, some of the results of large integrated or chain operations are beneficial to consumers. . . . But we cannot fail to recognize Congress' desire to promote competition through the protection of viable, small, locally owned businesses. Congress appreciated that occasional higher costs and prices might result from the maintenance of fragmented industries and markets. It resolved these competing considerations in favor of decentralization."

† Beginning in 1982, the Department of Justice began using a statistic called the Herfindahl index, rather than the concentration ratio, as the basis for its merger guidelines. The Herfindahl index is calculated by summing the squared percentage market shares of all firms in the market. The possible values of the Herfindahl index range between zero (for pure competition) and 10,000 (for pure monopoly). Higher values indicate greater concentration. For example, if a market contains five equal-size firms, its Herfindahl index is equal to 2,000 (= market share of 20 squared times 5); if the market contains ten equal-sized firms, the index is 1,000. The Justice Department defines a highly concentrated market as one with a Herfindahl index of 1,600 or higher. Under the new guidelines, a merger in which each firm had a 5 percent market share in a highly concentrated industry (rather than a 4 percent share as in the original guidelines) was just on the borderline of acceptability.

Table 13.1
Blockbuster horizontal mergers of the 1980s

ACQUIRING FIRM	ACQUIRED FIRM	VALUE (*Billions of dollars*)	HORIZONTAL OVERLAP
Standard Oil, CA (now Chevron)	Gulf Oil	$13.4	Refining/retailing of petroleum products
Texaco	Getty Oil	10.1	Refining/retailing of petroleum products
Campeau	Federated Department Stores	6.6	Retail trade
General Electric	RCA	6.4	Consumer and other electronics
Mobil Oil	Superior Oil	5.7	Refining/retailing of petroleum products
Philip Morris	General Foods	5.6	Food products

stations and a major refinery. Nonetheless, the attitude of both the courts and the federal enforcement agencies was undoubtedly more tolerant of horizontal mergers during the 1980s than at any time in the previous half century.

Table 13.1 shows some of the large horizontal mergers that took place during this period. Most of these would have been unthinkable only a few years before.

Vertical Mergers

Possible antitrust objections to horizontal mergers are straightforward: Because such mergers eliminate competition between the parties involved, they can lead directly to an increase in market power. There appears to be little economic basis for restrictions on vertical mergers, however. The arguments that once were advanced against such mergers by noneconomists (and even by some economists) have been shown either to be incorrect or to apply only in very rare circumstances. Two such arguments that influenced antitrust policy until recently are worth examining.

The **leverage theory** holds that a firm with market power in one market can use a vertical merger to extend that power into a vertically related market.

The Leverage Theory According to the **leverage theory**, a firm can use the "leverage" of market power in one market to obtain additional market power in vertically related markets. The argument is best illustrated by an example.

Suppose that the widget market is initially competitive but that all widget producers must obtain kryptonite, an indispensable input, from a monopolist whom we'll call Alpha. Now suppose that Alpha merges with one of the widget producers, say Beta, thereby creating a vertically integrated firm called AlphaBet. The leverage theory holds that AlphaBet, by cutting off the supply of kryptonite to any widget producer other than itself, could then monopolize widget production as well as kryptonite. The end result would be two monopolies where originally there was only one.

This argument is full of holes. First of all, it might well be more profitable for AlphaBet to continue to sell kryptonite to other widget producers than to monopolize the widget market. By refusing to sell kryptonite, AlphaBet would be sacrificing potential profits from its kryptonite monopoly, and those profits would not necessarily be offset by the profits gained by monopolizing the widget market. In fact, if other widget producers are more efficient than AlphaBet, the kryptonite would be worth more to them than to AlphaBet, and AlphaBet would be foolish not to sell it to them at a correspondingly high price.

But suppose for the sake of argument that AlphaBet does "leverage" its kryptonite monopoly into a widget monopoly. Will consumers pay a higher price for widgets as a result? The answer is not at all obvious. As a nonintegrated kryptonite monopolist, Alpha charged the monopoly price for kryptonite. Since kryptonite is an input in widget production, widgets were more costly to produce, and their price was correspondingly higher than if there had been no kryptonite monopoly. On the other hand, if a vertically integrated AlphaBet monopolizes widget production, it can obtain kryptonite at cost (It would hardly pay AlphaBet to charge itself a monopoly price for kryptonite!) and then set a monopoly price for widgets. Regardless of the degree of vertical integration, there is only one stage of production at which market power can be exercised: either at the kryptonite stage or the widget stage. The real question is whether the monopolistic widget price based on competitive cost of kryptonite would be higher than the competitive widget price based on monopolistic cost of kryptonite. In fact, it could go either way.

It is therefore not necessarily true *either* that the vertical merger would result in monopolization of the widget market, *or, even if it did*, that the result would be an increase in the price of widgets. Whatever market power AlphaBet possesses is based, not on the extent of its vertical integration, but on its kryptonite monopoly. If there is an antitrust objection, it should be to the kryptonite monopoly itself, not to the vertical merger.

Vertical Mergers and Exclusion Another argument advanced against some vertical mergers is that they can be used to exclude competitors from a market. According to this argument, for example, a manufacturer who sells through a number of independent retail outlets can exclude (or delay the entry of) other manufacturers by acquiring all of those retailers and refusing to carry the products of any new competitor. However, those competitors (including potential entrants) can open their own retail outlets or rely on the entry of independent retailers to carry their products. To exclude competitors at the manufacturing stage, therefore, the vertical merger must also block entry at the retailing stage. If it does not, the original manufacturer is left with excess retail capacity and higher costs than its competitors. Except in special circumstances, therefore, a vertical merger is an ineffective method of exclusion.

The Justice Department's original 1968 merger guidelines were nearly as restrictive regarding vertical mergers as they were on horizontal mergers. In recent years, however, antitrust policy has become increasingly tolerant of vertical mergers, even where they involve large firms in relatively concentrated markets. While some find this trend disturbing, to many economists it seems like a sensible policy.

Antitrust Policy and Single-Firm Monopoly

Like merger policy, antitrust policy toward single-firm monopoly has not been a model of consistency. For a half-century after the passage of the Sherman Act, the courts were generally tolerant of large size and market dominance when these were achieved through legitimate business practices. In 1945, however, a U.S. Court of Appeals overturned the "bigness is no offense" precedent by ordering the breakup of Alcoa Aluminum. Although the court recognized that Alcoa's large size had been maintained on the basis of superior efficiency, it nonetheless held that Alcoa's 90 percent share of the domestic aluminum market violated the Sherman Act's prohibition of monopoly.

The "bigness is badness" view inherent in the *Alcoa* decision set a precedent that held for almost 30 years. However, it was not a precedent without critics. These critics point out that where a single firm has achieved a position of market dominance by exploiting efficiencies not available to its rivals, its market power is limited by the extent of those efficiency advantages. Suppose, for example, that a firm achieves a position of market dominance based on its ability to produce at a cost of only $10 the same product that other firms can produce at a cost of no less than $11. Even if this firm were a virtual monopolist, it would not be able to charge a price greater than $11 without attracting entry (or face being undercut by smaller firms already in the market). Critics of the "bigness is badness" doctrine thus argue that large firm size achieved and maintained through superior efficiency should be tolerated under the antitrust laws, even if it is accompanied by some market power.

In recent rulings the courts seem to have accepted this view. In 1979, for example, a federal appeals court overruled an earlier decision in favor of the Berkey Photo Co., a film processor, in its suit against Kodak. Berkey had claimed that Kodak's size and methods of competition enabled it to maintain a near monopoly in film processing, but the court ruled that Kodak had not violated the Sherman Act. According to the court, Kodak was simply "reap(ing) the competitive rewards attributable to its efficient size."* In 1980 the FTC dismissed a complaint against DuPont on the grounds that the company's success was the result of intelligent planning and business foresight rather than unfair methods of competition. And, in 1982, the Department of Justice dropped its 13-year-old monopolization case against IBM.

On the same day it dropped the IBM case, the Justice Department also announced that it had reached an agreement with American Telephone & Telegraph, then the world's largest corporation, requiring AT&T to divest itself of all of its local telephone companies. However, the case against AT&T alleged that the company had maintained its monopoly position, not by superior efficiency,

* *Berkey Photo v. Eastman Kodak* (1979).

but by using its legally protected monopolies in regulated markets to exclude potential competitors from unregulated markets. For example, the government charged that the company had effectively excluded potential competitors from both the long-distance market and the telephone equipment market by making it difficult for them to connect their equipment to AT&T's legally protected local telephone monopolies.

The attitude of the courts in recent years toward large firm size attained through internal growth seems to be best summarized in a sentence taken, ironically, from the decision in the *Alcoa* case: "The successful competitor, having been urged to compete, must not be turned upon when he wins."

Vertical Restraints

A **vertical restraint** is a practice by which a firm restricts competition among vertically related firms.

Collusion and other practices that limit competition within a market (that is, among horizontally related firms) are examples of *horizontal restraints*. **Vertical restraints**, by contrast, restrict competition in markets at different stages in the same chain of production and distribution. For example, a manufacturer who prohibits retailers from discounting the retail price of its product is imposing a vertical restraint on those retailers. So also is a brewery that assigns each of its independent beer distributors an exclusive distribution territory so that they do not compete with one another.

Following a number of court decisions permitting vertical restraints in specific cases, the Department of Justice issued its own vertical restraint guidelines in 1985. According to these guidelines, most vertical restraints are to be presumed legal in most instances, and, in those special circumstances where they might adversely affect competition, they are to be evaluated under a rule of reason. In effect, the guidelines recognize that vertical restraints are frequently motivated by legitimate business concerns unrelated to the kind of restraint of trade that the antitrust laws are intended to prevent. A brief examination of the two practices just mentioned serves to illustrate the reasoning behind this position.

Resale Price Maintenance

Resale price maintenance (RPM) is the practice by which a manufacturer prevents retailers from discounting the price of its product.

The practice by which a manufacturer sets the minimum price at which retailers can resell its product is known as **resale price maintenance**, or RPM for short. In effect RPM eliminates price competition among retailers by preventing them from discounting the product. Perhaps because of confusion over the possible motives for using RPM, it has long been one of the most controversial business practices dealt with under the antitrust laws. Consider the following possible uses of RPM.

RPM and Horizontal Collusion RPM can be used as part of a manufacturers' price-fixing cartel. As we have seen, once the cartel is in place, each manufacturer has an incentive to cheat on the cartel agreement by shading price and expanding sales at the expense of its fellow colluders. However, if *all* manufacturers adopt resale price maintenance agreements, retailers are unable to pass along to final consumers any secret price cut by a cheating manufacturer; such a manufacturer is thus unable to increase sales; and the incentive to cheat on the cartel is correspondingly diminished.

RPM and the Supply of Promotional Services by Retailers In many cases, however, RPM is used by a *single* manufacturer independently of its competitors. What is the purpose of RPM used as such a purely vertical restraint?

Note that RPM does *not* enable a manufacturer to raise the price of the final product above what it would be in the absence of RPM. To see why, consider the following example. Suppose that Banana Computer sells its personal computers through a group of retailers whose competitive markup is $100. If Banana charges retailers a wholesale price of $1,900, competition establishes a retail price of $2,000. If instead Banana wants its computers to sell for $2,500 retail, it can raise the wholesale price to $2,400. Whatever market power Banana possesses can be exercised by adjusting the wholesale price; it need not resort to RPM simply to obtain a higher retail price. In fact, Banana would need RPM to support a retail price of $2,500 only if it charged retailers a wholesale price *below* $2,400—that is, only if it wants to increase its *retailers'* markup. What interest can a *manufacturer* have in guaranteeing its *retailers* a high markup?

One possibility is that the manufacturer may want retailer competition to take some form other than price cutting. Suppose, for example, that Banana Computer feels that the most effective way to promote its personal computer is for retailers to supply knowledgeable sales people who take the time to provide prospective buyers with detailed information and demonstrations of the product. But imagine what would happen if Banana were to give retailers the option of discounting the retail price of its computers. Some customers would obtain information, demonstrations, and other presale services from full-service retailers and then purchase their Banana computers from a discounter. Despite the fact that both Banana and its customers benefit from retailer-provided services, full-service retailers would be unable to meet the prices charged by discounters and would eventually be forced out of the market. RPM overcomes this problem by preventing discounters from free riding on the promotional efforts of full-service retailers. As such, it appears to be a legitimate marketing tactic and not at all contrary to the spirit of the antitrust laws.

RPM has been referred to as "vertical price-fixing," but this terminology is very misleading. There is a fundamental difference between collusive price-fixing among competitors and the purely vertical use of RPM. Nonetheless, RPM was held to be illegal per se in early court decisions. Congress even passed legislation in 1975 prohibiting manufacturers from setting minimum resale prices. Since 1981, however, the federal antitrust authorities have been reluctant to challenge resale price maintenance unless the evidence suggests that it is being used to promote horizontal collusion. Recent judicial rulings, such as the 1988 decision in favor of the Sharp Electronics Corporation, whose use of RPM had been challenged by one of its retailers, indicate that the courts may also be adopting a more tolerant attitude toward RPM.*

* *Business Electronics Corp. v. Sharp Electronics Corp.* (1988).

Exclusive Distribution Territories

Exclusive distribution territories exist when a manufacturer prevents competition among the distributors of its product by assigning each a separate distribution territory.

The practice of assigning **exclusive distribution territories** to independent distributors has been common in both the beer and soft drink industries. Because they eliminate competition among the distributors of a particular brand of beer or soft drink, exclusive territories sometimes arouse suspicion. Note, however, that the exclusive territories that Anheuser-Busch assigns to the distributors of its Budweiser beer do not protect either those distributors or Anheuser-Busch from competition from Miller, Strohs, and dozens of other beers in the same market.

What is it then that motivates a brewer or soft drink bottler to establish exclusive territories for its distributors? Here again, as in the case of RPM, the answer often lies in the nature of the services they wish to promote. Suppose, as is often the case, that the brewer or soft drink bottler wants its distributors to provide local advertising and other costly promotional services for its product. Without an exclusive territory, a distributor may be reluctant to do so, fearing that other distributors of the same product would then come into its territory and take advantage of its promotional efforts while incurring none of the costs. To the extent that exclusive distribution territories effectively prevent such free riding, they also appear to be a legitimate marketing tactic.

As with RPM, however, exclusive distribution territories can also be used to promote collusion. For example, they can lower the costs of collusion among distributors by reducing the total number of distributors in any given market. As with other vertical restraints, therefore, exclusive dealing should be evaluated under a rule of reason.

The Political Economy of Antitrust

As much of the preceding analysis suggests, the actual implementation of the antitrust laws has not always been consistent with the goals of economic efficiency and consumer welfare. In some cases—for example, in the treatment of vertical restraints until very recently—this inconsistency may have been the result of incomplete or incorrect economic analysis. The questions involved in many antitrust disputes are complex and can be resolved only on the basis of sophisticated economic analysis. Given the lack of formal economic training typical of judges, juries, and lawyers, we should be surprised if mistakes were *not* made.

As with other government policies, however, we cannot simply attribute all discrepancies between antitrust policy and the pursuit of economic efficiency to ignorance and mistakes. In particular, economists are beginning to realize that public choice theory applies to antitrust policy as well as to other areas of government action. As we have seen, that theory tells us that, in some cases, special interests can play as great or greater a role in determining policy as does the public interest. We may therefore ask what special interests can be served by antitrust policy. The answer is suggested by the fact that the vast majority of antitrust lawsuits—nearly 90 percent—are brought by private parties. In most of these suits, the private party is a business firm challenging the practices of its competitors as "unfair" or "predatory." It is extremely naive to ignore the possibility that many of these suits, perhaps most, are simply intended to protect competitors from competition.

As we have already noted, there has always been a body of opinion, especially among noneconomists, which holds that the goal of antitrust policy should be to protect competitors, particularly small businesses, rather than to promote competition. One former head of the Justice Department's Antitrust Division has suggested that the principal political constituency served by the antitrust laws has, in fact, been small businesses rather than consumers, and that constituency is largely responsible for those pockets of inefficiency that have persisted in antitrust policy.*

The Effects of Antitrust Policy

Given the conflicts over the goals of antitrust policy, the imperfect information with which it must often be implemented, and the various interest groups affected, it should come as no surprise that the actual effects of antitrust policy are mixed. On the one hand, by forcing overt cartels underground and making collusion more costly, the Sherman Act has almost certainly reduced its prevalence. Similarly, the laws have surely discouraged many horizontal mergers that would otherwise have achieved the same effects as a cartel.†

On the other hand, many of the potential mergers that were discouraged during the 1960s and 1970s may well have increased efficiency without significantly adding to market power. The same can probably be said about many of the purely vertical restraints dissuaded by the antitrust laws until very recently. In addition, the law's occasional protection of competitors from allegedly "unfair" prices and methods of competition have surely had the effect of stifling some desirable competitive behavior.

Whether the antitrust laws have been worth it in terms of their opportunity costs, including both the resources consumed by the enforcement process and the potentially desirable behavior that the laws may have discouraged, remains a question that is far from resolved. Although the vast majority of economists support the antitrust laws, few can be found who would not like to see their application changed in some way or another.

OLD STYLE INDUSTRIAL REGULATION

The so-called old style regulation of prices, profits, and entry conditions in specific industries has its roots in the latter part of the nineteenth century. It has been applied at the federal level to the interstate transmission of electricity, natu-

*William Baxter, "The Political Economy of Antitrust" in R. D. Tollison, Ed. *The Political Economy of Antitrust* (D. C. Heath & Co., 1980) pp. 3–49.

†George J. Stigler, "The Economic Effects of the Antitrust Laws" *The Journal of Law and Economics* (October 1966).

ral gas, telecommunications and broadcast signals, and at the state and local level to telephone service, electricity and natural gas distribution, cable television systems, and other local public utilities.

Natural Monopoly

A **natural monopoly** exists when a single firm can serve the entire market at lower cost than two or more firms.

The traditional economic rationale for industrial regulation is based on a special combination of economic and technological conditions known as **natural monopoly**. A natural monopoly exists when economies of scale are so significant relative to the size of the market that a single large firm can serve the market at lower unit (average) cost than two or more smaller firms.

The cost and demand conditions for a natural monopoly are illustrated in Figure 13.1 where *LRAC* is the long run average cost curve and *D* is the market demand curve. Scale economies are such that the natural monopolist's long-run average costs are still falling at the output rate at which the average cost curve crosses the market demand curve. A single firm can produce enough to satisfy the entire market at a cost of C_1 per unit, whereas two or more firms sharing the

Figure 13.1

Cost and demand conditions for a natural monopoly

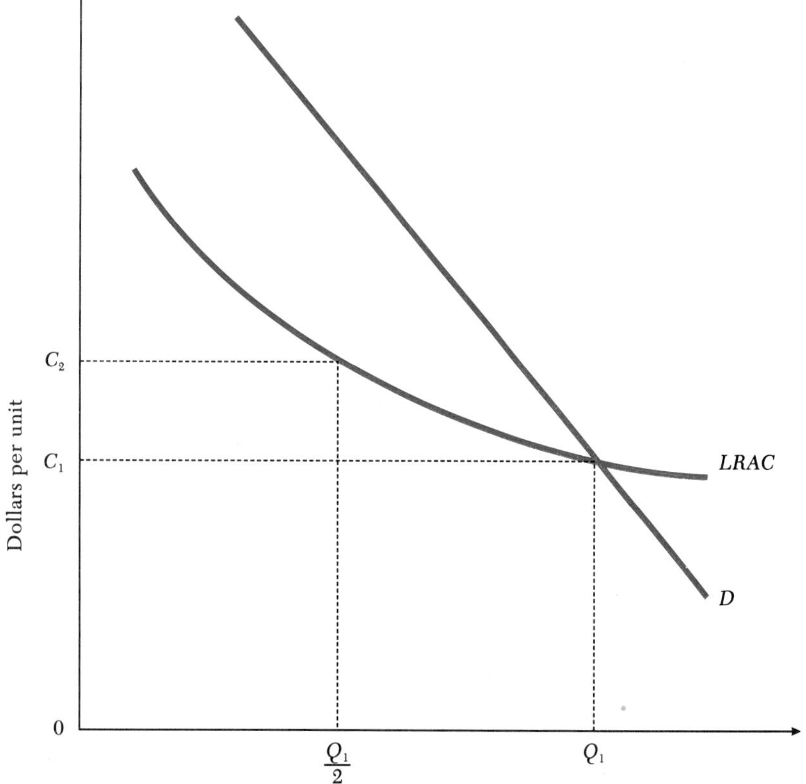

market have higher unit costs. For example, if the output of Q_1 is divided equally between two producers, it costs C_2 per unit to produce. Furthermore, the first of those two to expand output will lower its average cost, underprice its competitor, and ultimately force it out of the market. Monopoly is therefore the "natural" structure of this market because, under these cost and demand conditions, only one producer can survive in the long run.

The most frequently cited examples of natural monopoly are local public utility services. Two or more water or natural gas companies competing for customers in the same city, for example, would require unnecessary and wasteful duplication of water or gas mains in each neighborhood. Similarly, competing distributors of electricity or cable television signals would have to duplicate one another's main feeder lines, whereas a single feeder line is sufficient to supply the entire market. Accordingly, the city or utility district grants exclusive monopoly franchises to provide such utility services.

The economic rationale for then *regulating* those franchises is based on the further argument that, although a monopolist can serve the market at the lowest unit cost, the full benefits of those cost efficiencies are not realized if it simply maximizes profits. For example, the natural monopolist depicted in Figure 13.2

Figure 13.2

Profit maximization for a natural monopoly

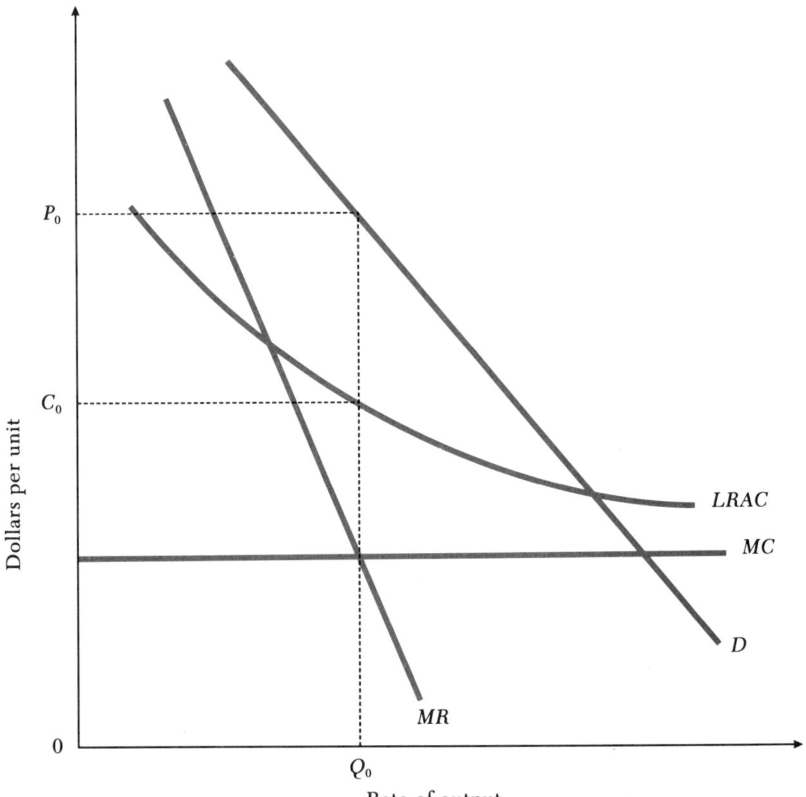

would maximize profits by restricting output to Q_0 units that would be produced at a cost of C_0 per unit and sold at a price of P_0 per unit. Consumers would end up paying a price in excess of average cost, and average cost in turn would not be minimized because of the monopolistic output restriction. The normative argument for regulation is therefore that government should insure that the natural monopoly's potential cost efficiencies are not lost as a consequence of monopolistic pricing and output restriction.

Regulation in Practice: "Fair Return on a Fair Value"

Rate-of-return regulation attempts to limit the regulated firm's revenues to an amount just sufficient to cover all of its costs, including the opportunity cost of its capital.

Regulation of local public utilities is carried out primarily by state agencies. Although details of the regulatory process vary from state to state, the basic approach common to all is known as **rate-of-return regulation**. The purpose of rate-of-return regulation is to prevent the regulated firm from earning pure economic profits, while at the same time allowing it sufficient revenues to cover all of its costs, including the cost of attracting capital.

Implementing rate-of-return regulation involves a number of steps. First, the regulatory agency must determine the regulated firm's operating costs. These include such things as labor costs and the cost of intermediate goods purchased from other firms. Next, the regulators must determine a level of accounting profit sufficient to allow the regulated firm to attract the financial capital needed to maintain and, if necessary, to expand its plant. The guiding legal principle in determining allowable profits is that of a *fair return on a fair value*. The *fair value*, also known as the *rate base*, is the value of the firm's plant and other capital assets; the *fair return* is the percentage rate of return to be applied to the rate base in calculating allowable accounting profit. For example, if the regulators determine that 10 percent is a fair return on investment and that the value of the regulated firm's rate base is $250 million, then its allowable accounting profit is $25 million per year.

The regulated firm is then allowed to set prices that bring in just enough revenues to cover its operating costs plus its allowable accounting profit. If the fair return accurately reflects the opportunity cost of the capital invested in the regulated firm, and if the fair value accurately reflects the value of its capital assets, then rate-of-return regulation leaves the firm with zero economic profit.

Criticisms of the Natural Monopoly Argument for Regulation

Economists have levelled a number of criticisms at the traditional, natural monopoly argument for regulation. Some of these criticisms focus on the practical implementation of rate-of-return regulation. Other, more fundamental criticisms have been directed at the concept of natural monopoly itself and the relatively narrow view of competition it implies. Finally, many economists who accept rate-of-return regulation in some circumstances—as applied to local public utilities, for example—have been critical of its extension to industries that cannot, by any stretch of the imagination, be considered natural monopolies.

Problems with Rate-of-Return Regulation

One criticism of rate-of-return regulation is that the fair return on a fair value as determined by regulators often bears little resemblance to the true opportunity cost of capital. In part, this reflects the difficulty of measuring fair return and fair value. Perhaps more importantly, however, it also reflects the fact that regulation is fundamentally a political process in which the regulatory authorities view their role as mediators among conflicting interest groups rather than as agents of economic efficiency.

Another criticism involves the adverse effect of rate-of-return regulation on the firm's incentives to control costs. A regulated monopoly that simply reports its costs and is then allowed sufficient revenues to cover those costs, has little incentive to keep costs down. Moreover, so long as demand is inelastic, any increases in cost can simply be passed on to the firm's customers via higher prices. And, because of its exclusive monopoly franchise, the regulated firm need not fear any adverse competitive consequences.

Are There Really Any Natural Monopolies?

In applying industrial regulation, government rarely uses any kind of market test to determine whether the regulated industry would in fact become monopolized if it were free of regulation. Instead it guarantees that this will be the case by granting one firm an exclusive and permanent monopoly franchise. There is ample evidence, however, that many such markets are not natural monopolies at all and would actually be competitive in the absence of regulatory entry restrictions. For example, it comes as a surprise to most people—including some economists—that in the early 1980s there were nearly 30 cities in the United States served by competing suppliers of electricity—perhaps the classic textbook example of natural monopoly.* There are also many local markets served by competing suppliers of cable TV services, an industry with many of the same technological characteristics as the distribution of electricity.†

Moreover, what qualifies as a natural monopoly changes with technological progress. For example, although we can make a plausible argument that long-distance telephone service was a natural monopoly when signals were carried by wire, this is hardly so in the age of microwave transmissions. Because microwaves transmit signals through space rather than over wires, suppliers of long-distance phone service can compete with one another without the need to duplicate a costly network of wires and cables.

Many economists believe that market competition, not government fiat, should determine what, if anything, qualifies as a natural monopoly. If competition weeds out all but one supplier, that is evidence of natural monopoly. If natural monopolies so discovered are then to be regulated, however, regulation

* Walter J. Primeaux, Jr., "Total Deregulation of Electric Utilities: A Viable Policy Choice," Chapter 5 in Robert W. Poole, Ed., *Unnatural Monopolies* (Lexington Books, 1985).

† See Thomas Hazlett, "Private Contracting versus Public Regulation as a Solution to the Natural Monopoly Problem," Chapter 4 in Robert W. Poole, Ed., *Unnatural Monopolies* (Lexington Books, 1985).

should not restrict entry into the market, for changes in technology may make competition a feasible alternative to regulation in the future.

Even where there are true natural monopolies, however, some economists believe that the argument for their regulation is based on too narrow a view of competition. Specifically, conditions of natural monopoly preclude competition *within* a market; they do not rule out competition *for* the market. This distinction suggests an alternative to rate-of-return regulation for dealing with natural monopoly. In particular, it has been suggested that exclusive, but time-limited, rights to serve natural monopoly markets be auctioned off to the firm that offers to serve the market at the lowest price.* For example, a city might solicit competitive bids on a franchise to supply its residents with water service for a period of, say, 10 years, with the franchise then awarded to the low-price bidder. At the end of 10 years the franchise would again be put up for bids. Because the winning bidder will always be the one offering to provide the service at the lowest price, such a system provides incentives for efficiency that are largely absent under rate-of-return regulation.

The main practical problem with this proposal is that of transferring the fixed capital from one firm to another whenever the franchise changes hands. One possibility is for the city or utility district to own the facilities and lease the right to manage and operate them via the competitive bidding process. In the case of some utilities, however, there is little fixed capital involved. For example, in 1985 when the city of San Jose, California awarded its garbage collection franchise to Waste Management Systems on the basis of its low-price bid, the previous incumbent, Browning-Ferris Industries, literally drove away in its capital, which consisted mainly of garbage trucks.

The Record of Regulation: Unnatural Monopolies

Whatever the merits of the natural monopoly concept as a justification for regulation, it is virtually impossible to reconcile it with the actual pattern of government regulation that we have observed in practice, particularly at the federal level. This pattern was set more than a century ago with the creation of the federal Interstate Commerce Commission (ICC) to regulate interstate railroad traffic. It was then repeated over and over again in the ensuing decades as federal regulation was extended to more and more industries. The development of the alphabet soup of federal industry regulation is chronicled in Table 13.2 on page 318. The most striking characteristic of this chronology is that, with few exceptions, the regulated industries cannot reasonably be classified as natural monopolies. Virtually any interstate trucking route can support a number of competing truckers, and most airline routes can support more than one air carrier. The spectrum of broadcast frequencies can be divided among many broadcasters, both radio and television, in each local market, and the technology of satellite and microwave transmission has opened up the possibility of a national market with a virtually unlimited number of suppliers. In the energy area, while we might argue that the pipeline *distribution* of natural gas qualifies as a natural monopoly,

*Harold Demsetz, "Why Regulate Utilities?" *Journal of Law and Economics* (1968).

Table 13.2

A chronology of the "old style" industrial regulation

YEAR	EVENT
1887	Interstate Commerce Commission (ICC) established to regulate interstate rail transportation
1913	Federal Reserve System founded to regulate commercial banking
1930	Federal Power Commission (FPC) founded to regulate electricity generated by interstate waterways
1932	Federal Home Loan Bank established to regulate interest rates and entry into the savings and loan industry
1934	Federal Radio Commission (later Federal Communications Commission, FCC) established to regulate radio transmission and telecommunications
1934	Securities and Exchange Commission (SEC) established to regulate securities markets
1935	ICC regulatory authority extended to cover interstate trucking as well as railroads
1938	Federal Power Commission begins regulating pipeline rates for natural gas distribution
1938	Civil Aeronautics Board (CAB) begins regulating interstate airlines
1960	Federal Power Commission begins regulating the wellhead price of natural gas
1977	Department of Energy (DOE) created to replace Federal Power Commission; obtains authority to regulate pricing and allocation of oil in addition to electricity and natural gas

we would be hard pressed to make that argument about its *production*. Nor do any of the regulated financial services such as banking, securities and commodities trading, and home loan institutions remotely resemble natural monopolies.

Indeed, it appears that in most cases the causation has run in precisely the opposite direction: Federal regulation was typically applied to what would otherwise have been a competitive industry and converted it into a virtual cartel. It did so by suppressing price competition, limiting entry, and, whenever possible, extending regulatory authority to potentially threatening new technologies. The price and entry regulation of the airline industry by the Civil Aeronautics Board (CAB) and the response of the Federal Communications Commission (FCC) to the changing technology of broadcasting and telecommunications typify the regulation of these "unnatural monopolies."

Airlines In the 50 years between 1938 and 1978, the CAB enforced uniform air fares on all routes, thereby effectively preventing airlines from competing via price. In addition, it completely prevented the entry of any new "trunk" (long-distance) airlines, while allocating routes among existing airlines in a way that limited the amount of competition on any given route. About the only way airlines could compete at all with one another was through the quality of their service. But as the overall quality of service rose, fares also rose to cover the higher costs, and air travelers who would have preferred lower priced, less lavish, service had no option but to pay the higher fares.

Broadcasting and Telecommunications When the FCC was established in 1934, broadcasting consisted only of radio transmissions. When television became a commercial reality in the late 1940s, the FCC responded in a way that favored the then dominant radio networks that it already regulated. It extended its authority to the new medium and allocated only a small portion of the broadcast spectrum for television transmission. In most local areas, licenses were granted for fewer than six television stations, and the bulk of those licenses went to stations owned by (or affiliated with) the three major radio networks—ABC, CBS, and NBC. In the 1950s, as the demand for television programming boomed, cable television networks began to expand to fill the void left by the FCC's artificial restriction of broadcast channels. By 1962, however, the major broadcast networks had persuaded the FCC to extend its regulatory authority to cable systems. Until 1977, when a federal court curtailed that authority, the FCC systematically retarded the growth of cable by imposing a variety of restrictions on cable operators.

The FCC behaved much the same way in responding to the changing technology of long-distance telecommunications. Originally that industry consisted solely of AT&T's "long lines" system that carried signals by wire. The development of microwave relay technology in the 1940s created an alternative means of communication by radio beams. The FCC, however, refused to allow anyone other than AT&T build or operate such systems until it was forced to do so by the courts in the late 1960s.

The Political Economy of Regulation

In the light of this kind of record, economists have long since abandoned the presumption that the government regulation of industry always serves the public interest. Here again, the public choice perspective provides an alternative explanation that is more consistent with the facts. The theory recognizes that regulation, like all government authority, is a valuable resource: It can protect the firms in an industry from new competition; it can determine whether a new technology will be given a chance to succeed in the market; or it can be used to promote economic efficiency and consumer welfare. Regulation is also a scarce resource, however, because it cannot be used to accomplish all of these things at once. How regulation is actually used depends on the way in which its benefits and costs are reflected in the political process.

As an example, consider again the case of airline regulation. In the heyday of regulation, the airlines and the labor unions representing their employees were well organized and politically effective interest groups, whereas consumers were generally unorganized and politically ineffective. The result was that the political marketplace allocated regulatory authority in a way that favored the airlines and their employees at the expense of consumers in general. Much the same circumstances apply to the regulation of telecommunications, trucking, taxicabs, securities trading, banking, broadcasting, and dozens of other industries.

The Trend Toward Deregulation

Public choice theory also tells us, however, that if the costs imposed by special interests become large enough and visible enough, those interests will begin to lose their political influence. This seems to have happened in the regulatory sphere during the past two decades. As the substantial costs of regulation became more and more apparent—thanks in large part to many dozens of studies conducted and published by economists—political pressures mounted for the partial or complete deregulation of many industries. As you can see from Table 13.3, deregulation began slowly in the late 1960s, gathered momentum during the

Table 13.3

The trend toward deregulation

YEAR	EVENT
1968	Supreme Court allows non-AT&T equipment to be hooked up to the Bell System, the national telephone monopoly
1969	Independent microwave long-distance networks are allowed to connect to the local Bell telephone companies
1975	Securities Act amendments end fixed brokerage fees and begin to promote competition in securities markets
	Truckers and railroads are permitted to propose rates independent of industry rate bureaus
1977	Supreme Court limits authority of the FCC and encourages development of nonnetwork (cable) television services
	Air cargo is deregulated; airlines are given more freedom in pricing
1978	Airline Deregulation Act begins deregulation of interstate airlines; CAB is to be phased out by January 1, 1985
	Natural Gas Policy Act proposes to end all regulation of natural gas prices by 1989
1980	Motor Carrier Act begins deregulation of railroads and interstate trucking
	Monetary Control Act begins deregulation of banking and other financial services
	FCC eliminates most federal regulation of cable TV
1981	Crude oil prices decontrolled
	FCC eliminates much radio regulation
1982	Intercity bus companies allowed to change routes and fares without federal approval
1984	Ocean shipping companies allowed to compete on rates and service

1970s, and continued into the 1980s. Its impact on the airline industry is instructive.

The Airline Deregulation Act of 1978 eliminated the CAB as of January 1, 1985. Even before the CAB went out of business, however, it substantially eased restrictions on entry on most routes and allowed airlines to cut prices without its approval. Between 1976 and 1987, average real air fares declined by 30 percent, and by 1989 about 90 percent of all passengers flew on discount tickets with an average discount of 60 percent off the regular fare.* In addition, a number of smaller, more specialized carriers entered the market. Some of these new entrants offered commuter service between major cities in direct competition with established national airlines. Others provided service on low-density routes between smaller communities which major airlines, with their wide-bodied jet fleets, found it unprofitable to serve. Some new entrants offered no-frills service at discount fares, while others continued to offer services such as in-flight movies and cocktails. One new entrant, Regent Air, offered fine food, spacious lounges, private staterooms, and even an on-board hairdressing salon for those who were willing to pay up to four times the standard Los Angeles-to-New York air fare! (Apparently not many people were, for Regent was out of business within a year.)

At the same time, many established airlines had difficulties in the more competitive environment. A few went bankrupt and others became takeover targets—evidence that inefficient, poorly managed airlines had survived under regulation only because it provided them with a protective shield against the rigors of competition. Moreover, despite the publicity given a few major crashes and near misses, air travel became more safe during the period of deregulation. For example, the accident rate was 26 percent lower in the 8 years following deregulation than it had been in the 7 years immediately preceding it.†

Mergers and a lack of airport facilities for new entrants have recently increased levels of concentration in the airline industry beyond what proponents of deregulation had anticipated. Although this situation has raised antitrust concerns in some quarters, it nonetheless appears that on balance consumers have clearly been beneficiaries of airline deregulation. Similar stories can be told about the effects of deregulation in industries ranging from trucking to securities trading.

It is difficult to predict how far the movement toward deregulation will proceed. Indeed, it is uncertain whether even the steps described here will be seen through to their ultimate conclusions or reversed. Many interest groups—among them the previously regulated industries and their employees—were still pressing for reregulation as the decade of the 1990s began.

* "Airline Deregulation: Boon or Bust?" *Economic Commentary*, Federal Reserve Bank of Cleveland (May 1, 1989).

† Murray L. Weidenbaum, "Liberation Economics: The Benefits of Deregulation," *Policy Review* (Summer 1987). Note however that, although the narrowly economic regulation of the CAB was eliminated, the federal agency directly responsible for regulating airline safety, the Federal Aviation Administration (FAA), was not significantly affected by deregulation.

NEW STYLE ENVIRONMENTAL, HEALTH, AND SAFETY REGULATION

The same economic activity that delivers the goods and services we all enjoy as consumers often generates undesirable side effects as well. The more serious of these are environmental pollution and hazards to our health and safety—both as consumers and as employees in the workplace. Because they result in the sacrifice of valuable alternatives—a cleaner environment, greater health and safety—these unintended spillovers are a real opportunity cost of economic activity. As we saw in Chapter 5, economists call them external costs. Unlike other costs, external costs are not fully registered in the marketplace and therefore may not be accurately weighed in economic decisions. For example, the automobile owner who is not charged for the air pollution caused by driving is not likely to take the costs of that pollution into account when purchasing a car or when deciding whether to drive to work each day. The weekend gardener who is unaware that the blade of a power lawn mower can fly off and cause serious injury is not likely to add the expected medical costs to the purchase price when deciding whether to buy that mower or some other brand. In both of these examples, decisions are made on the basis of an incomplete or inaccurate comparison of benefits and costs.

Although spillovers such as these are to some extent inevitable, government has often been called on to reduce (or redistribute) the external costs they impose. It was not until the 1970s, however, that the federal government assumed primary responsibility for the economywide regulation of health, safety, and environmental quality. Its response has produced what has come to be called the "new style" social regulation, which is primarily a product of the 1970s.

The Clean Air Act of 1970 and the Clean Water Act of 1972, both administered by the Environmental Protection Agency (EPA), laid the foundation for a national environmental policy. The Occupational Safety and Health Act of 1970 created the Occupational Safety and Health Administration (OSHA) and established the federal government as the final arbiter of health and safety standards in the workplace. The Consumer Product Safety Commission (CPSC), created in 1972, extended government's concern with the health and safety effects of consumer products from food and drugs to virtually all consumer goods. In addition, other agencies were created to contend with more specific concerns, ranging from the safety characteristics of automobiles to the protection of commodity futures traders. A chronology of this new style regulation is given in Table 13.4.

Command-and-control regulation establishes an across-the-board regulatory standard applicable to all firms, and punishes violations of that standard with fines.

While economists generally agree that government regulation can, in principle, reduce the costs of environmental pollution and of hazardous products or working conditions, they are almost unanimous in their criticism of the principal approach that the federal government has actually adopted to deal with these problems. Economists call that approach **command-and-control regulation**: The regulatory agency issues a *command*, usually in the form of some minimum standard of pollution control, product safety, workplace safety, or whatever, and then exerts its *control* by fining or shutting down those who do not meet the

Table 13.4

A chronology of the "new style" regulation

YEAR	EVENT
1938	Food, Drug, and Cosmetic Act is established to promote the safety of those products before they reach the market
1965	Motor Vehicle Air Pollution Act becomes the first federal legislation to control air pollution
1969	Consumer Credit Protection Act mandates truth-in-lending
1969	National Environmental Policy Act requires environmental impact statements for all federal government projects
1970	Clean Air Act sets standards and timetables for reducing air pollution
1970	Occupational Safety and Health Act establishes OSHA to regulate safety in the workplace
1972	Consumer Product Safety Act creates the CPSC to regulate the safety of consumer products
1972	Water Pollution Control Act sets standards for clean water
1972	Noise Pollution Control Act is established to regulate noise levels of products and transportation vehicles
1974	Commodity Futures Trading Commission is set up to protect traders in futures markets

standard. Environmental regulation by the EPA is typical of the command-and-control approach.

Command and Control by the EPA

The EPA uses a command-and-control approach to set and enforce maximum allowable emissions standards applicable to various sources of air and water pollution. This approach is subject to two major criticisms. First, it provides no incentive to reduce pollutants below the (usually arbitrary) threshold set by the EPA. The polluter avoids a fine by simply meeting the standard; it gains nothing by going beyond the standard. By accepting all pollution below its maximum allowable level, the EPA is in effect treating that pollution as though it imposes no cost. Second, the standards approach is generally a more costly means of achieving any given amount of pollution reduction than alternative approaches favored by many economists. Among these alternatives are *effluent charges* and *marketable pollution rights*.

Effluent Charges

An **effluent charge** is a tax levied on polluting emissions.

Effluent charges are essentially taxes levied on each unit of pollution (effluents) emitted into the air or water. As such, they convert what is otherwise an external cost into a private cost that must be borne by the polluter itself: The more pollution released into the air or water, the greater the polluter's tax liability.

Table 13.5

The costs of pollution reduction: an example

POLLUTANTS ELIMINATED *(Tons per Month)*	MARGINAL COST TO: *Aquasludge*	*Hydrogunk*
First ton	$100	$150
Second ton	$120	$170
Third ton	$140	$190
Fourth ton	$160	$210
Fifth ton	$180	$230

The advantages of the effluent charge approach over the standards approach are best illustrated by means of a numerical example. Table 13.5 shows the marginal costs of reducing water pollutants by two firms, Aquasludge and Hydrogunk. According to the table, pollution reduction is less costly for Aquasludge than for Hydrogunk. For example, it costs Aquasludge only $100 to eliminate 1 ton of water pollutants per month, whereas it costs Hydrogunk $150 to achieve the same reduction. It costs Aquasludge an additional $120, but Hydrogunk an additional $170, to eliminate the second ton of pollutants, and so on.

Suppose that the EPA, using its command-and-control approach, sets a uniform standard requiring each polluter to eliminate 3 tons of water pollutants each month. It will cost Aquasludge $360 per month (= $100 + $120 + $140) to meet that standard and Hydrogunk $510 per month (= $150 + $170 + $190). The total cost of eliminating 6 tons of pollutants per month will therefore be $870 per month (= $360 + $510).

Now suppose that, rather than mandating a standard reduction of 3 tons of pollutants per firm per month, we achieve the same total 6-ton reduction with an effluent charge. A charge of $175 per ton will do the trick. Faced with that charge, Aquasludge has an incentive to eliminate 4 tons of pollutants because each of its first 4 tons can be eliminated at a cost less than the $175 tax savings that result. (It would not be worth it for Aquasludge to eliminate the fifth ton of pollutants because the additional $180 cost would exceed the $175 tax savings.) The same $175 effluent charge would give Hydrogunk an incentive to eliminate 2 tons of pollutants. Total reduction of pollutants would therefore be 6 tons, the same as under the standards approach. However, the total cost under the effluent charges would only be $840 per month ($520 for Aquasludge and $320 for Hydrogunk), which is $30 less than under the command-and-control standards approach. Costs are less because effluent charges create incentives that shift more of the burden of pollution reduction to the firm for which it is less costly.

We could achieve any given total reduction in pollution, and therefore match any given command-and-control standard, simply by adjusting the effluent charge. For example, if we wanted a total reduction of 7 tons of pollutants per month rather than just 6, we could raise the effluent charge to $185 per ton. With the effluent charge set at that level, Aquasludge would eliminate 5 tons per month and Hydrogunk, 2 tons for a total reduction of 7 tons.

Moreover, in addition to minimizing the cost of achieving any given level of pollution reduction, effluent charges also create incentives to develop new technologies for reducing pollution even further because any reduction is rewarded with a reduced tax liability. Such incentives are almost completely absent under the command-and-control approach.

A Market in Pollution Rights

While some European countries—most notably, West Germany and France—use effluent charges as their principal means of controlling large-scale environmental pollution, that approach has been virtually ignored in the United States. However, a different modification of the EPA's rigid command-and-control approach, and one used on a small scale since 1978, was announced in 1989 as the cornerstone of the Bush Administration's Environmental Policy. (As yet, however, it has not been adopted by Congress.) That modification would establish **marketable pollution rights**, whereby a firm can exceed its basic EPA emissions standard, but only if it pays other firms to take up the slack.

Marketable pollution rights are permits, which can be exchanged among firms and other parties, to emit a certain amount of pollutants.

We can again use Table 13.5 to illustrate how this would work. Suppose again that the EPA mandates that pollutants be reduced by a total of 6 tons per month. As under the basic standards approach, it initially orders Aquasludge and Hydrogunk each to reduce its emission of pollutants by 3 tons. Now, however, it permits them to deviate from their individual standards as long as the total 6-ton reduction in pollutants is maintained. Since Aquasludge can reduce pollutants by 1 more ton at a cost of only $160, and since Hydrogunk can save $190 by reducing its pollutants by 1 less ton, the stage is set for a trade. In particular, Hydrogunk can pay Aquasludge an amount between $160 and $190 to bear a greater share of the total reduction in pollutants. Such a payment would more than compensate Aquasludge for the extra cost ($160) of reducing pollutants by a fourth ton and, at the same time, be less than the amount Hydrogunk saves ($190) by avoiding the third ton of its own pollutant reduction. Both firms come out ahead, the same total level of pollution reduction is achieved, and cost of that reduction in pollution is minimized. Indeed, costs are exactly the same as under the effluent charge because the burden of the total 6-ton per month pollutants reduction is allocated in exactly the same way, namely, Aquasludge eliminates 4 tons and Hydrogunk 2.

The dynamic incentive effects of marketable pollution rights are also much the same as those of effluent charges. Because firms that find a way to lower the cost of pollution reduction can in effect sell pollution reduction to other firms, they have an incentive to reduce pollutants below the EPA's basic standards. They also have incentives to develop less costly ways of reducing pollution in order to reduce pollution still further. In addition, private environmental and conservation groups, such as the Sierra Club and Friends of the Earth, could reduce pollution below the EPA's basic standards by purchasing and retiring pollution rights.

Although the EPA has permitted only limited trading in pollution rights, a market already exists. In 1988, for example, the rights to emit 1 ton of pollutants per year in the Los Angeles area were being traded for about $5,000.* Moreover, the United Nations is considering a proposal by the United States to use marketable pollution rights in dealing with chloroflourocarbons, the chemicals suspected of deleting the earth's ozone layer.†

Effluent charges and marketable pollution rights have been criticized as granting a "license to pollute" to any polluter willing to pay the price. But a clean and healthy environment is not free. Does it not make sense to forego the name-calling and try to achieve it at the lowest possible cost?

CHAPTER SUMMARY

1. *Antitrust* policies are concerned with the degree of competition in the marketplace and with business conduct that might affect competition. Because the language of the basic antitrust laws—the Sherman, Clayton, and FTC Acts—is quite general, concrete antitrust policy is formulated mainly in the courts.
2. Economists generally agree that the role of antitrust policy should be to *promote competition*, not to *protect competitors*.
3. Economics suggests that those limitations of competition that simply increase market power with no offsetting benefits should be illegal *per se*, that is, illegal in and of themselves, regardless of the circumstances in which they occur. Those whose effect on competition can be beneficial, harmful, or neutral depending on the circumstances should be evaluated under a *rule of reason* in the light of the particular circumstances in which they occur.
4. Most economists agree that antitrust should prohibit only those *horizontal mergers* that lead to significant market power for the merged firm or that significantly increase the chances of collusion by further reducing the number of firms in a highly concentrated industry. Antitrust policy toward mergers has not always been guided by these principles, however.
5. Arguments that *vertical mergers* can be used to "leverage" market power in one market into other markets or to block entry usually apply only to extreme and unlikely situations. In recent years, the courts have recognized this and been quite tolerant of such mergers.
6. Recent antitrust policy toward single-firm monopoly tolerates large size as long as it is achieved through superior efficiency and not by illegal tactics.
7. Recognizing that *vertical restraints*, such as resale price maintenance and exclusive distribution territories, are frequently used as legitimate market-

*See Timothy Tregarthen, "Selling the Right to Pollute: Pioneer in the Market for Particulates," *The Margin*, April, 1988.
†Timothy Tregarthen, "The Warming of the Earth," *The Margin*, Nov/Dec 1988.

ing tactics, courts and enforcement agencies have begun to treat most of them under a rule of reason in recent years.

8. The overall record of antitrust is somewhat spotty. On the one hand, the laws have certainly forced overt cartels underground and discouraged horizontal mergers that would otherwise have achieved the same effects as a cartel. On the other hand, they have probably discouraged some mergers and vertical restraints that would have increased economic efficiency, and the laws have occasionally been used to protect competitors rather than competition.

9. *"Old style" industrial regulation* seeks to alter prices, profits, and entry conditions in specific industries.

10. *Natural monopoly*, which exists where economies of scale are so significant that a single large firm can serve the market at lower unit cost than two or more smaller firms, provides the economic rationale for traditional industrial regulation.

11. *Rate-of-return regulation* allows the regulated firm enough revenues to cover its operating costs plus a fair return on invested capital. It has been criticized on the grounds that the fair return rarely reflects the true opportunity cost of capital and that such regulation provides little incentive for the regulated firm to control costs.

12. The concept of natural monopoly has been criticized on grounds that it takes too narrow a view of competition. Specifically, it considers only competition *within* a market and not competition *for* a market.

13. Many economists who accept rate-of-return regulation as applied to local public utilities have been critical of its extension to "unnatural" monopolies—that is, industries that perform like monopolies or cartels only because they are regulated.

14. Public choice theory suggests that organized interest groups, such as the regulated industry itself or its unionized employees, often use regulation to further their own ends at the expense of consumers in general. The record of regulation provides many instances when this seems to be the case.

15. Deregulation, which began in the 1970s, on balance seems to have benefitted consumers.

16. *"New style" social regulation* addresses issues, such as environmental quality, health, and safety, that cut across industry boundaries.

17. "New style" regulatory agencies, such as the EPA and OSHA, tend to rely on a *command-and-control* approach that utilizes fines to induce people to meet regulatory standards. This approach has been criticized by economists for often setting arbitrary standards that ignore costs and benefits and for providing no incentives to go beyond the standards.

18. *Effluent charges* and *marketable pollution rights* can achieve the same clean air and water standards set by the EPA but at a lower cost than its command-and-control approach. They also provide incentives to go beyond the EPA's basic standards.

Key Terms and Concepts

antitrust policy
old style industrial regulation
new style social regulation
per se illegality
rule of reason
horizontal merger
vertical merger
leverage theory
vertical restraint
resale price maintenance
exclusive distribution territories
natural monopoly
rate-of-return regulation
command-and-control regulation
effluent charges
marketable pollution rights

Questions for Thought and Discussion

1. In evaluating horizontal mergers, the Justice Department and the FTC often find that the merger partners' competitors oppose it. Should such opposition weigh in favor of the merger or against it?
2. "Predatory pricing" is a practice whereby a firm—the "predator"—prices goods below cost to drive out competitors and ultimately monopolize its market. It is illegal under the antitrust laws, but applying the law raises a number of issues.
   a. Below whose costs would the predator's price have to be, its own or its competitors'?
   b. Which measure of cost would you use to define "below cost"?
   c. How would the potential success of predatory pricing be affected by entry conditions in the market?
   d. Giving away free samples is certainly selling below cost and also draws business away from competitors. Is it "predatory"?
   e. In some antitrust cases, a firm has been able to convince the court that it is a victim of predatory pricing simply by demonstrating that the alleged predator's prices are below its own and that it has suffered losses as a result. As a legal precedent, is this sound antitrust policy?
3. We have argued that RPM imposed on retailers by manufacturers can be used either to promote a manufacturers' price-fixing cartel or to induce retailers to provide promotional services for the manufacturers' products. What kind of evidence would enable you to distinguish between these uses of RPM in court?
4. State "fair trade" laws impose resale price maintenance by law on entire industries. For example, a California law once prevented retail liquor stores from discounting

beer, wine, and liquor prices. Do you think such laws served a legitimate purpose, such as inducing retailers to provide point-of-sale service? Who do you think considered such laws "fair"; that is, from whom do you think they drew the most support?

5. Suppose that Zapco, a municipal electric utility, has $750 million invested in its electrical distribution system. The system provides 1 million customers with an average of 5,000 kilowatt-hours per year of electricity. The average, net-of-capital cost of distributing electricity is $0.10 per kilowatt. Zapco must pay 10 percent interest to attract financial capital in the bond market.

a. What is a "fair return on a fair value" for Zapco stockholders?

b. How much annual revenue should Zapco be allowed if it is subject to rate-of-return regulation?

c. Assuming no price discrimination, what price will Zapco be allowed to charge? What unit cost measure does this price equal? Is it the most efficient price from the standpoint of efficient resource allocation?

6. Once upon a time, truckers wanting to carry a certain type of cargo on a certain route had to obtain a certificate issued by the ICC. The certificate, which limited the number of competing truckers on any given route, had to be obtained either from the ICC itself or purchased from another trucker who already owned it. Depending on the cargo and the route, the purchase price ranged from a few thousand dollars to well over a million dollars. Why do you think these certificates were so valuable? What do you think happened (and why) to the value of these certificates when trucking was deregulated and entry was no longer restricted? Do you think this was "fair" to a trucker who might have paid thousands of dollars for a certificate?

7. What arguments would you make to an environmentalist who opposes marketable pollution rights as a "license to pollute that is sold to the highest bidder?"

8. What is the parallel between effluent charges and deposits on returnable bottles?

9. What would be the equivalent of the environmental effluent charge as a means of controlling safety in the workplace?

10. The federal Food and Drug Administration (FDA) requires that all new drugs be thoroughly tested and certified before they can be introduced to the market. What are the benefits and costs of this kind of regulation? For what kinds of drugs do you think that the costs are highest relative to the benefits? For what kind do you think that the costs are lowest relative to the benefits?

CHAPTER 14

Factor Markets and the Distribution of Incomes

What income do you expect to earn after you graduate? What determines anyone's income? Why do some people—rock stars, professional athletes, the presidents of major corporations—earn millions of dollars per year while others in our society live in poverty? To what extent are such differences the result of diligence and hard work? Of differences in innate abilities? Of just plain luck? Are they "fair?" What standard of fairness can we use to answer that question? Can government policies alter the distribution of income if people feel that it's not fair? What are the side effects of such policies?

In this chapter we attempt to provide some answers to—or, perhaps more accurately, a way of thinking about—questions like these. To do so, we examine the workings of the economy's *factor markets*, the markets in which productive resources (factors of production) and their services are exchanged.

By far the most important productive resource that most of us own is our *human capital*, our own personal mix of abilities, talents, knowledge, skills, and experience. We use our human capital to supply human productive services, or more mundanely, labor, in return for *wages and salaries*. Some of us also own nonhuman productive resources such as capital goods, land, and other natural resources. The services of these nonhuman resources generate income in the form of *rent* (if a contractual claim) and *profit* (if a residual claim). Finally, many of us own financial assets such as savings accounts and corporate bonds. Although these assets are not themselves literally factors of production, the process of saving by which we acquire them is genuinely productive. As we have seen, saving provides the credit for investment in new capital goods. The *interest* income we earn from our financial assets is essentially a claim on the additional output made possible by those capital goods.

Our incomes thus depend on two fundamental elements: first, the amounts and kinds of productive resources we own, and second, the prices (wages, rents, profit, and interest) that the factor markets place on the services of those resources. Accordingly, in our analysis of income and its distribution, we first examine the pricing of productive services in the factor markets and then turn our attention to the determinants of resource ownership.

THE BASIC ECONOMICS OF FACTOR MARKETS

We can distinguish between a productive resource itself—for example, a skilled worker, an acre of farm land, a computer—and the flow services it generates—an hour of skilled labor, a year's use of the farm land, a day of computing time. It is somewhat arbitrary whether we approach the factor markets by asking what determines the market value of productive resources or by asking what determines the value of their services. Since our main concern is the distribution of income, which is the payment for productive services, we shall focus primarily on the prices of factor services.

The Derived Demand for Productive Resources and Their Services

The **derived demand** for a productive resource is derived from the demand for the final goods that it can be used to produce.

The demand for a productive resource and its services is a **derived demand** because it depends on the final goods that the resource is used to produce. The demand for farm land is derived from the demand for the food and other products that can be made with the crops grown on the land. The demand for a hydroelectric generating plant is derived from the demand for electricity to light homes and to power stereos and television sets. The demand for a college professor's lectures is derived from students' demand to learn, which in turn is derived (at least in part) from employers' demands for educated employees, which ultimately is derived from consumer demands for the final goods that those educated employees can produce.

We can illustrate the nature of derived demand by means of a simple example. Table 14.1 on the next page summarizes the operations of Samantha's Sweats Shop, a hypothetical manufacturer of sweatshirts. The first column of the table shows the number of people Samantha may employ; the second column shows her corresponding daily output rate; and the third column shows the marginal product of Samantha's workers. (The fall in the marginal product as Samantha's level of employment rises reflects the effects of diminishing returns.)

Table 14.1

Samantha's Sweats Shop

Employees	*Total Output*	*Marginal Product*	*Value of Marginal Product (Price = $10)*
0	0	—	—
1	20	20	$200
2	38	18	180
3	54	16	160
4	68	14	140
5	80	12	120
6	90	10	100
7	98	8	80
8	104	6	60
9	108	4	40
10	110	2	20

The **value of the marginal product** is the market value of the marginal product of a resource.

Samantha will hire an additional worker only if it is profitable to do so—that is, only if that worker adds at least as much to Samantha's revenues as to her costs. The amount an additional worker adds to Samantha's costs is the wage that she must pay to obtain his services. His contribution to Samantha's revenues is the **value of his marginal product**, which is equal to his marginal product times the price at which Samantha sells her sweatshirts. The fourth column of Table 14.1 shows the value of labor's marginal product based on a price of $10 per sweatshirt. (We assume Samantha is a price taker.)

At a wage of $75 per day, Samantha would hire seven workers because the value of the marginal product of each of the first seven more than covers that wage. Samantha would not hire an eighth worker because his $60 contribution to her revenues would not cover his $75 wage. If the wage were $90 per day, Samantha would hire only six workers because the value of the seventh worker's marginal product would be less than the $90 wage. These employment decisions are illustrated graphically in Figure 14.1. Since the curve (or, in this simplified example, the step-shaped line) showing value of the marginal product tells us how much labor Samantha would hire at each wage, it constitutes her *derived demand curve* for labor.*

*The condition that a profit-maximizing producer will hire labor up to the point at which the wage equals the value of the marginal product is equivalent to the condition, derived and illustrated in Chapter 3 and again in Chapter 9, that a profit-maximizing producer will supply output up to the point at which the marginal cost of an additional unit of output is equal to its price. To see why, we can write the condition for profit-maximizing employment as $W = MP \cdot P$. Dividing both sides by the marginal product gives the equivalent expression, $W/MP = P$. The ratio of the wage to the marginal product is just another way of expressing the marginal cost of additional output. For example, if one more employee must be paid a wage of $100 ($= W$), and that employee contributes an additional ten units of output ($= MP$), then those additional units of output have a marginal cost of $10 each ($= W/MP$).

Figure 14.1

The value of labor's marginal product in Samantha's Sweats Shop

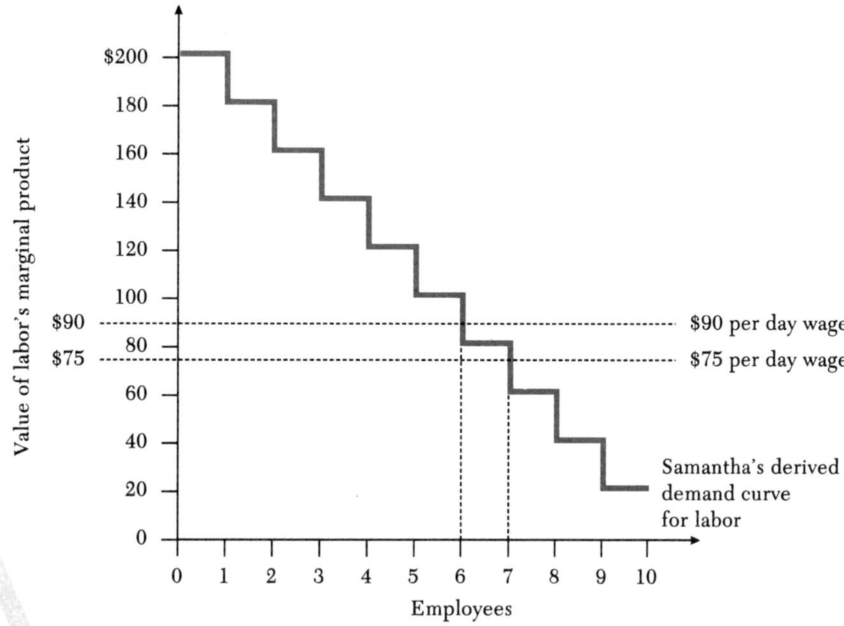

For an individual price taker like Samantha, the demand price for labor falls as more labor is employed because diminishing returns reduce labor's marginal product. When we shift from the individual firm's demand for labor to the market demand (or from the case of a price taker to that of a price setter), the fall in the marginal product is reinforced by the fall in the market price of the final product. Specifically, if more labor is used to produce sweatshirts (or anything else), the market supply will increase and, by the law of demand, the market price will fall. Correspondingly, so will the value of labor's marginal product, even if there are no diminishing returns to labor in sweatshirt production. Thus the derived market demand curves for productive services, like the market demand curves for final goods, must be downward sloped.

Elasticity of Derived Demand

The elasticity of demand for productive resources depends on the elasticity of demand for the final goods they produce. Specifically, the more elastic the demand for a final good, other things being equal, the more elastic will be the demand for the productive resources used in its production.

Derived demands are also more elastic in the long run than in the short run. In the short run, a rise in the price of a resource leads producers to substitute away from it, but only within the framework of existing technology; in the long run, however, they can develop and utilize new technologies that further economize on the higher priced resource.

Changes in Derived Demand

As is the case with final goods, changes in things other than the price of the productive services themselves shift the derived demand curve. As we have seen, the demand price for a productive service is equal to the value of its marginal product, which in turn is equal to its physical marginal product times the value of the final good produced. Accordingly, anything that changes the marginal product of a resource or the relative marginal values of the final goods it can be used to produce shifts its derived demand curve.

Changes in Marginal Product Other things being equal, an increase in the marginal product of a resource increases the demand for that resource and its productive services; a decrease in marginal product does the reverse. Changes in the marginal product, which typically reflect more general changes in overall resource productivity, can be the result of changes in the quality of the resource itself, changes in the technology by which its services are combined with other resources, or changes in the productivity of those other resources. For example, the demand for the services of agricultural land increases when the land is irrigated. The demand for your labor services increases when you acquire new job skills and experience that raise your productivity. The demand for personal computers increased as technological progress made them faster, more reliable, and easier to use. Improvements in computer software, a resource complementary to computer hardware, also increased the demand for computers by raising their productivity.

Changes in Relative Marginal Values of Final Goods An increase in the demand for any final good increases the derived demands for the resources used in its production; a decrease in the demand for a final good decreases the corresponding derived demands. For example, other things being equal, an increase in the demand for fine wine increases the demand for agricultural land in the Bordeaux region of France and in California's Napa Valley. An increase in the demand for computer games increases the demand for computer engineers, programmers, and technicians. A decrease in the demand for horseback riding decreases the demand for blacksmiths.

The Supply of Productive Resources and Their Services

Using the services of any productive resource in one endeavor means sacrificing its use in others. Working one more hour means sacrificing an hour of leisure, or sleep, or study time. Producing new capital goods or searching for new deposits of raw materials diverts resources from current consumption; using the services of existing capital goods and natural resources results in depreciation and depletion, thereby sacrificing future production and consumption. Holding financial assets also means sacrificing current consumption. The supply prices of productive resources and their services must cover the opportunity costs of these foregone alternatives.

Moreover, the opportunity costs of productive resources and their services typically rise at the margin with the quantity supplied. For example, the more labor supplied, the less leisure available; the less leisure available, the greater its marginal value and the greater the opportunity cost of another hour of labor. The more land used in the production of food, the less land is available for housing; the less housing available, the higher its marginal value and the greater the marginal cost of land used in food production. Whether in total or in the production of particular goods, therefore, the supply price for productive services rises with the amount supplied.*

Like the demand for productive services, the supply tends to be more elastic in the long run than in the short run. In the short run, a rise in price calls forth more services from a given stock of productive resources; in the long run, it also encourages investment that adds to that stock. For example, if the salaries of accountants rise, more college students will invest in the human capital necessary to become accountants. If the rental rate for office space rises, more office buildings will be built. If the price of gasoline rises, oil companies will invest in exploration for new reserves. All of these investments come to fruition and add to the flow of productive services only after a period of time.

The Role of Factor Prices

In factor markets as in markets for final goods, price adjustments are the coordinating mechanism. In effect, the market continuously compares the quantities of each productive service supplied and demanded and adjusts the factor price so that the market clears and productive services are allocated to their most valuable uses.

We can best illustrate this process by means of a simple example. Suppose that labor can be used to produce either of two final goods, food or clothing. ure 14.2 on page 336 shows the supply and demand curves for labor services in the food market. As we have seen, the demand curve shows the value of labor's marginal product in food production, whereas the supply curve shows its marginal cost. Since the best alternative use of labor is in the production of clothing, the marginal cost reflects the value of labor's foregone marginal product in clothing production. Suppose that initially only L' hours of labor services are employed in food production. At that level of employment, the $12 value of labor's marginal product in food production exceeds the $8 value of its marginal product in clothing production. Allocating one more hour of labor to food production therefore results in $12 worth of additional food at a cost of only $8 worth of clothing. The result is a net gain of $4 in the overall value of final output.

The market implicitly makes, and acts on, comparisons such as these as it moves toward equilibrium, which, in Figure 14.2, is achieved at a wage of $10

*A theoretical possibility that we shall ignore here is the "backward bending" supply curve of labor services according to which, at high wage rates, the supply of labor services falls with further wage increases. The reason is that if the wage becomes high enough, workers will respond to further increases by "buying" more leisure and working less.

Figure 14.2

Equilibrium in the market for labor services

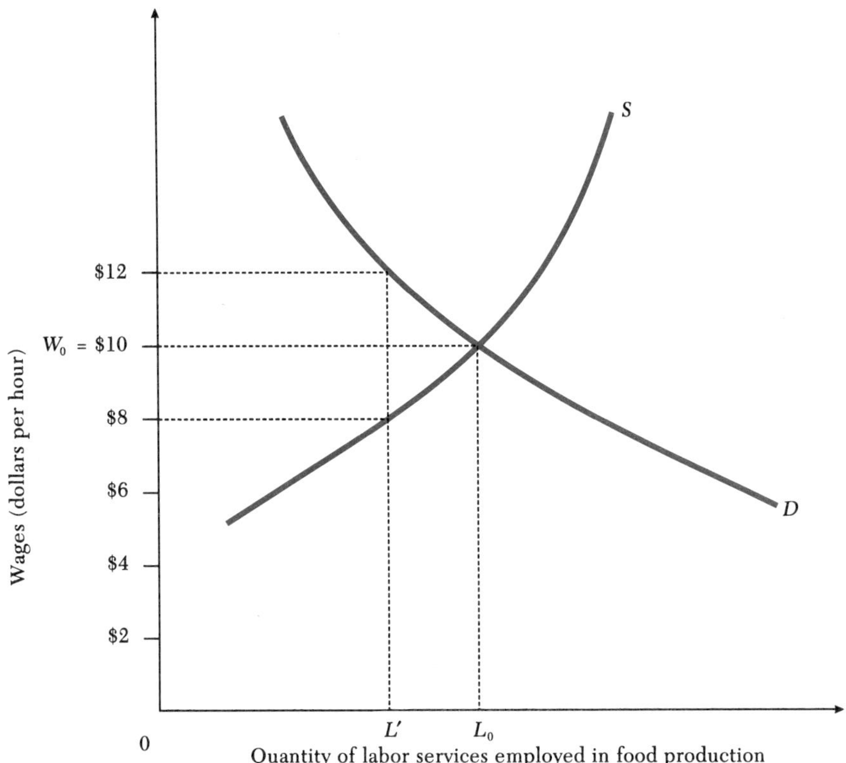

per hour with L_0 hours of labor used in food production. More importantly, the market does this continuously and automatically as economic conditions change. For example, if the demand for food increases, so also does the derived demand for labor in food production. The result is depicted in Figure 14.3(a). The increase in derived demand bids up the wages of food-producing labor, increases employment by food producers, and increases the quantity of food supplied. On the other hand, if the demand for clothing increases, the opportunity cost of labor employed in food production rises. This is reflected in an upward shift of the supply curve as depicted in Figure 14.3(b). The wage rises to reflect the higher opportunity cost as labor is bid out of food production and into clothing production. In each case, the outcome is just what the final consumer ordered!

The truly remarkable thing about the factor markets is that they continuously perform reallocations of this sort not just for one productive service and two final goods, but for literally millions of each.

Some Applications

The best way to appreciate the explanatory power of our basic factor market model is to apply it to some of the issues, questions, and policies related to the pricing of productive services. Although our examples focus mainly on the mar-

Figure 14.3

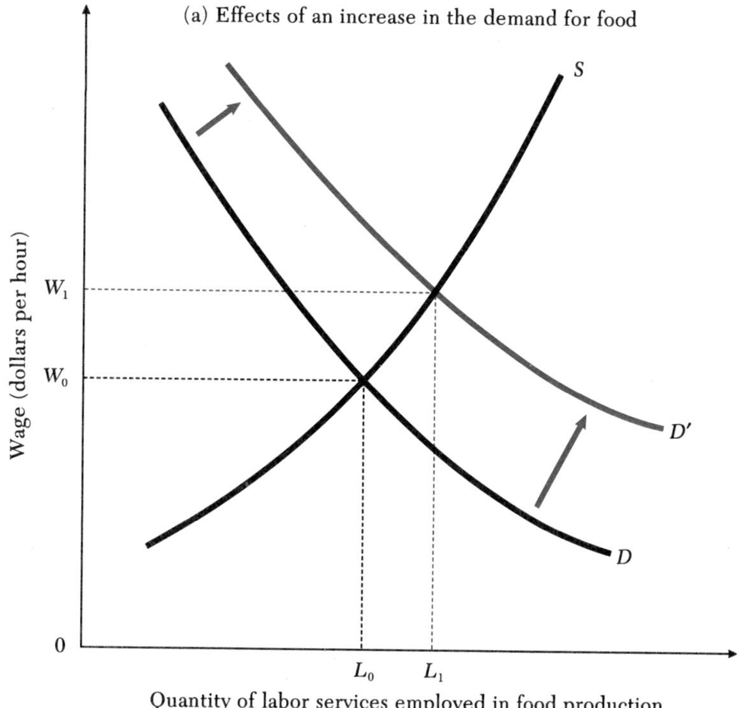

(a) Effects of an increase in the demand for food
S
D′
D
W1
W0
0
L0
L1
Wage (dollars per hour)
Quantity of labor services employed in food production

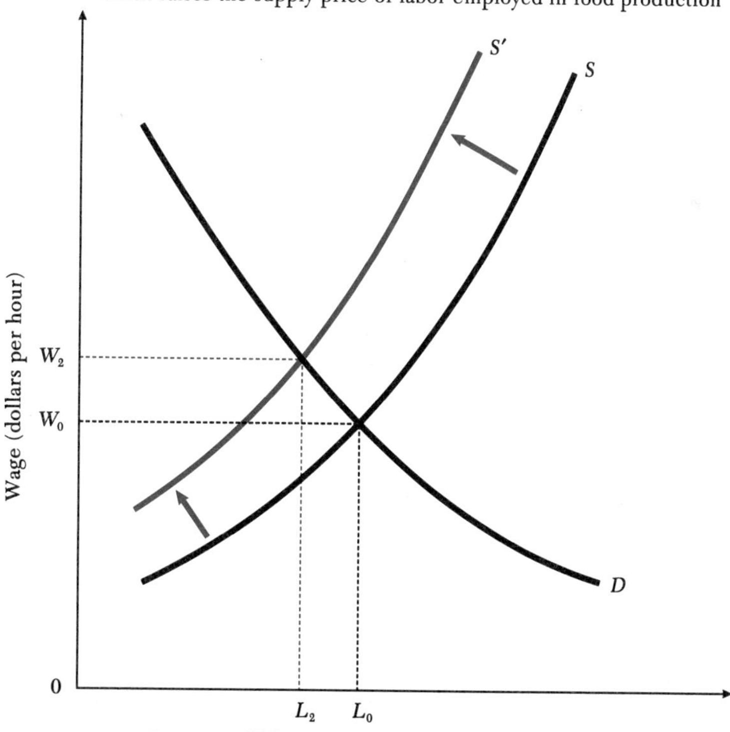

(b) Effects of an increase in the demand for clothing
which raises the supply price of labor employed in food production
S′
S
D
W2
W0
0
L2
L0
Wage (dollars per hour)
Quantity of labor services employed in food production

ket for labor services, nearly all of the analysis pertains equally to the markets for other productive services as well.

Compensating Wage Differentials

A **compensating wage differential** is the amount by which the wage must rise to compensate for the unpleasant or costly attributes of a particular type of employment, and thus to attract workers to that type of employment.

Because jobs differ with respect to their conditions of employment, the supply price of labor varies from job to job. Other things being equal, jobs that are dirty, hazardous, or otherwise unpleasant must pay higher wages to attract workers than jobs with more pleasant characteristics. Since the higher wage compensates the worker for the unpleasant attributes of the job, it is known as a **compensating wage differential**. Such differentials explain, for example, why oil workers in Alaska earn more than oil workers in Texas and why police officers in large cities with high crime rates earn more than their counterparts in rural areas where risks are lower. They also explain why coal miners, who work in a dirty and hazardous environment, earn more than other workers with similar levels of education, skills, and abilities but whose work environment is not nearly so unpleasant. Wage differentials also compensate for any costly training that must be borne by the worker. Compensating wage differentials are therefore the market's way of persuading people to accept less attractive, but socially productive, jobs and to invest in the human capital required to perform other jobs.

Comparable worth is a way of determining wages on the basis of "objectively" comparable job characteristics rather than on the basis of a job's market value.

Some critics of the market feel that wage differentials are sometimes arbitrary and unfair. They typically point to the lower wages in occupations that have traditionally attracted women, such as secretarial work, nursing, and teaching, as evidence of this. These critics claim that such jobs are essentially no different from many higher paying, male-dominated jobs, and they argue that it would be more fair to determine pay on the basis of **comparable worth**.

The typical comparable worth proposal would determine wages on the basis of certain "objective" differences in job characteristics as measured and evaluated by a panel of experts. These characteristics might include the mental and physical demands of the job, the amount of education and skills required, the amount of responsibility the job entails, and so on. The proponents of comparable worth argue that jobs deemed "comparable" according to these criteria should receive equal pay. For example, the state of Washington once decided that, on the basis of comparable worth, and contrary to the market, secretaries should earn the same amount as electricians, and librarians should earn more than chemists.

Such comparable worth proposals would inevitably lead to shortages and surpluses whenever the panel of experts disagrees with the market. If comparable worth says that secretarial services are worth the same as the services of electricians, for example, but the market says otherwise, then the comparable worth wages will create a surplus of secretaries and a shortage of electricians.

Comparable difficulty, or comparable educational or skill requirements, has nothing to do with comparable worth. Just as the most careful, objective analysis of the physical and chemical properties of apples and oranges cannot tell us which is worth more, there simply exists no viable alternative to the market in deciding the worth of labor services. When the market sets wage differentials, it is indeed measuring comparable worth in the only way that makes sense—that is, by allowing the final consumer to evaluate the outputs, not the inputs, of various types of labor services.

The Gender Gap

The catalyst for most comparable worth proposals is a belief that lower earnings in female-dominated professions are a reflection of gender discrimination. After all, average female earnings are only about 60 percent of average male earnings. Comparing these averages can be very misleading, however, for the average woman in the labor force is quite different from the average man. In particular, she is younger, has less experience in her current job, works fewer hours, and is more likely to leave the labor force for child rearing. When these differences, along with occupational differences, are taken into account much—but not all—of the male-female wage differential disappears.

It may well be that any remaining differences are the result of discrimination. However, the discrimination hypothesis must confront a difficult question: Why don't employers without gender prejudice (and surely there are many) take advantage of the wage differential by hiring low-cost women rather than high-cost men? Not only would this increase their profits, but the competitive pressures would drive up female wages relative to male wages until the two were equal (after allowing, of course, for experience, occupational differences, and so on).

One explanation is that some employers mistakenly regard women as less capable of performing certain tasks. For example, suppose employers believe that women do not make good electrical engineers. Because of this prejudice, women who invest in the human capital necessary to become electrical engineers obtain a lower return on their investment than men who make similar investments. As a result, at least some women who otherwise would have chosen to become electrical engineers do not invest in the necessary human capital; instead they become, say, teachers and earn less than electrical engineers. Note that according to this argument, gender prejudice *causes* the productivity differences that are typically used to *explain* the gender gap.

Minimum wage laws, which are on the books of the federal government and most state governments, prevent employers from offering, and workers from accepting, wages below some minimum level. In 1989 the federal minimum wage was raised from $3.35 per hour to $4.25 per hour.

We can use Figure 14.4 to analyze the impact of minimum wage laws. It shows the supply curve for labor services and two demand curves. The demand

* Some of the material in this section draws on "Boosting the Minimum Wage," *The Margin*, Sept/Oct 1988, and "Demand for Labor: The Federal Minimum Wage," Chapter 21 in Robert Paul Thomas, *Microeconomic Applications: Understanding the American Economy* (Wadsworth, 1981).

Figure 14.4

Effects of minimum wage laws

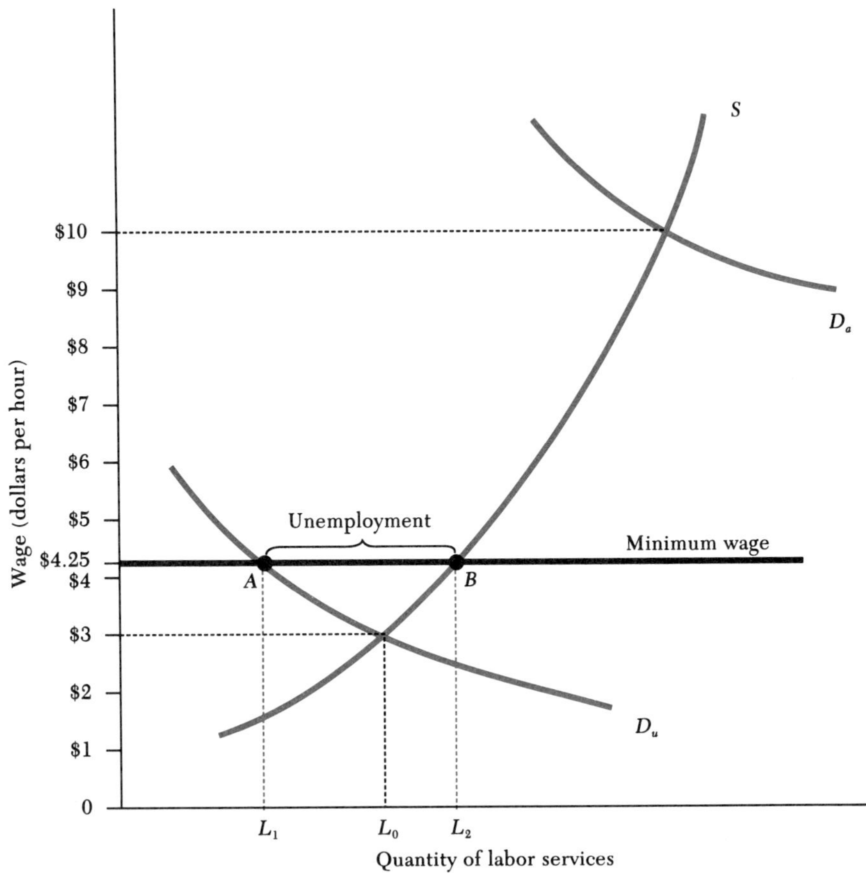

curve labelled D_u represents the demand for the services of unskilled labor, whereas that labelled D_a represents the demand for the services of labor with average skills. Because unskilled labor is less productive than average labor, D_u lies below D_a. The average wage is $10 per hour and the market-clearing wage for unskilled labor is $3 per hour.

Now suppose that the government makes it illegal for anyone to offer or accept employment at any wage below $4.25 per hour. Since the average market wage is well above the legal minimum anyway, workers with average and above average skills are not directly affected. (We see below how they may be affected indirectly.) In the market for unskilled labor, however, the law becomes a price floor that keeps the wage above its market-clearing level. As with any effective price floor, the result is a surplus. In labor markets the surplus, represented by the distance *AB* in the diagram, takes the form of unemployment.

Minimum wage unemployment is borne mainly by those workers whose productivity is so low that it is not profitable for employers to hire them at the legal minimum. Such workers are sometimes categorized as "unemployable," but this term is very misleading; anyone is employable if he or she is willing to accept a wage commensurate with his or her productivity. Minimum wage laws deny this option to the least skilled members of the labor force, telling them, in effect, that no wage is better than a low wage.

Who are the unskilled, low-productivity workers displaced by the minimum wage? Most studies have focused on teenagers, whose incomplete formal education and lack of work experience places them near the bottom of the productivity scale. These studies typically show that each 10 percent rise in the minimum wage leads to a reduction in teenage employment of between 1 and 3 percent. Another study, however, found the greatest impact of the minimum wage to be on unskilled, adult women. This study concluded that increases in the minimum wage have such a negative impact on employment within this segment of the labor force that they actually reduce its total earnings.

The employment effects of the minimum wage are greater in the long run when employers have time to substitute other resources, such as capital or skilled labor, for unskilled labor. After the minimum wage was increased by Congress in 1978, for example, the fast food industry, a major employer of teenage labor, initially responded by cutting back on working hours. In time, however, the industry gradually adopted production techniques, such as automated cooking equipment and centralized commissaries, that enabled them to economize still further on the use of unskilled labor.

Perhaps even more important is the law's impact on the ability of teenagers to acquire valuable job skills and on-the-job experience. Entry-level jobs not only enable teenagers to earn incomes but also teach them promptness, responsibility, and other basic job skills that are a critical component of human capital. By eliminating entry-level jobs and making it more expensive for employers to provide on-the-job training, the minimum wage delays or eliminates this investment in human capital and makes it more difficult for today's unskilled workers to move up to better jobs in the future.

Much of the organized support for raising the minimum wage comes from labor unions. On the surface this may seem puzzling. After all, union workers are typically highly skilled workers earning wages far above the minimum. Why should a labor union whose members are already earning $15 or $20 per hour support an increase in the minimum wage to, say, $5 per hour?

Although union spokespersons inevitably attribute their support for high minimum wages to a magnanimous concern that "every American is entitled to a just and living wage," there may be another, less altruistic, explanation. Anything that raises the price of unskilled labor increases the demand for substitutes, including substitutes in the form of skilled, union labor. (The substitution sometimes occurs in mysterious and indirect ways. For example, although we may not think of skilled electronics technicians as substitutes for teenage fast food workers, the increase in the minimum wage that prompted the fast food industry to replace teenagers with automated technologies for preparing food almost certainly increased the demand for skilled technicians to repair and maintain the new equipment.) By raising the demand for skilled, union workers, the minimum wage also raises their earnings and employment. One study found, for example, that the 1974–75 increase in the minimum wage raised the average earnings of union workers by $600 per year.

Superstars, Personal Attributes, and Economic Rent

At the opposite end of the earnings spectrum from the unskilled minimum wage worker is the "superstar" earning millions of dollars per year. Superstars come in a variety of styles, from rock stars like Bruce Springsteen, to sports stars like Michael Jordon, to entertainment stars like Bill Cosby. Although all of these superstars have undoubtedly honed their human capital through years of practice and experience, their huge earnings are more the result of the natural scarcity of their unique talents and abilities. You can bet that if plumbers' earnings were in a class with Michael Jordon's, people would be falling all over themselves to become plumbers, and the increase in the supply of plumbers would soon drive their earnings down to opportunity costs. However, very few of us are born with the size and physical talent to star in professional basketball, and all of the hard work and determination in the world isn't going to change that fact.

The income of these superstars greatly exceeds their opportunity costs as measured by their potential earnings in other occupations. (Can you imagine, for example, how much less Bill Cosby, who has an advanced degree in education, would earn as a teacher or school administrator than he does as a television star?) As we saw in Chapter 9, earnings in excess of opportunity costs for scarce and nonreproducible factors of production are called *economic rents*. The income of the typical superstar therefore consists mainly of economic rent.

Figure 14.5 illustrates the relation between scarcity and economic rent in the factor market. Although the analysis is essentially the same for rock stars or high-fashion models, we assume it is the market for professional basketball players. Suppose that there are only 300 men with the size and athletic ability to play professional basketball, and assume for simplicity that all of them have the same opportunity cost, namely, earning $30,000 per year in some other occupation. These assumptions imply that the supply curve of professional basketball players looks like a backwards L. The supply of professional basketball players jumps from 0 to 300 at the $30,000 salary necessary to cover their opportunity cost, but salaries above $30,000 have no effect on supply because of the natural scarcity of talent. Given the demand for the services of professional basketball players (which is derived from consumer demand for basketball games), the market clears at a salary of $500,000 per year. Each player thus earns $470,000 per year in economic rent, and the total rent earned by all professional basketball players is represented by the shaded area in the diagram.

The mere possession of some unique talent is not sufficient to generate economic rent; there must be a demand for that talent as well. You may be the only person in the universe who can wiggle your ears while standing on your head and whistling "Dixie," but if there is no demand for your exceptional talent, you will not earn a penny of economic rent. In terms of Figure 14.5, unless the

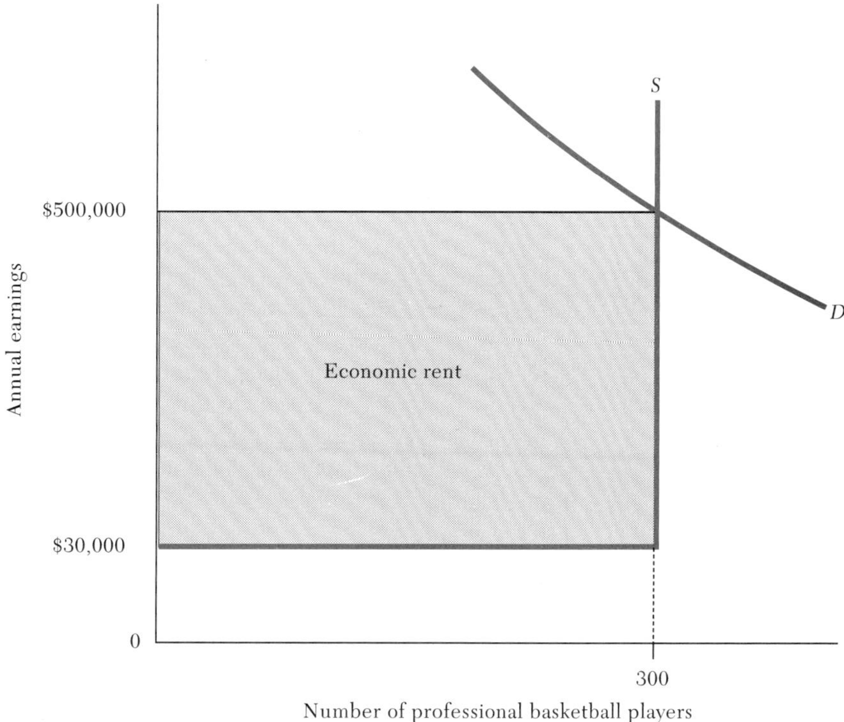

Figure 14.5

Economic rent of superstars

demand curve is high enough to intersect the supply curve in its vertical range, there will be no economic rent. (Imagine how many large and agile people had the misfortune to be borne before professional basketball became a popular form of entertainment!)

You do not have to be a literal superstar, however, to earn at least some economic rent. Almost any little personal advantage will do. If your ability to inspire loyalty and confidence in others makes you a particularly effective manager, or if your winning personality makes you a better salesperson than others, then part of your earnings will be economic rent. We are all individuals, and to the extent that our unique and inimitable qualities have market value, they enable us to earn economic rent.

Contrived Scarcity and Factor Market Monopoly

Earnings in excess of opportunity costs are not always due to natural scarcity; sometimes they are the result of artificial, or contrived, scarcity which, as we have seen, is the essence of monopoly. This is as true in the factor markets as in the markets for final goods, as a few examples will illustrate.

Labor Unions and Their Effects

A labor union is a workers' organization formed to promote the economic interests of its members. Because of their virtual exemption from the antitrust laws, unions are permitted to act as monopoly suppliers of labor services. (This monopoly power is of course limited by such things as competition from non-unionized producers, foreign producers, and the ability of employers to substitute other inputs for union labor.) Let us consider some of the consequences of this form of factor market monopoly.

Figure 14.6 shows the demand and supply curves in some segment of the labor market. The competitive wage in this market is W_c and employment under competitive conditions is L_c. Suppose, however, that the workers in this market have formed a union to bargain as an exclusive supplier of their services. Using its monopoly power, and perhaps the threat of a strike, the union is able to obtain a wage of W_u for its members. At this higher wage, there is a potential surplus of union labor equal to the distance *AB* in the diagram. The union must find some a way to eliminate the surplus if it is to prevent a portion of its membership from becoming unemployed. Typically it does so by adopting a membership quota, charging members dues and initiation fees, and requiring them to satisfy a long period of apprenticeship. In addition, the union may make total employ-

Figure 14.6

Effects of a labor union

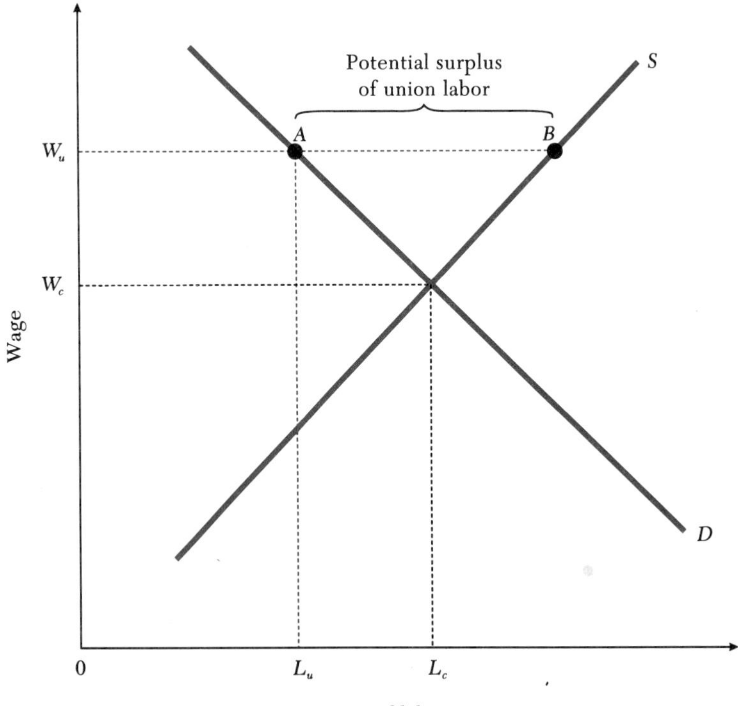

ment a subject of negotiations with the employers. For example, the airline pilots' union has negotiated agreements with airlines requiring the latter to maintain a cockpit crew of three persons in planes designed to be flown by only two. (The practice of using more workers than necessary to perform a task is sometimes called *featherbedding*.)

All things considered, the success of labor unions in raising wages above competitive levels has been mixed and has varied from union to union and from time to time. Even if every union succeeds in raising wages, however, we cannot conclude that they raise the average wage in the economy as a whole because those workers displaced from the unionized sector of the economy by higher wages (represented by the difference between L_c and L_u in Figure 14.6) must find employment in the nonunionized sector where they add to supply and depress wages. To the extent that unions effectively reallocate labor from higher marginal product employment to lower marginal product employment, they reduce average labor productivity, and thus the average level of real wages, in the economy as a whole.

On the other hand, union membership may provide a sort of quality assurance on which employers can rely as a certification of the productivity of workers. Just as consumers are willing to pay premium prices for brand-name products in a world of imperfect information, employers may well be willing to pay higher wages simply to obtain this kind of quality assurance in their labor force. To the extent that union membership is a low-cost and reliable means of conveying information about the quality of workers, therefore, it can raise average real wages.

In any case, it is not true, as some people apparently believe, that only labor unions stand between greedy employers and subsistence wages for workers. Indeed, in a competitive labor market, the "greed" of employers bids wages up, not down. Suppose, for example, that you are employed in Firm A where the value of your marginal product is $10 per hour. If the value of your marginal product in Firm B is $12 per hour, then Firm B's "greedy" quest for profits would lead it to offer a wage between $10 and $12 to obtain your services. Only collusion between the two firms would prevent your wage from rising.

Occupational Licensure

Another potential source of contrived scarcity in labor markets is *occupational licensure*. In dozens of occupations—from architecture to acupuncture, from barbering to brain surgery—practice is limited to those who have obtained a license issued by the state. Sometimes, as in the case of brain surgery, the license is a certification of the practitioner's training and qualifications. In a world of costly information, where consumers find it difficult to distinguish between competence and incompetence, such certification can have substantial economic value. Moreover, the members of an occupation do have an incentive to exclude "quacks" whose shoddy performance damages the reputation of legitimate practitioners. (Of course, if consumers could easily distinguish between competence and incompetence, then neither they nor the legitimate practitioners would have anything to fear from quacks!)

Often, however, the license is simply a means of raising wages in a particular occupation by limiting competition. The typical method of granting licenses is for a panel of incumbent practitioners—who better qualified?—to determine how many new licenses are to be granted and who is to obtain them. We therefore end up with a situation in which existing practitioners determine how many new competitors they will allow into the market. Whatever their good intentions in assuring professional competence, one must admit that this is a little like letting the fox guard the hen house.

Labor Market Monopsony

Monopsony is a market condition in which there is a single buyer or in which collusion among buyers eliminates competition.

Collusion among employers leads to a market condition known as **monopsony**. Monopsony, literally a "single buyer," is to the buyers' side of the market what monopoly is to the sellers' side. Just as monopoly raises the price above the competitive level by limiting or eliminating competition among sellers, monopsony lowers the price below the competitive level by limiting or eliminating competition among buyers. The "company town" in which all workers depend on the same firm for their employment is the classic example of factor market monopsony.

One high profile labor market in which elements of monopsony regularly surface is the market for professional athletes. The owners of team sports franchises have historically used a variety of methods to try to keep the salaries of professional athletes below what they would be in a competitive market. Until recently, for example, major league baseball's monopsony was institutionalized in its "player reserve system." Under the reserve system, when a team signed a player it acquired the exclusive right to his services for the rest of his career. If his original team traded him, the new team acquired the same exclusive right. The reserve system effectively prevented a player from seeking or accepting competitive bids for his services.

Baseball's reserve system survived numerous legal challenges, but it was finally overturned in 1975 by an arbitrator who had been appointed jointly by the players and team owners. The arbitrator ruled that players could become "free agents" after some minimum number of years in the major leagues. (A free agent is literally free to offer his services to the highest bidder.) With the demise of the reserve system, baseball players soon went from the lowest paid professional athletes to the highest. The owners' response to this trend was apparently covert collusion. At least that was the conclusion of two independent arbitrators who found that the owners had agreed not to bid against one another for free agents after the 1985 and 1986 playing seasons.

Chance, Choice, and the Ownership of Productive Resources

Our theory of the pricing of productive services tells only half of the story of the market distribution of income. For the other half, we must ask what determines the pattern of ownership of the productive resources that supply those services.

Our particular ownership of productive resources is determined by a combination of factors, some of which are, and some of which are not, under our personal control. In other words, our ownership of productive resources reflects the effects of both *chance* and *choice*. The choices we make can either reinforce or offset the effects of chance; they can help us to overcome the severest of handicaps, but they also leave us free to squander our wealth and talents.

Chance

One can hardly deny that chance plays a role in the distribution of wealth and income. Indeed, since some of our most important human capital is literally carried in our genes, ownership of productive resources is often just an accident of birth. Some, but very few, of us are born with the talents and abilities of superstars; others, tragically, are born with handicaps that severely limit their earning potential. Of course, the vast majority of us fall somewhere in between. Our varying physical, intellectual, and temperamental endowments undoubtedly stagger the starting lines in the race for economic success.

Family status is another important accident of birth. Those lucky enough to be born into a wealthy family generally inherit productive resources. These resources include not only nonhuman wealth, such as financial assets or the family business, but also superior human capital acquired through education at the best and most expensive schools. By contrast, those born into a family environment of poverty and ignorance may inherit little productive wealth of any form. Here again, most of us fall somewhere between these two extremes: Our families provide us with varying amounts of the initial human and nonhuman capital with which we take our first steps as productive members of society.

Other accidents of birth that unfortunately can also affect income are gender and race. On average, women and some minorities, particularly blacks, earn less than white males. (Some minorities, such as Asian-Americans, however, earn more.) Many of these income differentials reflect differences in education, experience, and factors other than the effects of outright prejudice and discrimination. Nonetheless, some differentials still remain after adjusting for differences in human capital. Moreover, as we already noted, the generally lower levels of education and experience of some minorities may itself be the result of prejudice and discrimination.

Arbitrary discrimination on the basis of gender or race is costly not only to its victims but also to the employers who discriminate. If a firm hires a less productive white worker when it could hire a more productive black at the same wage, its prejudice carries a cost in the form of lower profits. Moreover, such discrimination will put it at a disadvantage relative to its competitors who do not discriminate. Indeed, where competition is intense and productivity is easily observable, as in professional sports, racially discriminatory pay differentials tend to disappear.*

*James Gwartney and Charles Haworth, "Employer Cost and Discrimination: The Case of Baseball," *Journal of Political Economy* (June 1974).

Of course, chance can operate through channels other than accidents of birth. Unforeseeable changes in market conditions can also alter the value of one's productive resources. Had you been a geologist or a petroleum engineer in the mid-1970s, for example, you would have experienced a substantial rise in the value of your human capital as the rising price of crude oil dramatically increased the demand for your skills. On the other hand, had you attempted to cash in on this boom by studying geology or petroleum engineering in the late 1970s, you would have watched the value of your human capital depreciate rapidly as world oil prices collapsed in the early 1980s.

Choice

The ownership of productive resources is by no means set in stone by the vagaries of chance and fate, for a market economy provides numerous opportunities to either offset or reinforce the effects of chance. Most of these opportunities involve investment choices which, as we know, represent choices between present and future. We can add to our stock of productive resources, and thus to our future income, only by sacrificing current consumption. We do this, for example, when we use our savings to acquire financial assets such as corporate stocks and bonds. For most of us, however, by far the most important investment decisions are those that affect our stock of human capital. Your choice to attend college provides a good example of such an investment.

If you are one of those students who simply enjoys learning for the sake of learning—or, for that matter, if you are majoring in partying!—then at least part of your college experience is current consumption. For most students, however, a college education is primarily an investment in the future. Some of the fruits of this investment, such as an understanding of history or an appreciation of literature, can provide a lifetime of personal satisfaction but may have little value in the job market. But a college education also represents an investment in marketable human capital. In 1987, for example, the average college graduate earned about 60 percent (roughly $12,000 per year) more than the average high school graduate.

THE DISTRIBUTION OF INCOME

The outcome of the market choices and random elements that determine our individual incomes is summarized in the economy's *income distribution*. Unfortunately, this terminology is somewhat misleading, for it conjures up an image of someone handing out incomes the way a card dealer might distribute cards from a deck. This is certainly not the way incomes get "distributed." As we have seen, incomes are the result of voluntary exchange—specifically, of some people exchanging their money for the productive services rendered by others. People who, by chance or by choice, own substantial productive wealth, and who use that wealth to provide services that others value greatly, earn large

Table 14.2

Income distribution in the United States. Percentage of total income earned by families in each quintile

Quintile	1947	1955	1965	1975	1987	1987 *Break Point*
			Year			
Lowest	5.1	4.8	5.2	5.4	4.6	
						$14,450
Second	11.8	12.2	12.2	11.8	10.8	
						$25,100
Third	16.7	17.7	17.8	17.6	16.9	
						$36,600
Fourth	23.2	23.4	23.9	24.1	24.1	
						$52,910
Highest	43.3	41.8	40.9	41.1	43.7	

Source: *Statistical Abstract of the United States* (various years).

incomes; people who own little productive wealth, or whose wealth provides services with little market value, earn small incomes.

The Statistical Distribution of Income

One standard statistical summary of income distribution ranks families by income level, divides the ranking into five equal segments called *quintiles*, and shows the percentage of all incomes earned by families within each quintile. Table 14.2 uses this method to summarize the U.S. income distribution for selected years since World War II. (The table also shows the incomes representing the dividing lines between each pair of quintiles for 1987. In that year, 20 percent of all families earned less than $14,450, 20 percent earned between $14,450 and $25,100, and so on.)

The remarkable thing about these data are how little the percentage distribution of income has changed over the past four decades. Give or take a couple of percentage points, the 20 percent of all families in the lowest quintile of the income distribution continues to account for about 5 percent of all incomes, whereas the 20 percent of all families in the highest quintile continues to account for just over 40 percent.

Beyond Statistics: What the "Raw" Data Do Not Tell Us

Although economists differ regarding the precise contribution of innate ability, education, family background, inheritance, discrimination, and the many other factors affecting income distribution, they generally agree that differences in human capital are the primary source of the income differentials reflected in Table 14.2. They also generally agree that raw data of the kind presented in the table tend to overstate the degree of income inequality.

A **transfer** is a grant or payment for which nothing is given in return.

For one thing, those data do not reflect the effects of government taxes and **transfers**. A government transfer is a direct government grant; it is just the opposite of a tax. The government takes a portion of the tax revenues it collects from some families and transfers it to other families as supplements to their incomes. These income supplements can take the form of cash or of transfers *in kind,* such as food stamps, medicaid, and public housing. A disproportionate share of government transfers go to families with low incomes. This, coupled with the fact that the overall tax system is moderately progressive (the higher a family's income, the larger the fraction of its income the government takes as taxes) means that the overall impact of the tax-transfer system is to reduce the net incomes of those in the higher quintiles of the distribution relative to those in the lower quintiles.

In addition, because the data in Table 14.2 represent a snapshot of the income distribution at a given point in time, they tell us nothing about the dynamics of how it changes over time. To see how this can be misleading, consider a family headed by a medical intern. His current income is very low, probably placing the family in the lowest quintile of the income distribution. However, by any reasonable standard our hypothetical intern is far from poor; he has acquired very valuable human capital that will almost certainly place his family in the top quintile when he becomes a full-fledged doctor in the near future.

As this example illustrates, lifetime earnings are a better indicator of whether someone is rich or poor than is current income. Figure 14.7, which shows average income by age of householder in 1987, suggests that the typical lifetime earnings profile is hardly flat. Income is typically low for young families just beginning in the work force, rises as they acquire skills, experience, and other human capital, reaches a peak when the family's wage earners are in their mid-40s to mid-50s, and then declines as they age further and finally retire. By lumping together in the lowest quintiles those families who will remain poor because

Figure 14.7

Income by age of householder, 1987

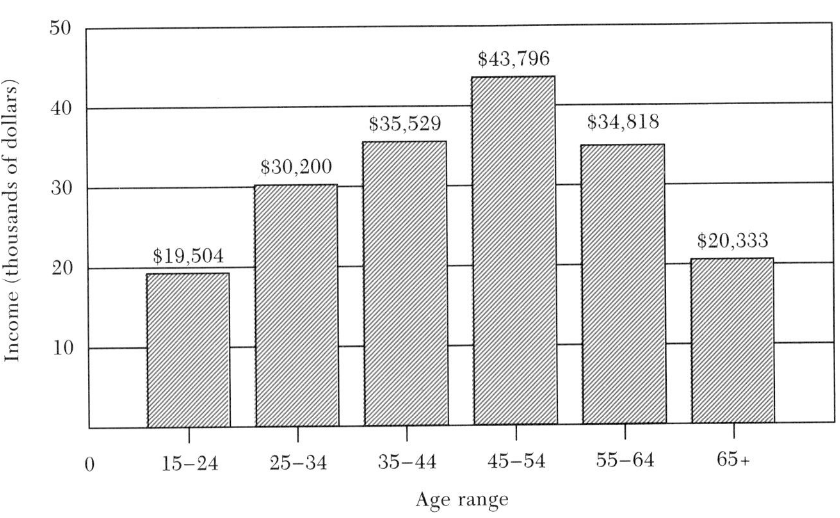

(Source: *U.S. Statistical Abstract, 1990*)

they lack the human capital and other productive resources to move up in the income distribution and families who are temporarily "poor" but who will eventually move into the higher quintiles, the data in Table 14.2 obscure the dynamics of income mobility.

Recent research covering the period from 1971 to 1978 suggests that such mobility is far from trivial.* More than half the families who started the period in the top quintile had moved down to a lower quintile by its end. About half the families who started in the lowest quintile moved up to a higher one during the period; about one in four moved up through at least two quintiles. About two-thirds of the families in each of the middle three quintiles moved in one direction or the other.

There also appear to be considerable intergenerational changes in the distribution of income. Among the offspring of families in the top quintile of the income distribution, for example, only one-third remained in that position among newly formed families. Fewer than half of the offspring of the families in the bottom quintile remained in that quintile among newly formed families.

This research strongly suggests that economic status is not chiselled in stone, and that it is misleading to think of "the rich" and "the poor" as fixed and unchanging groups of people. As a generalization, the old adage that "the rich just get richer and the poor get poorer" is simply not true.

Some Normative Issues

Measuring and explaining the distribution of income is an exercise in positive economics. Sooner or later, however, almost all discussions of the income distribution enter the normative realm. The central normative issue is that of "distributive justice." It usually boils down to questions about whether and to what extent inequality in the distribution of income is fair. In asking such questions and analyzing their implications, it is useful to distinguish between two normative standards of equality, namely, *equality of opportunity* and *equality of results*. Using the analogy of a foot race, the former implies that everyone has the same starting line; the latter, that everyone finishes in a tie.

Equality of Opportunity?

Equality of opportunity is an appealing standard, especially for Americans in whose history and cultural traditions it occupies a central role. Of course, literal equality of opportunity is impossible. We are simply not all born with the same chance to sing at the Metropolitan Opera, win the Nobel Prize in physics, or become Miss America. What we really mean by equality of opportunity is the absence of artificial and arbitrary restrictions on how we can use our natural talents and abilities. Racial discrimination is an example of an arbitrary restriction that denies equal opportunity in employment; requiring that college professors have a Ph.D is not.

*Greg Duncan et al., *Years of Poverty, Years of Plenty* (Ann Arbor: Institute for Social Research, University of Michigan, 1984).

As appealing as equality of opportunity is to most people as a normative standard, it nonetheless raises some difficult questions. For example, is it fair that inheritance enables some people to start with better-than-equal opportunities? Should inherited wealth be confiscated to better equalize the starting lines? Should this apply only to inheritance in the form of real and financial assets, or should it also apply to human capital? Specifically, is it fair that rich families can invest more heavily in their children's education than poor families? Is it fair that some families—rich, poor, and in the middle—choose to make sacrifices specifically to give their sons and daughters *better* opportunities than others?

We do not pretend to have the answers to these questions (although we do have our own opinions). We merely raise them to show that the concept of equality of opportunity is not always as simple as it may seem on the surface.

Equality of Results?

Equality of final results is quite a different standard from equality of opportunity, and one that is not as likely to win general acceptance. As we have seen, much income inequality is the result of individual choice. Some people earn more than others because they have chosen to invest more in human capital, or to work harder and longer, or to work at less appealing jobs. Are inequalities that reflect these kind of choices fair? Should they be allowed to stand, or should they be levelled by a "Robin Hood" system that taxes the rich and transfers a portion of their incomes to the poor? Or should income differences due to choice be allowed to stand, but those due to chance be eliminated? If so, how are we to disentangle the effects of choice and chance in an uncertain world? What if you *choose* to acquire skills that by *chance* become obsolete? Should you suffer the consequences of your choice or be compensated for your bad luck? If a risky, but successful, business venture pays you large profits, should you be entitled to keep them as a reward for your entrepreneurship and foresight, or should they be taxed away as a mere windfall? Again, questions without answers.

Philosophers have been searching for the meaning of distributive justice for centuries without reaching a consensus. We should not expect more of economists. Economics can, however, make a modest contribution to the debate. It tells us that the market's distribution of income can be altered only at some cost, and that this cost takes the form of diminished incentives. In particular, taxing away incomes of those who earn much to supplement the incomes of those who earn little reduces incentives of both groups to supply productive services. The result is a reduction in the aggregate of all incomes.

Attempts to redistribute income have been likened to attempts to redistribute water using a leaky bucket: We can move it from one place to another but we lose some in the process.* Economics tells us that the bucket leaks; in principle, it can even measure the size of the leak. But it cannot tell us whether the result is worth it.

*Arthur M. Okun, *Equality and Efficiency: The Big Tradeoff* (Washington, D.C.: The Brookings Institution, 1975).

Poverty

Regardless of our feelings on the issue of equality and inequality in the distribution of income, we surely all agree that poverty is an evil. Poverty is not the same as inequality. We can imagine—indeed, we can observe—societies in which everyone is equally poor. We can also imagine societies in which income is distributed unequally between the rich and the very rich. The point is that equality and inequality are relative concepts, whereas poverty is an absolute. Specifically, it is the inability to afford the basic necessities of life.

The **poverty line** is the annual income level below which a family is officially classified as poor.

The **poverty rate** measures the percentage of all families whose incomes fall below the poverty line.

Since 1955, the U.S. government has attempted to define and measure the **poverty line** below which income is not sufficient to provide the basic necessities. In 1988, the official poverty line was $6,024 for an individual and $12,092 for a family of four. The **poverty rate** is the percentage of the population below the poverty line. Figure 14.8 shows the poverty rate for the years 1959 to 1988. As you can see, after a substantial drop in the early 1960s the poverty rate remained relatively stable until the early 1980s when it rose as a consequence of a major economic recession. Since 1983, the rate has been falling back toward its prerecession level.

There is some irony in comparing the falling poverty rate during the late 1950s and early 1960s with its relative stability from the late 1960s to about 1980 because it was in the mid-1960s that the federal government declared its massive "war on poverty" and began a dramatic increase in programs designed

Figure 14.8

Poverty rate, 1959–1988

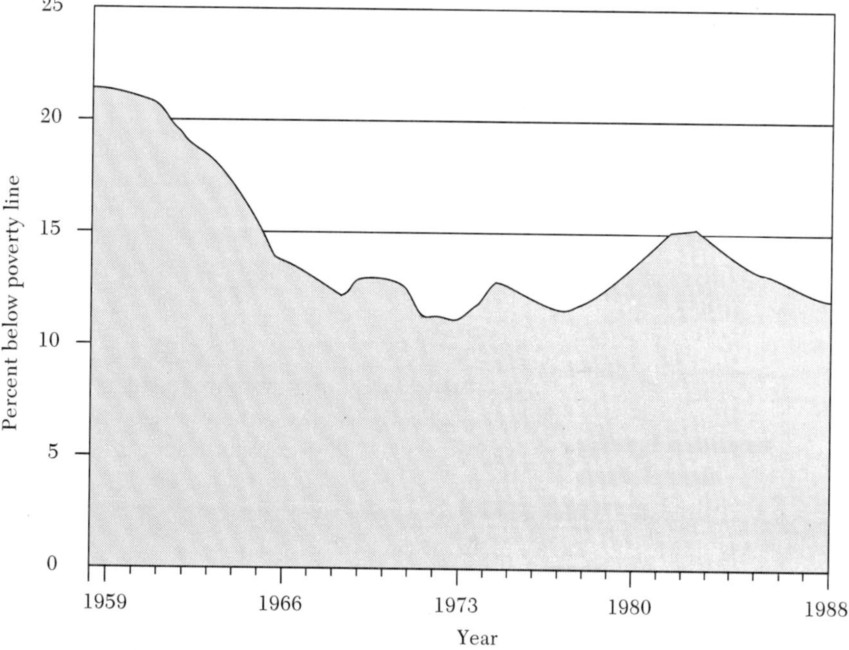

(Source: *U.S. Statistical Abstract, 1990*)

Figure 14.9

Cash and noncash benefits to persons with limited incomes, 1987 (Billions of $)

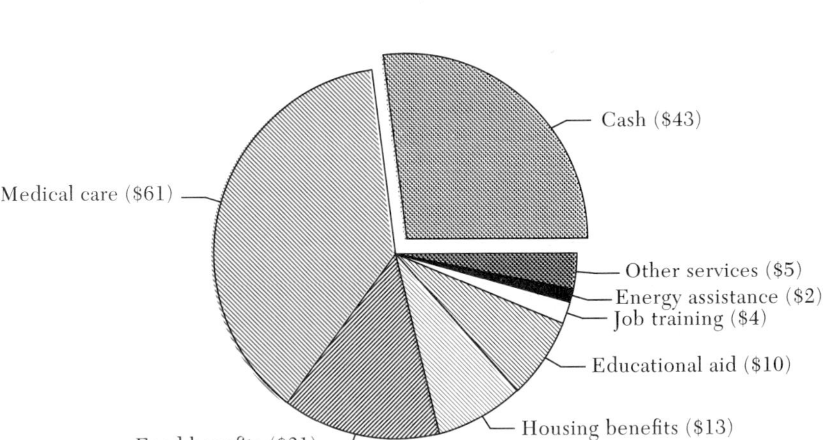

(Source: *U.S. Statistical Abstract, 1989*)

to eliminate poverty. Are we to conclude that these programs have been a total failure?

There are those who would answer yes to this question.* We should note, however, that the data underlying Figure 14.8, and indeed the government's entire approach to measuring poverty, has been subject to considerable criticism. Some of these criticisms are similar to those levelled at the raw data on the income distribution. For example, the poverty data, like the data on the income distribution, do not take into account the effects of in-kind government transfers such as food stamps and public housing, programs that have increased substantially in relative importance in recent years. Figure 14.9 shows federal cash and noncash (in-kind) benefits for "persons with limited incomes" in 1987. As you can see, noncash benefits accounted for more than two-thirds of the total. Indeed, the poverty rate appears to be about 50 percent less when the market value of these benefits is taken into account. For example, when adjusted for the value of in-kind transfers, the 1987 poverty rate of 13.4 percent falls to 8.5 percent.†

The High Cost of Escaping Poverty

One reason that federal programs have failed to make more of a dent in poverty is that they frequently increase the cost of escaping poverty. If this sounds paradoxical, consider the following example.‡ In 1983, a single mother with two children living in the state of Pennsylvania was actually better off earning $4,000

*The most convincing case for the failure of federal antipoverty programs is contained in Charles Murray, *Losing Ground: American Social Policy, 1960–1980* (New York: Basic Books, 1984)

†*Statistical Abstract of the United States, 1989*, Table 742.

‡This example is taken from James Gwartney and Thomas S. McCaleb, "Have Antipoverty Programs Increased Poverty?" *Cato Journal* (Spring/Summer, 1985).

The **marginal tax rate** on additional earnings is the percentage by which those earnings are reduced by a combination of rising taxes and falling government transfers.

than earning $9,000. If she earned $4,000, she had $9,214 in spendable income after receiving all of the government transfers to which she was entitled. If she earned $9,000, however, she lost most of her transfers, had to pay taxes on the extra earnings, and was left with spendable income of only $8,798. For her efforts to earn an additional $5,000, she ended up with $416 *less* to spend! In cases like this it hardly pays a poor person to work more, look for a better job, or invest in more human capital because the effective **marginal tax rate**—which includes not only the extra taxes on additional earnings but also the loss of eligibility for government transfers—is simply too high.

The Negative Income Tax

The **negative income tax** would provide poor families with cash grants ("negative taxes") and only partially reduce those grants if family earnings increased.

Many economists argue that the best way to reduce the high marginal tax rates on the earnings of the poor is to replace the current web of federal antipoverty programs with a much simpler **negative income tax**. A negative income tax would provide poor families with a cash transfer (a "negative tax") if their income fell below some predetermined level. The transfer would then be reduced if their earnings increased, but only by a fraction of the additional earnings.

Under most negative income tax proposals, the government would choose both the minimum guaranteed income and the amount by which it would be reduced for each dollar earned. The latter determines the effective marginal tax rate. Table 14.3 shows how this works with a guaranteed minimum income of $8,000 per year and a 50-cent reduction in the government transfer for each dollar earned. As you can see, the cash transfer falls by half of each increment in earnings and is eliminated entirely once earnings rise to $16,000 per year. Families with annual earnings of more than $16,000 pay positive income taxes just like anyone else.

To contrast the negative income tax with the current system of antipoverty programs, let us return to our foregoing example of our hypothetical mother of

Table 14.3

The negative income tax: an example. Assumptions: minimum income level is $8,000 per year. Marginal tax rate on earnings is 50%; that is, cash grant is reduced by 50 cents for each $1.00 earned.

ANNUAL EARNINGS	CASH TRANSFER (NEGATIVE TAX)	TOTAL ANNUAL INCOME
$ 0	$8,000	$ 8,000
2,000	7,000	9,000
4,000	6,000	10,000
.	.	.
.	.	.
.	.	.
9,000	3,500	12,500
10,000	3,000	13,000
12,000	2,000	14,000
14,000	1,000	15,000
16,000	0	16,000

two. If she is currently earning $4,000 per year, her total annual income under the negative income tax is $10,000, consisting of the $4,000 in earnings plus a $6,000 cash transfer from the government. If she increases her earnings to $9,000 per year, her cash grant will fall by $2,500, but her total income will rise to $12,500 (= $9,000 in earnings plus a $3,500 transfer). In effect, she gets to "keep" all but $2,500 of the $5,000 increase in earnings so that her effective marginal tax rate is only 50 percent. Clearly, the reward for working harder and earning more is much greater under the negative income tax system than under current antipoverty programs.

The Political Economy of Antipoverty Programs

Despite its widespread appeal among economists, there appears to be little political support for a negative income tax approach to the poverty problem. Public choice theory provides a possible explanation for this lack of support.

For one thing, the very simplicity of the negative income tax threatens a whole range of interest groups. Among those with a clear vested interest in the current web of antipoverty programs are the government employees who administer them. As with any other government bureaucracy, the incentives of this "welfare bureaucracy" are not so much to accomplish a specific social goal—in this case the elimination of poverty—as to perpetuate and expand the programs it administers. A negative income tax would substantially pare back those programs and the size of the bureaucracy that administers them.

Moreover, the current antipoverty system, with its emphasis on in-kind transfers, also benefits a number of private sector interests. Farmers, for example, benefit from the increased demand for food generated by the food stamp and school lunch programs; landlords benefit from rent subsidies to low-income tenants; the construction industry benefits from construction of public housing; doctors and other medical professionals benefit from medical aid; technical schools benefit from job training subsidies. The influence of these interest groups is suggested by the fact that the coverage of most of the noncash benefit programs listed in Figure 14.9 has been expanded well beyond the official poor. In 1987, for example, only 42 percent of those receiving Medicaid, 40 percent of those receiving food stamps, 27 percent of those receiving federally subsidized school lunches, and 19 percent of those occupying public housing were below the poverty line.*

Nearly everyone agrees that the current approach to dealing with the poverty problem is wasteful and inefficient. It has been estimated that it would take only about $50 billion per year, an amount less than one-third the cost of the programs depicted in Figure 14.9 and only about one-seventh of the total of all government transfer spending, to bring everyone above the official poverty line. Only when we take into account the influence of interest groups other than the poor themselves can we understand why the negative income tax and other proposals to reform and streamline the system have found so little political support.

* *Statistical Abstract of the United States, 1990*, Table 579.

CHAPTER SUMMARY

1. The derived demand for a productive service is determined by the *value of its marginal product*, which is equal to its marginal product multiplied by the price of the final good it is used to produce. The supply of a productive service is determined by its opportunity cost, which is its value in alternative uses.

2. The factor markets continuously compare the quantities of each productive service supplied and demanded, and adjust factor prices so that markets clear and productive services are allocated to their most valuable uses.

3. *Compensating wage differentials* are the market's way of persuading people to accept less attractive, but socially productive jobs, and to invest in the human capital required to perform other jobs.

4. *Comparable worth* proposals would circumvent the market and attempt to set wages on the basis of objective job characteristics as evaluated by a panel of experts. To the extent that "comparable worth" differed from "market worth," it would inevitably lead to shortages and surpluses in the labor market.

5. To the extent that legal minimum wages exceed market wages, they lead to unemployment. Minimum wage unemployment falls mainly on those workers whose productivity is so low that it is not profitable for employers to hire them at the legal minimum.

6. In addition to those unskilled workers who remain employed at the minimum wage, skilled workers also benefit from minimum wage laws because, by raising the price of unskilled labor, the minimum wage increases the demand for substitutes in the form of skilled labor.

7. "Superstars" earn economic rent because of the natural scarcity of their abilities and talents. If those abilities and talents could be easily reproduced, their earnings would be reduced to their opportunity costs.

8. To obtain higher wages for their members, *labor unions* must limit entry into unionized sectors of the labor market. To the extent that this effectively reallocates labor from more productive to less productive employment, it reduces average labor productivity and thus average real wages in the economy as a whole. On the other hand, to the extent that union membership is a low-cost and reliable means of conveying information about the quality of workers, unions raise real wages.

9. A similar argument can be made concerning the effects of *occupational licensure*: To the extent that licensure restricts entry, it is inefficient; to the extent that it conveys valuable information about quality, it is efficient.

10. *Monopsony* is to the buyers' side of the market what monopoly is to the sellers' side. Just as monopoly raises the price above the competitive level by limiting or eliminating competition among sellers, monopsony lowers the price below the competitive level by limiting or eliminating competition among buyers.

11. Our particular ownership of productive resources is a reflection of both *chance* and *choice*. Chance largely determines our inheritance of productive resources, human as well as nonhuman, and choice determines how much we invest in additional resources.

12. Statistical measures of society's *income distribution* suggest that it has not changed much over time. However, such measures typically overlook the effects of government taxes and transfers, fail to consider patterns of lifetime earning, and say little about the mobility of individuals and families within the distribution.

13. The basic normative issue surrounding income distribution is to what extent income inequality is fair and just. Judging fairness on the basis of *equality of opportunity* usually leads to different conclusions from judging it on the basis *equality of results*.

14. Although economics itself cannot tell us what constitutes a fair and just distribution of income, it can and does tell us that attempts to redistribute income also diminish incentives and lower total income.

15. *Poverty* is not the same as inequality. Equality and inequality are relative concepts, whereas poverty is an absolute—namely, the inability to afford the basic necessities of life.

16. One of the reasons that poverty has been so persistent in the face of government programs to eliminate it is that those programs themselves often raise the cost of escaping poverty by effectively taxing the earned income of the poor at very high marginal tax rates.

17. Many economists favor a *negative income tax* as an alternative to current government antipoverty programs. Such a plan would reduce the cost of fighting poverty, while at the same time reducing the high marginal tax on the earnings of the poor.

Key Terms and Concepts

derived demand
value of the marginal product
compensating wage differential
comparable worth
monopsony
transfer
poverty line
poverty rate
marginal tax rate
negative income tax

Questions for Thought and Discussion

1. What is the relation between the value of the productive services provided by a resource and the value of the resource itself?

2. In acquiring a college education, you are investing in human capital that will increase your future earning capacity. In 1987, for example, the average college graduate earned about $12,000 more than the average high school graduate. However, this future earning capacity does not come free.

   a. What costs, both explicit and implicit, should you consider as part of your investment in the college education component of your human capital?
   b. In principle, how would you determine whether, in narrow economic terms, your college education is a good investment?
   c. Is it possible to convert some of the future earnings that your college education will enable you to earn into current income to help you pay for that education? How?
   d. Is it possible for someone who chooses not to go to college to make up some or all of the future income disadvantages he faces? How?

3. Why do you think the average worker in the United States earns so much more than the average worker in, say, Brazil or India? Is it because he works harder and is more diligent? Or are there other reasons?

4. A multinational corporation pays workers in its U.S. plants $10 per hour and workers in its Mexican plants $3 per hour. How do you explain the wage differential? Is it fair to the Mexican workers?

5. Suppose that the market has set the annual salary of a doctor at $65,000 per year and that of a nurse at half that, or $32,500 per year. The following table shows the value of the marginal product of each additional doctor and nurse employed by the To-Your-Health Medical Clinic. Use this information to answer the following questions.

	VALUE OF MARGINAL PRODUCT	
Number	*Doctors*	*Nurses*
1	$120,000	$45,000
2	100,000	40,000
3	75,000	35,000
4	50,000	25,000
5	20,000	15,000

   a. Is a doctor "worth" more than a nurse? Can you think of any circumstances in which another nurse would be worth more than another doctor to the To-Your-Health clinic? Would the clinic have to pay more for another nurse than for another doctor in those circumstances?
   b. What would happen if a panel of experts convinces the clinic's management that the jobs performed by nurses and doctors have "comparable worth," and that each should be paid $50,000 per year?

6. Reasoning that it is just as difficult to obtain a Ph.D. in English or philosophy as in electrical engineering or finance, and that all faculty members work equally hard, a

university administrator decides that the English and philosophy faculty should be paid the same as the electrical engineering and finance faculty. Have you any advice for him?

7. One could hardly help but notice the many "Help Wanted" signs in the windows of fast food restaurants in many metropolitan areas during the summer of 1989. Does this contradict the argument in the text that minimum wages cause teenage unemployment? [Hint: The federal minimum wage in effect in 1989 had not been raised since 1981.]

8. John and Marsha are both lucky enough to have beautiful voices, and each earns $75,000 per year singing for the New York Metropolitan Opera. If John's voice gave out, he would drive a taxi and earn $30,000 per year; if Marsha's gave out, she could fall back on her MBA degree and earn $60,000 per year.

   a. Does either John or Marsha earn any economic rent?
   b. Which of the two has the higher supply price to the Metropolitan?
   c. Why does the Metropolitan have to pay John as much as Marsha?

9. We have argued that the prevalence of in-kind assistance to the poor (e.g., food stamps and medical and housing subsidies) can be at least partially explained by the fact that, unlike cash assistance, in-kind payments also benefit other interest groups (e.g., farmers and the health care and housing industries). It can also be argued that the political appeal of these in-kind assistance programs is based on normative value judgments that go beyond economic efficiency. What kind of value judgments do you think we have in mind?

10. Mr. Poor earns $500 per month in wages. In addition, his family receives $200 worth of federal food stamps each month, as well as $100 per month in cash assistance and a $150 per month housing allowance from the county. If Mr. Poor takes a job that pays him $800 per month, the family will lose half its federal food stamps, half its housing subsidy, and all of its cash assistance. What is the Poor family's marginal tax rate?

CHAPTER 15

A Prelude to Macroeconomics

In this chapter we preview the *macro*economic perspective on the economy. Because macroeconomics is concerned with the big picture, its theories provide the broad brush strokes through which we interpret and explain the overall historical performance of economic systems. To gain a perspective on that history and an appreciation for the fundamental questions addressed by macroeconomics, we begin with a review of the performance of the U.S. economy during the twentieth century. We then examine the normative goals by which we traditionally judge that performance and introduce the macroeconomic policies through which we hope to achieve those goals. Finally, we introduce the two major schools of thought that have shaped modern macroeconomics, the *classical* and the *Keynesian*.

THE U.S. ECONOMY IN THE TWENTIETH CENTURY

Our review of the U.S. economic performance requires the use of some important *economic aggregates*, variables that summarize, in a single number, the outcome of economic processes involving millions of individual economic decisions and market transactions. These aggregates, each of which we discuss in much greater detail in subsequent chapters, include national product and national income, the general price level, and the labor force, employment, and unemployment.

National Product and National Income

One way to measure a nation's overall level of economic activity is to sum the monetary values of all of the goods and services it produces during a year. Another is to add up all of the incomes earned in the production of those goods and services. The first approach leads to an economic aggregate called **national product**; the second leads to an aggregate called **national income**. As we shall see in Chapter 16, national income and national product are conceptually identical, for they represent but two alternative ways of measuring aggregate economic activity. In 1989 the U.S. national income and product were more than 5.2 trillion dollars, by far the highest of any nation in the world.

National product is the total value of all goods produced by a nation's economy during a year.

National income is the total of all incomes generated by a nation's economic activity during a year.

The goods and services included in national product, as well as the wages and other factor payments that make up national income, are valued at their market prices. Changes in these aggregates therefore reflect changes in both the *real quantities* of goods and services produced and in the *money prices* at which they are exchanged. For example, had the goods and services included in the 1989 U.S. national product been sold at their 1976 prices instead of their actual 1989 prices, their market value would have been just about half of what it actually was. Put another way, the average level of prices more than doubled between 1976 and 1989.

Measures of national income, national product, and other aggregates that have been adjusted to net out the effect of changing prices are called *real* measures; measures that have not been adjusted to eliminate such effects are called *nominal* measures. Figure 15.1 shows the long-term (or *secular*) behavior of both real and nominal U.S. national product since 1900.* As you can see from the graph, the nominal measure has risen more rapidly than the real measure. This reflects a general upward trend in prices. However, even after allowing for rising prices, real national product has increased almost fifteenfold—or an average of about 3 percent per year—since the turn of the century.

Economic growth is reflected in the long-term increase in real national product and national income.

This long-term rise in real national product reflects the effects of **economic growth**. Part of this growth is the result of a growing population and labor force. However, even after adjusting for population growth, real national product *per capita*—that is, per person—has also risen over time. This rise has been due primarily to investment, including investment in new capital goods that expand the productive capacity of the economy, investment in research and development that lead to improvements in technology, and investment in education, training, and other forms of human capital that increase the productivity of the labor force. Table 15.1 shows some recent estimates of the percentage contribution of each of these factors to the long-term growth of real national product.

*The vertical axis of Figure 15.1 is a *ratio scale*. On such a scale, the *distance* between two numbers reflects their *ratio*. Thus the distance between 50 and 100 is the same as the distance between 500 and 1,000.

Figure 15.1

Real and nomimal national product

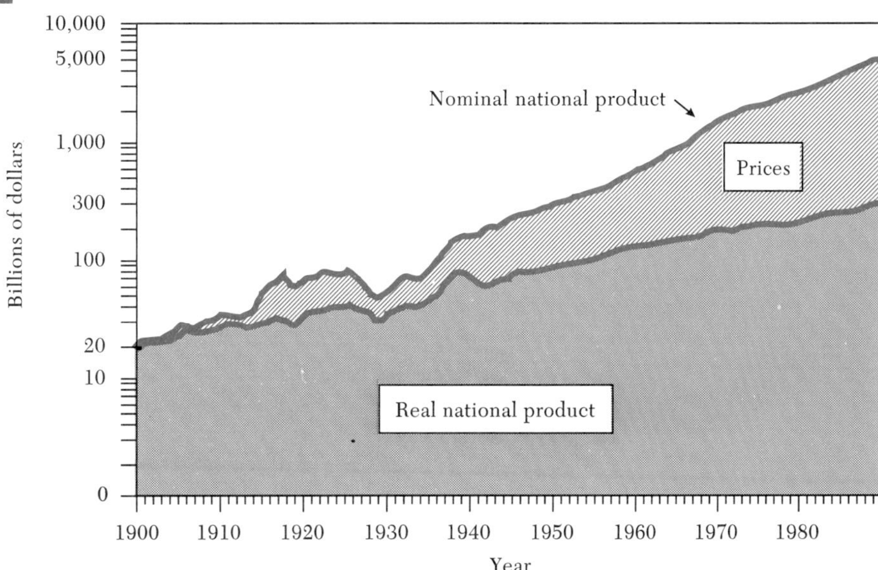

Table 15.1

The sources of economic growth

CONTRIBUTING FACTOR	PERCENTAGE CONTRIBUTION
Growth of labor inputs	32%
Increases in education per worker	14
Growth of the capital stock	19
Technological progress	28
Other factors	7
Total	100%

Source: Edward F. Denison, *Trends in American Economic Growth, 1929–1982* (The Brookings Institution, Washington, D.C., 1985), p. 30.

The Price Level and Inflation

The **price level** is the average nominal price of all goods and services in the national product.

As we just noted, the fact that nominal national product has increased more rapidly than real national product implies that prices have tended to rise over time. This implication is confirmed by Figure 15.2(a) on the next page. It shows the increase in the **price level** since 1900. The price level is a measure of the average price of all goods and services in national product. It is measured, not as a dollar amount, but as an *index number* that expresses each year's price level as a percentage of its value in some *base year*. The base year for the price index in Figure 15.2(a) is 1982. Thus the price level for each year shown in the graph

Figure 15.2

The price level and inflation

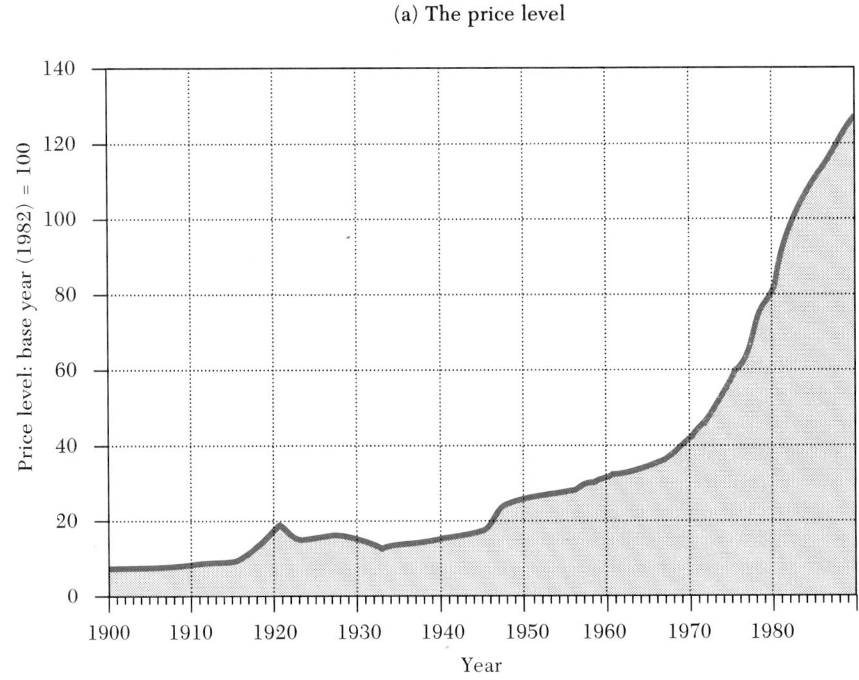

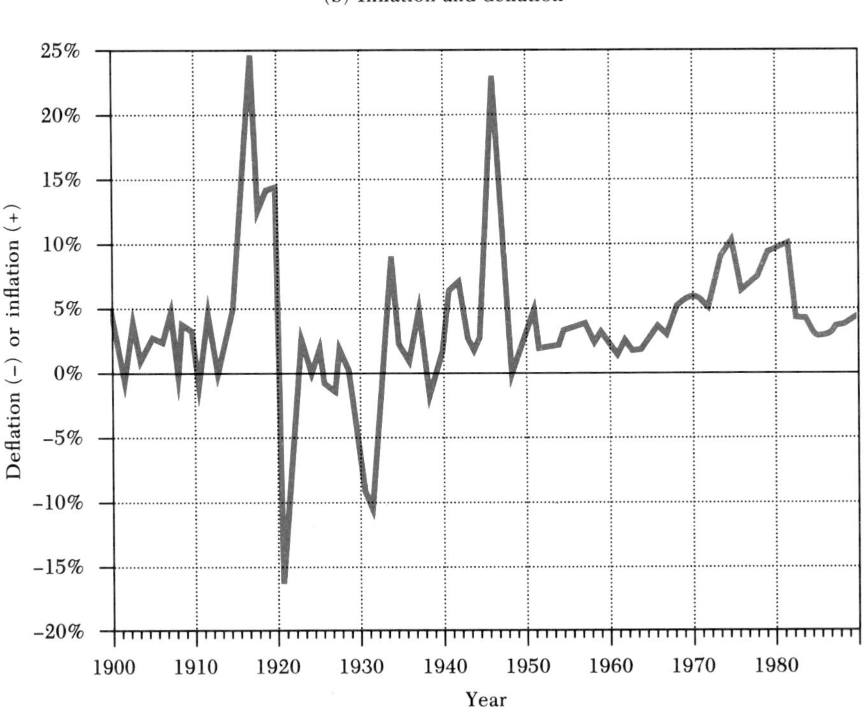

is expressed as a percentage of the 1982 price level. For example, the 1989 price level of 126 implies that prices were about 26 percent higher on average in 1989 than in 1982. Similarly, the 1973 price level of 50 indicates that prices in 1973 were, on average, only about half of what they would be in 1982. The price level for the base year, 1982, is 100 percent of itself.

Inflation means a rise in the economy's price level over time.

Deflation means a fall in the economy's price level over time.

The **rate of inflation** is the annual percentage increase in the economy's price level.

Inflation and **deflation** are the respective terms we apply to increases and decreases in the price level over time. Note that these terms apply to *changes* in the price level, not to how high or low it is in absolute terms. The price level itself could be low and rising and we would still have inflation; it could be high and falling and we would have deflation. The **rate of inflation** is the annual percentage change in the price level. For example, the increase in the price index from 121 in 1988 to 126 in 1989 represents about a 4 percent rate of inflation. A negative rate would, of course, imply deflation.

Figure 15.2(b) shows annual rates of inflation since 1900. As you can see, these rates have been positive in most years, including all years since the late 1940s. However, there have also been periods of comparative price level stability—from the early 1950s to the early 1960s, for example—and even some periods of substantial deflation—most notably during the early 1920s and again during the 1930s.

It is also important to distinguish chronic and persistent inflation from a one-shot rise in the price level. Our experience with oil price shocks provides a good example of this distinction. During the 1970s, the underlying inflation rate in the United States remained between 5 and 6 percent. However, twice during that decade—once in 1974–5 and again in 1979–81—the rate jumped abruptly, but temporarily, to 10 percent or more as the economy absorbed dramatic increases in the price of OPEC crude oil. Then, when oil prices collapsed in 1986, the rate of inflation temporarily dropped virtually to zero before again resuming its underlying rate of about 4 percent. Although the massive changes in oil prices led to sudden, once-and-for-all increases in the general price level, they themselves had no permanent effect on the underlying rate of inflation.

Finally, we must once again emphasize the difference between inflation in the *general* price level and changes in the *relative* prices of particular goods and services. If *all* nominal prices rise at the same rate, say, 5 percent per year, then we have a 5 percent rate of inflation with no change in relative prices. On the other hand, if some nominal prices increase while others fall just enough to offset that increase, relative prices change but there is no inflation. As we saw in Chapter 3, the price changes that we observe in practice almost always reflect a mixture of the effects of both inflation and relative price adjustments; however, the conceptual distinction between the two is very important.

The Labor Force, Employment, and Unemployment

As we shall see, the economy's aggregate labor market plays a particularly important role in macroeconomics. Although we examine this market in detail in Chapter 19, a few basic definitions are sufficient for our purposes here.

An **employed** person is working for pay.

An **unemployed** person is not working, but is actively seeking work.

The **labor force** includes everyone who is either working (employed) or actively seeking work (unemployed).

The **unemployment rate** is the percentage of the labor force that is unemployed.

A person is **employed** if he is working for pay; he is **unemployed** if he *is not* working but *is* actively looking for work. The **labor force** includes all persons who are either employed or unemployed, that is, all persons who are either working or looking for work. Persons who are neither working nor looking for work—retirees and full-time students, for example—are not in the labor force and are therefore not considered unemployed. To be unemployed, a person must not only be without a job, he must also be actively looking for one. The **unemployment rate** is the percentage of the labor force that is unemployed.

In 1989, the U.S. labor force averaged 125.5 million people, or just over half the total population of about 249 million. On average, 119.0 million were employed and 6.5 million unemployed, leading to an unemployment rate of 5.2 percent (= 6.5/125.5).

Figure 15.3(a) shows the U.S. labor force and employment since 1900 and Figure 15.3(b) shows the behavior of the unemployment rate over the same period. As you can see, the unemployment rate has been much more volatile than either the labor force or employment. For the most part, however, it has remained in a range between 4 percent and 10 percent of the labor force. Although it rose to 25 percent in 1933 and remained above 10 percent throughout the decade of the 1930s, it was not until 1982, and then only for a few months, that unemployment again reached 10 percent.

The Business Cycle

Business cycles are short-term fluctuations in economic activity.

As we have already noted, one of the most prominent features of our economic history has been a long-term trend of rising real output. Closer inspection reveals that superimposed on this long-term trend of economic growth have been periodic episodes of economic contraction and falling real output. These recurrent fluctuations in economic activity reflect the short-term influence of the **business cycle**. The rollercoaster pattern of the business cycle, which has been repeated twenty times since the turn of the century, is chronicled in Table 15.2 and is depicted graphically as deviations from the long-term growth trend in Figure 15.4. Although the term *cycle* usually carries a connotation of regularity and predictability, both the table and the figure show that the timing, duration, and magnitude of the business cycle have by no means been regular and predictable. Explaining these cyclical fluctuations in economic activity has been the central focus of macroeconomic theory since the 1930s.

Anatomy of a Recent Business Cycle

To understand what goes on during a typical business cycle, let us dissect a recent one. Figure 15.5 plots quarterly data—that is, data recorded at three-month intervals—on real national product, unemployment, and the rate of inflation from 1981 through 1989. As you can see from both the table and the figure, real national product reached a *peak* during the third quarter (between June and September) of 1981, began falling in the fourth quarter of that same year, and continued to fall through the third quarter of 1982 when it reached the low point,

Figure 15.3

Labor force, employment, and unemployment

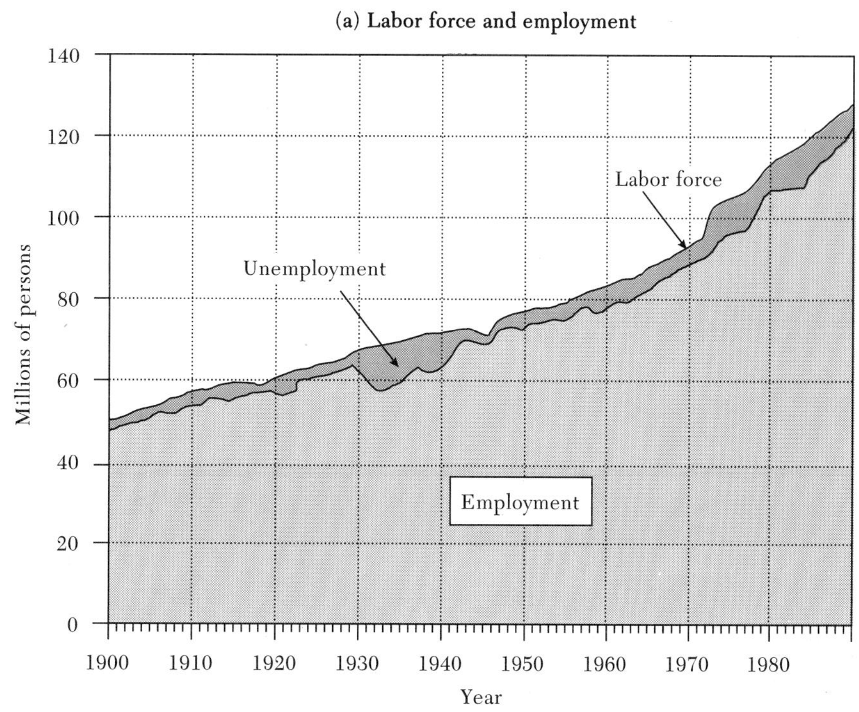

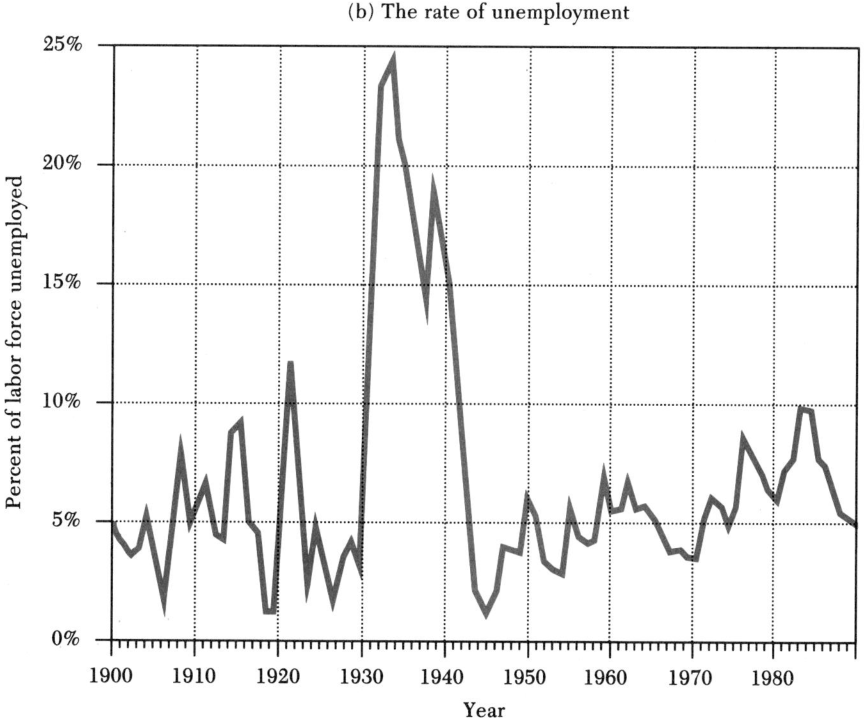

Table 15.2
Twentieth-century business cycles

DATE OF PEAK	DURATION OF RECESSION (MONTHS)	DATE OF TROUGH	DURATION OF RECOVERY/ EXPANSION (MONTHS)
June 1899	18	December 1900	21
September 1902	23	August 1904	33
May 1907	13	June 1908	19
January 1910	24	January 1912	12
January 1913	23	December 1914	44
August 1918	7	March 1919	10
January 1920	18	July 1921	22
May 1923	14	July 1924	27
October 1926	13	November 1927	21
August 1929	43	March 1933	50
May 1937	13	June 1938	80
February 1945	8	October 1945	37
November 1948	11	October 1949	45
July 1953	10	May 1954	39
August 1957	8	April 1958	24
April 1960	10	February 1961	106
December 1969	11	November 1970	36
November 1973	16	March 1975	58
January 1980	6	July 1980	12
July 1981	16	November 1982	?

Source: *Statistical Abstract of the U.S.* (various years).

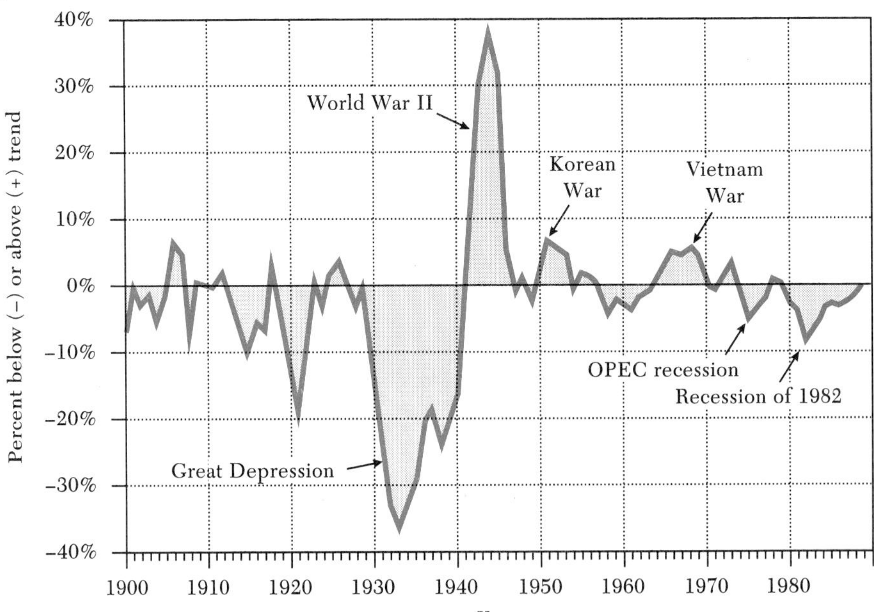

Figure 15.4
Business cycles, 1900–1989

Figure 15.5

Recession and recovery: 1981–89

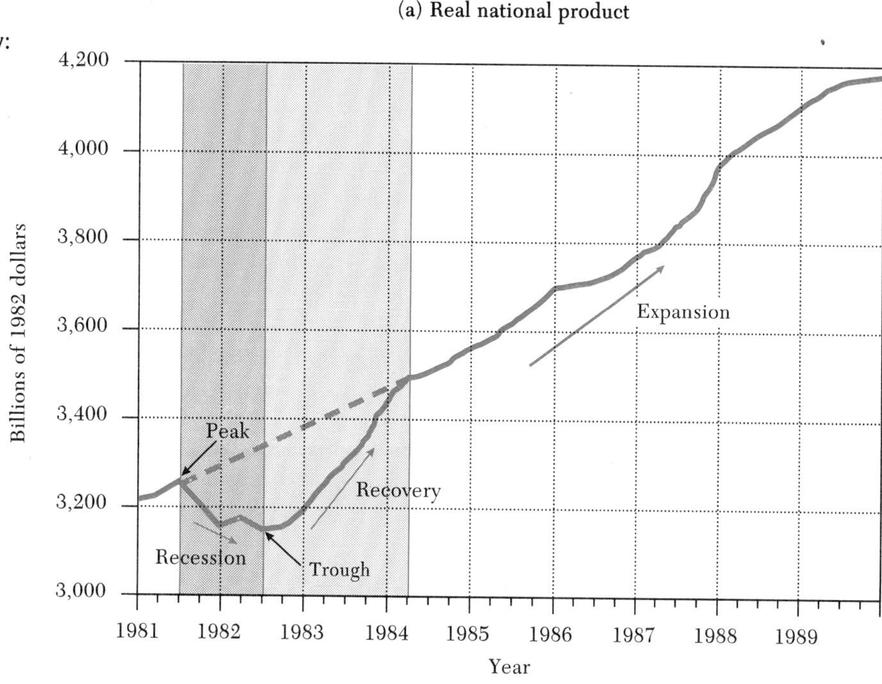

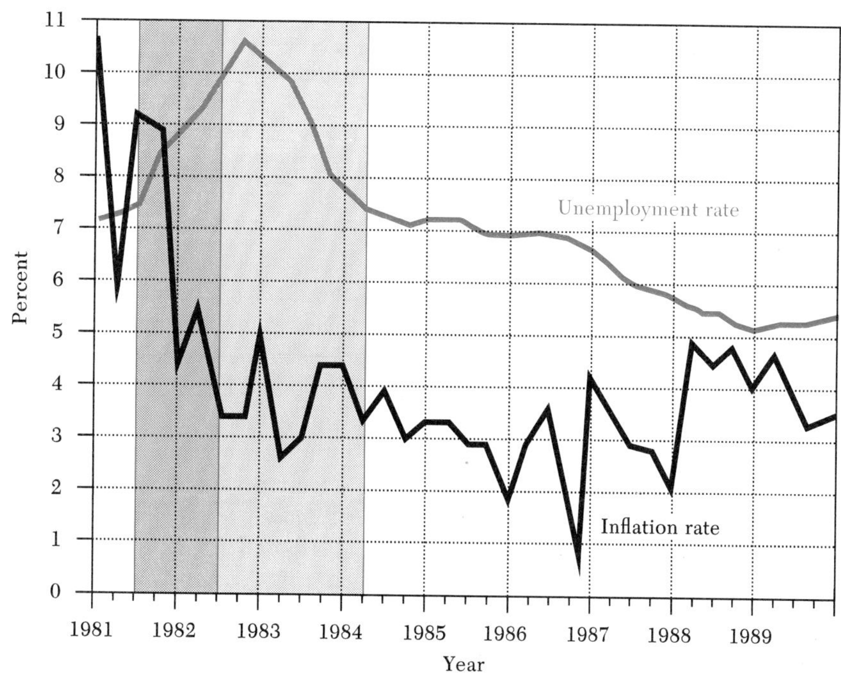

A **recession** is a decline in real national income and product that lasts for at least two calendar quarters.

or *trough*, of the cycle. This phase of the business cycle, during which economic activity is contracting and real national product is falling, is called a **recession**. Economists generally consider a recession to have occurred whenever real national product has fallen for at least two consecutive calendar quarters.

By the fourth quarter of 1982, real output had begun to increase again as the economy entered the *recovery* phase of the cycle. By the third quarter of 1983, real output had surpassed its previous peak and economic *expansion* resumed. As this expansion continued through mid-1990, it became the longest in recorded U.S. peacetime history. Like all expansions, however, it almost certainly will eventually come to an end. Perhaps even as you read this the economy will have experienced another recession.

Figure 15.5(b) shows how unemployment and inflation were affected by the cycle. During the recessionary phase, the rate of unemployment rose by more than a third, from 7.5 percent of the labor force to 10.6 percent in December 1982. At the same time, the annual rate of inflation dropped from its prerecession high of more than 10 percent to less than 3 percent. During the recovery phase of the cycle, the rate of inflation levelled off and the rate of unemployment gradually declined until it had fallen well below its prerecession level.

The Great Depression of the 1930s

One twentieth-century business cycle must be singled out for special attention: the *Great Depression* which engulfed not only the United States but most of the rest of the world during the 1930s. In less than 4 years, between the end of 1929 and 1933, the real national product of the United States fell by nearly one-third, completely wiping out a decade of strong economic growth. Accompanying the decline in real output was a falling price level: A basket of goods that had cost $100 in 1929 cost only about $75 by 1933. However, this 25 percent drop in prices was little consolation to the average family, whose income was cut in half over the same period. By 1933 one person out of every four who wanted to work was unemployed. That was more than double the highest unemployment rate ever recorded in the United States before or since.

The economy gradually began to recover after 1933, but in 1937, just as it approached its predepression level of real output, the roof fell in once more. Real output began falling again and unemployment rose back to nearly 20 percent of the labor force. In effect, there was a recession within a depression. The economy did not fully recover until the onset of World War II.

Despite the fears of many (including many economists) that depressed conditions might return after the war, the economy once again resumed its normal path of economic growth. Although that path has been interrupted by periodic recessions, none has even remotely approached the Great Depression in its severity. Indeed, the postwar recessions have been shorter and shallower on average than those that preceded the Great Depression.

In short, the Great Depression was a unique crisis the likes of which the industrialized world had never seen before and, thankfully, has not seen since. Our economic and political institutions still bear the scars of the unprecedented events of the 1930s. So also does economic theory. Indeed, it is no exaggeration to say that the questions raised by the Great Depression gave birth to modern macroeconomics. Many of those questions, as we shall see, have yet to receive a satisfactory answer.

THE GOALS AND TOOLS OF MACROECONOMIC POLICY

The economic growth and fluctuations just described reflect not only the workings of the private marketplace but also the effects of government policies. Indeed, the governments of virtually all industrialized market economies have adopted a variety of policies intended to influence both the short-term, or *cyclical* performance of the economy and its long-term growth. These policies tend to emphasize three principal normative goals: *full employment*, a *stable price level*, and sustained *economic growth*. As we see in the chapters that follow, economic analysis plays an important role in assessing our ability to achieve these goals, in analyzing possible trade-offs among them, and in suggesting the kinds of policies that might be used to promote each. In this preliminary excursion into the world of macroeconomics, however, we concentrate on clarifying the meaning of these goals and explaining why each is considered normatively desirable. We also introduce the two major categories of macroeconomic policy, namely, *monetary policy* and *fiscal policy*, and take our first look at an important dispute over the appropriate use of these policies.

Full Employment

Because the supply of labor services is by far the largest source of income in a market economy, the economy's ability to generate employment opportunities, and to provide incentives for people to take advantage of those opportunities, is an important dimension of its economic performance.

As a policy goal, however, the pursuit of full employment does *not* mean that unemployment should be reduced literally to zero. To see why, consider the three reasons why people look for work—that is, why they become unemployed. Some are labor force *entrants* who are either looking for their first job or returning to the labor force after a period of absence. Others are *job leavers* who have voluntarily quit one job to look for another. Still others are *job losers* who have been fired or laid off from a previous job. Voluntary job switches and labor force entry are inevitable in an economy in which people are free to choose among employers and to enter and leave the labor force as they see fit. In addition, many firings and layoffs reflect the normal and continuous reallocation of labor among employers as the economy adjusts to new technologies and shifting demands. Thus, even under the best of conditions, there is a continuous flow of job losers, job leavers, and labor force entrants.

If all of these job seekers found work instantly, there would be no unemployment. Unfortunately, however, information about the job market is inevitably incomplete and costly for job seekers to acquire. Thus, even if there is an acceptable job offer waiting for each and every one of them, most have to search for a time to find that offer. While they search, they are officially counted as unemployed.

The **natural rate of unemployment** is the rate associated with normal job turnover and labor market entry.

The unemployment associated with normal job turnover and labor market entry determines what economists call the **natural rate of unemployment**. As we shall see in our subsequent analysis, the natural rate of unemployment is the lowest rate consistent with a stable price level. For that reason, it is generally accepted as the benchmark for full employment.

The natural rate of unemployment appears to be about 5.5 percent in the U.S. economy as we enter the 1990s. This rate is not chiselled in stone, however. The natural rate rose steadily from about 4 percent of the labor force in the early 1960s to about 6 percent in the late 1970s through the mid-1980s. Recently, it has apparently begun a gradual decline. We examine the reasons for this in Chapter 19.

A Stable Price Level

If you ask the proverbial man in the street how inflation affects him, he will probably tell you that it makes him poorer by raising his "cost of living." He may point out, for example, that he has seen a 5 percent increase in his wage income during the past year eaten up by a 5 percent increase in the cost of the goods and services he consumes. What he fails to realize, however, is that the same inflationary forces that lead to higher prices for the goods and services he buys also contribute to the higher wages he receives for the labor services he sells. As a result, the real amount of work he has to do—or equivalently, the amount of leisure he must sacrifice—to obtain those goods and services is not affected by inflation. Since a true increase in the cost of living implies an increase in the real alternatives one must sacrifice to achieve a given living standard, inflation itself does *not* increase the real cost of living.

No doubt our hypothetical man in the street considers the increase in his wage to be a just reward for his hard work, while viewing the increase in prices as the result of forces beyond his control. However, the two phenomena are part and parcel of the same inflationary process. Inflation simply shrinks the monetary yardstick by which we measure the economic value of all goods and services, those we sell as well as those we buy.

This is not to say that inflation is harmless. It can create very serious social and economic problems through its haphazard and unpredictable effects on the distribution of a society's wealth and through the real costs people incur in attempting to avoid those effects.

A couple of examples illustrate what we mean.

Inflation and Wealth Redistribution

Suppose you borrow money to buy a car, agreeing to pay the lender back over a period of years. Who gains and who loses if inflation unexpectedly doubles the price level before your loan is paid off? Clearly, you come out ahead. You still have the same car as you would had there been no inflation, but since money is worth only half as much, you end up sacrificing only half as many real goods and services when you make your loan payments. Of course the lender is on the other side of the fence: The money he is repaid buys only half as much as he anticipated when he made the loan.

As another example, suppose that you invest your life savings in bonds issued by the U.S. Treasury and blue-chip corporations. Despite the fact that the risk of default on your bonds is nil, you will nonetheless find your wealth depleted if unexpected inflation reduces the purchasing power of money before you redeem your bonds. On the other hand, the Treasury and the corporations that issued those bonds come out ahead because they can pay you back with less valuable money than they borrowed when they sold the bonds in the first place.

These examples illustrate an important point: Unexpected inflation generally redistributes wealth from creditors to debtors. Note that we said *unexpected* inflation. The role played by expectations, or anticipations, in the redistributive effects of inflation is crucial.

The Role of Anticipations

As we saw in Chapter 4, the nominal interest rate increases by the expected rate of inflation. Thus, if inflation were correctly anticipated at the time of your car loan in the first example above, it would be reflected in a nominal interest rate giving the lender the same real return that he would have obtained in the absence of inflation. Similarly, had the bond markets correctly anticipated inflation when you purchased your bonds, their prices would have been appropriately discounted to compensate you in advance for the effects of expected inflation. (Remember the market value of a bond is the present value of future bond payments discounted at the nominal rate of interest. Thus, as inflationary expectations push up the nominal interest rate, they simultaneously pull down the prices of bonds.)

It is not simply the fact that people expect inflation, however, that eliminates its redistributive effects. Unless those expectations turn out to be *correct*, inflation will still create gainers and losers. If borrowers and lenders expect a 5 percent rate of inflation, for example, and the actual rate of inflation turns out to be greater than 5 percent, then borrowers will gain at the expense of lenders; if it turns out to be less than 5 percent, lenders will gain at the expense of borrowers. It is not so much the rate of inflation itself, therefore, but its *stability and predictability* that determine its redistributive consequences.

The Real Costs of Inflation

The redistributive effects of inflation are not themselves a real economic cost; they simply represent a transfer of wealth, whereby one person gains what another loses. However, attempts to avoid, or take advantage of, those effects do result in real costs. By increasing the risk associated with borrowing and lending, saving and investing, unpredictable inflation discourages the kind of credit transactions that play an important role in a dynamic, forward-looking economy. In addition, inflation distorts incentives and diverts people's time and effort away from genuinely productive activity and into finding ways to protect themselves from its capricious and arbitrary effects. If it becomes severe and unpredictable enough, inflation can strain the very fabric of society.

Hyperinflation

The costs of inflation are most graphically illustrated by the extreme case of *hyperinflation*. Hyperinflation is very rapid inflation—so rapid that it quickly renders money virtually useless. Indeed, during hyperinflation money's purchasing power often becomes less than the cost of printing it!

The most famous hyperinflation of this century is that which struck Germany following World War I. Millions of people who held their life savings in the form of savings accounts and other monetary assets found their entire wealth wiped out almost overnight as the German price level rose over a trillionfold between May 1921 and November 1923. (That's right, folks, a *trillion*fold!) Prices were not just rising, they were rising so fast that bargains struck in the morning would have to be renegotiated by the same afternoon. Toward the end of the German hyperinflation, it literally took a wheelbarrow to carry enough money to the store to buy a loaf of bread. It should come as no surprise that a monetary system ultimately breaks down completely under such conditions as people forsake money for barter to carry out their everyday transactions.

Hyperinflation is an extreme and comparatively rare phenomenon, but the costs imposed on society by even a moderate inflation, especially one that varies unpredictably, are sufficient to make price level stability a macroeconomic goal worth pursuing.

Economic Growth

Economic growth, specifically growth of per capita real national product, is the primary source of increases in our material standard of living. Over and above its effects on living standards, however, economic growth contributes importantly to social cohesion. Without it, the size of the economic pie would be fixed, and the only way for one person to get a bigger slice would be at the expense of someone else. Although redistribution of a fixed amount of output can be accomplished legitimately through government taxes and subsidies, it weakens the link between effort and reward and tends to create resentment between losers and gainers. In a growing economy, by contrast, everyone can share in the benefits of the increased production. Economic growth is thus an indispensable social lubricant in a society in which people continually aspire to better living standards.

Monetary and Fiscal Policies

Monetary policies are policies that influence macroeconomic performance via their impact on the supply of money.

The federal government influences macroeconomic performance through its monetary and fiscal policies. **Monetary policies** are carried out by the nation's central bank. In the United States the central bank is called the *Federal Reserve System*, or the *Fed* for short. As we see in subsequent chapters, the basic function of the Fed is to control the nation's supply of money. The money supply in turn affects the aggregate flow of spending, either directly through the amount of money people have available to spend, or indirectly through its effects on interest rates and credit conditions.

The Fed is an independent government agency whose key policy makers are appointed by the president and confirmed by Congress. Once confirmed, however, they are not under the direct control of either. As a result, the Fed is an extraordinarily powerful body with considerable independence in formulating and implementing its monetary policies.

Fiscal policies are policies that use the government budget to achieve macroeconomic goals.

Fiscal policies involve the use of the federal government's budget to achieve macroeconomic goals. As we shall see, the level of government expenditures, the level and structure of taxes, and the extent of government borrowing all have important macroeconomic consequences. Like monetary policies, some fiscal policies act primarily through their effects on the overall flow of spending in the economy. Others, especially those on the tax side, exert their influence through effects on incentives to work, save, and invest.

Fiscal policy is formulated and implemented in a distinctly political arena, namely, that in which the President, Congress, and a myriad of interest groups thrash out budget issues. By its very nature, therefore, the use of fiscal policy to pursue macroeconomic goals must often be subordinated to the political realities of the budgetary process.

The Policy Activism Debate: Rules versus Discretion

Our ability to maintain full employment, a stable price level, and healthy long-term growth depends to a large extent on our approach to monetary and fiscal policy. Unfortunately, economists and policy makers do not always agree on just what constitutes the best approach.

On one side of the debate are those who believe that the best way to dampen the cyclical ups and downs of economic activity is to give policy makers the *discretion* to actively intervene, as they see fit, whenever economic performance appears to fall short of its normative goals. They contend that such active intervention, or economic fine tuning, can contribute to economic stability by heading off potentially destabilizing forces both within the economy and without. This discretionary approach to economic policy rests on a fundamental belief that government policy makers have the knowledge, the tools, and the incentives that enable them to improve on the economic performance of the private marketplace.

Opponents of the discretionary approach to policy contend that such a belief is based on a naive and unwarranted faith in government. They argue that, because of the difficulty of predicting the precise timing and effects of monetary and fiscal policies, even the most well intentioned of such policies have at least as much chance of *de*stabilizing the economy as of stabilizing it. They would therefore prefer to see the actions of policy makers circumscribed by strict policy *rules*. Such rules might require policy makers to always react in some predictable manner to a given set of economic conditions, or they might even require that policy makers stick to a particular course of action regardless of changes in economic conditions. Proponents of policy rules have argued, for example, that the best monetary policy is one that simply keeps the money supply growing at a constant rate. In the fiscal area, their suggestions involve variations on the central theme of a balanced federal budget. The rules approach to macroeconomic policy is based on an underlying view that the economy performs best when the government commits itself to stability and predictability in its policies.

In summary, the discretionary approach to macroeconomic policy doubts the ability of the private market to meet the goals of macroeconomic policy and so places its faith in government; by contrast the rules approach places much more confidence in the marketplace and much less in government as a means to achieving those goals. An evaluation of these conflicting positions must await our full discussion of macroeconomic policy.

ECONOMIC EVENTS AND ECONOMIC THEORY: THE DEVELOPMENT OF MODERN MACROECONOMICS

Twice during this century—first during the 1930s and again during the 1970s—historic events shook the faith of economists in their macroeconomic theories. Each time, they were forced to reconsider those theories in the light of new and apparently contradictory facts and, each time, the theory emerged more powerful and robust than before. Throughout this evolutionary process, two schools of thought—or traditions—continuously vied for supremacy, both as positive theories of macroeconomic behavior and as the normative bases for economic policy. These are the *classical tradition* and the *Keynesian tradition*, the latter named for John Maynard Keynes, the great British economist whose *General Theory of Employment, Interest and Money*, published in 1936, gave birth to modern macroeconomics. Although the classical tradition is more than 200 years old and the Keynesian at least 50, the most fundamental disagreements in contemporary macroeconomics still reflect the differences between these two schools of thought.*

The Classical Tradition

The **classical tradition** emphasizes the effectiveness of the market mechanism in promoting economic stability and adapting to change.

The **classical tradition** has its roots in Adam Smith's great work, *The Wealth of Nations*, published in 1776. Smith believed that the economy is a self-regulating system in which individuals motivated by their own self-interest are "led as if by an invisible hand" to promote harmony and the economic welfare of society. This theme, as developed by generations of economists in the two centuries since Smith, is the essence of the classical tradition. That tradition views the market

*Keynes himself did his most important work during the 1930s, hence the 50-year age of the Keynesian tradition. Many economists would argue, however, that the fundamental ideas in this tradition go back in time well before Keynes himself, perhaps as far back as the classical tradition itself.

economy as a fundamentally stable system in which relative price adjustments automatically achieve market-clearing equilibria. Applied to macroeconomics, this view implies that business cycles are primarily a reflection of the transition from one equilibrium to another as the economy responds to external disturbances, or "shocks." In other words, it implies that recession and unemployment are temporary and ultimately self-correcting phenomena.

The Keynesian Revolution

The cataclysmic events of the Great Depression led Keynes to break with the classical tradition, a tradition in which he himself had been trained. He argued that prices and wages are too "sticky" for classical market adjustments to return the economy to normal within an acceptable period of time, and he dismissed as irrelevant arguments that such adjustments may succeed in the long run with his famous phrase, "In the long run we are all dead."

Keynes abandoned classical economics with its emphasis on prices and markets and constructed a revolutionary new theory of his own, emphasizing relations among economic aggregates. By focusing almost exclusively on these aggregates, Keynes virtually invented macroeconomics. (He still accepted the classical theory for microeconomic analysis, however.) We examine the details of the Keynesian theory and its implications for economic policy in the chapters to come. Suffice it to say that it precipitated a genuine revolution in economic thinking, occupying the research efforts of a generation of economists who refined, elaborated, and extended it over the next four decades. As the **Keynesian tradition** evolved, its central theme stood in stark contrast to that of the classical tradition: For Keynesians, the market system is an inadequate mechanism for insuring economic stability because many prices and wages fail to respond, or respond too slowly, to changes in economic conditions.

The **Keynesian tradition** is skeptical of the market's ability to promote economic stability and adapt to change.

By the 1950s, Keynesian theory had become the dominant orthodoxy among macroeconomists, and Keynesian influence had begun to shape the macroeconomic policies of governments. Not surprisingly, Keynesians tend to favor discretionary government policies to augment (or supercede) the market in pursuing the macroeconomic goals of full employment and a stable price level. This activist approach to policy appeared so successful during the 1960s that in 1968, after nearly 8 years of uninterrupted economic expansion, the president of the American Economic Association was led to pronounce the business cycle dead. Ironically, the high tide of Keynesian economics was about to recede.

The Stagflation of the 1970s

According to the original Keynesian theory, unemployment and inflation were an either-or phenomenon: an economy could experience one or the other, but not both simultaneously. Keynes's successors went beyond this simple view of unemployment and inflation and argued instead that there existed a trade-off between the two phenomena. In particular, they believed that we could reduce unemployment if we were willing to tolerate a higher rate of inflation, and that

Figure 15.6

A hypothetical Phillips curve

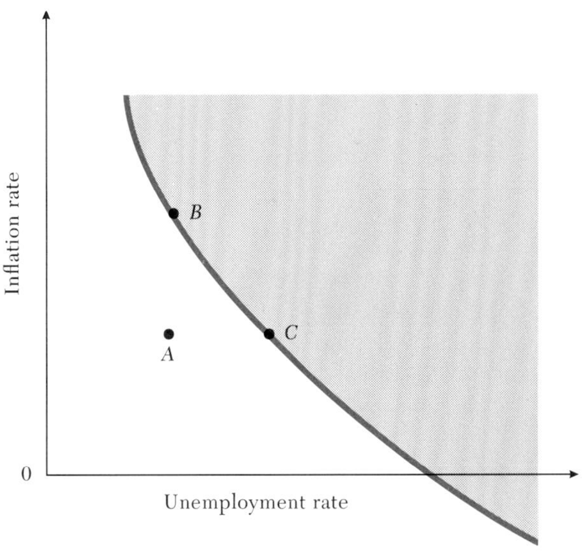

The **Phillips curve** is a curve purporting to show a trade-off between unemployment and inflation.

we could reduce inflation if we were willing to tolerate a higher rate of unemployment. These trade-offs were usually depicted in a diagram called a **Phillips curve**.*

A hypothetical Phillips curve is shown in Figure 15.6, with the rate of inflation measured on the vertical axis and the rate of unemployment on the horizontal. According to the Keynesian economics of the 1960s, although we could not achieve combinations of inflation and unemployment "inside" the Phillips curve, such as point *A*, we could choose among those that lay along the curve, such as points *B* and *C*. In effect, the Phillips curve presented policy makers with a menu of alternative combinations of inflation and unemployment.

Figure 15.7 plots the actual inflation and unemployment rates for the U.S. economy from 1960 through 1989. Looking at the data for the 1960s alone, it is easy to see why economists once accepted the notion of an inflation–unemployment trade-off, for throughout that decade a steadily falling rate of unemployment was accompanied by a steadily accelerating rate of inflation. However, in 1970 when policy makers attempted to reverse this trend and move the economy "back down the Phillips curve" to a lower inflation rate, the result was a rude surprise: Although unemployment increased as expected, the inflation rate just kept rising! And that was just the beginning. As the diagram shows, evidence from the 1970s and 1980s hardly supports the idea of a stable and predictable trade-off between inflation and unemployment.

*The curve is named after A. W. Phillips, an Australian economist whose empirical work on prices, wages and unemployment first hinted at such a relationship.

Figure 15.7

Inflation and unemployment, 1960–89

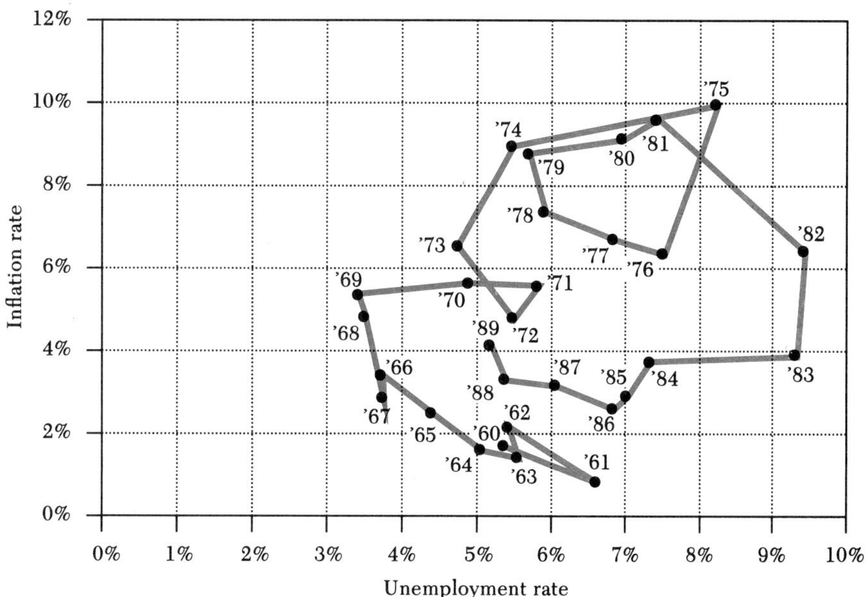

Even more puzzling was the fact that twice during the decade—in 1970 and again in 1975—inflation actually accelerated as the economy slipped into a recession. During every other recession on record, the rate of inflation had fallen rather than risen. As a whole, the decade of the 1970s was a period of abnormally slow real growth—a "stagnant" economy—combined with high rates of inflation. This unhappy combination came to be known as **stagflation**.

Stagflation is a combination of unacceptably high inflation and stagnant economic growth.

The economy of the 1970s thus behaved in a manner quite inconsistent with what economists trained in the Keynesian tradition had come to expect. It also provided those economists with many lessons (perhaps not the least of which is the value of humility!), and it sent them back to the drawing board to develop new theories and to search for new approaches to macroeconomic policy.

Although no new general theory has come along since 1970 to revolutionize macroeconomics as Keynes did a half-century ago, economists have discovered a number of fruitful avenues of investigation that were relatively neglected during the heyday of traditional Keynesianism. Together they define modern macroeconomics and distinguish it from the macroeconomics of only a generation ago.

The Keynesian and Classical Traditions Today

Modern macroeconomics has been shaped by, and continues to reflect, the classical and Keynesian traditions. Building primarily on the foundation originally laid by Keynes, but with a new appreciation for the importance of many classical ideas, are today's *new Keynesian* economists. In the Keynesian tradition, they emphasize the importance of sticky prices and wages in preventing smooth market adjustments. Unlike Keynes, however, they try to explain this stickiness on the basis of rational microeconomic behavior. In particular, they tend to emphasize the transactions costs of frequent price and wage changes and the role of long-term contracts in avoiding those costs.

Drawing principally on the classical tradition, but in light of the Keynesian contribution, are today's *monetarists* and *new classical* economists. Like their classical predecessors, they regard prices and wages as fundamentally flexible and argue that their apparent stickiness is due only to the fact that they are often set on the basis of outmoded and incorrect information.

As we shall see, both new Keynesian and new classical theories have contributed important insights into the way the economy works. Despite the fundamental differences between the two schools of thought, there are nonetheless many areas in which they can be fruitfully viewed as complementary, rather than conflicting, theories.

CHAPTER SUMMARY

1. The economy's *real national income and product*, its *price level*, and its *labor force* and *employment* have all exhibited a long-term, secular upward trend. The secular rise in real income and product represents *economic growth*, while the rise of the price level represents *inflation*.
2. Superimposed on these long-term, secular trends are variations in real output, inflation, and employment which reflect the impact of the *business cycle*.
3. The goals of macroeconomic policy are *full employment, a stable price level*, and *economic growth*. *Monetary policies* are carried out by the Federal Reserve, the nation's central bank, and *fiscal policies* are implemented through the political process.
4. The debate over policy activism pits those who favor a *discretionary* approach to macroeconomic policy against those who favor a *rules* approach to macroeconomic policy.
5. Economists in the *classical tradition* consider the market economy to be a stable system in which relative price adjustments automatically achieve market-clearing equilibria. According to this view, recession and unemployment are temporary and ultimately self-correcting phenomena.
6. Economists in the *Keynesian tradition* consider the market system to be an inadequate mechanism for insuring economic stability because many prices and wages fail to respond, or respond too slowly, to changes in economic conditions.

Key Terms and Concepts

national product (real and nominal)
national income (real and nominal)
economic growth
price level
inflation
deflation
rate of inflation
employed
unemployed
labor force
unemployment rate
business cycle
recession
natural rate of unemployment
monetary policy
fiscal policy
classical tradition
Keynesian tradition
stagflation
Phillips curve

Questions for Thought and Discussion

1. Based on the information in the graphs in this chapter, how would you characterize U.S. economic performance during the 1920s? The 1950s? The 1960s?
2. Using the data in Table 15.2, compare the average duration of recessions and recoverys/expansions in the pre- and post-World War II periods. (Do not count the 80-month expansion that accompanied the war or the expansion that began in November 1982.)
3. Using the basic supply–demand market model, how would you expect the effects of a recession caused by a general fall in demand to differ from those of a recession caused by a general fall in supply?
4. Suppose we discovered a policy whereby we could force the unemployment rate literally to zero without the danger of inflation. Would you have any second thoughts about using that policy?
5. In January 1987, the *Los Angeles Times* reported the following in a syndicated story: "The U.S. inflation rate rose only 1.1 percent last year, the Department of Commerce said Wednesday. . . . (The increase) was the smallest since 1961, when prices rose just 0.7 percent." The story's headline was "Inflation Rose 1.1% in 1986." If you were an editor, what corrections would you have made and why?
6. We have given examples—a car loan, investment in bonds—of how unexpected inflation arbitrarily redistributes wealth. Using the same examples, show how unexpected *de*flation also redistributes wealth. What would happen in each example if deflation were expected?
7. Which pattern of inflation would be the least costly: (a) an inflation rate which fluctuates unpredictably between moderate inflation and moderate deflation but which averages zero over the long run; (b) an inflation rate which fluctuates between 2 percent and 6 percent and averages 4 percent over the long run; (c) an inflation rate which remains constant at 8 percent over the long run?

8. Why don't we state the economic growth goal of macroeconomic policy as the attainment of "maximum possible" growth?
9. In 1969, then-President Richard Nixon, in an attempt to reduce inflation, imposed wage and price controls on nearly all markets. From what you know so far about the classical and Keynesian traditions, which would be more sympathetic to such a policy?

CHAPTER 16

Measuring Economic Activity: National Product, National Income, and the Price Level

The **national income and product accounts** provide the accounting framework for measuring national income and product.

In any given year in our economy, hundreds of millions of people produce, exchange, and consume billions of goods and services worth trillions of dollars. Economists summarize the outcome of this incredibly complex process in a system of **national income and product accounts**, or just "national income accounts" for short. These accounts, kept by the Bureau of Economic Analysis in the U. S. Department of Commerce, provide the framework within which we measure the value of all the goods and services produced during the year and of all the incomes earned in producing them. As such, they are about as close as we can get to assigning a number—or more accurately, a set of numbers—to that elusive concept we call "aggregate economic activity."

Our goal in this chapter is to gain an understanding of the U.S. national income and product accounts as well as an appreciation of their limitations. We begin by examining the fundamental concepts on which the accounts are based and then see how these concepts are applied to specific categories of economic activity to measure national income, national product, and other important economic aggregates. We also see how the economy's price level is measured and how the result is used to correct nominal economic variables for the effects of inflation.

ISSUES IN THE MEASUREMENT OF NATIONAL INCOME AND NATIONAL PRODUCT

Stocks and Flows

A **stock** is a variable with no time dimension because it is measured at a point in time.

Variables measured at a point in time are called **stocks**. Economic stocks include wealth and its various components such as money and other financial and real assets. If someone asks you how much money you have in your wallet, or what the balance in your savings account is, for example, you need only reply with a dollar amount; no time dimension is needed.

A **flow** is a variable with a time dimension because it is measured over an interval of time.

The national income accounts measure economic activity, not in terms of stocks, but in terms of **flows**. Unlike stocks, flows have a time dimension and must be expressed as a rate per unit of time. To say that your income is $1,000, for example, is meaningless unless you specify a time period: $1,000 per week is clearly not the same income as $1,000 per year. Production is also a flow (a firm produces 10,000 widgets *per day*), as are expenditure (a family spends $100 *per week* on food), saving (a person saves $50 *per month* out of her paycheck), and depreciation (a piece of machinery depreciates at the rate of 10 percent *per year*).

Note the difference between money and income. We often ask a person how much "money" he makes when we really want to know what his income is. This simply reflects the fact that monetary units—dollars, pesos, yen, or whatever—mark the yardstick by which we measure income and other economic flows. Money itself, however, is a stock.

Final Goods, Intermediate Goods, and Value Added

The typical production process is one in which each of a number of separate firms contributes to the value of some final product. As an illustration, consider the bread you used for your morning toast. That slice of bread was the result of efforts by wheat farmers, flour mills, a bakery, a grocer, and many other firms. Table 16.1 depicts, in a simplified way, the process that links all of these firms together. It begins with a farmer who, we assume, produces wheat worth $100. A miller buys this wheat from the farmer and mills it into flour which he in turn sells to a baker for $150. The baker then uses the flour to bake bread which she sells to a grocer for $225. Finally the grocer brings the bread to his retail store where he sells it to consumers for $250. The $250 worth of bread on the grocer's shelf is therefore the *final product* of this step-by-step process.

As this example makes clear, the value of the final product reflects the contributions of many producers. The contribution of an individual producer is not,

Table 16.1

Value added

PRODUCER	PRODUCT	SALES REVENUES	INTERMEDIATE PURCHASES	VALUE ADDED
Farmer	Wheat	$100	n.a.	$100
Miller	Flour	150	$100	50
Baker	Bread (wholesale)	225	150	75
Grocer	Bread (retail)	250*	225	25
Total		$725	$475	$250*

*Final output.

however, simply the value of what it sells. We can see this by noting that sum of the sales revenues of all producers in the preceding example is $725, which considerably overstates the $250 value of the final product. It does so because it counts the contributions of some producers more than once. If we add the farmer's revenues to those of the miller, for example, we count the farmer's contribution to the value of the final product twice, once as the value of the wheat he sells and again as part of the value of the flour sold by the miller. Similarly, adding the baker's revenues to those of the farmer and the miller counts the farmer's contribution three times, the miller's two times, and so on.

Value added is the difference between the value of a producer's output and the value of the intermediate goods used up in producing that output.

To obtain an individual producer's contribution to the value of the final product, we must deduct from the value of his output the value of the intermediate goods he uses up in producing that output. The result is a measure called **value added**. In this example, the miller's value added is the $50 difference between the $150 worth of flour that he sells and the $100 worth of wheat he purchases from the farmer.

The fourth column of Table 16.1 shows each producer's purchases of intermediate goods. (For simplicity, we have assumed that the farmer purchased no intermediate goods—perhaps he started with his own seeds.) The last column of the table shows each producer's value added. Note that the sum of the values added is equal to the value of the final product, which is no accident: Because each producer's value added is his individual contribution to the value of the final product, the sum of the values added of all producers must equal the total value of the final product. This relation holds not only for a single production process but also for the economy as a whole. National product is therefore equal to the sum of all values added in the economy.

Value Added and Income

To see where value added comes from and where it goes, we must examine more closely the productive activity that takes place within a single firm. Suppose this firm is the Yum Yum Bakery, one of many that operates at the baking stage in

Table 16.2A

PRODUCTION STATEMENT FOR YUM YUM BAKERY

Costs		*Production*	
Wages	$ 40,000	Sales	$155,000
Rent	25,000		
Interest	3,000		
Ingredients	80,000		
Recipe consultant	2,000		
Total costs	$150,000	Total output	$155,000
Profit	5,000		
Total	$155,000	Total	$155,000

Table 16.2B

VALUE ADDED STATEMENT FOR YUM YUM BAKERY

Incomes		*Value Added*	
Wages	$ 40,000	Sales	$155,000
Rent	25,000	Intermediate purchases	− 82,000
Interest	3,000	(Ingredients 80,000)	
Profit	5,000	(Recipe consultant 2,000)	
Total incomes	$ 73,000	Value added	$ 73,000

the production of your morning toast. Table 16.2 summarizes the operations of the Yum Yum Bakery during a recent year. Table 16.2A is Yum Yum's production statement. The right-hand side shows that Yum Yum produced and sold $155,000 worth of bakery products during the year. The left-hand side shows that Yum Yum incurred total costs of $150,000, including $40,000 in wages, $25,000 in rental payments, $3,000 interest on a loan used to purchase capital equipment, $80,000 for ingredients, and $2,000 paid to an independent recipe consultant. It also shows that Yum Yum earned (accounting) profits of $5,000, which is simply the difference between the $155,000 worth of goods it produced and the $150,000 of costs it incurred. By defining profit in this way and placing it on the left-hand side of the production statement, we guarantee that the two sides of the statement are equal.*

Table 16.2B shows Yum Yum's value added statement. To obtain the value added statement we deducted Yum Yum's purchases of intermediate goods—namely, $80,000 worth of ingredients and $2,000 worth of consulting services—from both sides of its production statement. On the right-hand side, this leaves a value added of $73,000. What remains on the left-hand side is a list of

*To obtain a measure of *economic* profit, we would have to deduct the implicit opportunity cost of the labor and capital supplied by the owner. This is not done in the National Income Accounts.

all the incomes earned as a result of Yum Yum's productive activity, including the profits earned by Yum Yum's owners. Because we deducted the same $82,000 worth of intermediate purchases from both sides of the production statement, the sum of the incomes on the left-hand side of the value added statement must equal the value added on the right-hand side. To generalize, the value added at each stage in the production process is equal to the total income created at that stage. This identity between value added and income holds not only at the level of the individual producer but also at the aggregate level as well. National income is therefore also equal to the sum of all values added in the economy.

The **basic national income accounting identity** says that national product is always equal to national income.

Finally, because national product and national income are each equal to aggregate value added, they must also be equal to one another. Indeed, they are but two different ways of viewing the same productive activity. The conceptual equivalence of national income and national product is known as the **basic national income accounting identity**.

Income as Earnings

The income components of value added, and thus of national income, include only *payments for current productive services*. As such, they exclude many payments and receipts that may be considered "income" for purposes other than those of the national income accounts. If your rich aunt dies and leaves you $10,000, for example, you must report that to the Internal Revenue Service as taxable "income," but is not part of national income because it is not a payment for your current productive services (unless perhaps you were especially diligent in mowing your rich aunt's lawn and washing her car every week just before she died!). "Income" from the sale of existing assets, such as stocks and bonds, 1985 Chevrolets, and houses built 10 years ago, is excluded from national income for the same reason. Unemployment compensation, social security benefits, and welfare payments are also excluded because they are not payments for productive services. In general, we can determine whether any particular receipt is a part of national income for any given year simply by asking whether it was *earned as a result of productive services supplied during that year*. If the answer is yes, it is part of national income; if the answer is no, it is not.

Capital Goods: Final or Intermediate?

Economic activity produces capital goods as well as consumer goods. Unlike intermediate goods, such as the flour and other ingredients our hypothetical baker uses up in the production of bread, capital goods such as the baker's oven are only partially "used up" each year as they depreciate with use. This poses a dilemma for the national income accounts: Are they to treat capital goods as final goods or as intermediate goods in calculating national product?*

*Note that if the accounting period were longer than the useful life of all capital goods, this dilemma would not exist. Capital goods would simply be intermediate goods.

Gross national product (GNP) measures the aggregate value of all final goods produced during the year, including all new captial goods with no allowance for depreciation.

Net national product (NNP) is equal to gross national product minus depreciation.

The national income accounts resolve the dilemma by defining two different measures of national product: **gross national product**, or GNP, and **net national product**, or NNP. GNP includes all currently produced capital goods with no allowance for depreciation, thereby treating all new capital goods as final goods. To obtain a measure of NNP, the national income accounts deduct depreciation (or capital consumption) from GNP, in effect treating the capital used up during the year as an intermediate good. Put another way, *gross* national product includes *gross investment*, whereas *net* national product includes only *net investment*, that is, new investment net of depreciation.

Because it allows for the depreciation of the capital stock, net national product is theoretically a better measure of value added than gross national product. Unfortunately, however, the estimates of depreciation used to calculate NNP are notoriously unreliable. Because of this, GNP is the more widely used measure of national product.

What the National Income Accounts Don't Count

With minor exceptions, the national income and product accounts reflect only that economic activity for which an actual monetary transaction is recorded. Thus, although they include most market exchanges and tax-financed government purchases, the accounts ignore a substantial portion of economic activity for which no money changes hands or which, for other reasons, goes unrecorded. Such activity includes household production, transactions in the "underground economy," and transactions that are illegal.

Household Production

One sector of the economy in which a great deal of genuine productive activity takes place, but which is almost entirely overlooked in the national income accounts, is the household sector. If a family pays a maid to prepare its meals and clean house, a gardener to tend the yard, and a professional handyman to provide minor maintenance and repairs, those productive activities are all included in measured national income and product. However, the identical services are ignored if they are performed within the household by members of the family. (To illustrate the arbitrariness of this treatment of household production, economists frequently use the example of a man who reduces national income and product by marrying his housekeeper.)

In a few special cases, the accounts assign, or *impute*, a market value to household production. For example, that portion of a farmer's output that he and his family consume themselves is assigned its market value and included in national product. Similarly, the owner of a house is treated as though she pays herself rent to live in that house, and the imputed rent is included in national income. Such imputations are the exception, however, and they capture only a small fraction of total household production. It has been estimated that measured GNP would be about 25 percent, or more than a trillion dollars per year, higher if it included the value of household production.

The Underground Economy

The national income accounts also account for only a small portion of the economic activity that takes place in the "underground economy," where people resort to unrecorded barter and cash transactions to avoid taxes. If a plumber writes a check to an auto mechanic for a tune-up on his car, chances are that the payment and tune-up will be included in measured national income and output. However, if the same plumber repairs the mechanic's leaky pipes in return for his tune-up, the transaction goes unrecorded, not only for the purpose of the Internal Revenue Service but also for that of the national income accountant. While estimates of the size of the underground economy vary widely, some claim that its inclusion might add as much as 30 percent to national income and product.*

Illegal Activity

Finally, the national income and product accounts exclude incomes from illegal activities such as prostitution and dealing in illegal drugs. This exclusion can lead to an element of inconsistency, for the definition of what is legal and what is not varies from time to time and place to place. For example, the production of alcoholic beverages is included in today's GNP but was excluded during prohibition. Similarly, bookmakers (the kind who handle bets, not the kind who produced the book you're reading) who ply their trade in Nevada or Atlantic City contribute to measured national income and product but their counterparts in areas where bookmaking is illegal do not. According to one recent estimate, the activities of organized crime alone would add about 6 percent to our measures of aggregate economic activity.†

Despite these and other limitations, the national income and product accounts probably provide us with the best measures of as complex and slippery a concept as "aggregate economic activity" that we can realistically hope for.

THE ACTUAL NATIONAL INCOME AND PRODUCT ACCOUNTS

The national income and product accounts estimate GNP via two separate approaches, an *expenditures* approach and an *incomes* approach. These approaches correspond to the two ways of looking at value added: The expenditures approach views GNP in terms of expenditures on final output, whereas the incomes approach views it in terms of the incomes generated in producing that output. Because the two approaches rely on different sets of data and different statistical sampling techniques, they rarely produce identical results in practice. However

* "Unearthing the Underground Economy," *The Wall Street Journal*, February 4, 1985.

† See James Cook, "The Invisible Enterprise," *Forbes*, September 29, 1980.

the "statistical discrepancy" between the two is generally quite small, usually in the range of 1–2 percent or less.

The Expenditures Approach to GNP

There are four sources of expenditures on final goods and services: consumption expenditures by households, investment (capital) expenditures by business firms, government purchases of goods and services, and foreign expenditures to purchase exports. We can express GNP as the sum of these four expenditure categories, namely,

$$Y = C + I + G + X$$

where Y is the standard macroeconomic symbol for GNP, C is consumption expenditure, I is investment expenditure, G is government purchases, and X is net exports.

Table 16.3 shows the expenditure estimate of GNP for 1987.

Table 16.3

The expenditure approach to GNP, 1989

EXPENDITURE CATEGORY	AMOUNT IN BILLIONS OF DOLLARS	
Consumer expenditures		
a. Durables	474	
b. Nondurables	1,122	
c. Services	1,874	
Total		**3,470**
Investment expenditures		
a. Plant and equipment	513	
b. Residential construction	235	
c. Net inventory change	29	
Total		**777**
Net Exports		
a. Exports	624	
b. Imports	675	
Total		**−51**
Government purchases		
a. Federal	404	
b. State and local	633	
Total		**1,037**
Gross National Product		**5,233**

Source: *Economic Report of the President, 1990.*

Consumer expenditures consist of household purchases of all currently produced consumer goods and services. These include durable consumer goods such as automobiles, furniture, and appliances, nondurable consumer goods such as food and clothing, and services such as entertainment, medical care, and education.

Investment expenditures also consist of three main components. The first is business purchases of new plant and equipment, including buildings, machinery, and other fixed capital. The second component of investment is purchases of new residential structures such as houses and apartment buildings. Note that a house is the only final good typically purchased by a household that the national income accounts classify as a capital good rather than a consumer good. The third component of investment is the net change in business inventories. Additions to inventory are treated as investment because inventories, like machinery and other capital goods, are a source of *future* revenues for the producer. Note that it is the *change* in inventories (a flow), and not the absolute *level* of inventories (a stock), that is part of GNP. This change is positive if current production exceeds current sales; it is negative if current sales exceed current production.

Unlike the other components of investment, inventory changes are not entirely under the control of firms. If sales turn out to be slower than anticipated, firms experience an unexpected increase in inventories. Conversely, if sales turn out to be more brisk than anticipated, firms may have to draw down inventories to meet demand. Inventories thus act as a *buffer* that absorbs the initial impact of unanticipated changes in demand. This buffer function of inventories plays an important role in our analysis of the business cycle.

Government purchases include purchases of currently produced goods and services by federal, state, and local governments, as well as the wages and salaries these governments pay their employees. Because governments rely primarily on taxes, rather than on market exchanges, to finance their purchases, the government purchases component of GNP does not directly measure the market value of final output. In effect, government output is valued at its cost of production. Whether on balance the value of national defense, interstate highways, public libraries, police and fire services, and other publicly provided goods and services is greater or less than the costs of providing them, and thus whether national income accounts understate or overstate government's contribution to national product, is an open question.

It is also important to realize that the government purchases component of GNP does *not* include all government spending. A substantial portion of government expenditures—indeed, about half of all federal expenditures—are *transfer payments*. As we have seen, government transfers include such things as unemployment compensation, social security benefits, and various forms of welfare payments. Since transfer payments entail neither factor payments nor expenditures on currently produced goods and services, they are not part of GNP.

Net exports, the fourth and final category of GNP, is equal to the difference between exports and imports. As a measure of total production, GNP must include goods produced for export as well as those sold domestically. On the other hand, some expenditures made by domestic consumers, businesses, and governments represent purchases of goods and services imported from other countries. The consumer expenditures just described, for example, include purchases of television sets and automobiles produced in Japan. Because these goods are not part of our own production, expenditures on them must be deducted from GNP. The net export component of GNP captures these elements of foreign trade. The fact that it was negative in 1989 means that total imports of goods and services exceeded total exports of goods and services during that year.

The Incomes Approach to GNP

Table 16.4 shows the incomes estimate of GNP for 1989. The first five entries in the table are the components of national income.

Compensation of employees, or labor income, includes all wages, salaries, bonuses, and other payments for labor services.

Rental income of persons includes not only the earnings of individual property owners (including the rents imputed to those who occupy their own houses) but also the earnings from "intellectual property" such as an author's royalties.

Net interest represents the business payments for the services of capital goods financed by borrowing from households. Because households also pay interest to

Table 16.4

The incomes approach to GNP, 1989

INCOMES AND OTHER CLAIMS AGAINST VALUE ADDED	AMOUNT IN BILLIONS OF DOLLARS	
Compensation of employees	3,146	
+ Rental income of persons (net of housing depreciation)	+ 8	
+ Net interest	+ 461	
+ Corporate profits	+ 298	
a. Profit taxes		129
b. Dividends		122
c. Retained earnings		36
d. Adjustments		11
+ Proprietors' income	+ 352	
= **National Income**	= **4,265**	
+ Indirect business taxes (and statistical discrepancy)	+ 416	
= **Net National Product**	= **4,681**	
+ Capital consumption allowances (depreciation)	+ 552	
= **Gross National Product**	= **5,233**	

Source: *Economic Report of the President, 1990.*

businesses (on consumer loans, charge accounts, and the like), the interest earnings component of national income is the *net* flow of interest from businesses to households. (The interest payments from government to households on government debt is not counted as part of national income but as a transfer payment. This is somewhat arbitrary, since at least some government borrowing is used to finance public capital goods such as roads, bridges, and harbors.)

Corporate profits represent the earnings of the stockholders who supply (and legally own) the capital used by corporations. As Table 16.4 shows, a portion of these earnings is used to pay corporate profits taxes and the remainder is either distributed to stockholders as dividends or kept within the corporation as retained earnings. (The "adjustments" component of corporate profits represents a correction made for profits and losses that are not the result of current production. For example, the accounts exclude any profits or losses that are the result of changes in the market value of inventories produced in previous years.)

Proprietors' income includes the earnings of independent professionals, such as doctors and lawyers, and of unincorporated businesses. Because the owners, or proprietors, of such businesses typically work in the business and simply keep for themselves whatever is left after meeting expenses, it is virtually impossible to separate their wages from their profits. Accordingly, the national income accounts lump together all of their income in one category.

The official measure of *national income* is the sum of these five earnings categories. That it differs from the incomes estimate of GNP at the bottom of the table does not, however, invalidate the basic national income accounting identity. It simply reflects the fact that, in practice, some claims on value added are not factor incomes. For example, some of the value of final output is claimed by government as taxes rather than paid out as income to the factors of production. These *indirect business taxes* include sales taxes, excise taxes, and property taxes. Technically, they are not part of national income because they are not payments for productive services. They are part of national product, however, because as part of producers' expenses they must ultimately be covered in the prices of final products. We thus add indirect business taxes to national income to obtain a measure of net national product. Finally, we then obtain the incomes approach estimate of GNP at the bottom of Table 16.4 by adding estimated depreciation (capital consumption allowances) to NNP.

Personal Income, Disposable Personal Income, and Personal Saving

Table 16.5 on the following page illustrates the relation between GNP, national income, and some other economic aggregates. We proceed from GNP to national income by reversing the steps we just went through. We then make two adjustments to national income. First, we deduct those parts of national income that are not paid directly to households. These include the portion of wages and salaries deducted from paychecks as contributions for social insurance (Social Security taxes) and the portion of corporate profits not paid to households as dividends. Second, we add transfer payments to households, nearly all of which

Table 16.5

Derivation of personal income, disposable personal income, and personal saving, 1989, in billions of dollars

Gross National Product	**5,233**
− Capital consumption allowances	−552
= **Net National Product**	**4,681**
− Indirect business taxes	−416
= **National Income**	**4,265**
− National income not paid to households	−665
+ Transfer payments to households (including household interest on national debt)	+829
= **Personal Income**	**4,429**
− Personal taxes	−649
= **Disposable Personal Income**	**3,780**
− Personal outlays for consumption and interest	−3,574
= **Personal Saving**	**206**

Source: *Economic Report of the President, 1990.*

Personal income includes all income paid directly to persons (households) rather than to businesses or government.

Disposable personal income is after-tax personal income, which can be either saved or consumed.

Personal saving is disposable personal income minus personal expenditures for consumption and interest. It equals the net increase in household assets during the year.

are from government. The result is an aggregate called **personal income**. It is the income that ends up literally in the hands of persons, or households, rather than businesses or governments.

If we then deduct personal taxes (mainly income taxes) from personal income, we end up with the after-tax income of households. We call this **disposable personal income**. It is the income that households can either spend or save at their discretion.

As you can see from the table, most disposable income is used for consumer outlays, including both current consumer expenditures and interest payments on consumer debt. Households can use what remains to acquire assets or to reduce liabilities—that is, to increase their wealth. We call this increase in household wealth **personal saving**. It includes household acquisitions of financial assets such as stocks, bonds, and savings account balances, as well as the repayment of household debt. (Selling assets or acquiring liabilities—that is, going into debt—is negative saving. Thus personal saving can be negative, but this is almost never the case in the aggregate.)

The definition of saving as the acquisition of assets or the reduction of liabilities is perfectly general. It applies not only to household saving but also to saving by businesses, government, and foreigners as well. For example, corporate retained earnings are a form of business saving because they are used by the corporation to acquire both real and financial assets. On the other hand, depreciation is a form of negative business saving because it represents a decline in the value of the real assets (capital goods) owned by firms.

Saving and Investment

The relation between saving and investment in the national income accounts tells us something about the sources of the funds available for investment. To examine this relation, let us begin with a simplified economy in which there is no government sector and no foreign trade. In such an economy, GNP includes only consumer expenditures and investment expenditures. Furthermore, with no taxes, all income is either spent on consumption or saved. Thus we can write the basic national income accounting identity for this simplified economy as

$$C + I = C + S_p$$

where C and I are again consumer and investment expenditures, respectively, and S_p is total private (household *and* business) saving. Deleting consumer expenditures from both sides of the equation leaves the basic relation between saving and investment, namely,

$$I = S_p$$

In this simple economy, therefore, saving and investment are equal. Put another way, all private saving finds its way into investment. Note, however, that part of that investment may take the form of unintended changes in business inventories. A simple example illustrates how this can occur.

Suppose that businesses themselves plan to spend \$200 for investment and expect households to spend \$800 on consumer goods. They therefore produce \$200 worth of capital goods and \$800 worth of consumer goods and, in the process, generate \$1,000 worth of income. If households then decide to save \$250 of that income and spend only \$750 on consumer goods rather than the \$800 that businesses anticipated, then \$50 worth of consumer goods will go unsold and be added to producers' inventories. This change in inventories is a part—albeit an unplanned part—of business investment. Adding it to the originally planned investment of \$200 results in actual investment of \$250, the same as total saving. In general, therefore, inventory changes automatically guarantee that *actual* investment is always equal to saving even when *planned* investment is not.

The equality between saving and investment is preserved in a slightly more complicated form when we add a government sector to our simple economy. In particular, using G to represent the government purchases component of GNP, T_x to represent taxes, and T_r to represent government transfer payments, we can rewrite the basic national income accounting identity for an economy with a government sector as

$$C + I + G = C + S_p + T_x - T_r$$

where the left-hand side is national product and the right-hand side is national income. (T_r appears with a minus sign on the right-hand side of the equation because transfer payments are not part of national income.) Again deducting consumer expenditures from both sides of the equation and then rearranging terms, we find the following expression for investment spending:

$$I = S_p + (T_x - T_r - G)$$

The term in parentheses is government tax receipts minus total government spending, both transfers and purchases. In other words, it is the government's budget surplus (if positive) or deficit (if negative). A budget surplus means that the government is taking in more in tax revenues than it is spending; it therefore represents government saving. A budget deficit means that the government is taking in less in tax revenues than it is spending. To finance the difference, the government must increase its liabilities by borrowing, or equivalently, selling bonds. A government budget deficit is therefore negative saving. Thus, labelling government saving as S_g, we can rewrite the relation between investment and saving as

$$I = S_p + S_g$$

Including government in the economy therefore leaves the basic equality between saving and investment intact.

We complete the saving–investment picture by including the foreign sector in our economy. We do this by adding net exports, X, to expenditures on GNP and rewrite the national income accounting identity as

$$C + I + G + X = C + S + T_x - T_r$$

Again deleting consumer expenditures and government purchases from both sides and rearranging terms, we obtain the following expression for investment in an economy with both a government and a foreign sector:

$$I = S_p + S_g - X$$

In 1989 the value of net exports was minus \$51 billion. In other words, we paid foreigners \$51 billion more for imports than they paid us for our exports. What did foreigners do with that extra \$51 billion which we paid them? They used it to purchase U.S. assets: Treasury bonds, shares of stock in U.S. corporations, and hotels in Las Vegas. Because the difference between imports and exports is used by foreigners to acquire U.S. assets, it represents foreign saving in the United States. Conversely, net exports—the difference between exports and imports—is the negative of foreign saving. In symbols, $S_f = -X$, where S_f represents foreign saving. In an economy with a foreign sector, we can therefore write the relation between saving and investment as

$$I = S_p + S_g + S_f$$

This expression reveals the three sources of saving used to finance investment: private, domestic saving; government saving; and foreign saving. In recent years government saving has been negative thanks to large federal budget deficits. Government borrowing to finance these deficits has diverted funds away from private investment, but this trend has been partially offset by substantial foreign saving in the United States due to the large excess of imports over exports. In effect, the foreign sector has been helping to finance our federal budget deficits by accepting U.S. debt, rather than currently produced goods and services, in exchange for the goods and services foreigners are selling in the United States.

MEASURING THE PRICE LEVEL AND INFLATION

As we saw in Chapter 15, changes in GNP reflect changes in the economy's price level as well as in its output of goods and services. To eliminate the effects of changes in the price level, national income accountants evaluate each year's GNP not only in that year's prices but also in the prices that prevailed in some *base year*. The choice of the base year is somewhat arbitrary since it serves only as the basis for comparison. Currently, the national income accounts use 1982 as the base year.

Nominal GNP is gross national product evaluated in current prices.

Real GNP is gross national product evaluated in base year prices.

We refer to GNP valued at actual market prices as **nominal GNP** and GNP valued at base year prices as **real GNP**. We can illustrate the distinction using data for 1989. In our tour through the national income accounts, we have seen that 1989 GNP was $5,233 billion. Because that figure was computed using the actual market values of goods and services produced in 1989, it represents that year's nominal GNP. In addition, the national income accountants have determined that if the same real goods and services produced in 1989 had been sold at their 1982 prices instead of their 1989 prices, their value would have been only $4,143 billion. Real GNP in 1989 was therefore $4,143 billion in base year (1982) prices.

The GNP Deflator

Because the current year's output is used to calculate both nominal and real GNP, the two differ only to the extent that current prices differ from base year prices. The ratio of nominal GNP to real GNP for any given year thus provides us with a measure of the change in prices since the base year. This ratio is called the **GNP deflator**. It is the price index that measures the average price of all goods and services in current GNP relative to their prices in the base year. For example, the GNP deflator for 1989 relative to the 1982 base year was 1.263 (= 5,233/4,143), indicating that prices were 26.3 percent higher on average in 1989 than in 1982. Index numbers such as the GNP deflator are often multiplied by 100 to convert them to percentages. Accordingly, the 1989 GNP deflator might also be written as 126.3.

The **GNP deflator** is a measure of the price level obtained by dividing nominal GNP by real GNP.

Table 16.6 shows nominal GNP, real GNP, and the (percentage) GNP deflator

Table 16.6

Nominal GNP, Real GNP, and the price level: 1960–89

YEAR	NOMINAL GNP *(Billions of Dollars)*	REAL GNP *(Billions of 1982 Dollars)*	GNP DEFLATOR *(1982 = 100)*	RATE OF INFLATION *(Percent per Year)*
1960	515	1665	30.9	1.6
1961	534	1709	31.2	1.0
1962	575	1799	31.9	2.2
1963	607	1873	32.4	1.6
1964	650	1973	32.9	1.5
1965	705	2088	33.8	2.7
1966	772	2208	35.0	3.6
1967	816	2271	35.9	2.6
1968	893	2366	37.7	5.0
1969	964	2423	39.8	5.6
1970	1016	2416	42.0	5.5
1971	1103	2485	44.4	5.7
1972	1213	2609	46.5	4.7
1973	1359	2744	49.5	6.5
1974	1473	2729	54.0	9.1
1975	1598	2695	59.3	9.8
1976	1783	2827	63.1	6.4
1977	1991	2959	67.3	6.7
1978	2250	3115	72.2	7.3
1979	2508	3192	78.6	8.9
1980	2732	3187	85.7	9.0
1981	3053	3249	94.0	9.7
1982	3166	3166	100.0	6.4
1983	3406	3279	103.9	3.9
1984	3772	3501	107.7	3.7
1985	4015	3619	110.9	3.0
1986	4232	3718	113.8	2.6
1987	4524	3854	117.4	3.2
1988	4881	4024	121.3	3.3
1989	5233	4143	126.3	4.1

Source: *Economic Report of the President, 1990.*

for the years 1960 to 1989. (The notation "1982 = 100" tells us that the base year for the GNP deflator is 1982; the base year value of any index number is always 100 percent.) Over the period shown in the table, nominal GNP increased more than tenfold from $515 billion to $5,233 billion. This increase in nominal GNP, however, reflected only about a two-and-one-half-fold increase in real GNP from $1,665 billion to $4,143 billion. The remainder of the increase in nominal GNP reflects the effects of persistent inflation which raised the price level more than fourfold from 30.9 to 126.3 over the same period. The annual rates of inflation, as measured by the annual percentage increase in the GNP deflator, are shown in the last column of the table.

Deflating a Nominal Value to Get a Real Value

To **deflate** a variable is to divide its nominal value by a price index to obtain a measure of its real value (i.e., its value in base year prices).

Using Y to denote nominal GNP, Q to denote real GNP, and P to denote the price level (decimal value), the definition of the GNP deflator is $P = Y/Q$. Alternatively, we can state the relationship among the three variables as $Q = Y/P$. This illustrates the process of **deflating** the nominal value of a variable to obtain its real value. (Perhaps you have been wondering about the significance of the terminology, GNP "deflator.") Deflating is just another word for dividing a nominal value by a (decimal valued) price index. It adjusts the nominal value for changes in the price level by converting it into dollars of base year purchasing power. For example, suppose that your nominal earnings increased from $300 per week in 1983 to $350 per week in 1989, and you want to know how your real earnings changed as a result. We can answer that question by deflating both nominal amounts to the same base year purchasing power and then comparing them. From Table 16.6, the decimal value of the GNP deflator for 1983 is 1.039 and for 1989 is 1.263. Using these to deflate your nominal earnings converts each to real 1982 purchasing power, namely, $288.74 (= $300/1.039) for 1983 and $277.12 (= $350/1.263) for 1989. In this hypothetical example, therefore, your real earnings—that is, your purchasing power—has fallen.

The Consumer Price Index

The **consumer price index (CPI)** is a price index that tracks the average price of a market basket of consumer goods.

The **consumer price index**, or CPI, is another closely watched measure of prices. The CPI tracks the prices of a "market basket" of goods and services purchased by a typical urban household. Because this market basket includes only consumer goods, the CPI is more narrowly focused than the GNP deflator. Its primary importance lies in its widespread use in determining automatic cost-of-living adjustments (COLAs) for social security recipients, federal government employees, the members of labor unions, and many other groups. Whenever the CPI rises, the incomes of the people in these groups are increased in proportion to compensate for changes in their "cost of living."

CHAPTER SUMMARY

1. The *national income and product accounts* measure the nation's aggregate annual *flows* of income and output.

2. The *value added* by an individual producer is that producer's contribution to the value of final output. As a measure of the aggregate value of final output, national product equals the total value added in the economy during the year.

3. For the purposes of the national income accounts, income includes only payments for current productive services. Moreover, since the income created at each stage in a production process is equal to the value added at that stage, national income is also equal to the total value added in the economy during the year.

4. Since national product and national income are each equal to aggregate value added, they also equal one another. The equivalence of national income and national product is known as the *basic national income accounting identity*.

5. *Gross national product*, or *GNP*, includes all currently produced capital goods with no allowance for depreciation, thereby treating all new capital goods as final goods. *Net national product*, or *NNP*, nets out the depreciation (or capital consumption) of existing capital goods, in effect treating it as an intermediate good.

6. The national income accounts do not measure the substantial economic activity that takes place in the household, the "underground economy," or illegal markets.

7. Actual GNP is measured in two ways: The *expenditure approach* sums annual consumer expenditures, business investment expenditures, government purchases (which do not include government transfer payments), and net exports. The *incomes* approach sums all incomes earned during the year.

8. Aggregate *personal income* includes all national income that actually ends up in the hands of persons (as distinct from corporations and government) plus transfer payments to persons. *Disposable personal income* is personal income minus personal taxes.

9. The portion of disposable personal income not spent on consumption is *personal saving*. As a residual, it includes the purchase of any nonconsumption assets.

10. Investment in any given year must be equal to total saving, which is the sum of personal saving, government saving (the government budget surplus), and foreign saving (the negative of net exports).

11. The *GNP deflator* is the broadest measure of a nation's price level. It is calculated as the ratio of *nominal GNP* (GNP in current prices) to *real GNP* (current year GNP valued in *base year* prices). The *consumer price index* is a narrower measure of the price level. It tracks the average price of a "market basket" of consumer goods.

Key Terms and Concepts

national income and product accounts
stock
flow
value added
basic national income accounting identity
gross national product (GNP)
net national product (NNP)
personal income
disposable personal income
personal saving
nominal GNP
real GNP
GNP deflator
deflate
consumer price index (CPI)

Questions for Thought and Discussion

1. A bakery produces $1,000 worth of cookies. It pays $400 for flour, $300 for other ingredients, $200 for wages, and keeps $100 as profit. What is the bakery's value added?
2. Which of the following receipts of income would be considered part of 1990 national income?
   a. The amount over and above his regular salary that each employee of the Megabux Corp. receives as part of the company's 1990 profit sharing plan.
   b. A widow's 1990 receipts from her deceased husband's life insurance policy.
   c. That portion of a worker's earnings that are deducted from her paycheck in 1990 as contributions to the social security fund.
   d. That portion of its 1990 profits kept by a corporation in the form of retained earnings.
3. Per capita GNP in the United States in 1984 was $15,380; in Mexico it was $1,795; in the Sudan it was $230 (all measured in constant 1983 prices). Do you think that these figures accurately portray the economic gulfs separating these countries?
4. Use the information in the following table to compute the values of *gross national product, net national product*, and *national income*.

Consumer expenditures	= 1500	Imports	= 300
Gross investment expenditures	= 500	Government transfer payments	= 700
Government purchases	= 600	Depreciation	= 400
Exports	= 200	Indirect business taxes	= 100

5. Is "consumer expenditure" the same thing as "consumption?"
6. Suppose that 1982 GNP valued in 1982 prices is $2,000, 1990 GNP valued in 1982 prices is $3,000, 1982 GNP valued in 1990 prices is $4,000, and 1990 GNP valued in 1990 prices is $5,000. What is the (percentage) value of the *GNP deflator for 1990* relative to *base year 1982*? What is the value of the *1982 GNP deflator* relative to *base year 1990*?

CHAPTER 17

Money, Banking, and the Federal Reserve

Money, like wine, must always be scarce.
ADAM SMITH *

As your parents have undoubtedly told you many times over, "Money doesn't grow on trees." But have they told you where it does come from? Probably not. In this chapter we fill this gap in your knowledge by examining the nation's *money supply*—what it is, where it comes from, and how it changes. As we see in subsequent chapters, variations in a nation's money supply are an important determinant of its overall macroeconomic performance.

WHAT QUALIFIES AS MONEY?

If you're like most people, when you think of money you probably think of little green pieces of paper printed by the government and embossed with fancy engraving and presidential portraits. In the United States, these little pieces of paper are called *Federal Reserve notes* because they are issued by the Federal Reserve System, or Fed, the U.S. central bank. They are indeed part of the money supply, but as we shall see, only a relatively small part.

* *The Wealth of Nations* (Modern Library Edition), p. 406.

The Functions of Money

History shows that money can take many forms other than paper. It also demonstrates that money exists not because the Fed or some other government agency wills it into existence, but rather because people find it useful. As we saw in Chapter 2, transactions costs are substantially reduced when a common and generally accepted *medium of exchange* replaces barter as a means of obtaining goods. This common medium of exchange is money, and it enables people to engage in trade without a "double coincidence of wants," that is, without a costly search for trading partners whose wants exactly complement their own. In a money economy, a carpenter who wants a steak for dinner doesn't have to find a butcher who wants a house built. He simply sells his carpentry services for money and uses the money to buy the steak; the butcher then can use the money to buy whatever he wants.

In principle, anything commonly accepted as means of payment can serve as the medium of exchange. At various times and in various places, things as diverse as shells, fishhooks, salt, beads, gold, and other precious metals have served as media of exchange. In prisoner-of-war camps during World War II, prisoners found it convenient to use cigarettes as their medium of exchange. When the government decrees its little pieces of paper to be "legal tender," therefore, it is simply backing their general acceptability with the force of law. Money itself would exist in one form or another whether or not the government ran its printing presses.

With money used in all exchanges, it is only natural to also use it as the common denominator for measuring and comparing the values of the goods that are exchanged. Accordingly, money serves not only as the medium of exchange but also as the *unit of account*. As such, it enables us to compare the values of apples and oranges, of Volkswagens and Van Goghs, and anything else that is exchanged for money.

Finally, money is an asset, a form in which people can hold their wealth. In this capacity, money is said to serve as a *store of value*.

An asset's **liquidity** depends on the transaction cost of converting it into something usable in exchange and the stability of its monetary value; the lower the transactions cost and the more certain its monetary value, the greater the asset's liquidity.

Demand deposits are deposits in banks and other financial institutions that are payable on the demand of the depositor, usually by honoring the depositor's check.

Defining Money: Liquidity

The characteristic that distinguishes money from other assets is its **liquidity**. The more liquid an asset, the lower the transaction cost of exchanging it for other goods and the more stable its monetary value. Figure 17.1 on the following page ranks various assets according to their liquidity. *Currency*, which consists of coins and Federal Reserve notes, is the most liquid of all. The monetary value of currency is fixed almost by definition, and about the only transaction cost of using it is the effort of reaching into your pocket or purse. Close behind currency in terms of liquidity are *checkable deposits*. These include balances in ordinary checking accounts, or **demand deposits**, so-named because their owners can withdraw them on demand simply by writing a check. A few strokes of a pen, perhaps showing a driver's license or other identification, and payment is made. Other checkable deposits, including those that pay interest, are subject to restric-

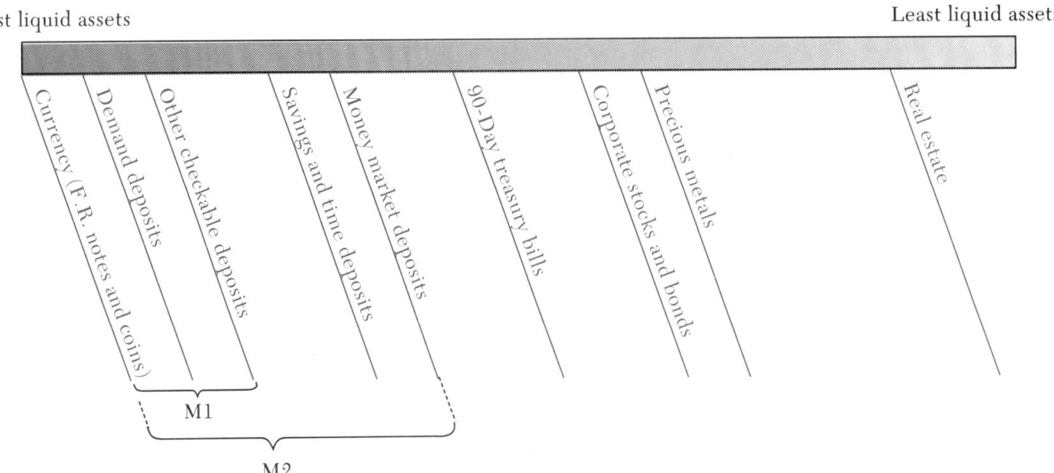

Figure 17.1

The liquidity spectrum

tions such as minimum balance requirements or limitations on the number or size of checks that can be written against them. They are very liquid, but not quite as liquid as standard demand deposits.

Time deposits are deposits in banks and other financial institutions for which the institution can legally require notice (usually 30 days) before withdrawal.

Next come savings account balances, or **time deposits**. Before they can be spent, the depositor may have to make a trip to the bank or savings and loan to convert them to cash or telephone to transfer them to a checking account. Less liquid still are assets such as bonds and shares of stock, which require the payment of brokerage fees before they can be converted into spendable cash or checking account balances, and whose monetary value can fluctuate on a daily basis. Finally, real assets such as land, antiques, and capital goods may impose substantial transactions costs when their owners convert them into spendable assets—that is, when their owners *liquidate* them.

The Official Definitions of Money: M1 and M2

M1 is the narrowly defined money supply consisting of currency and demand deposits in the hands of the nonbank public.

Where along this spectrum should we draw the line separating money from other assets? Actually, the Fed has chosen to draw more than one line and, as a result, has provided us with more than one definition of money. The narrowest one, officially known as **M1**, emphasizes money's role as a medium of exchange. As such, it includes only those assets that are directly acceptable as means of payment, namely, *currency, checkable deposits, and travelers' checks*. The value of M1 was $798 billion at the end of 1989. As Figure 17.2 shows, demand deposits and other checkable deposits accounted for nearly three-fourths of that amount, with the remaining one-fourth consisting of currency. (Travelers' checks are such a small portion of M1 that we can safely ignore them in our discussion of the determinants of the money supply.)

Figure 17.2

The composition of M1 in billions of dollars: 1989. Total M1 = $798 billion

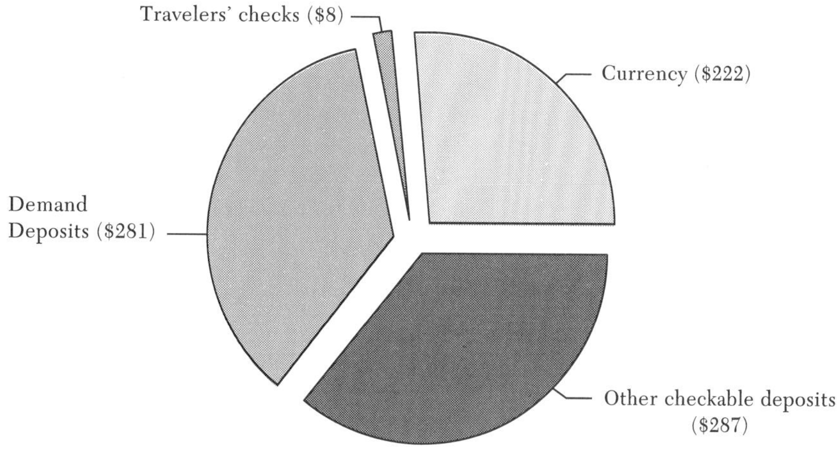

Figure 17.3

The composition of M2 in billions of dollars: 1989. Total M2 = $3,217 billion

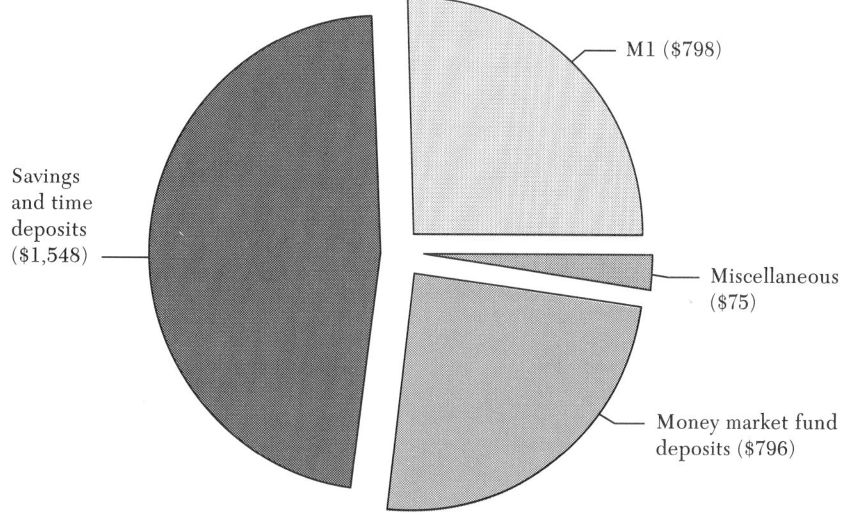

M2 defines a money supply consisting of M1 (currency plus demand deposits), savings and small time deposits, and deposits in money market funds.

Because funds held in savings accounts, other small time deposits, and money market funds can be so easily converted into currency or checkable deposits, they are almost as liquid as checkable deposits. The Fed therefore includes them in a broader definition of the money supply known as M2. *M2 includes everything in M1 plus savings and small time deposits and deposits in money market funds.* M2 was $3,217 billion at the end of 1989. Figure 17.3 shows its composition.

It is important to note that only liquid assets held by the general public outside of banks and other "depository institutions," such as savings and loans, count as part of the money supply. The reason is quite simple. Suppose you were to take a $100 bill to your bank and deposit it in your checking account. What you have done is exchanged one form of money (currency) for another (a checking account balance). However, if we were to count the extra $100 that the bank now has in its vault as part of the money supply, we would be counting it twice, first as the new $100 balance in your checking account and, second, as a $100 bill in the bank's vault. We avoid this by excluding assets held by banks and other depository institutions from our definitions of money.

The Value of Money

As the preceding discussion makes clear, our money supply consists almost entirely of pieces of paper and bookkeeping entries that keep track of balances in banks and other depository institutions. Contrary to popular belief, none of this money is backed by gold, silver, or any other precious metal. In other words, our money supply is made up almost entirely of **fiat money**. Fiat money's acceptability is based not on its intrinsic value, which is virtually nil for paper money, but rather on its special legal status. This status is made explicit in the words, "This note is legal tender for all debts, public and private" printed on every Federal Reserve note. (Although coins are not pure fiat money, their value in exchange also far exceeds the intrinsic value of the metal they contain.)

Fiat money is money whose value in exchange is determined by its legal status rather than by its intrinsic value.

It may seem strange to you that Federal Reserve notes and bookkeeping entries can be exchanged for things obviously worth many times their intrinsic value. Does this mean that our monetary system is a house of cards built on a foundation of sand? What, if anything, makes fiat money worth anything at all?

A simple application of supply and demand can answer the second question—although it may not dispel the concern implied by the first. People demand fiat money because, as legal tender, it is useful in reducing the transactions costs of exchange. Given this demand, the value, or price, of money—like that of any other useful good—is determined by the available supply.

But, you may ask, isn't the price of a dollar . . . well . . . just a dollar? Ah yes! But remember, supply and demand determine the *relative* prices, or exchange ratios, among goods. The relative price of money thus reflects the other goods for which money can be exchanged—in other words, its *purchasing power*. As long as the supply of money is limited relative to the demand, the value of money, and thus its purchasing power, will be maintained.

This simple supply-and-demand analysis points to a potential problem with fiat money. As with any good, if the supply of money increases relative to the demand, its value will fall. As we saw in Chapter 15, a fall in the purchasing power of money is just another name for a rise in the price level, or inflation. If those responsible for supplying those fancy little pieces of paper get carried away and run their printing presses too fast, therefore, the result is inflation. Indeed, the kind of hyperinflation we described in Chapter 15 is invariably the result of extraordinarily rapid increases in a nation's money supply.

This danger has led many thoughtful people, including some economists, to argue that **commodity money** would be preferable to fiat money. More accu-

Commodity money is money that is backed by a commodity with intrinsic economic value such as gold or silver.

rately, they favor a commodity-backed monetary system in which every dollar of paper money would be backed by a certain amount of some real commodity, say, 1/100 of an ounce of gold. The natural scarcity of the underlying commodity would limit the supply of paper money and thus prevent runaway inflation. Many proponents of a commodity-backed system propose a return to the *gold standard* on which, in one form or another, the monetary systems of the United States and other industrial nations were based until 1971.

Tying the supply of money to that of some particular commodity is not without problems, however. For one thing, the opportunity cost of commodity-backed money is generally higher than the opportunity cost of paper. Gold in Fort Knox cannot be used to make wedding rings or watch bands; silver used to back paper money cannot be used to coat photographic film or fill teeth. Indeed, the very evolution of paper money itself reflects attempts to economize on the use of more costly monetary commodities.

Also, and perhaps more importantly, the supply of gold, silver, or any other commodity is not systematically related to the economy's demand for money. Capricious fluctuations in the supply of the monetary commodity could contribute to economic instability by causing similar fluctuations in the supply of money. Discoveries of gold and silver in the New World in the sixteenth century, for example, flooded the economies of Europe with new money and led to a prolonged period of high inflation.

Finally, if we don't trust the government to exercise restraint in running its monetary printing presses, why should we trust it with the authority to arbitrarily determine how much commodity backing money should have? After all, reducing the amount of gold required to back a dollar from 1/100 of an ounce to 1/200 of an ounce would have the same effect as doubling the output of fiat money from the printing press.*

We have more to say about the gold standard and other proposals for commodity-backed money in our subsequent discussion of monetary policy. We simply note here that, for better or for worse, the United States and other industrial nations have adopted fiat monies, thereby implicitly choosing to rely on the not-always-so-reliable discretion of governments to preserve the value of those monies by limiting their supplies.

MONEY AND THE BANKING SYSTEM

Because most money is held as deposit balances in banks and other financial institutions, a knowledge of banking basics is essential for understanding how the money supply is controlled and managed by the Fed.

*A reduction in the amount of the commodity backing of money is called "devaluation." The numerous instances of devaluation during the period when most of the industrial world was on the gold standard should make us suspicious of the ability of commodity backing alone to guarantee monetary stability.

Once upon a time, not very long ago, there were some pretty clear distinctions between commercial banks and other depository institutions. Commercial banks were the only ones that could hold checkable deposits, and those deposits were confined to non-interest-bearing demand deposits; savings and loans, mutual savings banks, and credit unions could hold only savings deposits. Moreover, all interest-bearing deposits were subject to interest rate ceilings. There were no deposits in money market funds because there were no money market funds. Commercial bank loans were mainly business and personal loans; savings and loan associations extended only mortgage credit to home buyers; and credit unions only made small personal loans for items like cars and furniture.

All this was changed by an act of Congress. The Monetary Control Act of 1980 allowed all depository institutions to hold checkable deposits, lifted restrictions on the kinds of loans various types of financial institutions could make, eliminated interest rate ceilings on deposits, and brought all depository institutions under the authority of the Federal Reserve System. In effect, it virtually eliminated the distinctions between commercial banks and other depository institutions. We therefore simply refer to all such institutions generically as banks.

The Bank's Balance Sheet

The basic operations of a bank are best understood by examining its balance sheet. Table 17.1 shows selected items on the balance sheet of the hypothetical Greenback National Bank. The first item on the asset side of Greenback's balance sheet is the currency, or cash, that it keeps in its vault. (Remember, this vault cash is not part of the money supply because it is not in the hands of the nonbank public.)

The second item on the asset side, "Deposits at the Fed," requires more explanation. Because the Fed provides services for banks similar to the services that banks provide for their customers, it helps to think of the Fed as a "bankers' bank." For example, just as banks hold deposits for households and businesses, the Fed in turn holds deposits for banks; just as households and businesses can borrow from banks, banks can borrow from the Fed. The "Deposits at the Fed" entry on Greenback's balance sheet reflects the balance in its account at the Fed. Only banks that are members of the Federal Reserve System (which includes all

Table 17.1

Balance sheet of Greenback National Bank in millions of dollars

ASSETS		LIABILITIES AND NET WORTH	
Vault cash	1	Deposits of customers	60
Deposits at the Fed	5	Discounts at the Fed	2
Loans to customers	44	Other	3
Other	20	Net Worth	5
Total	70	Total	70

banks chartered by the federal government) are required to have an account with the Fed; most other banks have one anyway. In any case, a bank's deposits in its account at the Fed earn no interest.

The third item on the asset side of the balance sheet reflects the loans Greenback has made to its customers. When Greenback extends a loan, it receives in return a promise from the borrower to repay the loan at some future date. That promise, or IOU, is an asset for the bank because it is a claim to future payment.

The "Other" category on the asset side of Greenback's balance sheet includes its holdings of government and corporate bonds, as well as its physical assets such as buildings, computers, and other capital equipment.

The first item on the liability side of the balance sheet is the total of all balances in the accounts of Greenback's depositors. These balances are liabilities for Greenback because its depositors can claim them by making withdrawals or, in the case of checkable deposits, by writing checks against them. In effect, Greenback owes these balances to its depositors.

The next item on the liability side of Greenback's balance sheet, "Discounts at the Fed," is the amount Greenback owes the Fed as a result of its borrowing. The terminology comes from the fact that bank borrowing from the Fed is called *discounting* and the *discount rate* is the interest rate which the Fed charges banks for their loans.*

Finally, the right-hand side of Greenback's balance sheet includes its other liabilities and its net worth, which is the difference between its assets and its liabilities.

Reserve Requirements and Deposit Expansion

Bank reserves include bank holdings of vault cash and deposits at the Fed that satisfy the Fed's reserve requirement.

The **required reserve ratio** is the minimum fraction of a bank's deposits that it must hold as reserves.

The Fed requires all banks to hold **bank reserves** against their deposit liabilities. *Vault cash and deposits at the Fed are the only assets that qualify as reserves; their sum must equal some minimum fraction of the bank's deposit liabilities.*† This fraction, called the **required reserve ratio**, is set by the Fed and varies according to the type of deposit and the size of the bank. At the beginning of the 1990s, required reserve ratios ranged from 3 percent on most savings deposits and small time deposits to 12 percent on checkable deposits in large banks.

Contrary to widely held belief, the function of the reserve requirement is *not* to make sure that banks have enough cash on hand to pay off their depositors in the unlikely event that they all want to withdraw funds at the same time. Given that a bank's reserves are only a small fraction of its total deposit liabilities, and that it holds only a small fraction of those reserves as cash, reserves clearly do not make the bank a "currency warehouse" for its depositors. Rather the prin-

*The term *discounting* comes from the way in which these loans are made. To obtain a loan from the Fed, the bank puts up assets as collateral and receives a loan equal to the present discounted value of those assets.

†Banks that are not members of the Federal Reserve System may choose to hold their reserves as deposits at other banks rather than at the Fed. For our purposes, we can ignore this technicality.

cipal function of the reserve requirement is to limit the amount of credit that the banking system can extend.

To see how the reserve requirement limits bank credit, let us simplify by assuming that the required reserve ratio is a uniform 10 percent on all deposits. According to the numbers in Table 17.1, Greenback National Bank has just enough reserves to meet this 10 percent reserve requirement: The sum of its $1 million in vault cash and $5 million balance in its Fed account equals exactly 10 percent of its $60 million deposit liability.

Now suppose that one of Greenback's customers, we'll call her Alice, deposits $10,000 in cash into her account. Greenback now has an additional $10,000 of deposit liabilities, against which it must hold an additional $1,000 in required reserves. However, Greenback also has an additional $10,000 cash in its vault, all of which is new reserves. As a result of Alice's deposit, therefore, Greenback now has $9,000 of **excess reserves**, that is, reserves over and above those required by the Fed. These changes in Greenback's balance sheet are summarized in Step 1 of the monetary expansion process depicted in Table 17.2.

A bank's **excess reserves** are reserves over and above the minimum required by the Fed.

Excess reserves, whether held as vault cash or as deposits at the Fed, earn nothing, so Greenback National Bank will want to put those reserves to work. It can do so by making a loan. To see how this works, suppose that Ben, another of Greenback's customers, wants to borrow $9,000 to buy a used car. With $9,000 in excess reserves, Greenback is in a position to make such a loan. It does so by accepting Ben's IOU and adding $9,000 to his checking account balance. (If Ben does not already have a checking account at Greenback, the bank will open one for him with an initial balance of $9,000, the amount of the loan.) The effect of the loan on Greenback's balance sheet is reflected in Step 2 of Table 17.2. The $9,000 added to Ben's checking account is new money created by the extension of bank credit. When banks have excess reserves, they use those reserves to expand credit and, in effect, create new money. (Note that the extra $10,000 in Alice's account is *not* new money; she simply exchanged $10,000 in currency for a $10,000 deposit balance.)

Of course, Ben didn't take out his loan just to hold the funds in a checking account and pay interest on them. Thus we can safely assume that the $9,000 in Ben's account won't be there long. When he writes a check to buy his car, the $9,000 balance in his account is extinguished; however, it does not disappear from the money supply. In fact, it allows the money supply to expand even further.

To see why, suppose Ben buys the car from Carl's Autorama. Carl takes Ben's check for $9,000 and deposits it in his account at Wampum Bank. Now the check must *clear*. Check clearing is a service provided for most banks by the Fed. It involves a bookkeeping operation that adjusts bank reserve accounts to reflect the flow of money between banks. In our example, Ben's check represents a withdrawal of $9,000 from Greenback National Bank, so that amount is deducted from Greenback's account at the Fed. Since the check was deposited in Wampum Bank, $9,000 is added to Wampum's account at the Fed. Step 3 in Table 17.2 shows the situation in both banks after the check has cleared. Ben now has a zero balance in his account at Greenback National, and Greenback is

Table 17.2

The process of monetary expansion

STEP 1

GREENBACK NATIONAL BANK

Assets		*Liabilities*	
Vault cash	+ 10,000	Deposits of customers:	
		Alice	+ 10,000
Total reserves	+ 10,000		
Required reserves	+ 1,000		
Excess reserves	+ 9,000		

STEP 2

GREENBACK NATIONAL BANK

Assets		*Liabilities*	
Vault cash	+ 10,000	Deposits of customers:	
Loans to customers:		Alice	+ 10,000
Ben	+ 9,000	Ben	+ 9,000

STEP 3

GREENBACK NATIONAL BANK

Assets		*Liabilities*	
Vault cash	+ 10,000	Deposits of customers:	
Deposits at the Fed	− 9,000	Alice	+ 10,000
		Ben	0
Net change in reserves	+ 1,000		
Loans to customers:			
Ben	+ 9,000		

WAMPUM BANK

Assets		*Liabilities*	
Deposits at the Fed	+ 9,000	Deposits of customers:	
		Carl's Autorama	+ 9,000
Total reserves	+ 9,000		
Required reserves	+ 900		
Excess reserves	+ 8,100		

left with a net increase in reserves of $1,000 ($10,000 more in vault cash from Alice's initial deposit, but $9,000 less in its account at the Fed). At the 10 percent reserve requirement, this is just enough to hold against Alice's $10,000 deposit. With no excess reserves, Greenback cannot make any more loans; in banking parlance, it is *loaned up*.*

Not so for Wampum Bank, however. After he deposits Ben's check, Carl has an additional $9,000 in his account at Wampum Bank, against which Wampum must hold an additional $900 in reserves. However, Wampum had $9,000 added to its reserve account at the Fed when Ben's check cleared. Thus Wampum now has excess reserves of $8,100 which it can lend. When it does, the money supply will increase by another $8,100.

We could continue the story indefinitely, changing only the numbers for each round of new loans. Someone will borrow the $8,100 from Wampum, write a check for that amount, and the check will be deposited in some other bank. That bank will then have an additional $8,100 in deposit liabilities and an additional $8,100 in its account at the Fed. Of that amount, $810 will be required reserves and the remainder, $7,290, will be excess reserves. This will make possible another loan and a further increase in the money supply by $7,290, which will be deposited in some other bank, and so on.

Table 17.3 illustrates the cumulative effect of this process of monetary expansion. The first four rounds, which we have traced, led to a cumulative deposit expansion of $34,390, of which all but the first $10,000 represents new money. By the tenth round, deposit expansion has reached $65,132, and by the twenty-fifth round it has reached $92,821. It will have reached $100,000 of new deposits and $90,000 of new money by the time the process has worked its way completely through the banking system.

Can you see how the expansion of deposits is related to both the initial change in bank reserves and the required reserve ratio? The banking system got an extra $10,000 in reserves as a result of Alice's deposit of cash. With a 10 percent required reserve ratio, each dollar of those new reserves will support $10 of new deposit liabilities, or a total of $100,000. If the required reserve ratio were 20 percent instead of 10 percent, each dollar of new reserves would support only $5 new of deposits and total deposit expansion would have been only $50,000. In this example, therefore, the maximum total deposit expansion is equal to the initial change in bank reserves divided by the required reserve ratio (or multiplied by its reciprocal).

The same process works in reverse. If Alice had withdrawn $10,000 cash from her account, Greenback would have lost reserves and been forced to reduce its deposit liabilities. It would do so by allowing existing loans to be paid off faster than new loans are made, thereby building up its reserves relative to its deposit liabilities until it reached a legal reserve position. The money used to pay off the Greenback loans would be withdrawn from other banks, which would

*Can you see why Greenback cannot lend Ben more than $9,000? If it does it will be left with less than $1,000 in net new reserves when Ben's check clears, and thus it will not have enough reserves to hold against Alice's deposit. As a rule, therefore, a bank can safely lend no more than its excess reserves.

Table 17.3
Total deposit expansion

ROUND #	NEW DEPOSITS (* = NEW MONEY)	CUMULATIVE NEW DEPOSITS
1	$ 10,000	$ 10,000
2	9,000*	19,000
3	8,100*	27,100
4	7,290*	34,390
5	6,561*	40,951
.	.	.
.	.	.
.	.	.
10	3,487*	65,132
.	.	.
.	.	.
.	.	.
25	718*	92,821
.	.	.
.	.	.
.	.	.
All remaining rounds	7,179*	$100,000
Total deposit expansion =	$100,000	
New money =	$ 90,000	

lose some of their reserves, be forced to curtail their lending, and so on. The process would continue until the banking system's $10,000 loss of reserves was matched by a $100,000 reduction in its total deposit liabilities.

The Money Multiplier

The **money multiplier** measures the change in bank deposits per dollar change in bank reserves.

The change in bank deposits per dollar change in bank reserves is known as the **money multiplier**.* In the foregoing example, where a $10,000 change in reserves led ultimately to a $100,000 change in deposits, the money multiplier was 10, which is simply the reciprocal of the required reserve ratio. In reality, however, things are a little more complicated. For one thing, there is not just one, but a number of required reserve ratios applicable to different types of deposits and different sizes of banks. The money multiplier is therefore affected by the

*Technically, this is really a "deposit multiplier." The money multiplier is usually defined as the change in the money supply per dollar change in reserves *plus* publicly held currency. Since we consider only the effects of reserve changes, this technicality is unimportant for our purposes.

allocation of money among different types of deposit accounts and among deposit accounts in banks of different sizes. The greater the fraction of their deposits people hold in accounts with high-reserve requirements, the smaller the money multiplier, and vice versa.

Our simple example of deposit expansion also assumed that banks immediately lend all of their excess reserves. Although they certainly have an incentive to do so since idle reserves earn nothing, they must first find suitable borrowers. Because this typically cannot be done instantaneously, the banking system always operates with some excess reserves. Though a very small amount in relation to total reserves—usually much less than 1 percent—average excess reserve holdings also affect the relation between reserve changes and money supply changes. In particular, the more excess reserves held by banks, the smaller the impact of a reserve change on deposit expansion and thus the smaller the money multiplier.

Finally, our example of deposit expansion did not take into account the *currency drain*. In particular, people typically hold a portion of their money as currency, and money held as currency does not serve as bank reserves. To illustrate the impact of the currency drain, suppose that in the second round of our example Carl had deposited only $5,000 of the $9,000 he received from Ben into his Wampum Bank account. Wampum would then have had only $4,500 instead of $8,100 in excess reserves to lend. As a result, the amount of new loans by Wampum in the next round, and by all other banks in successive rounds of the expansion process, would have been less. The greater the currency drain, therefore, the lower the value of the money multiplier.

Only one of the factors affecting the money multiplier, namely, required reserve ratios, is under the direct control of the Fed. The proportion of their deposits people hold in high-reserve accounts relative to low-reserve accounts, the proportion of their money people wish to hold as currency, and the amount of excess reserves held by the banking system are determined by choices made by the general public and the banking system.

Figures 17.4(a) and (b) show the behavior of the money multipliers for M1 and M2 (calculated as the ratio of M1 and M2, respectively, to total bank reserves) since 1985. As you can see, after relatively sharp declines in the mid-1980s, both multipliers began to rise again during the latter part of the decade.

Money versus Credit

As the preceding discussion makes clear, there is a close relation between monetary expansion and credit expansion. Money and credit are not the same thing, however, and monetary expansion is only one means by which credit can be extended. The relationship between money and credit is an important one, and one that deserves closer examination.

In a modern monetary economy, we can obtain goods in a simultaneous exchange for money or in exchange for the *promise* of a future payment of money. The latter type of exchange is of course a credit transaction. Both money and

Figure 17.4

Money multipliers

(a) The M1 money multiplier (M1/reserves)

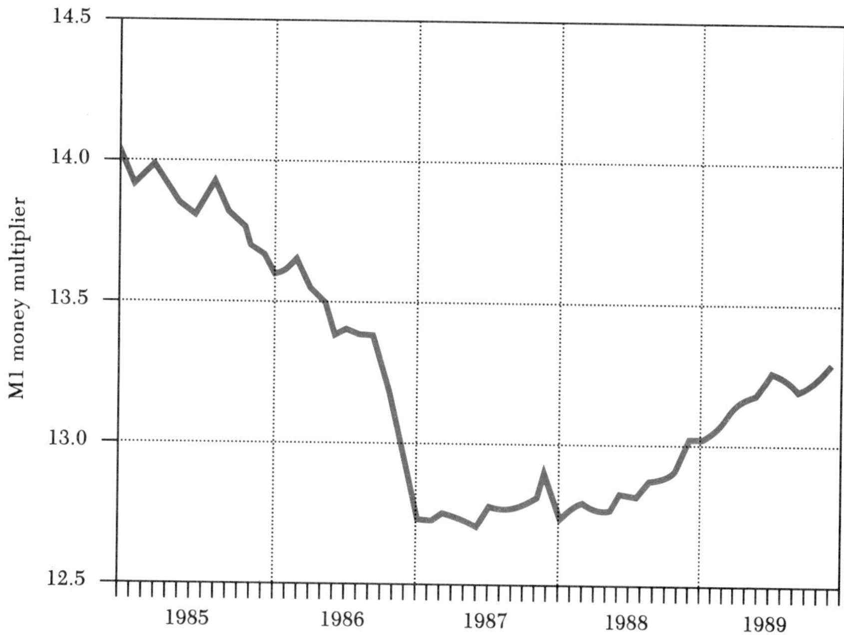

(b) The M2 money multiplier (M2/reserves)

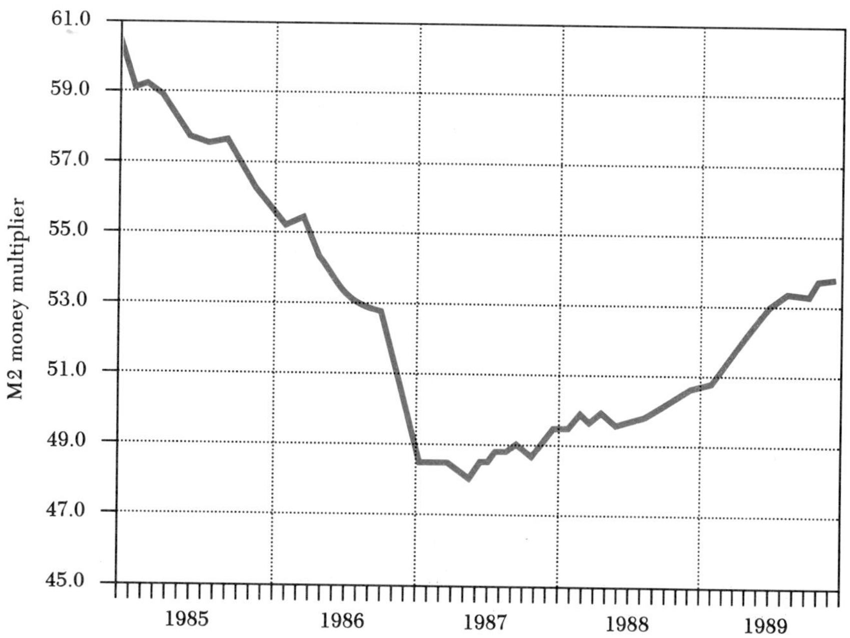

credit are therefore media of exchange, and, as such, both reduce transactions costs. We have seen how money reduces transactions costs by eliminating the necessity for a "double coincidence of wants." Credit goes a step further, reducing transactions costs by allowing buyers and sellers to consolidate many small payments into a single transaction and to coordinate payments with receipts of income. As an illustration, consider the billing practices of the utility companies that provide your electricity and water. These companies typically bill their customers each month for services consumed during the previous month, in effect extending them a month's worth of credit. Imagine how much more costly it would be for *both* the utility company and its customers if transactions were on a pay-as-you-consume basis. A transaction would have to take place each time someone turned on a light or flushed a toilet!

Money and credit are substitutes in any particular transaction—you can "pay now or pay later." However, they are also complements in exchange for, without the use of money to eventually settle debts, credit transactions would have almost all of the disadvantages of other barter transactions. The essential difference between money and credit is that money is a stock that can be used over and over again in a series of exchanges, whereas credit is a flow that arises in the context of a specific transaction. This distinction is best illustrated by means of a simple example.

Suppose you head to your local Wiltingdale's Department Store with the intent of refurbishing your entire wardrobe. After splurging on $1,000 worth of new clothes and accessories, you realize that you do not have enough money—either in cash or in your checking account—to pay for them on the spot. You do, however, have two credit options: You can either take out a consumer loan from your bank or use your Wiltingdale's charge card. Let's contrast the effects of these two credit alternatives.

When your bank uses some of its excess reserves to lend you the $1,000 for your splurge, the money supply increases by that amount. When you write the $1,000 check, you transfer the new money to Wiltingdale's, which will use it to pay its employees, who in turn will use it to make other purchases, and so on. The $1,000 of new money created through your credit transaction with the bank continues to circulate through the economy indefinitely.

If you use your Wiltingdale's charge card, no new money is created. The credit simply reflects an agreement between you and Wiltingdale's to defer the payment of money which already exists, but which is not yet in your possession. In general, therefore, credit extended through charge cards, installment contracts, and finance companies supports only the specific transaction for which it is created; it does not create any additional money that can be used in other exchanges.

The demand for and the supply of credit, which we analyzed in Chapter 4, are therefore not synonymous with the demand for and the supply of money. Moreover, the interest rate is the price of credit, not the price of money. These distinctions are particularly important in understanding the macroeconomics of money and monetary policy.

THE FED AND MONETARY POLICY

As the central bank of the United States, the Federal Reserve System is responsible for carrying out monetary policy. The system consists of twelve regional Federal Reserve Banks, each responsible for the banks and other depository institutions in its region.* The Fed's *Board of Governors* is responsible for the main regulatory guidelines, including required reserve ratios, applicable to these institutions. The Board consists of seven members, each appointed by the President and confirmed by the Senate to serve 14-year terms. To preserve the independence of the Fed from direct political tinkering, the terms are staggered so that no President can appoint more than a few members of the Board. Each President, however, does have an opportunity to appoint one of the Board members to a 4-year term as a chairman. The chairman, in turn, must report regularly to Congress on the general goals of monetary policy. Given the pressures that can be exerted by Congress and the President, the Fed's actual independence from politics is perhaps more theoretical than practical.

Open Market Operations: How the Fed Controls the Money Supply

The Fed body most directly involved in the making of monetary policy is the *Federal Open Market Committee*, or FOMC, which consists of the seven members of the Board of Governors, the president of the New York Federal Reserve Bank, and presidents of four of the other regional Federal Reserve Banks on a rotating basis.

Open market operations are the Fed's purchase and sale of government securities in the open market. Fed purchases of government securities increase bank reserves and permit monetary expansion; Fed sales of government securities reduce bank reserves and force monetary contraction.

As we have seen, changes in the money supply are directly linked to changes in bank reserves. The FOMC uses this linkage to control the money supply through its **open market operations**. Open market operations involve the Fed's purchase and sale of U.S. government securities—Treasury bills and bonds—in the open market—that is, the same market that is open to you, me, or anyone else who wants to trade in government securities. The Fed is the largest trader in that market, as well as the largest single holder of government securities. Its open market policy is determined by the FOMC, whose buy-and-sell orders are executed through an office at the New York Fed. Open market purchases of government securities by the Fed add to bank reserves, thereby allowing the money supply to expand; open market sales of government securities absorb bank reserves, thereby forcing the money supply to contract.

We can illustrate how this works by means of a simple example. Suppose the Fed purchases $100 million worth of government securities in the open market. The people who sold the securities receive checks from the Fed which they then cash or deposit in their bank accounts. Since the public now has an additional

*The regional banks are in Boston, New York, Philadelphia, Atlanta, Richmond, St. Louis, Kansas City, Chicago, Cleveland, Minneapolis, Dallas, and San Francisco.

$100 million in currency and deposits that it did not have before the Fed's open market purchase, the money supply has increased by $100 million. This is not the end of the story, however. When the banks into which the Fed's checks have been deposited present them to the Fed for clearing, the Fed credits their reserve accounts. Although some of these new reserves must be held against the banks' new deposit liabilities, most are excess reserves. If all $100 million of the Fed's checks are deposited in banks, the banks have $100 million of new deposit liabilities and $100 million of new reserves. With a 10 percent required reserve ratio, for example, $90 million of those new reserves are excess reserves that can be used to make new loans and expand the money supply still further. The total amount of monetary expansion resulting from this open market operation depends on the money multiplier. If the money multiplier has a value of 10, then the $100 million open market purchase ultimately leads to a $1 billion increase in the money supply.

When the Fed sells government securities, the same process works in reverse. Suppose, for example, that the Fed sells $100 million worth of government securities. The people who buy the securities pay for them by writing checks on their bank accounts. The reduction in the public's checking account balances represents an immediate $100 million reduction in the money supply. With $100 million less in deposit liabilities, banks can get by with $10 million less in reserves. However, the Fed has deducted $100 million from their reserve accounts when the checks cleared so that banks have actually lost more reserves than is justified by the decline in their deposit liabilities. As a result, they must curtail their lending activities, and that causes the money supply to shrink still further. The total decrease in the money supply is equal to the size of the Fed's open market sale times the money multiplier.

Other Fed Tools: Discount Policy and Changes in Required Reserves

If a bank has no excess reserves but still wants to make a loan, it must borrow the necessary reserves. It can borrow them from the Fed—use the "discount window" in banker talk—and pay interest determined by the Fed's **discount rate**. Alternatively it can borrow reserves in the **federal funds market**, a market in which banks that need reserves borrow them for short periods of time from banks that have excess reserves. The interest rate on these interbank loans is called the **federal funds rate**. Despite the terminology, the federal funds rate is *not* set by the Federal Reserve; rather it is determined by supply and demand in the federal funds market.

The **discount rate** is the interest rate the Fed charges on loans to banks.

The **federal funds market** is the market in which banks borrow and lend reserves among themselves.

The **federal funds rate** is the interest rate set by the supply of and demand for bank reserves in the federal funds market.

When a bank borrows reserves from the Fed, the result is a net addition to total bank reserves. Bank discounting thus allows the money supply to expand. In federal funds market transactions, by contrast, the reserves obtained by the borrowing bank are offset by the reserves given up by the lending bank so there is no net change in either total bank reserves or the money supply.

In theory, if the Fed wanted the money supply to expand, it could set the discount rate low relative to the federal funds rate, thereby encouraging banks to use the discount window. Conversely, if it wanted to restrict monetary expansion, it could set the discount rate high relative to the federal funds rate, thereby channelling bank borrowing into the federal funds market. In practice, however, banks are generally reluctant to borrow from the Fed, and when they do it is only in special circumstances and for a very brief time. Moreover, the Fed is quite selective in its lending, so that the discount window isn't really available to just any bank that would rather pay the discount rate than the federal funds rate. Thus changes in the discount rate, though always banner headlines in the financial pages, usually have little real impact on the money supply. They are mainly symbolic indicators of the Fed's intentions.

While we're on the subject, we should dispel one widely held myth about the discount rate. Often an increase in the discount rate is reported in the news media as an "increase in the cost of the funds banks need to make loans," the implication being that this cost will be passed along as higher interest rates to businesses and consumers. While an increase in the discount rate often *accompanies* a general increase in market interest rates, it rarely *causes* the latter. Indeed, if there is any causality, it usually runs in the opposite direction as the Fed tries to keep the discount rate in the same ballpark as market interest rates. Given the relatively small amount of borrowing by banks at the Fed's discount window, the federal funds rate provides a much better indicator than the discount rate of the marginal cost of funds to the banking system.

Another tool in the Fed's monetary toolbox, and one which is potentially powerful but also very blunt, is a change in required reserve ratios. By lowering these ratios, the Fed can instantly convert required reserves into excess reserves, thereby allowing the money supply to expand. Conversely, by raising the required reserve ratios, the Fed can instantly throw banks into a deficit position, force them to curtail their lending, and thus shrink the money supply. Because changes in reserve requirements can have such a dramatic impact on the money supply, they are rarely used as an instrument of monetary policy. For the ongoing process of monetary management, the Fed much prefers the finer control afforded by open market operations.

How Much Control Does the Fed Really Have?

The reserve changes brought about by the Fed's open market operations are transmitted to the money supply through the money multiplier. However, as we have seen, the required reserve ratios set by the Fed are only one factor in determining the value of the money multiplier; the others are beyond the Fed's control. Variations in the currency drain and in the allocation of bank deposits among different types of accounts introduce a great deal of slippage and uncertainty into the process of monetary control and greatly complicate the Fed's task. Suppose, for example, that the Fed is trying to slow money growth through open market sales while at the same time people are unexpectedly shifting funds from checking deposits with high-reserve requirements into savings deposits with low-reserve requirements. The public's reallocation of its deposit balances would at least partially offset the Fed's open market policy, as would an unexpected shift of deposits from large banks to small banks, or a decision by the public to hold less of their money as currency and more as bank deposits. Over time, the Fed can recognize such changes and react accordingly, but they make the short-term conduct of monetary policy as much an art as a science.

Unpredictable fluctuations in the value of the money multiplier at least partially explain the Fed's persistent difficulty in hitting the monetary growth targets it is required by law to announce each year. In recent years its task has been made even more difficult by the sweeping and more-or-less continuous changes in financial institutions and their regulatory environment. Nonetheless, there are those who feel that, despite the inevitability of short-term slippage, the Fed should be able to do a much better job of monetary control than it has.

Can the Government Print Money to Pay Its Bills?

Well, can it? More specifically, if the federal government's tax revenues fall short of its expenditures, can it simply print money to make up the difference?

To answer this question, we must recognize that paying the government's bills is the responsibility of the U.S. Treasury, while "printing money" is the responsibility of the Federal Reserve System.* The Treasury and the Fed are separate agencies, and neither the Secretary of the Treasury nor his boss, the President of the United States, can legally force the Fed's Board of Governors to create money. However, this does not mean that there is no relation between Treasury deficits and the money supply.

When the Treasury finances a budget deficit, it sells new government bonds. Were it to sell those bonds directly to the Fed, the Fed would credit the value of the bonds to the Treasury's checking account. (The Treasury is the only institution besides banks that can hold an account at the Fed.) The Treasury would then write checks on that account to pay defense contractors, welfare recipients, U.S. Senators, and all others parties with a claim on government expenditures. These checks would then become new money when cashed or deposited in the bank accounts of their recipients. In effect, the Fed would have created new money for the Treasury to spend. Moreover, the deposit of Treasury checks into the banking system would add to bank reserves and allow the money supply to expand still further.

In reality, the Fed is prohibited by law from buying all but an insignificant amount of new government bonds directly from the Treasury, so the preceding scenario cannot literally take place. However, this does not mean that the Fed and the Treasury, acting together, cannot create money to cover a government deficit; it just means that to do so requires a more roundabout process. In particular, suppose that for every *new* bond the Treasury sells to private individuals and businesses, the Fed buys an *already existing* government bond on the open

*The Treasury does have the authority to mint coins, but they are such a tiny part of the money supply that we can ignore them here.

market. There is nothing illegal about this; it's just an ordinary, everyday open market operation by the Fed. Yet the effect is exactly the same as if the Treasury had sold its new bonds directly to the Fed! In each case government borrowing is initially matched by an equal increase in bank reserves and the money supply; in each case the latter can then expand still further via the money multiplier.

Monetizing a government deficit involves a combination of actions by the Treasury and the Fed which, in effect, allows the government to create money to cover a budget deficit.

This kind of cooperation between the Treasury and the Fed allows the government to **monetize its deficit**, that is, to finance it through money creation. (It is also sometimes referred to as an *accommodating* monetary policy because it literally accommodates the Treasury's need for new money to spend.) We should emphasize that there is nothing that legally requires the Fed to pursue such a policy; as an independent agency it can choose whether, and to what extent, it will monetize the government's deficit. Thus, although government deficits *can* lead to money creation, they need not if the Fed's Board of Governors chooses not to accommodate the Treasury.

We examine this and other aspects of the relationship between the Fed and the Treasury more closely in subsequent chapters in the context of the relationship between monetary and fiscal policy.

CHAPTER SUMMARY

1. As a common *medium of exchange*, money reduces transactions costs by eliminating the need for a double coincidence of wants in exchange. It also serves as a common measure of value, or *unit of account*, and, as a *store of value*, it provides one form in which to hold wealth.

2. The narrow *M1* definition of money, which stresses its use as a medium of exchange, includes currency and checkable deposits (as well as travellers' checks). The *M2* definition includes everything in M1 plus savings and small time deposits and deposits in money market funds.

3. Most of our money is *fiat money*, which consists of paper and bookkeeping entries with little or no intrinsic value. Fiat money has value (purchasing power) only because it is generally accepted as means of payment and only to the extent that its supply is limited relative to the demand.

4. Banks are required to hold *reserves*, in the form of vault cash and deposits at the Fed, equal to some minimum fraction of their deposit liabilities. This fraction, known as the *required reserve ratio*, is set by the Fed.

5. Reserves over the minimum required are called *excess reserves*. Banks can use their excess reserves to make loans.

6. The *money multiplier* determines the amount of new money that can be created per dollar of additional reserves injected into the banking system. Its value depends on the required reserve ratios set by the Fed, the proportion of their money people wish to hold as currency, the proportion of their

deposits people hold in high-reserve accounts relative to low-reserve accounts, and the amount of excess reserves held by the banking system.

7. Although there is a close relation between monetary expansion and credit expansion, money and credit are not the same thing. Money is a stock that can be used over and over again in a series of exchanges; credit is a flow that arises in the context of a specific transaction.

8. The Fed uses *open market operations* to control bank reserves and, ultimately, the money supply. Open market purchases of government securities add to bank reserves, thereby allowing the money supply to expand; open market sales of government securities absorb bank reserves, thereby forcing the money supply to contract.

9. A bank can borrow additional reserves from other banks at the *federal funds rate* or from the Fed at the *discount rate*. The Fed's discount rate is mainly a symbolic indicator of its intentions, with little real impact on monetary policy. The Fed's other tool, changes in reserve requirements, is rarely used.

10. Variations in the currency drain and in the allocation of bank deposits among different types of accounts introduce a great deal of slippage and uncertainty into the process of monetary control.

11. Although the U.S. Treasury cannot literally print money to pay the government's bills, a Federal Reserve policy of *monetizing* new government debt accomplishes virtually the same thing.

Key Terms and Concepts

liquidity
demand deposits
time deposits
M1
M2
fiat money
commodity money
bank reserves
required reserve ratio
excess reserves
money multiplier
open market operations
discount rate
federal funds market
federal funds rate
monetizing a government deficit

Questions for Thought and Discussion

1. Visa and MasterCard are accepted as means of payment nearly everywhere. Why do we not consider them to be media of exchange and thus part of the money supply?

2. Suppose that you cash a check for $100. What is the immediate effect on the money supply? On your bank's reserves? How do these immediate effects differ from the ultimate effects of your transaction?

3. Your best friend wants to borrow $500 to buy a new stereo. What happens to bank reserves and the money supply if you take $500 in cash out of your piggy bank and lend it directly to your friend? What happens if you write a check for $500 and give it to her? What happens if you deposit $500 in cash into your bank account and the bank then lends her the $500?

4. You deposit $1,000 in your bank account. In terms of the effect on bank reserves and the money supply, does it make any difference whether you took the money from under your mattress or got it from the Fed in return for a U.S. government bond?

5. During the Great Depression of the 1930s, there were "runs" on a number of banks during which the public clamored to withdraw their bank deposits in the form of cold, hard cash. In response, many banks sought to build up their reserve positions, holding abnormally high amounts of excess reserves to protect themselves from a run. Assuming that the Fed did not actively try to add to bank reserves (it actually allowed reserves to shrink), what effect do you think this had on the nation's money supply?

6. Why would the U.S. or any other government want to "monetize" its deficit? Is this a real danger, or just a theoretical possibility? (Hint: Public choice theory may provide a clue.)

7. We argued that money can serve as a medium of exchange, a unit of account (a common way of measuring and comparing values), and a store of value (a form of wealth). In which sense is the word "money" used in each of the following familiar proverbs?

   a. "Remember that time is money." (Benjamin Franklin)
   b. "A fool and his money are soon parted." (Anonymous)
   c. "(Health is) a blessing that money cannot buy." (Izak Walton)
   d. "The love of money is the root of all evil." (*The New Testament*) Or, if you prefer, "Lack of money is the root of all evil." (George Bernard Shaw)

CHAPTER 18

The Roots of Modern Macroeconomics: The Classical System and the Keynesian Challenge

The ideas of economists and political philosophers, both when they are right and when they are wrong, are more powerful than is commonly understood. Indeed, the world is ruled by little else. Practical men, who believe themselves to be quite exempt from any intellectual influences, are usually the slaves of some defunct economist. Madmen in authority, who hear voices in the air, are distilling their frenzy from some academic scribbler of a few years back.

JOHN MAYNARD KEYNES*

Modern macroeconomics is not a neat package of settled issues. The differences between the classical and Keynesian traditions introduced in Chapter 15 are still the basis for continuing disagreement among economists on matters of both analysis and policy. In this chapter we therefore lay the foundations for our study of modern macroeconomics with an analysis of its classical and Keynesian roots. As we shall see, many of the issues raised here reappear in contemporary form in later chapters.

*John Maynard Keynes, *The General Theory of Employment, Interest and Money* (Harcourt, Brace & World, Harbinger Edition, 1964) p. 383.

AN OVERVIEW OF THE ISSUES

The Classical Economics of Keynes's Day

When Keynes used the term "classical economics" in his *General Theory*, he was referring to a tradition that reflected the contributions of economists from Adam Smith, who published his monumental *Wealth of Nations* in 1776, to Alfred Marshall, the great Cambridge University economist who died in 1924 and whose prize pupil was none other than Keynes himself.

Although the scores of economists who lived and wrote during the 160 years between Smith's *Wealth of Nations* and Keynes' *General Theory* disagreed on many points, there was a common theme that characterized the classical economics of Keynes's day. It was that a market economy was a fundamentally stable system in which relative price adjustments would automatically achieve market-clearing equilibria.

Consider, for example, the classical view of unemployment. Involuntary unemployment reflects a surplus in the labor market—that is, a condition in which workers offer to supply more labor than employers demand. As we have seen, a surplus puts downward pressure on price, which in the labor market is the wage. The falling wage encourages employers to hire more workers, discourages some potential workers from seeking employment, and eventually eliminates the surplus of labor. Once a market-clearing wage is attained, the amount of labor demanded by firms is just sufficient to absorb the amount supplied by workers. Classical labor market equilibrium is therefore a full-employment equilibrium. (More on this in a moment.)

But what if people don't want to buy all of the goods that can be produced by a fully employed labor force? Can there be a situation in which there is simply not enough demand for final goods to warrant employing everyone who wants to work? The classical economists dismissed this possibility of over production—or, as they called it, a general "glut" of goods—as illogical. They argued that people offer to *sell* their labor and other productive services only to earn income with which to *buy* other goods and services they wish to consume. The supply of labor therefore reflects an underlying demand for final goods. Indeed, whether an exchange involves labor services or anything else, an offer to supply one thing is always motivated by a demand to obtain something else in return. The *supply* of any good or service is thus fundamentally motivated by a matching *demand* for some other good or service. This famous classical proposition is known as **Say's Law** (after J. B. Say, an eighteenth-century French classical economist). It implies that a *general* deficiency in the demand for final goods and services is impossible. Moreover, as long as the price system works effectively to clear markets, labor and other resources that might become unemployed in markets where *relative* demand has fallen will be absorbed into markets where relative demand has risen. For example, if people decide to spend a smaller share of their incomes on food and a greater share on housing, then wage adjustments will insure that workers who become unemployed in the food market will find employment in the housing market.

Say's Law holds that a general deficiency of aggregate demand is not possible because the supply of any good or service is always motivated by a demand for some other good or service.

But, you may ask, what becomes of Say's Law when people save? Surely some people earn income to save rather than spend. Not to worry, said the classical economists. If people decide to save part of their income rather than spend it on consumer goods, then the interest rate (which, you will recall from Chapter 4, is also a relative price) will insure that all of those savings are channelled into expenditures on capital goods via the credit market.

The classical economists recognized that the wage, price, and interest rate adjustments required to keep the economy on an even keel might not be instantaneous. In that respect, they did not argue that unemployment and recession could not occur, but rather that, if they did occur, they would tend to be self-correcting and temporary.

The Keynesian Revolution

As we have seen, the inability of classical economics to explain the staggering economic events of the 1930s led Keynes to develop his own revolutionary new theory. Keynes identified the cause of the Depression as a lack of *effective demand*. As we have seen, as long as prices—including wages and interest rates—adjust quickly to clear product, labor, and capital markets, Say's Law tells us that unemployment due to insufficient demand for final goods and services is impossible. Keynes' assertion that some prices, particularly wages, tend to be downwardly rigid, or at least "sticky," led him to question the relevance of Say's Law.

To illustrate the essence of the Keynesian argument, let us consider a simple economy in which only three things are traded: labor services, widgets, and money. Figure 18.1 depicts economic activity in such an economy as a circular flow between households and business firms. Households sell labor services to firms, and firms use those labor services to produce widgets that they sell to households. As a result, there is a continuous flow of money from firms to households in payment for labor services, and back again from households and firms in payment for widgets.

Now suppose the flow of spending is interrupted. In particular, suppose that households take half the money they receive as wages and stuff it into mattresses and cookie jars. With only half as much money being spent on widgets, firms must either charge lower prices, produce fewer widgets, or both. If they can convince households to accept half as much money in wages, they can charge half the original price for their widgets and still continue to produce the same amount. Although households will receive only half as much in wages, they are no worse off because they will also have to pay only half as much for their widgets. If households refuse to accept lower money wages, however, firms will have no choice but to meet the drop in spending by cutting back on production and employment. Given downward rigidity of wages, therefore, the interruption in the flow of household spending leads to recession and unemployment.*

*Keynes argued further that once unemployment arrives, it may persist even if prices and wages *do* eventually fall because households without employment do not have incomes. Without incomes they

Figure 18.1

Circular flow in a simple economy

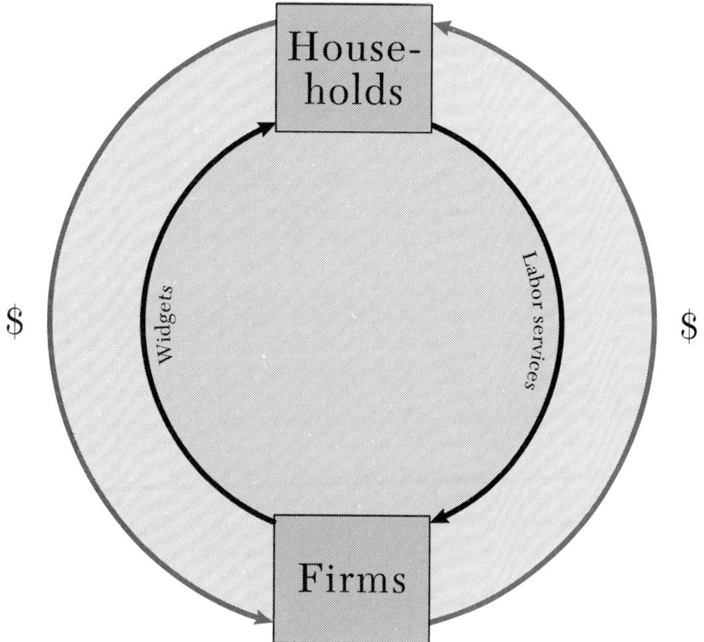

It should be clear from this brief discussion that a central issue in Keynes's break with his classical predecessors was his more skeptical view of the ability of wages to perform their coordinating, market-clearing function in the labor market. Accordingly, we begin our macroeconomic analysis with a simple model of the labor market and its relation to the economy's output of real goods and services.

Real Output, Employment, and the Labor Market

Over the long term, the economy's aggregate real output (real GNP) depends on its labor force, its capital stock, and its stock of technological knowledge. All of these inputs grow over time but, compared with the swings in economic activity over the business cycle, their growth is quite gradual. In analyzing the short-run, *cyclical* behavior of real output, it is therefore a useful approximation to assume

---

cannot pay for widgets, and, if they cannot pay for widgets, then firms have no incentive to hire them to produce widgets. Note that if households have access to money from sources other than current income—for example, if they can borrow against future earnings—then a persistent lack of effective demand is unlikely. However, the failure of wages and prices to adjust immediately to a fall in spending can still precipitate a fall in output and employment. When this occurs, the surest way—and perhaps the only way—to restore health to the economy is to find a way to stimulate total spending.

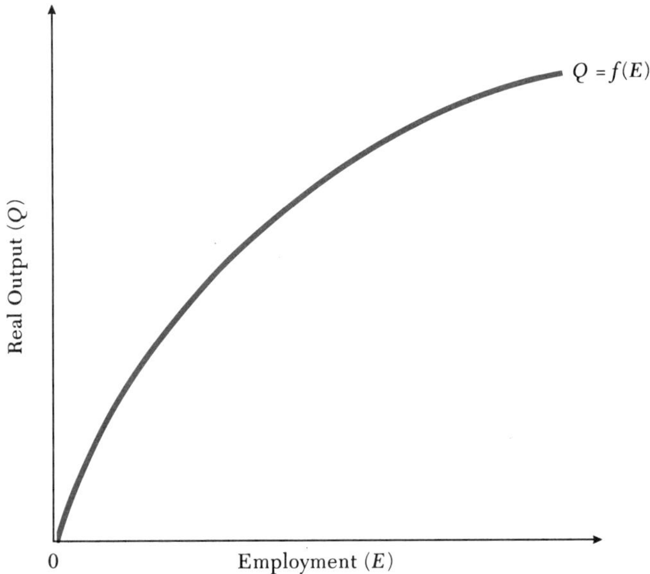

Figure 18.2

The aggregate production function

that all inputs are fixed except one. The one variable input is the economy's input of labor services, or total employment. In particular, we assume that fluctuations in real output over the business cycle are due primarily to variations in the level of employment.

Figure 18.2 shows this relation graphically in the form of the economy's *aggregate production function*, relating its aggregate real output Q to its total employment E. The curve's positive slope tells us that an increase in employment leads to an increase in real output.*

The Labor Market

At any given time, the economy's level of employment, and thus its rate of real output, is determined by demand and supply in the labor market. We assume that both the demand for labor and the supply of labor depend on the *real wage*, which is equal to the nominal wage deflated by the price level. In symbols, if W is the nominal wage and P is the price level (the GNP deflator expressed as a decimal number), then W/P is the real wage.

Note that the real wage can change as a result of changes in either the nominal wage or the price level. For example, suppose the price level is initially 1.0, the nominal wage is \$100 per day, and the real wage is also \$100 per day (= \$100/1.0). If the nominal wage doubles to \$200 while the price level remains the

*Its convex shape, implying that successive increases in employment each add less to total output, is a reflection of diminishing returns to labor.

same, the real wage also doubles to \$200 (= \$200/1.0) of base year purchasing power. If the price level rises by 25 percent to 1.25 while the nominal wage remains at \$100, the real wage falls by 25 percent to \$80 (= \$100/1.25). If both the nominal wage and the price level change in the same proportion, the real wage is unaffected. For example, if both increase by 50 percent, to \$150 and 1.5, respectively, the real wage remains at \$100 of base year purchasing power.

The demand curve for labor as a function of the real wage is negatively sloped. Economically, this is because a fall in the real wage—which is equivalent to a rise in output prices relative to wage costs—makes it profitable for firms to expand output and employment. Conversely, a rise in the real wage reduces the amount of labor demanded because it raises input costs relative to output prices, thereby giving producers an incentive to cut back on output and employment.

The supply of labor also depends on the real wage, for it is the real wage—not the nominal wage—that measures the reward for working. In particular, an increase in the real wage increases the amount of labor supplied because it makes market employment more attractive relative to nonmarket alternatives such as leisure or household production. A decrease in the real wage makes market employment less attractive and so reduces the amount of labor supplied. The supply curve for labor as a function of the real wage is therefore positively sloped.

In Figure 18.3, we plot both the demand for labor D_L and the supply of labor

Figure 18.3

Labor market equilibrium

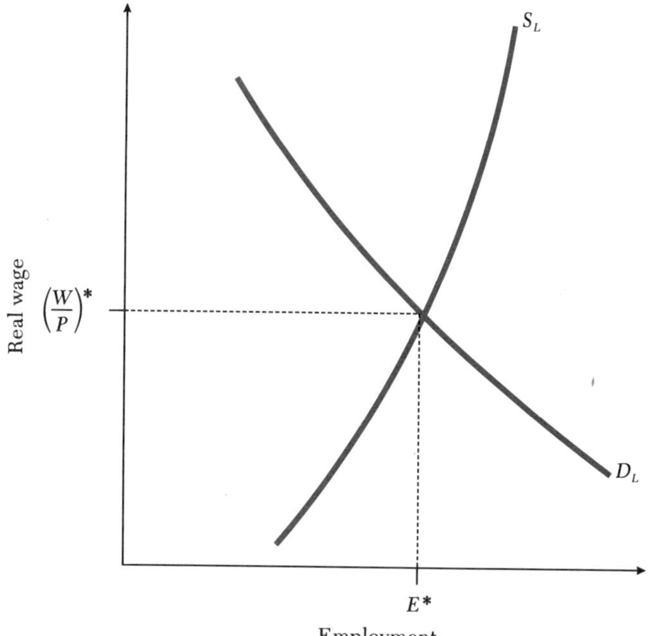

S_L as functions of the real wage. According to the diagram, the labor market clears at a real wage of $(W/P)^*$ and a corresponding level of employment E^*.

Note: Throughout our macroeconomic analysis we use an asterisk (*) to signify values associated with market-clearing conditions.

THE BASIC CLASSICAL THEORY

Let us first use the foregoing analysis to derive the basic classical theory of employment, output, and the price level. We then use the same analytical framework to examine the original Keynesian version of the story.

Classical Labor Market Equilibrium

The classical theory of the labor market held that the flexibility of the *nominal* wage would keep the *real* wage at its market-clearing level whenever the price level changed. Figure 18.4 illustrates how this adjustment process works for a rise in the price level; Figure 18.5 shows how it works for a fall in the price level. In each case, we assume a market-clearing real wage of \$100, which is initially achieved by a price level of 1.0 ($= P_0$) and a nominal wage of \$100 per day ($= W_0$).

According to Figure 18.4, a 25 percent increase in the price level from 1.0 to 1.25 ($= P_1$) with no change in the nominal wage reduces the real wage to \$80

Figure 18.4

Classical labor market adjustment to a rise in the price level

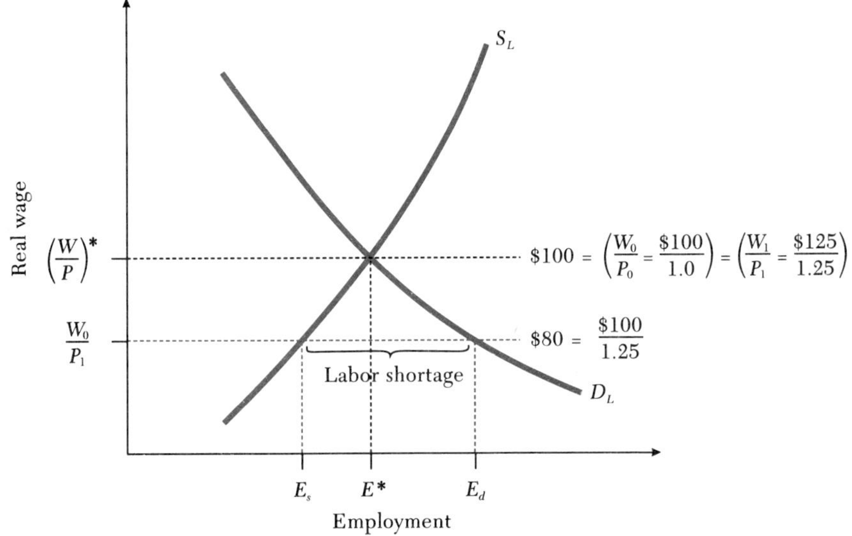

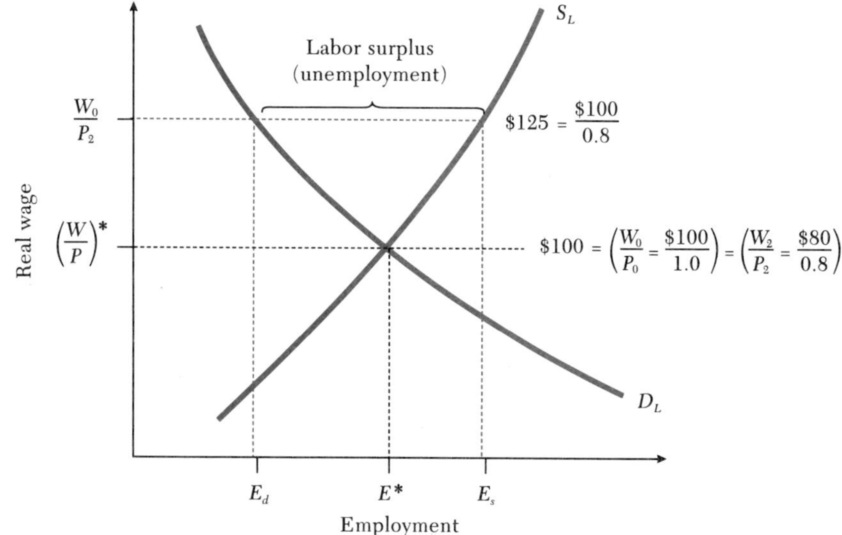

Figure 18.5

Classical labor market adjustment to a fall in the price level

(= \$100/1.25 = W_0/P_1). This creates a shortage of labor equal to distance $E_d - E_s$ and forces firms to offer higher nominal wages to fill job vacancies. The nominal wage continues to rise, pulling up the real wage, until the shortage is eliminated. In particular, the nominal wage has to rise by 25 percent to \$125 (= W_1) to restore the real wage to its market-clearing level.

Figure 18.5 shows the effects of a fall in the price level from 1.0 to 0.8 (= P_2). With no change in the nominal wage, this raises the real wage to \$125 (= \$100/0.8 = W_0/P_2) and creates a surplus of labor equal to distance $E_s - E_d$. This surplus represents an excess of the number of people offering to work at the higher real wage over the number employers are willing to hire at that wage. In other words, it represents *unemployment*.

According to the classical theory, unemployed workers will offer to work for lower nominal wages rather than remain unemployed. (Remember that the price level has fallen so that offering to work for a lower *nominal* wage is not equivalent to accepting a cut in *real* purchasing power.) Just as an increase in the price level creates a shortage of labor that raises the nominal wage, therefore, a decrease in the price level creates a surplus of labor that lowers the nominal wage. In particular, the fall in the price level from 1.0 to 0.8 leads to a proportionate fall in the nominal wage from \$100 to \$80 (= W_2), which restores the real wage to its market-clearing value of \$100 (= \$80/0.8). To the extent that unemployment can exist at all in the classical theory, downward flexibility of the nominal wage insures that it will be only temporary.

Figure 18.6 shows the joint determination of employment and output in the classical model. Part (a) shows supply-and-demand conditions in the labor market, and part (b) shows the production function. By lining up the two parts of the figure and measuring employment along the horizontal axis of each, we can

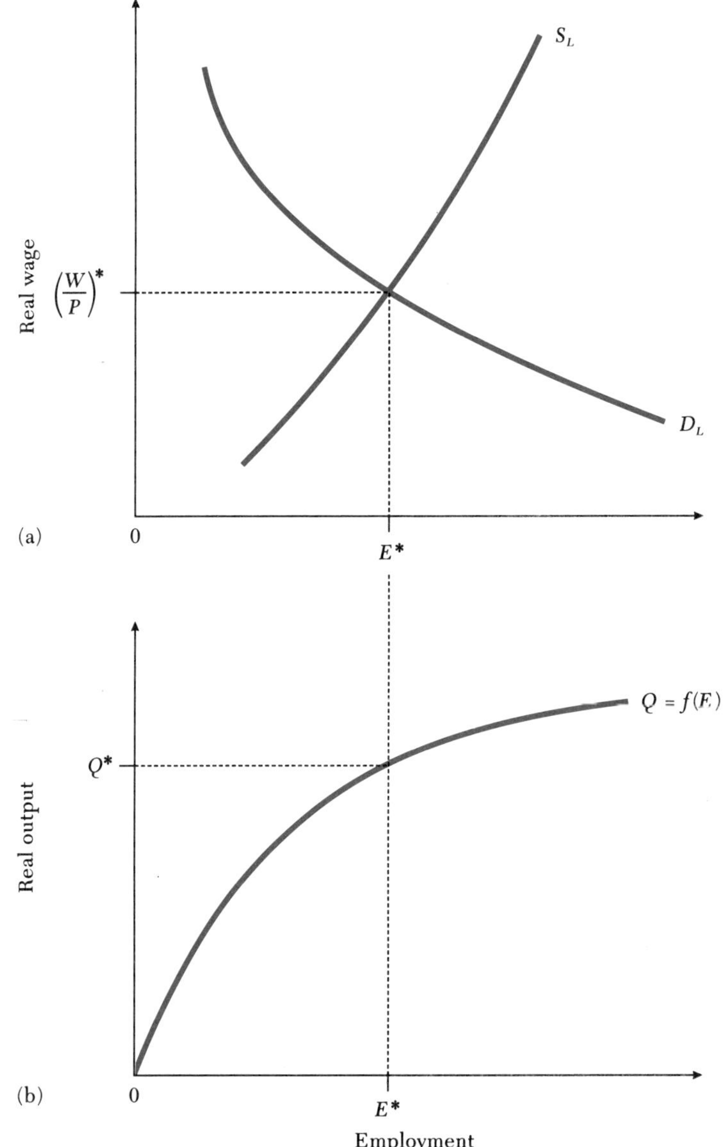

Figure 18.6

Classical output determination. (a) Labor market and (b) Production function

The **natural rate of real output** is the real output rate corresponding to market-clearing conditions in the labor market.

project any level of employment in the labor market onto the production function to find the corresponding level of real output. For example, the production function in part (b) shows that the real output corresponding to employment E^*, and thus to the real wage $(W/P)^*$, in part (a), is Q^*. We refer to Q^*, the rate of real output determined by market-clearing conditions in the labor market, as the **natural rate of real output**.

The Classical Aggregate Supply Curve

The **aggregate supply curve** is a curve showing how the supply of aggregate real output varies with the general price level, other things being equal.

An **aggregate supply curve** shows the relation between the price level and the aggregate amount of real output supplied. Because the rate of real output is determined by the level of employment, the shape of the aggregate supply curve reflects an underlying theory of the labor market. As we have seen, the classical theory held that the nominal wage adjusts to any change in the price level to maintain the market clearing level of employment. Because changes in the price level have no effect on employment in the classical theory, they also have no effect on real output. Aggregate supply is therefore independent of the price level in the classical theory. Graphically, this means that the classical aggregate supply curve is simply a vertical line whose position is determined by the natural rate of real output as illustrated in Figure 18.7.

It is very important that you understand the difference between the *aggregate* supply curve for the economy as a whole and the *market* supply curves introduced in Chapter 3. A market supply curve shows what happens to the supply of a particular good when its price changes *relative to the prices of other goods.* Market supply curves have a positive slope because an increase in the price of one good relative to the prices of other goods (and thus relative to opportunity costs) makes it profitable for firms to produce more of that good. The aggregate supply curve, by contrast, shows what happens to the supply of *all goods* (real GNP) when the overall *price level* changes. In principle, the price level can change without any change in relative prices, and thus without any change in outputs. For example, if the prices of all goods and services double, the price

Figure 18.7

Classical aggregate supply curve

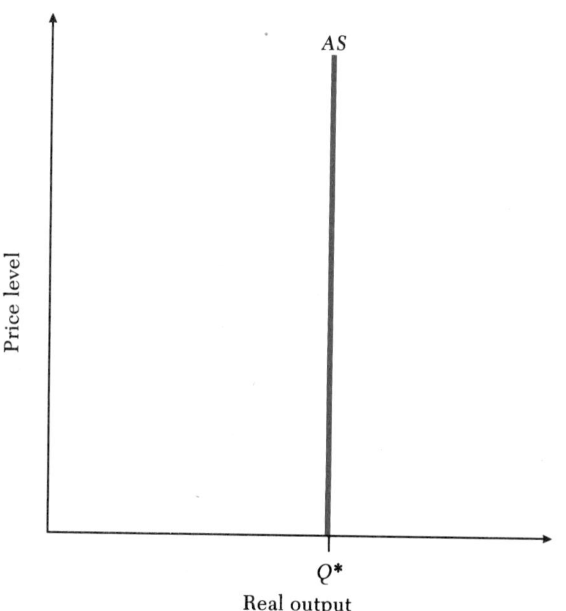

level doubles but relative prices and all outputs remain unchanged. In the classical theory, the real wage is the critical relative price, and it does not change when the price level changes.

The Classical Theory of Aggregate Demand

The **aggregate demand curve** is a curve showing how the demand for aggregate real output varies with the general price level, other things being equal.

The **equation of exchange** is an identity stating that the money stock times its velocity must always equal the price level times aggregate real output, or $MV = PQ$.

The **velocity** of money is the annual rate at which the stock of money turns over in the purchase of final goods.

Just as a market supply curve has its macroeconomic counterpart in the economy's aggregate supply curve, so also does a market demand curve have its counterpart in the economy's **aggregate demand curve**, which shows the relation between the price level and the aggregate amount of real output demanded by buyers of final goods and services.

The classical economists developed a *monetary theory of aggregate demand* based on a relationship called the **equation of exchange**. The equation of exchange can be written as

$$MV = PQ$$

where P and Q again represent the price level and aggregate real output, M represents the amount of money in circulation, and V represents its **velocity**. The velocity of money is the rate at which money turns over each year in the purchase of final goods. The money *stock* times its velocity thus equals the aggregate annual *flow* of expenditures on final goods and services. For example, a money stock of \$500 billion circulating with a velocity of 6 results in an expenditure flow of \$3,000 billion per year.* The equation of exchange simply says that the aggregate flow of money expenditures on final goods and services in any given year ($= MV$) is equal to that year's nominal national product ($= PQ = Y$). Indeed, MV and PQ are simply two ways of expressing aggregate expenditures on final goods and services, and thus nominal national product. The equation of exchange is therefore a definitional identity that must hold for all values of M, V, P, and Q.

The classical economists converted the equation of exchange from a definitional truism into a *theory* of aggregate demand by maintaining that velocity was independent of the stock of money, the price level, and the level of aggregate real output. Its value, they argued, was determined by the characteristics of the economy's financial institutions. Moreover, because such institutions change only gradually over time, the classical economists considered velocity to be quite stable, at least in the long run. As an *approximation*, we regard it as constant in our discussion of the classical theory.†

*We define velocity to reflect only those turnovers of the money stock that involve purchases of *final* goods and services. Were we to consider *all* transactions, including purchases of intermediate goods, financial assets, real assets produced in previous periods, and so on, measured velocity would be much higher. The velocity of money in the purchase of final goods is sometimes referred to as *income velocity* to distinguish it from the *transactions velocity* which applies to all monetary transactions.

†We examine the actual behavior of velocity more carefully when we consider the demand for money in Chapter 21.

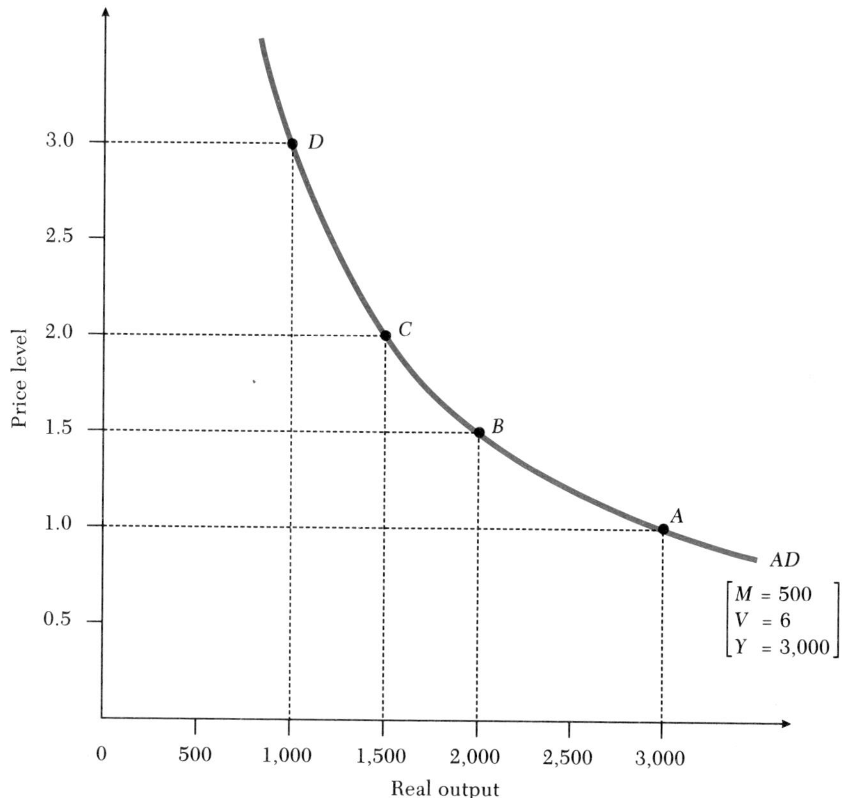

Figure 18.8

A classical aggregate demand curve

In Figure 18.8, we have drawn a classical aggregate demand curve for a money stock of \$500 billion and velocity of 6. Since this combination of money and velocity implies nominal expenditures of \$3,000 billion per year, the product of the price level and real output must equal \$3,000 billion at each point on the curve. For example, at a price level of 1.0, the nominal expenditure flow of \$3,000 billion implies a demand for \$3,000 billion worth of real output (point *A*); at a price level of 1.5, the same \$3,000 billion flow of nominal expenditure implies a demand for \$2,000 billion worth of real output in base year prices (point *B*); and at a price level of 2.0, it implies a demand for \$1,500 billion worth of real output (point *C*).

With velocity constant (or at least independent of the money stock), the equation of exchange implies that aggregate demand is directly proportional to the size of the money stock. Figure 18.9 on the next page shows two aggregate demand curves, both assuming a velocity of 6, but one (AD_0) drawn for a money stock of \$500 billion and the other (AD_1) for a 50 percent larger money stock of \$750 billion. For each value of the price level, the quantity of real output demanded along AD_1 is 50 percent greater than along AD_0. Alternatively, for each level of

Figure 18.9

A shift in the classical aggregate demand curve

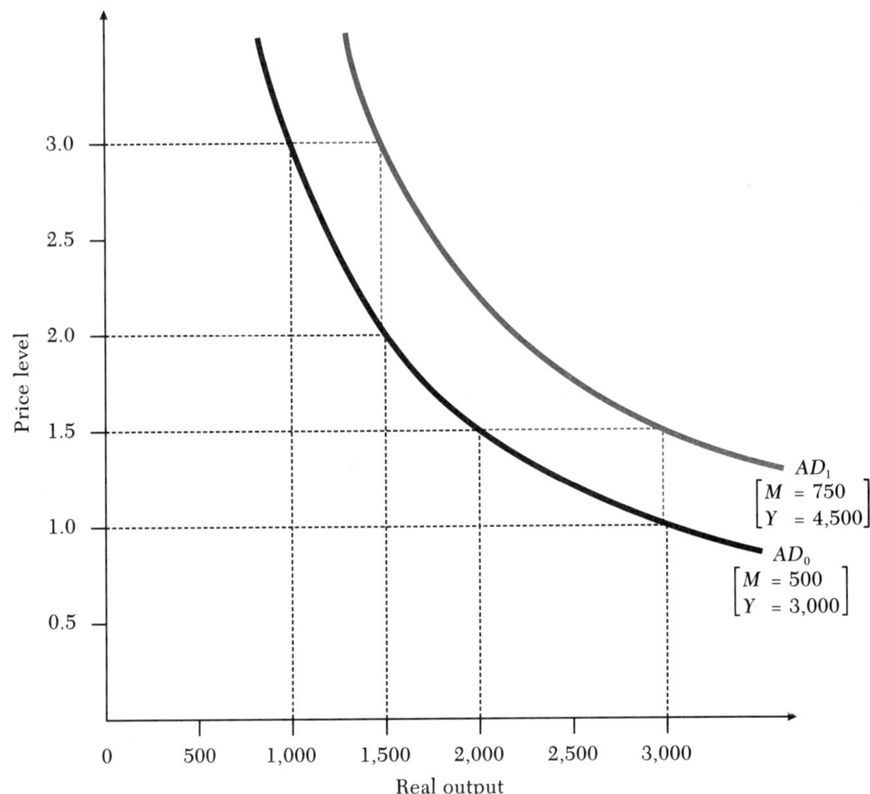

real output demanded, the price level along AD_1 is 50 percent higher than along AD_0. In the classical theory, therefore, an increase in the stock of money can be interpreted as a proportional rightward, or upward, shift of the aggregate demand curve. A reduction in the money stock has just the opposite effect, shifting the aggregate demand curve proportionally downward and to the left.

Classical Product Market Equilibrium and Its Implications

The classical aggregate demand and aggregate supply curves are plotted together in Figure 18.10. The price level at which these two curves intersect, P_0, is the only one for which the total amount of real output demanded is equal to the total amount supplied. At a lower price level, such as P_1, the flow of nominal expenditures would exceed the nominal value of real output and the result would be upward pressure on prices. At a higher price level, such as P_2, the nominal expenditures would be less than the nominal value of real output and there would be downward pressure on prices. The classical product market is therefore in

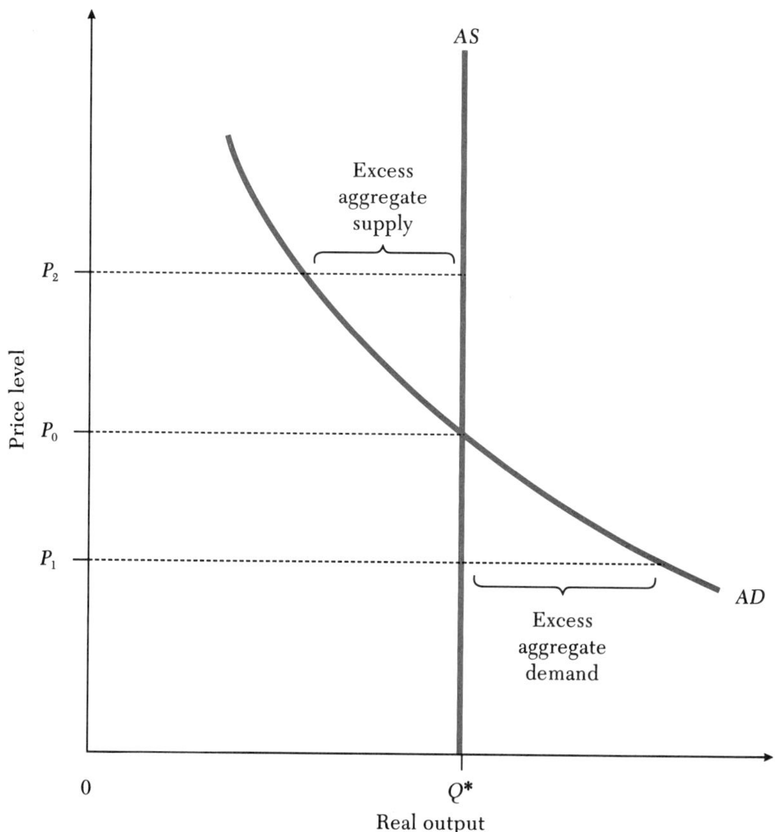

Figure 18.10
Classical equilibrium

equilibrium only at the price level P_0 and real output rate Q^*, which, as we have seen, is the only output rate consistent with classical labor market equilibrium.

Figure 18.11 on the next page illustrates the effects of a change in aggregate demand in the classical model. The increase in aggregate demand from AD_0 to AD_1 raises the equilibrium price level from P_0 to P_1. Given the classical theory of the labor market, however, nominal wages would rise right along with prices, thereby maintaining a constant real wage so that neither employment nor real output would change. The level of aggregate demand thus has no effect on output in the classical model; it is, however, the sole determinant of the price level.

Aggregate Demand Changes and the Vertical Aggregate Supply Curve: A Closer Look

The classical conclusion that a change in aggregate demand affects only the price level may seem paradoxical, especially in light of our microeconomic analysis of market supply and demand. After all, we know that an increase in the *market* demand for a particular good generally leads to an increase in both its price *and*

Figure 18.11

An increase in aggregate demand in the classical model

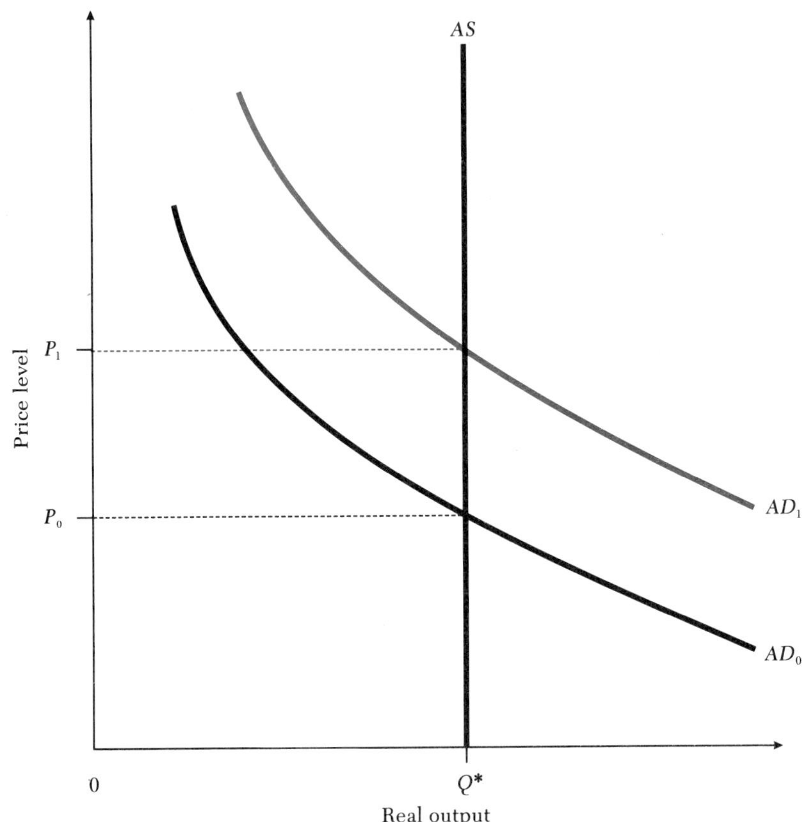

quantity supplied. Why then doesn't an increase in *aggregate* demand lead to an increase in the quantities of all goods supplied, and thus to an increase in real national product, as well as to an increase in the price level? A very good question, indeed!

To resolve the apparent paradox, we must be very clear about the meaning of a change in aggregate demand. Aggregate demand reflects the flow of expenditures on *all* final goods and services. Other things being equal, therefore, a *pure* change in aggregate demand changes all market demands in proportion. A 10 percent increase in aggregate demand, for example, means a 10 percent increase in the demand for automobiles, a 10 percent increase in the demand for T-bone steaks and Big Macs, for entertainment and medical care, and for every other final good and service in national product. It also implies a 10 percent increase in the nominal opportunity costs of producing each of those goods and services.

We can best illustrate the implications of this fundamental point by means of a simple example. Imagine an economy in which there are only two final goods, widgets and gizmos, and assume that the same productive resources needed to produce one widget could instead be used to produce two gizmos. The real mar-

Figure 18.12

Market effects of an increase in aggregate demand

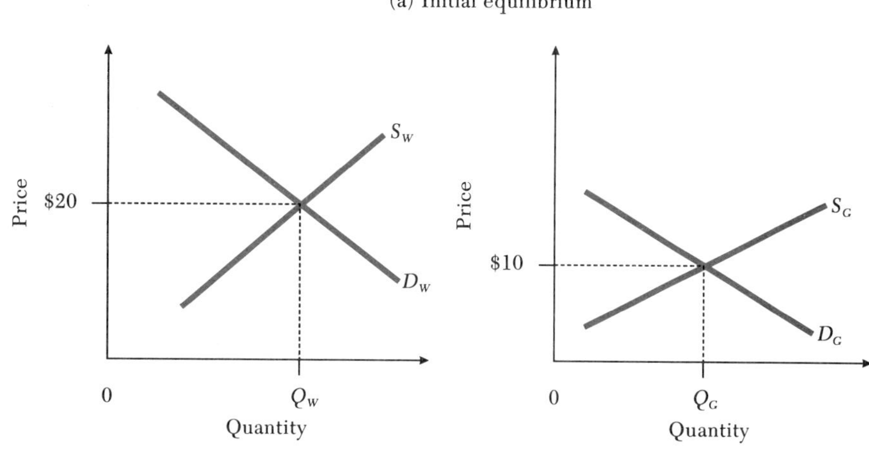

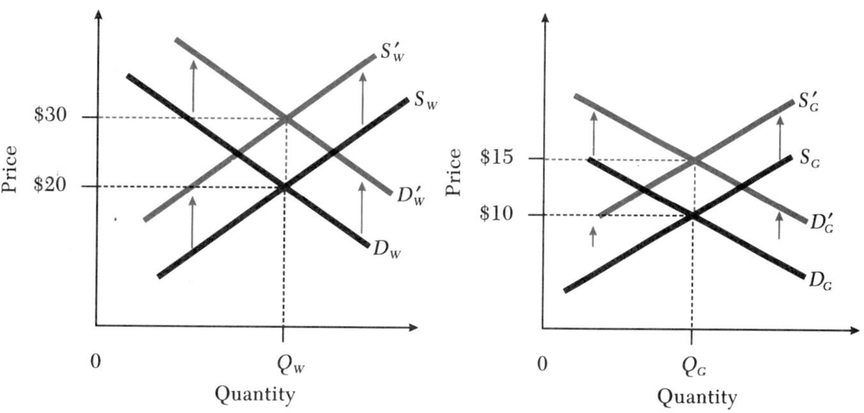

ginal cost of a widget is therefore two gizmos, and the real marginal cost of a gizmo is half of a widget. Suppose that aggregate demand is initially such that the nominal demand price for a widget is $20, and the nominal demand price for a gizmo is $10. Since supply prices are determined by marginal costs, it follows that the nominal supply price of a widget is $20 (= the value of the two gizmos that must be sacrificed to produce a widget) and the nominal supply price of a gizmo is $10 (= the value of the half of a widget that must be sacrificed to produce a gizmo). With the supply price of each good equal to its demand price, both the widget market and the gizmo market, and therefore the economy as a whole, are in equilibrium. This initial equilibrium is depicted in Figure 18.12(a).

Now suppose that aggregate demand increases by 50 percent. This shifts the market demand curves for both widgets and gizmos upward by 50 percent as shown in Figure 18.12(b). At the original output rates, the new nominal demand price of a widget is $30 and that of a gizmo is $15. However, the nominal supply price of a widget has also risen to $30 because the two gizmos that must be sacrificed to produce that widget are now worth $15 each. Similarly, the nominal supply price of a gizmo has risen to $15, half the value of a $30 widget. This increase in supply prices, represented by the upward shifts of the market supply curves in Figure 18.12(b), just matches the increase in demand prices represented by the upward shifts of the market demand curves. In the new equilibrium, therefore, the nominal prices of both widgets and gizmos are higher by 50 percent—the same as the percentage increase in aggregate demand—but the output of each good is unchanged.

In general, when a change in aggregate demand is registered uniformly in all markets—including the markets for labor and other productive inputs whose prices determine production costs and supply prices—all nominal prices are changed in proportion, leaving relative prices and real outputs unaffected. In focusing on wages, the classical economists were simply emphasizing the most important cost element in the supply price of real output. The classical aggregate supply curve therefore reflects the argument that changes in aggregate demand will affect both market demand prices and market supply prices (costs) in the same proportion.

Changes in the Stock of Money: The Classical Quantity Theory

The classical argument that changes in aggregate demand affect only the price level can also be expressed in terms of the equation of exchange. In particular, if velocity is not affected by changes in the money stock, and if labor market adjustments insure that real output remains at Q^*, then the equation of exchange can be written as

$$M\bar{V} = PQ^*$$

The **quantity theory** holds that because real output is determined by nonmonetary factors, and because velocity is independent of changes in the money supply, changes in the money supply lead to proportionate changes in the price level.

where the bar over the V indicates a constant value. With V and Q determined by factors other than the stock of money, any change in M on the left-hand side of the equation must be matched by a proportional change in P on the right-hand side. For example, suppose that velocity is 6 and real output in base year prices is $3,000 billion. If the money stock is initially $500 billion, then the price level will be 1.0 (because $500 × 6 = 1.0 × $3,000). If the money stock then rises by 20 percent to $600 billion, the price level will also rise by 20 percent to 1.2. ($600 × 6 = $3,000 × 1.2) Other things being equal, therefore, the price level is proportional to the stock of money in the classical model. This classical theory of the price level is known as the **quantity theory** because it implies that the quantity of money determines the general level of prices.*

*The theory is technically known as the *quantity theory of money*. However, that is somewhat of a misnomer because it is really a theory of the *price level*. We refer to it simply as the "quantity theory."

Figure 18.13

Inflation in the classical model

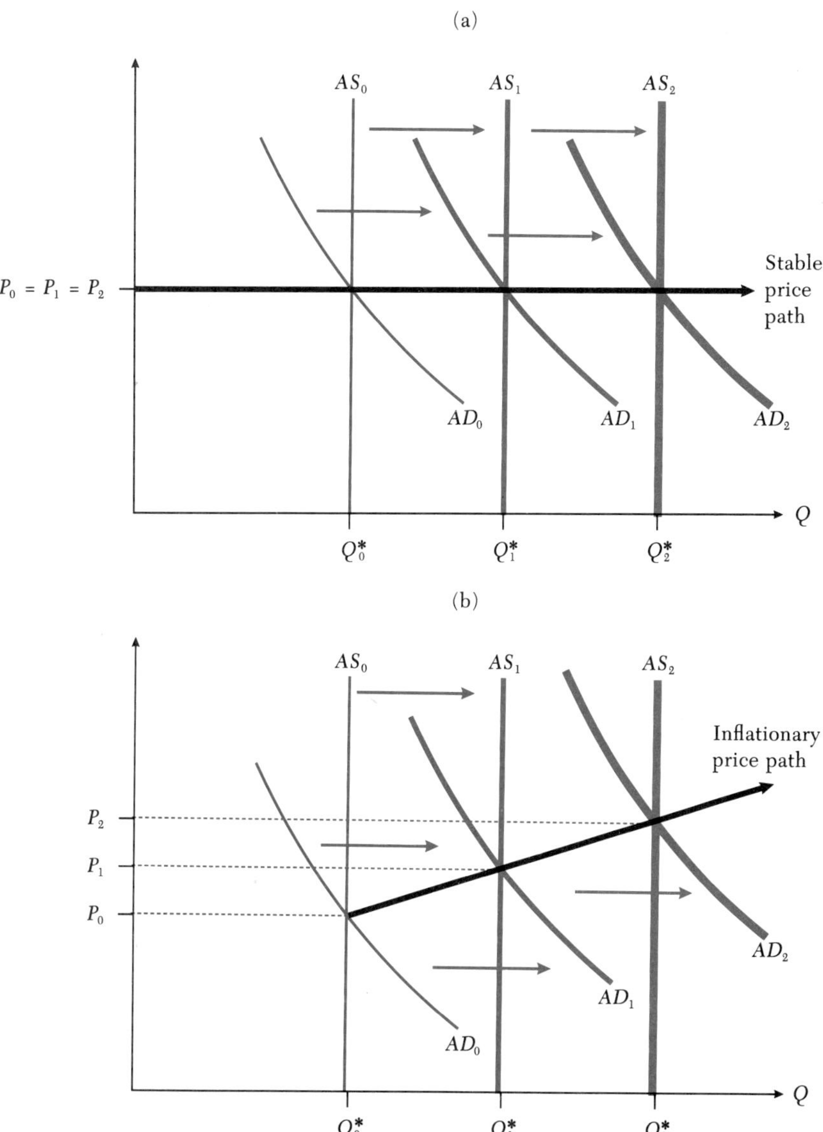

Inflation in the Classical Theory

The quantity theory can be easily converted from a static theory of the price level to a simple, dynamic theory of inflation. In particular, suppose that the natural level of real output grows over time as the labor force grows, the capital stock expands, and technology progresses. We can interpret this real economic growth as a steady, rightward movement of the vertical aggregate supply curve as illustrated in Figures 18.13(a) and (b). The real output rate Q_0^* and the corresponding aggregate supply curve AS_0 represent supply conditions in year 0; Q_1^* and AS_1 represent supply conditions in year 1; and so on. If the money stock were to increase at the same annual rate as real output, the aggregate demand curve would shift to the right each year by the same amount as the aggregate supply curve, and the equilibrium price level would remain constant. In other words, there would be no inflation or deflation. This case is illustrated in Figure 18.13(a) where the black arrow indicates the time path of the price level.

Figure 18.13(b) shows what happens if the money stock grows faster than real output. The equilibria in successive years are at higher and higher price levels as shown by the upwardly sloped black arrow. The upward trend in the price level is, of course, inflation. In the classical theory, therefore, ongoing inflation is the result of the stock of money growing faster than natural real output.*

Unemployment in the Classical Theory

As we have seen, nominal wage adjustments insure that the labor market clears in the classical theory. The classical economists recognized that wage adjustments are not instantaneous and that there might be some temporary unemployment during the adjustment process. They also recognized that there would always be some "frictional" unemployment among people temporarily between jobs or people entering the labor force for the first time. However, unemployment in excess of that amount will not persist in the classical theory unless something prevents the nominal wage from falling when the real wage is above its market-clearing level. Minimum wage laws, for example, can lead to unemployment in the classical theory.

Classical Theories of the Business Cycle

Real theories of the business cycle view fluctuations in aggregate supply, rather than aggregate demand, as the source of the business cycle.

Because the classical economists did not claim that nominal wages would always adjust instantaneously to a change in the price level, they left open the possibility that fluctuations in aggregate demand could account for temporary fluctuations in output and employment. However, their explanations of more significant fluctuations in aggregate economic activity were based on **real theories of the business cycle**. According to these theories, factors related to in the economy's real productive capacity were the source of economic boom and bust.

Suppose, for example, that a plague or famine were to reduce the population and thus the supply of labor. The result would be a reduction in the equilibrium levels of employment and output and a leftward shift of the aggregate supply

*We can illustrate the same point using the equation of exchange. Assume again that $V = 6$, while the initial values of the other three variables in the equation are $M = \$500$ billion, $P = 1.0$, and $Q^* = \$3,000$ billion. Now suppose that Q^* grows by 10 percent to \$3,300 billion after 1 year. If the money stock also grows by 10 percent to \$550 billion, the level of nominal expenditures will be \$3,300 billion ($= MV = 6 \times \$550$ billion) and the equilibrium price level will not change. On the other hand, if the money stock grows by 20 percent from \$500 billion to \$600 billion, the price level will have to rise by approximately 9 percent to absorb the excess of nominal expenditures (\$3,600) over real output (\$3,300) because \$600 billion $\times$ 6.0 = 1.09 $\times$ \$3,300 billion.

curve. A reduction in labor productivity—perhaps due to a sudden scarcity of some crucial raw material, such as OPEC oil in the 1970s—would reduce the demand for labor and also shift the aggregate supply curve to the left. On the other hand, a dramatic technological breakthrough with widespread application that increased productivity would shift the aggregate supply curve to the right, leading to a boom in real output while lowering the price level. Note that these real theories of the business cycle imply that, given the level of aggregate demand, real output and the price level move in opposite directions over the course of the business cycle.

The Classical Theory and the Facts

The test of any theory is its ability to explain the facts. The classical theory does a pretty good job of explaining some facts but not a very good job of explaining others. The classical explanation of the price level is generally consistent with the long-term relation between monetary growth and inflation, as well as the shorter term but more extreme case of hyperinflation. (The classical theory fares less well, however, in accounting for cyclical variations in the inflation rate around its long-term trend.)

The classical theory is less useful as an explanation of the business cycle. Although some cyclical fluctuations in real output and employment reflect the economy's response to changes in real factors—the recessions of 1974–75 and 1979–80 are recent examples—it is almost impossible to escape the conclusion that fluctuations in aggregate demand are a significant factor in most business cycles. Indeed, the typical cyclical pattern is for real output and the price level (or at least the rate of inflation) to move in the same direction, declining together during recession and then rising together during recovery and expansion. Moreover, many recent recessions—and certainly the Great Depression—have been so severe and so prolonged that they cannot be explained within the classical framework without stretching that framework beyond recognition. In sum, classical business cycle theory as it existed in the 1930s left much to be desired.

THE BASIC KEYNESIAN THEORY

As we have seen, it was the inability of the classical theory to provide a satisfactory explanation of business cycles in general, and the Great Depression in particular, that prompted Keynes to supply his own explanation. As we have also seen, that explanation identified the culprit as insufficient aggregate demand. Indeed, Keynes believed that aggregate demand was the key to macroeconomic performance: Too little aggregate demand and there would be recession and unemployment; too much and there would be inflation.

Aggregate demand is of paramount importance in the Keynesian theory precisely because the aggregate supply curve implied by Keynesian theory differs fundamentally from that of classical theory.

The Keynesian Aggregate Supply Curve

The essential difference between the Keynesian and classical theories of aggregate supply is to be found in differing views of the labor market. In the opening pages of his *General Theory*, Keynes dismissed the nominal wage flexibility of the classical theory with the assertion that workers would resist a cut in the nominal wage, even if the alternative was unemployment. Although he granted that the nominal wage would rise if there were an excess demand for labor, Keynes felt that it would be rigid, or at least "sticky," in the face of an excess supply of labor.

The substitution of the Keynesian assumption of a downwardly rigid nominal wage for the classical assumption of a flexible nominal wage, as innocuous as it may seem, leads to a fundamentally different view of aggregate supply. With the *nominal* wage W downwardly rigid, a fall in the price level raises the *real* wage (W/P) above its market-clearing level and thus reduces employment and output.

Figure 18.14 illustrates the derivation of a Keynesian aggregate supply curve. Part (a) shows demand-and-supply conditions in the labor market, part (b) shows the production function, and part (c) shows the aggregate supply curve. (Once again, the horizontal axes of parts (a) and (b) both measure employment, so we can project any employment level in the labor market directly onto the production function.) Our starting point is an initial equilibrium in which the nominal wage is W_0, the price level is P_0, and the corresponding real wage (W_0/P_0) clears the labor market. Employment is E^* and the corresponding aggregate real output in part (b) is Q^*. The combination of the initial price level P_0 and natural real output Q^* is shown as point A on the aggregate supply curve in part (c).

First consider the effects of a rise in the price level from P_0 to P_1. Other things being equal, the rise in the price level reduces the real wage, creates a shortage of labor, and leads firms to bid up the nominal wage. The process continues until the labor market again clears at a new nominal wage of W_1, where $(W_1/P_1) = (W_0/P_0)$. In the Keynesian theory as in the classical theory, therefore, an increase in the price level in an economy already at its natural rate of real output affects neither employment nor output. Thus, point B on the Keynesian aggregate supply curve in part (c) of Figure 18.14 shows that the same real output Q^* is supplied at the price level P_1 as at the price level P_0.

Next, consider the effects of a fall in the price level from P_0 to P_2. According to the Keynesian theory, the nominal wage does *not* fall in response, so that the real wage rises to W_0/P_2 as shown in Figure 18.14(a). The rise in the real wage reduces employment to E_2 (the quantity of labor demanded at higher real wage) and leads to unemployment equal to the distance RS. According to the production function in part (b) of Figure 18.14, the fall in employment from E^* to E_2 reduces real output from Q^* to Q_2. Point C on the aggregate supply curve thus tells us that real output Q_2 will be supplied at the price level P_2. A further decline in the price level to P_3 reduces employment to E_3 (and increases unemployment to $R'S'$) in the labor market and reduces the supply of real output to Q_3. This is shown by point D on the aggregate supply curve. In summary, therefore, a decline in the price level leads to a decrease in employment and a rise in unem-

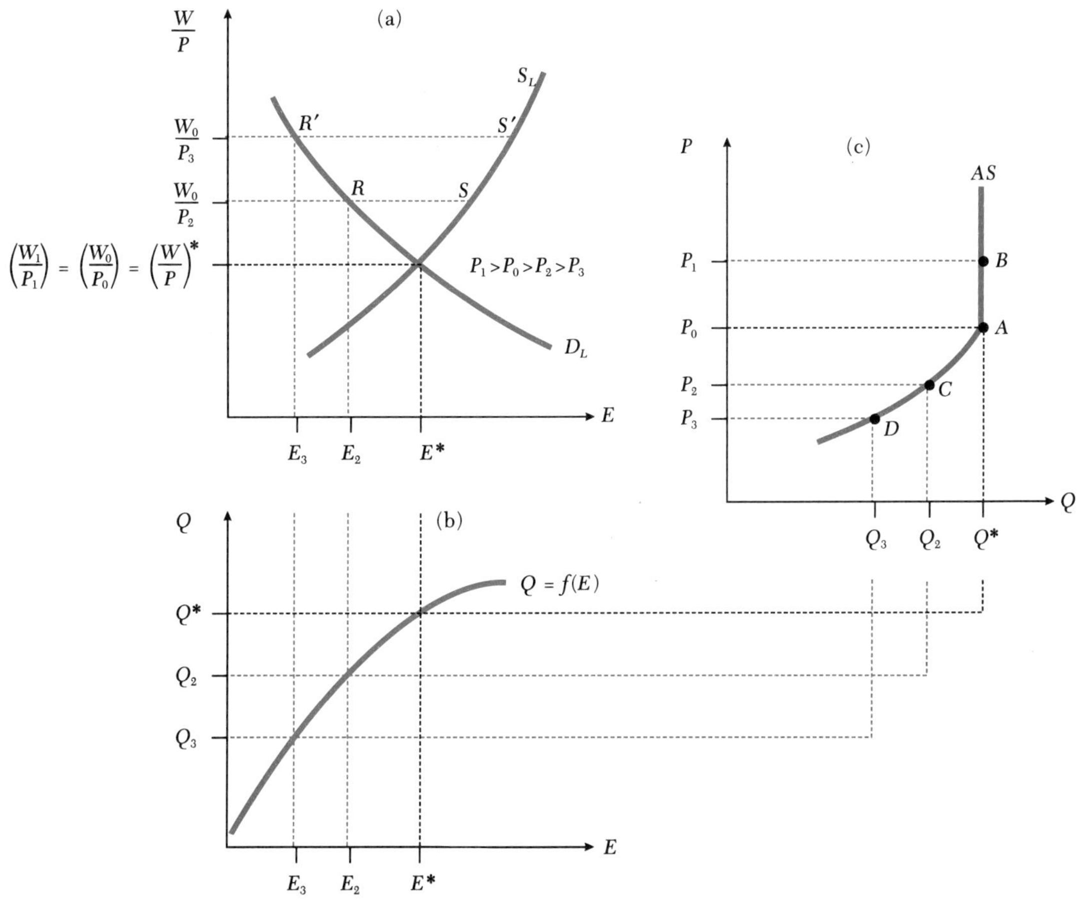

Figure 18.14

Derivation of a Keynesian aggregate supply curve. (a) Labor maket, (b) Production function, and (c) Aggregate supply

ployment in the labor market and a fall in real output along the Keynesian aggregate supply curve.

The Role of Aggregate Demand in the Keynesian Theory

As we have seen, the classical economists held a *monetary* theory of aggregate demand in which the *stock* of money determines the *flow* of expenditures via a stable velocity of money. In contrast, the Keynesian theory of aggregate demand is an *income-expenditure* theory in which the *flow* of income determines the *flow* of expenditures. We examine this income-expenditure theory of aggregate demand, along with modern monetary theories of aggregate demand, in subsequent chapters. For our purposes here, however, the particular theory underlying the aggregate demand curve is not important. What is important is that changes in

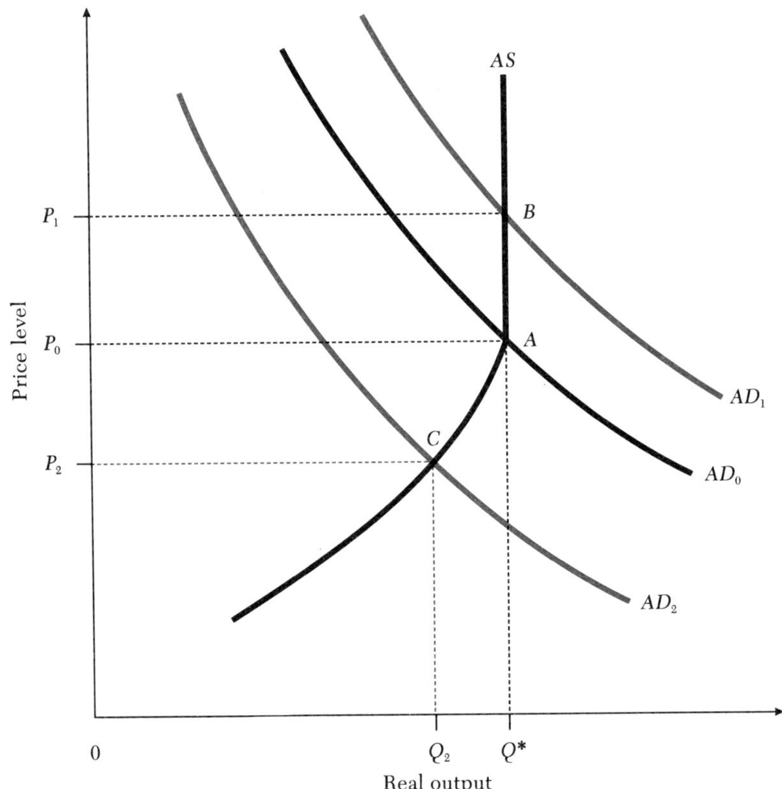

Figure 18.15

Changes in aggregate demand: Keynesian case

aggregate demand, whatever their source, have different effects in the Keynesian theory from the ones they have in the classical theory.

To illustrate, suppose that the economy is initially in equilibrium with a price level of P_0 and natural real output of Q^* in Figure 18.15. If aggregate demand increases to AD_1, the equilibrium price level rises to P_1 but real output is not affected. Thus, starting at the natural rate of real output, an increase in aggregate demand has the same effect in the Keynesian theory as in the classical theory—namely, an increase in the price level with no effect on real output.

The story is quite different, however, for a fall in aggregate demand. If aggregate demand decreases from AD_0 to AD_2, a new equilibrium is established at point C with a price level of P_2 and real output of Q_2. Thus a decrease in aggregate demand in the Keynesian theory causes a fall in both the price level and real output; in other words, it causes a recession.

We hope you know that shifting curves on a graph is no substitute for understanding! It is therefore important that you understand the *economics* of why a drop in aggregate demand leads to a fall in output and employment in the Keynesian theory. As prices fall in response to falling aggregate demand, the *real* wage rises because of the downwardly rigid *nominal* wage. The rising real

Figure 18.16

The great depression à la Keynes

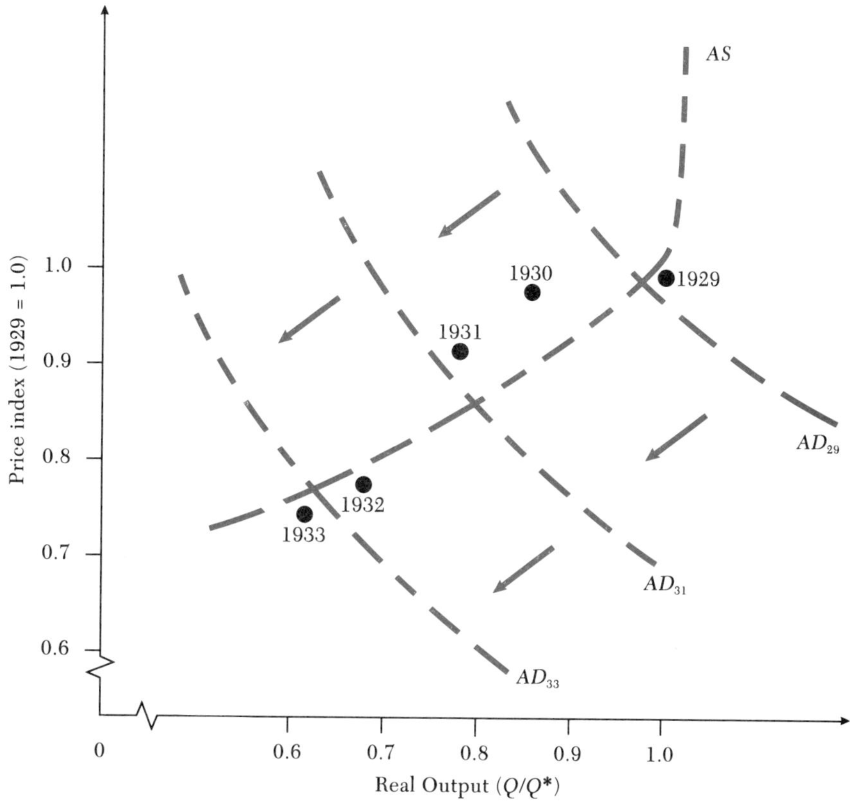

wage reduces the amount of labor demanded, leading to falling employment and output. Moreover, the higher real wage is accompanied by a surplus of labor—unemployment—in the labor market. In other words, point C in Figure 18.15 represents an **unemployment equilibrium**.

An **unemployment equilibrium** is a Keynesian equilibrium in which a combination of downwardly rigid wages and insufficient aggregate demand lead to persistent unemployment.

This, in a nutshell, was the Keynesian explanation of the Great Depression: It was the result of a severe drop in aggregate demand, and it persisted because no actions were taken to restore aggregate demand to its pre-Depression level. Figure 18.16 illustrates the appeal of this explanation. The diagram plots real output and the price level (both as percentages of their 1929 values) for each year between 1929 and 1933. If we interpret the dashed lines as hypothetical Keynesian aggregate demand and aggregate supply curves, they appear to be quite consistent with the Keynesian hypothesis that a massive drop in aggregate demand was responsible for the Great Depression.

Inflation in the Keynesian Theory

According to the Keynesian theory, inflation is caused by the same general conditions as in the classical theory—namely, aggregate demand that is excessive relative to the economy's real productive capacity. Looking back at Figure 18.15, for example, we can see that the price level rises from P_0 to P_1 when the aggregate demand curve increases from AD_0 to AD_1. Whereas the price level would stabilize at P_1 if there were no further changes in aggregate demand, inflation would persist if aggregate demand continued to increase. Or, more realistically, inflation would persist if aggregate demand continued to grow more rapidly than Q^* over time. The only real difference between the Keynesian and classical theories of inflation is that the former did not identify increases in the stock of money as the sole source of increases in aggregate demand.

Some Problems with the Keynesian Theory

Because the Keynesian theory seemed to provide a plausible—and much needed—explanation of recession and unemployment, it rather quickly won acceptance among most economists. By the 1960s it provided the intellectual foundation for macroeconomic policies in the United States and other industrialized market economies. (However, some economists contend that Keynes himself would not have recognized as his own what came to be known as "Keynesian economics" in the 1960s.)

There is certainly substantial agreement among modern economists that a sudden and dramatic drop in aggregate demand did precipitate the Great Depression (although there is less agreement about the source of that drop in aggregate demand). Moreover, economists are confident in their belief that fluctuations in aggregate demand are an important factor in most ordinary, garden variety business cycles. (Here again, however, they often disagree about what causes fluctuations in aggregate demand and what, if anything, can be done to alleviate them or mitigate their consequences.) However, the Keynesian theory was much less successful in accounting for the kind of stagflation that the United States and other industrial, market economies experienced during the 1970s. While the theory suggests that inflation is the result of excessive aggregate demand, and unemployment the result of insufficient aggregate demand, the combination of simultaneously rising unemployment and accelerating inflation was beyond its explanatory power.

In addition to these empirical shortcomings, many economists—including many Keynesian economists—were troubled by an apparent theoretical gap in the Keynesian theory. Look again at Figure 18.14(a). According to the Keynesian theory, the fall in the price level from P_0 to P_2 raises the real wage to (W_0/P_2) and reduces employment to E_2. At that employment level, however, the demand price (nominal wage) firms are willing to pay for additional workers exceeds the supply price at which those workers are willing to accept employment. Thus firms and unemployed workers could reach mutually beneficial wage agreements that would eliminate unemployment. *Keynesian unemployment can persist, therefore, only if firms and workers persistently fail to exploit potential gains from trade*. To many economists, this failure seems to be at odds with the fundamental economic postulate of rational behavior. Realizing this, many modern-day Keynesians have constructed theories that attempt to explain sluggish wages (and prices) as the result of rational choice. We examine these "new Keynesian" theories in the chapters that follow.

Summary and Preview

The quotation at the beginning of this chapter was taken from the conclusion of Keynes *General Theory*, published more than 50 years ago. The influences to which he referred were those of classical economists. It is prophetically ironic that, from the perspective of yet another half century, many modern economists have come to view the lingering influence of many Keynesian ideas in much the same way that Keynes viewed the influence of his classical predecessors. Among today's "academic scribblers," however, neither classical nor Keynesian ideas are "defunct," for both have strongly influenced the development of modern macroeconomics. We are about to see this influence in Chapter 19 where we introduce the modern theory of employment and unemployment, and in Chapter 20 where we construct the modern theory of aggregate supply and demand.

CHAPTER SUMMARY

1. The view of classical theory was that a market economy is a fundamentally stable system in which price adjustments automatically achieve market-clearing equilibria. The main tenet of the Keynesian attack on classical theory is that some prices—particularly, wages—are too "sticky" for this to be the case.

2. *Say's Law* argues that since the supply of productive services is motivated by a demand for final goods, a general deficiency of demand is impossible. Keynes argued that Say's Law did not hold when wages were downwardly rigid.

3. In classical theory, the flexible *nominal wage* keeps the *real wage* at its market-clearing level when the price level changes. As a result, the classical *aggregate supply curve* is vertical at the *natural rate of real output*.

4. The classical economists held a *monetary theory* of *aggregate demand*. Specifically they argued that aggregate demand is determined by the stock of money times its *velocity*, which is independent of the money stock.

5. In the classical theory, the level of *aggregate demand* determines the price level but has no effect on real output. Moreover, since aggregate demand is proportional to the money supply, so also is the price level. This is the classical *quantity theory* of the price level. In dynamic terms, it implies that

ongoing inflation is the result of the money supply growing faster than natural real output.

6. Classical *real theories of the business cycle* held that factors related to the economy's real productive capacity are the source economic of boom and bust.

7. The classical theory provides a pretty good explanation of long-term inflation, but it is less useful as a theory of the business cycle.

8. In the Keynesian theory, the assumption of a downwardly rigid nominal wage leads to an aggregate supply curve along which reductions in the price level lead to reductions in real output and employment.

9. In the Keynesian theory, recessions and depressions are the result of insufficient aggregate demand; inflation is a result of excessive aggregate demand.

10. Although the Keynesian theory provides a more useful theory of the business cycle than does the classical theory, it has a difficult time explaining stagflation.

Key Terms and Concepts

Say's Law
natural rate of real output
aggregate supply curve
aggregate demand curve
equation of exchange
velocity
quantity theory
real theories of the business cycle
unemployment equilibrium

Questions for Thought and Discussion

1. According to the classical theory, what would prevent a fall in aggregate demand if households suddenly decided to save more of their incomes and spend less on consumption goods?
2. Say's Law is often stated as, "Supply creates its own demand." Granted that this is an oversimplification, what is the grain of truth in stating it like this?
3. Is there a difference between the application of Say's Law in a barter economy and in a money economy?
4. What would happen to the velocity of money if people suddenly decided to keep more cash in their wallets and larger balances in their bank accounts? What would happen to aggregate demand?
5. Use the classical theory to trace through the effects of each of the following changes on the real wage, employment, output, and the price level:

a. A technological improvement that raises both labor productivity and the demand for labor (i.e., shifts both the production function upward and the demand curve for labor upward).

b. An increase in the supply of labor (i.e., an outward shift of the labor supply curve.

c. A decrease in velocity.

6. Apply the Keynesian theory to predict the effects of a decrease in velocity.

CHAPTER 19

Employment, Unemployment, and the Labor Market

Unemployment and its cyclical fluctuations are facts of life in all modern, market economies. That such fluctuations occur, and that during their course unemployment often persists for years at high levels as it did during the Great Depression and in major post-World-War-II recessions, is a puzzle that economists have grappled with for more than half a century. Recent attempts to solve that puzzle have relied on a much more sophisticated view of the labor market than the simple supply-and-demand model that we introduced in the previous chapter. In this chapter we develop that view by introducing some important characteristics of the labor market and seeing how they fit into the modern theory of employment and unemployment.

THE CHARACTERISTICS OF EMPLOYMENT AND UNEMPLOYMENT

In Chapter 15 we introduced some preliminary definitions of employment, unemployment, and the labor force. Although those definitions sufficed for a general discussion of the historical behavior of employment and unemployment, our analysis here requires a much more detailed picture of the labor market.

Table 19.1

Population, labor force, and employment

YEAR	1989*	1983 *(Recession Year)*	1933** *(Great Depression)*
Total Population (millions)	248.8	234.8	125.6
Minus: persons younger than 16 and persons in institutions	62.4	60.6	37.5
Equals: **Age-Eligible Population**	186.4	174.2	88.1
Minus: persons not in the labor force	60.9	61.0	36.5
Equals: **Labor Force**	125.5	113.2	51.6
Minus: **Employed**	119.0	102.5	38.8
Equals: **Unemployed**	6.5	10.7	12.8
Unemployment Rate (= unemployed/labor force)	5.2%	9.5%	24.9%
Labor Force Participation Rate (= labor force/age-eligible population)	67.3%	65.0%	58.6%
Employment Rate (= employed/age-eligible population)	63.8%	58.8%	44.0%

Source: *Economic Report of the President, 1990.*

*Preliminary.

**Prior to 1947 the age-eligible population was defined to include all persons over 14 years of age. For purposes of direct comparison with 1989 and 1983, the age-eligible population for 1933 was corrected to include all persons over 16 years of age. Labor force figures for 1933 do not include resident armed forces; those for 1989 and 1983 do.

The Labor Force, Employment, and Unemployment

Table 19.1 shows the relationships among the population, labor force, employment, and unemployment in 1989. For purposes of comparison, we have also included data for 1983, a recent recession year, and 1933, the historical "worst case." Starting with total population at the top of the table, we make two adjustments to obtain a measure of the labor force. First we deduct the number of persons under the age of sixteen; according to the official statistics they are too young to be in the labor force. This leaves the *age-eligible population.** Next

*In addition to those under 16, persons confined to an institution, such as a prison or hospital, are also excluded from the age-eligible population. For that reason, the age-eligible population is sometimes referred to as the *noninstitutional population*. However, since the number of persons younger than 16 vastly exceeds the number institutionalized, the terminology "age-eligible" seems more appropriate.

we deduct those members of the age-eligible population who choose not to participate in the labor market. These include people who work in the home rather than in the marketplace (homemakers), students over sixteen who choose not to work, retirees, and other adults who are neither working nor looking for work. These people are not considered unemployed; they are simply not in the labor force. Deducting their number from the age-eligible population leaves the *labor force*. The labor force thus consists of everyone 16 years of age and older who is either working for pay or actively seeking work. Those working for pay are considered *employed*, while those not working but actively seeking work are considered *unemployed*. In 1989 the labor force averaged 125.5 million people, of whom 119 million were employed and 6.5 million were unemployed.*

Determining Labor Force Status

To determine who is employed, who is unemployed, and who is not in the labor force, the Bureau of Labor Statistics (BLS), an agency of the U.S. Department of Labor, conducts a monthly survey of about 60,000 households representative of the U.S. population as a whole. The basic structure of the survey, which is designed to reveal the labor force status of all adults in the household, is illustrated in Figure 19.1.

The BLS survey counts anyone who is *working for pay*, whether part time or full time, as in the labor force and *employed*.† Among adults not working for pay, the survey counts as in the labor force and *unemployed* anyone who is currently *available for work* and who either has *actively sought work within the past 4 weeks* or is on *temporary layoff* waiting to be recalled to a job. Anyone else—that is, anyone over 16 who is not employed, not actively seeking work, and not waiting to be recalled to a job—is classified as *not in the labor force*.

The BLS survey also tries to determine whether people not in the labor force would prefer to be working. It does this by asking them whether they want a job. Typically, about nine out of ten say they *do not* want a job—most for reasons related to household responsibilities, schooling, or retirement. Those who say they *do* want a job are asked why they are not actively looking for one. (Remember, if they *were* looking, they would be classified as unemployed rather than not in the labor force.) Most cite the same factors—namely, household and school responsibilities—cited by those who say they do *not* want a job! Some, however, say they are not seeking work because they feel that they would be unable to find a job. These people are often referred to as "discouraged workers," and, although they are not counted among the unemployed because they are not part of the labor force, some economists argue that they are nonetheless

* We have included members of the armed forces residing in the United States in our measures of the labor force and employment. Employment and unemployment statistics are also reported for the *civilian* labor force exclusive of resident armed forces. All of the figures in this chapter include military personnel as employed members of the labor force. Since military service is currently voluntary, it makes no more sense to exclude them from the labor force than it would to exclude, say, postal employees. Were military service compulsory, this inclusion might be questionable.

† Anyone working in a family business, even if not for pay, is also considered employed.

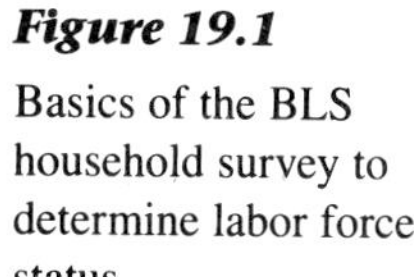

Figure 19.1

Basics of the BLS household survey to determine labor force status

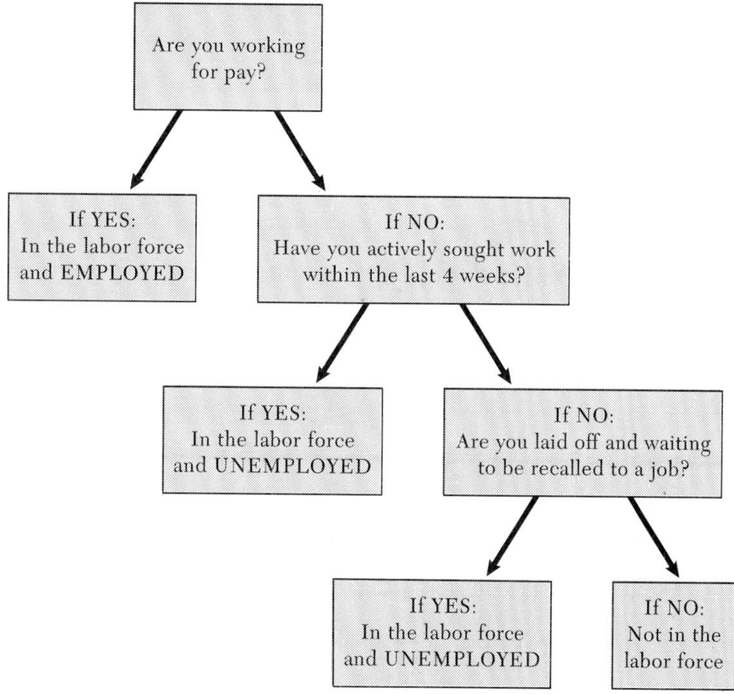

part of the social problem of unemployment. Others argue that simply claiming to want a job, without actually looking for one, implies little or nothing about an individual's real desire to work.

The Unemployment Rate, the Employment Rate, and the Labor Force Participation Rate

Table 19.1 also shows three important ratios: the unemployment rate, the employment rate, and the labor force participation rate. The *unemployment rate* is the most widely publicized labor force statistic. It represents the proportion of the labor force that is unemployed. The unemployment rate of 5.2 percent for 1989, for example, represents the ratio of the 6.5 million unemployed persons to the 125.5 million in the labor force.

The **labor force participation rate** is the percentage of the age-eligible population that is in the labor force, either employed or unemployed.

The **employment rate** is the percentage of the age-eligible population that is employed.

The **labor force participation rate** is the proportion of the age-eligible population that is in the labor force, and the **employment rate** is the proportion of the age-eligible population that is employed. As Table 19.1 indicates, just over two-thirds of the age-eligible population was in the labor force in 1989, and nearly 64 percent was employed. (Note that the employment rate is not simply the complement of the unemployment rate since the former is measured as a percentage of the age-eligible population and the latter as a percentage of the labor force.)

Figure 19.2

Labor force participation rate and employment rate, 1950–89

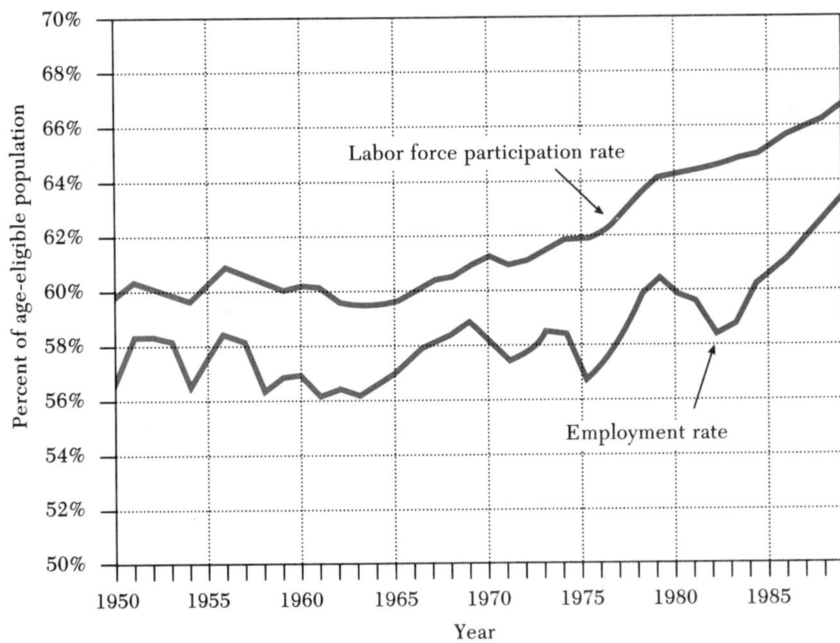

Figure 19.2 shows how both the labor force participation rate and the employment rate have risen during the past three decades. The upward trend in labor force participation implies that the labor force has grown more rapidly than the adult population, and the upward trend in the employment rate indicates that the economy has successfully absorbed most of that labor force growth.

The Dynamics of Labor Force Status

It is useful to think of the labor force in terms of stocks and flows as depicted in Figure 19.3. The large outer box represents the entire age-eligible population, which is in turn distributed among the smaller, internal boxes representing employment, unemployment, and people who are not in the labor force. The number of people in each of these boxes at any given time is a stock, while the arrows connecting the boxes represent continuous flows of people between them. (You might even think of little people marching between boxes in the direction of the arrows.) These flows tell us that the number and identity of the people in each box is in a constant state of flux.

The arrows labelled 1 and 2 represent flows that affect the entire age-eligible population. Flow 1 consists of people entering the age-eligible population as they reach the age of 16 and flow 2 consists of those departing for the big retirement home in the sky. The difference between flow 1 and flow 2 determines the rate at which the age-eligible population grows.

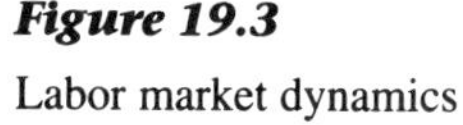

Figure 19.3

Labor market dynamics

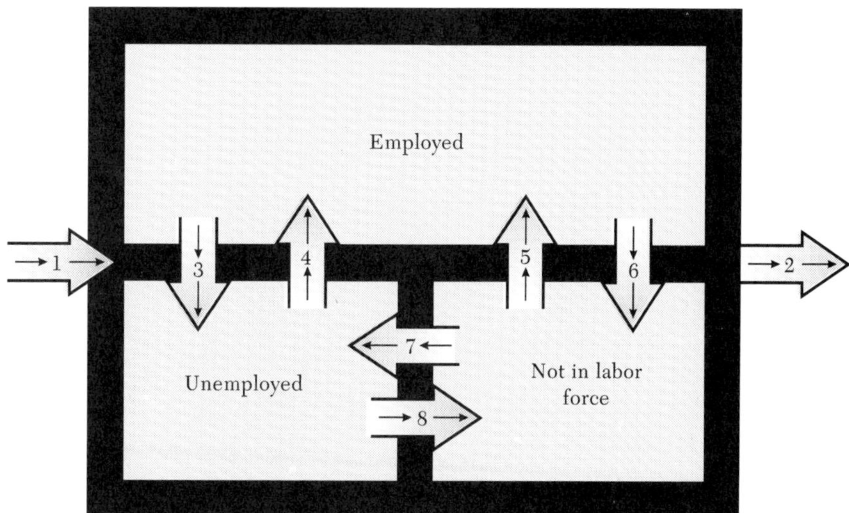

Arrows 3 and 4 represent the flows between employment and unemployment. Flow 3 consists of people becoming unemployed by either losing or quitting a job; flow 4 consists of people finding and accepting jobs after a period of unemployment. Other things being equal, unemployment will rise if flow 3 exceeds flow 4 and fall if the reverse is the case.

Arrows 5 and 6 represent the flows of people between employment and not in the labor force. Flow 5 is made up of people accepting job offers without having actively sought work. (Had they sought work, they would have been classified as unemployed before becoming employed, and so followed a path combining flows 7 and 4.) Flow 6 represents people who have lost or left jobs but are not looking for new employment. It includes people who are entering retirement, for example.

Arrows 7 and 8 represent flows between unemployment and not in the labor force. Flow 7 is made up of people entering the labor force to look for work; flow 8 is made up of those leaving the labor force after unsuccessfully looking for work. It includes the "discouraged workers" noted earlier.

This simple stock-flow model provides a useful framework for analyzing some important issues in the measurement and meaning of our labor force statistics.

How People Become Unemployed

As you can see from Figure 19.3, people become unemployed via either flow 3 or flow 7. Flow 3 includes both *job losers*, who have been discharged, fired, or laid off from a job, and *job leavers*, who have voluntarily quit one job to look for another. Flow 7 is made up of *labor force entrants*, including both *new*

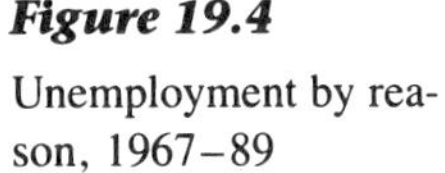

Figure 19.4

Unemployment by reason, 1967–89

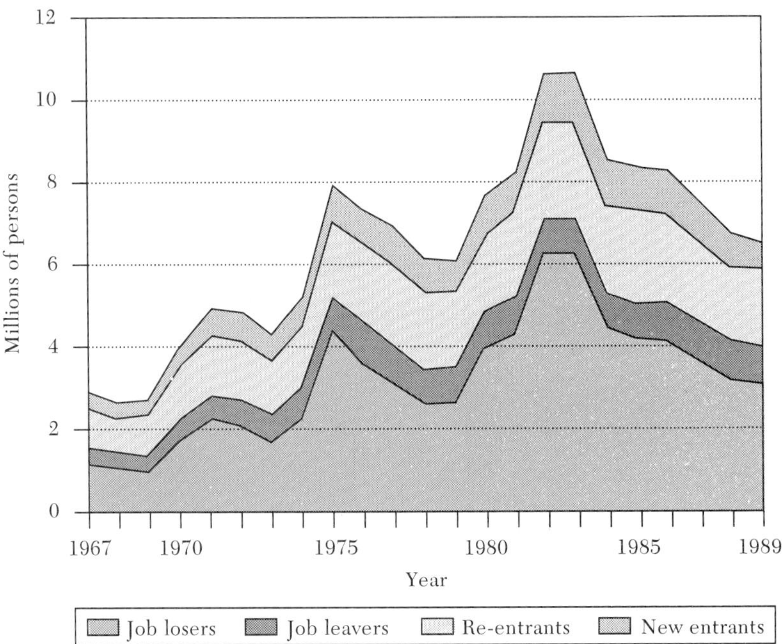

entrants who are looking for their first job and *re-entrants* who are returning to the labor force after a period of absence.

Figure 19.4 shows the composition of total unemployment by job losers, job leavers, and labor force entrants since 1967. Table 19.2 presents the same information in more detail for 1979 and 1989, 2 years of relatively low unemployment, and 1975 and 1983, 2 recession years. As you can see from the table, except during periods of recession, most unemployment is not the result of lost jobs but rather of decisions to leave a job or to enter the labor force. Even during a recession as severe as that of 1982–83, fewer than three out of five unemployed persons were unemployed because they had lost their jobs.

Simultaneous Changes in Employment and Unemployment Rates

In 1983 the U.S. economy recorded its highest *unemployment* rate since the Depression. In that same year, however, the *employment* rate was virtually the same as it had been in 1969, the year in which unemployment was at its lowest level since World War II. We can reconcile these seemingly contradictory facts and interpret their significance with the help of our stock-flow model.

Recall that the employment rate is the fraction of the age-eligible population that is employed, whereas the unemployment rate is the fraction of the labor force that is unemployed. Because these two rates are not simple complements, they can increase or decrease simultaneously depending on the flows in Figure 19.3. Given the age-eligible population, entry into the labor force via flows 5

Table 19.2

Unemployment by reason and duration

YEAR	**1975**		**1979**		**1983**		**1989**	
UNEMPLOYMENT RATE	**8.3%**		**5.8%**		**9.5%**		**5.2%**	
Reason	***Number in Thousands***	***Percent***	***Number in Thousands***	***Percent***	***Number in Thousands***	***Percent***	***Number in Thousands***	***Percent***
Job losers	4386	55.3	2635	42.9	6258	58.4	2983	45.7
Job leavers	827	10.4	880	14.3	830	7.7	1024	15.7
Re-entrants	1892	23.9	1806	29.4	2412	22.5	1843	28.2
New entrants	823	10.4	817	13.3	1216	11.4	677	10.4
Total	7929	100.0	6137	100.0	10717	100.0	6527	100.0
Duration (weeks)								
Mean	14.2		10.8		20.0		11.9	
Median	8.4		5.4		10.1		4.8	

Source: *Economic Report of the President, 1990.*

and 7 increases the employment rate as long as *any* of those entrants find jobs. However, the unemployment rate also rises if unemployment is higher among the new entrants than within the labor force as a whole.

To illustrate, suppose that there are 150 million people in the age-eligible population and that 100 million of them are initially in the labor force. If 95 million of those are employed and 5 million are unemployed, then the employment rate is 63 percent (= 95/150) and the unemployment rate is 5 percent (= 5/100). Now suppose that 10 million people who were in the age-eligible population but not in the labor force decide to enter the labor force. If only half of them find jobs, the unemployment rate will rise to 9.1 percent (= 10/110) at the same time that the employment rate rises to 67 percent (100/150).

Lower unemployment among the new entrants than within the labor force as a whole lowers the unemployment rate while raising the employment rate. For example, if all 10 million new entrants in the preceding example find jobs, the employment rate will rise to 70 percent (= 105/150) and the unemployment rate will fall to 4.5 percent (= 5/110).

Increases in both the age-eligible population and the labor force participation rate led to rapid growth in the U.S. labor force from the late 1960s through the mid-1980s. This growth, although accompanied by a rising employment rate, also contributed to a rising unemployment rate. In fact, more than two million new jobs would have had to be created each year during that period just to keep the unemployment rate steady. (More on this in a moment.)

Unemployment Rate or Employment Rate?

Cyclical variations in labor force participation often lead to short-run changes in unemployment that are largely unrelated to the availability of jobs. In particular, the net flow of persons into the labor force (flows 5 and 7) tends to increase during periods of recession. This implies that the increase in the unemployment rate overstates the reduction in job opportunities during a recession.* Many economists thus feel that the employment rate is a better indicator of labor market conditions, particularly on the demand side, than the unemployment rate. Nonetheless it is still the unemployment rate that grabs the headlines.

The Duration of Unemployment

During 1989 flows 3 and 7 together encompassed 22.7 percent of the labor force. Thus, since everyone who becomes a part of these flows is unemployed, more than a fifth of the labor force experienced some unemployment during 1989. Yet the unemployment rate for 1989 was only 5.2 percent. How can the unemployment rate be 5.2 percent when 22.7 percent of the labor force experiences some unemployment during the year?

The answer to this question lies in the fact that not all of those who were unemployed during 1989 were unemployed at the same time or for the entire year. In fact, the average duration of unemployment in 1989 was 11.9 weeks, or about 0.23 of a year. This implies that on average only 0.23 of the 22.7 percent, or 5.2 percent, were unemployed at any given time. If the same 22.7 percent of the labor force had been unemployed for an average of 13 weeks, or one-fourth of a year, the average unemployment rate would have been 5.7 percent (= 1/4 of 22.7). In general, the unemployment rate for any given year is equal to the total percentage of the labor force experiencing some unemployment during that year times the average duration of unemployment. Other things being equal, therefore, the rate of unemployment is directly related to the duration of unemployment.

The bottom part of Table 19.2 illustrates this relationship for the years 1975, 1979, 1983, and 1989. As you can see, changes in the duration of unemployment are an important contributor to cyclical variations in the unemployment rate. Indeed, as we shall see, a theory of the duration of unemployment is central to the modern theory of unemployment fluctuations.†

A "Dual" Labor Market?

As our stock-flow model makes clear, the labor force, employment, and unemployment are not made up of static, unchanging groups of people. Unemploy-

*See Michael Keeley, "Unemployment versus Employment," Federal Reserve Bank of San Francisco, *Weekly Letter*, September 21, 1984.

†One of today's preeminent macroeconomists, Robert Hall of Stanford University, has declared that "a theory of the unemployment rate is largely a theory of the duration of job seeking." (Robert E. Hall, "Is Unemployment a Macroeconomic Problem?" *American Economic Review: Papers and Proceedings*, May 1983, p. 221.)

ment, especially, is in a continuous state of flux. Between 1968 and 1984, for example, the flow of people entering the labor force to look for work (flow 7 in Figure 19.3) averaged 1.3 million per month, whereas the flow of unemployed people dropping out of the labor force (flow 8) averaged 1.5 million per month. These flows alone represent a monthly turnover of between 20 and 25 percent among the unemployed.* Adding flows 3 and 4 suggests an even more rapid turnover. Indeed, recent research has shown that a typical spell of unemployment (ending in either a job or withdrawal from the labor force) lasts less than a month, and that a significant portion of total unemployment is accounted for by a relatively small number of people repeatedly moving into and out of the labor force and between unemployment and short-term jobs lasting only a few months.†

By contrast, most employed persons are in jobs they have held longer than 3 years, and jobs lasting longer than 15 years account for more than half of all employment.‡ The appropriate picture of the labor market is therefore one that combines a large and stable core of employed persons with a fringe of persons who move continuously into and out of the labor force and, while they are in the labor force, between employment and unemployment.

THE NATURAL RATE OF UNEMPLOYMENT

All of the flows depicted in Figure 19.3 reflect, at least in part, the normal workings of a market economy. We have already seen that population growth and increasing labor force participation have led to a continuous flow of entry into the labor force. In addition, changing technologies and shifting demand patterns—while opening new employment opportunities in some sectors of the economy—also lead to a continuous flow of layoffs and discharges in other sectors. Finally, the freedom of workers to choose among employers, and the labor force mobility it implies, leads to a continuous flow of voluntary quits among workers seeking better jobs.

If all of these labor force entrants, job losers, and job leavers found new employment instantaneously, there would be no unemployment. However, finding a job without any intervening period of unemployment is the exception rather than the rule. Because information about what jobs are available, where, and at what wages is typically incomplete and costly, most job seekers must search for a period of time until they find an acceptable offer of employment. Some unem-

*See Michael Keeley, "Unemployment versus Employment," Federal Reserve Bank of San Francisco, *Weekly Letter*, September 21, 1984.

†See Kim B. Clark and Lawrence H. Summers, "Labor Market Dynamics and Unemployment: A Reconsideration," *Brookings Papers on Economic Activity*, 1:1979 and Robert E. Hall, "Employment Fluctuations and Wage Rigidity," *Brookings Papers on Economic Activity*, 1:1980.

‡See Robert E. Hall, "Is Unemployment a Macroeconomic Problem?" *American Economic Review: Papers and Proceedings*, May 1983, p. 221.

ployment is therefore inevitable regardless of the overall level of economic activity. To have it otherwise would not only prevent the market from continuously reallocating labor from less productive to more productive jobs but would also deny people the freedom to choose their employers and to enter or leave the labor force as they wish.

The **natural rate of unemployment** is the rate corresponding to the normal flow of job losers, job leavers, and labor force entrants, combined with the normal duration of job search.

The normal flow of entry into the labor force and the continuous reallocation of workers among jobs, combined with the normal duration of search for a new job, determine the **natural rate of unemployment**. As we saw in Chapter 15, most economists consider this rate to be about 5.5 percent in today's economy. One way to arrive at this figure is to note that during a typical nonrecessionary year following a period of relatively steady economic growth, about 22 percent of the U.S. labor force experiences some unemployment, and the duration of that unemployment averages about 13 weeks, or one-fourth of a year. This combination implies about a 5.5 percent unemployment rate (one-fourth of 22 percent).

Changes in the Natural Rate of Unemployment

The natural rate of unemployment is not engraved in stone. Although, by definition, it is independent of short-term, cyclical fluctuations in economic activity, it is influenced by longer term factors. During the period from the early 1960s to the mid-1980s, for example, demographic trends, sectoral adjustments to changes in world markets, and government policies raised the natural rate from about 4 percent of the labor force to about 6 percent.

Demographic Factors The rise in the birthrate following the end of World War II created the so-called baby boom generation. The influx of baby boomers into the labor force, which began during the early 1960s, contributed to a rising natural rate of unemployment in two ways. First, it raised the flow of new labor force entrants. Second, it increased the proportion of teenagers and young adults in the labor force. Those groups tend to switch jobs more often and remain unemployed for longer periods of time than their adult counterparts.

Increasing labor force participation by women also contributed to the rise in the natural rate of unemployment. In the early 1950s, for example, only one-third of all age-eligible women were in the labor force; by the late 1980s, this proportion had risen to more than one-half. The high rate at which women were entering the labor force thus reinforced the effects of the rapid entry by baby boomers.

Sectoral Shifts During the 1970s and 1980s, the U.S. economy was buffeted by several dramatic changes in world oil prices and by increased foreign competition in many markets. Adjustments to these shocks led to a substantial reallocation of the labor force out of energy intensive sectors of the economy and out of sectors such as automobiles, steel, and consumer electronics, which were especially vulnerable to foreign competition. By one estimate, these sectoral shifts added more than a percentage point to the natural rate of unemployment.*

Government Policies Extensions in the coverage and duration of government unemployment compensation programs have also raised the natural rate of unemployment by reducing the costs of unemployment and encouraging longer periods of job search. Other income maintenance (welfare) programs, most of which were enacted between 1965 and 1975, have had similar effects.

The upward trend in the natural rate of unemployment has begun to reverse itself in recent years. The baby boom generation has largely been absorbed into the labor force, and the "baby bust" generation that followed will soon be maturing. It also appears that the labor force participation rate among women has begun to stabilize. According to the Bureau of Labor Statistics, these trends should slow the rate of entry into the labor force from its peak of more than 2.5 million persons per year during the 1970s to less than 1.0 million per year by the early 1990s. They will also mean less job turnover as the average age and experience of the labor force begins to increase. As a result, the natural rate of unemployment may decline significantly in the economy of the 1990s.

CYCLICAL FLUCTUATIONS IN UNEMPLOYMENT

Economics views employment and unemployment as it views other social phenomena, namely, as the outcome of individual choice. People can choose whether or not to participate in the labor force, whether to remain in a job or quit to look for another, and, if unemployed, whether to accept job offers that become available or to continue looking for something better. Like all economic choices, these depend on both the personal preferences of those doing the choosing and the alternatives that are available to them. In the case of labor force status, the alternatives are determined by labor market conditions—job openings, wage rates, and the like—and the information people have about those conditions.

(Saying that labor force status is largely a matter of choice is *not* equivalent to saying that people who are unemployed, or who are discouraged workers, are happy with their choices. Economics says only that people make the best choice they can from among the available alternatives; it does not claim that those alternatives themselves are always satisfactory. Certainly they are not satisfactory for the unemployed head of a household whose only choices are to accept a low-paying job or drop out of the labor force.)

*David M. Lilien, "Sectoral Shifts and Cyclical Unemployment," *Journal of Political Economy*, August 1982.

In attempting to explain unemployment as a consequence of rational choice, economics has focused on two important aspects of the labor market, namely, *job search* and *contracting*. In effect, these two approaches reflect the dual nature of the labor market that we noted above. Job search theories emphasize the continuous turnover among unemployed persons, whereas contract theories emphasize the stability of long-term employment relationships.

Job Search Theory

How long will an unemployed person search for a job? Before you answer "Until he finds one," you should know that most unemployed people in fact find—and reject—many job offers before they accept one (or drop out of the labor force). By the same token, employers rarely hire the first warm body that rolls into the personnel office to apply for a job opening. Both the job seeker and the potential employer usually find it worthwhile to examine a number of alternatives—that is, to *search*—before making a decision. Economists analyze this search process in terms of its benefits and costs.

The Benefits and Costs of Job Search

It is unlikely that a skilled auto mechanic would accept a job as a fry cook just because it happens to appear in the want ads on the day he becomes unemployed. Given his skills and experience, he knows that he can probably do much better if he invests some time searching for a job that is more rewarding and better suited to his skills and experience. In general, the longer he searches, the better the job offer he can expect to find.

This fundamental benefit of job search is a consequence of the job seeker's incomplete information. If he already knew everything about all of the job offers available to him, there would be no need for search. He would simply pick the best offer and go back to work. In effect, search expands the job seeker's alternatives by providing him with valuable information about what the labor market has to offer. In that sense, it is as much a search for information as it is a search for employment.

Employers also benefit from search. Screening many job seekers prior to hiring one not only enables the employer to find the worker best suited to his job vacancy but also provides him with information about supply conditions in the labor market. If he already knew everything about the skills and experience of all job seekers, their aptitudes for the type of employment he is offering, and the wages they are expecting, search by the employer would also be unnecessary.

On the cost side, however, job search consumes time, effort, and other resources. In addition, the job seeker incurs the opportunity cost of foregone income whenever he rejects a job offer in favor of continued search. Similarly, the employer's search costs include not only the costs of help wanted ads and interviews by the personnel office but also the production foregone as long as a job remains unfilled.

Figure 19.5

Balancing the benefits and costs of job search

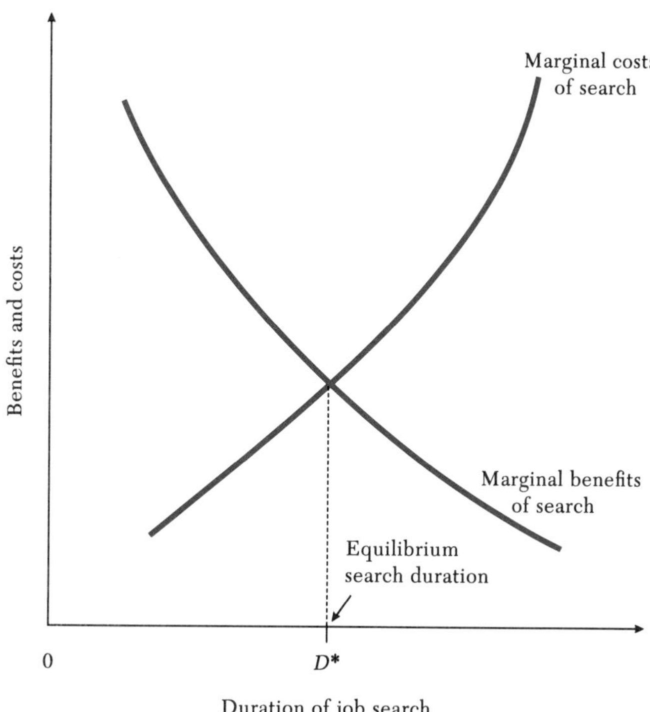

To maximize the net gain from search, the job seeker or potential employer continues searching only as long as the expected marginal benefits from further search exceed the marginal costs. This balancing of benefits and costs at the margin is illustrated in Figure 19.5. The marginal benefit curve is negatively sloped because, other things being equal, the longer the duration of search, the less new information there is left to uncover. The marginal cost curve is positively sloped because the longer the search, the better the options that have already been found and thus must be turned down to continue searching. The intersection of the marginal benefit and marginal cost curves thus determines the equilibrium search duration D^*.

Job Search and Unemployment Differentials

Differences in unemployment rates among various subgroups within the labor force often reflect differences in the benefits and costs of job search. For example, because teenagers are typically supported by their parents, they tend to have relatively low search costs. As a result, they can afford to search longer and more frequently and be more "choosey" than the average job seeker in deciding whether to accept offers of employment. This at least partially explains why the unemployment rate among teenagers is about double that for the labor force as a whole. By contrast, family responsibilities make search costs relatively high for married men with families, so they tend to search less frequently and for shorter periods of time than other members of the labor force. As a result their unemployment rate is typically less than half that for the labor force as a whole.

Reservation Wages, Wage Offers, and Search Duration

Our major concern here is not with differences in unemployment rates among various occupations and categories of the labor force but with fluctuations in the unemployment rate for the labor force as a whole. We can address this question with an extension of our basic job search model.

The typical job seeker does not search in an informational vacuum. She has first-hand knowledge of her own skills, experience, and other qualifications, and she can rely on a variety of sources, such as want ads and discussions with fellow workers, for additional information about her value in the labor market. On the basis of this information, the job seeker determines the lowest wage at which she will accept employment. We call this her **reservation wage**. In principle, the reservation wage includes not only actual dollar pay but also the monetary value of other job characteristics, such as location and work environment. Thought of in this way, it summarizes the job seeker's minimally acceptable conditions for employment.

A person's **reservation wage** is the minimum wage at which that person will accept employment.

The job seeker may start with a high reservation wage, hoping to get lucky and land a good job quickly. However, as the duration of her search lengthens and the costs of search mount, she will become less "choosey" and begin to lower her reservation wage. This is illustrated by the negatively sloped reservation wage curve labelled *RW* in Figure 19.6. On the other hand, the longer the duration of her search, the higher the *wage offer* the job seeker can expect to find. This is illustrated by the positively sloped wage offer curve labelled *WO* in the same diagram.

Because the job seeker continues to search until she finds a wage offer at least as high as her reservation wage, the intersection of the reservation wage curve and the wage offer curve determines her expected search duration. Thus the job seeker's expected search duration in Figure 19.6 is D^* and the (nominal) wage at which she expects to be hired is W_0. Note that the D^* in Figure 19.6 is the same search duration as that determined by the marginal benefits and costs of job search in Figure 19.5 because a rational job seeker will adjust her reservation wage so that her expected search duration is that which equates the marginal benefit and marginal cost of search.

We should emphasize that D^* and W_0 are *expected* outcomes. Some job seekers who expect to search for D^* weeks and land a job at a wage of W_0 will be lucky and find a higher paying job in a shorter period of time; others with the same expectations, but worse luck, will search longer and end up accepting a lower wage. However, if all job seekers search on the basis of correct information about wage offers, the good luck and the bad luck cancel and *average* search duration is D^*.

Figure 19.6

Reservation wages, wage offers, and the duration of job search

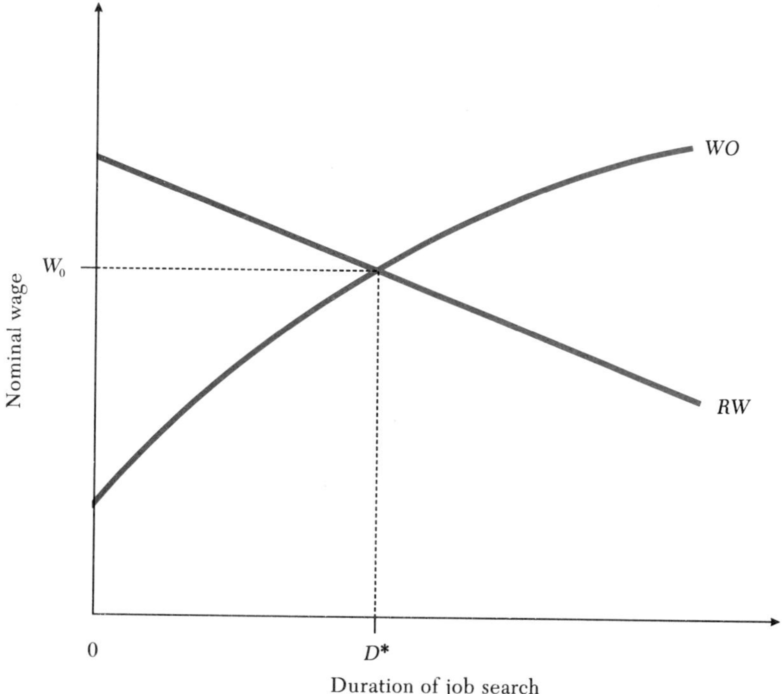

Since we are interested primarily in changes in *aggregate* unemployment, we interpret the reservation wage and wage offer curves in Figure 19.6 as averages for the economy as a whole. In this context, D^* represents average search duration for the economy as a whole when the labor market is in equilibrium. In other words, D^* is the search duration associated with the natural rate of unemployment.

Job Search and Unemployment Fluctuations

Job search theory attributes cyclical fluctuations in unemployment to imperfect information on the part of job seekers. In particular, when job seekers fail to recognize a change in labor market conditions, they search for a longer or shorter time than they would if they knew the true state of the labor market. It is these variations in search duration that lead to unemployment fluctuations in the job search model.

We can illustrate the argument with the aid of Figure 19.7 on page 468. Part (a) shows reservation wages and wage offers and their relation to search duration; part (b) shows the relation between search duration and the rate of unemployment u. The positive slope of the line in part (b) indicates that, other things being equal, an increase in search duration leads to an increase in the unemployment rate.

Figure 19.7

The effects of a fall in the demand for labor on search duration and unemployment

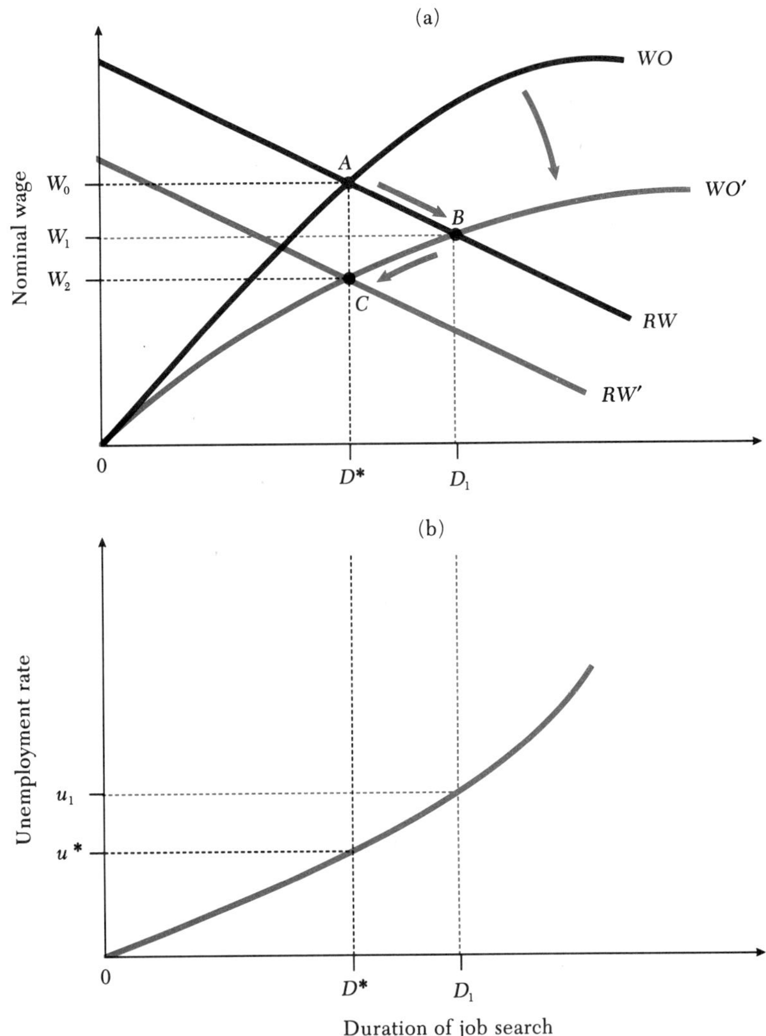

We start from an initial equilibrium at point A, with job seekers finding employment at a wage W_0 after a search duration of D^* which, as we noted earlier, corresponds to the natural rate of unemployment u^* in part (b) of the diagram.

Now suppose there is a fall in the demand for labor. Because employers are offering fewer jobs at lower wages than before, the actual wage offer curve in Figure 19.7(a) shifts down to WO'. If job seekers are unaware of the change in labor market conditions, however, they will continue to set their reservation wages on the basis of the original—but now incorrect—wage offer curve WO. With the reservation wage fixed, there will be a temporary movement to point B. Job seekers *expect* to obtain a wage of W_0 after a period of search equal to

D^*, but because they expect more than the labor market has to offer, they *actually* end up searching longer (D_1) and accepting lower wages (W_1). The increase in search duration from D^* to D_1 causes the unemployment rate in Figure 19.7(b) to rise from u^* to u_1.

The story doesn't end here, however. Although job seekers may initially think that their failure to find another good job as quickly as anticipated is simply due to bad luck, their prolonged search will eventually teach them that it is really the result of diminished alternatives. Realizing this, they will revise their reservation wages downward rather than continue to bear the high costs of longer search. This is illustrated in Figure 19.7(a) by the downward shift of the reservation wage curve from *WR* to *WR'*. In the final equilibrium at point *C*, the wage paid for new job hirings has fallen to W_2, and search duration has returned to its equilibrium length D^*. Finally, with search duration back in equilibrium, unemployment has returned to its natural rate in part (b) of the diagram.

Figure 19.8 on the following page illustrates the case of an increase in the demand for labor that shifts the *actual* wage offer curve up from *WO* to *WO'*. If job seekers are initially unaware of the increase in demand, the *expected* wage offer curve will remain at *WO* and the reservation wage curve at *RW*. As a result, search duration will fall and unemployment will drop temporarily below its natural rate. However, as job seekers begin to realize that their ability to find jobs more quickly and at higher wages than expected is not the result of luck but of an improvement in labor market conditions, they will raise their reservation wages. The upward shift of the reservation wage curve from *RW* to *RW'* will lead to still higher wages, a return of search duration to its equilibrium length, and a return of unemployment to its natural rate.

In summary, job search theory attributes both fluctuations in unemployment about its natural rate and lags in wage adjustment to the time it takes to learn about a change in labor market conditions. If all workers were fully informed about a change in the demand for labor as soon as it occurred, they would adjust their reservation wages immediately to reflect that change. In terms of Figures 19.7 and 19.8, the reservation wage curve would shift simultaneously with the wage offer curve, wages would adjust immediately to W_2, and neither search duration nor unemployment would be affected. According to job search theory, therefore, incomplete information is the culprit responsible for both lagging wage adjustments and fluctuations in unemployment about its natural rate.

Contract Theory*

As we have already noted, the majority of the labor force consists of people in the midst of long-term employment relationships, or what we usually refer to as *careers*. In contrast to job search theory's emphasis on labor market turnover,

*This section draws on Charles L. Schultze, "Microeconomic Efficiency and Nominal Wage Stickiness," *American Economic Review* (March 1985), Robert Hall, "Employment Fluctuations and Wage Rigidity," *Brookings Papers on Economic Activity* 1:1980, and Benjamin Klein, "Contract Costs and Administered Prices: An Economic Theory of Rigid Wages," *American Economic Review* (May 1984).

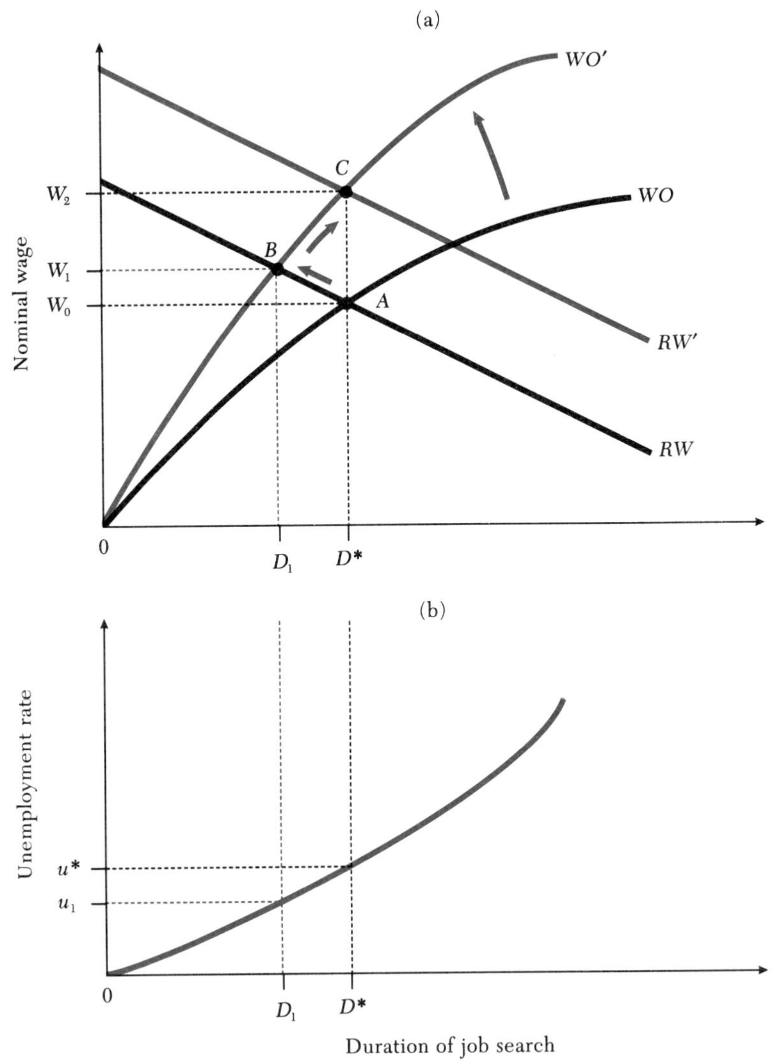

Figure 19.8

The effects of a rise in the demand for labor or search duration and unemployment

the contract theory of the labor market focuses on the stability and continuity of career employment.

The Mutual Gains from Long-Term Employment

If all workers were identical and interchangeable, it would make little difference to an employer whom he hired, or for how long. By the same token, if all employers were identical, no worker would have much incentive to remain with a particular employer for any length of time. In reality, however, neither workers nor employers are perfectly interchangeable, and it is this fact that provides the "glue" that binds employers and workers together in the career labor market.

Career employment not only provides workers with relatively certain and stable jobs but also enables employers to avoid the costs of repeatedly training new workers, while at the same time providing them with a work force whose abilities and productivity they can count on. Long-term employment is also the source of the on-the-job experience that makes a worker uniquely valuable to a particular employer. Once a good match has been found, it therefore pays both sides to preserve it.

They can do so by entering a formal contract, such as the collective bargaining agreements between firms and labor unions. About 20 percent of the U.S. labor force is covered by such agreements. However, formal contracts are not always necessary to preserve long-term employment relationships. In many instances, employer and worker simply find it advantageous to continue an arrangement from which each benefits and which neither has an incentive to violate despite the absence of any formal penalties for doing so. Such informal bonds constitute an **implicit contract**.

An **implicit contract** is an informal, unwritten agreement based on mutual advantage.

Implicit contracts have certain advantages over formal, written contracts. For one thing, they avoid costly, prior negotiations over how to deal with every conceivable contingency that may affect the employment relation in the future. Instead they rely on the common interests of both parties to handle those contingencies as they arise. As a result, implicit contracts can be more flexible and cheaper to enforce than explicit contracts. This is the reason that implicit contracts are so much more prevalent in the career labor market than explicit contracts of the collective bargaining type.

Wage and Employment Adjustments under Long-Term Contracts

Wage payments under a long-term employment contract are similar to the payments on an installment contract. When someone buys a new car, for example, he typically takes out a loan and agrees to make fixed monthly payments until the car is paid for. The present value of those payments, which reflects both the purchase price of the car and the interest rate on the loan, is the price that adjusts to clear the market at the time of purchase. Subsequent changes in the market that alter car prices or interest rates do not affect the monthly payments on an existing installment contract.

By analogy, the expected *present value* of the flow of future wages in long-term employment contracts adjusts to clear the labor market *at the time such agreements are entered in to*. Subsequent, short-term fluctuations in labor market conditions do not affect those wages. Instead they are absorbed through variations in employment. This has certain advantages. It eliminates the need to renegotiate wages every time there is a blip in demand. It also provides a certain and stable wage that most workers prefer to an uncertain and fluctuating wage. (For example, workers typically prefer a contract promising a straight $10 per hour through thick and thin to one promising $12 per hour when the sales are above normal and $8 per hour when sales are below normal, even though the average wage would be the same under each contract.) Finally, the fixed wage reduces any incentive the employer may have to exploit his position at the expense of his workers. If he could vary wages, he might be tempted to claim that weak demand warrants a wage cut when that is really not the case. This kind of opportunistic behavior is less likely to occur when temporary fluctuations in demand are absorbed through variations in employment because reductions in employment, unlike wage cuts, reduce the employer's output and revenues as well as his wage costs. As such, they impose costs on the employer as well as on the worker.

None of this means that wages in long-term employment contracts are fixed forever. Such contracts must allow for wage revision in the event of *permanent* changes in labor market conditions. This is the reason that explicit contracts, such as collective bargaining agreements, are typically renegotiated every 3 years. Implicit contracts must also allow for wage adjustments; otherwise the relation between the employer and his career workers would become strained and eventually break down, to the detriment of both, under the weight of economic change.

The important point is that contract theory suggests that there is an element of stickiness in wage adjustments. It takes time to determine whether a change in labor market conditions is the result of random and temporary factors that can be accommodated within an existing wage agreement or whether it reflects more permanent factors that warrant a change in that agreement. Only when the latter proves to be the case will wages eventually adjust to clear the market.

The contract theory of the labor market thus concludes that fluctuations in unemployment about its natural rate are the result of contractual wage stickiness in the face of changes in the demand for labor.

Job Search and Contract as Complementary Theories

Because contract theory explains unemployment fluctuations on the basis of sticky wages, it falls within the Keynesian tradition of macroeconomic analysis. Job search theory, by contrast, holds that wages are fundamentally flexible; it is only incomplete information that prevents them from adjusting immediately to a change in labor market conditions. Job search theory therefore falls within the classical tradition.

It is nonetheless useful to think of job search and contract theories as complementary. The continuous flow of people between employment and unemployment, which encompasses a relatively small percentage of the labor force but which accounts for a large share of unemployment, is probably best analyzed within the job search framework. On the other hand, the implications of the long-term employment relationships that characterize most of the labor force are best analyzed within the contract framework. Moreover, neither theory can ignore the implications of the other. It is through job search and labor market turnover, for example, that the wages paid to new employees begin to adjust and eventually establish the conditions for renegotiation of wages in the long-term contracts of career employees. By the same token, the variations in employment that occur when wages are fixed by contract affect the flow of job searchers and the duration of search. For example, although temporary layoffs themselves account for a relatively small portion of all unemployment, many career workers look for stop-gap jobs while on temporary layoff. This makes it more difficult for other job searchers, especially unskilled new entrants, to find jobs and thus increases the duration of their search.

What job search theory and contract theory—and indeed all of modern macroeconomics—have in common is a view that employers and workers often commit themselves to courses of action based on incomplete information. They do so, not because they are irrational, but because information is costly and they do not have perfect foresight. In the next chapter, we extend this insight as we develop the modern theory of real output and the price level.

CHAPTER SUMMARY

1. The *labor force* includes everyone in the *age-eligible population* who is either working or actively seeking work. The remainder of the age-eligible population—namely, people over 16 years of age who are neither working nor seeking work—are not in the labor force.

2. The *unemployment rate* is the percentage of the labor force that is unemployed; the *employment rate* is the percentage of the age-eligible population that is employed; the *labor force participation rate* is the percentage of the age-eligible population that is in the labor force.

3. People become unemployed for three reasons: *job losers* include those who have been discharged, fired, or laid off from a job; *job leavers* include those who have voluntarily quit one job to look for another; *labor force entrants* include both new entrants who are looking for their first job and re-entrants who are returning to the labor force after a period of absence.

4. Most of the fluctuations in the unemployment rate are the result of fluctuations in the average duration of unemployment. Other things being equal, the longer the duration of unemployment, the higher the unemployment rate.

5. The labor market appears to be a dual one, combining a large and stable core of employed persons with a fringe of persons who move continuously into and out of the labor force and, while in the labor force, between employment and unemployment.

6. The normal flow of entry into the labor force and the continuous reallocation of workers among jobs, together with the normal duration of search for a new job, determine the *natural rate of unemployment*. Demographic factors, sectoral changes in the economy, and government policies combined to raise the natural rate of unemployment during the 1960s and 1970s, but it now appears to be falling.

7. *Job search theories* of employment and unemployment emphasize the continuous turnover among unemployed persons, whereas *contract theories* emphasize the stability of long-term employment relationships.

8. The equilibrium duration of job search is that which equates the marginal benefits and marginal costs of further search.

9. According to job search theory, incomplete information is responsible for fluctuations in unemployment about its natural rate. When unemployed workers search for work on the basis of overly optimistic information, search duration increases and unemployment rises above its natural rate; when they search on the basis of overly pessimistic information, search duration decreases and unemployment falls below its natural rate.

10. Contract theory starts with a recognition of the mutual gains to employers and employees from long-term, *career employment*. It concludes that wages set in contracts, whether explicit or implicit, tend to be sticky in the face of short-term changes in labor market conditions.

11. It is best to think of job search and contract as complementary theories. Job search theory better explains the continuous flow of people between employment and unemployment, wheras contract theory better explains the long-term employment relationships that characterize most of the labor force.

Key Terms and Concepts

labor force participation rate
employment rate
natural rate of unemployment
reservation wage
implicit contract

Questions for Thought and Discussion

1. Which of the following are in the labor force and employed, which are in the labor force and unemployed, and which are not in the labor force?
   a. A 14-year-old with a paper route.
   b. A 19-year-old who has been laid off and decides to return to college full time.
   c. A college student seeking a part-time job.
   d. An upwardly mobile young professional (a.k.a. "yuppie") who has quit a $75,000-a-year job to look for one that pays at least $100,000.
   e. A retired person who keeps busy doing volunteer work.
   f. An aspiring actor who waits on tables while waiting for a big break.
   g. An executive who lost his job and is using his severance pay to take a vacation in the Bahamas.

2. Suppose that the age-eligible population of the imaginary nation of Concordia is 110 people. During a recent year this population was divided into three (mutually exclusive) categories: 60 million people held jobs without interruption during the entire year; 20 million people were either working or actively seeking work at any time during the year; 30 million people neither worked nor sought work during the entire year. In addition, the average length of job search for the people in the second category was 3 months. What were Concordia's average unemployment rate, average employment rate, and labor force participation rate for the year?
3. Can unemployment ever be "too low"? Would it be "good" if we could push unemployment below its natural rate?
4. It is sometimes said that our full-employment goal should be the elimination of all "involuntary" unemployment? Is there a difference between "voluntary" and "involuntary" unemployment?
5. Other things being equal, what do you think would be the impact of each of the following on the natural rate of unemployment?
   a. An increase in the proportion of multiple-earner families.
   b. An increase in the birthrate (distinguish between the immediate and longer term effects).
   c. A law that raises the level and coverage of the government's unemployment compensation.
   d. A computerized, national job information bank that provides centralized information about jobs available all over the country.
6. Other things being equal, do you think that the average duration of search would be higher in occupations with large wage variations or in occupations with small wage variations?
7. As we have already noted, there is evidence that labor force participation tends to rise during recessions. Is this evidence consistent with the hypothesis that there are more discourage workers during recessions?

CHAPTER 20

Aggregate Supply and Aggregate Demand: The Modern Theory

Does more spending lead to more real output and employment or just to inflation and higher prices? Is it true, as Keynes argued, that when people spend less they are also eliminating other people's opportunities for employment? If so, must they then spend more to restore those opportunities? Are fluctuations in spending the principal cause of the business cycle? Are they the only cause? Are there trade-offs between real and nominal variables? For example, can we have less unemployment if we are willing to accept more inflation? Less inflation if we are willing to accept more unemployment?

The theory of aggregate supply and aggregate demand that we develop in this chapter summarizes the most recent attempts by economists to answer such questions. That theory builds on the classical and Keynesian foundations introduced in Chapter 18, incorporates the labor market analysis developed in Chapter 19, and adds another crucial ingredient—namely, the affect of expectations or anticipations on people's behavior. Indeed, the emphasis on foresight in economic decision making is one of the defining characteristics of modern macroeconomics.

THE BASIC MACROECONOMIC MODEL

Changes in the level of total spending on final goods—what we have called *aggregate demand*—must be absorbed by changes in prices, changes in quantities supplied, or a combination of the two. In symbols, aggregate demand determines nominal national product Y and, by definition, $Y = PQ$. It follows that a change in aggregate demand must lead to a change in P, a change in Q, or both.

There is substantial agreement among economists that by the time a change in aggregate demand has been fully incorporated into all economic decisions, it will have changed all prices and other nominal variables in proportion, with no lasting effect on real variables such as output and employment. In other words, the economy's long-run aggregate supply curve, like the classical aggregate supply curve of Chapter 18, is vertical.

By contrast, empirical evidence strongly suggests that changes in aggregate demand *do* have Keynesian-type, short-run effects on real output and employment. The key to understanding these short-run effects, and therefore the key to understanding the business cycle, is to be found in people's expectations of the future and the implications of those expectations for current economic decisions.

Every production and employment decision made today reflects at least an implicit expectation of the future. People enter the labor force, search for jobs, and accept employment in anticipation of the real goods and services they will be able to buy with their wages in future weeks and months. Firms hire and fire workers, order materials, stock inventories, print price lists, and make dozens of decisions every day on the basis of their expectations of future market conditions. Often these expectations lead to commitments, such as when a worker enters into a career employment relation with a firm, or when one firm agrees to supply another with components or raw materials over a period of time. As we saw in Chapter 19, these commitments may be spelled out in formal, written contracts, or they may be based on implicit contracts that rely solely on the mutual interests of the affected parties for their enforcement.

When economic conditions change, firms and workers adjust their expectations and revise their commitments accordingly. The time it takes them to do so provides the basis for the macroeconomic distinction between the *long run* and the *short run*. In particular, we define the long run as a period of time long enough for people to fully adjust their expectations and revise their commitments in response to changing economic conditions. In the short run, by contrast, we consider expectations—and by implication, the commitments based on those expectations—to be fixed.

A word of warning! Although it is convenient to think of the difference between the short run and long run in terms of calendar time, it is important to remember that the logical distinction is based not on time but on the adjustment of people's expectations. Indeed, if economic change were fully and accurately anticipated and incorporated into people's expectations without delay, and if all commitments could be immediately and costlessly revised when expectations change, then the short run would disappear entirely. It is precisely because this is almost never the case, however, that the distinction between the short run and the long run is a useful one.

Long-Run and Short-Run Aggregate Supply

The economy's **long-run aggregate supply curve** shows how fully anticipated changes in the price level affect aggregate real output.

In the theory of aggregate supply, the distinction between the long run and the short run is based on the relation between the *actual price level* and the *expected price level*. In particular, the **long-run aggregate supply curve** shows what happens to real output when changes in the actual price level are matched by changes in the expected price level. When firms and workers make their decisions on the basis of correct expectations, relative prices and real wages clear all markets regardless of the general level of nominal prices. The long-run aggregate supply curve is therefore just a vertical line whose position is determined by the natural rate of real output Q^*. Such a curve is labelled *LRAS* in Figure 20.1, where the vertical axis measures the *actual* price level.

It is important to emphasize that the vertical long-run aggregate supply curve is an *other-things-equal* concept: It does *not* imply that real output is fixed in the long run, only that it is not affected by changes in the price level. The natural rate of real output, and therefore the position of the long-run aggregate supply

Figure 20.1

Long-run and short-run aggregate supply curves

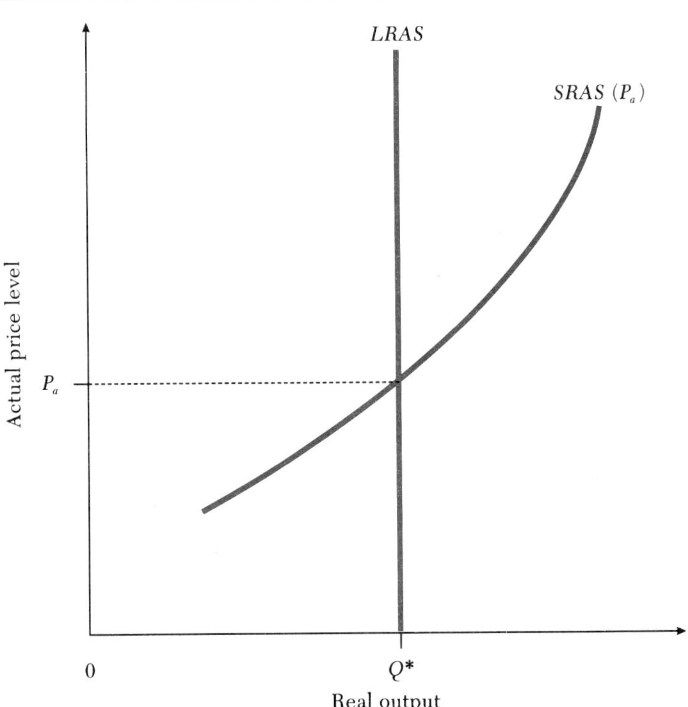

curve, does change with changes in such *real* factors as the labor force, the capital stock, and technology.

The economy's **short-run aggregate supply curve** shows how unexpected changes in the price level affect aggregate real output.

The **short-run aggregate supply curve** shows what happens to real output when the actual price level varies while the expected price level remains fixed. The curve labelled $SRAS(P_a)$ in Figure 20.1 is a short-run aggregate supply curve. The parenthetical P_a indicates that the curve is drawn for an expected price level of P_a. Whenever we draw a short-run aggregate supply curve, we must specify the expected price level for which it is drawn. Moreover, the short-run aggregate supply curve must always intersect the long-run aggregate supply curve at that expected price level because the economy is in long-run equilibrium, and thus on the long-run aggregate supply curve, only when price level expectations are fulfilled. The only point that a short-run aggregate supply curve and the long-run aggregate supply curve can have in common, therefore, is the point at which the actual price level matches the expected price level.

The positive slope of the short-run aggregate supply curve tells us that real output rises above (falls below) its natural rate whenever the actual price level rises above (falls below) the expected price level. Let us postpone for the moment an in-depth discussion of why this should be the case and first examine some of its implications.

An Increase in Aggregate Demand: Inflationary Boom

Suppose that aggregate demand is initially given by the curve labelled AD_0 in Figure 20.2 on the following page. Point A is a point of long-run equilibrium because it reflects a price level P_a that is consistent with both the expenditure plans of buyers (it is on the aggregate demand curve) *and* with the expectations of firms and workers (it is also on the long-run aggregate supply curve).

Now suppose that aggregate demand increases from AD_0 to AD_1. With the expected price level fixed at P_a in the short run, the increase in aggregate demand moves the economy from point A to point B along its short-run aggregate supply curve, raising the actual price level to P_b. However, if firms expect the overall price level to remain at P_a, each will interpret the increase in the price of its own product as an increase in *relative* price. Because an increase in the relative price of a good makes it profitable to produce more of that good, firms will attempt to expand production, and thus employment. As they do, they will bid up the nominal wage. If workers also expect the price level to remain at P_a, they will interpret the increase in the *nominal* wage as an increase in the *real* wage and respond by supplying more labor. As long as price level expectations are fixed for both firms and workers, therefore, the increase in aggregate demand leads to a short-run increase in output and employment as well as prices.

In the long run, expectations will adjust to the higher prices. In particular, when workers realize that the price level has risen, they will demand still higher wages to compensate for the loss of purchasing power. This will raise production costs and supply prices and shift the short-run aggregate supply curve upward.

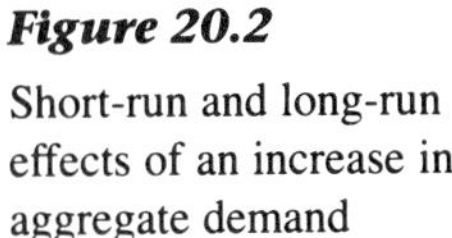

Figure 20.2

Short-run and long-run effects of an increase in aggregate demand

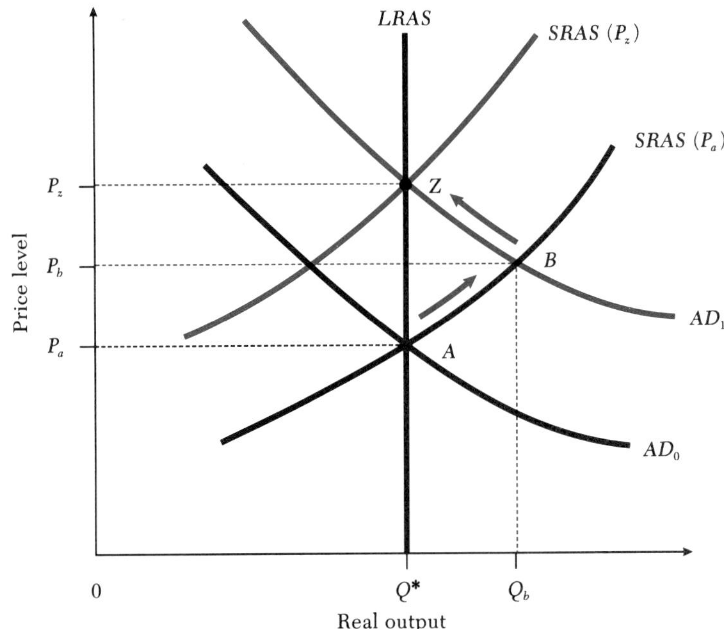

Note that whereas an increase in the *actual* price level results in a movement along a given short-run aggregate supply curve, such as that from point *A* to point *B* in Figure 20.2, an increase in the *expected* price level shifts the curve upward. This is because expectations of higher prices on the part of workers and other input suppliers lead to higher production costs and thus higher supply prices for any given level of real output.

Once the expected price level has risen to P_z, the short-run aggregate supply curve will have shifted upward to *SRAS*(P_z), real output will have returned to its natural rate, and the economy will be back in long-run equilibrium at point *Z*. (We postpone for the moment a more complete discussion of the adjustment process that carries us from point *B* to point *Z*.)

During the **demand pull** phase of the inflationary process, an increase in aggregate demand pulls up the prices of final goods before it affects wages and other costs.

During the **cost push** phase of the inflationary process, expectations of continuing increases in the price level push up wages and other costs.

The Inflationary Process: Demand Pull and Cost Push

The adjustment to an increase in aggregate demand includes a period of inflation as the price level rises from P_a to P_z. The initial increase in prices from P_a to P_b, which reflects the effects of the increase in aggregate demand before it affects wages and other costs, represents the **demand pull** phase of the inflationary process. The further increase from P_b to P_z, which is the result of rising wages and other costs pushing up supply prices as expectations adjust to higher prices, represents the **cost push** phase of the inflationary process.

Both the demand pull and cost push phases of inflation are part of the process initiated by the increase in aggregate demand. Although, as we shall see, a shift in the aggregate supply curve can cause a one-shot increase in the price level, most economists believe that inflation cannot persist in the absence of continuously increasing aggregate demand. In particular, they reject arguments that "greedy" labor unions or business firms can start and sustain an inflationary wage–price spiral without accompanying increases in aggregate demand.

A Decrease in Aggregate Demand: Recession and Recovery

We can simply reverse the preceding analysis to examine the consequences of a fall in aggregate demand. This is illustrated in Figure 20.3 where points A and Z again represent the initial and final long-run equilibria, respectively. When aggregate demand falls from AD_0 to AD_1, the short-run effect is to decrease the actual price level to P_b. With the expected overall price level fixed at P_a in the short run, each firm will interpret the fall in the nominal price of its own product as a decrease in its relative price and respond by cutting output and employment. The result is a fall in real output to Q_b and a corresponding drop in employment. The decline in output and employment constitutes a recession.

Eventually, as workers and firms realize that their expectations are inconsistent with actual economic conditions, wages and other input prices will begin to fall, the short-run aggregate supply curve will shift downward, and real output will begin to rise. The economy will have entered the recovery phase of the cycle, which is represented by the movement from point B to point Z in Figure

Figure 20.3

Short-run and long-run effects of a decrease in aggregate demand

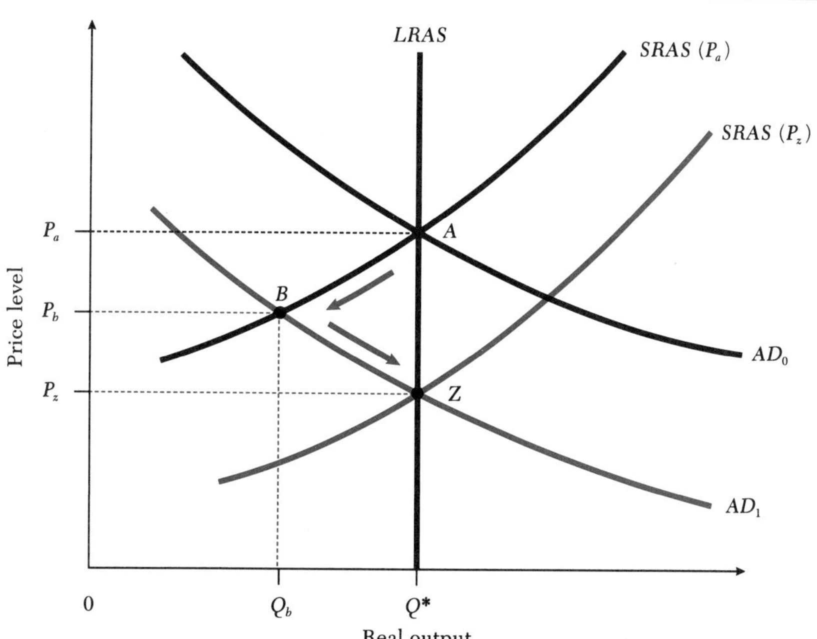

20.3. Once the process has reached point Z, the economy will be back in long-run equilibrium with real output back at its natural rate and the price level lowered to P_z.

Expectations Adjustment: The Transition from the Short Run to the Long Run

To make explicit the expectations adjustment process that gets us from the short run to the long run, let us consider two possibilities, namely, *adaptive* expectations and *rational* expectations.

Adaptive Expectations

Adaptive expectations are formed by extrapolating past experience into the future without inquiring into the cause-and-effect relationships between the two.

Suppose you are planning a picnic for tomorrow and you want to know what the weather will be like. If you forecast that it will probably be sunny and warm tomorrow simply because it has been sunny and warm all week, then you are forming **adaptive expectations** of tomorrow's weather. Adaptive expectations are expectations formed by simply extrapolating past experience into the future without inquiring into the cause-and-effect relation between the two.

To illustrate the macroeconomic implications of adaptive expectations, let us consider a simple case in which people expect tomorrow's price level to be the same as today's.* Figure 20.4 depicts the resulting adjustment to an increase in aggregate demand. Once again point A represents an initial long-run equilibrium, AD_0 is the initial level of aggregate demand, and AD_1 the final level. With the expected price level initially at P_a, the increase in aggregate demand moves the economy from point A to point B along the short-run aggregate supply curve, $SRAS(P_a)$, increasing real output to Q_b and raising the actual price level to P_b. Once workers observe the higher price level, they expect it to continue, so they demand higher wages. The upward pressure on costs shifts the short-run aggregate supply curve upward to $SRAS(P_b)$—where P_b has now become the new expected price level. As a result, real output falls to Q_c while the actual price level rises to P_c. The expected price level is therefore revised upward once again, this time to P_c; the short-run aggregate supply curve shifts up to $SRAS(P_c)$; and the actual price level rises still further to P_d.

As you can see, the actual price level stays one step ahead of the expected price level, but the gap between the two shrinks as the adjustment process continues. Once it reaches point Z, that gap will have disappeared altogether and the economy will be back in long-run equilibrium.

Rational Expectations

Many economists are uncomfortable with the hypothesis of adaptive expectations because it is often inconsistent with the fundamental economic postulate of ratio-

*Adaptive expectations need not be nearly so naive as this. For example, rather than simply using today's price level as a forecast of tomorrow's, adaptive expectations might use an average of a number of past price levels.

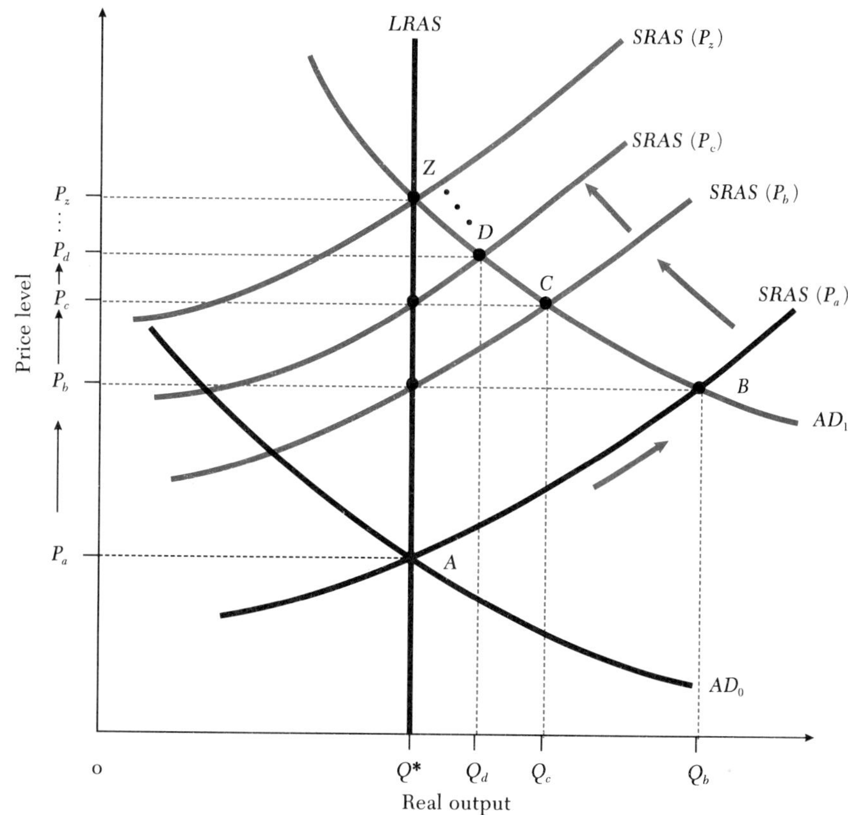

Figure 20.4

Adjustments to an increase in aggregate demand: the case of adaptive expectations

nality. Specifically, it implies that people do not learn from experience. Economists have therefore begun to explore the macroeconomic implications of an alternative hypothesis, namely, that of **rational expectations**. Rational expectations are expectations formed on the basis of all available information, including information about the cause-and-effect relations between past observations and future events.

Rational expectations are based on all available information, including information about cause-and-effect relations between past experience and future events.

To illustrate the nature of rational expectations, consider again the example of forecasting tomorrow's weather. Instead of simply assuming that it will be sunny and warm tomorrow because it has been sunny and warm all week, you might rely on additional information about the cause-and-effect relations linking today's weather to tomorrow's. For example, knowing that a falling barometer often precedes a change from sunny skies to cloudy skies, you might look at today's barometer reading before forming your expectation of tomorrow's weather. Better yet, you can switch on your radio or television set to get information from an expert weather forecaster. Such an expert can provide you with the information you need much more cheaply than you can obtain it yourself. Of course, for all their expertise, the forecasters can be wrong. Rational expectations are *not* always correct; they are just the best that you can do with the available information.

Rational Expectations with Complete Information and Zero Transactions Costs

We can apply the hypothesis of rational expectations to the effects of an increase in aggregate demand. In particular, it seems reasonable to assume that if people repeatedly observe the pattern of price and output adjustments we described for the case of adaptive expectations, they will eventually realize that the initial change in the price level is just the beginning of an adjustment process that ultimately leads to still higher prices. Such a realization, in itself, alters the nature of the adjustment process.

To illustrate, let us first consider an extreme, but instructive, example. Suppose once again that aggregate demand increases, but now let us assume that all of the following conditions hold: Firms and workers correctly anticipate the increase in aggregate demand and know that it will be permanent; they know enough to accurately predict the new long-run equilibrium price level P_z; and the transactions costs of revising all contracts and other commitments are zero. The result is shown in Figure 20.5. Because the expected price level jumps directly from P_a to P_z when aggregate demand increases from AD_0 to AD_1, the short-run aggregate supply curve shifts immediately from $SRAS(P_a)$ to $SRAS(P_z)$. As a

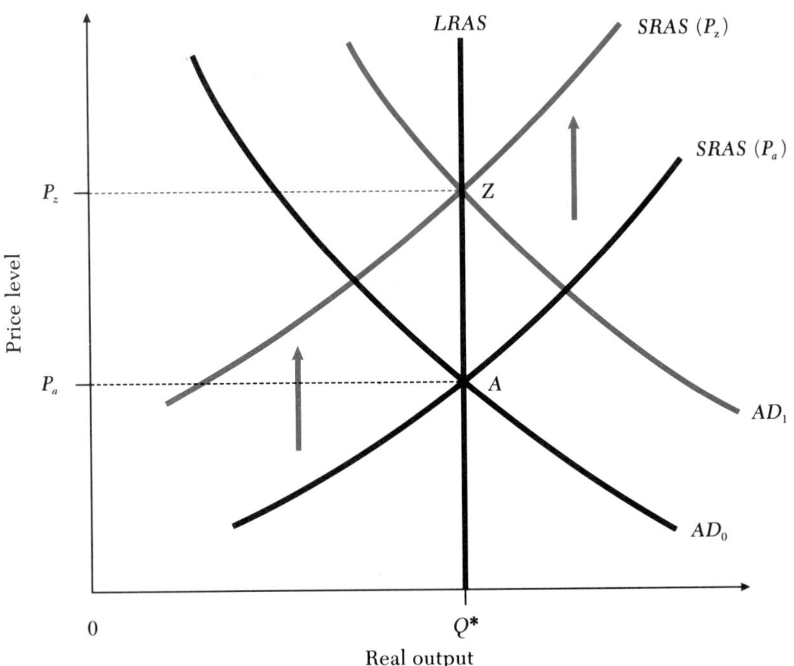

Figure 20.5

Adjustment to an increase in aggregate demand: the case of rational expectations result, only the price level is affected; there is no effect, either short-run or long-run, on real output.

Because it is virtually impossible for all three conditions we have assumed here—namely, correct anticipation of a change in aggregate demand, accurate prediction of its final effects, and zero transactions costs—to be satisfied in practice, most economists regard this kind of rapid, price-only adjustment as little more than an interesting theoretical possibility. Nonetheless, it does highlight an important implication of rational expectations, namely, that anticipated changes in aggregate demand have smaller effects on real output and employment than unanticipated changes.

WHY ARE PRICES "STICKY" IN THE SHORT RUN?

Since changes in aggregate demand are never fully and accurately anticipated, our model implies that they will be absorbed in the short run by a combination of price and output changes. Put another way, since the price level adjusts completely to a change in aggregate demand only in the long run, prices appear to be "sticky" in the short run. In trying to figure out why this should be the case, economists have focused on two sets of factors: one is related to the role of incomplete information in output, employment, and pricing decisions, and the other is related to the prevalence of markets in which prices seem to be set by implicit contract.

Incomplete Information

Suppose that there is an increase in aggregate demand. From the perspective of the individual firm, this appears to be an increase in the market demand for its own product. Firms therefore respond by trying to increase output as well as prices. To increase output, they must increase employment, so the result is a general, economywide rise in wage offers. If job seekers knew about the general increase in prices and wage offers, they would increase their reservation wages accordingly. As a result, search duration would remain the same and employment and output would not be affected. Because job seekers are unaware of the general increase in prices and wage offers, however, they continue to set reservation wages on the basis of their original expectations. As a result, they find jobs more quickly than anticipated, average search duration shortens, and employment and output rise. It is the incomplete information available to firms and workers that leads to the increase in output and employment. This is only a short-run phenomenon, however, because once workers realize that prices and wage offers have risen, they increase their reservation wages accordingly. When they do, wages and prices rise still further, but search duration rises and employment and output return to their natural levels.

We can tell a parallel story about the effects of a decrease in aggregate demand. Firms initially perceive the fall in spending as a reduction in market demand and respond by reducing output and employment as well as prices. Job seekers, unaware of the general decline in wage offers, continue to search for employment on the basis of the original, but now overly optimistic, reservation wages. As a result, search duration increases and employment and output fall. Eventually, as firms and workers accumulate better information about falling prices and wages, their expectations adjust to the lower level of aggregate demand, and the economy reaches a new equilibrium at its natural rate of real output but at a lower price level.

Customer Markets and Auction Markets

Have you ever wondered why restaurants print menus that are unchanged for months at a time? After all, they know that the prices of the meat, fish, produce, and other ingredients that go into the meals they serve fluctuate from week to week, and even from day to day, altering unpredictably the costs of providing those meals. They also know that there are sure to be some unexpectedly busy days when they could charge higher prices and still have all the business they could handle. Why then do they commit themselves in advance to the prices printed on a menu?

One reason is that printing new menus is costly: It simply wouldn't be worth the cost of printing a new menu just to change the price of a prime rib dinner every time the price of beef rises or falls. An even more important reason is that most restaurants depend on repeat business from customers who are not in the market for major surprises when it comes to their dinner bill. In a sense, the restaurant is implicitly saying to those customers through its menu, "Look, we will absorb the small but inevitable weekly and daily fluctuations in costs and demand, and thus provide you with known quality at predictable prices, if you will reward us with your continued patronage."

A **customer market** is one in which the relationship between buyers and sellers is (implicitly or explicitly) contractual and based on the mutual advantages of long-term stability.

The market linking the restaurant and its patrons is an example of a **customer market.** Customer relationships are to the product market what career relationships are to the labor market. They exist because they reduce transactions costs for both buyer and seller, especially in markets where products are not standardized and buyers must shop among various sellers to obtain information about the prices, products, and services offered by each. Such shopping, like job search, is costly, so once a buyer has found a seller on whom he can rely for a satisfactory product at a predictable price, he has an incentive to continue to patronize that seller. By the same token, the seller has an incentive to retain such customers as a source of repeat business and a steady and predictable flow of sales. Like the employer and worker in the career labor market, buyer and seller can mutually benefit from the long-term continuity of a customer relationship. Although there may be no explicit, written agreement to continue such a relationship, those mutual benefits make it at least implicitly contractual.

Not all markets rely on customer relationships. Indeed, in many markets the buyer and seller never even meet and are completely unaware of one another's

An **auction market** is an impersonal market in which a standardized product is traded through an intermediary, and in which price adjusts rapidly to changes in demand and supply.

identity. Such markets are called **auction markets** because transactions are carried out through an intermediary, the auctioneer. The markets for most primary agricultural products are auction markets. If you want to buy a bushel of wheat, for example, you need only call a commodities broker and place your order; you will get your wheat without the slightest idea of the seller's identity. And why should you care? After all, a bushel of wheat is a bushel of wheat is a bushel of wheat. And with a single market price, which is known to all buyers and sellers, there is no reason for you to seek out any particular seller.

Unlike customer markets, auction markets are strictly impersonal. They are feasible only where commodities are standardized and where there is no need for the buyer to physically inspect the product or to negotiate with the seller over its price or other characteristics. In addition to the markets for agricultural commodities, there are auction markets for primary metals such as aluminum, copper, and scrap steel; for textiles such as burlap, wool, and satin; and for hundreds of other standardized commodities from lumber to crude oil to rubber. Prices in these markets respond very rapidly—in some cases, literally within minutes—to changes in demand and supply.

Price Changes in Customer Markets

Because the essence of the customer relationship is continuity and predictability, prices do not respond nearly as quickly in customer markets as they do in auction markets. Were the seller to change the price in response to every fluctuation in demand, the customer relationship would break down and the buyer would have an incentive to shop elsewhere. Moreover, where prices are subject to negotiation, it is uneconomical for the buyer and seller to renegotiate price in response to every minor change in demand or cost. Firms in customer markets therefore rely on inventories, variations in delivery time, and other forms of non-price rationing, rather than on price adjustments, to meet short-term fluctuations in demand. In effect, the customer relationship replaces the "invisible hand" of market price adjustments with an "invisible handshake" by which buyer and seller agree to price stability.

If a change in conditions persists, however, firms eventually adjust prices, but they need to convince their customers that they are acting in good faith. This often means citing a change in costs as the justification for a price change. When a firm announces that it is raising its price because of an increase in costs, both the firm and its customers appear to be victims of circumstances beyond their control. Accordingly, the price increase appears "fair" in the context of their implicit, long-term contract. By contrast, a firm that increases its price because of an increase in demand appears to be gaining at the expense of its customers. In effect, it is telling them, "I have found someone who is willing to pay more than you are, so you must either meet that price or shop elsewhere." Such behavior may be construed by the customer as an opportunistic violation of the implicit contract on which the customer relationship is based.

Even price decreases are more in the spirit of the customer relationship when they are the result of cost reductions than when they are the result of a drop in demand. The firm appears to be telling its customers, "My costs have fallen, so I will share the benefits with you by charging a lower price." This apparent goodwill on the part of the firm may simply reflect a realization that competition from other firms whose costs have also fallen would cost it some of its customers if it did not cut its own price. The fact remains, however, that both the buyer and seller share in the benefits of a price reduction based on a fall in cost. The same cannot be said of a price cut based on a fall in demand, which appears to benefit the buyer at the expense of the seller.

Because of considerations like these, prices in customer markets typically adjust more quickly and completely to changes in costs than to changes in demand.

Customer Markets, Auction Markets, and Changes in Aggregate Demand

To see the macroeconomic significance of all this, let us tell the story of an increase in aggregate demand from the perspective of a particular set of markets, namely, those related to the production and distribution of automobiles. Keep in mind, however, that adjustments similar to those we describe occur simultaneously in all other markets as well.

The first people to feel the impact of an increase in aggregate demand are new car dealers, who suddenly find more people, willing to spend more money, in their showrooms. Although the increased demand does not immediately affect the manufacturers' sticker prices, it allows dealers a higher markup and thus increases the final sales prices of new cars. In addition, the higher rate of sales reduces dealer inventories, leading them to increase the rate at which they place new orders with manufacturers. Because the relationship between a car manufacturer and its dealers is typically a customer relationship, manufacturers respond to the increased orders by increasing output rather than prices. To do so, they have to increase the amount of labor and other inputs they use in production.

Automobile manufacturers and their employees have a contractual relationship based on explicit collective bargaining agreements. These agreements allow manufacturers to vary employment at fixed wages until the contract is renegotiated. In addition, car manufacturers enjoy customer relationships with most of their suppliers, so the latter initially meet the manufacturers' increased demand for sheet metal, tires, windshields, and other inputs by drawing on inventories and increasing production rather than by raising prices. The principal, short-run impact of the increase in aggregate demand is therefore on real output and employment rather than on prices.

Eventually, however, the chain of new orders reaching from new car dealers through car manufacturers to input suppliers will extend down into the auction markets for metals, crude oil, fabrics, rubber, and scores of other primary raw materials. As these markets begin to experience increases in demand from other sectors of the economy as well—remember, we are dealing with an increase in *aggregate* demand, not just the demand for new cars—there will be an across-the-board increase in the prices of raw materials and other auction market commodities. This increase will in turn mean higher production costs for the automobile industry's suppliers, and because rising costs justify price increases in customer markets, these costs will be passed along to car manufacturers in the form of higher prices for everything from tires to sheet metal to windshields. In addition, as long-term employment contracts are renegotiated, wages will begin to rise, reinforcing the upward pressure on costs and prices. Finally, the increase in car manufacturing costs due to higher wages and other input prices will be passed along from manufacturers to dealers in the form of higher wholesale prices for the new cars and higher sticker prices to consumers. Eventually, the increase in aggregate demand that precipitated this chain of events will be absorbed entirely in higher prices with little or no residual impact on real output or employment.

This process would be reversed for a decrease in aggregate demand. In particular, with prices in customer markets and wages in the career labor market fixed by both implicit and explicit contracts in the short run, a fall in aggregate demand must be absorbed initially by falling output and employment. Only when the reduction in demand reaches back to the auction markets for primary raw materials, and only when long-term labor contracts are revised, will costs and prices begin to fall significantly and real output return to its natural level.

Classical versus Keynesian Theory Once Again

Modern economists in the classical tradition—so-called *new classical economists*—tend to emphasize imperfect and incomplete information in explaining short-run fluctuations in output and employment due to changes in aggregate demand. Economists in the Keynesian tradition—so-called *new Keynesian economists*—tend to emphasize contractual wage and price rigidities such as those that characterize career labor markets and customer product markets. However, both explanations imply essentially the same adjustment process. According to both, changes in aggregate demand are absorbed through a combination of price and output adjustments in the short run but by price adjustments alone in the long run. For our purposes, therefore, it is probably best to think of them as complementary, rather than mutually exclusive, theories.

USING THE MODEL TO EXPLAIN ECONOMIC EVENTS

We can use our basic aggregate demand–aggregate supply model to explain and interpret many of the major events of recent macroeconomic history. As we saw in Chapter 15, these include the acceleration of inflation in the late 1960s, the stagflation of the 1970s, and major recessions in 1974–75 and 1982–83.

Inflationary Expectations and Aggregate Supply

Before embarking on our analytical excursion through recent economic history, however, let us note that we can express the short-run aggregate supply relation in terms of actual and expected *rates of inflation* as well as actual and expected price levels. This way of viewing the relation between prices and real output is more descriptive of actual events in an economy like that of the United States, which has experienced persistent inflation in recent years.

Suppose that the initial price level (index) is 1.00 but that people expect it to be 1.05 one year from now. This is equivalent to saying that they expect a 5 percent rate of inflation over the coming year. If the actual rate of inflation turns out to be greater than expected, then the actual price level will rise above the expected price level. For example, if inflation turns out to be 8 percent, then the actual price level will rise to 1.08. Conversely, if inflation turns out to be less than 5 percent, then the actual price level will fall below the expected price level. Our short-run aggregate supply relation therefore implies that real output rises when inflation turns out to be greater than expected and falls when inflation turns out to be less than expected.

Long-Term Dynamics: Economic Growth and Equilibrium Inflation

Since the cyclical events of our recent economic history are superimposed on secular trends of economic growth and rising prices, it is useful to begin with an analysis of the implications of our basic model for the relation between long-term growth and inflation.

As we have already noted, the long-run aggregate supply curve, like any other supply or demand curve, is an other-things-equal concept. Although its vertical shape means that changes in the price level have no effect on the natural rate of real output, other factors can and do change Q^* over time. Among these factors are those that contribute to the long-term growth of the economy's productive capacity, namely, expansion of its capital stock, improvements in technology, and a labor force that is growing in both numbers and skills. These factors continuously increase the natural rate of real output, thereby shifting the long-run aggregate supply curve to the right over time. This is illustrated in Figures 20.6(a) and (b) where Q_1^* is the natural rate of real output in year 1, Q_2^* in year 2, and so on.

If aggregate demand grows at the same rate as natural real output—that is, if the aggregate demand curve is shifting to the right at the same rate as the long-run aggregate supply curve—then the price level will remain constant. This is illustrated in Figure 20.6(a). If aggregate demand grows more rapidly than aggregate supply, then the price level will rise as shown in Figure 20.6(b). As long as the rising level of aggregate demand is fully anticipated and accurately incorporated into all wage and price decisions, real output will not deviate from its natural growth path. The resulting rise in prices will therefore be an **equilibrium rate of inflation**. For example, if real output grows at a constant rate of 3 percent

The **equilibrium rate of inflation** is the rate implied by fully anticipated growth in aggregate demand.

Figure 20.6

Long-run growth and inflation

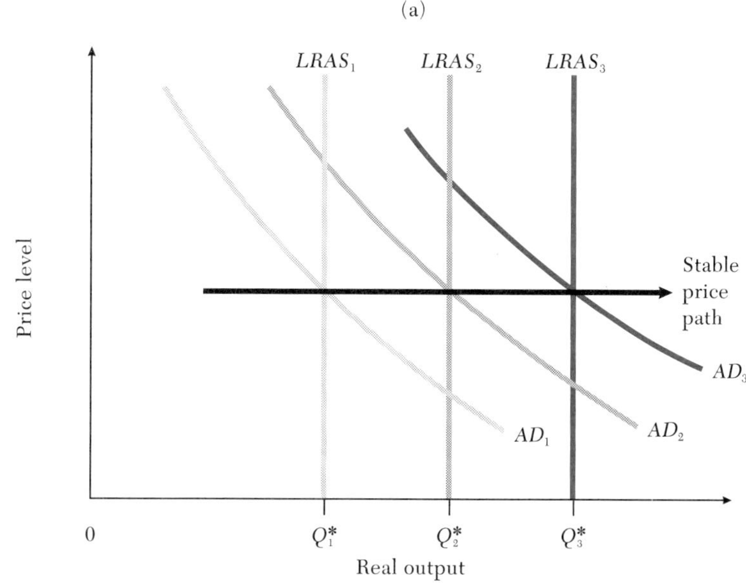

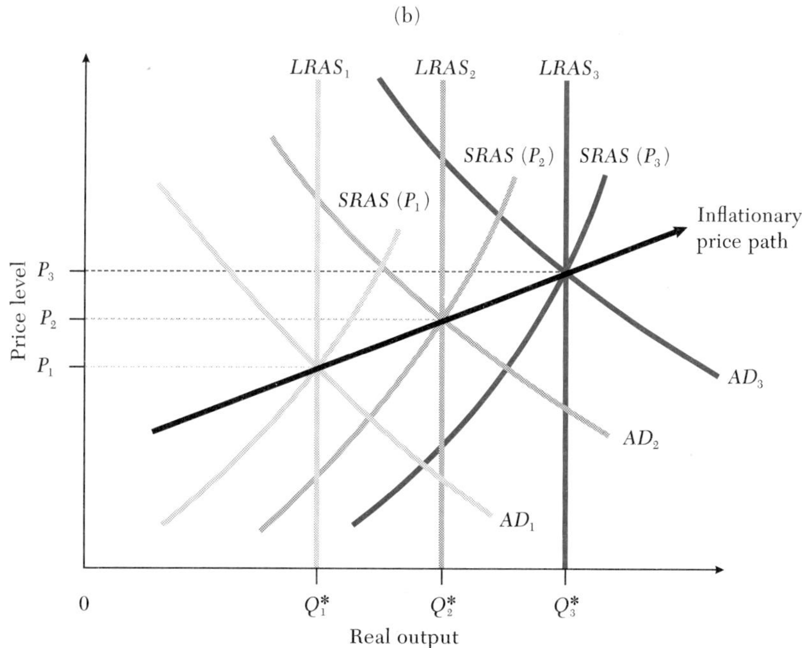

per year and aggregate demand at a constant and fully anticipated rate of 5 percent per year, then the equilibrium rate of inflation will be 2 percent per year. If the rate of aggregate demand growth changes unexpectedly, however, real output may deviate from its natural real growth path as inflation adjusts to the new aggregate demand conditions. The period between 1965 and 1969 provides a good example of such an adjustment process.

Accelerating Inflation during the 1960s

In 1965 the economy was operating at just about its natural rate and had been experiencing an average rate of inflation of about 2 percent since 1950. Since the actual rate of inflation rarely fell outside of the 1.5 to 2.5 percent range during that period, it is reasonable to assume that an inflation rate of about 2 percent had come to be expected by the mid-1960s. Between 1965 and 1969, however, an accelerating money supply, along with rising government spending on both the Vietnam War and expanding social welfare programs, began to increase aggregate demand more rapidly than people anticipated. As a result, real output rose above its natural growth path and unemployment fell below its natural rate, which was then about 4 percent, to only 3.5 percent of the labor force. At the same time, the inflation rate rose to more than 5 percent.

We can interpret these events with the help of Figure 20.7. For the sake of

Figure 20.7

An unanticipated acceleration in aggregate demand

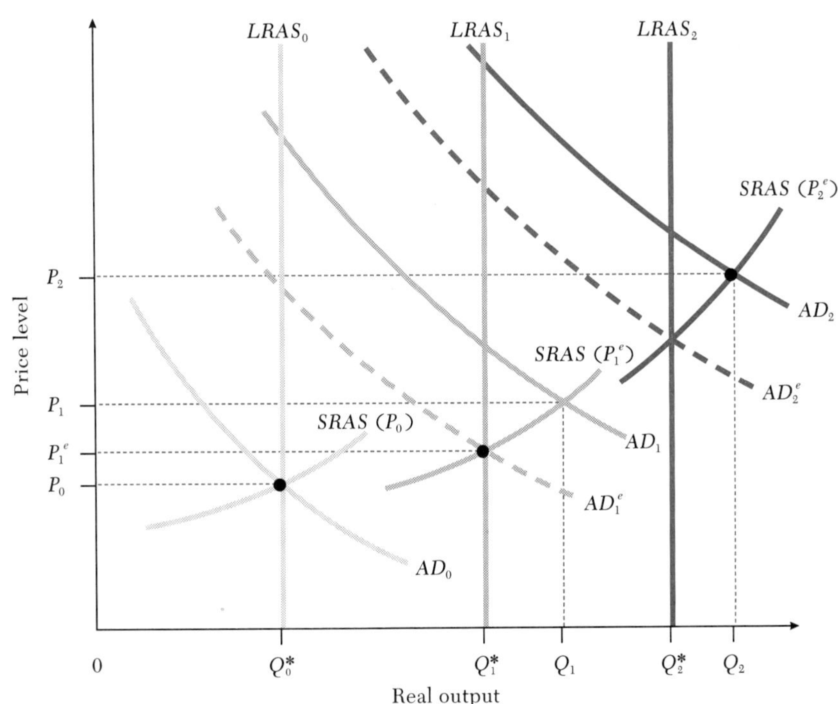

simplicity, let us begin with an economy in long-run equilibrium in year 0 with a price level of P_0, no inflation, and real output at its natural level Q_0^*. The dashed AD^e curves show the *expected* growth of aggregate demand beyond year 0, whereas the solid AD curves show its *actual* path. Recalling that the short-run aggregate supply curve always intersects the long-run aggregate supply curve at the expected price level, we have drawn each year's short-run aggregate supply curve through the point at which the expected (dashed) aggregate demand curve intersects the corresponding long-run aggregate supply curve. The intersection of each short-run aggregate supply curve with the corresponding actual aggregate demand curves determines the actual price level and real output in each year. Thus, while the expected price level in year 1 is P_1^e, the actual price level for that year turns out to be higher, namely, P_1. In other words, inflation turns out to be greater than expected and, as a result, real output rises above its natural level Q_1^*, to Q_1. In year 2, aggregate demand again rises more than expected, again inflation accelerates, and real output remains above its natural level. As long as the increases in aggregate demand continue to exceed expectations, real output will remain above its natural level and inflation will continue to accelerate. This is a reasonably accurate description of what happened in the U. S. economy between 1965 and 1970.

The Inflationary Recession of 1970

An **inflationary recession** occurs when an unexpected fall in aggregate demand is added to inflationary expectations, resulting in a combination of recession and continued inflation.

In 1970, after 5 years of accelerating inflation, there was an unexpected slowdown in the growth of aggregate demand. The result was an **inflationary recession** during which the rate of inflation continued to rise as real output dropped and unemployment jumped above its natural rate.

Figure 20.8 on the next page shows what happened in terms of our basic model. Starting from an initial equilibrium in year 0 (point *A*), people expected aggregate demand in year 1 to rise to the level shown by the dashed curve labelled AD_1^e. This determines the expected price level P_1^e and thus the location of the short-run aggregate supply curve for year 1, which we have labelled $SRAS(P_1^e)$. When the growth of aggregate demand turned out to be lower than anticipated (the solid curve labelled AD_1 rather than the dashed curve), real output fell below its natural level to Q_1 while the price level continued to rise to P_1. This is essentially what happened during the recession of 1970: Inflationary expectations kept the price level from falling—in fact, the rate of inflation rose slightly—despite the recession brought on by a fall in aggregate demand growth.

Supply Shocks and the Recessions of 1973–75 and 1979–80

A **supply shock** results from an unexpected change in the conditions underlying aggregate supply.

In 1973 and again in 1978, the industrialized world experienced **supply shocks** brought on by the actions of the OPEC oil cartel. These shocks took the form of dramatic increases in the price of crude oil, from less than \$3 per barrel to more than \$10 per barrel in 1973–74, and from about \$12 per barrel to more than \$30 per barrel in 1978–79. Each time, the result was a temporary drop in the economy's productive capacity as firms diverted a substantial share of their resources

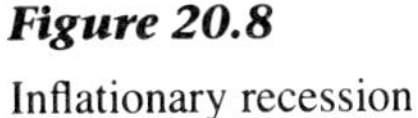

Figure 20.8

Inflationary recession

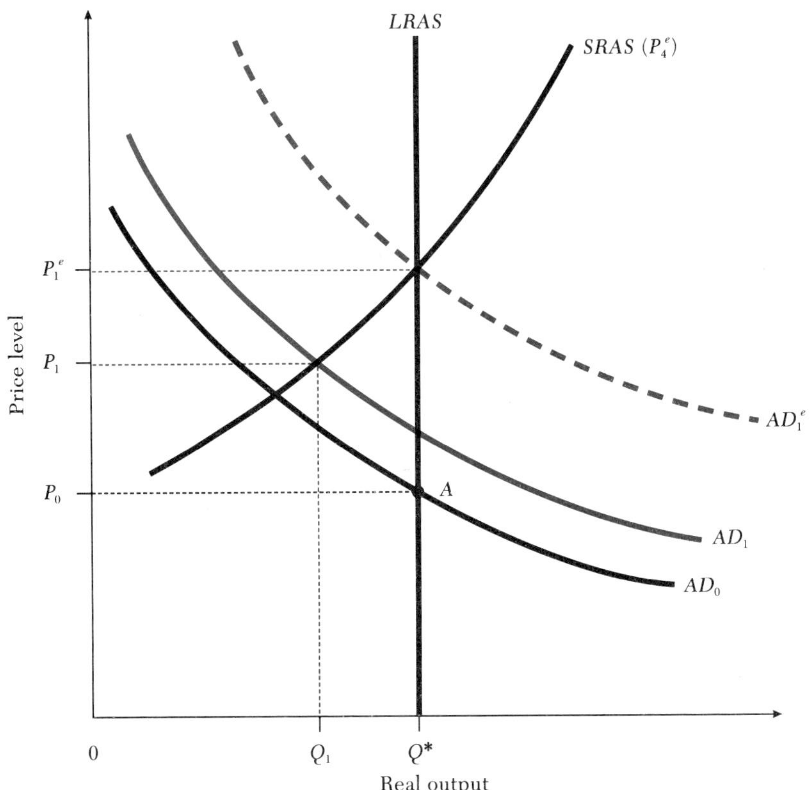

from normal production to developing energy-saving technologies and incorporating them into their production processes. In the automobile industry, for example, production slowed as engines and car bodies were redesigned for greater fuel efficiency and as factories converted to more efficient energy sources. Similar adjustments were made in other industries throughout the economy.

The effects of such a negative supply shock are illustrated in Figure 20.9. When natural real output falls from Q_0^* to Q_1^*, the long-run aggregate supply curve shifts from $LRAS_0$ to $LRAS_1$. Assuming for simplicity that aggregate demand remains constant, the short-run result is a rise in the price level to P' and a fall in real output to Q'. As the economy continues to adjust to the negative supply shock, the price level eventually rises to P_1 and real output falls to Q_1^*.

The events of 1973–75 and 1979–80 illustrate this kind of adjustment process. During each of these periods, real output fell as inflation temporarily accelerated from about 6 percent (approximately its equilibrium rate during the 1970s) to about 10 percent. In each case, once the OPEC supply shock had been absorbed, the rate of inflation then declined back to about 6 percent. Note that although the OPEC actions raised the price level, they did not permanently increase the rate of inflation.

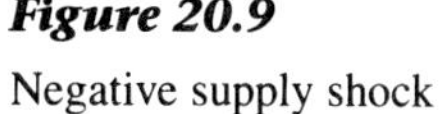

Figure 20.9

Negative supply shock

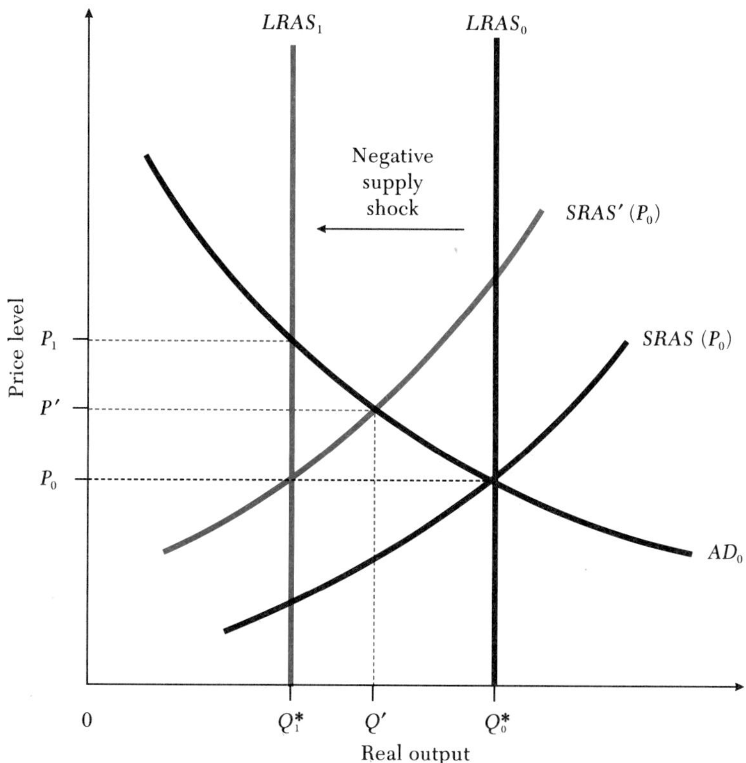

Thus the 1970s, which began with an inflationary recession, experienced two major supply shocks, each of which resulted in a recession accompanied by (temporarily) accelerating inflation. Is it any wonder that the decade gave birth to the term *stagflation*?

Disinflation: Recession and Recovery, 1981–1990

In 1979, after a decade and a half of rising and unstable inflation due both to the erratic behavior of aggregate demand and to the supply shocks just described, the Federal Reserve System adopted policies that ultimately led to a substantial slowdown in the growth rate of aggregate demand. By late 1981, aggregate demand had slowed enough to precipitate a recession. Accompanying this recession was a fall in the rate of inflation from 9.7 percent in 1981 to 6.4 percent in 1982, and ultimately to as low as 2.6 percent in 1986 as the economy recovered.

We can interpret these events as a move from point *A* to point *B* along the economy's short-run aggregate supply curve in Figure 20.10 on the following page. With the expected price level initially at P_0, the fall in aggregate demand

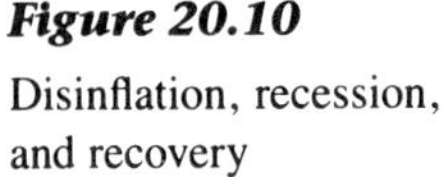

Figure 20.10

Disinflation, recession, and recovery

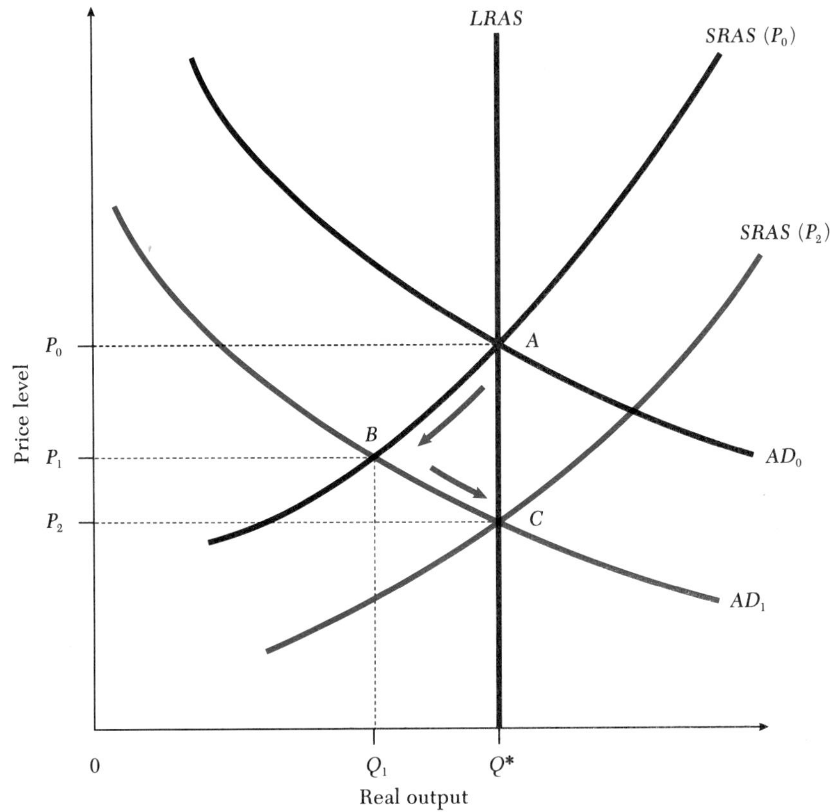

led, through a lower rate of inflation, to a price level of P_1. Because this level was below expectations, it was accompanied by a fall in real output to Q_1.

With restraint on aggregate demand continuing through 1983 and 1984, price level expectations began to adjust to the lower rates of inflation. The result was a rise in real output as the economy recovered from the recession, accompanied by a further drop in the rate of inflation to only 4.1 percent by 1984. In terms of Figure 20.10, expectations of lower inflation were shifting the short-run aggregate supply curve downward and moving the economy along its aggregate demand curve to a point like *C*. By the end of 1988, the inflation rate had stabilized at about 4.5 percent and the economy had rebounded to about its natural level of real output where it remained as of mid-1990.

The Phillips Curve Revisited, or, Is There a Trade-Off between Inflation and Unemployment?

Figure 20.11(a) shows the combination of unemployment and inflation for each of the years between 1960 and 1969. Looking at those data, it is easy to see why

Figure 20.11

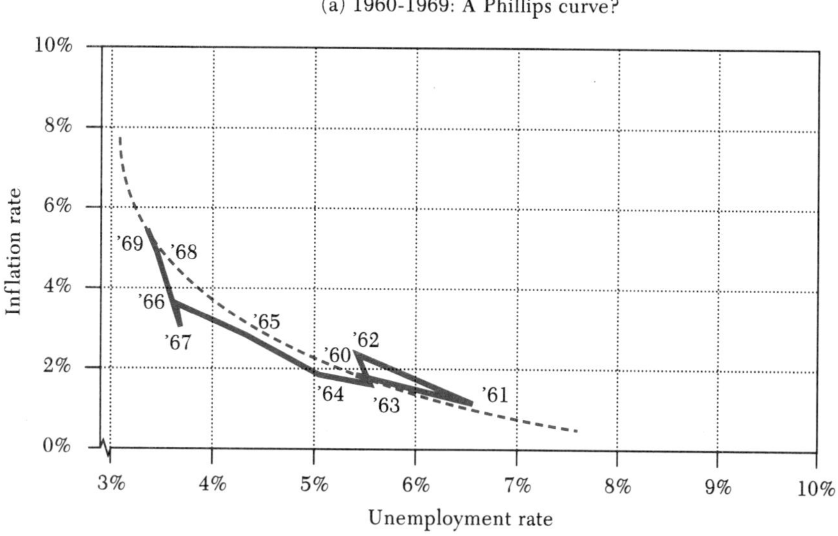

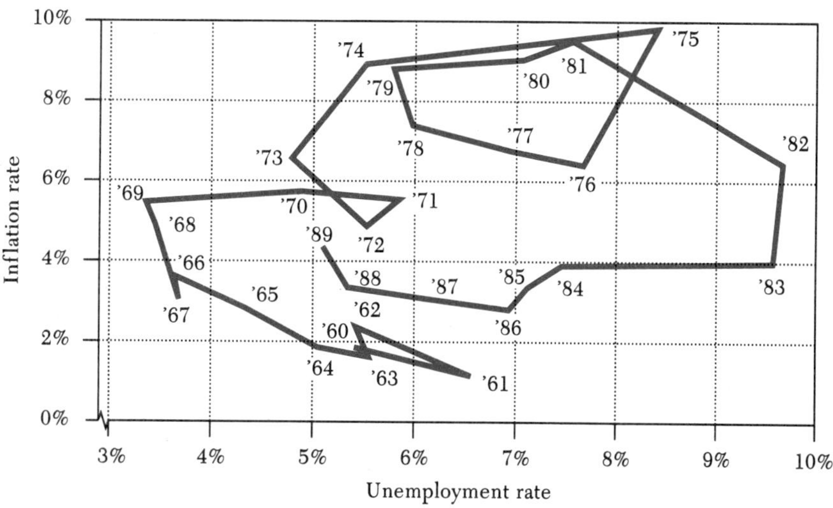

economists concluded that there was a trade-off between unemployment and inflation. As we saw in Chapter 15, that trade-off was embodied in the concept of a *Phillips curve*. The Phillips curve, which is represented by the dashed line in the diagram, implies that the higher the inflation rate, the lower the rate of unemployment, and vice-versa.

If a picture is worth a thousand words, then Figure 20.11(b) speaks volumes about why economists have pretty much abandoned the idea of a stable and predictable trade-off between inflation and unemployment. It shows that inflation and unemployment can move not only in opposite directions, as implied by the Phillips curve, but also in the same direction. For example, both inflation and unemployment increased in 1969–70, 1974–75, and 1979–80; they simultaneously decreased in 1975–76 and 1983–84, 1984–85, and 1985–86. This is not to say that there is no relation between inflation and unemployment, just that the relation is not nearly as simple as economists once thought.

Our basic model tells us that other things being equal, an increase in aggregate demand raises the economy's equilibrium price level and thus leads to inflation. Moreover, if this inflation is unanticipated and not incorporated into contractual commitments, it will be accompanied by a rise in real output and a temporary fall in unemployment below its natural rate. It is not the inflation itself that leads to the fall in unemployment, however; it is the mismatch between expectations and reality. In particular, unemployment falls below its natural rate only when inflation turns out to be higher than expected, and it rises above its natural rate only when inflation turns out to be lower than expected. To the extent that a Phillips curve trade-off exists at all, therefore, it is a short-run trade-off relating changes in the unemployment rate to *unexpected* changes in the rate of inflation.

The **short-run Phillips curve** shows the effect on the rate of unemployment of unexpected changes in the rate of inflation.

Figure 20.12 shows a **short-run Phillips curve** for an expected inflation rate of 4 percent. If the actual inflation rate rises above 4 percent to, say, 6 percent,

Figure 20.12

Long-run and short-run Phillips curves

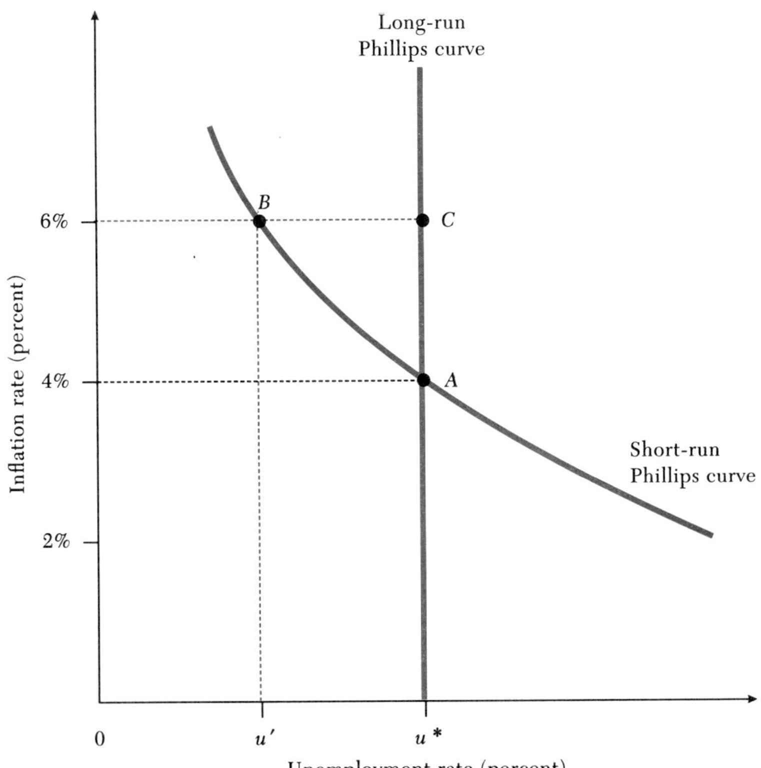

unemployment will temporarily fall below its natural rate to, say, u'. In terms of the diagram, the economy moves from point A to point B along the short-run Phillips curve.

Once the 6 percent rate of inflation comes to be expected, however, unemployment will return to its natural rate and the economy will settle at point C in the diagram, with a higher rate of inflation but the same (natural) rate of unemployment with which it began. In the long-run, therefore, there is no trade-off between inflation and unemployment. In effect, the **long-run Phillips curve** is a vertical line at the natural rate of unemployment.

The **long-run Phillips curve** shows the effect on the rate of unemployment of fully anticipated changes in the rate of inflation.

This analysis has some important implications. First, it suggests that the more quickly and completely expectations adjust to a change in the rate of inflation, the smaller the effect of that change on unemployment. Second, it tells us that we cannot use higher rates of inflation to "buy" permanently lower unemployment, or vice-versa. Finally, it implies that in the long run the natural rate of unemployment can coexist with any rate of inflation. These conclusions have very important policy implications which we explore in later chapters.

Preview

In this chapter we have developed some important macroeconomic tools and showed how they can be used to explain the recent performance of the U. S. economy. Do not be too impressed, however, for there are many things that our model does *not* tell us. It is one thing to look at historical data and say, for example, that a past recession can be explained by an unexpected decrease in aggregate demand. It is quite another to say in advance why and when aggregate demand will fall and to predict the timing and magnitude of the effects on real output, employment, and the price level. Unfortunately, macroeconomics in its current state is not quite as impressive at performing the latter task as it is at performing the former. Nonetheless, economists have made great strides in the past two decades, and the result is a theory that provides useful explanations of inflation, recession, stagflation, and many other interesting and important phenomena.

Until now we have concentrated primarily on the behavior of aggregate supply and, although we have talked about changes in aggregate demand, we have said little about the *source* of such changes. In the following chapters, therefore, we turn our attention to theories of aggregate demand and their important implications for macroeconomic policy.

CHAPTER SUMMARY

1. In macroeconomics, the *long run* is a period of time long enough for people to fully adjust their expectations and revise their commitments in response to changing economic conditions. In the *short run*, expectations, and the commitments based on those expectations, are assumed to be fixed.

2. According to the basic aggregate demand–aggregate supply model, changes in aggregate demand are absorbed by a combination of price level and real output changes in the short run, but they affect only the price level in the long run.

3. In the short run, the aggregate supply of real output rises when the actual price level rises above the expected price level and falls when the actual price level falls below the expected price level.

4. The inflationary process resulting from an increase in aggregate demand is composed of an initial *demand pull* phase, during which both the price level and real output are rising, followed by a *cost push* phase, during which the price level continues to rise but real output falls.

5. *Adaptive expectations* are expectations formed by simply extrapolating past experience into the future without inquiring into the cause-and-effect relation between the two. *Rational expectations* are expectations formed on the basis of all available information, including information about the cause-and-effect relations between past observations and future events. Rational expectations imply that anticipated changes in aggregate demand have smaller effects on real output and employment than unanticipated changes.

6. *Customer relationships* reduce transactions costs for both buyer and seller by providing stable prices in markets where products are not standardized and information costs are high. Whereas prices in *auction markets* change very quickly, in customer markets they tend to be sticky, changing only when costs change.

7. Stated in terms of inflation rather than the price level, the short-run aggregate supply relation implies that real output rises when inflation turns out to be greater than expected and falls when inflation turns out to be less than expected.

8. The *equilibrium rate of inflation* is that which results when increases in aggregate demand in excess of aggregate supply are fully anticipated and accurately incorporated into all wage and price decisions. When inflation is at its equilibrium rate, real output is on its natural growth path.

9. During an *inflationary recession*, the rate of inflation rises as real output drops. It is the result of aggregate demand growing more slowly than anticipated.

10. *Supply shocks* result from sudden changes in the economy's productive capacity.

11. To the extent that a *Phillips curve* trade-off exists, it is a short-run trade-off relating changes in the unemployment rate to unexpected changes in the rate of inflation. Specifically, unemployment falls below its natural rate when inflation turns out to be higher than expected and rises above its natural rate when inflation turns out to be lower than expected.

Key Terms and Concepts

long-run aggregate supply curve
short-run aggregate supply curve
demand pull
cost push
adaptive expectations
rational expectations
customer market
auction market
equilibrium rate of inflation
inflationary recession
supply shock
short-run Phillips curve
long-run Phillips curve

Questions for Thought and Discussion

1. This chapter began with a series of questions about the relationships between various nominal and real variables. How would you now answer those questions?
2. We have used OPEC price increases as examples of negative supply shocks. What might cause a positive supply shock? What would be the cyclical effects of a positive supply shock on output, employment, and inflation?
3. Under what circumstances can we have each of the following conditions?
   a. Booming real output combined with accelerating inflation.
   b. Booming real output combined with falling inflation.
   c. A recession combined with falling inflation.
   d. A recession combined with accelerating inflation.
4. A popular textbook states that "the costs of recession are largely the costs of disappointed expectations." What do you think the author means?
5. During the pro football season, most major newspapers publish point spreads showing which teams are favored to win the next week's games and by how many points. These spreads are set to equalize the amount of money bet on the opposing teams. Do you think the information that establishes point spreads is based on adaptive expectations or rational expectations?
6. As we see in subsequent chapters, the Federal Reserve can adopt policies to control the growth of aggregate demand. Suppose that in the midst of accelerating inflation the Fed announces that it intends to bring inflation down by restraining the growth of aggregate demand. Does it make any difference whether people really believe the Fed will do so?
7. Suppose the rate of inflation falls from 8 percent to 4 percent. Do you think that this fall will have a greater negative impact on employment if prices have been rising at 8 percent per year for some time or if inflation has recently fallen from 12 percent to 8 percent?

CHAPTER 21

The Money Market and the Economy

At its inception in 1913, and for nearly 20 years thereafter, the Federal Reserve took a relatively narrow view of its mission. It believed its charge was simply to regulate the banking system and to insure that the general public had enough liquidity to carry on its everyday business. This view began to change dramatically in the years following the Great Depression. Today we pretty much take it for granted that the Fed's control of the money supply is an important ingredient in the economy's overall performance. In this chapter we see why. In particular, we see how the supply of money interacts with the demand for money in the money market and how events in that market ripple through the entire economy. We also take our first look at the ongoing debate between Keynesians and monetarists.

VELOCITY AND THE DEMAND FOR MONEY

Money, Velocity, and Aggregate Demand

Money is a *stock*. When it is spent on final goods, it creates the *flow* of expenditures we call aggregate demand. The *equation of exchange*, which we introduced in Chapter 18, provides a useful way of thinking about the relation between money and aggregate demand.

To refresh your memory, the equation of exchange is

$$MV = PQ$$

where M is the stock of money, V is its velocity of circulation (the average number of times per year each dollar turns over in the purchase of final goods), P is the price level (the GNP deflator), and Q is real GNP. Given the definition of the GNP deflator, the term PQ is simply nominal GNP, which we continue to denote as Y. Accordingly, we can also write the equation of exchange as

$$MV = Y$$

Recall also that the equation of exchange is an identity, a truism that must always hold simply because of the way its variables are defined. Specifically, money times velocity must always equal nominal GNP because velocity itself is defined as the ratio of nominal GNP to the money stock. Furthermore, since the number of dollars in circulation multiplied by the number of times per year each dollar is spent equals the total flow of spending during the year, MV is just one way of expressing aggregate demand. For example, in 1989 the money stock of about \$800 billion turned over about 6.5 times, thereby generating about \$5,200 billion (= \$800 billion × 6.5) of aggregate demand. This flow of spending is what purchased the \$5,200 billion of final goods that made up 1989 nominal GNP.*

The equation of exchange makes it clear that the effect of a change in the money stock on aggregate demand depends critically on money's velocity. For example, a \$10 billion increase in the money supply adds \$70 billion to aggregate demand when velocity is 7, but only \$60 billion when velocity is 6.

The Demand for Money

The **demand for money** is a demand to hold the specific liquid assets that make up the money supply.

Velocity is closely related to—indeed, is the mirror image of—the **demand for money**. We must be very clear here about what we mean by the "demand for money." In everyday language the term "money" is often used as a synonym for income or wealth. ("How much money do you make?" "She has all her money in real estate and the stock market.") As we have seen, however, money has a more precise and technical meaning in economics. Specifically, it includes only very liquid assets held by the public in the form of currency and checking account balances.† The demand for money is therefore a demand for a stock of these specific, liquid assets.

To illustrate, imagine that a rich uncle has died and left you \$1 million in cash. Of course you will be deliriously happy that your wealth has increased by \$1 million, but you will undoubtedly have far more money than you demand! If you need to be convinced, think for a moment about what you would do with

*The \$800 billion was the approximate value of the M1 money stock in 1989. Throughout this chapter we shall use that narrow definition of money. Where the use of the broader *M2* measure would make a difference in our analysis or conclusions, we point out the difference in a note.

†And, in the case of the broader *M2* definition, money also includes balances in savings accounts and money market funds.

your $1 million windfall. Would you hold it all as cash or as a balance in your checking account? Almost certainly not! You would probably buy yourself a new Porsche, maybe even a modest yacht, and invest a lot in stocks, bonds, and real estate. So you see, your willingness to accept a $1 million inheritance is not equivalent to a demand for that much money; rather it reflects a demand for all of those other goodies that money can be exchanged for. When we ask why people demand money, therefore, we are really asking why they would choose to hold some of their wealth in the form of currency and bank deposits.

When money is held, it has a zero velocity; when it is spent, it has a positive velocity. Accordingly, *the greater the demand for money* relative to the demand for the things money can buy, the more money people will choose to hold rather than spend and *the lower will be money's velocity*. Conversely, *less the demand for money* relative to the demand for the things money can buy, the faster money will be spent and *the greater its velocity*. Other things being equal, therefore, a decrease in the demand for money is equivalent to a rise in velocity, and an increase in the demand for money is equivalent to a decline in velocity.

The Determinants of Money Demand

The **transactions demand** for money is a demand to hold money balances for use in transactions.

The **asset demand** for money is a demand to hold money as an asset.

As we have seen, money serves both as a medium of exchange and as a very liquid form of wealth. Accordingly, it is useful to think of the demand for money in terms of two separate components: a **transactions demand** for money as a medium of exchange and an **asset demand** for money as a store of value.

Transactions Demand

Let us introduce the concept of transactions demand in the context of a simple model of receipts and expenditures. In particular, suppose your monthly income is $2,000, paid on the first day of each month. On that day you take your employer's check to the bank, deposit some of it in your checking account, and keep the rest in cash. Your money balances are therefore $2,000 on the first of each month. Those balances then decline over the remainder of the month as you spend them on groceries, rent, and a variety of other items, until, on the last day of each month, your money balances have fallen to zero: You have no cash left in your wallet and a zero balance in your checking account. Then the next day is payday and the process begins all over again, repeating itself month after month. If your expenses are spread evenly throughout the month, the time profile of your money holdings would look like the one depicted in Figure 21.1(a). With your actual money balances fluctuating between $0 and $2,000, your average money holdings would be $1,000. This amount represents your transactions demand for money—literally, the amount you hold, on average, for ordinary, everyday transactions.

This simple model suggests a number of factors that may influence the transactions demand for money. The most obvious of these is income. Other things being equal, higher levels of income and expenditures mean more transactions, and thus result in a greater transactions demand for money. For example, if your monthly income and expenditures in the preceding example had been \$3,000 rather than \$2,000, your money balances would have fluctuated between \$0 and \$3,000 and thus averaged \$1,500 rather than \$1,000.

Another important determinant of transactions demand is the timing of receipts and expenditures. In particular, anything that leads to closer synchronization of receipts and expenditures tends to reduce the transactions demand for money. For example, suppose that you receive your \$2,000 monthly income, not in a single payment, but in two \$1,000 paychecks, one on the 1st of the month and one on the 15th. On each of those days you hold money balances of \$1,000. Those balances then decline as you pay your bills, reaching zero just before the next payday, when they are replenished with a new paycheck and the cycle begins again. The resulting time profile of your money balances is shown in Figure 21.1(b). As you can see, the more frequent receipt of income reduces your average money balance to only \$500. In effect, you can get by with less money on average because you don't have to stretch a single paycheck over as long a period. (Note that we said less money, not less income. Your income is still \$2,000 per month.)

Credit cards such as Visa and Mastercard also reduce the transactions demand for money by allowing us to economize on the use of money in everyday transactions. To take an extreme example, imagine what would happen to your transactions demand for money if you could make *all* of your purchases with a credit

Figure 21.1

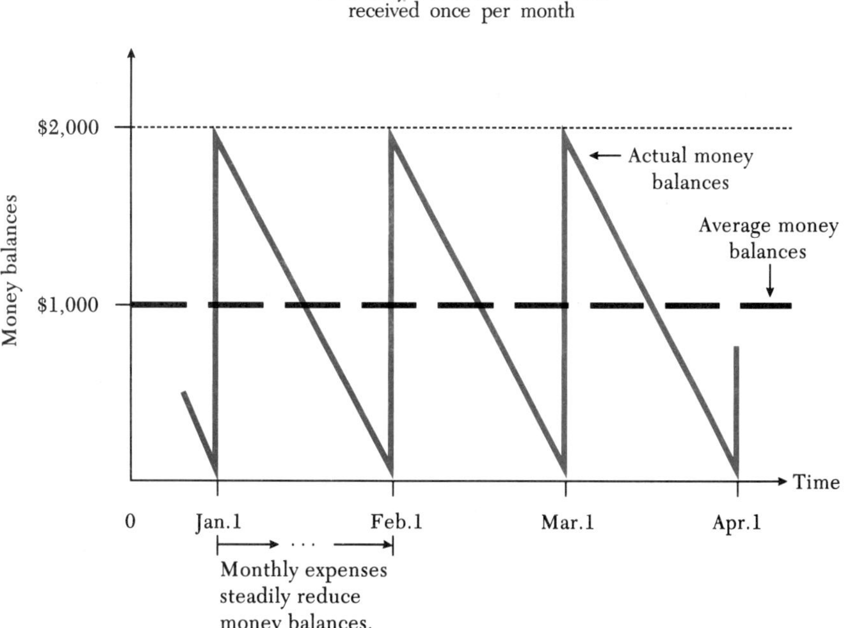

Figure 21.1

(continued)

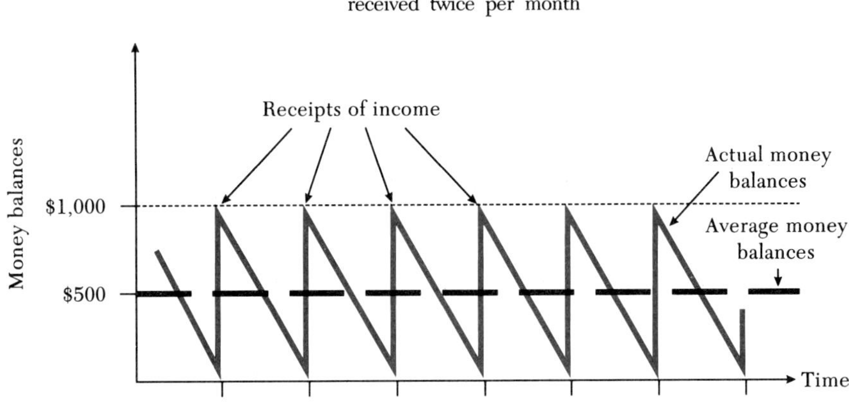

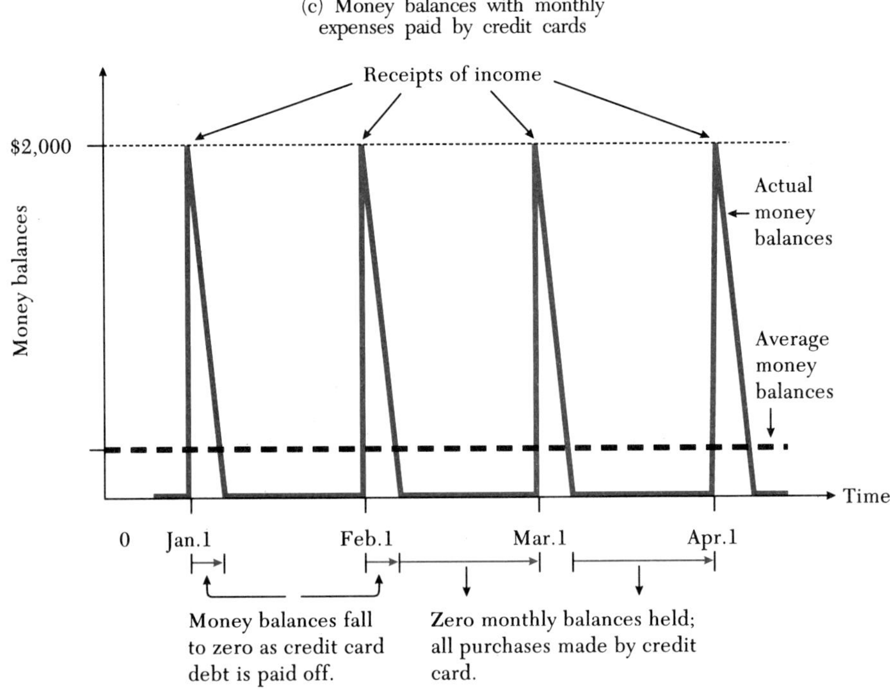

card and pay off the balance once each month immediately after you received your pay check. Figure 21.1(c) shows how this would affect the time profile of your money balances. Except for a very brief period of time between depositing your check and paying off your credit card bill each month, you would hold no money balances at all. As a consequence, your average money holdings over the month would be very low. Although no one uses credit cards for literally all purchases, credit cards do enable people to get by with lower money balances than would otherwise be the case. Other things being equal, therefore, the increasing use of credit cards in recent years has reduced the transactions demand for money.*

Less frequent billings also reduce the transactions demand for money. The fact that your landlord, your utility company, and many other businesses bill you monthly rather than daily, for example, allows you to get by on lower average money balances. In effect, monthly billings, like credit cards, allow you to enjoy a month's worth of consumption with only a single money payment.

The average length of the pay period, the use of credit cards, the billing practices of firms, and other factors affecting the synchronization of receipts and payments typically change only gradually over time. Accordingly, we would expect their effects to show up as long-run trends in the demand for money. Variations in income, on the other hand, can have a significant short-run, cyclical impact on transactions demand.

The Asset Demand for Money

The asset demand for money is a demand for money balances over and above those needed for ordinary, everyday transactions. People choose to hold money for asset purposes because of its near-perfect liquidity. As we have seen, a liquid asset is one that can be exchanged for other assets or consumable goods at low cost, and whose value in exchange is relatively stable and predictable. These advantages are considerable in an uncertain world. For one thing, holding extra money balances enables us to meet unforseen contingencies, and to take advantage of unexpected opportunities, at much lower cost than if we held all of our wealth in less liquid forms. Imagine how costly it would be, for example, if you had to borrow against your real estate holdings each time your car needed emergency repairs, or if you had to sell some of your stock portfolio each time you wanted to take advantage of a special sale at your local department store.

In addition, except in the extreme case of hyperinflation, the value of money is relatively stable and predictable over time. Although its purchasing power varies inversely with changes in the general price level, such changes are almost never as sudden, as frequent, or as extreme as changes in the value of other assets. People who fear a fall in the value of nonmoney assets, or who simply

*Since a decrease in the demand for money is equivalent to a rise in velocity, we can restate all of these examples in terms of velocity. In the case of more frequent pay periods, velocity increases because money balances lie idle for at most 2 weeks rather than a month; in the case of credit cards, velocity increases because money received is immediately spent to pay last month's bills, rather than held and spread over next month's.

wish to avoid the risk of sudden changes in their wealth, may therefore choose to hold some of that wealth in the form of money even though they do not expect to use that money for transactions.

The Opportunity Costs of Holding Money

In choosing how much money to hold, people consider the costs as well as the benefits. As with all costs, the cost of holding money is the opportunity cost of foregone alternatives, and the alternative to holding money is to spend it. Money can be spent either on other financial assets or on real goods.

Consider first the cost of holding money rather than other financial assets. Currency and most demand deposits earn no interest at all; even interest-bearing checkable deposits earn less interest than other, less liquid financial assets.* The opportunity cost of holding money rather than other financial assets is therefore foregone interest. This cost is best measured by the nominal rate of interest, which compensates holders of nonmoney assets for the expected effects of inflation.

The opportunity cost of holding money rather than spending it on real goods is foregone consumption, or, more accurately, postponed consumption, since money held today can still be used to purchase goods for consumption in the future. As we saw in Chapter 4, the positive rate of subjective time preference implies that there is a real cost to postponing consumption, and that cost is reflected in the real rate of interest. Moreover, if money's purchasing power falls as a result of inflation, then real consumption opportunities are not simply postponed by holding money; they are also diminished. The expected future rate of inflation is thus another cost to be considered in the decision to hold money. Since the sum of the real rate of interest and the expected rate of inflation is the nominal rate of interest, the latter also measures the opportunity cost of holding money rather than spending it on real goods.

We can therefore summarize the opportunity cost of holding money in a single variable, namely, the nominal rate of interest.

The Money Demand Function

The foregoing discussion suggests that the demand for money is determined by the levels of income and nominal interest rates and by a variety of other factors—such as credit card usage—that affect the synchronization of receipts and payments. Because these latter factors change only slowly over time, we focus our attention on the role of income and interest rates in determining the short-run, cyclical behavior of the demand for money. In particular, we assume that people choose to hold money balances equal to some fraction of their income, and that fraction, which we shall call **fluidity**, is inversely related to the level of nominal interest rates. Assuming for simplicity a single nominal interest rate,

Fluidity is the amount of money demanded per dollar of income.

*The savings and money market deposits included in *M2* also generally earn less interest than other, less liquid financial assets.

Figure 21.2

Equilibrium in the money market

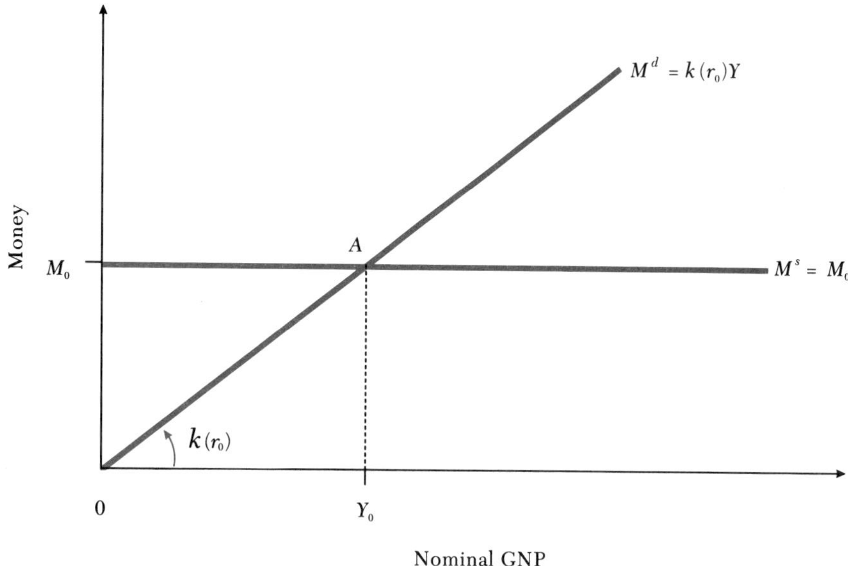

and recognizing that aggregate income is equal to nominal GNP, we can express the total demand for money as

$$M^d = k(r)Y$$

where M^d is the amount of money demanded, Y is nominal GNP, r is the nominal interest rate, and k is fluidity. The expression $k(r)$ is functional notation telling us that fluidity depends on the nominal interest rate: The higher the nominal interest rate, the lower fluidity; the lower the nominal interest rate, the higher fluidity.*

Monetary Equilibrium

Equilibrium in the money market, as in any other market, requires that demand and supply be equal. Such an equilibrium is illustrated graphically in Figure 21.2, where we assume that the interest rate is equal to r_0. Given that interest rate, the amount of money demanded at each level of nominal GNP is shown by the line labelled $M^d = k(r_0)Y$. The horizontal line labelled $M^s = M_0$ tells us that M_0 is the amount of money supplied by the Fed. The money market is in equilib-

*Economists often refer to the k in the demand for money function as "the Cambridge k" after a theory of the demand for money developed by classical economists associated with Cambridge University in England early in this century. We use the term *fluidity* because it is simpler and more descriptive. Just as *liquidity* is often measured by the ratio of money to the *stock* of all assets, *fluidity* is the ratio of money to the *flow* of income. We owe this terminology to Michael Darby, *Intermediate Macroeconomics* (McGraw-Hill, 1979).

rium at the level of nominal GNP equal to Y_0, which equates the demand for money with its supply.

Note the relation between fluidity and velocity. In equilibrium, fluidity is equal to the ratio of the money stock to GNP (i.e., $k = M/Y$). Since velocity is the ratio of GNP to the money stock ($V = Y/M$), it follows that fluidity is simply the reciprocal of equilibrium velocity ($k = 1/V$).

MONEY AND AGGREGATE DEMAND

In principle, money market equilibrium can be achieved in either of two ways. One way is for the Fed to adjust the supply of money to meet whatever demand is generated by current levels of nominal GNP and interest rates. The other is for the Fed to determine the money supply independently, thereby forcing demand to adjust to that supply through changes in GNP and interest rates. In the first case, the Fed is passively responding to current economic conditions; in the second, it is actively trying to alter those conditions. We consider the implications of these alternative approaches to Fed policy later. Here we focus on how active changes in the money supply affect the economy.

Monetary Disequilibrium and the Flow of Spending

Imagine what would happen if the Fed increased the money supply and all of the new money was simply hoarded—stuffed in cookie jars and held as idle balances in bank accounts. It would be as though the Fed threw a party and no one showed up! *New money affects the economy only when it is spent.*

Changes in the money supply influence the flow of spending by creating a disequilibrium—either an excess supply or an excess demand—in the money market. To see how this works, let us consider first the case of an increase in the money supply. The process begins with an open market purchase of government securities by the Fed. As we have seen, this puts excess reserves into the banking system and allows banks to make loans they would otherwise not have been able to make. Suppose, as a concrete example, that those additional reserves make it possible for you to borrow $10,000 to buy a new car. When your bank makes the loan, it uses its excess reserves to create $10,000 of new money, which it credits to your checking account. Of course, you didn't borrow $10,000 to hold as money in your checking account; you borrowed it to buy a new car. In other words, at the moment you receive your loan from the bank, you are personally holding a $10,000 excess supply of money.

You eliminate your personal excess supply of money when you exchange it for your new car. But then the car dealer has an additional $10,000 in his bank account. He also has one less car in his inventory and an obligation to pay one more sales commission. Since the dealer would rather have a full inventory and a happy salesman than $10,000 sitting idle in his bank account, *he* now holds an excess supply of money. When he uses that money to pay his salesman's commission and replenish his inventory by ordering another car from the manufacturer, the excess supply of money is passed on to the salesman and the car manufacturer. They in turn will respond by increasing their spending, the salesman perhaps taking his family out to dinner and the car manufacturer paying some of its parts suppliers.

By now you probably get the picture. Each successive recipient of the new money—you, the car dealer, the salesman, the manufacturer—eliminates a personal excess supply of money by spending it. From the perspective of the economy as a whole, however, the excess supply is not eliminated; like a hot potato, it simply passes from hand to hand. As it does so, it adds to the total flow of spending in the economy.

Direct and Indirect Effects on Aggregate Demand

The increase in spending affects aggregate demand, which includes only spending on *new final goods*, via two paths: a path by which new money enters the flow of spending on new final goods *directly*, and a path by which it enters that flow *indirectly* through its impact on asset prices and interest rates. These two paths are depicted schematically in Figure 21.3.

Although the direct and indirect effects of a change in the money supply work together in practice, they are logically distinct, and it is useful to consider each separately.

Figure 21.3

Direct and indirect effects of money supply changes

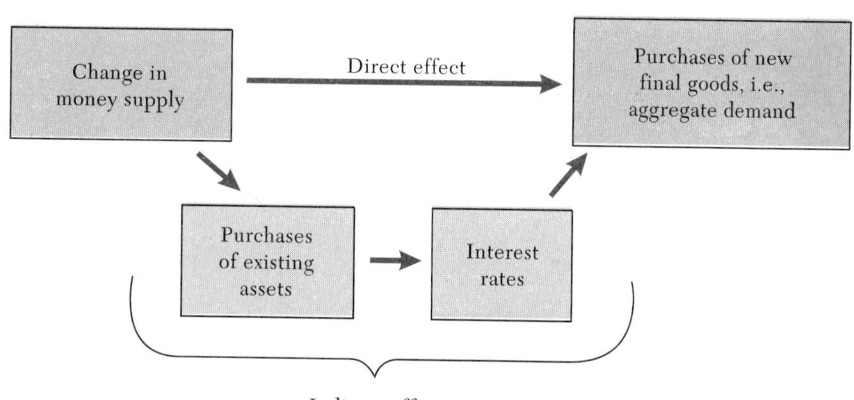

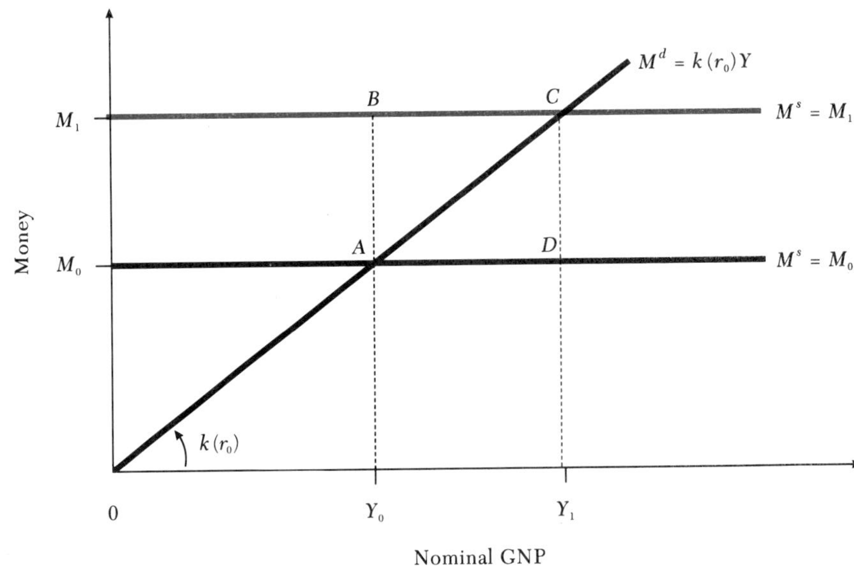

Figure 21.4

The direct effect of an increase in the money supply

The Direct Effect

Figure 21.4 illustrates the direct effect of an increase in the money supply on aggregate demand and nominal GNP. Starting from point A, with a money supply of M_0 and a corresponding equilibrium GNP of Y_0, the Fed increases the money supply to M_1. This shifts the money supply line upward and creates an initial excess supply of money equal to distance AB. When the new money enters the flow of spending on new final goods, it adds directly to aggregate demand and nominal GNP. The rising level of GNP increases the amount of money demanded, moving the economy along the money demand line to point C where, with GNP equal to Y_1, the money market is back in equilibrium.

Since money spent directly on new final goods does not affect the prices and yields of existing assets, interest rates are unaffected. Accordingly, fluidity, and thus the slope of the money demand line, remains fixed at $k(r_0)$. The change in nominal GNP is therefore equal to $1/k(r_0)$ times the change in the money supply, or, equivalently, to equilibrium velocity times the change in the money supply.

An illustration may help to clarify this point. Suppose the initial money supply is \$750 and equilibrium velocity is 6 (fluidity $= 1/6$). The initial equilibrium level of nominal GNP is therefore \$4,500 ($= 6 \times 750 = MV = Y$). If the money supply then increases by \$50 to \$800, the equilibrium level of nominal GNP will increase by \$300 to \$4,800 ($= 6 \times 800$).

Note that actual velocity (which is simply the ratio of Y to M) departs from its equilibrium value during the adjustment process. For example, with GNP initially at \$4,500 in our numerical illustration, the jump in the money supply from \$750 to \$800 temporarily reduces velocity from its equilibrium value of 6

(= 4,500/750) to 5.6 (= 4,500/800). Then, as the flow of spending adjusts to the higher money supply and nominal GNP rises to its new equilibrium value of $4,800, velocity rises back to its equilibrium value of 6 (= 4,800/800). In general, therefore, an increase in the money supply temporarily reduces velocity.

The direct effect on aggregate demand and nominal GNP works in reverse for a decrease in the money supply. When the Fed reduces the money supply, it creates an initial excess demand for money. People respond to this excess demand by reducing their rate of spending on new final goods to rebuild their money balances. As they do, aggregate demand and the level of nominal GNP fall, thus reducing the amount of money demanded until it is equal to the new, lower supply.

The Indirect Effect

Now let us consider the indirect effect of a change in the money supply. This effect depends on a change in the money supply altering spending on existing assets, such as government bonds, corporate stock, and used cars. Although spending on existing assets is not part of aggregate demand, a change in the demand for such assets indirectly influences aggregate demand via its impact on interest rates. Let's first see how this works when changes in the money supply do *not* affect inflationary expectations.

Suppose that the Fed increases the money supply with an open market purchase. As we have seen, this initially puts excess reserves into the banking system and excess money balances into the hands of the public. When people exchange some of their excess money balances for other financial assets—say, bonds—the increased demand for bonds raises bond prices. As we saw in Chapter 7, this rise in bond prices is equivalent to a fall in bond yields. For example, a bond maturing 1 year from now with a face value of $100 and selling today for $90 yields 11.1 percent interest [= (100 − 90)/90]. If its price is bid up to $95, its yield falls to only 5.3 percent [= (100 − 95)/95).

Just as the public is attempting to exchange its excess money balances for bonds, banks are also attempting to exchange their excess reserves for other financial assets, namely, the IOUs of borrowers. The drop in bond yields will thus be accompanied by a decline in interest rates on bank loans as banks with excess reserves compete for borrowers. The result is a general decline in interest rates, which encourages credit-financed spending by businesses on new capital goods and by households on new cars, furniture, and other consumer durables. These expenditures, the indirect effect of the increase of the money supply on interest rates, all add to the flow of aggregate demand.*

The indirect effects are reversed when the money supply decreases. A decrease in the money supply creates an initial excess demand for money, to which

*Excess money balances could also be used to buy existing *real* assets, such as used cars and houses built in previous years. As in the case of financial assets, the increased demand for real assets raises their prices and reduces their yields (as measured by their flow or real services relative to their prices). The rise in prices and decline in yields on existing assets raises the demand for their newly produced counterparts—new cars and houses, for example—and the increased spending on those new assets also adds to aggregate demand.

people respond by selling bonds and other assets in an attempt to rebuild their money balances. This drives asset prices down and interest rates (yields) up, the higher interest rates discourage credit-financed purchases of new final goods, and the result is a fall in aggregate demand and nominal GNP.

The Complete Adjustment to a Change in the Money Supply with Fixed Inflationary Expectations

The complete adjustment to a change in the money supply is illustrated in Figure 21.5. We begin with the economy in equilibrium at point *A* with a money supply of M_0, nominal GNP equal to Y_0, a nominal interest rate equal to r_0, and fluidity of $k(r_0)$. The Fed then increases the money supply from M_0 to M_1. This creates an initial excess supply of money represented by distance *AB*. As part of the new money enters directly into the flow of aggregate demand, it begins to raise the level of nominal GNP. At the same time, the increased spending on existing assets reduces the nominal interest rate from r_0 to, say, r_1. As we have just seen, the lower interest rate stimulates credit-financed spending, which adds indirectly to aggregate demand and nominal GNP. However, the lower interest rate also reduces the opportunity cost of holding money and thus raises fluidity. This is represented in the diagram by the upward rotation of the money demand line from $k(r_0)$ to $k(r_1)$. The falling interest rate and rising GNP combine to increase the quantity of money demanded until, at point C', it is once again equal to the amount supplied and equilibrium is restored.

Note that the rise in fluidity limits the increase in nominal GNP to Y_1' rather

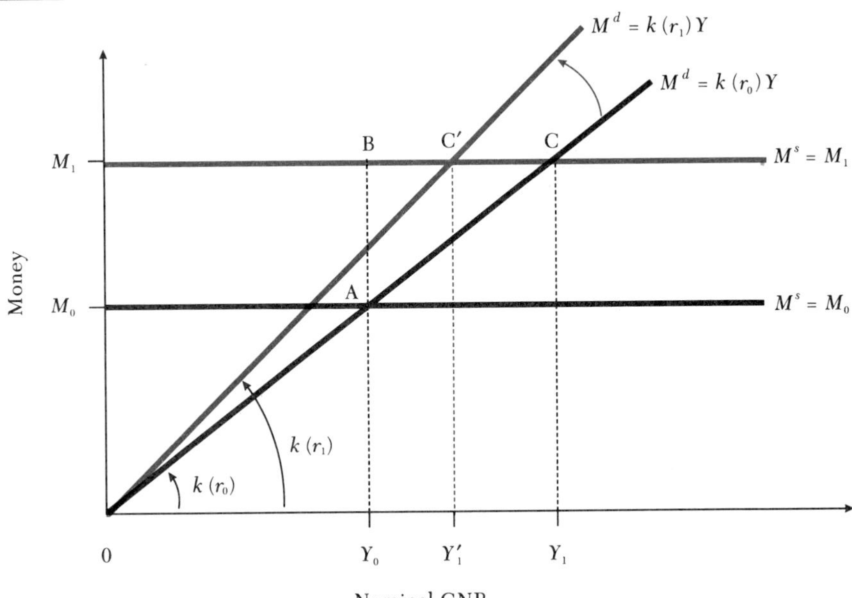

Figure 21.5

The complete adjustment to an increase in the money supply

than Y_1. In effect, the rise in fluidity is equivalent to a fall in velocity, which partially offsets the impact of the increase in the money supply on aggregate demand and GNP.

The same adjustment process works in reverse for a decrease in the money supply. In particular, a downward shift of the money supply line creates an initial excess demand for money. This decreases aggregate demand and nominal GNP. At the same time, the rising interest rate reduces fluidity. The reduction in fluidity and the fall in nominal GNP combine to decrease the demand for money until it has fallen enough to match the decrease in supply. In the new equilibrium, fluidity is lower and velocity higher due to the higher interest rate.

Money and Interest Rates with Variable Inflationary Expectations

Up to this point, we have simplified our analysis by assuming that the expected rate of inflation is unaffected by a change in the money supply. As we have just seen, however, changes in the money supply alter aggregate demand, which plays a critical role in determining the price level and inflation. Accordingly, let us now consider what happens when a change in the money supply *does* lead to a change in inflationary expectations.

In discussing its indirect effect on aggregate demand, we argued that an increase in the money supply lowers the nominal rate of interest. Recall, however, that the nominal rate of interest is equal to the real rate of interest plus the expected rate of inflation. An increase in the money supply can therefore *raise* the nominal interest rate if it raises inflationary expectations sufficiently. Moreover, a rising nominal interest rate increases the opportunity cost of holding money, thereby reducing fluidity and raising equilibrium velocity—just the opposite of what we concluded in the case of fixed inflationary expectations. In this case, the impact of an increase in the money supply on aggregate demand is reinforced, rather than offset, by the change in velocity. By the same token, a decrease in the money supply that reduces inflationary expectations can reduce nominal interest rates. This leads to a rise in fluidity and a fall in velocity, which reinforces the impact of the fall in the money supply.

Depending on its impact on inflationary expectations, therefore, a change in the money supply can lead to an offsetting change in velocity, a reinforcing change in velocity, or no change in velocity. Accordingly, the resulting changes in aggregate demand and nominal GNP can be proportionately smaller than, greater than, or the same as the change in the money supply.

MONEY, REAL OUTPUT, AND THE PRICE LEVEL

To analyze money's impact on the price level and inflation, we must integrate our theory of the money market with the theory of aggregate supply that we developed in Chapter 20. The equation of exchange provides a useful framework for such an integration: Our theory of the money market tells us how changes in the supply of and demand for money affect aggregate demand on the left-hand (MV) side of the equation, whereas our theory of aggregate supply tells us how those changes are divided between the price level and real output effects on the right-hand (PQ) side.

We first consider the effects of one-time-only changes in the supply of money and the demand for money. That analysis will then provide the foundation for a dynamic analysis of the relations among monetary growth, inflation, and real output growth.

One-Shot Changes in the Supply of Money

Figure 21.6 depicts long-run and short-run aggregate supply curves like those developed in Chapter 20. The short-run aggregate supply curve is drawn for an expected price level of P_0. This is also the equilibrium price level when aggre-

Figure 21.6

Aggregate demand, aggregate supply, and changes in the supply of money

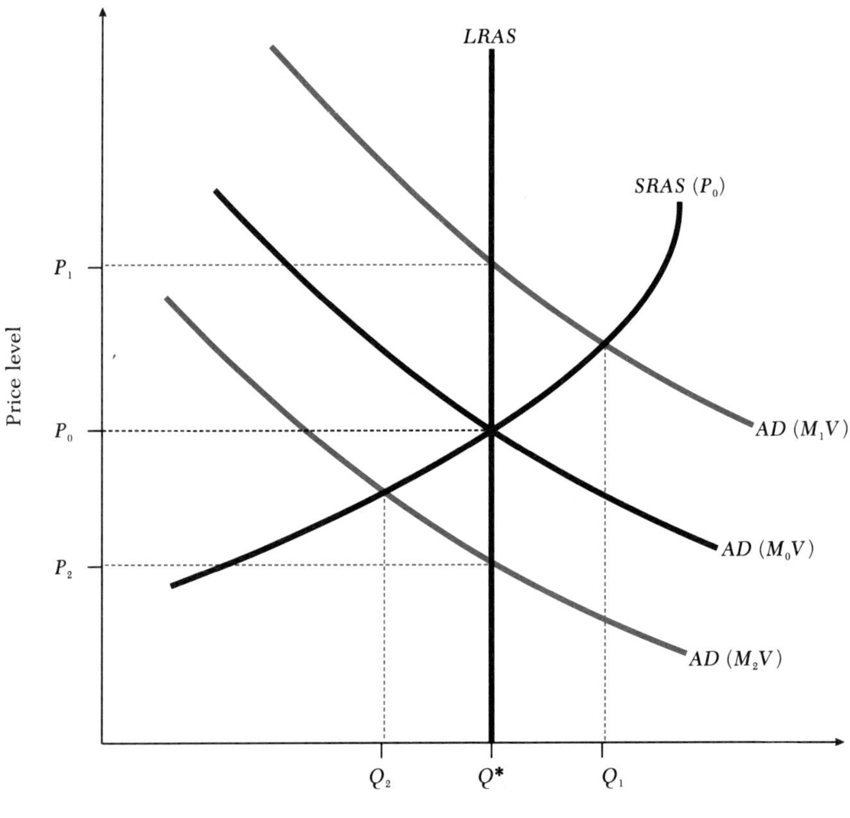

gate demand is $AD(M_0V)$, which we assume is the level of aggregate demand when the money supply is M_0 and velocity is V.

Starting from this initial equilibrium, suppose the Fed increases the money supply to M_1. The additional money adds to total spending, thereby raising the aggregate demand curve to $AD(M_1V)$. In the short run, information lags and contractual wage and price rigidities prevent the price level from fully adjusting to the higher level of aggregate demand. As a result, the increase in aggregate demand is partially absorbed through a short-run rise in real output from Q^* to Q_1. In the long run, as expectations adjust and contracts are rewritten, real output will return to its natural level and the price level will continue to rise to a new equilibrium of P_1. The higher price level will have also raised nominal GNP just enough so that the amount of money demanded now matches the greater supply and equilibrium is also restored in the money market.

Our theory of aggregate supply also tells us that the more sudden and unexpected the increase in the money supply, the greater its impact on real output and the smaller its short-run effect on the price level (that is, the flatter the short-run aggregate supply curve). Conversely, the more accurately anticipated the increase in the money supply, the smaller its short-run impact on real output and the more rapid its ultimate effect on the price level.

A one-shot decrease in the money supply from M_0 to M_2 would have just the opposite effect. Aggregate demand would fall from $AD(M_0V)$ to $AD(M_2V)$, and the result would be a short-run recession as real output declined to Q_2. This would be followed in the long run by an economic recovery in real output and a continuing deflation in the price level to P_2 as expectations adjust to the lower level of aggregate demand. At the lower price level, nominal GNP will have fallen just enough so that the quantity of money demanded just matches the lower supply. Moreover, the more sudden and unexpected the decline in the money supply, the more severe the short-run recession. Conversely, the more accurately it is anticipated, the quicker the deflation in prices and the less severe the recession.

One-Shot Changes in the Demand for Money

Now let us consider the effects of independent shifts in the demand for money. Other things being equal, an increase in the demand for money relative to income (that is, an increase in fluidity) lowers velocity and leads to a reduction in aggregate demand. In terms of the equation of exchange, if M remains fixed while V falls, then aggregate demand MV will also fall. Conversely, a decrease in the demand for money raises velocity and, other things being equal, also the level of aggregate demand.

Figure 21.7 on the next page shows the effect of changes in the demand for money when the supply of money is held constant. Suppose the economy is initially in equilibrium with a price level of P_0 and a level of aggregate demand corresponding to velocity of V_0, namely, $AD(MV_0)$. Then something happens that leads people to demand higher money balances relative to their incomes. The resulting fall in velocity is accompanied by a drop in aggregate demand to $AD(MV_1)$.

Figure 21.7

Aggregate demand, aggregate supply, and changes in the demand for money

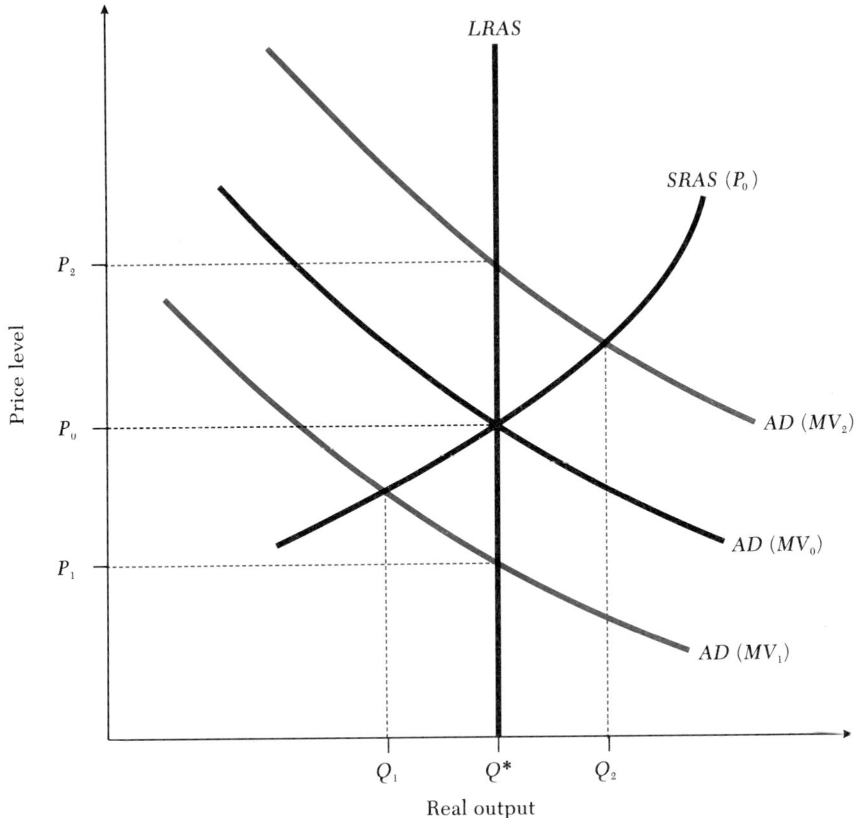

The short-run result is a recession as real output falls to Q_1; in the long run, real output returns to its natural level and the price level continues to fall until it reaches P_1. The effects of an *increase* in the *demand* for money are therefore much the same as those of a *decrease* in the *supply* of money. Conversely, a decrease in the demand for money and a rise in velocity have the same effect as an increase in the supply of money. In Figure 21.7, a rise in velocity from V_0 to V_2 raises aggregate demand from $AD(MV_0)$ to $AD(MV_2)$, leads to a short-run surge in real output to Q_2, and initiates an inflation that ultimately raises the price level to P_2.

If the Fed could correctly anticipate such changes in the demand for money, it could use its control of the money supply to offset the resulting variations in velocity and thus maintain a stable level of aggregate demand. Unfortunately, as we shall see, this is easier said than done.

Dynamics: Money, Growth, and Inflation over Time

Now let us add a time dimension to our analysis. The best way to do so is to once again invoke the equation of exchange, but in a slightly different, dynamic form. In particular, let us make use of the mathematical property which says that *the growth rate of the product of two variables is equal to the sum of their respective individual growth rates.** Since aggregate demand can be expressed as the product of the money supply and its velocity, it therefore follows that the growth rate of aggregate demand is equal to the growth rate of the money supply plus the growth rate of velocity. Similarly, since nominal GNP is equal to the product of the price level and real GNP, the growth rate of nominal GNP is equal to the growth rate of the price level—or equivalently, the rate of inflation—plus the rate of real economic growth. Using lower case letters to denote annual rates of change, we can therefore write the *dynamic version of the equation of exchange* as

$$m + v = p + q$$

where m is the growth rate of the money supply, v is the growth rate of velocity, p is the rate of inflation, and q is the growth rate of real GNP. Like the static form of the equation, this identity must always hold. Simple arithmetic therefore tells us that any combination of money supply growth and velocity growth that exceeds the growth rate of real output must necessarily be accompanied by inflation. For example, if the money supply grows at 6 percent per year, velocity at 2 percent per year, and real output at 3 percent per year, then inflation will be 5 percent per year (because $6 + 2 = 5 + 3$).

Long-Term Dynamics

As we have seen, the long-term growth rate of real output is determined by factors such as technological progress and the growth of the capital stock and labor force. In addition, the long-term trend of velocity is largely determined by the evolution of our credit and financial institutions. For example, economists believe that factors such as the increasing use of credit cards, automatic transfers between savings and checking accounts, and the development of electronic banking have all contributed to a long-term rise in velocity.

Given the long-term growth rates of real output and velocity, monetary growth is the principal determinant of the long-term, or secular, rate of inflation. For example, during the period between 1960 and 1982, both real output and velocity grew at just under 3 percent per year while the money supply grew at about 5.5 percent per year. Since the increase in real output almost exactly offset the rise in velocity, the average rate of inflation was just about equal to the rate of monetary growth, namely, 5.5 percent.

Short-Run Dynamics

The dynamic relations among money, velocity, real output, and the price level are more complex in the short run. From our theory of aggregate supply, it follows that an acceleration of money growth typically leads to a temporary, short-run acceleration in the growth rate of real output before it is fully absorbed

*This holds exactly only when growth rates are continuously compounded. When they are compounded annually or monthly, it provides only a close approximation.

into a higher secular inflation rate. By the same token, a sudden deceleration of monetary growth would initially slow the growth of real output, and perhaps even cause a recession (negative q), before it is fully reflected in a lower secular rate of inflation.

The short-run relation between monetary growth and inflation becomes more complicated still when we recognize that factors other than monetary change itself can cause unanticipated fluctuations in real output and velocity. To see the implications of this, suppose that the growth rate of the money supply remains steady at 5 percent per year. If real output and velocity each grow at a steady 3 percent rate, inflation will also remain steady at 5 percent. However, if either real output or velocity deviates unpredictably from their long-term growth paths, the result will be short-run swings in the rate of inflation. For example, if a negative supply shock pushes real output into a −2 percent nosedive, inflation will accelerate from 5 percent to 10 percent (because $5 + 3 = 10 - 2$). As we have seen, this is exactly what happened when inflation temporarily accelerated into the double-digit range during the OPEC supply shock recessions of the 1970s. In addition, deviations in velocity from its long-term growth path will be reflected in short-run instability of aggregate demand and lead to cyclical fluctuations in real output growth as well as the rate of inflation.

In a nutshell, therefore, although monetary growth is the principal determinant of the long-term, secular rate of inflation, the short-run relations among monetary growth, inflation, and real output are quite complicated. This complexity has some very important implications for the Fed's conduct of monetary policy.

Monetary Policy: An Introduction

Monetary policy involves the Fed's use of open market operations and its other policy tools to influence the level of aggregate demand. Although we examine overall macroeconomic policy in detail in Chapter 23, it is useful to introduce the basics of monetary policy here while the links between the money market and aggregate demand are still fresh in mind.

An **expansionary monetary policy** is one that increases the supply of money relative to the demand.

A **contractionary monetary policy** is one that decreases the supply of money relative to the demand.

The Fed can stimulate aggregate demand by allowing the money supply to grow relative to the demand for money. This constitutes an **expansionary monetary policy**. Conversely, the Fed can restrain aggregate demand by restricting the growth of the money supply relative to the demand for money. This constitutes a **contractionary monetary policy**. Note that it is not the behavior of the money supply per se that determines whether monetary policy is expansionary or contractionary, but its behavior relative the demand for money, or equivalently, relative to the behavior of velocity. For example, the money supply can be rising, but we would properly consider monetary policy contractionary if the demand for money were rising faster, or equivalently, if velocity were falling faster, than the money supply is rising.

There is a consensus among economists, and considerable evidence to support that consensus, on two important points regarding monetary policy. The first of these is that, since the rate of money growth is the principal determinant of the long-term rate of inflation, monetary policy is the key to achieving and maintaining a low and stable secular rate of inflation. The second point of consensus is that, because monetary policy operates primarily through aggregate demand, it has little if any impact on real output and employment in the long-run. The consensus tends to break down, however, on the use of monetary policy for purposes of short-run stabilization. In particular, there is disagreement among economists about what, if anything, monetary policy can or should do to offset the effects of short-run fluctuations in aggregate demand. To get at the sources of this disagreement, let us focus on the variables that link the Fed's policy actions to changes in aggregate demand.

The Fed's principal policy tool, open market operations, operates directly on bank reserves; a change in bank reserves leads to a change in the money supply; and a change in the money supply alters total spending and aggregate demand. This causal chain is summarized in Figure 21.8. The upper row shows the successive variables affected by monetary policy: bank reserves, the money supply, and aggregate demand. The lower row shows the links among these variables: The money multiplier is the link between bank reserves and the money supply, and velocity is the link between the money supply and aggregate demand. These links are relatively tight and predictable in the long-run so that the Fed's open market operations provide it with a good tool for controlling long-run inflation. However, both links are subject to considerable uncertainty in the short run. Although the money multiplier is partially determined by the Fed's reserve requirements, it also varies as people switch their money balances between currency and bank deposits and among different types of deposit accounts. Moreover, as we have seen, velocity varies inversely with changes in the demand for money relative to income. If the Fed could correctly anticipate changes in the money multiplier and velocity, it could use its open market purchases to keep aggregate demand on a stable growth path—ideally, one matching that of the natural rate of real output. In the absence of supply shocks, the result would be high employment without inflation.

As you may suspect, this is easier said than done. As we shall see in our more complete discussion of macroeconomic policy in Chapter 23, the Fed's task is complicated not only by the unpredictability of fluctuations in the money multi-

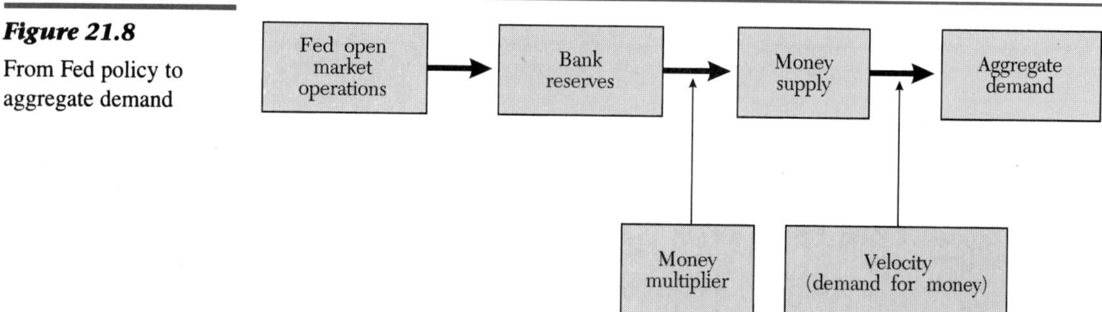

Figure 21.8
From Fed policy to aggregate demand

plier and velocity and by periodic supply shocks but also by a considerable amount of uncertainty regarding the timing of its policy actions. In addition, the feedback information with which the Fed attempts to ascertain whether its policies are having an expansionary, contractionary, or neutral impact on the economy is often ambiguous and difficult to interpret.

Whether the Fed is up to the task of actively using monetary policy to offset short-run fluctuations in aggregate demand—indeed, whether it should even try—is at the center of the debate between Keynesians and *monetarists*.

MONETARIST VERSUS KEYNESIAN

Theoretical Differences

In Chapter 18, we introduced a classical theory of money and the price level called the *quantity theory*. According to the original quantity theory, changes in the money supply have proportional affects on the price level because they do not affect either velocity or real output. Double the money supply and the price level doubles; cut the money supply in half and the price level is cut in half.

Monetarism is a point of view that emphasizes the relative stability of the velocity of money and the primacy of the money supply in determining aggregate demand.

Modern day **monetarists** are lineal descendants of the classical quantity theorists. Indeed, it was the development of a modern and more sophisticated version of the quantity theory that gave birth to contemporary monetarism during the 1960s.* Like their classical predecessors, monetarists believe that the supply of money is the principal determinant of aggregate demand. They also believe that velocity (and thus the demand for money) does not bounce around erratically; rather it is a stable and predictable function of a relatively few variables. In the short run, the most important of these variables are the expected rate of inflation and the real rate of interest on nonmoney assets. In the long run, they are the slowly evolving characteristics of the economy's banking and financial institutions.

If velocity and the demand for money are stable and predictable, as the monetarists claim they are, then unstable aggregate demand must be the consequence of an unstable money supply. Accordingly, monetarists believe that short-run fluctuations in real output and inflation are more often than not the result of erratic and unpredictable changes in the behavior of the money supply. Indeed, many monetarists believe that the blame for most twentieth-century business cycles, including the Great Depression, rests squarely on the shoulders of the Fed.

While most Keynesians do not dispute the long-term relation between monetary growth and inflation, their interpretation of the short run differs considerably from that of the monetarists. For one thing, Keynesians believe that money plays

*The most famous of all monetarists, and the one who during the 1960s almost single-handedly revived interest in the quantity theory, is Milton Friedman. Friedman shared the 1976 Nobel Prize in economics.

a less important role—or perhaps more accurately, a less active role—in short-run fluctuations in aggregate demand. They claim that such fluctuations are more often the result of variations in other factors, including household thrift, profit expectations of businesses, foreign trade flows, and levels of government spending and taxing. To the extent that monetary changes affect aggregate demand, Keynesians believe that such changes work indirectly through their influence on these other variables.

Moreover, Keynesians also hold that aggregate demand can change without any change in the money supply. Since aggregate demand must equal the money supply times velocity, nonmonetary factors can affect aggregate demand only by altering velocity. Accordingly, far from being the paragon of stability it is in monetarist theory, velocity (and, by implication, the demand for money) passively adapts to changes in many other variables in Keynesian theory. As it relates to money's role in the economy, therefore, the fundamental theoretical dispute between the monetarists and Keynesians revolves around the short-run stability of velocity and the demand for money.

Monetary Policy Differences

Monetarists generally favor a *rules* approach to monetary policy. Such an approach would substantially reduce—perhaps entirely eliminate—the Fed's discretionary control over the money supply and replace it with a rule requiring the Fed simply to provide stable, perhaps even constant, monetary growth.

The monetarist argument for a rules approach to monetary policy follows naturally from the monetarist's belief in the fundamental stability of both velocity and, á la their classical predecessors, the real economy. If, as the monetarists claim, both velocity and real output would follow relatively stable and predictable growth paths in the absence of monetary disturbances, then a stable and predictable monetary growth path would lead to a stable and predictable rate of inflation. Deviations from a stable monetary growth path, on the other hand, would lead to short-run instability in both real output and the rate of inflation.

Keynesians favor a *discretionary* approach to monetary policy. Once again, this view follows directly from their theoretical conclusions. If, as the Keynesians believe, velocity and the demand for money are subject to substantial short-run instability, then the Fed must have the authority to offset this instability with discretionary changes in the money supply. Suppose, for example, that the demand for money suddenly increases and velocity drops. As we have seen, this will lead to a recession unless offset by an increase in the supply of money. Under these circumstances, according to Keynesians, a strict monetary policy rule would unwisely tie the Fed's hands, preventing it from supplying the additional money necessary to stave off the recession.

Empirical Evidence and Its Interpretation

The stability of velocity is an empirical question which, in principle, can be resolved by looking at the facts. The relevant facts are depicted in Figure 21.9, which plots the quarterly behavior of velocity (calculated as the ratio of nominal

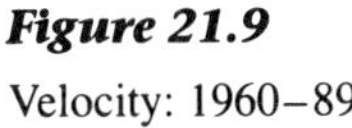

Figure 21.9

Velocity: 1960–89

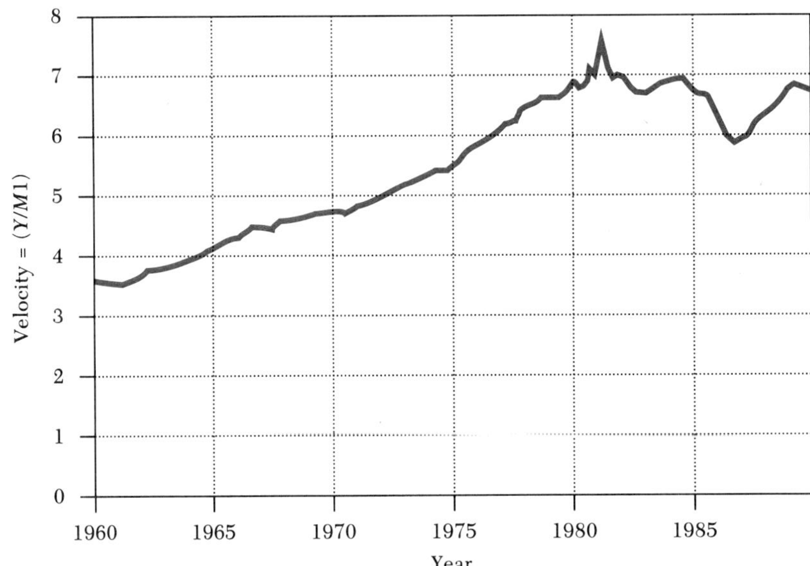

GNP to M1) for the years from 1960 to 1989. The data clearly indicate a long-term upward trend in velocity extending through 1981. This trend appears to have been broken beginning in 1982. The data also reveal relatively small, short-term fluctuations in velocity throughout the entire period. Keynesians interpret these fluctuations as evidence of the short-run instability of the demand for money, and they point to the break in velocity's upward trend following 1981 as the final, damning evidence against monetarism.

As you may suspect, monetarists interpret the same data somewhat differently. They point out that, just by simple arithmetic, measured velocity will temporarily depart from its equilibrium value whenever the money supply changes. We illustrated this when we showed how a lag in the adjustment of nominal GNP to an increase in the money supply temporarily lowers velocity. If the money supply behaves erratically, as the monetarists claim it has, then measured velocity will inevitably exhibit short-term ups and downs. According to the monetarists' interpretation of the facts, therefore, the short-run fluctuations that we observe in velocity are not evidence of an unstable *demand* for money. Quite the contrary, they are the result of an unstable *supply* of money.

Regarding the break in the upward trend in velocity after 1981, monetarists argue that it is the result of disinflation and falling nominal interest rates. They also argue that the extensive changes in banking and the financial markets that followed the Monetary Control Act of 1980 have temporarily introduced much greater uncertainty into the relation between nominal GNP and the money supply. The relation will again stabilize, they predict, once these changes have fully worked themselves out.

As you can see from the preceding discussion, the empirical data on the behavior of velocity do not conclusively support either side, although in recent years the burden of proof seems to have shifted more to the monetarists.

Further blow-by-blow descriptions of the monetarist–Keynesian debate and its policy implications require a thorough understanding of the Keynesian theory of aggregate demand. It is to that theory which we turn in the next chapter.

CHAPTER SUMMARY

1. In the equation of exchange, money times its velocity (*MV*) is equal to aggregate demand. The effect of a change in the money supply on aggregate demand therefore depends on velocity.
2. The *demand for money* is the demand to hold the specific, liquid assets of which the money stock is composed. Other things being equal, a decrease in the demand for money is equivalent to a rise in velocity, and an increase in the demand for money is equivalent to a decline in velocity.
3. The *transactions demand* for money is positively related to income. It is reduced by anything that leads to closer synchronization of receipts and expenditures.
4. The *asset demand* for money is based on money's liquidity relative to other assets.
5. The nominal interest rate provides a measure of the opportunity cost of holding money.
6. The overall demand for money is positively related to income and negatively related to nominal interest rates.
7. An increase in the money supply adds directly to aggregate demand to the extent that it is spent on new final goods; it adds indirectly to aggregate demand to the extent that it reduces interest rates and stimulates additional credit-financed spending on new final goods.
8. Depending on the effect of an increase in the money supply on inflationary expectations, it may lead to either lower or higher interest rates. Specifically, an increase (decrease) in the money supply can raise (lower) interest rates if it raises (lowers) inflationary expectations.
9. An unanticipated one-shot increase (decrease) in the money supply raises (lowers) real output and employment in the short run, but only increases (decreases) the price level in the long run.
10. A one-shot increase (decrease) in the demand for money lowers (raises) real output and employment in the short run, but only decreases (increases) the price level in the long run.

11. In its dynamic version, the equation of exchange says that the growth rate of the money supply plus the growth rate of velocity must equal the inflation rate plus the growth rate of real output. Thus, given the long-term growth rates of real output and velocity, monetary growth is the principal determinant of the long-term, secular rate of inflation.

12. In the short run, the relation between monetary growth and inflation is complicated by fluctuations in velocity and real output.

13. An *expansionary* monetary policy is one that allows the money supply to grow relative to the demand for money; a *contractionary* monetary policy is one that restricts the growth of the money supply relative to the demand for money.

14. Economists agree that, although monetary policy has little if any long-run impact on real output and employment, it is the key to achieving and maintaining a low and stable secular rate of inflation. They disagree about what, if anything, monetary policy can or should do to offset short-run fluctuations in aggregate demand.

15. Believing that velocity, the demand for money, and the real economy are inherently stable, *monetarists* favor a rules approach to monetary policy. Keynesians, believing that velocity, the demand for money, and the real economy are potentially unstable, favor a discretionary approach to monetary policy.

Key Terms and Concepts

demand for money
transactions demand
asset demand
fluidity
expansionary monetary policy
contractionary monetary policy
monetarism

Questions for Thought and Discussion

1. What do you think happens to fluidity and velocity during hyperinflation? Why?
2. Empirical studies of the effect of interest rates on the demand for money find that the demand for *M1* money balances is far more sensitive to interest rates than is the demand for *M2* money balances. Why do you think this is the case?
3. "Since money is a form of wealth, the Fed could increase everyone's wealth simply by printing new money and dropping it out of airplanes over large cities." What is the fallacy in this statement?

4. Suppose that velocity, which is initially equal to 6.0, changes by 0.25 for each 1 percentage point change in the nominal rate of interest. By how much will nominal GNP change when the money supply increases by $10 billion if the increase in the money supply leaves nominal interest rates unaffected? If the increase in the money supply reduces nominal interest rates by 2 percentage points? If the increase in the money supply raises inflationary expectations by 1 percentage point?

5. Distinguish between the short- and long-run effects of a one-shot increase in the money supply and a permanent increase in the *growth rate* of the money supply.

6. Use the dynamic form of the equation of exchange to tell what will happen to the long-term rate of inflation, other things being equal, under each of the following scenarios.

   a. The growth rate of the money supply increases by 3 percentage points.
   b. Real economic growth slows by 0.5 percentage points while the growth rate of velocity increases by 1 percentage point.
   c. The growth rates of both real output and the money supply rise by 1 percentage point.
   d. The growth rates of both the money supply and velocity rise by 1 percentage point.

CHAPTER 22

The Income-Expenditure Model of Aggregate Demand

An economic model is simply an analytical framework—a way of thinking about how some part of the economy works. In the preceding chapter, the equation of exchange provided us with a convenient and natural framework for thinking about the relation between money and aggregate demand. In this chapter we develop an alternative framework for thinking about aggregate demand, namely, the **income-expenditure model**. This model was initially developed by Keynes himself, and it continues to be the mode of analysis favored by most contemporary Keynesians. It is an especially useful framework for thinking about the effect on aggregate demand of such things as foreign trade, the government budget, and fluctuations in investment spending.

The **income-expenditure model** focuses on the relation between the level of nomimal GNP (national income) and the level of aggregate expenditure.

THE BASIC INCOME-EXPENDITURE MODEL

As its name suggests, the income-expenditure model focuses on the relation between income and expenditures. In particular, it postulates that, other things being equal, the higher people's income, the greater their expenditures. For the economy as a whole, this means that the higher the level of national income, or nominal GNP, the greater the sum of expenditures by households, businesses, foreigners, and government.

A word of caution! As we saw in Chapter 16, actual expenditures on final goods are by definition always equal to nominal GNP. Our concern here, however, is not with this definitional identity, but with the behavioral relation between people's current income and their expenditure *plans*. As we shall see, the two are not always consistent.

The **expenditure function** shows the level of aggregate, planned expenditures for each level of nominal GNP.

The **marginal propensity to spend** measures the change in aggregate expenditures per dollar change in GNP.

The Expenditure Function

The line labelled E in Figure 22.1 is an **expenditure function**. It shows the level of planned expenditures for each level of nominal GNP. Its slope is called the **marginal propensity to spend**. The marginal propensity to spend tells us by how much spending changes per dollar change in GNP. A basic assumption of the income-expenditure model is that the marginal propensity to spend is positive but less than 1, implying that as GNP increases, some, but not all, of the additional national income will be spent on new final goods. The remainder will be

Figure 22.1

The expenditure function and equilibrium GNP

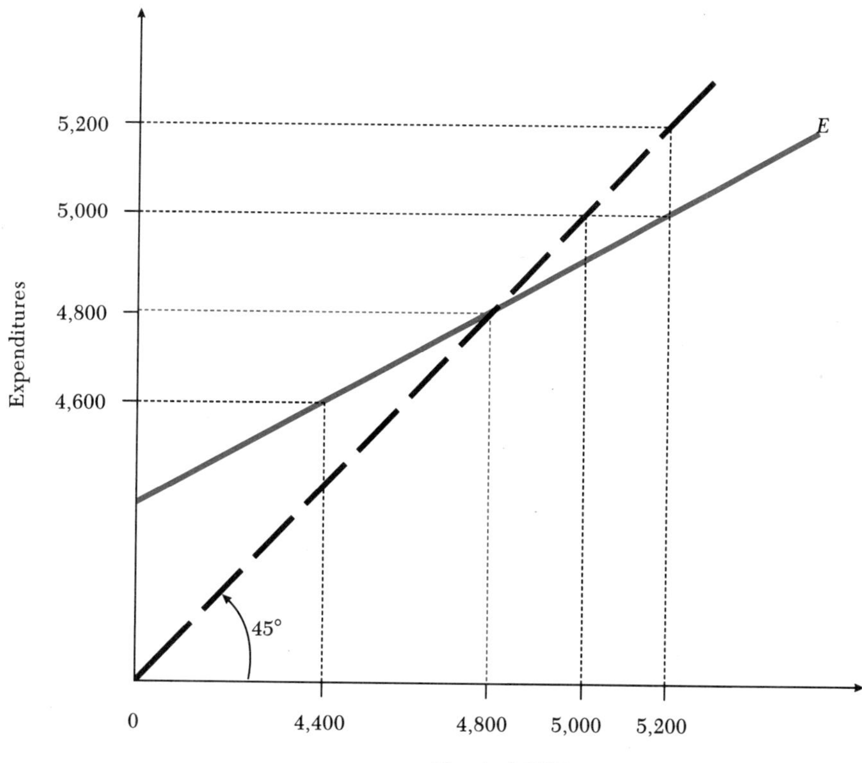

saved, used to pay taxes, or spent on existing assets. Similarly, when GNP falls, spending will also fall, but only by a fraction of the fall in GNP. The expenditure function in Figure 22.1 is drawn with a marginal propensity to spend of 0.5, so that each $1 change in GNP leads to a 50-cent change in spending in the same direction.

In addition to the expenditure function, Figure 22.1 also includes a dashed line drawn through the origin at an angle of 45°—that is, with a slope of +1. Points on this line are equidistant from the two axes. Thus, where GNP measures $5,000 (billion) on the horizontal axis, the vertical distance up to the 45° line is also $5,000; where GNP is $5,200, this distance is $5,200, and so on. Since the expenditure function shows total spending, it follows that the vertical gap between it and the 45° line represents the difference between GNP and total spending. For example, when GNP is $5,200, planned spending is only $5,000. The vertical gap between the 45° line and the expenditure function at that level of GNP thus represents the $200 excess of GNP over expenditures. Where the expenditure function lies above the 45° line—for example, where GNP is $4,400 and expenditures are $4,600—the gap between the two represents an excess of planned expenditures over GNP.*

Equilibrium in the Income-Expenditure Model

The economy is in income-expenditure equilibrium only when the current level of GNP generates a matching flow of expenditures. Graphically, this condition is satisfied at the level of GNP corresponding to the intersection of the expenditure function and the 45° line. In Figure 22.1, this occurs at the $4,800 level of GNP.

To see why this is an equilibrium, let us consider what would happen if GNP were at some other level. Suppose, for example, that GNP is initially $4,400 per year. According to the expenditure function in Figure 22.1, the income from this rate of production generates an expenditure flow of $4,600 per year. People are therefore spending at a rate that exceeds the current market value of the goods they are trying to buy. Clearly something must give! Either more goods must be produced, prices must rise, or both; in any case, nominal GNP must increase. As it does, the gap between expenditures and GNP will shrink, finally disappearing once GNP has risen to $4,800. At that level of GNP, the economy is in equilibrium because the expenditures of $4,800 just match the value of what is being produced.

Now let's reverse things. Suppose nominal GNP is initially equal to $5,200. The result is expenditures of only $5,000, which are not enough to purchase current GNP. Unless producers are willing to accumulate inventories indefinitely, therefore, they must either cut production, reduce prices, or both. In any case, nominal GNP must fall. As it does, the gap between GNP and expenditures will shrink, finally disappearing when GNP reaches its equilibrium level of $4,800.

*If you are wondering how spending can exceed GNP, remember that people can draw on credit as well as on current income to finance spending.

Changes in Equilibrium: The Autonomous Spending Multiplier

An **autonomous spending change** is a change in spending caused by some factor other than a change in nominal GNP.

Changes in spending due to changes in nominal GNP, such as the adjustments to equilibrium just described, move us along a given expenditure function. Changes in spending caused by factors other than a change in GNP shift the expenditure function and alter equilibrium. Such spending changes are called **autonomous spending changes**. We will examine the sources of autonomous spending change later. To illustrate their common effects, however, let us examine the impact of an autonomous \$100 increase in spending in the economy whose expenditure function we have been using in the foregoing examples. Figure 22.2 reproduces this expenditure function, now labelled E_0, along with a new one, labelled E_1, that lies \$100 above the original at each level of GNP. As you can see, the \$100 upward shift of the expenditure function raises the equilibrium level of GNP by \$200, from \$4,800 to \$5,000.

Whoa there! How can a \$100 increase in spending cause a \$200 increase in GNP? Are we pulling rabbits out of a hat? It seems that the adjustment to a new equilibrium bears closer examination.

Figure 22.2

A change in autonomous spending: the spending multiplier

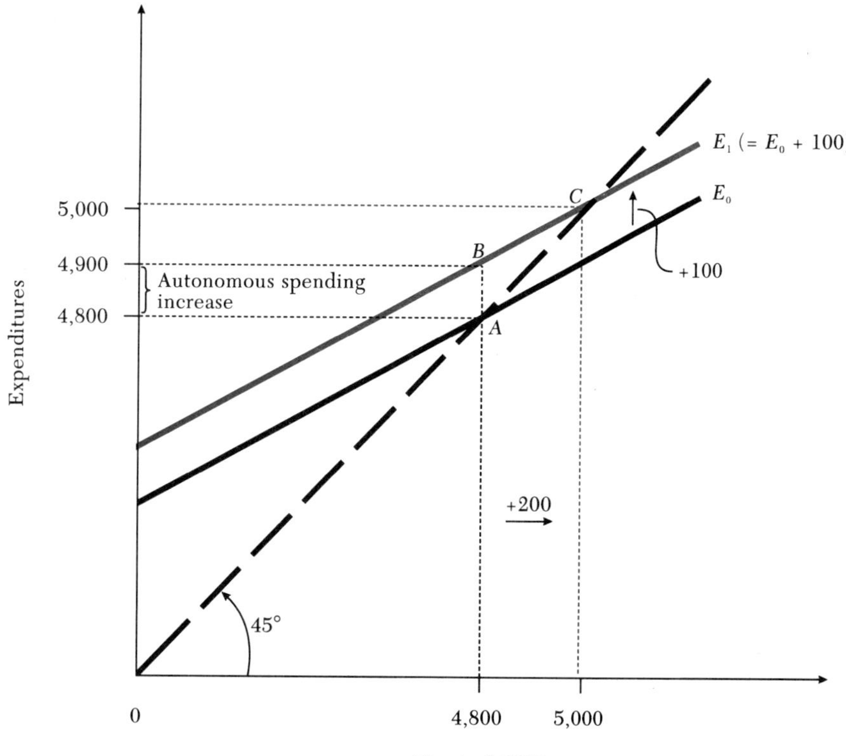

Table 22.1

The adjustment to a $100 autonomous increase in spending, assuming a marginal propensity to spend of 0.5

ROUND	CHANGE IN EXPENDITURE		CHANGE IN GNP AND INCOME	CUMULATIVE CHANGE IN GNP
1	+100.00*	⟶	+100.00	$100.00
2	+ 50.00	⟷	+ 50.00	150.00
3	+ 25.00	⟷	+ 25.00	175.00
4	+ 12.50	⟷	+ 12.50	187.50
5	+ 6.25	⟷	+ 6.25	193.75
.	.		.	.
.	.		.	.
.	.		.	.
All remaining rounds	+ 6.25		+ 6.25	$200.00

*Initial autonomous spending change.

While it is true that the $100 autonomous spending increase itself adds only $100 to GNP, it also starts a process that adds even more to both spending and GNP. To see why, note that the people who are the recipients of initial increase in spending have $100 of additional income. If their marginal propensity to spend is 0.5, then their spending will rise by $50. That will add another $50 to GNP and incomes, which in turn will generate another $25 of spending, add $25 more to GNP and incomes, and so on. This round-by-round ripple effect of the initial $100 autonomous spending increase is summarized in Table 22.1. Each successive increase in spending is equal to the marginal propensity to spend, which we have assumed to be 0.5, times the change in GNP and national income in the previous round. As you can see, the entire process leads ultimately to a cumulative $200 increase in GNP.*

As this example suggests, the effect on GNP of an autonomous change in spending depends on both the magnitude of that change and the marginal propensity to spend by which its effects are propagated through the economy. The following formula gives the precise relationship among these variables:

*We can also represent the adjustment process graphically using Figure 22.2. The initial increase in autonomous spending is represented by the jump from point *A* to point *B* as the expenditure function shifts upward. The secondary increase in spending as GNP rises to its new equilibrium is represented by the movement from point *B* to point *C* along the new expenditure function.

$$\begin{pmatrix}\text{change}\\ \text{in GNP}\end{pmatrix} = \left(\frac{1}{1 - MPS}\right) \times \begin{pmatrix}\text{change in}\\ \text{autonomous spending}\end{pmatrix}$$

where *MPS* is the marginal propensity to spend.*

The **autonomous spending multiplier** measures the change in equilibrium GNP per dollar change in autonomous spending.

The term 1/(1 − *MPS*) is the **autonomous spending multiplier**. It literally multiplies a change in autonomous spending to determine its effect on equilibrium GNP. In the preceding example, the marginal propensity to spend was 0.5, so the value of the multiplier was 2 [= 1/(1 − 0.5)]. That is why the $100 increase in autonomous spending led ultimately to a $200 increase in equilibrium GNP.

The spending multiplier works in both directions. Just as an autonomous increase in spending is multiplied into a greater increase in GNP, an autonomous decrease in spending is multiplied into a greater decrease in GNP.

Since the marginal propensity to spend is assumed to be between 0 and 1, the spending multiplier will always be greater than 1. Moreover, its value will be greater the higher the marginal propensity to spend. If the marginal propensity to spend were 0.75 rather than 0.5, for example, the multiplier would be 4 rather than 2. In that case, a $100 increase in autonomous spending would raise equilibrium GNP by $400 rather than $200.

Although the arithmetic of the multiplier is fairly simple, and the process by which it works is relatively straightforward, several conditions must be met if it is to describe accurately the impact of a change in autonomous spending.

First, the multiplier effect requires that the change in autonomous spending be maintained over time. Empirical studies of the impact of changes in autonomous spending typically conclude that it takes several years for the multiplier process to work its way through the economy. Thus an autonomous change in spending that lasts for only a few months would alter GNP only temporarily, and by less than the amount implied by the spending multiplier.

Second, the multiplier operates only on the *net* change in autonomous spending. If an increase in spending in one sector of the economy is accompanied by a decrease in some other sector, only the difference between the two is multiplied into a change in equilibrium GNP.

Finally, since total spending is equal by definition to the money supply times its velocity, a change in spending that is not accompanied by a change in the money supply must alter velocity in the same direction if it is to have a multiplier effect on GNP. To illustrate, suppose that in our preceding example the money supply remains fixed at $800 when autonomous spending increases by $100. If the multiplier effect increases GNP from $4,800 to $5,000 as it did in our example, simple arithmetic tells us that velocity must have risen from 6.0 (= $4,800/$800) to 6.25 (= $5,000/$800). The multiplier effects of spending changes *independent of changes in the money supply* therefore require that velocity passively adjust to any change in autonomous spending and GNP. We

*Mathematically, the successive changes in GNP form an infinite geometric series with a common ratio equal to the marginal propensity to spend. The sum of such a series with a first term of *A* and a ratio of *b*, where $0 < b < 1$, is equal to $A[1/(1 - b)]$. Hence the formula.

develop this point in some detail later when we consider the interaction between the income-expenditure flow and the money market.

Real Output, the Price Level, and the Spending Multiplier

We have said nothing yet about how the multiplier effects just described are divided between changes in real output and changes in the price level. To do so requires that we interpret the income-expenditure model in light of our aggregate supply–aggregate demand analysis of Chapter 20.

We can use Figure 22.3 to show how nominal GNP and expenditures are related to the aggregate supply-and-demand curves. Suppose that current real output is $2,800 in base year prices and the current price level (both actual and expected) is 1.5 relative to the same base year. At that price level, real output of $3,000 is demanded, so there is an excess of aggregate demand over aggregate supply.

To interpret these conditions in terms of nominal GNP and planned expenditures, recall first that nominal GNP is equal to the price level times real output.

Figure 22.3

Aggregate supply and aggregate demand disequilibrium

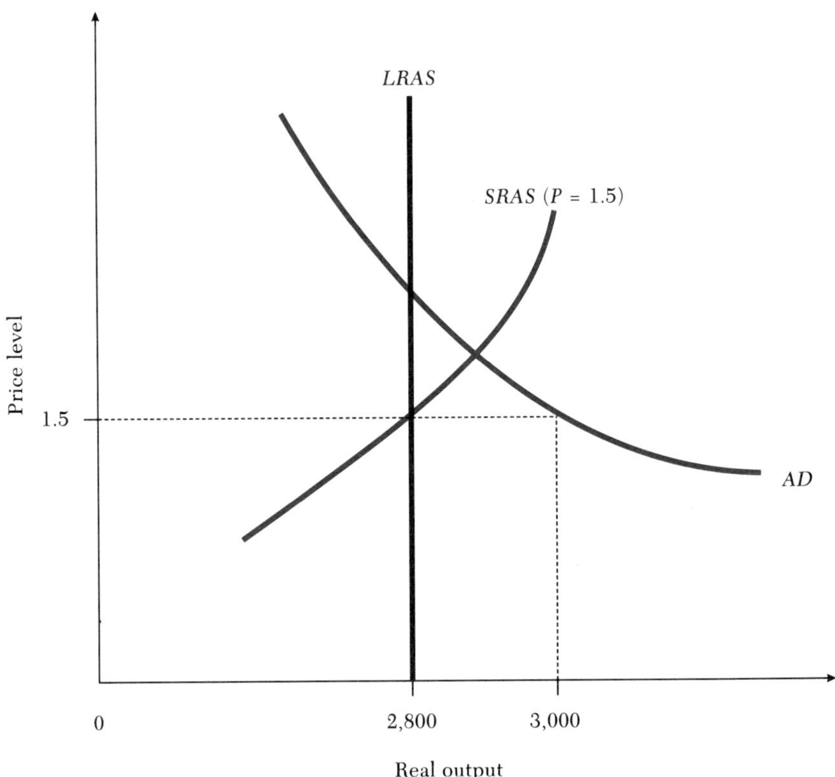

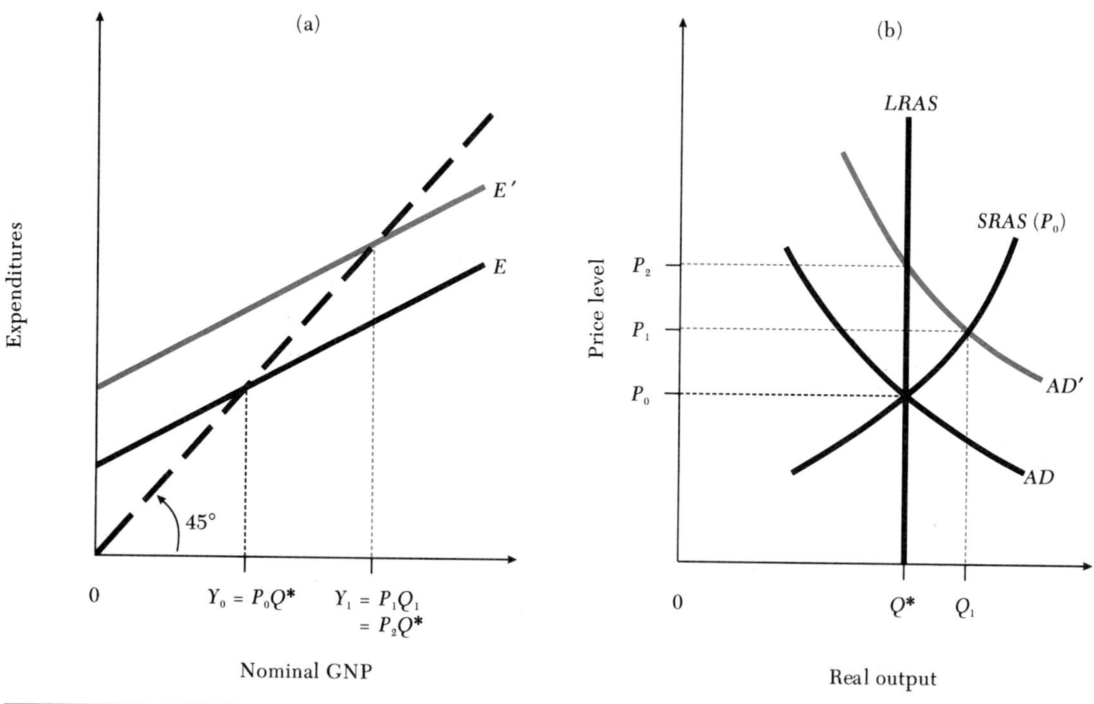

Figure 22.4

Two views of a change in aggregate demand

It is currently \$4,200 (= 1.5 × \$2,800). Planned expenditures, on the other hand, are the product of the price level and the amount of real output people demand, or \$4,500 (= 1.5 × \$3,000). Thus the excess of aggregate demand over aggregate supply is equivalent to an excess of planned expenditures over nominal GNP. Conversely, an excess of aggregate supply over aggregate demand is equivalent to an excess of nominal GNP over planned expenditures. It follows that aggregate supply and aggregate demand are equal only when nominal GNP and expenditures are equal.*

With this in mind, consider Figure 22.4, which interprets the effects of an autonomous increase in planned expenditures in the context of both the income-expenditure model (part (a)) and the aggregate supply–aggregate demand model (part (b)). Assume the economy is initially in equilibrium with real output at its natural level Q^*, a price level of P_0, and nominal GNP of Y_0 (= P_0Q^*). An autonomous increase in spending then simultaneously shifts the expenditure function upward from E to E' and the aggregate demand curve outward from AD to AD'. The income-expenditure model predicts an increase in nominal GNP via the multiplier effect from Y_0 to Y_1 in part (a). The aggregate supply–aggregate

*Note that the converse holds only in the short run. That is, if expenditures and nominal GNP *are* equal, we can conclude only that aggregate demand is equal to *short-run* aggregate supply. The price level and real output may or may not be in long-run equilibrium.

demand analysis in part (b) goes further. It tells us that in the short run, the increase in nominal GNP reflects the combined effects of a rise in the price level from P_0 to P_1 and a rise in real output from Q^* to Q_1, whereas in the long run it reflects a rise in the price level alone from P_0 to P_2.* Moreover, our theory of aggregate supply tells us that the relative timing and the magnitude of the effects on the price level and real output depend on the speed with which expectations adjust to the higher level of spending. If the autonomous spending change is correctly anticipated, its multiplier effect will be mainly on the price level, with little impact on real output. Conversely, if the autonomous spending change is unanticipated, it may have a substantial short-run multiplier effect on real output before dissipating itself in higher prices.

THE COMPONENTS OF TOTAL SPENDING

As a theory of aggregate demand and nominal GNP, the income-expenditure model focuses our attention on the nonmonetary factors underlying aggregate demand. These factors are best understood in their relation to the individual components of total spending, namely, *consumer expenditures* by households, *investment expenditures* by business firms, *net foreign expenditures on exports*, and *government purchases* of goods and services. In this section we examine some of the factors that affect spending in each of the first three of these categories. The role of government in the income-expenditure model is important enough to warrant separate treatment. Accordingly, we postpone until the following section our discussion of the government purchases component of total spending, as well as our analysis of the effect of government taxes and transfers on the other three components of spending.

Consumer Expenditures

If you were to enumerate the factors that influence your spending on food, housing, entertainment, transportation, and other consumer goods, your disposable income would surely be near the top of the list. There is also a close relation between disposable income and consumer expenditures for the economy as a whole. This relation is depicted in Figure 22.5, where each point shows the combination of aggregate disposable income and aggregate consumer expenditures for a selected year between 1929 and 1989. These points lie very nearly along a straight line with a slope of 0.9, suggesting that households spent about 90 cents of each additional dollar of disposable income on consumer goods over

*Technical note: The final price level P_2 would not be such that P_2Q^* is exactly equal to P_1Q_1 if changes in the price level affect spending. For example, an increase in the price level may discourage spending by reducing the real value of wealth held as nominal assets. This would shift the expenditure function down slightly during the transition to the long run, and the result would be a final equilibrium where P_2Q^* is slightly less than P_1Q_1.

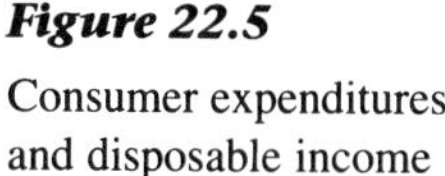

Figure 22.5

Consumer expenditures and disposable income

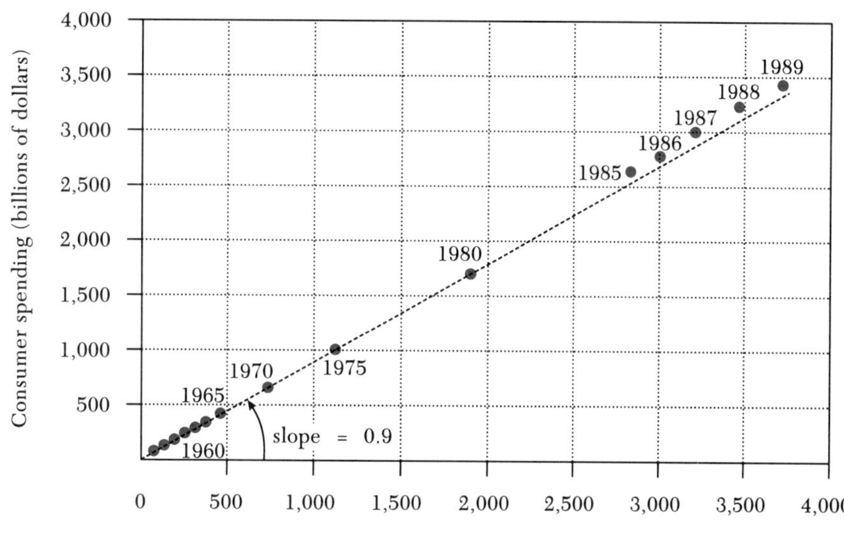

The **marginal propensity to consume** is the fraction of additional disposable income that is spent on consumption goods.

this time period. We call the proportion of additional income spent on consumer goods the **marginal propensity to consume**. Since consumption spending is by far the largest component of total spending on final goods, and since changes in disposable income tend to be closely correlated with changes in GNP, the marginal propensity to consume is the most important determinant of the more general marginal propensity to spend, and thus of the spending multiplier.

Although the data plotted in Figure 22.5, as well as data reconstructed from historical records going back well over a century, tend to confirm a long-run marginal propensity to consume of about 0.9, they also show that changes in disposable income have a smaller impact on consumer spending in the short run than in the long run. In particular, over the course of the business cycle, consumer spending typically changes by only about 60–75 cents for each dollar change in disposable income. The short-run, or cyclical, marginal propensity to consume thus appears to be between 0.60 and 0.75.

The Permanent Income Theory

The **permanent income theory** holds that consumption and saving depend on the disposable income households expect under normal conditions.

The most widely accepted reconciliation of the long-run and short-run differences in the marginal propensity to consume is provided by the **permanent income theory**. According to this theory, a household's permanent income is the income it has come to expect under normal conditions, and it is that income on which it bases its consumption and saving decisions. Since expectations are not always fulfilled, however, actual income can differ from permanent income during any given time period. When it does, according to the permanent income theory, households adjust their saving and borrowing as necessary to maintain a level of consumption consistent with their permanent income. In effect, the theory implies that households use the credit markets to smooth out consumption in the face of temporary fluctuations in their actual incomes.

A simple example illustrates how this works. Suppose Sally Saleswoman has decided to spend 90 percent of her permanent income on consumption and save the remaining 10 percent. Based on her skills, experience, and knowledge of the marketplace, she figures her permanent income to be about $30,000 per year. Accordingly, she expects to spend $27,000 and save $3,000 in a normal year.

Now suppose Sally has an unexpectedly bad year in which her actual income turns out to be only $25,000. As long as she considers the entire $5,000 shortfall just a temporary setback, neither her permanent income nor her consumption will change. Rather, she will borrow $2,000, or withdraw that amount from her savings, to maintain her consumption spending at $27,000. On the other hand, if Sally's disposable income turns out to be greater than expected, she will not go on a spending binge. Instead she will either save the extra income as a buffer against future bad years or use it to pay off debts incurred in past bad years. For example, if her actual income turns out to be $35,000, but if she considers the entire $5,000 in excess of her permanent income to be a temporary windfall not likely to be repeated in the future, she will add it to her normal $3,000 saving for a total saving of $8,000.

If Sally's expectations turn out to be correct, her income and consumption will average $30,000 and $27,000 per year, respectively. Moreover, her extra saving in good years will just offset the debts she incurs in bad years so that her saving will average $3,000 per year—just what she planned based on her permanent income. However, if her actual income turns out to be consistently above or below her permanent income, Sally will revise her expectations and adjust her permanent income and consumption accordingly. For example, if her income remains at $35,000 year after year, she will eventually become convinced that the extra $5,000 is not a windfall at all, but rather an increase in her permanent income. She will therefore increase her consumption spending to $31,500 (= 0.9 × $35,000).

Applied to the economy as a whole, the permanent income theory suggests that households will borrow or draw on past savings to maintain their consumption spending when disposable income falls temporarily during a recession. During economic booms, on the other hand, consumption spending will rise, but less than proportionally with income as households wait to see if the higher incomes will be permanent. The economy's short-run marginal propensity to consume thus remains relatively low as income changes over the course of the business cycle. Over the long run, however, the higher incomes generated by continued economic growth are incorporated into expectations and permanent income. As a result, consumption spending grows right along with income in the long run.

Interest Rates and Consumer Expenditures

We saw in Chapter 4 how a rise (fall) in interest rates—specifically, *real* interest rates—makes saving more (less) attractive relative to spending. Real interest rates are an especially important determinant of expenditures on new houses and consumer durables, such as cars, furniture, and major appliances, which households typically finance through credit. Other things being equal, a rise in real interest rates decreases such expenditures, shifts the expenditure function down, and, via the spending multiplier, lowers the equilibrium level of nominal GNP. A fall in real interest rates increases consumer spending, shifts the expenditure function up, and raises nominal GNP.

Investment Expenditures

Whether for the purchase of new capital goods such as buildings and equipment, or for additions to inventory for later sale, business investment expenditures are always made in anticipation of future profits. In particular, a business will make an investment only if the expected present value of the future profits from that investment exceeds its initial cost. Suppose, for example, that a business firm expects the cost savings generated by a new computer to add $50,000 to its profits each year for the next 10 years. It will invest in that computer only if its cost is less than the present value of $50,000 per year for 10 years.

This suggests that there are two key factors in any investment decision: *expectations of future profits*—often referred to as "the state of business confidence"—and the *rate of interest* used to compute present value. Since it is the real return that determines whether or not an investment will be profitable, both the expected future profits and the interest rate must be adjusted for inflationary expectations. In other words, it is expected *real* profits and the *real* rate of interest that matter for the investment decision.

Of course, neither future profits nor future inflation are known with certainty, so there is an inevitable element of risk in any investment decision. Nonetheless, after allowing for risk, more optimistic profit expectations and lower real interest rates stimulate investment spending by increasing the expected present value of current capital outlays. More pessimistic expectations and higher real interest rates do the reverse.

Investment Fluctuations and the Keynesian Theory of the Business Cycle

Just as a household may get by using its old car for one more year when times are tough, a business firm can continue production with its existing stock of capital goods when prospects for profitable new investment look bleak. The flow of productive services generated by that stock, like the flow of services provided by cars and other consumer durables, does not depend on current investment expenditures. Indeed, the productive services could continue indefinitely even if *net* investment were zero—that is, even if *gross* investment were just sufficient to offset depreciation and maintain the existing capital stock. For this reason, investment expenditures tend to be bunched together during periods of general business optimism and spread thinly over more pessimistic periods.

For Keynes, this volatility of investment spending was the key to the business cycle. He regarded the state of business confidence as fragile and unstable, driven by what he called the "animal spirits" of capitalism, and capable of changing from optimism to pessimism at the drop of a rumor. The volatility of investment was made more significant by the Keynesian spending multiplier, through which every $1 change in investment spending led to an even greater change in GNP. Combined with the assumption of wage and price rigidity, the result was a Keynesian view of the market economy as one inherently subject to pronounced fluctuations in real output and employment.

The effect of the Keynesian multiplier in magnifying fluctuations in investment spending contrasts sharply with the damping effects implied by the classical theory of the credit market. According to that theory, an initial drop in investment spending reduces the demand for credit. This leads to a fall in the real rate of interest, which in turn stimulates both investment and consumer spending. Thus a drop in investment spending is offset by the stimulative effect of lower interest rates. According to Keynes, however, these interest rate effects are relatively small and will be swamped by the effects of changes in the state of business confidence.

For modern Keynesians, the volatility of investment spending (and by implication the demand for money to finance that spending) is still the prime mover of the business cycle. This is in contrast to modern-day monetarists who, as we saw in the previous chapter, attribute most business cycles to fluctuations in the supply of money.

Foreign Trade and the Expenditure Function

Chapter 24 provides a full discussion of the determinants and effects of international trade. However, it is useful to examine here the more limited question of the relation between trade flows and aggregate demand.

Recall that net exports are equal to the difference between foreign expenditures on exports, which add to domestic aggregate demand, and domestic expenditures on imports, which reduce domestic aggregate demand. Net exports thus represent an addition to the flow of expenditures and aggregate demand when they are positive—that is, when there is a *trade surplus*—and a subtraction from that flow when there is a *trade deficit*.

Net exports depend in part on the state of the world economy. Other things being equal, the higher the levels of national income and output in foreign countries, the greater their demand for U.S. exports. An increase in gross world product therefore shifts the U.S. expenditure function upward and, via the multiplier effect, raises equilibrium U.S. GNP. Conversely, a decline in gross world product reduces the demand for U.S. exports and lowers U.S. GNP.

On the other side of the coin, the higher the level of U.S. GNP, the more BMWs, Sony TVs, and Chateau Lafite wine will be demanded by U.S. citizens. Other things being equal, this tendency for imports to rise with increases in domestic GNP reduces the effective marginal propensity to spend. For example, suppose that U.S. citizens spend 60 cents of each additional dollar of their national income. Were all of that spending for domestically produced final goods, the marginal propensity to spend would be 0.6 and the spending multiplier 2.5 $[= 1/(1 - 0.6)]$. However, if 10 cents of the 60 cents of additional spending is on imported goods, then the relevant marginal propensity to spend on goods produced in the United States is only 0.5, and the spending multiplier only 2.0.

GOVERNMENT IN THE INCOME-EXPENDITURE MODEL

The taxes and expenditures of government at all levels—federal, state, and local—have important implications in the income-expenditure model. Government purchases, whether of aircraft carriers or of the services of librarians in public libraries, add directly to aggregate demand. Government transfer payments, such as unemployment compensation and social security benefits, alter consumer spending via their impact on household disposable income. So also do income taxes, the major source of tax revenue for federal and state governments. Other taxes, such as those on corporate profits and capital gains, affect the level of investment spending, and still others, such as tariffs and other import duties, affect net exports.

Fiscal Multipliers

Fiscal multipliers tell how much GNP changes per dollar change in government spending or taxes.

We use the term **fiscal multipliers** to describe the multiplier effects of changes in government spending and taxes. All fiscal multipliers are derived from the basic spending multiplier. Indeed, the fiscal multiplier for a change in government purchases is exactly the same as the multiplier for any other autonomous spending change. In terms of multiplier effects, it makes no difference whether a $100 increase in autonomous spending reflects a business firm's purchase of a new computer, a foreigner's purchase of U.S. wheat, or a state government's outlays for highway maintenance. All are direct expenditures on new final goods and, if the basic spending multiplier equals 2, each ultimately adds $200 to nominal GNP.

Government transfer payments, by contrast, do not add directly to expenditures on new final goods; they do so only to the extent that they are spent by their recipients. As a result, the fiscal multiplier for transfers is generally less than that for government purchases. For example, suppose that the government disburses an additional $100 in unemployment compensation to households during a recession. If households have a marginal propensity to consume of 0.75, then only $75 of the $100 increase in transfer payments will be spent on new consumer goods; the rest will be saved or used to pay off past debts. As a result, the expenditure function will shift up by only $75, and, again assuming a basic spending multiplier of 2, GNP will increase by only $150. In effect, the fiscal multiplier for the $100 increase in transfer payments is only 1.5.

Tax changes have negative multiplier effects: An increase in taxes reduces spending and lowers the equilibrium level of GNP; a decrease in taxes raises both spending and GNP. Like transfer payments, however, taxes typically affect spending only indirectly and so have smaller absolute multiplier effects than changes in government purchases.

Taxes levied on households alter consumer spending via their impact on disposable income. To illustrate, suppose that a $100 cut in property taxes leaves households with an additional $100 of disposable income. If their marginal propensity to consume is 0.75, consumer spending will rise by $75 and, assuming a basic spending multiplier of 2, lead to a $150 increase in equilibrium GNP. In terms of their fiscal multiplier effects, the $100 *decrease in taxes* is thus equivalent to the $100 *increase in transfer payments* in the preceding example.

Changes in income tax rates not only shift the expenditure function, they also change its slope which, as we have seen, is the marginal propensity to spend. To see why, let us contrast the effect on spending of a $100 increase in GNP in an economy with, and one without, income taxes. For simplicity we assume that changes in income affect only consumer spending and that the marginal propensity to consume is 0.75. If there are no income taxes, then a $100 increase in GNP leads to an equal, $100 increase in disposable income and thus to a $75 increase in consumer spending. On the other hand, if income taxes take 20 percent of each additional dollar of income, then $20 of the $100 increase in GNP will be taxed away, leaving only an $80 increase in disposable income, of which $60 (= 0.75 × $80) will be spent on consumption. In effect, the 20 percent income tax decreases the marginal propensity to spend from 0.75 to 0.60 and correspondingly lowers the spending multiplier from 4 [= 1/(1 − 0.75)] to 2.5 [= 1/(1 − 0.6)]. If the income tax rate were raised from 20 percent to 33 percent, the marginal propensity to spend would fall to 0.5 and the spending multiplier to 2.0. (Can you see why?) Other things being equal, therefore, a rise in the income tax rate leads to both an autonomous drop in spending (via its impact on disposable income) and a fall in the value of the multiplier (via its impact on the marginal propensity to spend).

Investment spending is also influenced by taxes. For example, an investment tax credit—a tax provision that makes a portion of investment expenditures tax deductible for businesses—encourages investment, shifts the expenditure function upward, and raises equilibrium GNP. Taxes on the corporate profits tend to discourage investment spending, shift the expenditure function downward, and lower GNP.

Finally, net export spending is influenced by the tax treatment of exports and imports. Other things being equal, for example, an increase in import tariffs—which are simply taxes on imports—reduces imports and raises net exports. A reduction in tariffs does the reverse.

We can summarize the general properties of the fiscal multipliers as follows:

1. **Direction** Changes in government spending, including both government purchases and transfers, have positive multiplier effects: An increase (decrease) in spending leads to an increase (decrease) in equilibrium GNP. Tax changes (unless they are import tariffs) have negative multiplier effects: An increase (decrease) in taxes leads to a decrease (increase) in equilibrium GNP.

2. **Magnitude** The multiplier effect of a change in government purchases is the same as that of a change in any other component of autonomous spending; changes in taxes and transfer payments have smaller multiplier effects, which depend on how they affect spending.

Fiscal Policy: An Introduction

Fiscal policy involves the federal government's use of its budget to pursue macroeconomic goals.

The existence of these fiscal multipliers suggests that the government may attempt to systematically influence aggregate demand through changes in its expenditures and taxes. To do so would be to pursue macroeconomic **fiscal policies**.

In focusing on the budgetary aggregates, fiscal policy abstracts from the many microeconomic decisions that determine the sources and composition of total federal tax revenues and the allocation of those revenues among various government programs. Although it is not always clear where to draw the line between microeconomic budget decisions and macroeconomic fiscal policy, for some purposes it is useful to think in terms of overall budgetary aggregates. Since this view of fiscal policy emphasizes the multiplier effects of those aggregates, it is natural to introduce it here in the context of our discussion of the fiscal multipliers. We put off until the following chapter a discussion of the implications of a somewhat more disaggregated, microeconomic view of the budget process.

The Structural and Cyclical Components of the Budget

The state of the government's budget is determined by the difference between total tax revenues and total government spending, including both government purchases and transfer payments. In symbols,

$$B = T_x - G - T_r$$

where T_x is tax revenues, G is government purchases, and T_r is government transfer payments. A positive B represents a budgetary *surplus*; a negative B represents a *deficit*.

The state of the government budget at any given time depends not only on the tax rates and expenditure programs enacted into law but also on the state of the economy. Given the level of tax rates, for example, tax revenues—especially those from personal and corporate income taxes—are positively related to the level of GNP. Many government transfers, on the other hand, most notably those for unemployment compensation and various income maintenance (welfare) programs, are inversely related to the level of GNP. During a recession, therefore, the budget deficit increases (or the surplus decreases) as revenues from income and profits taxes decline and transfer payments rise. During periods of recovery and economic growth, the deficit falls (or the surplus rises) as tax revenues increase and transfer spending decreases.

The actual budget surplus or deficit at any given time can therefore be viewed as the sum of two components, a *structural* component reflecting legislated tax and spending programs, and a *cyclical* component reflecting the state of the

The **structural budget** is the surplus or deficit that exists under legislated tax rates and government spending programs in an economy operating at its natural rate of real output.

The **cyclical budget** reflects the additional surplus or deficit in the government budget due to variations in economic activity over the course of the business cycle.

economy. The **structural budget** (also referred to as the "cyclically adjusted budget") is the surplus or deficit that would exist if the economy were at its natural level of real output. Because it is adjusted to eliminate the influence of short-run variations in economic activity, it reflects only the tax and spending legislation passed by Congress and signed by the President. The **cyclical budget** reflects the state of the economy; it is assumed to be zero when the economy is operating at its natural rate of real output and employment.

We can illustrate the difference between the structural and cyclical components of the budget with the aid of Figure 22.6. The upper part of the diagram shows how tax revenues and government spending are related to nominal GNP. The line showing tax revenues is positively sloped because, given the tax rates set by law, tax revenues tend to rise as GNP rises and fall as GNP falls. The negative slope of the line relating government spending to the level of GNP reflects primarily the impact of transfer payments. The lower panel of the diagram consolidates the tax and spending information into a single budget line. This line plots the difference between taxes and government spending at each level of GNP, and so shows the relation between GNP and the budgetary deficit (if negative) or surplus (if positive).

Since we assume that cyclical influences on the budget are absent when the economy is at its natural rate of real output and employment, we can determine the remaining structural surplus or deficit with reference to the corresponding level of nominal GNP. In particular, suppose that, given the current price level, the natural level of real output corresponds to a nominal GNP of Y_0. The lower part of Figure 22.6 then tells us that current tax and spending legislation calls for a *structural deficit* equal to distance *OA*.

Now suppose that a recession lowers GNP to Y_1. The recession adds a *cyclical deficit*, *AB*, to the structural deficit, *OA*, and the result is an actual, total deficit equal to distance *OB*. The cyclical component of the deficit reflects the impact of the recession in lowering tax revenues and increasing transfer payments. If GNP were above its natural rate, there would be a cyclical surplus. The result would be an actual deficit less than the structural deficit, or even an actual surplus.

The Structural Deficit and Discretionary Fiscal Policy

Because the structural budget reflects the tax and spending legislation passed by Congress and approved by the President, it provides a better measure of the intentions of policy makers than does the actual deficit or surplus, which includes the impact of cyclical factors beyond their control. We can therefore classify as discretionary fiscal policies those which, through legislative and executive action, change the structural deficit or surplus.

An **expansionary fiscal policy** is one that attempts to stimulate aggregate expenditure by increasing government spending or decreasing taxes.

According to our discussion of the fiscal multipliers, a decrease in taxes or an increase in either of the components of government spending—in short, anything that reduces the structural surplus or raises the structural deficit—will increase the equilibrium level of GNP. Such actions thus constitute an **expansionary fiscal policy**. Conversely, an increase in taxes or a decrease in government spend-

Figure 22.6

Structural and cyclical budget components

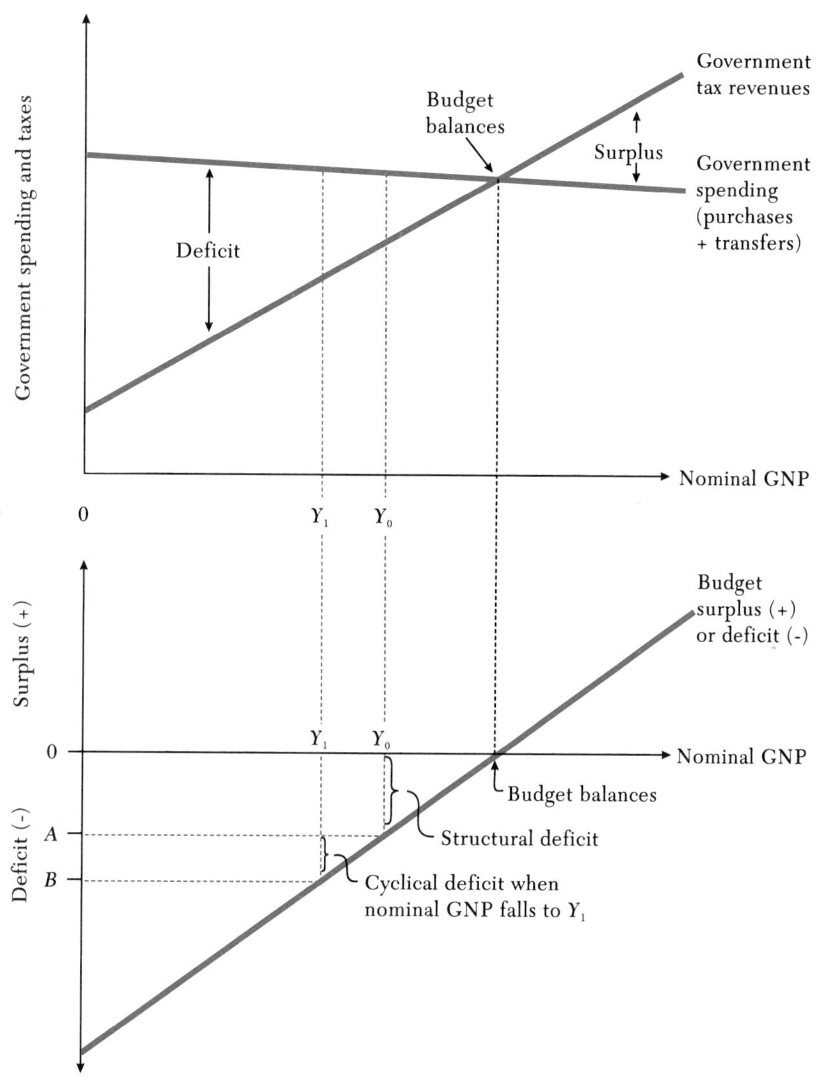

A **contractionary fiscal policy** is one that attempts to retard aggregate expenditure by decreasing government spending or increasing taxes.

ing—in short, anything that raises the structural surplus or lowers the structural deficit—will decrease the equilibrium level of GNP. Such actions thus constitute a **contractionary fiscal policy**.

Countercyclical Fiscal Policy

The idea that government can use fiscal policy to stabilize aggregate demand is a distinctly Keynesian contribution to macroeconomics. Keynes himself argued that massive increases in government spending financed by borrowing or by creating money were the only way out of the Great Depression. Latter day Keynesians, armed with statistical estimates of the fiscal multipliers, went even further. They argued that the effects of changes in government spending and taxes were predictable enough that fiscal policies could be used to offset fluctuations in private spending and thereby maintain a level of aggregate demand consistent with high employment and low inflation. The discretionary use of the government budget in the pursuit of economic stability became known as **countercyclical fiscal policy**. Let us illustrate how it would work in an ideal world.

Countercyclical fiscal policy involves the discretionary use of the government budget to offset fluctuations in private sector spending.

Suppose that economists (or other soothsayers) predict that the level of aggregate demand consistent with achieving natural real output and stable prices next year is $5,000 billion, but that an impending decline in private investment spending is about to reduce actual aggregate demand to only $4,850 billion. The result will be a recession unless the $150 billion shortfall in aggregate demand can be headed off with an appropriate expansionary fiscal policy. Suppose further that economists have estimated the fiscal multipliers to be +2.0 for a change in government purchases and −1.5 for a change in taxes. As we have seen, this means that aggregate demand and nominal GNP will increase by $2.00 for every $1.00 *increase* in autonomous government purchases and by $1.50 for every $1.00 *decrease* in autonomous tax revenues. It follows that the $150 billion demand deficiency can be eliminated by either a $75 billion increase in government purchases (since +2.0 × $75 = +$150) or a $100 billion tax cut (since −1.5 × −$100 = +$150). Alternatively, it could be eliminated by a combination of $45 billion of additional government spending and a $40 billion tax cut [since (+2.0 × $45) + (−1.5 × −$40) = +$150]. Indeed there are in theory an infinite number of combinations of spending changes and tax changes that would achieve the desired result. All that is needed to avoid recession is to convince the Congress and the President to adopt one of them.

It is instructive to list the assumptions, both explicit and implicit, on which the preceding example rests. First, it assumes that policy makers are able to forecast both actual and ideal levels of future aggregate demand. Second, it assumes that they know the fiscal multipliers and the timing of the multiplier effects of government spending and tax changes. Finally, it assumes that policy makers can overcome the political constraints inherent in the federal budgeting process to make the appropriate spending and tax changes in a timely fashion.

If you suspect that all of this is a tall order, your suspicions are hereby confirmed. As we see in the next chapter, discretionary, countercyclical fiscal policy is beset by all of the problems of discretionary monetary policy, and then some. It is also complicated by the fact that fiscal actions often have side effects that spill over into the money market. To see the implications of this, we must examine the role of money in the income-expenditure model.

MONEY IN THE INCOME-EXPENDITURE MODEL

In the previous chapter, we used the equation of exchange to show how changes in the supply of money alter expenditures and nominal GNP. In terms of the income-expenditure framework, changes in the money supply shift the expenditure function. Since expenditures change in the same direction as a change in the money supply, the shift is upward for an increase in the money supply and downward for a decrease.

Beyond simply providing an alternative interpretation of how changes in the money supply affect GNP, however, the income-expenditure model raises some important issues regarding the relation between money and spending. In particular, because nominal GNP is, by definition, equal to the money stock times its velocity, the multiplier effects of autonomous spending changes must logically be accompanied by simultaneous changes in the money supply, velocity, or both.

Mixed Monetary-Expenditure Changes

When an autonomous change in spending is accompanied by changes in the money supply, the direction of its impact is unambiguous. If the Fed increases the money supply in response to an autonomous increase in spending, for example, it is in effect creating the money necessary to support higher levels of aggregate demand and nominal GNP without an increase in velocity. On the other hand, if a fall in autonomous spending is accompanied by a fall in the money supply, both contribute to a fall in aggregate demand and nominal GNP. In each case, the change in nominal GNP will be divided between changes in real output and the price level according to our theory of aggregate supply. The only ambiguity regarding the effects of a mixed monetary-expenditure change is the size of its impact on nominal GNP. We return to this point later.

Pure Autonomous Spending Changes

A **pure fiscal policy** is one that is not accompanied by a change in the money supply.

The effects of changes in autonomous spending that are not accompanied by changes in the money supply are more complex. We illustrate these effects in the context of a **pure fiscal policy**, that is, a fiscal policy that is not accompanied by a change in the money supply. In particular, suppose that the government decides to increase its expenditures or cut its taxes at a time when the Fed is determined to keep the money supply from growing. To finance the additional structural deficit resulting from this expansionary fiscal policy, the government must turn to the credit markets where it offers to sell new Treasury bonds. The increased supply of bonds, which is equivalent to an increase in the demand for credit, leads to a fall in bond prices and a rise in market interest rates. The higher interest rates have two effects.

First, they increase the opportunity cost of holding money, thereby reducing fluidity, the amount of money people demand relative to their incomes. As we saw in the previous chapter, this is equivalent to a rise in velocity. In effect, the higher interest rates induce people to exchange some of their money balances for the low-cost, high-yield Treasury bonds used by the government to finance its additional fiscal deficit. When money is transferred from idle currency and deposit balances into the flow of government spending, its velocity rises. To the extent that this occurs, the rise in velocity allows aggregate demand and GNP to rise, even though the money supply has not increased.

Crowding out refers to the tendency of a pure, expansionary fiscal policy to discourage private spending by raising interest rates.

Second, the higher interest rates discourage, or **crowd out**, some private spending. Business investment spending and household spending on consumer durables are likely to be particularly affected because they are typically financed by credit. The higher interest rates also force state and local governments to cancel or postpone some of their own bond-financed public projects and encourage foreigners to spend their dollars on high-yield U.S. financial assets rather than on U.S. goods.

The higher interest rates caused by an expansionary pure fiscal policy thus work in two directions. To the extent that they induce people to hold smaller money balances, the resulting rise in velocity permits an expansion of aggregate demand and nominal GNP. However, to the extent that higher interest rates crowd out credit-financed spending in other sectors of the economy, the expansion in GNP will be less than that predicted by the simple fiscal multipliers.*

These effects work in reverse for a contractionary pure fiscal policy. With a constant money supply, a fall in the structural deficit (or rise in the surplus) reduces the demand for credit and lowers interest rates. The lower interest rates increase the amount of money demanded relative to income and thus decrease money's velocity; they also stimulate credit-financed spending in other sectors of the economy. The net impact of the fiscal action on GNP depends on the relative magnitudes of these opposing effects. In any case, it is again likely to be smaller than the simple multiplier effects that ignore the money market.

Monetarist versus Keynesian Again

The foregoing analysis raises a number of issues over which there is still some disagreement among economists. As you may expect, the battle lines once again reflect the continuing debate between monetarists and Keynesians. In analyzing their differences regarding the relation between the money market and the income-expenditure flow, we shall draw a rather sharp contrast. Although this is useful in highlighting the central issues in the debate, we must emphasize that the actual differences between the two schools are rarely so stark. Rather they typically boil down to subtle shades of emphasis and matters of degree.

As we have seen, the essence of modern monetarism is a belief in the fundamental, long-run stability and reliability of the relation between the money supply and nominal GNP. Monetarists believe that money is a very special asset, and one for which nonmoney assets such as bonds are poor substitutes. Accordingly, they believe that changes in interest rates have relatively little impact on the long-run demand for money relative to income—on velocity, that is. If so, an expansionary pure fiscal policy must ultimately displace a nearly equal amount of private spending. According to monetarists, therefore, the multiplier

*We would reach the same conclusion regarding pure autonomous changes in private spending. For example, an autonomous increase in investment spending would be financed by an increase in the supply of new corporate bonds. The effect on the credit markets and interest rates would be the same as those of a pure expansionary fiscal policy: Interest rates would rise, thus raising velocity but also discouraging other private and public expenditures. The impact of the increase in investment spending on GNP would therefore be less than predicted by the simple spending multiplier.

effects of pure fiscal policies are likely to be small or nonexistent. Put another way, monetarists regard changes in the supply of money as both sufficient *and* necessary for changes in aggregate demand and nominal GNP.

Keynesians, by contrast, place their faith in the relative stability and reliability of the autonomous spending multiplier. Since a stable spending multiplier implies a passive and unstable velocity, this puts them in diametric opposition to the monetarists. The Keynesian view of velocity is based on a theory of the demand for money that emphasizes the substitutability between money and nonmoney assets. According to this view, people will readily reduce their money balances to obtain the higher yields offered by nonmoney assets whenever interest rates rise. Thus when a pure expansionary fiscal policy (or an increase in autonomous private spending) starts pushing up interest rates, velocity will rise enough to permit a substantial multiplier effect on aggregate demand and nominal GNP. For Keynesians, therefore, a change in the money supply may be sufficient, but it is not necessary, for a change in GNP. Indeed, Keynesians tend to regard nonmonetary factors as the principal sources of fluctuations in GNP. The emphasis placed on the volatility of investment spending in the Keynesian theory of the business cycle is perhaps the preeminent example of this.

Regarding mixed monetary-expenditure changes, both monetarists and Keynesians agree that they will change aggregate demand and nominal GNP in the same direction. However, they disagree about the fundamental source of that change in GNP and its magnitude relative to the monetary-expenditure change. Take, for example, an increase in government purchases accompanied by a simultaneous expansion of the money supply. Both monetarists and Keynesians agree that the result will be an increase in nominal GNP. However, monetarists argue that it is the increase in the money supply, not the expansionary fiscal policy, that is the source of the increase in GNP; Keynesians argue just the reverse. Moreover, monetarists argue that the increase in equilibrium GNP will equal the increase in the money supply times its velocity; Keynesians argue that it will equal the increase in government spending times the spending multiplier.

We can illustrate these differences with a simple numerical example. Assume that velocity is equal to 6 and that the simple autonomous spending multiplier is 2. Now suppose $10 (billion) of additional government purchases is financed by a simultaneous creation of $10 (billion) of new money. A monetarist would predict an ultimate $60 (= 6 × $10) increase in GNP, while a Keynesian would predict a $20 (= 2 × $10) increase.

The Empirical Evidence

As we saw in Chapter 1, theoretical disagreements such as those between monetarists and Keynesians can, in principle, be resolved by empirical test. Unfortunately, economists do not have access to a neat, controlled experiment that tells us whether the views of monetarists or of Keynesians are more consistent with reality. The only "laboratory" available to test their opposing theories is the real world, a dynamic environment in which everything is always changing at the same time, including the money supply, numerous categories of spending, the myriad of interest rates, technology and productivity, people's expectations, and so on. The problem of disentangling these changes and determining what is cause and what is effect is an extraordinarily difficult one. It is also one for which there is no single, "correct" solution. Since a theory is a guide for gathering and interpreting facts, it should come as no surprise that monetarists and Keynesians, working within different theoretical frameworks, use different approaches in attempting to answer the questions raised by their debate. Perhaps not surprisingly, the different approaches yield different answers to the same questions.

The Keynesian approach tends to confirm the multiplier effects of pure changes in autonomous spending. Although the estimated magnitude of the autonomous spending multiplier depends on the particular empirical investigation, Keynesians usually find its value to be somewhere in a range between 2 and 4. By contrast, the monetarist approach yields far smaller estimates of the autonomous spending multiplier, usually finding that is substantially less than one. Interestingly, both monetarist and Keynesian approaches conclude that whatever the size of the multiplier effect, it is both real and nominal in the short run but only nominal in the long run. This finding is quite consistent with our theory of aggregate supply.

Regarding the effects of a mixed monetary-expenditure change, one study based on the monetarist approach estimated that, given equal increases in government spending and the money supply, only about 4 percent of the resulting increase in GNP would be due to the increase in government spending, while 96 percent would be due to the increase in the money supply. In addition, the increase in GNP would be just about proportional to velocity, a conclusion quite consistent with monetarist theory.*

Given the state of our knowledge, none of these empirical results provides conclusive answers to the questions raised by the monetarist–Keynesian debate. As we see in the next chapter, these questions raise some critical issues for the conduct of macroeconomic policy.

CHAPTER SUMMARY

1. According to the income-expenditure model, total spending is positively related to the level of national income and nominal GNP. The *marginal propensity to spend* is the fraction of each additional dollar of national income that is spent on new final goods.

2. In the income-expenditure model, equilibrium is attained at the level of nominal GNP that generates an equal amount of total spending.

*For a survey of these and other monetarist empirical estimates, see the papers in *Review*, The Federal Reserve Bank of St. Louis, October 1986.

3. The *autonomous spending multiplier* tells us by how much GNP changes per dollar change in autonomous spending. The multiplier is equal to $1/(1 - MPS)$, where *MPS* is the marginal propensity to spend.

4. When total expenditures exceed (fall short of) nominal GNP, aggregate demand is greater than (less than) aggregate supply.

5. The *marginal propensity to consume* is the proportion of disposable income spent on new consumer goods.

6. Over the long run, the marginal propensity to consume has been about 0.9, but over the course of the business cycle, consumer spending typically changes by only about 60–75 cents for each $1 change in disposable income. This is explained by the *permanent income theory*, which holds that households use the credit markets to smooth out consumption in the face of temporary fluctuations in their actual incomes.

7. The most important determinants of investment spending are expectations of future profits and the rate of interest.

8. For Keynesians, the source of the business cycle lies in the volatility of investment spending and its effects on GNP via the autonomous spending multiplier.

9. Net exports represent an addition to the flow of expenditures and aggregate demand when there is a trade surplus, and a subtraction from that flow when there is a trade deficit.

10. The *fiscal multiplier* for a change in government purchases is the same as the autonomous spending multiplier. The fiscal multiplier for transfers is less than that for government purchases, as is the fiscal multiplier for taxes, which is also negative.

11. *Fiscal policy* involves the federal government's use of budgetary aggregates, such as total spending, total tax revenues, and the size of the surplus or deficit, to pursue macroeconomic goals.

12. The actual government budget surplus or deficit is the sum of a *structural* component, reflecting legislated tax and spending programs, and a *cyclical* component, reflecting the state of the economy.

13. *Discretionary* fiscal policies are those which, through legislative and executive action, change the structural deficit or surplus. They are *expansionary* when they increase the deficit (or decrease the surplus) and *contractionary* when they decrease the deficit (or increase the surplus).

14. The discretionary use of the government budget to offset fluctuations in private spending is known as *countercyclical fiscal policy*.

15. The multiplier effects of autonomous spending changes must logically be accompanied by simultaneous changes in the money supply, velocity, or both.

16. Pure fiscal policies are fiscal policies not accompanied by changes in the money supply. An expansionary pure fiscal policy raises interest rates. The rise in interest rates raises velocity but also *crowds out* some private spending, so that the expansion in GNP is less than that predicted by the simple fiscal multipliers.

17. Monetarists regard changes in the supply of money as both sufficient and necessary for changes in aggregate demand and nominal GNP; for Keynesians a change in the money supply money may be sufficient, but it is not necessary, for a change in GNP.

Key Terms and Concepts

income-expenditure model
expenditure function
marginal propensity to spend
autonomous spending change
autonomous spending multiplier
marginal propensity to consume
permanent income theory
fiscal multiplier
fiscal policy
structural budget
cyclical budget
expansionary fiscal policy
contractionary fiscal policy
countercyclical fiscal policy
pure fiscal policy
crowding out

Questions for Thought and Discussion

1. How much will an autonomous $100 increase in investment spending add to equilibrium nominal GNP if the marginal propensity to spend is 0.67? If it is 0.8?

2. GNP is currently in equilibrium and equal to $5,000, and the marginal propensity to spend is 0.75. What will happen as a consequence of the following simultaneous, autonomous changes in spending: investment rises by 45; exports rise by 15; and imports rise by 10?

3. What does your answer to the previous question imply about velocity if the money supply remains constant at $1,000 when the autonomous spending changes occur? If velocity does not change, how much additional money would the Fed have to supply for your answers to hold?

4. Suppose planned expenditures are $6,300, the current level of nominal GNP is $6,000, and the price level is 2.0.
    a. What are the quantities of real GNP supplied and demanded?
    b. Assuming that the economy is currently operating at its natural rate of real output, and that expenditures are not affected by changes in the price level, what is the long-run equilibrium value of the price level?

5. Suppose that your permanent income is $20,000 and your marginal propensity to consume out of permanent income is 0.9. What will happen to your consumption spending and your saving if your income this year rises to $25,000, of which you consider $2,000 to be a permanent increase?

6. Contrast the classical and Keynesian conclusions about how the economy would react to a drop in investment spending due to a more pessimistic "state of business confidence." Which view implies the more painful adjustment process?

7. Other things being equal, investment spending falls by $10 and consumption spending falls by $5 for every 1 percentage point increase in interest rates. Assuming a marginal propensity to spend of 0.5, how much private spending will be crowded out by a pure increase in government spending of $50 that pushes interest rates up by 2 percentage points? By how much will the increase in government spending raise the equilibrium level of nominal GNP.

8. Assume that the marginal propensity to spend is 0.5 and the marginal propensity to consume is 0.8. If the government gives consumers a $100 tax "rebate," by how much will autonomous spending rise and what will happen to equilibrium GNP? What is the fiscal tax multiplier implied by your answer?

9. Assume the following initial values: nominal GNP = $5,000; price level = 1.0; natural real output = $5,000; money supply = $1,000; velocity = 5.0; and marginal propensity to spend = 0.5. Now suppose that there is a $200 increase in government spending accompanied by a $100 increase in the money supply. What will be the new long-run equilibrium value for each of the following according to a dyed-in-the-wool monetarist? According to a dyed-in-the-wool Keynesian?

   a. Nominal GNP.
   b. Real GNP.
   c. The price level.
   d. Velocity.

CHAPTER 23

Problems of Macroeconomic Policy

The problem of government policy [*is*] *what to do when you don't know what to do—when available information does not point unequivocally to a certain policy as best.*

HERBERT STEIN*

Those with limited competence—such as governments—may be better off with simple, even naive policies than with sophisticated ones.

THOMAS MAYER†

It is probably safe to say that most of us take it for granted that the federal government has a responsibility to maintain an acceptable level of macroeconomic performance. If unemployment rises, if inflation accelerates, if a recession strikes, we almost instinctively demand Presidential leadership and Congressional action to remedy things.

Our purpose in this chapter is to subject this reflexive response to the critical scrutiny of economic analysis. In particular, we examine the extent to which the federal government has the tools to deal with macroeconomic problems, the knowledge of how best to use those tools, and the incentive to use them accordingly.

* *Agenda for a Study of Macroeconomic Policy*, American Enterprise Institute (1983).

† "The Keynesian Legacy: Does Countercyclical Policy Pay Its Way?" Chapter 4 in Thomas D. Willet, Ed. *Political Business Cycles* (Duke University Press, 1988).

POLICY GOALS AND POLICY APPROACHES

The Goals of Macroeconomic Policy

An ideal macroeconomic policy would accomplish three things. It would keep unemployment at its natural rate, real output on its natural, long-run growth path, and maintain a zero rate of inflation. Like so many other economic choices, however, macroeconomic policy is made in and for an imperfect world. As such, it is unrealistic to expect that it can satisfy all of these goals completely and simultaneously. It is therefore more fruitful to view macroeconomic policy as **stabilization policy**—that is, as policy that attempts to minimize the deviations of unemployment about its natural rate, real output about its long-run growth path, and inflation about some low and stable rate.

Stabilization policy is macroeconomic policy intended to minimize fluctuations in unemployment, inflation, and real output.

We can consider the stabilization of output and employment to be the *real goal* of macroeconomic policy and the stabilization of inflation to be its *nominal goal*. Although this distinction is useful, we must not forget that real and nominal policy goals are complementary rather than independent. For example, we have seen how employment and output stability can be achieved only when job search, labor contracts, and production and pricing decisions are based on accurate expectations of future inflation. Such accuracy in turn requires a stable and predictable inflation rate.

Rules versus Discretion

Macroeconomic policy actions are not a series of unrelated events; rather they are manifestations of an underlying policy process. Viewed as such, the critical issue of macroeconomic policy is whether that process should be guided by a set of *rules* constraining the actions of policy makers, or whether policy makers should have the *discretion* to use their policy tools as they see fit. The choice between rules and discretion—or, more accurately, where to draw the line between the two—is the crux of the continuing policy debate between economists in the classical and Keynesian traditions.

Like their classical predecessors, monetarists and new classical economists believe that the market economy, although buffeted from time to time by external shocks (including erratic policies), is a fundamentally stable and self-correcting system. Accordingly, economists in the classical tradition generally favor a policy based on a few, simple rules. If, as they believe, fluctuations in real output and employment are mainly the result of mismatches between expectations and reality, then such mismatches will be minimized by simple rules committing policy makers to a predictable and well-defined course of action. The most well known of these is a proposed monetary policy rule that would replace the Fed's discretionary authority with a law requiring it to pursue a constant rate of monetary growth. Many monetarists and new classical economists also argue that fiscal policy should be constrained by a rule requiring some form of a balanced budget. We discuss the specifics of these and other proposed policy rules later in our discussion of monetary and fiscal policy. Suffice it to say at this point that most economists in the classical tradition believe that the best way to promote economic stability is to minimize surprises and uncertainty by adopting a rules-based approach to policy.

The contrary Keynesian view is that the market economy is a fragile mechanism requiring constant supervision. Accordingly, Keynesians generally favor an active, discretionary approach to macroeconomic policy. They would leave policy makers much greater flexibility in adapting to changes in economic conditions, allowing them to continuously adjust their policies in the light of new information. Why, they ask, tie the hands of policy makers with rules that, in effect, prohibit them from using new information as it becomes available?

The answer to this question gets us to the very heart of the dispute. Monetarists and new classical economists believe that information is most effectively used by decentralized, private individuals who have direct and concrete knowledge of its relevance and whose actions are coordinated through the market. They argue that no government policy maker or set of policy makers, such as the U.S. Congress or the Open Market Committee of the Fed, can hope to digest, interpret, and effectively use all of the mass of information bearing on any significant question of macroeconomic policy. Consequently, discretionary policy actions are as likely to *de*stabilize the economy as to stabilize it.

A few new classical economists carry the argument against discretionary policy even further. To the extent that a change in aggregate demand is correctly anticipated, they argue, its impact on real output and employment will be diminished. Since most discretionary policies tend to focus on aggregate demand, such policies will therefore lose much (perhaps all) of their ability to influence real output and employment once the underlying policy process becomes evident.

Keynesians, of course, see it differently. Emphasizing contractual wage and price rigidities, they tend to be more skeptical of the market's ability to coordinate private economic decisions, especially in the short run. Keynesians believe that centralized policy makers, free from the kind of contractual commitments that bind private decision makers, can respond more flexibly than the latter to new information and should be allowed to do so.

One aspect of the debate is difficult, if not impossible, to resolve. Surely market economies do not self-destruct; yet just as surely they experience ups and downs in the inevitable process of economic change. The real issue, it seems, is the extent to which policy discretion promotes or hinders economic stability. This is the issue around which we organize our discussion of monetary and fiscal policy.

MONETARY POLICY

As we saw in Chapter 21, there is a general consensus among economists that monetary policy is the key to achieving a low and stable long-run inflation rate. Where there is disagreement, it is over the issue of how monetary policy can best promote short-run economic stability. In a perfect world, the Fed would use monetary policy to offset short-run fluctuations in aggregate demand, thereby eliminating their destabilizing influence on output, employment, and the price level. Unfortunately, in a real world that is inevitably far from perfect, this is much easier said than done.

Information Problems

The Fed's job is greatly complicated by the fact that it must always formulate its policies in the light of incomplete information. One informational problem is that of anticipating, or even recognizing the early stages of, the kinds of changes in economic conditions that call for a policy response. Even the best economists have proven to be not much better than anyone else—which is to say, not very good at all—at forecasting changes in economic activity, especially turning points such as the onset of a recession or the beginning of an economic recovery. Although the Fed collects and continuously scrutinizes a vast amount of statistical information, that information often sends conflicting signals and is subject to different interpretations by different observers.

To take a striking example of the difficulty of interpreting economic information, consider the predictions made in the aftermath of the great stock market crash of October 1987. Nearly all of the "experts" predicted that the massive destruction of paper wealth would cause people to tighten their belts and reduce spending, and it was widely anticipated that the resulting fall in aggregate demand would shortly bring about a recession. Yet, well after the market crash, total spending was still growing strongly, as were real output and employment. Indeed, during the year immediately following the market crash, unemployment fell to its lowest level in 20 years.

The Fed must also operate with imperfect knowledge of the links between its policy actions and aggregate demand. As we have seen, these links consist of the money multiplier—through which a change in bank reserves alters the money supply—and velocity—through which a change in the money supply alters aggregate demand. Although relatively predictable over long periods of time, both the money multiplier and velocity can vary substantially in the short run. Even if the Fed could correctly anticipate an aggregate demand shock, it would still have to make at best an educated guess at the appropriate open market operation or other policy response.

We can illustrate the potential magnitude of this problem by means of a simple example. Suppose that the Fed estimates the long-run values of the money multiplier and velocity to be 12.0 and 6.0, respectively. It can be relatively certain that in the long run a $1 billion open market purchase of government securities will add $12 billion to the money supply and $72 billion to total spending. Suppose, however, that in the short-run both the money multiplier and velocity can vary by 10 percent in either direction—the money multiplier between 10.8 and 13.2 and velocity between 5.4 and 6.6. Such variations are within the realm of possibility, and they imply that the Fed's $1 billion open market purchase could increase aggregate demand in the short run by as much as $87 billion (= $1 billion × 13.2 × 6.6) or by as little as $58 billion (= $1 billion ×

10.8 × 5.4). The nearly 50 percent difference between these possible outcomes is hardly insignificant.

Another information problem confronting the Fed is that of gauging the impact of its policy actions. The most obvious indicator, and the one to which we have alluded throughout our discussions of monetary policy, is the behavior of the money supply. If the money supply is growing, then monetary policy is expansionary; if it is shrinking, then monetary policy is contractionary. Right?

Unfortunately, it is not quite this simple. Remember, the important thing is not the behavior of the money supply itself but its behavior *relative to velocity and the demand for money*. If the supply of money is growing but the demand is growing (velocity is falling) faster, then monetary policy is effectively contractionary, or "tight." By the same token, even a falling money supply is expansionary, or "loose," if the demand is falling (velocity is rising) faster.

Given these ambiguities, some economists argue that interest rates, and not the money supply, are the best indicator of monetary looseness or tightness. They typically focus on the federal funds rate which, as we have seen, is the rate at which banks borrow and lend reserves among themselves. If the Fed is supplying just enough reserves to meet the current demand for money, then the price of borrowed reserves as reflected in the federal funds rate will be steady. On the other hand, the rate will rise if the Fed is not supplying enough reserves to accommodate the demand for money, and it will fall if the Fed is supplying more reserves than necessary to accommodate demand. A rising federal funds rate therefore signals that monetary policy is contractionary, and a falling federal funds rate signals that it is expansionary.

Interest rates can also be ambiguous indicators of monetary policy, however. Recall that all market interest rates incorporate a premium for expected inflation. To the extent that monetary growth raises inflationary expectations, therefore, high interest rates can be symptoms, not of a contractionary monetary policy, but of an excessively expansionary one.

The Timing Problem

Even if the Fed could overcome all of these informational problems, it would still be confronted with a most difficult timing problem. The policy actions that the Fed takes *now* will not affect the economy until *later*, and just how much later is quite uncertain and difficult to predict. The time lag between the implementation of a particular course of monetary policy and its ultimate effects on aggregate demand has been estimated to vary between 6 months and 18 months. The uncertain time lag makes the Fed like a baseball player who can't hit a curveball: it keeps swinging where the ball was rather than where it is.

To illustrate the significance of this problem for monetary policy, consider the following possibility. Suppose the Fed correctly interprets a rise in the inflation rate as a sign of excessive aggregate demand and promptly responds with a large open market sale to slow monetary growth and ultimately the growth of demand. Suppose also, however, the Fed's actions do not affect aggregate demand until 1 year later, and at that time the economy is experiencing a negative demand shock. The policy actions taken 1 year earlier to slow inflation will now reinforce the negative demand shock, turning a mild economic slow-down into a full-fledged recession.

Monetarists and Keynesians on Monetary Policy

Despite its uncertainties, Keynesians typically favor an activist, discretionary approach to short-run monetary policy. Indeed, for Keynesians, it is the very instability of the links between monetary policy actions and overall economic performance that necessitates constant adjustment of those policies by the Fed. Admittedly, such an approach requires caution, but Keynesians feel that discretionary actions can on balance improve economic stability. It is better to try, they believe, than to sit idly by as the economy is buffeted by aggregate demand shocks, some of which might lead to serious recessions in the absence of offsetting policy actions.

Monetarists strongly disagree with this view. Indeed, many monetarists believe that the Fed's discretionary monetary policies are more often the cause of economic instability than its cure. Some have even argued that the blame for most twentieth-century business cycles rests squarely on the shoulders of the Fed. They cite the following pattern as typical of discretionary monetary policy.

Believing that unemployment is too high, the Fed speeds up monetary growth. This initially stimulates real output and employment, but later begins to show up in an accelerating inflation rate. Dutifully pledging to contain inflation, the Fed then puts on the monetary brakes. The short-run result is a slowdown in economic growth or even a recession—which of course requires that the Fed once again step on the monetary accelerator. And so it goes as the cycle repeats itself over and over. Monetarists believe that this approach to monetary policy, however well intentioned, serves only to introduce an unnecessary source of instability into the economy.*

Monetarists also point out that, at least until the early 1980s, the Fed's policies exhibited a long-run inflationary bias, due perhaps to repeated attempts to use expansionary monetary policy to drive unemployment below its natural rate. (In the Fed's defense, it must be pointed out that the hypothesis of the natural rate of unemployment did not become widely accepted among economists until relatively recently.)

For these reasons, monetarists prefer that the process of monetary policy be guided by rules rather than left to the discretion of the Fed. Traditional, dyed-in-the-wool monetarists favor a rule requiring a constant rate of monetary growth. They argue that the rate should be just sufficient to support the long-run growth

*If you have ever played one of the many computer "flight simulator" games, you may have some feeling for the monetarists' view of the relation between monetary policy and economic instability. Because of the lags in the "airplane's" response to the controls, you almost always at first overshoot your desired compass heading when trying to steer the plane. Then when you try to correct, you overshoot the heading in the opposite direction. The result is a very erratic flight path that usually ends in a crash.

of real output and to accommodate any secular trend in velocity. If real output can grow at 3 percent per year and velocity increases at 2 percent per year, for example, a rule requiring a 1 percent annual growth of the money supply will eliminate any long-run inflation. According to most monetarists, such a rule will also substantially reduce short-run fluctuations in velocity and real output. The overall result, they argue, will be a much more stable economy.

Some Other Voices

Although few economists favor a rule requiring literally constant monetary growth, also few believe that the Fed should attempt to fine tune the economy by responding to every blip in the economic statistics with a new policy action. Most find themselves somewhere between these two extremes. Many economists who are hesitant to completely eliminate the discretionary powers of the Fed nonetheless find some merit in the monetarists' criticism of the Fed. Accordingly, they would like to see some kind of rule limiting the Fed's discretionary authorities. Some favor a modified money growth rule, such as one setting constant monetary growth but for only a limited period of time, say 6 months to 1 year. At the end of that period, the growth rate would be reviewed and adjusted if necessary to accommodate possible changes in the trends of velocity and real output. Others economists prefer to combine a basic monetary growth rule with provisions allowing the Fed to deviate from the rule whenever there appears to be a significant change in the economic environment.

Constant monetary growth is desirable only insofar as velocity is stable and predictable, and this has not been the case in recent years. Accordingly, some economists who favor a rules-based approach to monetary policy argue that the rule should focus on something other than the money supply. One of the most frequently mentioned candidates is gold.

The Gold Standard

The **gold standard** ties a nation's money supply to its stock of gold.

Some argue that the monetary policy rule should be a domestic **gold standard**. Under a gold standard, the Fed would stand ready to exchange money for gold at a price fixed by law. This would tie the nation's money supply to its stock of gold and effectively eliminate the discretionary powers of the Fed. For example, if the government had gold reserves of 2 billion ounces, setting the price of gold at $400 per ounce would limit the money supply to $800 billion. With the price of gold fixed, changes in the money supply would be proportional to changes in the nation's gold reserves. Proponents of the gold standard emphasize that the natural scarcity of gold would serve as a discipline that would prevent excessive monetary expansion.

The problem with the gold standard is that changes in a nation's gold reserves bear no necessary relationship to its demand for money. Suppose, for example, that the demand for money is increasing (velocity decreasing) at a time when the supply of gold is decreasing or the demand for gold for nonmonetary purposes is increasing. The consequent decrease in gold reserves would lead to a reduction in the money supply which, if sudden enough, could precipitate a recession.

In addition, if all industrial nations were on a gold standard, as they were prior to the 1930s, the world supply of gold would determine the world supply of money. As we see in the next chapter, however, the allocation of that money supply among nations would be determined largely by international economic transactions beyond the control of any one of them. In effect, a gold standard would require nations to subordinate their domestic monetary policies to international events over which they have little or no control.

Finally, a government whose proclivity to create money is so great as to require the restraint imposed by a gold standard is also probably a government that would circumvent such a standard by simply lowering the official price of gold whenever it wanted to create more money. Indeed, the history of the gold standard provides numerous examples of such behavior.

Monetary Policy in Practice

In practice, the Fed has been most reluctant to commit itself to these or any other policy rules, preferring instead to maintain its discretionary power to choose whatever targets and operating procedures it deems appropriate. These targets and procedures have evolved over time with changes in economic conditions, our knowledge of the economy, and the composition of the Fed's Board of Governors.

Until the late 1970s, the Fed's main policy concern was interest rate stability, which it considered essential for the maintenance of "orderly financial markets." The immediate focus of its policy approach was the federal funds rate. As inflation began to accelerate in the late 1960s, this approach to monetary policy proved to be destabilizing. Each time expectations of higher inflation increased the inflation premium in the federal funds rate and other interest rates, the Fed responded with open market purchases in an attempt to push interest rates back down. This added to the money supply, eventually led to even more inflation, and forced interest rates even higher. The Fed was like a dog chasing its own tail.

Partly because of the Fed's sorry performance during the late 1960s and 1970s, the monetarist position gained some influence over the conduct of monetary policy. In 1979, the Fed announced that it was moving away from its almost exclusive reliance on interest rate targets to focus more closely on the behavior of the money supply. Beginning in 1981, it also adopted a contractionary policy stance. This eventually led to a substantial reduction in the rate of inflation, but only at the cost of a severe recession during 1982–83.

The Fed has hardly become a bastion of monetarism, however. Although it establishes and reports monetary growth targets, which by law it must do, actual monetary growth has rarely remained within the target range. Critics of the Fed infer from this that it does not take its own monetary targets very seriously. The Fed denies this and claims that financial deregulation and changes in financial institutions have made the money multiplier so unstable that the targets are impossible to hit. Moreover, it readily admits that it uses a number of other indicators in addition to the money supply in formulating its policies. Statements by high-level Fed officials suggest that it continues to look at interest rates, com-

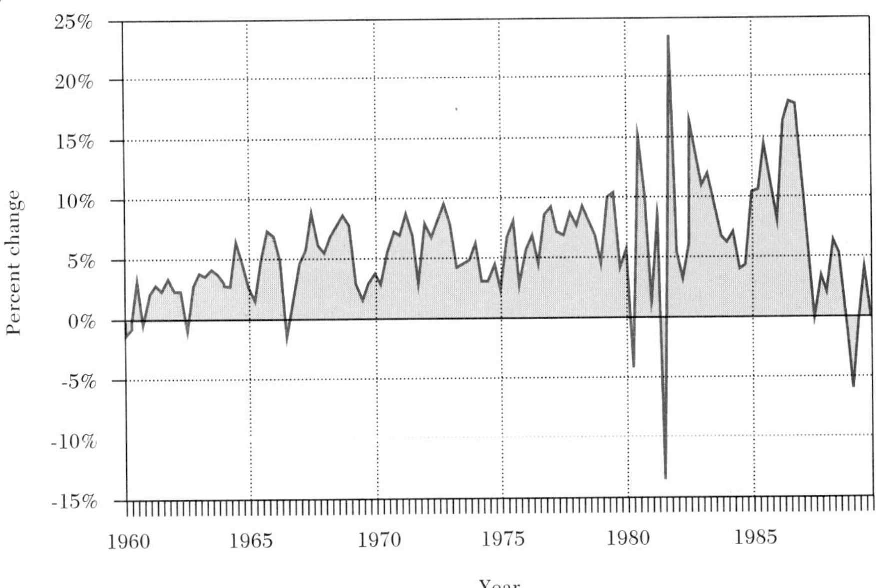

Figure 23.1

Quarterly growth rate of M1: 1960–89

modity prices, the value of the dollar relative to foreign currencies, and many other economic indicators. Rather than commit itself to any one policy rule, the Fed uses all of this information in a fundamentally discretionary—and, indeed, secretive—manner. Figure 23.1 shows the result in terms of the behavior of the money supply.

FISCAL POLICY

We saw in Chapter 22 how the government might use fiscal policies to influence aggregate demand. In particular, if the fiscal multipliers were known and stable, if their timing was predictable, if changes in private spending could be correctly anticipated, and if narrowly political constraints could be overcome, then the federal government could use changes in its spending and taxes to stabilize aggregate demand at a level consistent with full employment and a stable price level.

Although economists once had high hopes for such fiscal policies, those hopes have been dashed in recent years by a combination of theoretical and practical problems. This situation has left short-run demand management almost entirely in the hands of the Fed. As a result, the focus of fiscal policy has shifted away from its short-run impact on aggregate demand to its longer run implications for the growth of aggregate supply. Accompanying this shift in focus, and perhaps motivated by concerns over the massive federal deficits of the 1980s, has been an increasing interest in fiscal policy rules. Before turning to a discussion of these fiscal rules and the impact of fiscal policies on aggregate supply, however, it is worth examining some of the problems that have led to the virtual abandonment of discretionary, countercyclical fiscal policy as a viable, short-run stabilization tool.

Problems with Countercyclical Fiscal Policy

Just as discretionary monetary policy requires reliable, short-run estimates of the money multiplier and velocity, the success of discretionary fiscal policy depends on reliable estimates of the size and timing of the fiscal multipliers. The magnitude of these multipliers depends on how fiscal changes interact with the money market and how they affect expectations—both of which are difficult to predict.

Monetary Side Effects of Fiscal Policies

The effects of fiscal policies become much more complicated and uncertain than is implied by the simple fiscal multipliers when their monetary side effects are taken into account. For example, we saw in the previous chapter how a pure expansionary fiscal policy increases the demand for credit, thus putting upward pressure on interest rates. The higher interest rates reduce the demand for money (increase velocity) but also crowd out some private spending. An expansionary fiscal policy succeeds in stimulating aggregate demand, therefore, only to the extent that an increase in velocity compensates for the crowding out of private spending. Similarly, a contractionary fiscal policy succeeds in restraining aggregate demand only to the extent that a fall in velocity compensates for the stimulative effect of lower interest rates on private spending.

Because the relative magnitudes of these effects are difficult to predict, and because they depend on the kind of monetary policies simultaneously being pursued by the Fed, they introduce considerable uncertainty into conduct of discretionary fiscal policy. Moreover, to the extent that expansionary fiscal policies crowd out private investment spending, they leave the economy with a smaller private capital stock. In the long-run, this effect of crowding out is perhaps even more important than its short-run implications for aggregate demand management.

Fiscal Policy and Expectations

A fiscal policy that changes from expansionary in the face of recession to neutral when the economy is on an even keel, and to contractionary whenever inflation threatens, will soon be recognized and anticipated by the private sector. This has some important implications for the effectiveness of such a policy.

Suppose, for example, that the government were to rely on personal income tax changes to implement its fiscal policies, cutting taxes when it anticipates a recession due to insufficient aggregate demand and raising them when aggregate demand appears to be inflationary. Since business cycles are temporary and repetitive phenomena, these tax changes will eventually also come to be seen as temporary. The permanent income theory predicts that when they become viewed this way, they will lose their impact on consumer spending and aggregate demand.

Our experience with a 1969 tax increase intended to reduce aggregate demand in the face of accelerating inflation appears to confirm this possibility. That tax increase, explicitly announced as a temporary, 1-year "surtax" on incomes, failed to stem inflationary pressures because it had virtually no impact on consumer spending.*

As another example of the importance of expectations, consider a fiscal policy that relies on an investment tax credit—essentially a tax rebate for businesses based on their level of investment spending. During a recession, or when one appeared imminent, the tax credit would be raised to stimulate investment spending; during a period of excessive aggregate demand, it would be lowered or eliminated. Once businesses came to expect such variations in the investment tax credit, however, they would tend to postpone some investment spending until a recession allowed them to take advantage of the more favorable tax treatment. The resulting decline in investment spending during nonrecessionary periods could in itself start recessions prematurely, or even bring about recessions that would otherwise not have occurred.

Current Deficits as Future Taxes

Expectations can affect fiscal policy in another way as well. The changes in the deficit that accompany countercyclical fiscal actions alter future tax liabilities. To the extent that these effects are anticipated, they lead to changes in private spending that can offset the effects of the fiscal action.

To see how this works, let us consider the implications of an expansionary fiscal policy that increases government spending by $100 with no increase in current taxes. To finance the additional spending, the government must borrow $100, which it does by selling a new $100, 1-year Treasury bond on which it pays the market rate of interest, say, 10 percent. When the bond matures 1 year from now, the government will have two options. Either it can levy a tax of $110 to pay off both principal and interest, or it can "roll over" its debt by paying only the $10 interest and selling a new $100 bond to redeem the old one. Indeed, the government can roll over its debt indefinitely, paying only the annual interest and selling new bonds to redeem the old ones as they mature. Of course, all this means that if the $100 increase in government spending is not paid for with current taxes, it must be paid for with future taxes. Regardless of the timing of the tax payments, however, the present value of the increase in taxpayer liability is the same. Indeed, it is equal to the increase in government spending: The present value of $100 in taxes paid now is $100; the present value of $110 in

*A surtax is a tax on a tax. The temporary surtax of 1969 was a surtax on income taxes: Households were told to calculate their normal income taxes and then add an additional ten percent. A household that would ordinarily have paid $2,000 in income taxes thus paid $2,200.

taxes paid next year is $100 (= $110/1.10); and the present value of a perpetual $10 per year tax payment is $100 (= $10/0.10). An additional $100 of government spending leads to an additional $100 of tax liability, period. Deficit financing, therefore, does not allow the government to increase its spending without increasing taxes, but only to shift those taxes from the present to the future.

To the extent that households anticipate the future tax liabilities created by an expansionary fiscal action, their permanent income, and thus their consumption spending, will fall. Conversely, to the extent that they anticipate the future tax reductions implied by a contractionary fiscal policy, their permanent income and consumption will rise. In either case, the effects of the fiscal actions are partially offset by changes in private spending.

Sectoral Effects

There is no such thing as a neutral change in government spending. Spending changes necessarily involve more or less spending on educational subsidies, or highway construction, or military helicopters, or welfare payments, or any of the thousands of other programs funded by the federal government. Neither is there any such thing as a neutral change in taxes, only changes in personal income tax rates, or tax rates applied to capital gains, or the tax deductibility of consumer interest payments or charitable contributions, or the rates at which businesses can depreciate different types of capital equipment, or in the dozens of other elements in the overall tax base. Much more than monetary policies, therefore, fiscal policies tend to have a differential impact across various sectors of the economy. As a result, they almost always have microeconomic effects on the allocation of resources in addition to their macroeconomic effects on aggregate demand.

Repeated reallocation of resources in response to changes in the relative composition of government spending and tax revenues adds to economic instability. Suppose, for example, that fiscal policy relied solely on changes in defense spending to achieve its aggregate demand targets. Other things being equal (and to the extent that the timing of these spending changes was unanticipated), the result would be an increase in the unemployment rate as a periodic flow of workers shifts between defense and non-defense jobs. Unpredictable changes in the other components of government spending, or in the structure of taxes, would compound these effects.

Timing and Fiscal Lags

Timing is even more of a problem with fiscal policy than with monetary policy. In practice, fiscal policy—like monetary policy—must almost always react after the fact to changes in economic conditions. In addition, fiscal policy makers are confronted with a cumbersome budgetary process involving both Congress and the President and in which economic considerations more often than not take a back seat to political realities. The result makes the Fed look absolutely nimble in comparison.

Political Realities

Finally, any fiscal policy must come to grips not only with the question of *whether* government spending or taxes are to be changed but also with the far more difficult question of *whose* spending programs and taxes are to be affected. Here the fundamental political nature of the budgetary process becomes of the utmost importance. The President with his policy agenda and Congress with its regional and interest group constituencies are generally far more interested in how the budgetary pie is sliced than with its absolute size. Many economists believe that the use of the federal budget for macroeconomic stabilization is simply too much to expect of political institutions designed for other purposes. We will explore this possibility in more depth shortly.

Summary: The Limited Case for Countercyclical Fiscal Policy

Because of these difficulties just discussed, few economists today favor the kind of fiscal fine-tuning that many once advocated. Even Keynesians, who generally favor an activist discretionary approach to overall macroeconomic policy, today place much greater emphasis on monetary policy, and correspondingly less on fiscal policy, as the appropriate vehicle for the short-run control of aggregate demand. Although economists have not entirely abandoned the discretionary use of countercyclical fiscal policy, many prefer to hold it in reserve for severe recessions and other major economic crises. Many of them also believe that under normal conditions, discretionary fiscal policy should be replaced with fiscal rules.

Fiscal Policy Rules: Exercises in Budget Balancing

Those who prefer a rules approach to fiscal policy generally argue for some form of a balanced budget. However, to say only that the budget should be balanced begs a fundamental question, namely, over what period of time should tax revenues cover government expenditures?

The Annually Balanced Budget

An **annually balanced budget** fiscal rule would require that the federal budget be in balance each year.

Since the calendar year is the normal accounting period for most economic activities, one possibility is to require an **annually balanced budget**. This is probably what most people have in mind when they think of a balanced budget rule. However, it is a form of budget balancing favored by few economists, for it would tend to magnify, rather than dampen, any instability inherent in the economy. Under such a rule, government would presumably begin by setting taxes and expenditures so that there would be no deficit or surplus under normal economic conditions. In other words, it would balance the structural budget. If the economy were then to slip into a recession, the consequent fall in tax revenues and rise in transfer payments would create a cyclical deficit. The annually balanced budget rule would require the government to legislate a tax increase or a cut in government spending to restore a balanced budget within the accounting year, but such contractionary fiscal actions are just the opposite of what is called for during a recession. A fiscal rule requiring an annually balanced budget is, therefore, not just a mandate for a neutral, do-nothing approach to fiscal policy; rather it is one that would in effect often require *pro*cyclical rather than countercyclical fiscal actions.

The Cyclically Balanced Budget

A **cyclically balanced budget** fiscal rule would require that the federal budget deficits incurred during recession be offset by surpluses generated during recovery and expansion so that the overall budget remains in balance over the course of the business cycle.

One alternative to an annually balanced budget rule is a **cyclically balanced budget** rule. This rule would not try to offset cyclical deficits and surpluses as they occur, but it would require that they cancel one another out over the course of the business cycle. Unfortunately business cycles are not so regular and predictable that the cyclical deficits incurred during recessions are exactly offset by the cyclical surpluses generated during economic booms. Balancing the budget over the course of the cycle would most likely require at least some discretionary fiscal actions.

The Balanced Budget at High Employment

A **balanced budget at high employment** fiscal rule would require that the federal government's structural budget be in balance.

Still another candidate for the fiscal rule is one that requires only a balanced structural budget. Since the structural deficit is determined with reference to the natural rate of real output and employment, this rule is usually referred to as a **balanced budget at high employment**. Like the cyclically balanced budget, it would permit cyclical deficits and surpluses, thereby avoiding the destabilizing properties of the annually balanced budget rule. However, it would not require that cyclical surpluses exactly offset cyclical deficits.

One problem with this rule is that it assumes we know the natural rate of real output and employment at which the structural budget is to balance. As we have seen, the natural rate of real output is not something that we can easily measure. Rather it is a theoretical concept that would hypothetically emerge in the long run if, contrary to fact, the economy were not subject to periodic demand shocks and supply shocks. Moreover, even in theory, the natural rate of unemployment is not fixed and immutable but varies with demographic and policy changes—including fiscal policy changes. Nonetheless, a balanced budget at high employment is favored by many economists as the most practical and workable fiscal rule.

Intergenerational Fiscal Effects

Arguments favoring some form of a balanced budget are based on the premise that government programs should be funded on a pay-as-you-go basis. As such, they fail to distinguish between current and capital expenditures. Current expenditures, which include such budget items as the earnings of government employees and most transfer payments, yield only immediate benefits; capital expenditures, which include such things as highways, education, and environmental quality, provide a stream of benefits extending into the future. Some economists argue that such differences should be taken into account in any fiscal rule, which should accordingly attempt to coordinate the timing of tax payments and the receipt of benefits from government programs. This implies that government should finance current expenditures with current taxes and reserve deficit financing for capital expenditures. Since deficit financing shifts taxes to the future, the benefits of government capital expenditures would then be paid for as they were received.

A rule embodying this principal would prevent one generation of taxpayers from enjoying the benefits of government programs while shifting their costs to other generations, as is the case under current budgetary practice. It has been estimated, for example, that changes in the Social Security system in 1983 imposed a cost of about $12,000 (in present value terms) on the younger generation of taxpayers—meaning most of you who are reading this—to maintain the retirement benefits of the older generation. Intergenerational transfers like this not only raise questions of equity, they also pose potential problems of economic efficiency, for a generation of taxpayers that can shift the cost of government programs to other generations tends to support programs for which the total costs exceed the total benefits.

Incorporating these concerns into the fiscal rule would limit the structural deficit in the "high employment budget" to the level of government's capital expenditures.

Fiscal Policy in Practice

Figure 23.2 shows the federal government's structural budget for the years 1947–89. Using this as a measure of fiscal stimulus or restraint, you can see that fiscal policy has been quite volatile. The structural budget shifted from a large surplus in the late 1940s to a large deficit during the Korean War years of the early 1950s. It then remained roughly in balance until the early 1960s when it once again went into deficit. The structural deficit was again reduced during the 1970s but then grew dramatically during the 1980s.

Although various Presidents and legislators have paid lip service to one or the other of the fiscal rules described here—most frequently a balanced budget at high employment—it is pretty clear that fiscal policy has been essentially discretionary. Unfortunately, the discretion has not always been used in a countercyclical fashion. Indeed, one recent study of the effects of postwar fiscal policy found that it moved in the correct direction in only one-third of the instances calling for countercyclical actions; in the remaining two-thirds it moved in precisely the wrong direction.* This pattern may reflect mistakes resulting in the kind of information and timing problems we have already discussed. On the other hand, it

*Kieth M. Carlson, "Federal Fiscal Policy Since the Employment Act of 1946," *Review*, Federal Reserve Bank of St. Louis (December 1987). Using the change in the structural budget as the indicator of the direction of discretionary fiscal policy, the authors find that fiscal actions were countercyclical in only four of twelve instances where a change in fiscal policy was called for. In the remaining eight cases, fiscal policy moved in the wrong direction.

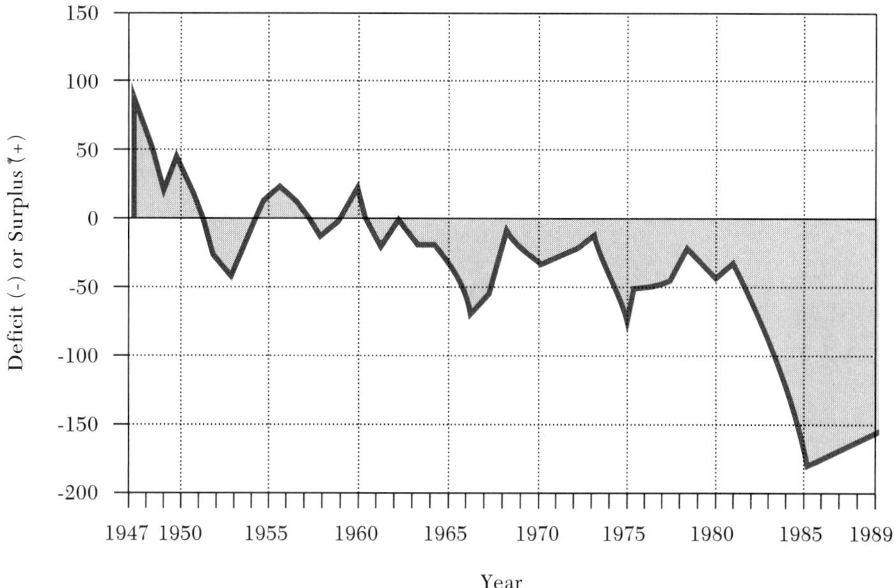

Figure 23.2

The structural budget, 1947–89

may not be the result of mistakes at all, but rather of systematic biases in our political institutions. We examine this possibility later. Before we do, however, let us conclude our discussion of fiscal policy by considering its potential impact on aggregate supply.

Supply-Side Fiscal Policies

To this point, our discussion of fiscal policy has focused almost exclusively on the relation between the government budget and aggregate demand. But fiscal policies also have potentially important effects on aggregate supply, or on what has come to be known popularly as the *supply side*. Supply-side fiscal policies emphasize the effects of the government budget on incentives to work, save, and invest. Unlike "demand-side" fiscal policies, they focus on the structure of tax rates, particularly the *marginal tax rates*, rather than on the overall level of tax revenues because marginal rates, which are the tax rates applied to additional earnings, have the greatest impact on incentives.

To take a simple illustration, suppose you are confronted by a choice at the margin between more work and more leisure. Your employer is willing to pay you up to $10 per hour, the market value of your hourly marginal product, for a few extra hours of work this week. If the marginal value to you of an hour of leisure time is only $8, then you and your employer can agree on a mutually acceptable wage—say, $9 per hour—for which you will work the extra hours. Suppose, however, that your additional earnings will be taxed at a marginal rate of 30 percent. Even if you can get your employer to pay you the full $10 per hour, it will not be worth it for you to work the extra hours because your maximum after-tax earnings of $7 will be less than the value you place on your leisure time. In effect, the tax drives a wedge between you and your employer and prevents the two of you from reaching a mutually beneficial agreement that would have increased both output and employment. The higher the marginal tax rate on earnings, the greater this detrimental impact of the tax system.

A similar argument applies to the effect of taxes on saving and investment. For example, suppose you are willing to save an extra $1,000, and thus supply that amount of additional loanable funds to the credit market, in return for an 8 percent rate of interest. Suppose further that a business firm has a prospective $1,000 capital investment that it believes will return 10 percent. The two of you can agree to a mutually beneficial and socially productive credit transaction in which you lend money to the firm at, say, 9 percent. (For simplicity we ignore the financial intermediaries that would typically act as brokers in this transaction.) If, however, your interest income is also subject to a 30 percent marginal tax rate, the credit transaction will not take place, you will consume rather than save the $1,000, and the future output from the capital investment will be lost. Saving and investment are even further discouraged when increases in the value of capital assets, or capital gains, are also taxed.

The supply-side approach to fiscal policy calls for reducing the marginal tax rates on work, saving, investment, and other productive activities. If successful, this will increase the economy's natural level of real output and shift the long-run aggregate supply curve to the right. It was this supply-side agenda that motivated the broad cuts in marginal tax rates enacted during the first Reagan administration. For example, during the early 1980s, the highest marginal tax rate on personal earnings was reduced from 70 percent to 33 percent, and on corporate earnings from 46 percent to 34 percent.

Despite the publicity touting the "supply-side revolution" of the 1980s, however, the basic ideas behind supply-side economics are hardly novel. Adam Smith pointed out more than 200 years ago the tendency of taxes to "obstruct the industry of people, and discourage them from applying to certain branches of business which might give maintenance and employment to great multitudes."* What was novel about the supply-side arguments of the 1980s was the magnitude of their claims. The most widely publicized of these was the "Laffer effect" (named after the economist, Arthur Laffer) by which a tax cut would expand output and employment so dramatically that the increase in the tax *base* would more than offset the cut in tax *rates*, thereby leading to an increase in total tax *revenues*. This did not happen, at least not as rapidly as the some of the supply-siders claimed it would, and the result was a massive increase in federal deficits during the 1980s. However, after 1982 the economy did embark on a prolonged and uninterrupted, but slow, path of expansion in real output and employment.

The role of the supply-side tax cuts in this expansion is still a matter of debate among economists. What consensus does exist can perhaps best be stated as

* *The Wealth of Nations* (Modern Library Edition), p. 778.

follows. The emphasis on aggregate supply correctly shifted the focus of fiscal policy away from short-run aggregate demand management toward a longer run concern with the impact of the tax structure on productivity and economic growth. However, the original supply-side arguments regarding the magnitude and timing of the effects of tax cuts on economic growth and tax revenues were overly optimistic. These arguments underestimated the effect of tax cuts in increasing the federal deficit and the negative impact of the deficit on economic growth. (Supply-siders argue, however, that slow growth during the 1980s was the fault of an overly cautious and restrictive monetary policy that prevented aggregate demand from expanding fast enough to take advantage of potential supply increases.)

THE POLITICAL ECONOMY OF MACROECONOMIC POLICY

Macroeconomic policy is not made by economic technocrats operating in a political vacuum; it is made by flesh-and-blood people in an essentially political environment. Some, such as the President and members of Congress, are elected politicians; others, such as the Chairman of the Fed's Board of Governors and the Secretary of the Treasury, are appointed and confirmed by those same politicians; still others are members of the permanent federal bureaucracy. Any discussion of macroeconomic policy that ignores these political realities and their implications is seriously deficient. It is simply naive to believe that the policy process is one in which political considerations are always, or even usually, subordinated to sound economics.

Interest Groups and Macroeconomic Policy

As we have seen repeatedly in our discussions of government policies, for better or for worse, interest groups play a prominent role in the democratic political process. That the interests of such groups are frequently at odds with sound macroeconomic policy should hardly be surprising, for they are inevitably more concerned with protecting and increasing their own share of the economic pie than with the conditions that promote its stable growth.

The impact of interest groups is most apparent in the budget process that culminates in government fiscal policies. This is true on both the expenditure side of the budget, where every federal program is the sacred cow of some organized interest group, and on the revenue side, where questions about the overall level of federal tax receipts typically take a back seat to interest group squabbles over whose preferential tax treatment is most deserved. Even in the heyday of activist fiscal policy, there were only two clear instances of fiscal change in which macroeconomic stabilization was the predominate concern—a 1964 tax cut and the 1969 income surtax that took more than a year to get through

Congress. As we remarked earlier, our democratic political institutions are simply not well suited to countercyclical fiscal policy.

Although the Fed is nominally independent of the President and Congress, it also is not immune from political pressures. Some of these pressures are the direct result of Presidential arm twisting—remember who appoints the Fed's Board of Governors—whereas others are brought to bear by Congress. The Fed can hardly ignore these pressures and at the same time realistically hope to maintain its cherished "independence." Moreover, the Fed has also been historically sensitive to banking and financial interests, which often conflict with sound macroeconomic policy.

The Political Time Horizon and Inflationary Bias

Another relevant characteristic of the political process is the short time horizon of many political decision makers, especially elected politicians. Presidential terms are only 4 years, U.S. Senators face reelection every 6 years, and members of the House of Representatives every 2 years. Since the re-election of incumbents often turns on the health of the economy, it is in their interest to make the economy look as good as possible at election time, even if the policy actions this requires lead to a postelection deterioration of economic performance. As a result, the short-run impact of a policy change often receives greater weight in the political process than do its long-term consequences.

One manifestation of this preoccupation with the short run has been the inflationary bias of postwar macroeconomic policy. The benefits of overly expansionary aggregate demand policies come early in the form of higher real output and lower unemployment; their costs come later in the form of higher inflation. With contractionary policies, the timing is reversed: The costs come early and the gains come later. Add to the timing of these economic trade-offs the observation that it is simply easier for politicians to vote for tax cuts and spending increases than to do the reverse, and it is easy to see why macroeconomic policy has exhibited an inflationary bias.

Figure 23.3 shows the average inflation rate, the average unemployment rate, and the average rate of growth of real output for each 5-year period between 1950 and 1989. With the exception of only one 5-year period, 1960–64, inflation accelerated continuously over the entire 30-year interval between 1950 and 1980. As the figure also shows, however, the expansionary policy bias largely responsible for this did not succeed in reducing unemployment or raising the rate of real economic growth. If anything, the contrary was the case. Although inflation abated during the recession of 1982–83 and remained relatively low through the late 1980s, it remains to be seen whether this represents a reversal of the long-term trend or just a temporary interruption.

A Political Business Cycle?

Some economists argue that macroeconomic policy itself is a cause of the business cycle rather than its cure. More than a simple recognition of the destabilizing potential of policy mistakes, their argument holds that the combination of

Figure 23.3

Inflation, unemployment, and growth

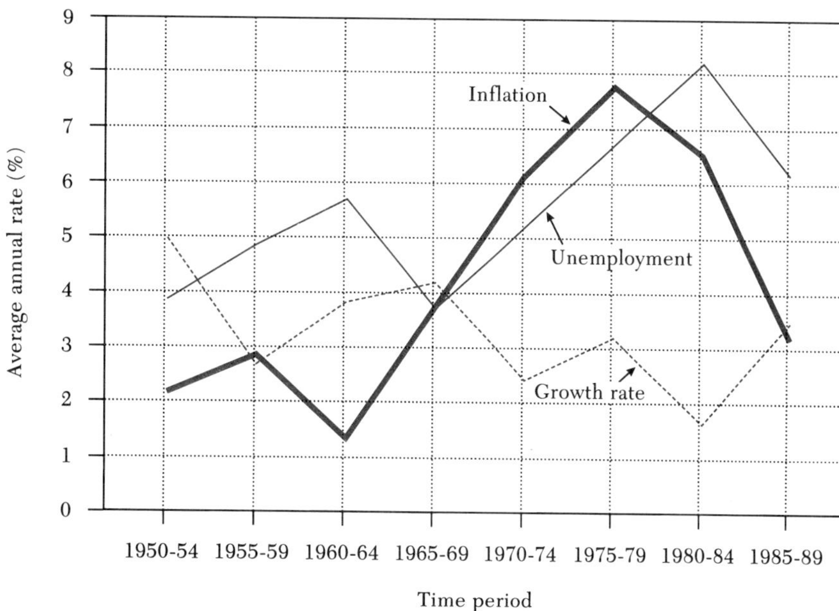

Political business cycles are cyclical fluctuations in economic activity brought about by policies that are economically destabilizing but politically appealing.

political incentives and economic realities confronting policy makers gives them an incentive to deliberately pursue what are, in effect, economically destabilizing policies. The result is a **political business cycle**.

The basic theory of the political business cycle recognizes that incumbent politicians (and the policy makers they appoint) can take advantage of favorable short-run trade-offs by overexpanding aggregate demand just before an election. The rising real output and falling unemployment that result will increase their chances for re-election (or reappointment), whereas the adverse inflationary consequences will not show up until safely after the election. Between elections, the political costs of curbing inflation may be low enough for contractionary policies to be adopted. Whether they are, or whether inflation is more tolerable politically than its cure, depends on just how much the rate of inflation has accelerated. In any case, there will be another expansionary policy burst just in time for the next election, and the process will begin all over again.

Figure 23.4 on the following page provides some evidence in support of the political business cycle hypothesis. It shows the average percentage point changes in unemployment and inflation from one year to the next over the 4-year Presidential election cycle for the period 1947–89. Along the horizontal axis, −1 represents the year before the election, 0 the election year, and so on. As you can see, on average both unemployment and inflation have tended to fall as the election year approaches and then rise again after the election.

The data behind these averages are also informative. During nine of the eleven Presidential election years between 1948 and 1988, the unemployment rate fell. Interestingly, in the only two election years in which the unemployment rate rose, 1960 and 1980, the party occupying the White House was defeated. Fur-

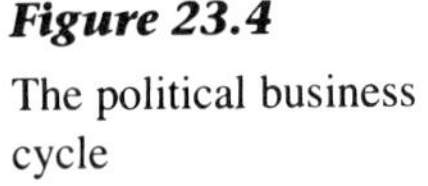

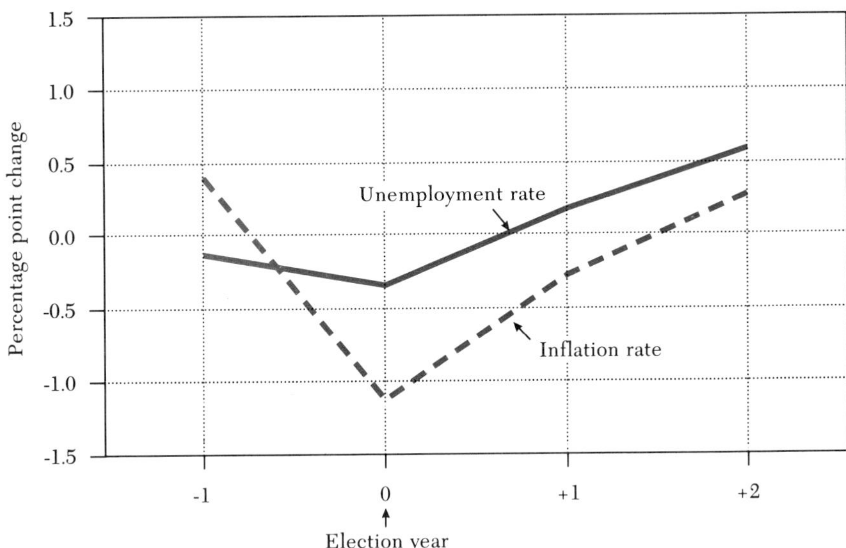

Figure 23.4

The political business cycle

thermore, in eight out of eleven cases (the exceptions being 1948, 1980, and 1984), the inflation rate rose during the 2-year period immediately following the election.

If the preceding pattern were regular enough and were repeated enough times, it would come to be expected, thereby reducing the ability for expansionary policies to achieve even short-run gains in real output and employment. The persistence over time of a political business cycle therefore depends on how well people learn from history.

Is the Cure Worse than the Disease?

Nearly all economists agree that monetary and fiscal policies have occasionally acted as destabilizing, rather than stabilizing, forces. The political business cycle hypothesis—indeed, the entire political economy of macroeconomic policy—raises a fundamental issue regarding the reasons for such destabilizing policy actions. Once we recognize that policy makers are flesh-and-blood people with their own personal interests, and that those interests may not always be consistent with the textbook prescriptions for the conduct of economic policy, then the presumption that macroeconomic policy actually *does* pursue economic stabilization is open to question. In short, we must recognize the possibility that macroeconomic policy can be a source of instability by design, as well as by mistake.

Economists believe, with varying degrees of confidence, that they know enough about the workings of the economy to suggest policies to avoid such major disturbances as the great German hyperinflation of the 1920s and the prolonged Depression of the 1930s. The really tough questions are whom to entrust with this policy power and how to circumscribe their authority to insure its prudent use during periods of relative economic normalcy.

CHAPTER SUMMARY

1. Macroeconomic *stabilization policy* attempts to minimize the deviations of unemployment about its natural rate, real output about its long-run growth path, and inflation about some low and stable rate.
2. Monetarists and new classical economists, believing that the market economy is a fundamentally stable and self-correcting system, favor a policy based on a few, simple rules. The Keynesians' view that the market economy is a fragile mechanism requiring constant supervision leads them to favor an active, discretionary approach to macroeconomic policy.
3. The Fed's job of conducting short-run monetary policy is complicated by incomplete information about changes in economic conditions and uncertainty regarding the behavior of the money multiplier and velocity. Monetary policy must also cope with a difficult timing problem, for the lag between Fed actions and their effects on the economy is long and variable.
4. Some Keynesians believe that the instability of the relations between monetary policy actions and economic performance necessitate the continual adjustment of monetary policy. Monetarists, by contrast, believe that discretionary monetary policies have often been the cause rather than the cure of economic instability in the short run and that these policies have exhibited an inflationary bias in the long run. They therefore favor a policy rule, such as one requiring a constant monetary growth rate. The views of many economists fall somewhere between these two positions.
5. Proponents of the *gold standard* argue that it would serve as a discipline preventing excessive monetary expansion. The major problem with the gold standard is that changes in a nation's gold reserves bear no necessary relationship to its demand for money.
6. Rather than commit itself to any policy rule, in practice the Fed continues to use its powers in an essentially discretionary manner.
7. Discretionary countercyclical fiscal policy is complicated by uncertainty regarding its monetary side effects, by its effects on peoples' expectations, by its differential microeconomic effects on resource allocation, by timing problems even worse than those encountered by monetary policy, and by the political realities of the budget process. Because of these difficulties, countercyclical fiscal policy has been virtually abandoned as a short-run stabilization tool.
8. As a fiscal rule, an *annually balanced budget* would probably tend to magnify, rather than dampen, any instability inherent in the economy.
9. The difficulty with a rule requiring a *cyclically balanced budget* is that business cycles are not regular and predictable enough to insure that the cyclical deficits incurred during recessions would be offset by the cyclical surpluses generated during economic booms.

10. A rule requiring a *balanced budget at high employment* implies that the structural deficit would be zero. Such a rule would permit cyclical deficits and surpluses, thereby avoiding the destabilizing properties of the annually balanced budget rule, but it would not require that cyclical surpluses exactly offset cyclical deficits.

11. The distinction between current and capital expenditures suggests that the structural deficit be limited to government's capital expenditures. This would promote equity and efficiency by insuring that the generations who are the beneficiaries of government programs also bear their costs.

12. In practice, fiscal policy has been essentially discretionary. Unfortunately, the discretion has often worked in the wrong direction.

13. The *supply-side* approach to fiscal policy calls for reducing the marginal tax rates on work, saving, investment, and other productive activities to increase the economy's natural level of real output and shift the long-run aggregate supply curve to the right.

14. In the political arena, sound macroeconomic policy is often subordinated to interest group politics. Moreover, the short time horizon of political decision makers leads to an inflationary bias in macroeconomic policy.

15. The combination of political incentives and economic realities confronting policy makers may give them an incentive to deliberately destabilize the economy for political gain. The result is what has been called a *political business cycle*.

Key Terms and Concepts

stabilization policy
gold standard
annually balanced budget
cyclically balanced budget
balanced budget at high employment
political business cycle

Questions for Thought and Discussion

1. The following table shows the average federal funds rate, the average rate of growth of *M*1, and the average rate of inflation over each 5-year interval between 1960 and 1980. Use it to answer the questions that follow it.

Period	*Federal Funds Rate*	*M1 Growth Rate*	*Inflation Rate*
1960–64	2.9%	2.8%	1.6%
1965–70	5.5	4.7	3.9
1971–74	7.1	6.1	6.3
1975–80	7.1	7.1	7.8

a. If you use the federal funds rate as a gauge, was monetary policy becoming more expansionary or more contractionary between 1960 and 1980?
b. If you use the growth rate of M1 as a gauge, was monetary policy becoming more expansionary or more contractionary between 1960 and 1980?
c. Which of your answers to parts a and b is more consistent with the trend in inflation over this period?

2. Some economists, disenchanted with both a monetary growth rule and the gold standard, have argued for a "commodity price rule." According to this rule, the Fed should attempt to stabilize an index of commodity prices. Because changes in commodity prices, which are set in auction markets, portend changes in the overall inflation rate, they could serve as an early warning signal for the Fed.

a. What advantages might such a rule have over a rule of constant monetary growth? Over a gold standard?
b. What problems might such a rule introduce?

3. During the Great Depression of the 1930s, when the federal government's budget started running cyclical deficits, tax rates were raised in an effort to rebalance the budget.

a. According to our definitions, would this increase in tax rates constitute discretionary fiscal policy? If so, was it in the appropriate direction?
b. With which of the three fiscal balanced budget rules would this tax increase be most consistent?

4. During the economic expansion that began in 1983, the federal government's budget deficits remained well above $100 billion per year, which is extremely large by pre-1980 standards.

a. Explain why the deficit itself is a problem. Is this problem confined to the short run, or does it have long-run ramifications as well?
b. What kind of monetary policy might the Fed be tempted to use to prevent these detrimental effects of the deficit? What is the danger of such a policy?
c. What would be the danger of attempting to reduce the deficit by a fiscal policy that substantially raises tax rates?

5. In 1985 Congress passed the Gramm-Rudman-Hollings bill in an attempt to cut the federal deficit. The bill mandated across-the-board cuts in federal spending if legislative action cutting specific federal programs or raising federal tax revenues was insufficient to meet its deficit reduction targets. Why do you think Congress would pass such a bill?

C H A P T E R 24

The International Economy

Visualize a simple routine that's part of your typical day. Perhaps you're dressed in jeans, a sweatshirt, and tennis shoes; you hop into your car, pop a tape into the tape deck, and head for class or work. How many countries can you count in this picture? Chances are pretty good that your jeans were made in Taiwan, your sweatshirt in Thailand, and your tennis shoes in Korea. Your car and its tape deck may have been made in Japan, its tires in France, and the gasoline in its tank refined from Saudi Arabian crude oil. The tape may have been recorded by a British rock group.

This vignette just hints at the great extent to which we all rely on the international economy to satisfy our daily economic wants. In this chapter we examine the network of international economic relations that makes this all possible.

WHAT MAKES INTERNATIONAL ECONOMICS DIFFERENT FROM "ORDINARY" ECONOMICS?

In Chapter 2 we introduced the concepts of specialization and exchange, the basic organizing principles of all economic activity. We saw how people gain from trade when they follow their comparative advantages as producers and then exchange the results for the things they value most as consumers. In Chapters 3 and 4, we saw how production and consumption activities involving thousands, millions, even hundreds of millions of people are coordinated through the market mechanism of supply, demand, and prices. Now envision such a large group of people and imagine an arbitrary line separating some of them from others. Would comparative advantage no longer matter in determining who produces what? Would mutually beneficial exchanges be confined only to people on one side of the line? Of course not! The basic principles of economic organization have no respect for our arbitrary dividing line.

Now suppose we call our dividing line an international border. This brings us into the realm of international economics and, although the fundamental principals governing production and exchange have not changed, the border and its implications do add some new elements to our analysis. The most important of these are international differences in comparative advantage, monetary units, and political systems.

International differences in comparative advantage reflect the different combinations of productive factors available within nations. Some of these differences are the result of distinct national endowments of natural resources, such as mineral deposits, climate, and terrain. Others—such as differences in national capital stocks or in the education, skills, and productivity of labor forces—are the result of past investment choices.

Nations are also distinguished by their use of different monetary units, or currencies. Dollars are the common medium of exchange in the United States; Canada and Australia also use dollars, but theirs are not the same as U.S. dollars. In Japan, the monetary unit is the yen; in Mexico, it is the peso; in England, it is the pound sterling or simply the pound; in Germany, it is the Deutschmark, or mark.

If you want to buy a Japanese stereo, you (or more accurately, the importer) must first buy yen with which to pay the Japanese manufacturer who, after all, cannot pay its workers with American dollars. International trade in goods thus requires international trade in currencies as well. The relative values of national currencies are determined within the international monetary system.

Finally, nations are distinct political entities with governments representing different constituencies through different political institutions. As such, they pursue different economic policies and respond to different economic interests. Most significantly, governments naturally tend to favor domestic interests over foreign interests when there is a conflict between the two. This fact is reflected in the historical enthusiasm with which they have embraced **protectionism**—that is, policies that protect domestic producers from foreign competition. As we shall see, such measures, although understandable from the public choice perspective, almost inevitably reduce overall economic welfare.

Protectionism is a policy of sheltering domestic producers from foreign competition.

These three elements—differences in comparative advantages, currencies, and political systems—together establish the economic significance of international boundaries. As such, they correspond to our three major topics in this chapter, namely, comparative advantage as the basis of international trade, the relation between international trade and the international monetary system, and the political economy of international economic relations.

THE ECONOMIC BASIS OF INTERNATIONAL TRADE

The basis for trade among nations is the familiar law of comparative advantage that we first encountered in Chapter 2. Indeed, it was in demonstrating the benefits of international trade that the economist, David Ricardo, originally stated the law back in 1817. In particular, Ricardo demonstrated that the citizens of any nation can gain by following their comparative advantages as producers and then trading with the citizens of other nations to obtain many of the goods they value as consumers.

Specialization and Trade in a Two-Nation, Two-Good World

To illustrate the fundamentals of this argument, let us first consider a simple world in which there are only two countries, Agraria and Industria, and two goods, food and clothing. Each of the countries has a population of one million people which, for simplicity, we assume is also its labor force. There the similarities end, however. Agraria is a relatively poor nation whose labor force is unskilled and equipped with little capital. By contrast, the people of Industria are highly educated and skilled and abundantly equipped with the most modern of capital goods. Because of these differences, an Agrarian worker can produce only 30 baskets of food or 20 articles of clothing per year, whereas his more productive Industrian counterpart can produce 40 baskets of food or 80 articles of clothing per year. These differences in productivity are summarized in Table 24.1.

In Figure 24.1 we have constructed the production possibilities curves (*PPC*s) for our two national economies. Consider first Agraria's *PPC*. If all Agrarians were engaged in food production, they would produce 30 million baskets of food per year (or 30*F*); if all were engaged in clothing production they would produce 20 million articles of clothing per year (20*C*). These two extremes are represented by the intersection points of Agraria's *PPC* on the vertical (food) and horizontal (clothing) axes, respectively. Intermediate production mixes lie along the straight line connecting these two points. For example, if half of Agraria's

Table 24.1

Labor productivities in Agraria and Industria (annual output per worker)

	BASKETS OF FOOD	ARTICLES OF CLOTHING
Agraria	30	20
Industria	40	80

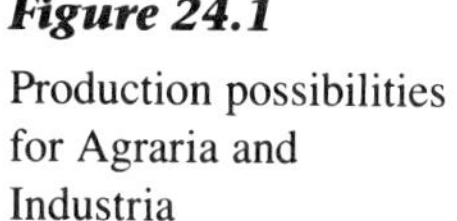

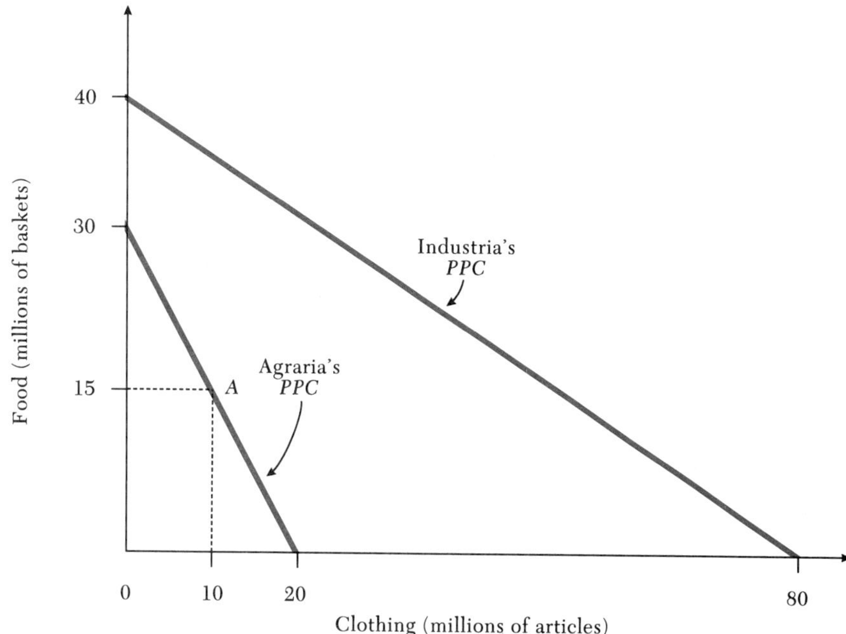

Figure 24.1

Production possibilities for Agraria and Industria

population were engaged in food production and half in clothing production, the result would be the combination of 15*F* and 10*C* represented by point *A* on Agraria's *PPC*.

Industria's *PPC* is plotted on the same diagram. If all Industrians were to produce food, the result would be 40*F* on the vertical axis; if all were to produce clothing, the result would be 80*C* on the horizontal axis. Intermediate combinations of food and clothing lie on the straight line *PPC* connecting these two points. The fact that Industria's *PPC* lies entirely above Agraria's tells us that Industria can produce more of either or both goods than Agraria. In other words, Industria has an *absolute advantage* over Agraria in the production of both food and clothing. However, it is *comparative advantages*, not absolute advantages, that establish the benefits of international trade.

A nation's comparative advantage is determined not by the absolute amounts of goods it can produce but by its opportunity costs of producing them relative to other nations. In our simple economy, these opportunity costs, which are summarized in Table 24.2, are determined by the production trade-offs between food and clothing. In particular, when an Agrarian produces food, 20 articles of clothing are sacrificed for each 30 baskets of food produced. The marginal cost of each basket of food produced in Agraria is therefore (2/3)*C*. In Industria 80 articles of clothing are sacrificed to obtain 40 baskets of food, so the marginal cost of a basket of food produced in Industria is 2*C*. Despite its lower absolute productivity, therefore, Agraria can produce a basket of food at lower opportu-

Table 24.2

Marginal costs in Agraria and Industria

	MARGINAL COST OF	
	Food	*Clothing*
Agraria	(⅔)C	(1½)F
Industria	2C	(½)F

nity cost than Industria. Agraria thus has a comparative advantage over Industria in food production. On the other hand, an article of clothing can be produced in Agraria at a marginal cost of (1-1/2)F, but in Industria at a cost of only (1/2)F. Industria therefore has a comparative advantage in the production of clothing.*

To see how these comparative advantages can be exploited for the mutual benefit of Agrarians and Industrians, let us begin with a situation in which there is no international trade and both nations are self-sufficient. We assume that Agraria initially produces a combination of 15F and 10C and Industria produces a combination of 10F and 60C. These output combinations are represented by point A on Agraria's *PPC* in part (a) of Figure 24.2 and point I on Industria's *PPC* in part (b) of the same figure. (The *PPC*s in Figure 24.2 are identical to those in Figure 24.1 except that they are plotted separately to keep the figure from becoming too cluttered.)

Now let us introduce international trade into the picture. According to the law of comparative advantage, Agraria should specialize in producing food and trade some of that food for clothing produced in Industria; by contrast, Industria should specialize in producing clothing and trade for food produced in Agraria. The first part of this strategy, specialization according to comparative advantage, moves Agraria up its *PPC* from point A to point X, and it moves Industria down its *PPC* from point I to point Y. Agraria is now producing 30F and 0C, while Industria is producing 80C and 0F. Note that total world output has increased as a result of specialization. Initially it consisted of 25F (15F produced by Agraria and 10F by Industria) and 70C (10C produced by Agraria and 60C by Industria); after specialization it consists of 30F (all produced by Agraria) and 80F (all produced by Industria).

The second part of the strategy requires that Agraria trade some of its food for clothing produced in Industria. We must therefore find a rate at which Agrarian food can be exchanged for Industrian clothing on the international market. This rate, called the *terms of trade* between the two goods, depends on the relative costs of production in the two countries. In particular, since it costs Agrarians (1-1/2)F to produce an article of clothing themselves, they would be

*You may recall from Chapter 2 that these marginal costs reflect the slopes of the production possibilities curves. For example, (minus) 1-1/2 slope of Agraria's *PPC* reflects the marginal cost of clothing produced in that nation while the (minus) 1/2 slope of Industria's *PPC* is the marginal cost of clothing produced there. The reciprocals of these slopes, 2/3 and 2, respectively, represent the marginal costs of food in the two countries.

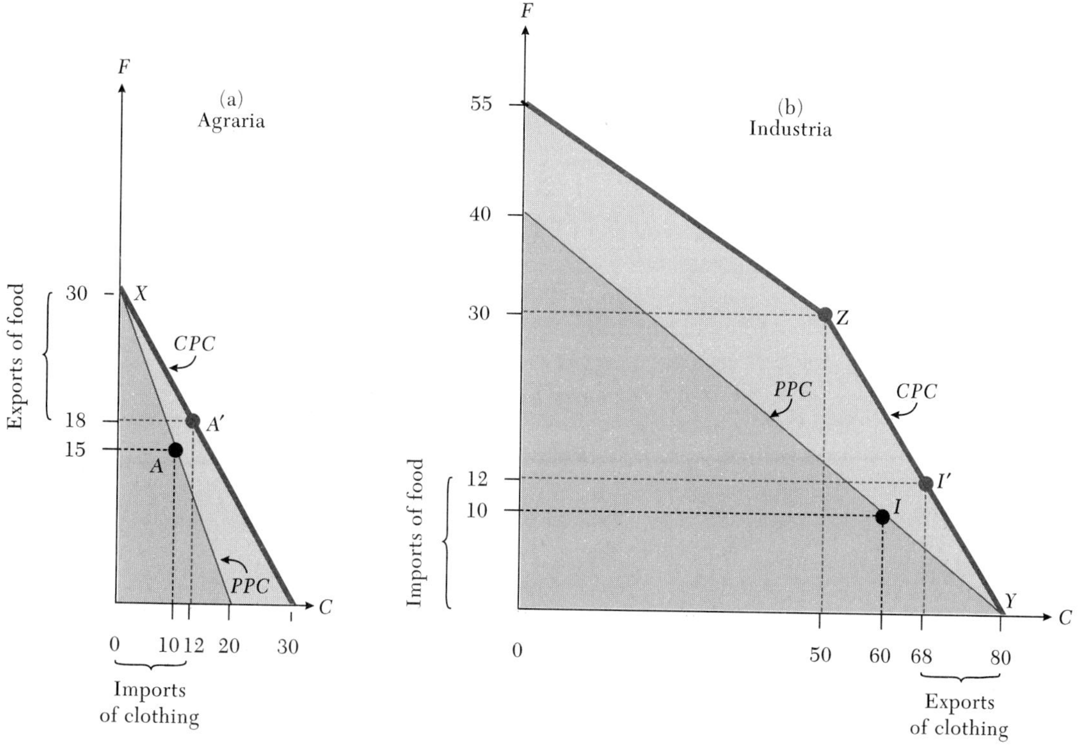

Figure 24.2

Consumption possibilities with international trade

willing to pay up to that amount, but no more, for each article of clothing they import from Industria. Industrians, on the other hand, would be willing to accept anything more than the (1/2)*F* it costs them to produce that article of clothing. Accordingly, Agraria and Industria would both benefit from exchange at the terms of trade anywhere between (1/2)*F* for 1*C* and (1-1/2)*F* for 1*C*. To keep the numbers simple, we assume that they have agreed to split the difference and trade food and clothing at the rate of 1*F* for 1*C*.

As Agraria trades its food for clothing, it moves away from point *X*, its point of specialization in Figure 24.2, down along the heavy line whose slope of -1 reflects the 1*C*-for-1*F* terms of trade. Since this line shows the consumption opportunities open to Agrarians when they specialize in food production and trade for clothing, we call it their **consumption possibilities curve**, or *CPC*. Agraria's *CPC* lies entirely above its *PPC*, indicating that Agrarians have more goods available for consumption through specialization and trade than through self-sufficiency. For example, if, after specializing in food production, Agrarians export 12*F* to Industria in return for 12*C*, they will be left with a consumption bundle consisting of 18*F* and 12*C*. With this consumption bundle, represented by point *A′* on Agraria's *CPC*, Agrarians have more of both goods than at the self-sufficient starting point of 15*F* and 10*C* on their *PPC*. The extra 3*F* and 2*C*

The **consumption possibilities curve** shows the consumption combinations available to a nation as a result of specialization and international trade.

is a measure of the gains from trade enjoyed by the Agrarians. Whether Agraria ends up at point A' or some other point on its *CPC* depends on the relative values its citizens place on food and clothing. If Agraria's climate is chilly and damp, for example, they might want to import more clothing and so end up below and to the right of A' on their *CPC*. But wherever they end up, they will be better off than if they were to remain self-sufficiently confined to their *PPC*.

Since specialization and trade are *mutually* beneficial, a similar argument must hold for Industria. Starting from point *Y*, the point of specialization on Industria's *PPC*, trade at the rate of 1*C* for 1*F* moves Industria upward and to the left along the heavy line segment *YZ* of its consumption possibilities curve. For example, when Industria imports 12*F* from Agraria in return for 12*C*, as in the preceding illustration, Industria ends up at point I' with 12*F* and 68*C*. This is more of each good than it had before trade with Agraria.

The kink in Industria's *CPC* at point *Z* reflects the fact that 30*F* is the upper limit on the amount of food it can import from Agraria, for that is the maximum amount that Agraria can produce. If Industria wants to consume more than 30*F*—that is, if it wants to move upward from point *Z* along its *CPC*—it will have to produce the additional food itself. The cost of producing its own food (2*C* for 1*F*) is more than it pays for imported food (1*C* for 1*F*), and this is reflected in the change in the slope of its *CPC* at point *Z*.

Just where Industria ends up on its *CPC*, whether at point I' or some other point, depends on the relative values its citizens place on food and clothing, respectively. If they place a high enough value on food relative to clothing, Industria might end up above point *Z* on its *CPC*, producing some food itself in addition to what it imports from Agraria. In any case, Industria gains by pursuing its comparative advantage in clothing production and relying as far as possible on imports for its food.

Some Extensions

While the preceding example illustrates the fundamental case for international trade based on comparative advantage, it is obviously simplified and somewhat artificial. Let us therefore see how the argument can be extended to take into account various real-world complications.

Nations Don't Trade, People Trade

The language in our simplified example may have left you with the impression that nations trade with nations. This is not the case. Although national governments can (and sometimes do) trade directly with one another, most international trade is carried out by individuals and business firms motivated by the same incentives that motivate them in domestic trade. If, for example, an enterprising Agrarian recognizes that an article of clothing costs 1-1/2 baskets of food when produced in her own country but only 1/2 basket of food when produced in Industria, she will find it profitable to import low-cost Industrian clothing for sale in Agraria. Similarly, profit-seeking Industrians will soon discover that they can import low-cost food from Agraria and resell it for a profit in their own country. If somebody makes a mistake—if our Agrarian entrepreneur decides to import food rather than clothing, for example—her shrinking bank account will soon provide a powerful incentive to change the way she does business. Thus there need be no government bureaucracy to ascertain that Agraria's comparative advantage is in food; no centralized authority must order Industria to produce clothing for export. The ordinary economic incentives of the marketplace are quite capable of accomplishing all of this in a decentralized fashion.

The Determinants of International Comparative Advantages

As we have already noted, international differences in comparative advantage reflect the different combinations of productive factors available within nations. For example, the abundance of fertile agricultural land in the United States gives it a comparative advantage in the production of many agricultural commodities. Its engineering and technical talent combined with a relatively skilled and well-educated labor force give it a comparative advantage in the development and production of goods on the cutting edge of technology, such as new chemicals, jet aircraft, and new generations of computer hardware and software. Japan, West Germany, and other Western European nations are in varying degrees similar in this respect. Countries such as Korea and Taiwan, with an abundance of unskilled and semiskilled labor, but with access to relatively modern capital, have a comparative advantage manufacturing of a variety of products from textiles to televisions. An abundance of petroleum reserves gives Saudi Arabia, Kuwait, and other Middle Eastern nations a comparative advantage in producing crude oil. The climate and terrain of Brazil and Columbia give them a comparative advantage in growing coffee; of France, in wine production; of the Caribbean nations, in tourism.

Comparative advantage can also reflect economies of large-scale production. In particular, the expansion of a domestic industry in which scale economies are important may give that industry a comparative advantage in world markets. The apparent comparative advantages of the United States, Japan, and West Germany in world automobile markets is, at least in part, a reflection of their large-scale production, as is the comparative advantage of the United States in the world market for commercial aircraft.

How Specialized?

In our preceding example, Agraria produced only food while relying exclusively on imports for its clothing; Industria did the reverse. However, there is nothing in the law of comparative advantage that says a country must specialize in producing one or a few goods; nor is there anything in the law that says it must rely entirely on imports for other goods. We ended up with complete specialization in our example only because of a simplifying assumption of constant marginal costs for both goods in each country. More realistically, marginal costs typically change with the level of output. If marginal costs increase as output expands, a country may have a comparative advantage in the production of some good up to a point, but a comparative *dis*advantage beyond that point. Alternatively, if economies of scale are important, comparative advantage may be attained only after some minimum scale of production is exceeded.

Economists have shown that when costs vary with output, comparative advantage may even lead a nation to export *and* import differentiated versions of the same product. For example, suppose there are three types of cars: compacts, family sedans, and luxury sports sedans. Suppose further that there are economies of scale in the production of each type. Under these conditions, one country—say, Japan—might specialize in the production of compacts, thereby reaping the economies of scale and the comparative advantage in that segment of the world market for cars. The United States might do the same in the production of family sedans, and Germany in the production of luxury sport sedans. If there is a demand for each type of car in each of these countries, then each will be both an importer and exporter of automobiles. The United States, for example, would import compacts and luxury sports sedans (which it does) and export family sedans (which it also does). A substantial portion of all international trade, including about 60 percent of all U.S. trade, represents such intraindustry trade.*

Other Effects of International Trade

The benefits of international trade often go beyond the fundamental gains from specialization and exchange. For one thing, trade increases the variety of goods available to consumers in each country. It allows Americans a choice between Sonys and Zeniths; among Toyotas, Mercedes, and Hyundais as well as Chevys and Fords; and between Heineken and Corona as well as Budwieser. It gives Germans and Japanese a choice between IBMs and Olivettis; between Reeboks and Nikes; and between U.S. beef and New Zealand lamb. Competition from foreign sources can also lower the prices charged by domestic producers by eliminating or reducing any market power they may have and by forcing them to operate as efficiently as possible. Finally, by expanding the markets in which all firms sell, international trade allows them to reap economies of large-scale production and distribution.

This is not to say that international trade does not occasionally impose costs. It does, and, as we see below, these costs frequently fall on vocal and visible interests who seek protection through the political process.

THE INTERNATIONAL MONETARY SYSTEM

Trade flows are accompanied by monetary flows going in the opposite direction. Exports generate a matching *inflow* of monetary payments *from* the rest of the

*Deborah Battles, "Trade Theory and Comparative Advantage: Is the Real World *Really* Like That?" (*The Margin*, Mar/Apr 1989) provides a good, understandable discussion of interindustry trade.

The **balance of payments accounts** provide the accounting framework for recording the monetary flows linking a nation's domestic economy to the rest of the world.

world; imports generate a matching *outflow* of payments *to* the rest of the world. Payment flows also accompany international exchanges of financial and other assets. The monetary flows linking a nation's domestic economy to the rest of the world are recorded in its **balance of payments accounts**.

The Balance of Payments Framework

The **current account** is the portion of the balance of payments accounts that summarizes current trade in goods and services and transfer payments.

The **capital account** is the portion of the balance of payments accounts that summarizes asset exchanges and credit flows.

The balance of payments accounts treat any payment flowing into the domestic economy from the rest of the world as a credit (+), and any payment flowing out of the domestic economy to the rest of the world as a debit (−). The accounts consist of two components: a **current account**, which reflects current trade in goods and services (as well as international transfer payments), and a **capital account**, which reflects international exchanges of assets. Since assets represent claims on future income, the capital account is essentially a record of international credit transactions.

The Current Account

Table 24.3 shows the U.S. balance of payments for 1988. As you can see, the current account consists of three components: merchandise trade, service trade, and transfer payments. In the terminology of international transactions, merchandise includes only physical goods. Thus the merchandise entry in the table reflects U.S. exports of IBM computers and Boeing 747s and imports of Toyota cars and French wine. Since U.S. exports generate an inflow of payments from

Table 24.3

U.S. balance of payments, 1988

CURRENT ACCOUNT		
Goods and services		
Merchandise (exports − imports)	−127	
Services (exports − imports)	+ 15	
Balance on goods and services		−112
Transfers (net)	− 14	
Balance on current account		−126
CAPITAL ACCOUNT		
Capital outflow (U.S. purchases of foreign assets)	− 82	
Capital inflow (foreign purchases of U.S. assets)	+219	
Balance on capital account		+137
Statistical discrepancy	− 11	
Total		+126

Source: *Economic Report of the President, 1990.*

the rest of the world to domestic producers, the value of merchandise exports is entered as a credit (+) in the current account. Merchandise imports, on the other hand, are entered as a debit (−) in the current account. The U.S. merchandise trade balance for 1988 showed a deficit of $127 billion, indicating that merchandise imports exceeded merchandise exports by that amount.

The services component of the current account reflects a variety of current transactions in which no physical goods cross international borders. For example, if a Korean business firm hires an American law firm to represent its interests in the U.S., its payment for those legal services is entered as a credit in the U.S. current account. Tourism is also considered a service, so that when a U.S. citizen travels abroad and consumes the services of foreign hotels, restaurants, and tour guides, her payments for those services are registered as debits in the current account. Expenditures for similar services by foreign tourists visiting the U.S. are registered as credits.

Investment income, which reflects payments for the services of U.S. capital invested abroad, is also included in the services component of the current account. For example, when a U.S. multinational corporation's manufacturing plant in Mexico earns dividends for its U.S. stockholders, those dividends are recorded as a credit in the services component of the U.S. current account. On the other hand, when an Arab sheik collects rent from the tenants in the high rise apartment building he owns in New York City, that rent is recorded as a debit in the U.S. current account. An excess of the earnings of U.S. investments abroad over foreign investments in the U.S. was largely responsible for the net $15 billion surplus in the services component of the 1988 current account.

Together the merchandise and services components of the current account determine the balance of trade in goods and services. As you can see from the table, the U.S. experienced a $112 billion deficit in its 1988 balance on goods and services.

The final component of the current account, transfers, includes payments for which no current goods or services are obtained. For example, pension payments to a retired American couple living in Mexico are entered as a debit in the transfer component of the current account. When that same couple sends a $25 birthday gift to their grandson back home, it is entered as a transfer credit.

Taking into account all current trade and transfers, the United States had a current account deficit of $126 billion in 1988.

The Capital Account

American purchases of foreign assets, such as bonds issued by foreign corporations or governments, result in a "capital outflow" and are recorded as debits in the capital account. Foreign purchases of U.S. assets represent a "capital inflow" and are recorded as a credit in the capital account. Net currency flows are also reflected in the capital account. If Americans exchange their dollars for French francs, for example, the result is a U.S. capital outflow (but a French capital inflow).

Why the Balance of Payments Must Always Balance

Suppose the United States imports $350 worth of merchandise and services and exports only $200 worth. Assuming for simplicity that net transfers are zero, the result is a $150 current account deficit. How do we finance this deficit? Or, to put it another way, how do we pay foreigners for the extra $150 worth of merchandise and services we have obtained from them? Certainly, they are not just going to give them to us.* Nor, apparently, do foreigners want another $150 worth of U.S. merchandise and services; otherwise our current account balance would have been zero. No, the $150 current account deficit indicates that foreigners have chosen to either hold U.S. dollars or use them to acquire assets such as U.S. Treasury bonds, stock in American corporations, or hotels in Las Vegas. In choosing to acquire U.S. assets rather than exchange their dollars directly for U.S. merchandise and services, foreigners have in effect extended us exactly enough credit on the capital account to cover our deficit on the current account. Conversely, if the United States had a current account surplus, it would use that surplus to acquire an equal amount of foreign assets (including foreign currencies) so that there would be a matching capital account deficit.

As this example illustrates, the balance of payments must always balance: Any deficit (surplus) in the current account must be exactly offset by a surplus (deficit) in the capital account.

Whoa there! Table 24.3 shows a current account deficit of $126 billion but a capital account surplus of $137 billion. Didn't we just say that the two must cancel? Yes, in principle they do, but in practice many international transactions inevitably simply slip through the cracks and are not recorded. (How many cocaine importers do you suppose file reports with the U.S. Department of Commerce, for example?) Thus the balance of payments must also report a "statistical discrepancy" to reconcile the current and capital accounts.

What About the "Balance of Trade?"

The figure that makes most of the headlines is something called the *balance of trade*, which does not appear in Table 24.3. The phrase "balance of trade" is somewhat ambiguous, but since it is used so frequently, let's look at some of its possible meanings. In the narrowest sense, the balance of trade refers to only the merchandise trade balance. A somewhat broader interpretation, and one that is consistent with a more general concept of trade, equates the balance of trade with the balance on goods and services. The broadest interpretation of all equates the balance of trade with the entire current account balance. It is this broad meaning that we have in mind when we use the phrase balance of trade.

*Note that if they did, the result would be a positive transfer of $150 and the current account balance would be zero.

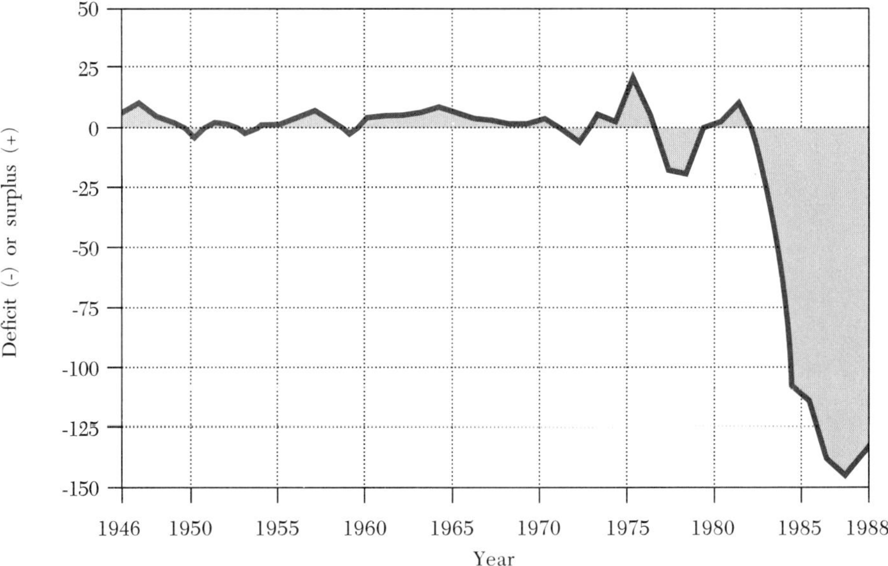

Figure 24.3

U.S. current account balance, 1946–88

The Sources and Consequences of Trade Deficits

Figure 24.3 shows the U.S. current account balance since the end of World War II. During most of this period, the nation showed a small but persistent trade surplus. This surplus, and the matching capital account deficit, reflected high levels of American investment overseas. Beginning in the early 1980s, however, the U.S. began running large trade deficits. Why has this change occurred and what are its implications?

To answer this question, it is useful to recall an accounting identity that we derived in conjunction with our analysis of the national income accounts in Chapter 16. The identity says that all domestic investment must be financed by saving, and that saving has three sources: the private sector, the government, and foreign sources. In the notation of Chapter 16,

$$I = S_p + S_g + S_f$$

where I is domestic investment, S_p is private saving, S_g is government saving (that is, the government budget surplus), and S_f is foreign saving in the United States. Since the latter represents foreign accumulation of U.S. assets, S_f is equal to the balance of the capital account, or equivalently, the negative of the current account balance. Since the preceding relation implies that $-S_f = S_p + S_g - I$, we can express the current account balance as

$$S_p + S_g - I$$

A current account deficit therefore occurs when domestic investment exceeds domestic saving, both private and public. As such, it may reflect a high level of domestic investment, a low (or negative) level of private saving, a low (or negative) level of government saving, or some combination of the three. Let's examine the implications of each.

Suppose that a high return on investment in the United States encourages foreigners to invest the dollars they receive from U.S. imports in the U.S. economy rather than spend those dollars on U.S. exports. In effect, the trade deficit becomes a source of financing for new capital goods and an expansion of U.S. productive capacity. Historically, rapidly growing economies, including the United States during the last half of the nineteenth century, have often financed high levels of domestic investment through current account deficits. The growing output and income generated by that investment enabled them to repay foreign investors and still enjoy higher levels of domestic consumption. To the extent that the U.S. current account deficit reflects a high return on domestic investment, therefore, it is accompanied by an increase in our real national wealth.

Low levels of private saving—or even negative saving—and correspondingly high levels of private consumption, can also be financed through a current account deficit. In effect, we can borrow from foreigners by exchanging IOUs, rather than exports, for the imported goods we wish to consume. Because those IOUs call for future principal and interest payments to foreigners, they become liabilities for domestic consumers. Using a current account deficit to finance consumption does not add to U.S. productive capacity and real wealth, however. To the extent that our current account deficit reflects low private saving, therefore, it is accompanied by a decrease in our national wealth.

Finally, suppose that the trade deficit is the result of negative government saving, that is, a government budget deficit. In effect, foreigners accept U.S. government debt, rather than currently produced goods, in return for their exports. Accordingly, U.S. citizens incur a future tax liability to foreigners. Whether domestic wealth increases or decreases in this case depends not so much on whether the budget deficit is financed with domestic or foreign funds but rather on how the government spends those funds. Specifically, to the extent that the government invests the funds in productive public capital, such as harbors or hydroelectric dams, the effect is to increase domestic wealth in much the same way as when the current account deficit finances private investment. On the other hand, to the extent that the government uses the foreign funds to cover its current operating expenses, the effect is similar to private dissaving, namely, a decrease in U.S. national wealth.

While the issue is far from settled, most economists believe that the large U.S. current account deficits of recent years reflect a combination of large federal budget deficits and high real returns on U.S. investment. Whether the portion of the federal deficit financed by foreign funds has added to our national wealth is a difficult question. As the foregoing discussion suggests, its answer depends on the kinds of federal spending that are being financed. However, *given the federal budget deficit and the pattern of federal expenditures that it reflects*, foreign sources of financing have augmented domestic saving and thus provided a source of financing for private, domestic investment. To the extent that this is the case, the current account deficits of the 1980s have contributed positively to U.S. national wealth. Of course, to the extent that those deficits have just financed a U.S. consumption binge, the reverse is the case.

Balance of Payments Equilibrium with Flexible Exchange Rates

The balance of payments must always balance—that is, sum to zero—because of the way its two components are defined. Saying that the current and capital accounts must always exactly offset one another is therefore a little like saying that quantity bought must always equal quantity sold. Balance of payments *equilibrium* goes beyond this accounting identity, however. It requires that the export and import plans reflected in the current account be consistent with the planned exchanges of assets reflected in the capital account. In the current world economic order, these plans are reconciled—and balance of payments equilibrium achieved—primarily through exchange rate adjustments.

An **exchange rate** is the price of one nation's currency stated in terms of another nation's currency.

Exchange rates are the relative prices of international currencies. As such they determine the international purchasing power of each country's monetary unit. For example, if the exchange rate between U.S. dollars and West German marks is $1 for 2 marks, then a dollar has the same purchasing power over German goods as 2 marks. By the same token, one German mark has the same purchasing power over U.S. goods as 1/2 of a U.S. dollar, or 50 cents. Moreover, if the exchange rate between dollars and Japanese yen is $1 for 150 yen, it follows that the exchange rate between marks and yen must be one mark for 75 yen.

Exchange rates determine the domestic prices of exports and imports. Suppose, for example, that a U.S. importer wants to buy television sets in Japan for resale in the United States. To do so, the importer must first exchange dollars for yen with which to pay the Japanese TV manufacturer. Assume that the exchange rate is $1 for 150 yen and that the price of a TV in Japan is 60,000 yen. Then the dollar cost of each TV to the U.S. importer is $400, for that is the amount of dollars necessary to purchase 60,000 yen at the exchange rate of $1 for 150 yen. By the same token, if beef sells for $3 per pound on the U.S. market, a Japanese beef importer has to pay 450 yen per pound for U.S. beef.

Exchange rates are determined by the supply of and demand for various national currencies on world currency markets. The equilibrium value of a nation's currency is in turn closely related to that nation's balance of payments. Indeed, balance of payments equilibrium and exchange rate equilibrium are but two sides of the same coin. When a nation such as the United States runs a current account deficit, the result is a net outflow, or supply, of dollars to the rest of the world. Unless that supply is matched by a net demand for dollars by the rest of the world to purchase U.S. assets on the capital account, neither the dollar's value nor the balance of payments is in equilibrium.

Figure 24.4

Foreign exchange value of the U.S. dollar, 1967–89

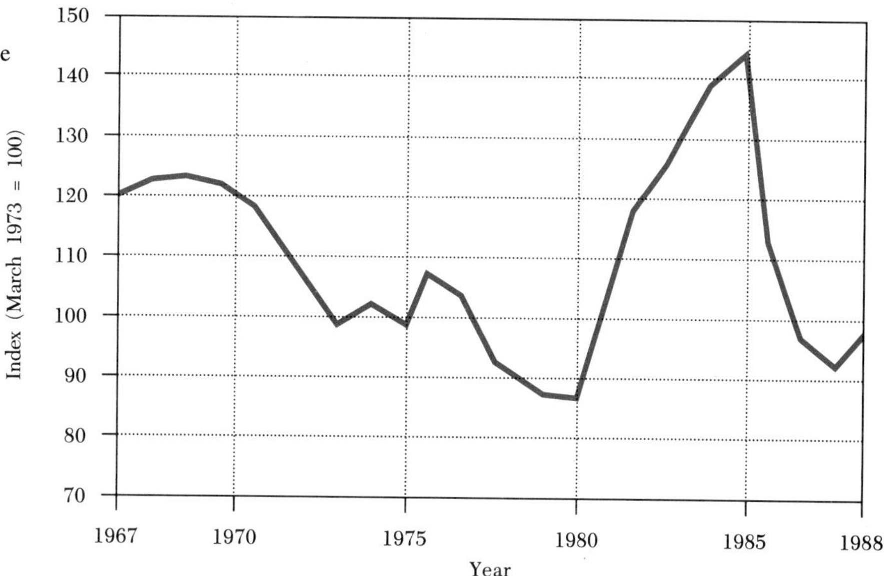

Suppose, for example, that the supply of dollars generated by the current account deficit exceeds the demand for dollars to buy U.S. assets on the capital account. As a result of the excess supply, the dollar falls in value relative to other currencies. This **currency depreciation** raises the price of imports to buyers in the United States and lowers the price of U.S. exports to the rest of the world. For example, if dollar depreciation lowers the exchange rate between dollars and yen from $1 for 150 yen to $1 for 125 yen, the TV importer in our foregoing example will have to pay $500 (= 60,000/125) rather than $400 for Japanese television sets. On the other hand, the price of U.S. beef exported to Japan will fall from 450 yen per pound to 375 yen per pound. Other things being equal, therefore, depreciation of the dollar discourages U.S. imports and stimulates U.S. exports. In so doing, it narrows the current account deficit and reduces the amount of dollars being supplied on world currency markets.* At the same time, dollar depreciation makes U.S. assets cheaper to foreigners and increases the amount of dollars they demand to purchase those assets on the capital account. Dollar depreciation thus eliminates the excess supply of dollars and simultaneously brings the value of the dollar and the balance of payments into equilibrium. Were there an initial excess demand for dollars instead of an excess supply, equilibrium would be achieved through **currency appreciation**, by which the value of the dollar would increase relative to foreign currencies. Figure 24.4 shows the fluctuations in the international value of the dollar in recent years.

Currency depreciation occurs when the value of a currency falls relative to other currencies on international markets.

Currency appreciation occurs when the value of a currency rises relative to other currencies on international markets.

*Actually, things are not quite so simple. The effect of a change in the exchange rate on the dollar flows of imports and exports—as opposed to their physical quantities—depends on the price elasticities of the demand for imports and exports and the initial level of expenditures on each.

Note that balance of payments equilibrium does not require that the current and capital accounts each show a separate balance of zero. It requires only that any supply of dollars generated by one account be matched by the demand for dollars generated by the other. This match can be achieved either with a current account deficit and a capital account surplus or with a current account surplus and a capital account deficit.

Purchasing Power Parity

The **purchasing power parity** principal says that the real purchasing powers of different national currencies must be approximately equal.

Exchange rate equilibrium, and thus balance of payments equilibrium, reflects a fundamental principle known as **purchasing power parity**. If the exchange rate between dollars and marks is $1 for 2 marks and between dollars and yen is $1 for 150 yen, then, according to the principle of purchasing power parity, $1, 2 marks, and 150 yen must all have about the same purchasing power. (We say "about" rather than "exactly" because different currencies cannot be used to purchase exactly the same bundle of goods. For example, you cannot buy a castle on the Rhine with dollars or a tour of the Grand Canyon with yen.)

We can illustrate the logic of purchasing power parity by considering what would happen if it did not hold. In particular, suppose that the exchange rate between dollars and yen is $1 for 150 yen but that a dollar buys more real goods in the United States than 150 yen buy in Japan. Under these circumstances, many Japanese would find it advantageous to trade their yen for dollars at the 150-for-1 exchange rate and then use those dollars to buy goods in the United States. The increased demand for dollars and the supply of yen would raise the value of the dollar relative to the yen until a dollar and its yen equivalent had the same real purchasing power.

We have to modify the principle of purchasing power parity somewhat when we recognize that a currency and the assets denominated in that currency (such as dollars and dollar-denominated U.S. Treasury bonds) are often held for future as well as current purchases. This means that the foreign exchange value of a currency reflects not only its current purchasing power but also its expected future purchasing power or, equivalently, the expected rate of inflation in the nation that issued it. In particular, since inflation reduces a currency's purchasing power, the currency of a nation that is expected to have a higher than average rate of inflation will be discounted accordingly in world currency markets.

Fixed versus Floating Exchange Rates

In a world in which nations independently determine their own monetary policies, actual and expected inflation can vary significantly over time and across countries. The behavior of exchange rates can therefore be a source of great uncertainty in economic decisions. For example, the volatility of exchange rates makes it difficult for a manufacturer who imports raw materials and components to make input decisions and predict production costs in advance. Or a manufacturer whose product competes with foreign imports may find it difficult to develop a pricing policy when competitors' domestic prices change with unpredictable fluctuations in the exchange rate.

To avoid this uncertainty, some governments and central banks prefer a system of **fixed exchange rates** to the system of flexible, or floating, exchange rates we have been describing. Under a fixed-rate system, the relative values of currencies are fixed by government fiat and changed only under extreme conditions. The world economy operated under such a system until 1973, and the historical experience is instructive.

A system of **fixed exchange rates** is one in which the relative values of national currencies are fixed by government fiat.

The International Gold Standard

Under the **international gold standard**, exchange rates among currencies are determined by the official prices of gold in terms of each nation's currency.

Prior to the Great Depression, most industrial nations were on the **international gold standard**. As we saw in our discussion of monetary policy, a nation on the gold standard fixed the value of its money relative to gold and thereby limited the size of its money stock to the amount of gold it owned. By restricting the power of governments to create money, the gold standard served the domestic function of preventing runaway inflation. Beyond this, however, it also had important implications for the international monetary system and for the way in which balance of payments equilibrium was achieved.

By fixing the prices at which they were willing to buy and sell gold, nations on the gold standard in effect also fixed the exchange rates among their currencies. For example, if the United States declared that an ounce of gold was worth $35 and Great Britain declared that an ounce of gold was worth 14 British pounds, then it followed that 1 British pound was worth $2.50 (= 35/14), or equivalently, $1 was worth 0.40 British pounds.

Under the gold standard, balance of payments equilibrium was achieved through adjustments in a nation's overall price level. A simple example illustrates how this worked. Suppose Great Britain was importing more than it was exporting and thus acting as a net supplier of British pounds to the rest of the world on the current account. If foreigners did not want to use all of their British pounds to acquire British assets on the capital account—that is, if there was an excess supply of British pounds—they would present them to Britain for redemption in gold at the official price. As a result, Britain would lose gold reserves, its money supply would shrink, and eventually its price level would fall. Falling British prices would stimulate British exports and reduce British imports, thereby reducing Britain's current account deficit and, with it, the international supply of pounds. The falling British price level would also make British assets more attractive as investments and thus increase the international demand for British pounds to purchase British assets on the capital account. Together, these adjustments would eventually restore equilibrium to the British balance of payments.

By contrast, an excess demand for British pounds would result in an inflow of gold into Britain in exchange for British pounds. The gold inflow would lead to an increase in the British money supply and a rise in the British price level. The rising price level would restore equilibrium by stimulating imports, reducing exports, and making British financial assets less attractive investments.

The critical point is that under the gold standard, a nation's control over its money supply, and thus its leverage in controlling fluctuations in its price level, was often subordinated to balance of payments adjustments. Unwilling to sacrifice their domestic monetary policies to international events over which they had little or no control, most nations abandoned the gold standard during the Great Depression.

The Bretton Woods System

The **Bretton Woods system** was an international monetary system in which governments fixed the prices of their currencies in terms of dollars, thereby also fixing their exchange rates in terms of one another.

Foreign exchange reserves are holdings of foreign currencies that a government uses to influence the international value of its own currency.

Currency devaluation is an official government act to reduce the international value of its currency.

After World War II, the world's major trading nations wanted to establish a system of fixed exchange rates without returning to the gold standard. The system they agreed on, called the **Bretton Woods system** after the small town in New Hampshire where the agreement was hammered out, lasted until 1973. Under this system, the U.S. dollar in effect took thc placc of gold. Thc cxchangc rates of all currencies were fixed in terms of dollars, and therefore relative to one another. In addition, the central bank of each nation held **foreign exchange reserves**—for the most part U.S. dollars—which it used when necessary to "defend" the value of its currency.

To see how this worked, suppose there was an excess supply of some currency, say Mexican pesos, at the official exchange rate. Under the Bretton Woods system, Mexico's central bank, perhaps in conjunction with the central banks of other countries, would use its dollar reserves to buy pesos, thereby adding to the demand. If successful, this strategy would stabilize the value of the peso at the official exchange rate. However, unless the fundamental source of disequilibrium—perhaps a high rate of Mexican inflation in the case of an overvalued peso—was eliminated, the central bank would soon run short of the reserves needed to "defend" its currency. When this happened, the government was forced into **currency devaluation**, whereby the value of the currency was officially reduced to a new exchange rate more consistent with its real purchasing power. (Note the difference between depreciation and devaluation: Depreciation is a market adjustment; devaluation is an official government act, which usually reflects market adjustments that are already well under way.) Moreover, mere expectations of devaluation can become a self-fulfilling prophecy. Fearing a devaluation of the Mexican peso, for example, holders of pesos may seek to exchange them for other currencies before it is too late. This exacerbates the excess supply of pesos and makes devaluation an even greater probability.

Anticipating such problems, the Bretton Woods agreement also established the *International Monetary Fund* (IMF) to make loans to governments trying to maintain the official values of their currencies. However, even the IMF could not solve the problems inherent in a system of fixed exchange rates. Since the currencies that became overvalued were usually those of countries pursuing inflationary domestic policies, the IMF repeatedly found itself having to choose between bailing out economically irresponsible governments or standing idly by while they devalued.

Moreover, under the Bretton Woods system, as under the gold standard, nations occasionally had to subordinate their domestic monetary policies to international considerations. A central bank forced to buy back its own currency, for example, is effectively contracting its money supply; one that is selling its currency is expanding its money supply.

Problems like these led to the abandonment of the Bretton Woods system in 1973, and today exchange rates are essentially free to fluctuate with market conditions. However, many nations still use their foreign exchange reserves, with varying degrees of success, in an attempt to keep those fluctuations within a relatively narrow range. Major trading nations also attempt to maintain exchange rate stability by coordinating their domestic monetary and fiscal policies, but again with varying degrees of success.

Although most academic economists favor the current regime of flexible exchange rates, the argument for fixed rates is not dead, nor is it entirely without merit. Fixed rates would be ideal *if* they could be maintained. The real question is how the fixed rates and the certainty and predictability they bring to international economic relations can be maintained in a world of constant change and divergent national economic policies.

THE POLITICAL ECONOMY OF TRADE AND PROTECTION

International trade has always been as much a political issue as an economic one. Perhaps this is inevitable, for in almost no other arena can politicians more successfully and convincingly wrap themselves in the flag while supporting politically influential special interests at the expense of the general welfare. What politician, after all, would not want to "protect American (or Japanese, or French, or Brazilian—pick your country) jobs and wages," "guarantee fair trade," "insure that the international playing field is level," and "keep the nation strong and independent," to borrow just a few of the high-sounding phrases that have been used to justify restrictions on international trade.

Almost all economists oppose restrictions on free international trade and they believe, with justification, that their arguments are convincing. But economists (at least most of them) are not naive. They recognize the timeless truth of Adam Smith's warning, made more than 200 years ago, that often "the interested sophistry of merchants and manufacturers confound(s) the common-sense of mankind."

Trade Surpluses and the Mercantilist Fallacy

Mercantilism is an economic fallacy that promotes trade surpluses as a means of acquiring a stock of precious metals.

National policies have long exhibited a bias in favor of current account ("trade") surpluses. To this end, they have systematically sought to promote exports and to discourage imports. This bias is probably in part a residue of **mercantilism**, a centuries-old economic fallacy that still occupies a place in our public consciousness.

In its original form, mercantilism held that a trade surplus was "good" because it enabled a nation to accumulate gold and other precious metals that were the common currencies of the day. Mercantilists identified a nation's wealth with its stock of precious metals. The fallacy in this argument is that the value of gold (aside from its minor value in ornamental jewelry and the like) lay in its general acceptability as a means of payment. In other words, gold was money, and, as money, its value was determined by what it could purchase. If the citizens of a nation want to exchange gold for imported food, clothing, and other goods, then that in itself is evidence that those goods are more valuable to them than gold. By discouraging or prohibiting such imports to accumulate more and more gold, therefore, mercantilist states actually reduced the real economic wealth of their citizens.

Mercantilist ideas have not disappeared with the passing of the international gold standard; they have just taken a new form. Today a surplus on the current account is often assumed to be "good" (and is almost always meaninglessly referred to in the news media as a "favorable" balance) because it allows a nation to acquire the assets of other countries on its capital account. Thus, for example, in recent years Japan has presumably gained because its "favorable" trade balance vis-à-vis the United States has enabled it to invest in U.S. assets. But we must ask what the purpose of this investment is. Do you suppose that Japanese investors just want to accumulate forever the U.S. dollars that these investments return to them? More concretely, do you think that they will be content to send us Toyotas and Sonys forever in return for little pieces of paper? Of course not! The dollars they receive from exports to, and investments in, the United States ultimately have only one real value, namely, their purchasing power over U.S. goods. When they are used for this purpose, U.S. exports will rise. In the long run, imports can only be paid for with exports; there is simply no way for one nation to run a trade surplus with the rest of the world forever. And of course it is logically impossible for all nations to simultaneously run trade surpluses even for a short time. But this does not keep them all from trying.

Protectionism

Another explanation of the persistent political bias in favor of trade surpluses is to be found in basic public choice theory. We have seen that policies that create benefits for organized interest groups and impose costs that are diffuse and difficult to identify are often adopted even if their total costs exceed their total benefits. As we are about to see, this is certainly the case with protectionist trade policies. First, however, let us examine some of the specific forms protectionist policies can take.

Types of Protectionist Policies

An **import tariff** is tax on imports.

Until recently, governments relied almost exclusively on **import tariffs** to protect domestic producers from foreign competition. Tariffs are simply taxes levied on imported goods. By adding to the cost of imports, they give domestic producers a cost advantage over their foreign competitors. U.S. tariff rates reached a peak of nearly 20 percent of the value of U.S. imports in 1932; today they average just under 4 percent.

An **import quota** is a limit on the amount of a good that can be imported.

As tariffs have declined in importance, various forms of nontariff protection have taken their place. Among these are **import quotas** that directly limit the amount of a good foreign producers can sell in domestic markets. In recent years, for example, the U.S. government has used quotas to limit imports of both television sets and cars from Japan. The quota on TVs was euphemistically referred to as an "orderly marketing agreement" (as if the TV market were "disorderly" before the quota was imposed!) and the car quota was called "voluntary" (the Japanese agreed to it because they feared even harsher measures if they did not). But whatever the language, a quota is a quota.

Governments also use *anti-dumping laws* to prevent foreign suppliers from selling at prices below the unit costs of their domestic competitors. In effect, such laws prevent consumers from taking advantage of lower cost foreign sources of supply. The U.S. government has used anti-dumping laws to protect domestic manufacturers of products as diverse as steel, shoes, and computer memory chips.

Finally, a domestic industry sometimes receives government *subsidies* to insure its survival in the face of foreign competition. It is doubtful, for example, whether the U.S. shipbuilding industry could survive in the world market without the combination of credit programs, special tax breaks, and direct subsidies that it receives from the federal government.

Although we have used examples from U.S. trade policy to illustrate this list of protectionist policies, we are by no means suggesting that such policies are more prevalent in this country than elsewhere. Indeed, in comparison with most other nations, the United States has been a veritable beacon of free trade.

The Costs of Protectionism

We can use Figure 24.5 on the following page to show the costs and benefits, and the distribution of those costs and benefits, that result from protectionist policies. The specific protectionist example we use is that of a tariff. However, we would reach the same general conclusions using other forms of protection as well.

Figure 24.5(a) shows the pretariff, free-trade market for widgets. S_d and D_d are the domestic supply and demand curves, respectively, for widgets, and S_f is the foreign supply. For simplicity we have assumed a horizontal foreign supply curve indicating that widgets are available on the world market at a constant price of P_f. If there were no foreign sources of supply, the domestic price of widgets would be P_d and consumption would be Q_2. With imports available at a price of P_f, however, consumption will rise to Q_3. Of this amount, domestic producers will supply Q_1 units because, up to that output rate, their lower marginal costs (supply prices) give them a comparative advantage over foreign suppliers. Beyond Q_1 domestic marginal cost is above the foreign supply price, so the remaining consumption, $Q_3 - Q_1$, consists of imports.

We can measure the gains from international trade by comparing the trade and no-trade situations. With foreign trade available, consumers pay a lower

Figure 24.5

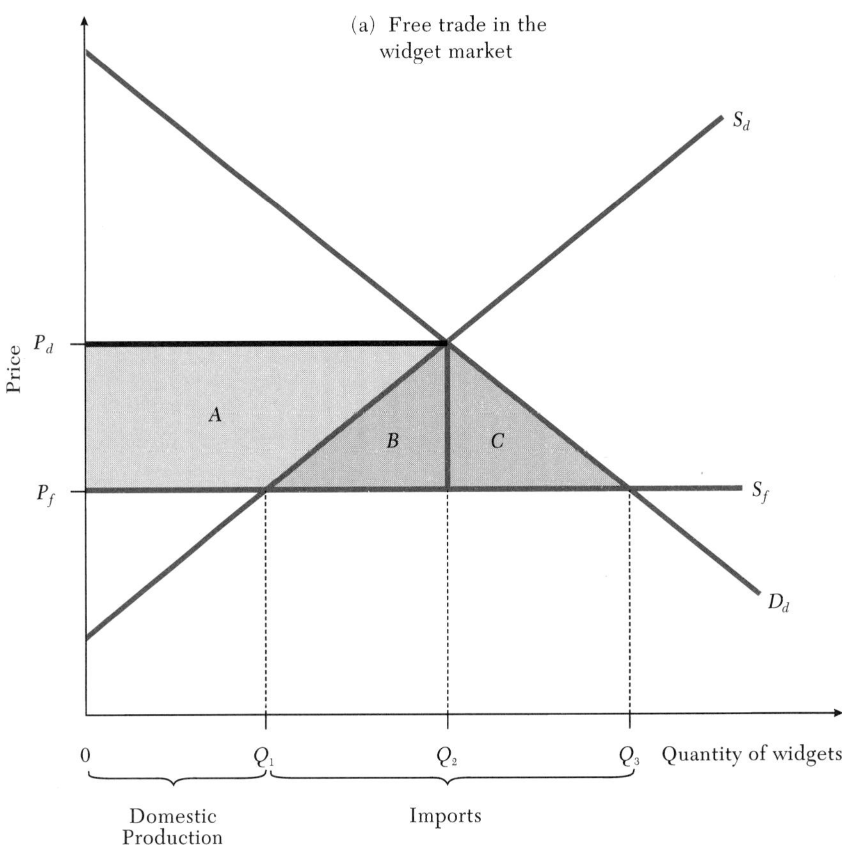

price, P_f rather than P_d. Thus they save an amount equal to area $A + B$ on the first Q_2 units they purchase. Moreover, the excess of consumers' marginal value over price on the additional units consumed can be represented by area C. The total gain to consumers—the increase in consumers' surplus—can therefore be represented by area $A + B + C$.

These gains are partially offset by a loss suffered by domestic producers. This loss of producers' surplus can be represented by the area A, which represents the excess of the domestic price over marginal costs on the Q_2 units that would be supplied by domestic producers in the absence of international trade. It includes not only lost profits for the owners of the domestic widget firms, but also any lost factor rents for the workers and other resources they employ. For example, if foreign competition forces a worker earning \$20 per hour in the domestic widget industry to shift to another line of work where he earns only \$15 per hour, the \$5 per hour difference is part of area A.

The net contribution of foreign trade to domestic economic welfare is the excess of the consumer gains ($A + B + C$) over producer losses (A). It is therefore represented by the area $B + C$ in the figure.

Figure 24.5
(*continued*)

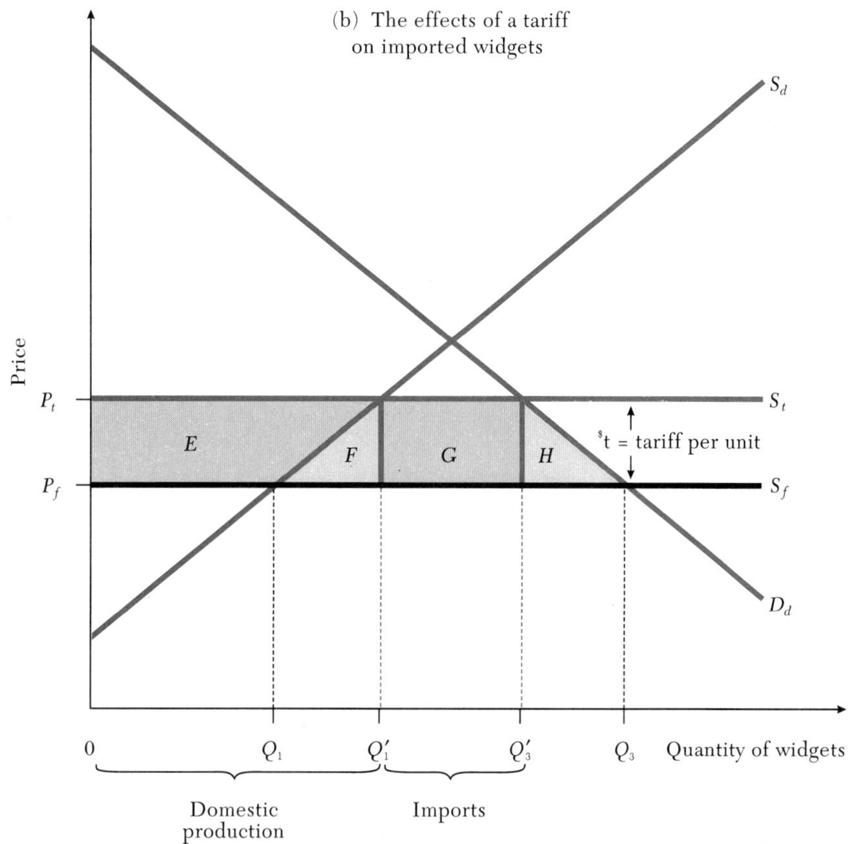

Now suppose that the government imposes a tariff of \$$t$ per unit on imported widgets. According to Figure 24.5(b), this tariff raises their foreign supply price from P_f to P_t and leads to a reduction in consumption to Q_3', of which Q_1' is produced domestically and the remainder imported. Domestic producers gain an amount of producers' surplus equal to area E, and the government collects tariff revenues equal to area G on the imports, but consumers' surplus falls by an amount equal to area $E + F + G + H$. The net effect of the tariff is therefore to reduce overall economic welfare by an amount equal to area F plus area H.

A similar analysis of the effects of import quotas and anti-dumping laws (which we spare you!) would lead to much the same conclusions. The main difference is that, under quotas or anti-dumping laws, the area G would represent additional payments to foreign suppliers rather than revenues collected by the government. It has been estimated, for example, that foreign producers gained nearly 40 percent of what U.S. consumers lost as a result of the import quotas on Japanese cars.

Our general conclusion is that trade restrictions impose costs on consumers, and those costs exceed the gains to domestic producers, as well as any gains that

Table 24.4

Annual costs of trade protection in selected industries

PROTECTED INDUSTRY	COSTS TO CONSUMERS Total (Millions)	Per Job Saved	GAINS TO PRODUCERS (Millions)	TARIFF REVENUE (Millions)
Book manu-facturing	$ 500	$ 100,000	$ 305	$ 0
Glassware	200	200,000	130	54
Orange juice	525	240,000	390	128
Canned tuna	91	76,000	74	10
Textiles and apparel	56,400	22–42,000	48,700	5,836
Carbon steel	13,120	240–750,000	7,900	1,406
Specialty steel	520	1,000,000	420	50
Footwear	930	30–55,000	340	401
Color TVs	420	420,000	190	77
Automobiles	5,800	105,000	2,600	790
Motorcycles	104	150,000	67	21
Dairy products	5,500	220,000	5,000	34
Meat	1,800	160,000	1,600	44
Fish	560	21,000	200	177
Petroleum	6,900	160,000	4,800	70

Source: Hufbauer, Gary Clyde, Diane T. Berliner, and Kimberly Ann Elliot. *Trade Protection in the United States: 31 Case Studies* (Institute for International Economics, 1986) as reported in Cletus C. Caughlin, K. Alec Chrystal, and Geoffrey E. Wood, "Protectionist Trade Policies: A Survey of Theory, Evidence and Rationale," *Review*, Federal Reserve Bank of St. Louis (January/February 1988).

accrue to the government in the form of tariff revenues or to foreigners in the form of higher prices. In the simplest possible terms, the bottom line on trade protection is negative.

Table 24.4 shows some recent estimates of annual consumer losses and producer gains due to the protection of various domestic industries. (It also shows the cost per job saved in the protected industry, which we discuss below.) As you can see, the costs to consumers are hardly trivial, running in many cases more than a billion dollars per year; and, as predicted by our analysis, they exceed the gains to producers in all cases.

Politics, Interest Groups, and Protection

It is not difficult to understand why trade protection is so prevalent despite its costs. Consumers are diffuse, unorganized, and largely unaware of the costs they bear as a result of trade protection. (Did you have any idea of the magnitude of these costs before looking at Table 24.4?) In addition, although the aggregate costs of trade protection are large, the costs *per consumer purchase* are relatively small. Under these conditions, it hardly pays for consumers to become informed about the costs of protectionist trade policies and to organize in political interest groups to oppose them. By contrast, the beneficiaries of trade protection are generally well organized and visible interest groups, with a large economic stake—per affected party, as well as for the group as a whole—in trade policy. They include domestic firms organized through industry associations and workers organized in labor unions. These interest groups contribute heavily to Congressional campaigns and maintain well-staffed Washington offices for lobbying purposes. Moreover, their interests are often effectively represented within government itself. U.S. government agencies such as the Department of Commerce, the Department of Labor, and the International Trade Commission frequently endorse protectionist measures to protect what they perceive to be their domestic constituencies.

Under these conditions, it should not be surprising that the beneficiaries of trade protection are generally more effective at using the political process to promote their interests than are the consumers who bear the costs of such policies.

Arguments in Favor of Protection

Of course, don't expect your congressman to declare that he supports this or that piece of protectionist legislation because he knows that consumers are ignorant of its costs and because the interest groups whom it will benefit have promised him a generous campaign contribution in return for his vote. His support for protectionism—a word he will avoid like the plague, incidentally—will inevitably be couched in terms of the public interest. He will drag out, and perhaps even believe, one or more of the plausible sounding arguments that are always invoked in the name of protection. Some of these arguments are simply wrong; others may, in rare cases, contain a grain of truth. In any case, they are recited so frequently, and are apparently believed by so many people, that we should not ignore them. Consider therefore the following claims for trade protection:

Import Restrictions Save Domestic Jobs Import restrictions do save jobs—but only in the protected industry, and only at a cost to the consumer that is usually greater than the value of the job. Look at the column in Table 24.4 that shows the consumer cost per job saved. Compare these ongoing, annual costs to the one-time cost of finding a new job. Are we to believe that a job saved in the domestic specialty steel industry is really worth $1 million per year? Or that a job in the color television industry is worth $420,000 per year? What answer do you think you would get if you asked someone employed in the color TV industry whether he would rather keep his job or give it up to look for another job with $420,000 in his pocket?

Moreover, for every job that import restrictions save in the protected industry, jobs are lost in other sectors of the economy where labor would be more productively employed. It is a fact that between 1982 and 1989, when the United States was running the largest trade deficits in its history, total employment in the United States grew at a much higher rate than it did in either Japan or Europe, both of which were running large trade surpluses vis-à-vis the United States, and at a much higher rate than it did in the 1970s when the United States itself generally ran trade surpluses. The argument that trade protection increases total employment by saving jobs is simply false.

Import Restrictions Are Necessary to Maintain High U.S. Wages This is also false. High wages in the protected industry may be maintained through protection, but wages in the economy as a whole fall as a result. Real wages are determined by labor productivity, and productivity is maximized when labor is allocated according to its comparative advantage. Put another way, a domestic worker's purchasing power is maximized only when he is employed where he is most productive and when he is allowed to spend his earnings on imported goods if those goods can be produced more cheaply abroad than at home.

High U.S. Wages Prevent Us from Competing with Low-Wage Countries Another version of the foregoing argument is that wages in the United States are too high for us to compete with low-wage countries such as Korea and Mexico. This ignores the fact that high U.S. wages are the result of high U.S. labor productivity. Indeed, a Korean or Mexican might—just as wrongly—reverse the preceding argument and claim that productivity in Korea (or Mexico) is too low for them to compete with high-productivity countries such as the United States. As our example of Agraria and Industria at the beginning of this chapter makes clear, absolute levels of productivity are irrelevant. Both Agraria, a low-productivity, and therefore low-wage, country and Industria, a high-productivity, high-wage country benefited from trade.

Protection Is Necessary for National Security The only protectionist arguments that may contain a grain of truth are those that apply to certain special cases. One such argument is based on the need to protect industries vital to the national defense. However, this argument usually ignores the possibility of importing and stockpiling military goods during peacetime or purchasing them from friendly countries during hostilities. Where mineral resources, such as oil, are involved, it ignores the fact that peacetime imports conserve domestic reserves for use in wartime emergencies. Even if we buy the general argument for protecting industries vital to defense, there is the practical problem of identifying the specific industries that legitimately qualify for such protection. In 1984, for example, the U.S. shoe industry, claiming that the military might have to go barefoot in the event of war, tried to convince Congress that reliance on imported shoes was "jeopardizing the national security of the U.S."*

We Must Protect Infant Industries Another argument that may contain a grain of truth in certain rare cases is the so-called *infant industry* argument. This calls for protection of a young (infant) domestic industry which, if allowed to mature, will eventually have a comparative advantage vis-à-vis the rest of the world. In recent years we have seen what is essentially the same argument applied to mature industries. For example, U.S. automobile producers, and before them steel producers, sought and received protection on the grounds that, if they were just given a respite from the pressures of international competition, they

*Reported in the *Wall Street Journal*, August 24, 1984.

would be able to modernize their facilities, streamline their operations, and become internationally competitive.

The problem with the infant industry argument and its variations is the practical one of identifying and confining protection to those industries that are legitimate candidates. Certainly every industry seeking protection would claim such privileged status. However, economic theory tells us that genuine infant industries are likely to be quite rare, and common sense tells us that industries that have been unable to compete internationally in the past are unlikely to do so in the future.

A **strategic trade policy** would have the government attempt to identify and promote industries that it believes can succeed in world markets.

We Need a Strategic Trade Policy In recent years, economists have developed theories of **strategic trade policy**. Although related to the infant industry argument, strategic trade policies typically do not rely on such traditional protectionist measures as tariffs and quotas to protect the status quo among domestic industries. Rather they establish government support for industries projected to be future winners in world markets.

The apparent success of Japan's Ministry of Trade and Industry (MITI) in promoting that nation's semiconductor industry is usually held up as the model of a successful strategic trade policy. MITI protected Japanese semiconductor firms with restrictive trade policies, while at the same time financing their research and development activities and other investments. As a result, Japanese firms now dominate the world semiconductor market.

Strategic trade policies raise two problems that make most economists—including many who developed the theoretical bases for such policies—hesitant to endorse their widespread use. First, arguments for strategic trade policy assume that government can successfully identify future winners in advance—and, implicitly, that it can do so with greater accuracy than private investors, who would otherwise privately supply the financing necessary for international competitiveness. Second, arguments for strategic trade policy overlook the practical implications of public choice theory. That theory suggests that the industries most likely to receive government support are not those based on new and emerging technologies, but those which already wield considerable political clout. History strongly suggests that governments are much more likely to protect the vested interests of the present than to promote the wave of the future.

The rarity of cases in which infant industry, national defense, strategic trade policy, and similar special case arguments for trade protection can be legitimately applied, and the obvious potential for such arguments to be abused, suggest that a general policy of free trade is realistically the best approach to international economic relations.

CHAPTER SUMMARY

1. Differences in comparative advantages, currencies, and political systems establish the economic significance of international boundaries.

2. Just as it provides the basis for trade among individuals, *comparative advantage* provides the basis for international trade. Specifically, regardless of their absolute productivities, all nations can gain by producing goods in which they have a comparative advantage and trading for goods in which they have a comparative disadvantage.

3. The monetary flows linking a nation's domestic economy to the rest of the world are recorded in its *balance of payments* accounts. The accounts, which consist of a *current account* and a *capital account*, treat any payment flowing into the domestic economy from the rest of the world as a credit (+) and any payment flowing out of the domestic economy to the rest of the world as a debit (−).

4. The current account (sometimes loosely referred to as the "balance of trade") consists of three components: merchandise trade, service trade, and transfer payments. The United States has been running large current account deficits in recent years.

5. The capital account records international purchases and sales of assets. Foreign purchases of U.S. assets represent a "capital inflow" and are recorded as a credit in the capital account.

6. The balance of payments must always balance: Any deficit (surplus) in the current account must be exactly offset by a surplus (deficit) in the capital account.

7. Current account (trade) deficits can reflect a high level of domestic investment, a low (or negative) level of private saving, a low (or negative) level of government saving, or a combination of the three. The first is usually accompanied by an increase in domestic wealth and the second by a decrease. The effect of financing negative government saving (budget deficits) with foreign funds depends on what the government does with the proceeds.

8. Balance of payments equilibrium is achieved through *exchange rate* adjustments that simultaneously insure that the supply of each nation's currency matches the demand for that currency, and that the export and import plans reflected in its current account are consistent with the planned exchanges of assets reflected in its capital account.

9. According to the principle of *purchasing power parity*, equilibrium exchange rates will be such that the purchasing power of each nation's currency will be about equal to the purchasing power of the foreign currencies for which it can be exchanged, after adjusting for expected inflation.

10. Under a system of *fixed exchange rates*, the relative values of currencies are fixed by government fiat rather than by the market.

11. The *international gold standard*, which most of the world observed prior to the Great Depression, was a fixed-rate system. Under the gold standard, balance of payments equilibrium was achieved through adjustments in a nation's money supply and its overall price level rather than the exchange

rate of its currency. As a result, a nation's control over its money supply and price level was often subordinated to balance of payments adjustments.

12. Under the *Bretton Woods system*, the U.S. dollar took the place of gold. The exchange rates of all currencies were fixed in terms of dollars, and therefore relative to one another, and the central bank of each nation held U.S. dollars as *foreign exchange reserves* which it used to "defend" the value of its currency.

13. Mercantilism held that a trade surplus was "good" because it enabled a nation to accumulate gold and other precious metals that were the common currencies of the day. Mercantilists incorrectly identified a nation's wealth with its stock of precious metals rather than with what could be purchased with those metals.

14. Public choice theory suggests that *protectionist* trade policies are adopted because they create benefits for organized interest groups and impose costs that are diffused among millions of unorganized consumers.

15. Most economists believe that protectionist trade policies do not save jobs or contribute to high U.S. wages. They are skeptical of arguments that such policies are necessary for national defense or that the *strategic trade policies* will work in practice.

Key Terms and Concepts

protectionism
consumption possibilities curve
balance of payments accounts
current account
capital account
exchange rate
currency depreciation
currency appreciation
purchasing power parity
fixed exchange rates
international gold standard
Bretton Woods system
foreign exchange reserves
currency devaluation
mercantilism
import tariffs
import quotas
strategic trade policy

Questions for Thought and Discussion

1. Imagine that you as an individual are a sovereign nation and everyone else with whom you trade comprises the "rest of the world."

   a. What do you "export" to pay for all the consumption goods you "import" from the bookstore, the grocer, the gas station, and so on?

b. How would each of the following affect your personal "balance of payments?" (If your answer is correct, your account should continue to balance—that is, the changes in your current account and those in your capital account should sum to zero.)
    i. You purchase a new stereo for $500.
    ii. You receive $20 as a birthday gift and use it to buy tickets to a rock concert.
    iii. You take your paycheck for $200 and deposit it in your savings account.
    iv. You use your $200 paycheck to buy a new outfit.

2. Suppose that the currency of Industria is the "indy" and the currency of Agraria is the "aggie." What affect will each of the following have on the exchange rate between indies and aggies?

a. Industria's inflation rate rises relative to that of Agraria.
b. Industrians decide that they do not want to buy as much food from Agraria as they have in the past.
c. Industrians decide that they want to invest in business ventures in Agraria rather than in Industria.

3. I have a brother-in-law who recently moved to Australia, whose currency is also the dollar (A$). In his letters, he tells us that the pay in Australia, where he is earning about A$ 40,000, is much better than in the United States, where he was earning about US$ 30,000 in the same occupation. He also reports, however, that the "cost of living" in Australia is about one-third higher than in the United States.

a. What do his observations suggest about the exchange rate between Australian and U.S. dollars?
b. Is he right about the "cost of living" in real terms?

4. According to Figure 24.4, the U.S. dollar depreciated dramatically against other world currencies between 1985 and 1989. Would you have gained or lost from this if you had found yourself in each of the following positions in 1985?

a. You were planning a trip to Europe.
b. You were planning to buy a Japanese stereo.
c. You owned bonds issued by a West German corporation.
d. You ran a business that catered to foreign tourists.
e. You ran an import business.

5. If you look at Figures 24.3 and 24.4 together, you see that the U.S. current account deficit began to rise at about the same time the exchange value of the dollar began to fall. What, if anything, is the connection between the two?

6. "Experts" repeatedly said the U.S. dollar was "overvalued" during 1982, 1983, and 1984. What do you think they meant? According to Figure 24.4, were they right? The same experts continued to say the same thing in 1985? Were they right then?

GLOSSARY

absolute (nominal) price: A price expressed in money terms.

accounting profit: The difference between a firm's revenues and its explicit costs. Unlike economic profit, accounting profit does not account for the implicit costs of owner-supplied resources used by the firm.

acquisition costs: The transactions costs of acquiring a capital good or other asset. These costs generally cannot be recovered if the asset is later sold.

adaptive expectations: Expectations formed by extrapolating past experience into the future without inquiring into the cause-and-effect relationships between the two.

agency costs: Costs of insuring that one's representative (agent) acts on one's behalf.

aggregate demand curve: A curve showing how the demand for aggregate real output varies with the general price level, other things being equal.

aggregate supply curve: A curve showing how the supply of aggregate real output varies with the general price level, other things being equal.

allocative efficiency: Efficiency which maximizes the value of the goods produced with scarce resources; satisfied only when resources are allocated in such a way that the marginal value of the last unit of each good produced is equal to its marginal cost.

annually balanced budget: A fiscal rule requiring that the federal budget be in balance each year.

antitrust policy: Policy concerned with the degree of competition in the marketplace and with business conduct that might affect competition.

artificial entry restrictions: Restrictions on entry unrelated to any cost or efficiency advantages of firms already in an industry.

asset: (1) Anything which generates future income or other benefits; e.g., a capital good, a bond, a bank account; (2) on a balance sheet, the value of something that is owned.

asset demand for money: The demand to hold money as an asset.

auction markets: Impersonal markets in which standardized products are traded through an intermediary, and in which prices adjust rapidly to changes in demand and supply.

autarky: An economic system in which people are self-sufficient.

autonomous spending change: A change in spending caused by some factor other than a change in national income (nominal GNP).

autonomous spending multiplier: The amount by which GNP changes per dollar change in autonomous spending.

average fixed cost: Fixed costs per unit of output; equal to total fixed cost divided by the output rate.

average total cost: Total cost per unit of output; equal to total cost divided by the output rate.

average variable cost: Variable cost per unit of output; equal to total variable cost divided by the output rate.

balance of payments accounts: The accounting framework for recording the monetary flows linking a nation's domestic economy to the rest of the world.

balanced budget at high employment: A fiscal rule requiring that the federal government's structural budget be in balance.

bank reserves: Bank holdings of vault cash and deposits at the Fed that satisfy the Fed's reserve requirement.

barter economy: An economy in which goods are exchanged directly for goods without the use of money.

basic national income accounting identity: National product is equal to national income.

bond: A financial instrument that promises the holder specified future payments at specified future dates. In making such promises, the seller of a bond incurs a debt.

Bretton Woods system: An international monetary system in which governments fix the prices of their currencies in terms of dollars, thereby also determining their exchange rates for one another.

business cycle: The short-term pattern of periodic recession and recovery superimposed on the longer term pattern of economic growth.

capital account: The portion of the balance of payments accounts that summarizes asset exchanges and credit flows.

capital goods: Productive resources that are themselves produced, e.g., buildings, machinery, computers and computer software, etc.

capital markets: Markets that coordinate saving and investment decisions and, in the process, determine how much of our productive capacity is to be used for current consumption and how much is to be used for adding to our capital stock. Capital markets consist of the **credit market** and the **equities market**.

capitalization: Obtaining the present value of a series of future payments or benefits by discounting each to its present value and summing them; the process by which the market evaluates a series of future payments or benefits.

cartel: An association formed to limit or eliminate competition among its members.

circular flow: A pictorial representation of the flow of real productive services from households to business firms in return for the flow of consumer goods from business firms to households.

classical tradition: A macroeconomic tradition emphasizing the effectiveness of the market mechanism in promoting economic stability and adapting to change.

collusion: An agreement to limit or eliminate competition.

command process: A process that relies on centralized authority to solve economic problems and coordinate economic activity.

command-and-control regulation: A form of regulation in which a government agency establishes an across-the-board regulatory standard applicable to all regulated firms and punishes violations of that standard with fines.

commodity money: Money that is backed by a commodity with intrinsic economic value, such as gold or silver.

comparable worth: A way of determining wages on the basis of "objectively" comparable job characteristics rather than on the basis of a job's market value.

comparative advantage: The efficiency advantage of lowest marginal cost provider of a good or productive service.

compensating wage differential: The amount by which a wage rises to compensate workers for the unpleasant or costly attributes of a particular type of employment.

competitive process: The dynamic, multidimensional process by which firms seek market advantages; includes competition via pricing, product characteristics, innovation, and all forms of entrepreneurial activity.

concentrated industry: An industry in which a small number of firms account for the bulk of sales.

concentration ratio: The percentage of industry sales accounted for by a small number (typically four or eight) of the largest firms in an industry.

constant cost industry: An industry in which the long-run supply price is constant (i.e., the long-run supply curve is horizontal); an industry in which entry and exit do not affect production costs.

constant returns to scale: A condition where changes in a firm's scale of operations have no affect on long-run average cost.

consumer price index (CPI): A price index that tracks the average price of a market basket of consumer goods.

consumers' surplus: The difference between the maximum amount buyers are willing to pay for a good and the amount they actually pay for it; a measure of the share of the gains from trade captured by buyers.

consumption possibilities curve: A curve showing the consumption combinations available to a nation as a result of specialization and international trade.

contractionary fiscal policy: A fiscal policy that attempts to reduce aggregate expenditure by cutting government spending or raising taxes.

contractionary monetary policy: A monetary policy that decreases the supply of money relative to the demand.

contractual claimant: One whose claim on some economic gain is promised by contract; e.g., in a business firm, the firm's employees typically have a contractual claim, in the form of wages and salaries, on the firm's revenues; a firm's creditors have a contractual claim to principal and interest payments.

corporate social responsibility: A normative view of the responsibility, if any, corporate managers owe to constituencies other than its stockholders.

corporate takeover: The acquisition of control over a corporation by purchasing 50+ percent of its voting stock.

corporation: A form of business organization that combines joint ownership by stockholders with professional management, limited stockholder liability, and marketable ownership rights (shares of stock).

cost push: The phase of the inflationary process during which expectations of higher prices push up wages and other costs.

countercyclical fiscal policy: The discretionary use of the government budget to offset fluctuations in private sector spending.

credit market: The market in which funds are loaned out in return for the promise of future repayment with interest.

cross elasticity: The ratio of the percentage change in the quantity demanded of one good to the percentage change in the price of a related good. Cross elasticity is positive for substitutes and negative for complements.

crowding out: The tendency of a pure, expansionary fiscal policy to raise interest rates and thereby discourage some private spending.

currency appreciation: A fall in the international value of a currency.

currency depreciation: A rise in the international value of a currency.

currency devaluation: A government action that reduces the official international value of its currency.

current account: The portion of the balance of payments accounts that summarizes current trade in goods and services and transfer payments.

customer market: A market in which there is a mutually advantageous, implicitly contractual relationship between buyers and sellers.

cyclical budget: The surplus or deficit in the government budget due to variations in economic activity over the course of the business cycle.

cyclically balanced budget: A fiscal rule requiring that the federal budget deficits incurred during recession be offset by surpluses generated during expansion and recovery so that the overall budget remains in balance over the course of the business cycle.

debt financing: Raising financial capital by selling new bonds (debt).

decisions at the margin: Decisions made by considering the effects of small ("marginal") changes on benefits and costs.

decreasing cost industry: An industry in which the long-run supply price falls as output increases (i.e., the long-run supply curve is negatively sloped); an industry in which entry of firms lowers production costs.

default risk: The risk that the borrower in a credit transaction will not fully repay his debt.

deflate: To divide the nominal value of a variable by a (decimal-valued) price index to obtain a measure of its real value (value in base year prices).

deflation: A fall in the economy's price level over time.

demand curve: A curve showing the quantity of a good demanded at each price when all factors other than the good's price are held constant; alternatively, a curve showing the demand price (marginal value) of a good for each quantity demanded.

demand deposits: Deposits in banks and other financial institutions that are payable on the demand of the depositor, usually by honoring the depositor's check.

demand elasticity: The ratio of the percentage change in quantity demanded to the percentage change in price, other things being equal.

demand for money: A demand to hold the specific liquid assets that make up the money supply.

demand price: The maximum price any buyer is willing to pay for each unit of a good. The demand price for any unit of a good is equal to the marginal value of that unit.

demand pull: The phase of the inflationary process during which an increase in aggregate demand is pulling up the prices of final goods before it affects wages and other costs.

derived demand: The demand for a productive resource (factor of production) that is derived from the demand for the final goods that it can be used to produce.

differentiated products: Products that are substitutes for one another but are not identical in the eyes of buyers.

discount factor: The factor by which a future amount is multiplied to obtain its present value. The discount factor for an amount payable t years from now when the current interest rate is r is equal to $(1 + r)^{-t}$.

discount rate: The interest rate the Fed charges on loans to banks.

diseconomies of scale: Factors that increase long-run average cost as the scale of a firm's operations increases.

disposable personal income: After-tax personal income, which can be either saved or consumed.

distribution: The problem of determining who gets what goods and in what amounts.

dividends: Corporate profits that are paid out to stockholders.

dynamic efficiency: Progress over time in the development of new products, new technologies, new information, and new forms of organization; the kind of progress resulting from entrepreneurial activities.

economic efficiency criterion: The normative criterion that holds that a something is desirable if its benefits exceed its costs.

economic growth: The long-term increase in real national product and national income.

economic profit: The difference between a firm's revenues and its opportunity costs, including both the explicit costs of resources purchased in the market and the implicit costs associated with owner-supplied resources.

economic rent: Income in excess of opportunity costs earned by specialized resources that are limited in supply.

economic system: A social system for coordinating individual choices in the face of scarcity.

economies of scale: Factors that decrease long-run average cost as the scale of a firm's operations increases.

effluent charge: A tax levied on polluting emissions.

elastic: A relationship between two variables in which the value of elasticity is greater than one, implying that a change in the independent variable leads to a more than proportionate change in the dependent variable.

elasticity: A measure of how sensitive one variable is to a change in another, related variable. It is equal to the ratio of the percentage (or proportionate) change in the dependent variable to the percentage (or proportionate) change in the independent variable.

empirical verification: Testing a theory or model to determine whether its predictions are consistent with available facts.

employed: Working for pay.

employment rate: The percentage of the age-eligible population that is employed.

enforcement costs: Costs of enforcing the terms of an exchange.

entrepreneurial competition: Competition through innovation and risk taking.

entrepreneurship: The undertaking of risk for the sake of possible profit.

equation of exchange: An identity stating that the money stock (M) times its velocity (V) must always equal the price level (P) times aggregate real output (Q); i.e., $MV = PQ$.

equilibrium: A state from which, unless distributed, no further change will occur.

equilibrium rate of inflation: The rate of inflation implied by fully anticipated growth in aggregate demand.

equities market: The market in which claims on future profits, such as shares of corporate stock, are exchanged; any market in which rights of ownership ("equity") are exchanged.

equity financing: Raising corporate financial capital by selling new shares of stock (equity).

excess reserves: Bank reserves over and above the minimum required by the Fed's required reserve ratio.

exchange rate: The price of one nation's currency in terms of another nation's currency.

exchange: The voluntary giving of one thing in return for another.

exclusive distribution territories: The practice by which a manufacturer prevents competition among the distributors of its product by providing each with a separate distribution territory.

expansionary fiscal policy: A fiscal policy that attempts to stimulate aggregate expenditure by raising government spending or cutting taxes.

expansionary monetary policy: A monetary policy that increases the supply of money relative to the demand.

expenditure function: A curve showing the level of aggregate expenditures for each level of national income (nominal GNP).

experience effects: The effect of past production experience in reducing costs; usually related to the cumulative volume of past production.

experience good: A good whose quality and other characteristics can be known only after it is purchased and consumed.

explicit costs: Costs for which there is an acutal market transaction, i.e., for which a payment actually changes hands.

external benefit: A benefit that is not reflected in market prices; a positive spillover effect of production or consumption.

external cost: A cost that is not reflected in market prices; a negative spillover effect of production or consumption.

externality: A benefit or cost that is not reflected in market prices; a positive or negative spillover effect of production or consumption. See **external benefit** and **external cost**.

factor markets: Markets in which productive resources (labor, capital, etc.) and their services are exchanged.

federal funds market: The market in which banks borrow and lend reserves among themselves.

federal funds rate: The interest rate in the federal funds market.

fiat money: Money whose value in exchange is determined by its legal status rather than by its intrinsic value, which is nil.

financial intermediary: A middleman that specializes in channelling funds from lenders/savers to borrowers/investors. Examples include banks, savings and loans, and stock brokerages.

financial investment: The purchase of financial assets, such as shares of corporate stock, corporate bonds, or savings account balances.

fiscal multipliers: Multipliers that tell how much GNP changes per dollar change in government spending and taxes.

fiscal policy: The use of the federal budget to pursue macroeconomic goals.

fixed costs: The short-run costs attributable to a firm's fixed inputs; costs that do not vary with a firm's output rate in the short run.

fixed exchange rates: A system in which the exchange rates among national currencies are fixed by government fiat.

flow: A variable measured over an interval of time.

fluidity: The amount of money demanded per dollar of income.

foreign exchange reserves: Holdings of foreign currencies that governments use to influence the international value of their own currencies.

free rider: A person who enjoys the benefits of a good while bearing little or none of the costs of providing it.

futures market: A market in which buyers and sellers agree now to a price at which they will exchange goods at some specified future date.

GNP deflator: A measure of the price level obtained by dividing nominal GNP by real GNP.

gold standard: A monetary rule that ties a nation's money supply to its stock of gold.

good: Anything that satisfies a human want.

gross national product (GNP): The aggregate value of all final goods produced during the year, including all new capital goods without allowance for depreciation.

homogeneous product: A product that is the same in the eyes of buyers regardless of its particular producer.

horizontal integration: Combining productive activities at the same stage in the production process within a single firm.

horizontal merger: A merger between competitors.

hostile takeover: A corporate takeover that is opposed by the corporation's incumbent managers.

human resources: People's abilities, skills, and knowledge available for use in production.

implicit contract: An informal agreement based on mutual advantage.

implicit costs: The opportunity costs associated with the use of owner-supplied resources within a firm; more generally, any opportunity costs for which there is no corresponding market transaction.

import quota: A limit on the amount of a good that can be imported.

import tariff: Tax on imports.

income elasticity: The ratio of a percentage change in demand to a percentage change in buyer income, other things being equal.

income-expenditure model: A macroeconomic model that focuses on the relation between the level of nominal GNP (national income) and the level of aggregate expenditure.

increasing cost industry: An industry in which the long-run supply price rises as output increases (i.e., the long-run supply curve is positively sloped); an industry in which entry of firms raises production costs.

industry: A group of firms selling products that are close substitutes for one another.

industry supply curve (long-run): Curve showing the quantity that will be supplied in the long run (i.e., after all entry and exit have taken place) at various market prices by all of the firms in an industry.

industry supply curve (short-run): Curve showing the quantity that will be supplied in the short run at various market prices by all of the firms in an industry.

inelastic: A relationship between two variables in which the value of elasticity is less than one, implying that a change in the independent variable leads to a less than proporationate change in the dependent variable.

inferior good: A good for which the demand decreases when buyer income increases; a good with a negative income elasticity.

inflation: An increase over time in the average level of all money prices (where the average level of prices is usually measured by a price index).

inflationary recession: A combination of recession and inflation brought about when an anticipated increase in aggregate demand is replaced by an unexpected fall in aggregate demand.

information costs: Costs of acquiring information useful in exchange.

inspection good: A good whose quality and other characteristics can be determined by inspection prior to purchase.

interest group: A group of citizens who share a common and well-defined position on some political issue.

intermediate goods: Goods used up in the production of other goods.

international gold standard: An international monetary system in which the prices governments set for gold determine the exchange rates among their currencies.

investment: The process of adding to the stock of productive resources.

Keynesian tradition: A macroeconomic tradition skeptical of the market mechanism's ability to promote economic stability and adapt to change.

labor force: Everyone who is either working (employed) or seeking work (unemployed).

labor force participation rate: The percentage of the age-eligible population that is in the labor force, either working or looking for work.

law of comparative advantage: The principle that the total output available from a given amount of resources is maximized when those resources are used according to their comparative advantage; or, equivalently, that the amount of resources necessary to produce a given amount of goods is minimized when those resources are used according to their comparative advantages.

law of demand: The principle that, other things being equal, more of a good will be demanded at a lower price than a higher price, and vice versa.

law of diminishing returns: The principle that holds that the marginal product of a variable input eventually declines as more of that input is added to a fixed amount of some other input.

lemons market: A market in which low-quality products ("lemons") come to predominate because consumers cannot distinguish such products from high-quality products.

leverage theory: A theory that holds that a firm with market power in one market can use a vertical merger to extend that power into other, vertically related markets.

liability: The value of something that is owed to someone.

limited liability: A provision that limits the liability of corporate owner/stockholders to the amount of their investment in the firm.

liquidity: A characteristic of an asset that depends on the transaction cost of converting it into money and the stability of its monetary value. The lower the transaction cost and the more certain its monetary value, the greater the liquidity.

long run: A period of time long enough for all adjustments to a change to work themselves out. In microeconomics, a period of time long enough for firms to vary all of their inputs and for firms to enter or exit from an industry; in macroeconomics, a period of time long enough for people's expectations to fully adjust to a change in economic conditions.

long-run aggregate supply curve: A curve showing how expected changes in the price level affect aggregate real output.

long-run industry equilibrium: Situation in which there is no entry into, or exit from, an industry; occurs when economic profit is zero if entry and exit are not artificially restricted.

long-run Phillips curve: A curve showing the effect on the rate of unemployment of fully anticipated changes in the rate of inflation rate.

M1: The narrow definition of the money supply that includes only currency and demand deposits in the hands of the nonbank public.

M2: A definition of the money supply that includes M1 (currency and demand deposits) plus savings and small time deposits and deposits in money market funds.

macroeconomics: The study of the relations among economic aggregates, such as the economy's total output, total level of employment, and average level of prices.

managerial coordination: Using managerial authority to coordinate production within a business firm.

marginal benefit: The benefit associated with a small change.

marginal cost: The cost associated with any small change; the cost of providing an additional unit of a good.

marginal product: The addition to total output that results when one more unit of a variable input is added to the production process.

marginal propensity to consume: The fraction of additional disposable income that is spent on consumption goods.

marginal propensity to spend: The fraction of an additional dollar of national income (nominal GNP) that is spent on final goods.

marginal revenue: The addition to a seller's revenue when one more unit is sold.

marginal tax rate: The percentage by which additional earnings are reduced by a combination of rising taxes and falling government transfers.

marginal value: The subjective value an individual places on an additional unit of a good; more generally, the value of some small change.

market coordination: Coordination of economic activity through market price adjustments to equate supply and demand.

market equilibrium: State of affairs that exists when there is no tendency for the market price to change; occurs at the market-clearing price when there are no restrictions on price adjustments.

market failure: The failure of a real-world market to achieve ideal economic efficiency.

market for corporate control: The market in which investors compete for control over corporations by acquiring 50+ percent of their voting stock, often with the intent of replacing corporate management.

market power: A seller's ability to control the price of its product; the ability of a seller to act as a price setter.

market process: A process that relies on decentralized individual choices and voluntary exchange to solve economic problems and coordinate economic activity.

market: The set of all contacts between buyers and sellers of a good.

market-clearing price: The price that equates the quantities demanded and supplied in the market; graphically, the price determined by the intersection of the market demand and supply curves.

marketable pollution rights: Permits, which can be exchanged among firms and other parties, to emit a certain amount of pollutants.

mercantilism: An economic fallacy that identified a nation's wealth with its stock of precious metals.

microeconomics: The study of the behavior and interaction of individuals, households, business firms and other decision-making units that make up the economy.

model: An abstract representation of some particular facet of reality; a way of thinking about the essential features of some facet of reality.

monetarism: A point of view that emphasizes the relative stability of the velocity of money and the primacy of the money supply in determining aggregate demand and the price level.

monetary policy: A policy adopted by the central bank to influence the supply of money.

monetizing a government deficit: The combination of actions by the Treasury and the Fed which, in effect, allows the government to create money to cover its budget deficit.

money multiplier: The change in bank deposits per dollar change in bank reserves.

monopolistic competition: A market structure in which there are large numbers of firms selling differentiated products and no significant restrictions on entry.

monopolistic efficiency loss: The net loss of economic benefits due to monopolistic output restriction.

monopoly: A single seller of a product with no close substitutes in a market with substantial entry costs.

monopsony: A market condition in which there is a single buyer; the equivalent, on the buyers' side of the market, of monopoly on the sellers' side.

national income and product accounts: The accounting framework for measuring national income and product.

national income: The total of all incomes generated in a nation's economy during a year.

national product: The total value of all goods and services produced by a nation's economy during the year.

natural cost advantages of incumbent firms: Factors that enable firms already in an industry to produce at lower cost than new entrants, e.g., economies of scale, experience effects, lower capital costs due to lower perceived risk.

natural monopoly: A set of conditions under which a single firm can serve an entire market at lower cost than can two or more firms.

natural rate of real output: The rate of aggregate real output corresponding to market-clearing conditions in the labor market.

natural rate of unemployment: The rate of unemployment corresponding to the normal flow of people between jobs and into and out of the labor force and the normal duration of job search.

natural resources: Productive resources available in the natural environment.

negative income tax: A program by which the government provides poor families with cash grants ("negative taxes") and gradually reduces those grants if family earnings increase.

negotiation costs: Costs of negotiating the terms of an exchange.

net national product (NNP): Gross national product minus depreciation.

net worth: The difference between assets (what is owned) and liabilities (what is owed).

new style social regulation: Government regulation concerned with environmental, health, and safety issues that cuts across industry boundaries.

nominal GNP: Gross national product evaluated in current prices.

nominal interest rate: An interest rate that includes a premium for expected inflation. It is equal to the sum of the real interest rate and the expected rate of inflation.

nominal price: See **absolute price**.

normal good: A good for which the demand increases when buyer income increases; a good with a positive income elasticity.

normative economics: An approach that attempts to evaluate economic conditions according to some subjective criterion. Such evaluation cannot be shown to be true or false in light of facts.

old style industrial regulation: Government regulation of prices, profits, and entry conditions in specific industries.

oligopoly: A market characterized by mutual interdependence among firms.

open market: A market with no restrictions on the entry of new competitors.

open market operations: The Fed's purchase and sale of government securities in the open market. Purchases increase bank reserves and permit monetary expansion; sales reduce bank reserves and force monetary contraction.

operating cost: The cost of operating a capital good.

opportunity cost: The value of the best alternative foregone when a choice is made.

partnership: A firm owned and operated by two or more individuals who personally receive all of its profits and bear all of its losses.

per se illegality: Illegal in and of itself without regard to particular circumstances.

perfectly elastic: A relationship between two variables in which the value of elasticity approaches infinity, implying that a very small change in the independent variable has a very large effect on the dependent variable.

perfectly inelastic: A relationship between two variables in which the value of elasticity is zero, implying that a change in the independent variable has no effect on the dependent variable.

permanent income theory: A theory that holds that households base their consumption spending on their permanent income, which is the income they have come to expect under normal conditions.

perpetuity: Something that generates periodic income payments forever.

personal income: Income that is paid directly to persons (households) rather than to businesses or government.

personal saving: Disposable personal income minus expenditures for consumption and interest; the increase in household assets (or reduction in household liabilities).

Phillips curve: A curve purporting to show a trade-off between unemployment and inflation.

political business cycle: Cyclical fluctuations in economic activity brought about by macroeconomic policies that are economically destabilizing but politically appealing.

positive economics: An approach that attempts to explain economic processes and verify the explanations in the light of facts.

possession cost: An opportunity cost in the form of foregone interest on funds tied up in capital goods or other assets.

poverty line: The annual income level below which a family is officially classified as poor.

poverty rate: The percentage of all families whose incomes fall below the poverty line.

present value: The value today of something available in the future; the amount that would have to be invested today, at today's interest rate, in order to have some specified future amount; the discounted value of some future amount.

price ceiling: A legal maximum price.

price discrimination: Multiple-part pricing in which price differentials do not reflect cost differentials.

price elasticity of demand: See **demand elasticity**.

price elasticity of supply: See **supply elasticity**.

price fixing: An agreement not to compete on the basis of price.

price floor: A legal minimum price.

price level: The average nominal price, expressed as an index number, of all goods and services included in national product.

price setter: A seller with some control over the price of its product.

price taker: A seller (or buyer) whose independent actions have no affect on market price.

private costs: Costs borne directly by the economic decision makers responsible for them.

private good: A good whose benefits are confined to a single consumer and from which other consumers can be excluded at low cost.

producers' surplus: The difference between the minimum amount sellers are willing to accept for a good and the amount they actually receive for it; a measure of the share of the gains from trade captured by sellers.

production function: The relation between the amount of inputs used in a production process and amount of output that results.

production possibilities curve: A curve showing the various combinations of two goods that can be produced when resources are used fully and efficiently.

production techniques: The problem of determining which combination of resources to use in the production of a good.

profit maximization: Decision making with the objective of increasing profits or reducing losses.

profit: See **economic profit** or **accounting profit**.

property rights: The legal rights regulating peoples' behavior with respect to goods, including the right of an owner to use goods and exclude others from their use and to transfer ownership to others.

proprietorship: A firm owned and operated by a single individual who personally receives all of its profits and bears all of its losses.

protectionism: A policy of sheltering domestic producers from foreign competition.

public choice theory: A positive economic theory of government behavior based on the observation that governmental authority is a scarce and valuable resource that must be allocated among alternative uses. It assumes that the actors in the political process which allocates that resource (voters, elected representatives, government bureaucrats) act rationally in their perceived self-interest.

public good: A good that provides indivisible and nonexclusive benefits, i.e., benefits that can be enjoyed jointly and simultaneously by a number of consumers, and from which those consumers cannot be excluded once the good is provided.

purchasing power parity: The principle that the real purchasing power of different national currencies must be appoximately equal.

pure competition: An economic model in which firms are assumed to be numerous and small in relation to the total market and produce a homogeneous product, in which all relevant information is costlessly available to all buyers and sellers, and in which there are no artificial restrictions on market entry or exit.

pure fiscal policy: A fiscal policy that is not accompanied by a change in the money supply.

pure rate of interest: The rate of interest determined by subjective time preference and the productivity of capital.

quantity theory: A theory that holds that because real output is determined by nonmonetary factors, and because velocity is independent of changes in the money supply, changes in the money supply lead to proportionate changes in the price level.

rate of inflation: The annual rate of increase in the economy's price level.

rate of return regulation: An approach to government regulation that attempts to limit the regulated firm's revenues to an amount just sufficient to cover all of its costs, including the opportunity cost of its capital.

rational expectations: Expectations based on all available information, including information about cause-and-effect relations between past experience and future events.

rational ignorance effect: Occurs when individual citizens find it rational to remain relatively uninformed about public policies and their effects because the costs of becoming informed are high relative to the benefits.

real GNP: Gross national product evaluated in base year prices.

real interest rate: The interest rate that would exist if no inflation were expected. It is equal to the difference between the nominal interest rate and the expected rate of inflation. (*Note*: the real interest rate cannot be observed directly.)

real investment: An addition to the stock of real capital.

real price: See **relative prices**.

real theories of the business cycle: Theories that view fluctuations in aggregate supply, rather than in aggregate demand, as the source of the business cycle.

recession: A decline in real national income and product that lasts at least two calendar quarters.

relative (real) prices: The trading ratios between goods; the real amounts of other goods that must be sacrificed to obtain a good.

rent seeking: Using scarce resources in an attempt to obtain exclusive monopoly rights and the economic rents that accompany such rights.

required reserve ratio: The minimum fraction of a bank's deposits that must be held as reserves.

resale price maintenance (RPM): The practice by which a manufacturer prevents retailers from discounting the price of its product.

reservation wage: The minimum wage at which a person will accept employment.

residual claimant: One whose claim on some economic gain takes the form of the residual, if any, that is left after all contractual claims are met; e.g., the owner of a business firm claims any residual—i.e., profit—that remains after all the firm's bills are paid.

resource allocation: The problem of determining how scarce resources are to be allocated among various goods.

retained earnings: The portion of corporate profits that is kept within the corporation rather than distributed to stockholders.

risk allocation: The problem of determining who will bear the unexpected gains and losses resulting from economic choices.

risk premium: An addition to the interest rate reflecting the possibility that a borrower might default; the greater the likelihood of default, the higher the risk premium.

rivalrous competition: Competition among identifiable rivals who are aware of their mutual interdependence.

rule of reason: An antitrust approach that determines the legal status of a business practice in the light of the particular circumstances in which it occurs.

Say's Law: The law that holds that a general deficiency of aggregate demand is not possible because the supply of any good or service is always motivated by a demand for some other good or service.

scale adjustments: Long-run adjustments in all inputs used in the firm; variations in the size of the firm's plant.

scarcity: The state that exists whenever available resources are insufficient to satisfy all wants or achieve all goals.

search costs: The costs of finding and taking advantage of the best price or other product characteristics.

short run: A period of time long enough for some, but not all, of the adjustments to a change to work themselves out. In microeconomics, some of a firm's inputs, as well as the number of firms in the industry, are fixed in the short run; in macroeconomics, people's expectations are fixed in the short run.

short-run aggregate supply curve: A curve showing how unexpected changes in the price level affect aggregate real output.

short-run Phillips curve: A curve showing the effect on the rate of unemployment of unanticipated changes in the rate of inflation.

shortage: The amount by which quantity demanded exceeds quantity supplied when the price is below its market-clearing level.

shut down: A situation in which a firm remains in business despite short-run losses, but minimizes those losses by producing nothing and thus avoiding its variable costs; occurs whenever revenues are not sufficient to cover variable costs.

social costs: The sum of private costs and external costs.

special interest: An interest which, when served, generates more total costs than benefits but concentrates large benefits on a relatively few persons while spreading the costs over many.

stabilization policy: Macroeconomic policy intended to minimize fluctuations in unemployment about its natural rate, real output about its long-term growth path, and inflation about some low and stable rate.

stagflation: A combination of high inflation and stagnant economic growth.

static efficiency: Efficiency at a given point in time, i.e., efficiency based on a set of given and unchanging resources, products, technologies, and information.

stock: A variable measured at a point in time.

stock option: The option of a corporate manager to purchase shares of stock in the corporation at some predetermined price.

stockholder equity: The aggregate value of the stock held by corporate stockholders.

strategic trade policy: A policy by which government attempts to identify and promote industries that can succeed in world markets.

structural budget: The surplus or deficit in the government budget generated by legislated tax rates and government spending programs in an economy operating at its natural rate of real output.

structuralist hypothesis: A hypothesis that the structure of an industry is the principal determinant of the competitive conduct and performance of its members.

subjective time preference: A preference on the part of most people to have goods available sooner rather than later.

sunk costs: Costs that are unavoidable and nonrecoverable bygones of past decisions. Such costs are not opportunity costs and should not affect future decisions.

supply curve: A curve showing the quantity of a good supplied at each price when all factors other than the good's price are held constant; alternatively, a curve showing the supply price (marginal cost) of a good for each quantity supplied.

supply curve of firm (short run): The portion of a price taking firm's marginal cost curve that lies above its average variable cost curve. It shows the amount the firm will supply at each market price.

supply elasticity: The ratio of the percentage change in quantity supplied to the percentage change in price, other things being equal.

supply price: The minimum price any seller is willing to accept for each unit of a good supplied. The supply price for any unit of a good is equal to the marginal cost of supplying that unit.

supply shock: An unexpected change in the conditions underlying aggregate supply.

surplus: The amount by which quantity supplied exceeds quantity demanded when the price is above its market-clearing level.

survivor principle: Principle that only those firms whose size and other characteristics are best suited to serve a market will survive in that market in the long run.

tacit collusion: Collusion based on implicit understanding rather than on an explicit agreement.

tax incidence: The division of the tax burden between the buyers and sellers of a good on which a tax is levied.

temporal allocation: The problem of choosing between the use of resources to satisfy current wants (consumption) and their use in expanding future opportunities (investment).

terms of trade: The international exchange rate between goods.

theory: A general explanation applicable to a wide range of particular circumstances.

time deposits: Deposits in banks and other financial institutions for which the institution can legally require a 30-day notice before withdrawal.

transaction costs: Costs that arise in the process of exchange.

transactions demand for money: The demand to hold money balances for use in transactions.

transfer: A grant, or payment, for which nothing is given in return.

unemployed: Actively seeking work.

unemployment equilibrium: A Keynesian equilibrium in which insufficient aggregate demand and downwardly rigid wages lead to persistent unemployment.

unemployment rate: Percentage of the labor force that is unemployed.

unitary elasticity: A relationship between two variables in which the value of elasticity is equal to one, implying that a change in the independent variable leads to an equal proportionate change in the dependent variable.

value added: The difference between the value of a producer's output and the value of the intermediate goods used up in producing that output.

value of the marginal product: The market value of the marginal physical product. It is equal to the marginal physical product times its market price per unit.

variable costs: The short-run costs attributable to a firm's variable inputs; costs that vary with a firm's output rate.

velocity: The rate at which the stock of money turns over each year in the purchase of final goods; calculated as the ratio of nominal national product to the money stock.

vertical integration: Combining productive activities at successive stages in a production process within a single firm.

vertical merger: A merger between firms in a buyer-seller relationship.

vertical restraint: Practice by which a firm restricts competition among vertically related firms; e.g., a manufacturer prevents retailers from discounting the price of its product.

A N S W E R S

FOR ODD-NUMBERED QUESTIONS FOR THOUGHT AND DISCUSSION

Chapter 1

1. Monetary costs of attending college include tuition, books, room and board, etc. Other, nonmonetary, opportunity costs include foregone earnings, foregone (or at least postponed) opportunities to acquire valuable job skills, leisure sacrificed in order to study, etc.
3. Not at all. Neither her altruism nor her apparent mistake are inconsistent with rational self-interest.
5. Lila's real opportunity cost of renting to Tom is the foregone opportunity of renting Tom's apartment to someone else. The fact that rents have been rising in Lila's neighborhood tells her that someone else is willing to pay more to rent Tom's apartment, and thus Lila's opportunity cost of continuing to rent to Tom has risen.
7. The fact of scarcity implies that the total of all goods and services desired exceeds the amount available. Since not everyone can have everything he or she desires, the economic system must include some way of rationing what is available. By implication, it must prevent people from getting at least some of the goods they desire.
9. Theories and models exist literally only in the mind. They are simply mental constructs for ordering and processing what, without them, would be an overwhelming body of information.

Chapter 2

1. The marginal cost of Stan's cooking a meal is 2 stints as dishwasher; the marginal cost of Ollie's cooking a meal is only 1-1/2 stints as dishwasher. Therefore Ollie has the comparative advantage as cook. Conversely, the marginal cost of Stan's doing the dishes is 1/2 a cooked meal; the marginal cost of Ollie's doing the dishes is 2/3 of a cooked meal. Therefore Stan has the comparative advantage as dishwasher.
3. Generally, no. Some faculty are relatively better at—i.e., have a comparative advantage in—teaching, and some have a comparative advantage in research. To the extent that the uniform standard forces all faculty to become "jacks-of-both-trades," the result is a point inside the *PPC* between teaching and research. To reach the

PPC, the university should encourage the relatively better teachers to devote more of their efforts to teaching and the better researchers to devote more of their efforts to doing research. (This answer assumes that teaching and research are substitutes; it is more complex to the extent that they are complementary as well.)

5. "It therefore concludes that trade will take place among people with different tastes."

7. The seller may have cut out the middleman, but he cannot cut out the need for the intermediary services (e.g., transportation, warehousing, distribution, etc.) that the middleman would otherwise have provided. If the seller himself can provide those services at lower cost than the middleman, then he may indeed be able to pass the savings on to his customers. On the other hand, if the seller's costs of providing the intermediary services are greater than those of the middleman, or if the customer must provide those services for himself, then cutting out the middleman will mean higher real costs to buyers.

9. The value of time to a teenager, especially one who is not employed, is probably less than its value to an employed young adult. The cost of waiting in line is therefore less for the teenager than for the young, employed adult. Conversely, the latter, because of greater earnings, often places a greater monetary value on the ticket than the teenager. Hence the exchange. In effect, the young adult "hires" the teenager to serve as middleman.

11. The price of transportation fell relative to the price of entertainment. The real prices of food and medical care increased; those of housing, transportation, and entertainment decreased.

Chapter 3

1. You shouldn't agree. First of all, "food" isn't a good; it's a category of goods, the amount demanded of any one of which is most likely quite responsive to its price. If the price of peas goes up, people will demand fewer peas and more green beans; if the price of steak goes down, people will demand more steak and less hamburger; etc. Second, very, very little of the water we consume is "vital for survival." Water is used to wash cars, hose down driveways, take 10-minute showers instead of 5-minute showers, water 50 plants rather than 20 plants, etc., all of which many people would willingly do without if the price of water were high enough.

3. It goes wrong where it says ". . . the lower price of gasoline will encourage more driving, thereby *increasing the demand for gasoline*." This part of the statement confuses a movement along the demand curve with a shift in the curve. Specifically, the power price will not increase the demand (shift the demand curve outward), it will only *increase the quantity demanded* until the market reaches a new equilibrium at a lower price.

5. Such predictions ignore the role of price in both supply and demand. In particular, where shortages begin to develop (or even become widely expected before they develop), the price would begin rising. The rising price would induce people to economize on the use of the resource and turn to substitutes, thereby reducing quantity demanded and flattening the slope of the line labelled "Demand" in the diagram. The rising price would also make it profitable for suppliers of the resource to search for and find more deposits. ("Known reserves" of any resource are not a measure of how much exists in total, but only of those deposits that it has paid to discover at past and current prices.) The rising price would thus increase the quantity supplied and make the line labelled "Supply" in the diagram steeper. Were there no restrictions on price adjustment, the "Demand" and "Supply" lines would converge and there would be no shortages.

7. *Not* allowing the price to rise when there is a shortage also means that some people—poor, rich, or both—will have to do without the good. Indeed, if the quantity supplied is at all responsive to price, there will be more "doing without" when the price is not allowed to rise than when it is. The argument that poor people are especially affected by the higher price may be true, but that is an objection to poverty, not to the price system.

9. As we emphasized in the text, it is the *marginal* cost, not the average cost, that must be covered. In the case of natural gas, the average cost of gas being pumped out of existing wells was considerably less than the marginal cost of finding and exploiting new wells. For supply to expand, the ceiling price would have had to have been high enough to cover that marginal cost, not just the average.

11. a. Demand for widgets falls (shifts to the left) as people switch to lower priced substitutes; price falls, quantity traded falls.
    b. The supply of widgets falls (supply curve shifts upward and to the left raising the supply price by the amount of the tax that is added to sellers' marginal costs); price rises, quantity traded falls.
    c. Marginal cost of widget production rises, increasing the supply price (decreasing the supply); price rises, quantity traded falls.
    d. Demand increases as people buy now to avoid expected higher future prices; current price rises, quantity traded rises.
    e. Demand and supply both increase; quantity traded rises, but the effect on price depends on which increases most.

Chapter 4

1. It should be just about impossible to identify literally everyone involved in the production of the shirt. The weaver who wove the cloth, the spinner who spun the thread for the weaver, the engineers who designed the weaving and spinning machinery, the teachers who taught the engineers, the trucker who shipped the shirt from the factory to the retailer, the people who made the trucker's truck, the carpenters who built the retail establishment, the people who made their hammers, etc. The point is that the process involved so many people that it is almost impossible to comprehend. Yet it happened!

3. It is not necessarily irrational for a country with a high population density to rely on labor-intensive production methods when more modern, capital-intensive methods are available. If labor is cheap relative to capital, which is likely to be the case in such a country, the use of labor-intensive methods may well be more efficient. The point is that what production method is economically efficient depends not just on what technology is more modern, but also upon the relative prices of inputs.

5. Most likely the 70-year old would have a higher rate of time preference because, given his life expectancy, he would discount the future more heavily than a 20-year old.

7. The baker can enter a contract with a speculator in which the speculator agrees to deliver wheat to the baker at some future date at a price agreed to now, say $3.00 per bushel. If the future price of wheat turns out to be $2.75, the speculator can buy it for that price and then sell it to the baker for the agreed-on $3.00, thus making a

profit of $0.25 per bushel. If the future price turns out to be $3.25, the speculator must buy wheat for that amount to resell to the baker for $3.00, thus losing $0.25 per bushel. In any case, the baker is guaranteed $3.00 per bushel and thus avoids the risk of price fluctuations.

Chapter 5

1. In a sense, and up to a point, the beach is a public good: a number of people can simultaneously enjoy it. However, exclusion is probably possible at relatively low cost (the city could charge admission) and, beyond some point, adding another consumer reduces the amount of beach available to others (the beach becomes congested).
3. Radio and TV broadcasts can be enjoyed simultaneously by a virtually unlimited number of consumers; anyone with a radio or TV can tune in and not reduce the amount available for others. Moreover, once the broadcast goes out over the airwaves, no one with a radio or TV set can be excluded from tuning in.

   Broadcasts can be produced by private networks because such networks can exclude advertisers from access to radio or TV advertising time. This enables them to charge for advertising time, which is not a public good, and thereby finance the broadcast.

   Like broadcast programming, cable programming can be enjoyed simultaneously by many viewers. However, cable programming is available only to those who subscribe to the cable service. Thus the nonexclusion characteristic of public goods does not apply to cablecasts.
5. Private costs of driving include the cost of gasoline and oil, wear and tear on the tires, engine, etc. Social costs include the air pollution that comes out of the tailpipe, the additional congestion that others suffer when the car is driven during rush hour, the potential damage to the life and limb of others due to the possibility of an accident.
7. Not at all. The EPA's budget is only a small fraction of the resources devoted to producing a cleaner environment. A far greater cost to society is borne by private businesses that must devote resources to modifying their production and waste disposal techniques to comply with EPA regulations. These costs are, of course, ultimately borne by the consumers who buy the products of those businesses.
9. The combination of the rationally ignorant voter and the economic advantages of interest groups suggests that many resources will be allocated to programs serving special interest groups. Given our definition of a special interest group, this implies that those resources would be socially more productive if used by the private sector. To the extent that this is true, government will tend to be too big.
11. Not necessarily. Better educated voters might be better able to understand and evaluate political information, but the costs would probably still be greater than the benefits for the average citizen. Moreover, better educated citizens might value their time more, thereby increasing the cost of becoming politically informed without measurably increasing the benefits.

Chapter 6

1. Slope = ($1.50 − $1.00)/(6,000 − 12,000) = −$0.50/6,000 = $0.000083 per rider. Elasticity = (6,000/9,000)/(0.50/1.25) = 15/9 = 1.67. Since demand is

elastic, revenues fall as a result of the fare increase. (Before the fare increase, revenues were ($1.00)(12,000) = $12,000 per week; after the fare increase they are ($1.50) (6,000) = $9,000.)

3. While there literally is no substitute for water itself, there are many substitutes for the things we do with water. An unwashed car is a substitute for a washed one; a short shower is a substitute for a long one; a swept-off driveway is a substitute for a hosed-down one; etc. In fact, the elasticity of demand for water has been estimated to be between about 0.15 and .20.
5. Yes. If we interpret the supply of Van Gogh paintings to include only those actually offered for sale at any given time, then the supply is not perfectly inelastic because some owners of Van Gogh paintings might offer them for sale at higher prices but not at lower prices.
7. Not very warmly. Since the supply of land is quite inelastic, the tax burden would have been borne almost entirely by landowners.

Chapter 7

1. The coach(es). The conductor.
3. In the vast majority of cases, it is not. Despite their legal status as owners of the firm, most stockholders view themselves as passive investors. They are undoubtedly at a comparative *dis*advantage relative to the corporation's professional management when it comes to determining how the firm should be run. Moreover, for most stockholders, the costs of even keeping up with corporate affairs, let alone the costs of actively participating in the corporation's management, far outweight the potential benefits.
5. You will get the present value of $100,000 available 5 years from now. Using the discount factor for 5 years at 7.5 percent, this present value equals $69,660 (= 0.6966 × $100,000).
7. The present value of the payments promised in the contract, and therefore the value of the contract, is $100,000 + $300,000 + ($300,000)(0.9091) + ($300,000)(0.8264) + ($200,000)(0.2394) = $968,530. Not even a paltry $1 million!
9. The people who demand a corporation's stock are implicitly betting that its price will rise; those who offer to sell that stock are betting that it will fall. Thus, when the stock market equates demand and supply, it is equating the bets that the price will rise with the bets that it will fall.

Chapter 8

1. a. The $2,000 in first-year depreciation is now sunk; also the insurance and license fee if already paid.
   b. The insurance and license fee are fixed costs; the depreciation and gasoline are variable costs because they depend on whether and how much you drive.
   c. Gasoline, insurance, and license fee are explicit costs; depreciation and foregone interest on its resale value are implicit costs.
   d. The marginal cost of driving another mile is 25 cents, the sum of the car's depreciation (20 cents) and the additional gasoline costs (5 cents).
   e. The total cost of driving 10,000 miles next year is:

Insurance and license:	$1,200	
Gasoline:	500	(500 gal @ $1/gal)
Depreciation:	2,000	(10,000 mi @ $.20/mi)
Foregone interest:	800	(10% of $8,000)
Total	$4,500	

The average total cost is therefore $0.45 per mile.

3. The marginal cost of the third unit is $14 (= $70 − $56). The $40 of costs that remain in a shut-down are the producer's fixed costs, so the total variable cost of 3 units is $70 − $40 = $30. The average variable cost of 3 units is therefore $30/3 = $10 per unit.
5. a. Explicit fixed costs: interest payments on a loan; property taxes; insurance premiums.
   b. Implicit fixed costs: foregone interest on the owner's capital.
   c. Explicit variable costs: employee wages, payments for materials and supplies; energy costs.
   d. Implicit variable costs: owner-supplied labor.
7. Your investment has grown by $15,000 (= $35,000 − $20,000). Your implicit costs are the $18,000 foregone salary and the $2,000 of foregone interest on your $20,000 investment for a total of $20,000. This implies that your economic profit is negative: a loss of $5,000.

Chapter 9

1. As individuals, we are a price takers in the markets for the vast majority of the consumer goods we purchase. We may be able to influence the price of goods, such as cars or houses, for which we negotiate with the seller.
3. A producer will find the most profitable output where marginal cost and marginal revenue are equal. In the short run, he will compare price with average variable cost to determine whether to produce or shut down. In the long run, he will compare price with average total cost to determine whether to continue production or exit from the market.
5. The increase in insurance rates does not affect marginal cost in the short run so it will have no effect on the industry's short-run supply curve. As a result, the market price and output will remain the same in the short run. But since total costs are higher, some firms will suffer losses and begin to leave the industry. This will continue, shifting the short-run supply curve to the left and raising prices until, in a new long-run equilibrium, the higher average total costs are covered.

   The increase in raw material prices does increase marginal costs in the short run so it will shift the short-run supply curve upward and raise the price in the short run. In addition, exit will proceed, further raising price until it covers the new, higher level of average total costs.

Chapter 10

1. For GM: large size, differentiated products. For the Mom-'n'-Pop grocery store: search costs, product differentiation (especially with respect to services). For the independent craftsman: product differentiation.
3. The publishers are pure monopolists only if you consider national newspapers (e.g., the *New York Times, USA Today,* etc.) and other sources of news (e.g., radio and

TV) to be very poor substitutes for the local newspaper. This is probably more likely to be the case from the perspective of an advertiser than from that of a reader.

5. a. Federal Express, United Parcel Service, fax service, telephone service.
b. Inter-city buses, cars, airplane travel.
c. Wood burning stoves, solar panels, camp stoves and heaters, wool sweaters.
d. Private schools, other school districts (a family can move or even falsify its address), education at home (as either a supplement or a substitute for the public schools).

7. No. If the buyer paid $40,000 for the patent, that would be equivalent to paying $5,000 per year for 17 years. (Recall that $40,000 is the present value of $5,000 per year for 17 years.) That cost would exactly offset the $5,000 per year in extra earnings by the patent holder.

9. $150 per day. Producing and selling 90 units at a price of $70 brings in daily revenues of $6,300; producing and selling 100 per day at a price of $65 brings in daily revenues of $6,500. The $200 difference less the $50 in extra materials' costs is the most the price setter would pay for the manager.

11. Whether or not Alcoa used its ownership of bauxite reserves to keep potential entrants out of the aluminum industry—e.g., by refusing to sell to them—such ownership did not give it a cost advantage. The opportunity cost of bauxite to Alcoa was not the internal cost of extracting it from the earth, but the price foregone by not selling it to anyone else. If a potential competitor was willing to pay $X per ton for bauxite, then that was the cost to Alcoa of using it itself, regardless of the "cost" of extracting it.

Chapter 11

1. It tells you virtually nothing. Most competition takes place within specific markets rather than across industries. General Motors, IBM, and Exxon are all among the 100 largest industrial corporations, for example, but they are direct competitors in very few product markets. In addition, the top 100 faced considerably more competition from foreign producers in 1987 than they did in 1970. Most economists would probably agree that, if anything, the U.S. economy is more competitive today than it was in 1970.

3. The oligopolist will be more reluctant to raise price if it believes its rivals will not respond because it will lose sales to its now relatively lower priced rivals. By contrast, its incentive to cut price is greater if it believes its rivals will not match the price cut because, in that case, it will attract more business from them. In other words, the oligopolist's demand is more elastic when rivals do not match price changes than when they do. (For elaboration on this, see the *kinked demand* section in the appendix to this chapter.)

5. a. Price = $3 (= marginal and average cost); total quantity = 90, with each firm producing 18 = 90/5; profits per firm = $0.
b. Price = $7 and total quantity = 50 (where $MR = MC =$ $3); quantity produced per firm = 10 = 50/5; profits per firm = $40 [= 10 × ($7 − $3)].
c. Approximately $4 = $7 − $3.

7. Yes, the absence of legal restrictions did invite the formation of many cartels, especially between the end of the Civil War and the passage of the Sherman Antitrust Act in 1890. However, very few of the cartels that were formed flourished for long; most soon collapsed as a result of internal bickering or entry by new competitors.

9. Imagine that it is the night before the exam. You know that if you put in just a little extra study time and your classmates do not, you will substantially improve your position on the curve. Do you think you might be tempted?

a. More likely to succeed in a small class because it is easier to monitor and detect cheaters and punish them (e.g., with ostracism by their classmates).
b. More likely to succeed if all students are residents of the same dorm for the same reason as in a.
c. Probably less likely to succeed on the final because it is more difficult to detect and punish cheaters after the class has broken up.

Chapter 12

1. When the car is new, it is usually safe for the buyer to assume that is has not been abused. By contrast, the potential buyer of a used car has little reliable information about how the owner has treated and maintained it.
3. One possible explanation is that reliance on repeat business in a metropolitan area induces the independent franchisee to provide high-quality service, which in turn reflects favorably on the gasoline company's brand name. The gas station on the rural highway, by contrast, relies very little on repeat business. Thus an independent franchisee might have an incentive to free ride on the company's brand name and provide poor service, perhaps even gouge customers needing repairs or other services. This would tarnish and devalue the company's brand name. To avoid this, the company owns and operates the rural stations itself.
5. Probably more dispersion of the prices of low-priced items like the pound of hamburger. The reason is that the higher prices of the "big ticket" items makes it more worthwhile to incur the search costs of shopping around. Thus a seller who is priced significantly above his competitors will more likely be found out and avoided.
7. You should advise them to introduce the 1-year battery to the market. They might sell only 1/4 as many in the long run, but the fourfold increase in price that buyers would pay would more than offset the twofold increase in costs. The potential profit of \$5 (= \$8 − \$3) on one 1-year battery is more than the profit of \$2 [=4(\$2 − \$1.50)] on four of the 3-month batteries.

Chapter 13

1. Generally, it should favor the merger. If the merger were likely to increase market power and raise prices, the competitors would benefit from the "umbrella effect." Put another way, were the merger to enable the merged firm to raise prices, the demand for competitors products would increase. On the other hand, competitors would certainly object if they believed that the merger would create a more efficient firm.
3. Evidence that *RPM* is being used to advance collusion would be that it is being used by many competing manufacturers, that retailer mark-ups are low (they would be high under the promotional services argument), and that point-of-sale service is unimportant. Evidence that it is being used to promote retailer services would include use by only one or a few competitors, high dealer mark-ups, and important point-of-sale service.
5. a. Using 10 percent as a "fair return" and Zapco's \$750 million investment as a "fair value" gives allowable accounting profit of \$75 million per year.
   b. Zapco would be allowed the \$75 million accounting profit plus \$500 million in

operating costs (= $.010 per kilowatt-hour times 5,000 million kilowatt-hours) for a total of $575 million.

c. Price = $0.1125 per kilowatt-hour = $575 million/5,000 million kilowatt-hours. This is equal to the *ATC*. No, the most efficient price is the marginal cost price of $0.10 per kilowatt-hour.

7. You would have to agree that it literally is a license to pollute and that such licenses are sold to the highest bidder. But you could point out that is so doing, the "license" minimizes the cost of achieving any given level of pollution reduction. You could also point out that under command-and-control approach, the EPA grants *free* "licenses to pollute" up to the maximum allowable standard. You might also tell your friend that the market in pollution rights enables him, perhaps through the environmental groups of which he is a member, to buy and retire pollution rights and thus to take direct action to reduce pollution even below the EPA's base standards. This is not possible under the command-and-control approach.

9. The equivalent of the effluent charge would be a tax levied on employers in proportion to the amount of work-related injuries suffered by their employees. A tax per day of work lost due to injury would be an example.

Chapter 14

1. The value of the resource is equal to the present value of the flow of future services it is expected to generate.

3. U.S. earnings are higher because U.S. workers are typically more productive, not because they work harder and are more diligent, but because they are generally better educated and have more nonhuman capital to work with.

5. a. According to the salaries set by the market, the market value of a doctor's marginal product ($65,000) is greater than the market value of a nurse's ($32,500). However, if the To-Your-Health clinic already employs four or more doctors and fewer than four nurses, another nurse would be worth more to the clinic than another doctor. If the clinic can hire nurses at the market wage, it would not have to pay more for another nurse, even though the nurse is "worth" more than another doctor.

b. The clinic will be able to hire as many nurses as it wants, but no doctors.

7. The argument is that a minimum wage *above* the market-clearing wage causes unemployment. Between 1981 and 1989, general inflation had probably pushed the (nominal) market-clearing wage for teen labor above the minimum in many metropolitan areas.

9. They might be based on judgements that people *should* use their assistance for things like food, medical care, and housing, but *should not* squander it on things like liquor, cars, or entertainment, as some do with their cash assistance.

Chapter 15

1. *The 1920s:* After an early recession during which unemployment surged and prices plummeted, the decade was one of high real growth, low unemployment, and a relatively stable price level.

The 1950s: A decade of relative stability on all fronts.

The 1960s: A decade of sustained real output growth accompanied by falling unemployment and moderately rising inflation.

3. A recession caused by a general fall in demand would be accompanied by a falling price level (deflation); one caused by a general fall in supply would be accompanied by a rise in the price level (inflation). (*Note*: applying the supply—demand market model to the macroeconomy is dangerous and sometimes misleading. In cases like this, however, it can provide worthwhile insight.)
5. The headline confuses inflation with the price level. *Inflation* did not rise 1.1 percent in 1986; quite the contrary, it fell from a level higher than that. The *price level* rose 1.1 percent. The headline should read either "Prises rose 1.1 percent" or "Inflation fell *to* 1.1 percent."
7. In principle, the constant inflation rate of 8 percent would probably be the least costly because it would soon become expected, thereby having the smallest redistributive effects.
9. The Keynesian, which downplays the importance of market price adjustments.

Chapter 16

1. The bakery's value added is $300 (= 1,000 − 400 − 300 = 200 + 100).
3. Although the differences are large, the per capita GNP figures probably overstate them because relatively more economic activity takes place in the household and underground sectors in economies like Mexico and Sudan, and such activity is not picked up in the accounts.
5. Consumer expenditures are not the same thing as current consumption. Consumer durables, and even some nondurables such as clothing, provide a flow of consumption that extends beyond the year in which they are originally purchased. For example, a new car will typically provide its owner with many years of transportation services. However, *consumption* of those services is not part of *consumer expenditures*, and thus not reflected in GNP, during the years following the initial purchase of the new car.

Chapter 17

1. Visa and MasterCard, like the hypothetical Wiltingdale's charge card in the text, are not really media of exchange. Rather they are only a means of deferring payment because you must eventually come up with money (e.g., a check) to pay for the purchases made on these cards.
3. If you lend your friend the $500 directly, there is no effect on either bank reserves or the money supply. If you write a check for $500 and give it to her, bank reserves, and ultimately the money supply, will fall. If you deposit the $500 in your bank account, bank reserves will have risen by that amount. Assuming a 10 percent reserve requirement, the bank will have only $450 of excess reserves that it can lend your friend so it will have to come up with another $50 in excess reserves. If it does, the money supply will increase by $500. The essential difference is that in this case you still have $500 to spend (as a balance in your checking account), whereas in the other two cases you do not. Moreover, in the case of the check written to your friend, bank reserves also fall.
5. It drastically shrank the money supply, partly because banks lost reserves. In addition, both the shift to currency on the part of the public and the increased holding of excess reserves by the banking system reduced the value of the money multiplier.

7. My best guesses:
   a. Unit of account (stating that the value of time can be compared with other values).
   b. Store of value (a fool is soon separated from his wealth).
   c. Medium of exchange.
   d. Store of value (wealth is probably what each means).

Chapter 18

1. The increase in saving would add to the supply of credit. This would lower interest rates in the credit market, and the lower interest rate would stimulate business investment spending. The drop in consumer spending would therefore be offset by a rise in investment spending, so that only the composition (not the level) of spending would change.
3. In a barter economy, labor (or any productive service) would be exchanged directly for some final good. Thus the supply of a productive service is *simultaneously* a demand for a final good. In a money economy, the productive service is exchanged for money. The supplier can then hold the money rather than spend it on a final good. The connection between supply and demand becomes more round about.
5. a. Real wage rises, employment rises, real output rises, price level falls.
   b. Real wage falls, employment rises, real output rises, price level falls.
   c. Same effect as a fall in the money supply, namely: real wage, employment and output unaffected; price level falls.

Chapter 19

1. a. Not in the labor force (too young to be in the age-eligible population).
   b. Not in the labor force (not working or seeking work).
   c. In the labor force and unemployed.
   d. In the labor force and unemployed.
   e. Not in the labor force (not working for pay or seeking work).
   f. In the labor force and employed.
   g. Not in the labor force.
3. Yes, unemployment could be too low from an economic efficiency standpoint. The natural rate of unemployment is the economically efficient rate—that is, the rate that people would choose on the basis of accurate information about labor market conditions. For unemployment to be below its natural rate would imply that people are accepting jobs that they would otherwise turn down in favor of further search if they had accurate information about job possibilities.
5. a. Increase (with multiple earners, unemployed family members can afford to search longer).
   b. Immediate effect, decrease (labor force exit would rise to care for children; search becomes more costly); longer term effect, increase (children eventually enter the labor force with effects similar to those of the baby boom).
   c. Increase (lowers the cost of prolonged search).
   d. Decrease (reduce duration of search).
7. Probably not. Other things being equal, an increase in the incidence of discouraged workers would tend to reduce labor force participation rather than raise it.

Chapter 20

1. a. More spending leads to higher real output and employment only in the short run, and then only to the extent that it is unanticipated. In the long run, it leads only to inflation and higher prices.
   b. When people spend less they may eliminate other people's employment opportunities, but again, only in the short run. Moreover, they need not increase spending to restore those opportunities; eventually changing expectations and revised contracts will do so automatically.
   c. Fluctuations in total spending are an important cause of the business cycle, but they are not the only cause. Supply shocks can also cause business cycles.
   d. Greater inflation leads to less employment only to the extent that it is unanticipated, and then only in the short run. We cannot permanently trade off unemployment for inflation.
3. a. Aggregate demand rising more rapidly than expected.
   b. A positive supply shock or expected inflation falling below actual inflation.
   c. Aggregate demand falling more rapidly than expected.
   d. A negative supply shock or expected inflation rising above actual inflation.
5. It is almost certainly based on rational expectations, for serious bettors try to obtain and interpret all possible information before risking their money. If it were based only on adaptive expectations, it would reflect mainly past records, including past games between the two teams. This is clearly not the case, for point spreads change from day to day on the basis of new information about injuries, weather, etc.
7. Unemployment will probably rise more if inflation has been at 8 percent for some time because then it will be built into people's expectations. If inflation has been falling, people might expect it to fall further and, to the extent that the reduction in inflation is anticipated, its impact on unemployment will be minimized.

Chapter 21

1. During a hyperinflation we would expect to see fluidity fall and velocity increase rather dramatically because the opportunity cost of holding money whose purchasing power is diminishing virtually over night is very high.
3. Unlike real wealth—such as gold, oil wells, and capital goods—money's value, and therefore its contribution to total wealth, is solely the result of its purchasing power. If money simply dropped from the sky, the price level would rise, each dollar would buy less, and real wealth would be unchanged.
5. A one-shot increase in the money supply will temporarily raise real output in the short run and permanently raise the price level, but it will have no long-run effect on inflation. A permanent increase in the rate of money growth will also temporarily increase real output in the short run, but it will also increase not only the price level but the long-run rate of inflation as well.

Chapter 22

1. $300; $500.
3. If the money supply remains constant, velocity must rise from 5 (= 5,000/1,000) to 5.2 (= 5,200/1,000). If velocity does not change, the Fed would have to increase the money supply by 40 (= 200/5) for equilibrium GNP to rise by 200.

5. Your consumption spending will rise from $18,000 to $19,800 and your saving from $2,000 to $5,200 (= $2,200 "permanent" saving + $3,000 windfall saving).
7. $30 of private spending ($20 of investment and $10 of consumption) will be crowded out. GNP will rise by 2 times the $20 net increase in spending, or by $40.
9.

	Monetarist:	Keynesian:
Nominal GNP	$5,500	$5,400
Real GNP	no change	no change
Price level	1.1 (= 5,500/5,000)	1.08 (= 5,400/5,000)
Velocity	5.0 (no change)	4.9 (= 5,400/1,100)

Chapter 23

1. a. The rising federal funds rate would imply increasing monetary contraction.
   b. The rising rate of growth of the money supply would imply increasing monetary expansion.
   c. The rising inflation rate would tend to confirm answer b, increasing monetary expansion.
3. a. Yes, it was a discretionary fiscal policy because the increase in tax rates raised the structural surplus. (Note, however, that it did not eliminate the cyclical deficit.) It was not in the appropriate direction; it was a contractionary fiscal policy when an expansionary policy was called for.
   b. Annually balanced budget.
5. Most people believe that the political pressures for deficit reduction were so great that Congress had to do something. When it became clear that the political obstacles to cutting specific programs or raising taxes were so great, Gramm-Rudman-Hollings seemed the only way out.

Chapter 24

1. a. If you are like most people, you "export" your labor services.
   b. i. Your current account falls by $500 because of the "import," and your capital account falls by $500 because of the capital outflow of currency.
      ii. $20 is added to transfers in your current account, and $20 is deducted from your balance on goods and services in the same account.
      iii. You add $200 for the "export" of labor services to your current account and deduct the $200 capital outflow from your capital account.
      iv. You add $200 to your current account for "exports" of labor services and subtract $200 from your current account for the "import" of the new outfit.
3. a. The exchange rate should be about 0.75 U.S. dollar for 1 Australian dollar (which it is as this is written).
   b. No. The "cost of living" is the same in real terms because the exchange rate apparently does reflect purchasing power parity.
5. If U.S. citizens decided to purchase more imported goods relative to what foreigners wanted to buy from us, the supply of dollars would rise pushing down the dollar's value, and at the same time the current account deficit would also rise.

INDEX

A 0
B 1
C 2
D 3
E 4
F 5
G 6
H 7
I 8
J 9